The Medical Library Association Guide to Finding Out about Heart Disease

The Best Print and Electronic Resources

Jeanette de Richemond
Terry Paula Hoffman

An imprint of the American Library Association

Chicago 2013

The information in this book is intended to help the reader locate information about heart disease. It is not intended to replace the advice of a qualified health care professional. While every effort has been made to ensure accuracy and currency of the facts presented, this information should not be used to make decisions about medical care. Please consult with your physician before making any decisions regarding medical treatment.

Contact information and URLs listed in the book were accurate at the time the manuscript went to press.

Published in cooperation with the Medical Library Association.

© 2013 by the Medical Library Association. Any claim of copyright is subject to applicable limitations and exceptions, such as rights of fair use and library copying pursuant to Sections 107 and 108 of the U.S. Copyright Act. No copyright is claimed for content in the public domain, such as works of the U.S. government.

Printed in the United States of America

17 16 15 14 13   5 4 3 2 1

Extensive effort has gone into ensuring the reliability of the information in this book; however, the publisher makes no warranty, express or implied, with respect to the material contained herein.

ISBNs: 978-1-55570-750-7 (paper); 978-1-55570-978-5 (PDF); 978-1-55570-980-8 (ePub); 978-1-55570-979-2 (Kindle).

Library of Congress Cataloging-in-Publication Data

De Richemond, Jeanette.
    The Medical Library Association guide to finding out about heart disease : the best print and electronic resources / Jeanette de Richemond, Terry Paula Hoffman.
        pages cm
    Includes bibliographical references and index.
    ISBN 978-1-55570-750-7 (alk. paper)
    1. Heart—Diseases—Bibliography. 2. Cardiovascular system—Diseases—Bibliography. 3. Diet in disease—Bibliography. 4. Heart—Diseases—Computer network resources. 5. Cardiovascular system—Diseases—Computer network resources. 6. Diet in disease—Computer network resources. I. Hoffman, Terry Paula. II. Medical Library Association. III. Title.
    Z6664.H3D38 2013
    [RC681]
    016.6161'2—dc23   2013011592

Cover design by Rosemary Holderby/Cole Design and Production.
Text design by UB Communications in the Minion Pro, Avenir, and Zapf Dingbats typefaces.
Composition by Scribe, Inc.

♾ This paper meets the requirements of ANSI/NISO Z39.48–1992 (Permanence of Paper).

Contents

Preface

H eart disease is the leading cause of death in the developed world. As physicians have increasingly limited time to spend with justifiably distressed patients and their families and friends, people are turning to the Internet for information and answers without knowing how to determine the credibility of online resources. A guide to reliable information resources for the public is necessary and important.

"I cannot give you a new heart." That's what one of the most preeminent physicians in a Midwestern state told my grandfather before discharging him as a patient in the early 1940s. While my mother was still in elementary school, my grandfather had a massive heart attack and spent nearly two years in bed. At that time, bed rest was the only treatment for heart disease. My grandfather took his health into his own hands and eventually got of bed, went back to work, and, luckily, lived long enough to play with me.

—Jeanette de Richemond

My dad died in his forties within minutes of having coronary thrombosis; he was slender and active. Back in 1964, my dad did not feel well for a few days. He went to his doctor for a checkup, but no serious cardiovascular results were identified. My dad died only a few days later. Both of my brothers, while in their fifties, developed classic symptoms and needed immediate quintuple bypasses. Both being slender and active, most likely, saved their lives. I am also slender and very active, and although symptomless, my LDL doubled in one year and my blood pressure jumped from a typical normal range to 150/100. It is safe to say that cardiovascular disease runs in my family. Understanding the importance of screening, preventive medicine, and lifestyle changes to lower my family's and my own risk of heart attack and stroke is vital.

—Terry Paula Hoffman

You are in the doctor's office. Your physician has just informed you that you have heart or cardiovascular disease and then asked, "Do you have any questions?" Regardless of whether your situation is immediately life-threatening or the beginning of a progressive disease, you might think of a few questions, your mind might go momentarily blank, or you might not feel informed enough to know what to ask. You say to yourself, "Tonight, I will go online and search the web."

When you begin your web search, you quickly discover there is an overwhelming amount of information about your condition on the Internet. Advertising-type websites pop up first; many of them cleverly resemble official medical sites. As you continue to scroll down or click from page to page, you ask yourself, "How do I know which are the reliable sites?"

The purpose of this book is to provide carefully selected, trustworthy, consumer-friendly resources that are easy to understand for patients and their families and friends; the related goal is to present knowledge that patients will need to be able to ask appropriate questions of their physicians. Included are sections on various types of heart and cardiovascular diseases, cardiac tests, treatments, including drug therapy and procedures, and related issues.

This book is intended to provide basic background information on heart and cardiovascular diseases, offering quality, vetted resources for librarians, health care personnel, and consumers. This information will allow consumers to be knowledgeable about heart basics and will assist in their consultations with physicians. Included are books (some in print, some as e-books), brochures, and websites.

Before changing careers to become a medical information specialist, I spent more than twenty years as a health/medical writer. During that time, I attended the scientific sessions of the American Heart Association and the American College of Cardiology for many years so I could report on the sessions for health professionals and for the general public. I also wrote a Coping column for a major newspaper on dealing with medical problems. I believed then as I believe now that "information is the antidote to anxiety."

—Jeanette de Richemond

I spent many years teaching secondary science as well as being a product development chemist before my career evolved toward becoming a medical information specialist. One might say educating, researching, and searching for information, as well as enabling others' empowerment through knowledge, is in my blood.

—Terry Paula Hoffman

Chapter 1

Introduction

How to Use This Book

The purpose of this book is to provide medical librarians, public library librarians, and laypersons with a basic understanding of heart disease and its treatment and management and to direct them to knowledgeable, accurate, and credible resources for further detailed information.

Within each chapter, each topic begins with a definition and description to explain any issues needed to further its clarification. This is followed by the section Resources for Further Information, which includes, if available and as current as possible, books; brochures, booklets, and other short print publications; carefully chosen websites; and patient support groups/organizations. Some chapters include just one resource section for the chapter overall and others provide separate condition-specific resource sections as well as a section for the chapter overall. Because the goal of this reference book is to be completely consumer friendly, each chapter can be viewed in any order and independently, and each contains its own set of instructions intended for the non-professional who is searching for relevant references.

The goal of this book was to identify books and websites that offer evidence-based health care information on heart and cardiovascular diseases. According to the Cochrane Library, evidence-based health care "is the conscientious use of current best evidence in making decisions about the care of individual patients or the delivery of health services. Current best evidence is up-to-date information from relevant, valid research about the effects of different forms of health care, the potential for harm from exposure to particular agents, the accuracy of diagnostic tests, and the predictive power of prognostic factors" (http://www.cochrane.org/about-us/evidence-based-health-care).

Authors' Note

This book is not intended to substitute for interaction with a patient's doctor or cardiologist. Learning about the aspects of heart disease will help patients discuss the issues of their disease with a doctor. Only a doctor can guide patients through the many steps needed to diagnose, treat, recover from, and live with heart disease.

Daily Evidence-Based Health News Updates

The physician-led **Insidermedicine Project** (http://www.insidermedicine.com/) "allows patients, doctors and medical students to keep up on the latest medical information by watching" videos created each weekday by their team of medical experts, allowing anyone to receive daily evidence-based health and medical updates. Previously created videos are available and free to view or download. Under the heading "Programs," click the category "By Disease or Symptom," scroll through the list of conditions, and click on a heart or cardiovascular topic. Also under the heading "Programs," click on "Universities and Hospitals" for links to "University and Hospital News Segments."

HealthDay—News for Better Living (http://consumer.healthday.com/) is a consumer-friendly expertly written health website that is updated several times a day. The HealthDay website also produces *HealthDay TV*, which provides a "daily [Monday through Friday] video recap of the latest consumer health research . . . for insight into the latest news published in major medical journals and new research presented at medical conferences . . . [in] short, easy-to-understand commentary that translates highly technical language into a concise and compelling report for medical consumers." Also available is a free, weekly *HealthDay* newsletter that can be customized for specific topics, such as heart health.

This first chapter explains how to use this book and its resources; it provides guidelines and strategies for conducting a heart disease reference interview, evaluating reference sources, and locating information. Chapter 2 explains how the heart works as part of the circulatory system. Many people are unaware they have a heart disease, and they often find out from a physician's diagnosis. Chapter 3 provides an understanding of the various types of heart and cardiovascular diseases. Chapter 4 provides an understanding of the various types of congenital heart disease. Chapter 5 describes diagnostic tests, treatments, and procedures. Chapter 6 describes the various types of risk factors and preventive measures. Chapter 7 describes lifestyle changes to help reduce risk or delay the onset of some heart diseases, as well as manage and control the progression or recovery of heart disease. Women have different heart problems and symptoms than do men; Chapter 8 explains women's heart issues. The book concludes with a glossary that provides the reader with basic definitions of heart and cardiovascular disease terminology.

Many references include animations, videos, audios, slide presentations, tutorials, and interactive charts. Many websites offer guides to what questions to ask your doctor, how to get a second opinion, latest clinical trials accepting patients, guides to health care costs and comparisons, patient discussions forums, and how to find the top doctors and top hospitals in cardiology your area, rated by the prestigious

U.S. News and World Report magazine; and several top U.S. hospital websites include an "Ask the Doctor" answered by a cardiologist or other heart specialist that you can call or e-mail. There are numerous free e-mail sign-ups for consumer-friendly, heart-healthy newsletters from trusted sites, such as the Hospital of the University of Pennsylvania, Harvard University–Harvard Medical School's *Harvard Heart Letter*, and the American College of Cardiology's CardioSmart.org. In addition, most of these trusted websites include links to their own social media, such as Facebook and Twitter accounts. There is also information specifically written for teens and for children. Included are links to consumer-friendly sections from Medicare.gov, the "Official U.S. Government Site for Medicare."

Because some heart conditions affect a higher percentage of the population than others do, such as high blood pressure and Marfan syndrome, the number of trusted references identified for each topic varies.

Although heart disease can be associated with other major diseases, such as diabetes, this book is limited to heart and cardiovascular diseases. However, exploring the resources

U.S. News and World Report's Top-Ranked U.S. Doctors and Hospitals for Cardiology and Heart Surgery

➢ U.S. News Best Hospitals: Cardiology and Heart Surgery. http://health .usnews.com/best-hospitals/rankings/ cardiology-and-heart-surgery. This list includes more than 700 hospitals with experience in treating difficult cases; the top 50 hospitals are ranked based on score and the rest are listed alphabetically.

➢ U.S. News Best Hospitals 2012–13: The Honor Roll. http://health.usnews .com/health-news/best-hospitals/ articles/2011/07/18/best-hospitals -2011–12-the-honor-roll. This list features 17 hospitals, most of which are household names, that scored in the top percentile in six or more of the Best Hospitals medical specialties.

➢ U.S. News Top Cardiologists: Top Doctors. http://health.usnews.com/ top-doctors/directory/best -cardiologists. This list includes 2,254 top cardiologists who were selected through a peer nomination process; 330 of them were also named to a highly selective list of America's Top Doctors.

See CHAPTER 5 for more detailed information on these rankings.

provided can lead to more information on directly related health care topics. For example, at the American Heart Association website (http://www.heart.org/), if you click on the category "Conditions" at the top of the screen, you will be directed to a website that contains a link to a list of heart and cardiovascular disease conditions, such as arrhythmia, high cholesterol, and heart attack. It also includes a link to more information on diabetes.

Recommended books are mostly for background information; however, because websites are continuously being updated with the latest information, user-friendly instructions are designed to help ensure you find these references, even if the original website address (URL, or uniform resource locator) changes. For example, currently at WebMD there is information on atrial fibrillation at http://www.webmd .com/heart-disease/atrial-fibrillation/default.htm. However, you can also find this webpage by going to WebMD's homepage at http://www.webmd.com/ and typing "atrial fibrillation health center" in the Search box at the top of the page. Likewise, whenever possible the various topics in this book are cross-referenced so you can find additional information relating to your primary topic in other sections.

Many complex terms are explained in the individual sections; the final section of this book also provides a glossary of terms. Many medical terms are composed of common phrases that might aid in comprehension. For example, *cardiac* refers to the heart, and *coronary* refers to the blood vessels and nerves associated with the heart. However, some terms that seem similar are not related. For example, *myocardial infarction* or *heart attack* is different from *heart failure*, which is also different from *sudden cardiac arrest.*

Heart Disease Reference Interview

Most medical librarians recognize a reference interview requires excellent listening skills, sensitivity, insight, tolerance, and discretion toward the user. For identifying the latest information, searching the Internet makes the most sense. Six basic steps are recommended:

- Establish a rapport with the user, and make good eye contact.
- Negotiate the question.
- Develop a successful search strategy and communicate it to the user.
- Locate the information and evaluate it.
- Provide information in a useful format (presentation of results).
- Ensure that the question is fully answered.

A patient, family member, or friend of the patient may likely be apprehensive, not fully informed, and uncertain as to what is wanted. Keeping users calm and reassuring them that you will be able to assist them in finding valuable resources will be helpful. Extracting key information from the users, such as symptoms, doctor's comments, or diagnosis, is a starting point. The librarian should provide only the information requested by the patient or family member and avoid providing negative information unless specifically requested to do so. Gently remind the user that you are a librarian and not a doctor; your goal is to offer the information, not analyze it. Never give advice, suggest a diagnosis, or recommend a particular treatment or physician. The librarian should be an impartial guide to the information needed to satisfy the user. For further details on working with patients and family members, refer to the Medical Library Association's policy of providing health care information to the public at the Consumer and Patient Health Information Section (CAPHIS) at http://caphis.mlanet.org/.

Websites in this guide were selected for their high quality and reliability. Although the selection of resources follows the Medical Library Association guidelines of CAPHIS, for evaluating the quality of health-related web resources users should always check on the applicability of any information with the physician who knows the patient's condition. This caveat applies to making lifestyle changes, such as diet and exercise, as well; the physician should be consulted before such changes are made. Most of the websites listed in this book hone in on a specific topic. Although the majority of these sites are written and developed for layperson use, included are a few clinical sites, such as Medscape and PubMed, which might assist the medical librarian in expanding on answers to a consumer's medical question, if needed, or aid health care professionals (e.g., physicians or nurses) who are looking for information for their patients. After the librarian guides the user to relevant websites and/or books, the interview can likely be closed.

Strategies for Locating Information

Searching for basic, background details about the user's question might be needed to enhance the search strategy for effectively finding the best information. Be sure to determine the correct spelling of the relevant search terms. The glossary and index of this book offer many terms, as do the specific chapters.

Jumping to Chapter 3 might be a good starting point for locating current information if answers about a specific condition, such as cardiomyopathy, are requested. Another option is going first to Chapter 6 if the user is interested in lifestyle changes for managing heart disease. Each chapter offers a wide variety of areas to peruse for patient-friendly information.

Providing nurses or physicians with information for a quick general overview may be sufficient, such as directing them to PubMed, MedlinePlus, drug suppliers' websites, and medical device suppliers' websites. Evidence-based websites that were used in searching for information on heart and cardiovascular diseases include MedlinePlus (http://www.medlineplus.gov/), the American Heart Association (http://www.heart.org/), the American College of Cardiology (http://www.acc.org/), the National Heart, Lung, and Blood Institute (http://www.nhlbi.nih.gov/), the Mayo Clinic (http://www.mayoclinic.com/), Medscape Reference (http://emedicine.medscape.com/), Medscape (http://www.medscape.com/), and PubMed (http://www.ncbi.nlm.nih.gov/pubmed/). The Medical

Library Association's CAPHIS also provides a list of the top 100 websites that can be trusted (http://caphis.mlanet.org/).

Guidelines for Evaluating Reference Sources

Numerous websites, journal and newspaper articles, and medical texts were examined. Heart disease is an expanding and ever-changing subject. New studies are published every day; websites containing medical information are updated on a regular basis. Therefore, cross-checking several sources will ensure the information is current and accurate. Remember that with various diagnostic screening tools, treatment options, and preventive measures recommended for heart and cardiovascular diseases, it is important for patients to discuss all information with their health care professionals.

Drug information is complex; consumer-friendly websites on drug treatments provide the detail to be able to understand a specific drug treatment's pros and cons. A drug treatment may be effective; however, its adverse effects might be too risky for a particular patient. Websites were also selected specifically for the non-medical professional for easy-to-understand descriptions of all areas discussed in this book.

See RESOURCES FOR FURTHER INFORMATION for general medical information in print (e.g., complete home medical guides, medical encyclopedias and dictionaries, overviews of medical conditions, and guidance on making informed medical decisions) as well as gateway websites to information about a disease, drug, or treatment that may be more useful to searching librarians. Websites listed in other chapters provide more specific, topic-driven information, such as on individual heart and cardiovascular diseases, which may be more beneficial to patients.

Resources for Further Information

Books

> American College of Physicians Staff. *American College of Physicians Complete Home Medical Guide.* 2nd ed. New York, NY: Dorling Kindersley, 2003. Print. Comprehensive and illustrated, this book provides information on taking control of your health, assessing your symptoms, your body and disease, and treating disease.

> American Medical Association. *American Medical Association Complete Medical Encyclopedia: A Brand-New A–Z Guide to More Than 5,000 Medical Terms with Up-to-Date Information on Symptoms, Diseases, Drugs, Treatments, and More.* New York, NY: Random House Reference, 2003. Print.

A solid reference filled with illustrations and pictures, this book is good to have on hand despite the utility of the Internet.

➤ Blakemore, Colin, and Sheila Jennett, eds. *The Oxford Companion to the Body.* London, England: Oxford University Press, 2002. Print.
This 778-page reference book on human anatomy and physiology is in alphabetical order, with more than 1,000 topics, including 150+ illustrations and 20 color plates. Carefully written for the professional and nonprofessional, the book features "full cross-referencing [and] comprehensive indexing."

➤ Chenzbraun, Adrian. *Heart Disease: The Facts.* New York, NY: Oxford University Press, 2010. Print.
Chenzbraun, a cardiologist who specialized in echocardiography at Stanford University Medical School, wrote this guide in a reader-friendly format that covers what heart disease is, types of heart disease, and treatment options.

➤ Delgado, Jane L. *The Latina Guide to Health: Consejos and Caring Answers.* New York, NY: Newmarket, 2010. Print.
This guide for Latinas in English and Spanish includes common conditions and medical decision making.

➤ Dorland. *Dorland's Illustrated Medical Dictionary.* 32nd ed. Philadelphia, PA: W.B. Saunders, 2010. Print; includes CD-ROM.
This seminal dictionary includes almost 124,000 medical terms and 1,525 illustrations. The e-book version contains 35,000 audio versions of medical terms.

➤ Engel, June, and Michael Evans. *Complete Canadian Health Guide.* Toronto, Ontario, Canada: Key Porter Books, 2005. Print.
This guide translates medical knowledge into clear terms. Key points are highlighted in orange boxes throughout the book. The index includes entries under both common and medical terms, suggests additional search terms, and directs readers to key pages for each topic.

➤ Gersh, Bernard J., ed. *Mayo Clinic Heart Book.* New York, NY: William Morrow, 2000. Print.
Editor Gersh's book includes information on the prevention, diagnosis, and treatment of cardiovascular disease, the number-one killer of women as well as men in the United States. Advances in minimally invasive surgeries; the risks and benefits of in-the-news topics, such as fish oil and margarine; insights about cardiac disease in women; the controversy surrounding appetite suppressants and heart damage; and even gene therapy are discussed in full, as are many more subject areas.

➤ McPhee, Stephen, Maxine Papadakis, and Michael W. Rabow. *Current Medical Diagnosis and Treatment 2012* (Lange Current Series). New York, NY: McGraw-Hill, 2012. Print.

This book lists relevant journal articles after discussions of diseases; it is updated and published annually.

> Mosby. *Mosby's Medical Dictionary*. 9th ed. Philadelphia, PA: Elsevier-Mosby, 2012. Print.
> While this dictionary is not as authoritative as others, it is useful as it explains medication terms in easy-to-understand language.

> Oster, Nancy. *Making Informed Medical Decisions*. Sebastopol, CA: Patient Center Guides, 2000. Print.
> Here are tools for health-information seekers who face critical health care decisions. This book guides readers through the world of medical information in print, on the Internet, and through contact with medical experts and other patients, and it gives practical advice on reading and understanding medical journal articles and understanding variations in standard treatments.

> Phibbs, Brendan. *The Human Heart: A Basic Guide to Heart Disease*. Philadelphia, PA: Lippincott Williams, 2007. Print.
> The book gives a comprehensive and accurate description of the heart and heart diseases and is helpful to readers from cardiovascular professionals to patients and families.

> Porter, Robert, et al., eds. *The Merck Manual Home Health Handbook*. 3rd home ed., unabridged. Whitehouse Station, NJ: Merck Research Laboratories, 2011. Print.
> This book, written by a diverse group of health care experts, provides a detailed overview of diseases and conditions for the consumer.

> Riegelman, Richard K. *Studying a Study and Testing a Test: How to Read the Medical Evidence*. 5th ed. Philadelphia, PA: Lippincott Williams and Wilkins, 2005. Print.
> This detailed guide by Riegelman provides information about how to understand medical journal articles, such as finding the limits to the study; understanding the results, data, and interpretations; and rating the study's value of evidence-based medicine. The book is arranged in a "step-by-step, active-participation approach to reading the medical evidence."

> Stedman, Thomas L. *Stedman's Medical Dictionary*. Philadelphia, PA: Lippincott Williams and Wilkins, 2005. Print.
> This 2,100-page comprehensive medical dictionary contains over 107,000 terms and definitions, with pronunciations, and includes about 1,500 images and illustrations. The book also features a list of common prefixes, suffixes, and other medical term fragments that compose "90 to 95% of medical vocabulary."

> Stedman, Thomas L. *Stedman's Pocket Medical Dictionary*. Philadelphia, PA: Lippincott Williams and Wilkins, 2010. Print.

Although bound to be pocket-sized, this 1,184-page book contains more than 38,000 defined terms derived from *Stedman's Medical Dictionary* and *Stedman's Medical Dictionary for the Health Professions and Nursing*. E-versions that include audio pronunciations are available.

➢ Younger-Lewis, Catherine, ed. *The Canadian Medical Association Complete Home Medical Guide*. 2nd ed. Toronto, Ontario, Canada: Dorling Kindersley, 2001. Print. Comprehensive and accurate, the *Canadian Medical Association Complete Home Medical Guide* was created in collaboration with the Canadian Medical Association to be an accessible source of up-to-date medical information for those who want to participate effectively in their own health care.

Gateway Websites

The following gateway sites will provide overall information about a disease, drug, or treatment and are likely to be useful to the searching librarian; websites in the other chapters provide specific, topic-driven information, such as individual heart and cardiovascular diseases, which will likely be more beneficial to a patient.

➢ BetterMedicine.com—"Heart, Blood, and Circulation." http://www.bettermedicine .com/category/heart-blood-and-circulation; alternate path: http://www.better medicine.com/, search for and then click on the title "Heart, Blood, and Circulation."

Online Search Tips

The following are brief, helpful, searching hints for accessing online resources:

- If you click on a link (e.g., a title) and nothing happens, try this: right-click on the link and then left-click on the option "Open in new window."
- If you experience problems with PDF documents, you can download the latest version of Adobe Reader for free at http://www.adobe.com/products/reader .html or by going to http://www.adobe.com/ and searching for "adobe reader."
- To view an animation, you might be asked to allow the installation of a common Internet plug-in called Shockwave Player by Adobe (http://www .adobe.com/products/shockwaveplayer/).
- Adobe Flash Player, required to view most short videos, is available as a free download at http://get.adobe.com/flashplayer/; alternate path: http://www .adobe.com/, choose the "Download" tab on the menu bar and select the Adobe Flash Player link.

Because the Internet is an ever-evolving resource, some direct links to resources may break over time. To help offset this, we provide alternate paths of access to the resources, but even these may change as websites modify their layout and content.

The Better Medicine website offers links to "Anatomy of the Heart," with separate links to "Heart, Blood, and Circulation Topics," and "Expert Advice from Harvard Medical School," which provides a Heart Disease Center with access to a range of heart disease articles; click on "Forums," scroll down to "Conditions," and click on "Heart Conditions." According to the Better Medicine website, "All content is medically reviewed by at least one medical professional. Our content is backed by evidence from sources, such as articles in peer-reviewed journals, government bodies, objective health organizations and medical groups of specialists. The name and credentials of the medical reviewer(s) are printed at the end of the article."

➢ CAPHIS (Consumer and Patient Health Information Section)—"Top 100 List: Health Websites You Can Trust." Medical Library Association. http://caphis .mlanet.org/consumer/.

The goal of this website is to offer a limited number of resources that meet CAPHIS's quality criteria for currency, credibility, content, audience, and so forth.

➢ MedlinePlus. U.S. National Library of Medicine and National Institutes of Health. http://www.nlm.nih.gov/medlineplus/; alternate path: http://www.nlm .nih.gov/, under "Databases," click on "MedlinePlus."

MedlinePlus, a component of the National Institutes of Health and produced by the federal National Library of Medicine, is updated regularly. This website is for patients and their families and friends to access information about diseases, conditions, and wellness issues in easily understandable language. MedlinePlus contains articles on the latest treatments, information on drugs and supplements, definitions of terms, and medical videos and illustrations. It provides links to the latest medical research and clinical trials on all manner of diseases and conditions.

➢ National Heart, Lung, and Blood Institute (NHLBI). U.S. Department of Health and Human Services, National Institutes of Health. http://www.nhlbi.nih.gov/.

There is a light blue box in the lower center of the homepage. Choose the left-hand column under "Public" to search the disease and conditions index. Choose from the search results. Each page on a disease has information on the nature of the condition, types, causes, risk factors, signs and symptoms, diagnosis, treatments, living with the condition, clinical trials, key points, and links to additional information. The homepage also has links to a variety of important topics under the "Public" Search box. As a federal government agency, the NHLBI's website is the gateway for the information provided on heart, lung, and blood diseases. To access the "Heart and Vascular Diseases" webpage, the URL is http://www.nhlbi.nih.gov/health/public/heart/index.htm. NHLBI provides global leadership for research, training, and education programs to promote the prevention and treatment of heart, lung, and blood diseases and enhance the health of all individuals.

➤ WebMD—"Heart Disease Health Center." http://www.webmd.com/heart-disease/
default.htm; alternate path: http://www.webmd.com/, search for "heart disease
health center," and click on "Heart Disease Health Center Guide."
This consumer-oriented website offers the latest information on heart disease,
using articles, slide presentations, videos, FAQs, discussions groups, and expert
blogs. According to the website, "WebMD News is an independent media service
designed to provide news, information, and educational material to consumers
and physicians. News content created by WebMD is free from influence by sponsors, partners, or other sources."

➤ WebMD—"Medscape Topics." http://www.medscape.com/medscapetoday/resource;
alternate path: http://www.medscape.com/, in lower left column under "Other Sites,"
click on "Medscape Today," and then at top right of the new page click on "More."
WebMD's alphabetical gateway has information on many diseases and related
topics. Users must register and registration is free. Topic portal pages have the latest
news on the topic and links to pages on specific issues on the topic. The information
is geared more toward physicians or those with a deeper knowledge of medicine.

➤ WebMD, Medscape Reference—"Drugs, Diseases, and Procedures." http://
emedicine.medscape.com/.
The Medscape Reference gateway leads to clinical references for a variety of diseases and medical specialties. The information is geared more toward physicians
or those with a deeper knowledge of medicine. Its specific webpages are very
thorough and are written by physicians knowledgeable in their subject areas.

Databases

➤ CINAHL Plus with Full Text. EBSCO Publishing. http://www.ebscohost.com/
academic/cinahl-plus-with-full-text; alternate path: http://www.ebscohost.com/,
click on "Public Libraries," and then under "Products" scroll down and click on
any of the CINAHL databases. Paid subscription; available at some hospitals or
public libraries.
According to the website, "This is the world's most comprehensive nursing and
allied health research database, providing full text for more than 770 journals."

➤ Embase Biomedical Answers. Elsevier. http://www.embase.com/. Paid subscription.
This database has citations to more European and drug studies than PubMed/
MEDLINE, and according to the Embase website, it contains indexed records
from more than 7,600 peer-reviewed journals.

➤ MEDLINE/PubMed Resources Guide. U.S. National Library of Medicine and
National Institutes of Health. http://www.nlm.nih.gov/bsd/pmresources.html;
alternate path: http://www.nlm.nih.gov/, search for and then click on the title
"MEDLINE/PubMed Resources Guide." Free.

Produced by the U.S. National Library of Medicine, the MEDLINE database is widely recognized as the premier source for bibliographic and abstract coverage of biomedical literature. MEDLINE provides information from the fields of medicine, nursing, and dentistry, as well as coverage in the areas of allied health, biological and physical sciences, humanities and information science as they relate to medicine and health care, communication disorders, population biology, and reproductive biology. The database contains more than 12 million citations from 4,600 biomedical journals published in the United States and other countries.

> Ovid MEDLINE. Ovid Technologies. http://www.ovid.com/. Paid subscription.
Ovid is a database service available at hospitals and some public libraries. According to Ovid, the website contains "more than 4,500 ebooks, including 60 book collections, including archive collections of critical historical material, publisher collections, and topical collections; over 1,200 premium, peer-reviewed journals—with no embargoes! Plus 50 journal collections, including archive collections and packages based on publisher or subject; and over 100 bibliographic and full-text databases."

> PsycINFO. American Psychological Association. http://www.apa.org/pubs/ databases/psycinfo/; alternate path: http://www.apa.org/, at top click on "Publications," and then click on "Databases." "PsycINFO" is one of the databases from which to choose. Paid subscription.
According to the website, PsycINFO "is an expansive abstracting and indexing database with more than 3 million records devoted to peer-reviewed literature in the behavioral sciences and mental health, making it an ideal discovery and linking tool for scholarly research in a host of disciplines." Subscription databases are available at hospitals and public libraries. This is a database of literature on behavioral health.

> PubMed. U.S. National Library of Medicine and National Institutes of Health. http://www.ncbi.nlm.nih.gov/pubmed/; alternate path: http://www.nlm.nih.gov/, under "Databases," click on "PubMed/MEDLINE." Free.
Available via the National Center for Biotechnology Information (NCBI) Entrez life sciences retrieval system, PubMed was developed at the National Library of Medicine, located at the U.S. National Institutes of Health. Entrez is the text-based search-and-retrieval system used at NCBI for services including PubMed, Nucleotide and Protein Sequences, Protein Structures, Complete Genomes, Taxonomy, OMIM, and many others. PubMed provides access to bibliographic information that includes MEDLINE and OLDMEDLINE. PubMed coverage also includes out-of-scope citations (e.g., articles on plate tectonics or astrophysics) from certain MEDLINE journals, primarily general science and chemistry journals for which the life sciences articles are indexed for MEDLINE. A PubMed overview

page and a tutorial page are available. Check out the main page (http://www.nlm
.nih.gov/) for additional databases.

Webliography

American College of Cardiology. "CardioSource." Accessed January 29, 2013. http://
www.acc.org/.
American Heart Association. Accessed January 18, 2013. http://www.heart.org/.
CAPHIS: Consumer and Patient Health Information Section. "MLA Annual Meet-
ing and Exhibition." Updated October 26, 2012. http://caphis.mlanet.org/.
The Cochrane Collaboration. "Evidence-Based Health Care and Systematic Reviews."
Updated November 9, 2012. http://www.cochrane.org/about-us/evidence-based
-health-care.
Mayo Clinic. Accessed January 29, 2013. http://www.mayoclinic.com/.
MedlinePlus. Updated January 29, 2013. http://www.nlm.nih.gov/medlineplus/.
Medscape. "News, Perspectives, and Full-Text Journal Articles." Updated January
29, 2013. http://www.medscape.com/.
Medscape Reference. "Drugs, Diseases, and Procedures." Accessed January 29,
2013. http://emedicine.medscape.com/.
National Heart, Lung, and Blood Institute. Accessed January 29, 2013. http://www
.nhlbi.nih.gov/.
PubMed. "Entrez: The Life Sciences Search Engine." Accessed January 29, 2013.
http://www.ncbi.nlm.nih.gov/sites/gquery/.
WebMD. "Atrial Fibrillation Health Center." Accessed January 29, 2013. http://www
.webmd.com/heart-disease/atrial-fibrillation/default.htm.

Chapter 2

How the Heart Works

Before discussing the various problems and diseases that can occur with the heart, it is helpful to understand the basic anatomy and function of the heart. At its simplest, the heart consists of several systems:

- Heart vasculature (or blood supply to the heart)
- Heart chambers (atria and ventricles)
- Heart valves (between the chambers and the major blood vessels, pulmonary artery, and aorta)
- Heart's electrical system

The heart is part of the circulatory system, which also includes the blood and blood vessels. Blood vessels are of three types: the arteries, which carry blood from the heart to the body; the capillaries, where the blood interacts with body cells; and the veins, which carry blood back to the heart. The blood is a mixture of blood cells, various chemical compounds, and liquids. The heart is the pump that moves the blood through the blood vessels to provide oxygen and energy to the body cells and to carry away carbon dioxide and other waste products to the lungs, liver, and kidneys.

The heart is central to the circulatory system. In the average adult, the heart beats at about 72 beats per minute or 38 million beats per year. To achieve this, the circulatory system and the various systems of the heart must work together correctly. If they do not, a variety of heart diseases can occur. Some heart diseases are congenital and occur during fetal growth. Some develop over time to certain parts of the heart or to the entire heart.

The fetal heart is slightly different from the adult heart, as explained in a later section in this chapter (*see* THE FETAL HEART). Some specific parts (e.g., pericardium, myocardium, endocardium) of the heart are discussed in other chapters under sections concerning their specific diseases.

Heart Vasculature

To explain cardiac procedures, it's necessary to understand a few anatomical facts. The heart, like any other organ in the body, is supplied with blood through the cardiac (or coronary) arteries and drained of blood by the cardiac (or coronary) veins. For the most part, cardiac veins are not likely to have problems. Cardiac arteries, however, can become narrowed or blocked by emboli (such as blood clots or pieces of loose fat), plaque deposits, or thickening of the artery walls through disease processes.

To learn more, visit the **National Heart, Lung, and Blood Institute** of the National Institutes of Health at http://www.nhlbi.nih.gov/health/health-topics/topics/hhw/anatomy.html (alternate path: http://www.nhlbi.nih.gov/, search for and click on the title "Anatomy of the Heart"). This webpage features the article "Anatomy of the Heart," which includes useful diagrams of the human heart's external and internal anatomy. Images illustrating the interior anatomy of the heart include arrows that show the direction of blood flow through the heart to and from the lungs and body.

There are three main cardiac arteries, each of which serves a specific function:

- The right coronary artery feeds blood to the right side of the heart.
- The left coronary artery feeds blood to the left side of the heart.
- The circumflex branch of the left coronary artery encircles the heart and joins with the branches of the right coronary artery at two points. This branching helps keep the heart supplied with blood should an artery become blocked or damaged.

To learn more, visit the **Johns Hopkins Medicine Health Library** at http://www.hopkinsmedicine.org/healthlibrary/conditions/cardiovascular_diseases/coronary_heart_disease_85,P00207/ (alternate path: http://www.hopkinsmedicine.org/, search for "circumflex artery" and click on "Coronary Heart Disease—Johns Hopkins Medicine Health"). This webpage includes a diagram of the coronary arteries that shows exits from the aorta and the two junctions of the left and right arteries outlining the circumflex artery.

The right and left coronary arteries are connected to the aorta just above the aortic valve. If these arteries become narrowed, the heart will not function as it should because the heart muscles are not getting enough oxygen and energy. If the arteries become blocked, sections of the heart may die in the resulting myocardial infarction or heart attack.

Heart Chambers

The heart has four chambers and four valves to cause the blood to be pumped in one direction through the heart. The blood moves through the heart in a wave of contraction of the heart chambers as follows: blood from the vena cava fills the right atrium. As the right atrium contracts, blood is pumped through the tricuspid valve into the right ventricle. Blood returning from the lungs through the pulmonary vein collects in the left atrium. As the left atrium contracts, blood is pumped through the mitral valve into the left ventricle. As the left ventricle contracts, blood is pumped through the aortic valve and the aorta and the body. As the right ventricle contracts (a short time after the left ventricle), blood is pumped through the pulmonary valve and pulmonary artery to the lungs. Once the heart has fully contracted, it relaxes, and the cycle starts again.

Heart Valves

Each valve is a collection of flexible leaves that open and close depending on the pressures in the heart chambers. The tricuspid, pulmonary, and aortic valves have three leaves; the mitral valve has only two. The pulmonary and aortic valves are the outlet from the atria and act like flappers or one-way valves in a pipe: when there is backflow, they close. The tricuspid and mitral valves work the same way but are tethered by muscles and tendons to the inside of their respective ventricles. As a ventricle contracts, the pressure forces the blood into the associated major blood vessel and its downstream resistance. This pressure could force the leaves of the valves to bulge into the atria if the muscles were not present.

To learn more, visit the **MedlinePlus Medical Encyclopedia** at http://www.nlm.nih.gov/medlineplus/ency/imagepages/18093.htm (alternate path: http://www.nlm.nih.gov/medlineplus/, search for "18093" and click on "Heart Valves—Superior View (Image)"). The diagram on this webpage shows the heart valves as seen from above. Note the coronary arteries above the aortic valve (superior view).

Electrical System of the Heart

To make the heart beat in the proper way to pump the blood to the lungs and body, an array of nerves in the heart—also called the heart's electrical system—is composed of three major sections. Nerves run from the sinoatrial (SA) node (the first section) near the top of the right atrium over to the left atrium and down to the center of the heart to the atrioventricular (AV) node (the second section) near the bottom center of the right atrial septum. The AV node is connected to the bundle of His at the top of the ventricular septum. This bundle runs down the septum and separates into the left and right bundle branches, which spread through the ventricle walls via the Purkinje fibers (the His-Purkinje system comprises the third section).

To learn more, visit the **Children's Hospital of Wisconsin** at http://www.chw.org/display/PPF/DocID/24698/router.asp (alternate path: http://www.chw.org/, click on "Health Information," under "Conditions" click on "Cardiovascular Disorders," then click on "The Heart," and then click on "Anatomy and Function of the Electrical
(Continued)

(*Continued*)

System"). This webpage provides discussion of the anatomy and function of the electrical system of the heart, complete with a diagram. To view an animation of the heart's electrical system at work, visit the **National Heart, Lung, and Blood Institute** at http://www.nhlbi.nih.gov/health/health-topics/topics/hhw/electrical .html (alternate path: http://www.nhlbi.nih.gov/, search for and click on the title "Your Heart's Electrical System"); click the "Start" button to begin the animation.

The nerve impulses start at the SA node and cause the atria to contract and force blood into the ventricles. This corresponds to the P wave on an electrocardiogram (ECG or EKG). (For information on the electrocardiogram test, *see* ELECTROCARDIOGRAPHY in Chapter 5.) When the nerve impulse reaches the AV node, there is a slight pause (the PQ segment of the wave) to allow the ventricles to fill as the nerve impulse travels to the bundle of His. From there, the impulse travels down the left and right bundle branches and Purkinje fibers, causing the left ventricle to contract, followed a brief moment later by the right ventricle. The contraction of the left ventricle corresponds to the QR section of the ECG graph, and the RS section corresponds to the contraction of the right ventricle. When the nerve impulse has reached all of the heart muscles and caused them to contract, the muscles then relax. The relaxation of the heart corresponds to the ST segment of the ECG graph. After a short rest, the heart contracts again, once about every 0.8 seconds.

The heart is also affected by the body's central nervous system (i.e., sympathetic nervous system). For example, when a person is afraid, in love, exercising, or engaging in any of a range of other acts, the brain causes chemicals from various glands to be poured into the bloodstream. These chemicals affect the function of the heart. However, a discussion of this subject is beyond the scope of this book.

The Fetal Heart

The fetal heart differs from the adult heart because the fetal lungs are not yet working. Most fetuses have a blood vessel called the ductus arteriosus that connects the pulmonary artery with the descending aorta. Most fetuses also have a foramen ovale, which is a hole between the left and right atria. Both of these shunts allow blood to bypass the lungs. Instead of the lungs, the placenta provides the needed nutrients and gases and carries waste products away from the fetus. These shunts typically close shortly after the baby is born.

Resources for Further Information

Books

➤ Ascheim, Robert, and Deborah Ascheim. *Heart Health: Your Questions Answered.* New York, NY: DK Publishing, 2009. Print.
This straightforward book includes sections on understanding your heart, risk factors, heart problems, and heart problem diagnosis.

➤ Caster, Shannon. *Heart* (Body Works Series). New York, NY: PowerKids Press, 2010. Print.
Using 3-D diagrams and detailed full-color photographs, the text explains what the heart does, what can go wrong, and how to keep the heart healthy and strong. This book is written for 8- to 12-year-olds.

➤ Cleveland Clinic, Eric Topol, and Michael Eisner. *Cleveland Clinic Heart Book: The Definitive Guide for the Entire Family from the Nation's Leading Heart Center.* New York, NY: Hyperion, 2000. Print.
This book translates medical information into a layperson's language and comprehension level. It demystifies diagnostic and treatment procedures with clear, detailed descriptions and illustrations.

➤ Curry, Don L. *How Does Your Heart Work?* (Rookie Read-About Health Series). New York, NY: Children's Press, 2004. Print.
Written for children from kindergarten through fourth grade, this is a good introduction to the dynamics of the heart.

➤ Editors of *The Johns Hopkins Medical Letter: Health After 50* and Simeon Margolis, eds. *The Johns Hopkins Complete Home Guide to Symptoms and Remedies.* New York, NY: Black Dog and Leventhal, 2004. Print.
This book covers a variety of heart problems. Information includes what each condition is, its symptoms, how it's diagnosed, the latest treatment options, prevention strategies, and when to call your doctor.

➤ Gersh, Bernard J. *The Mayo Clinic Heart Book.* New York, NY: William Morrow, 2000. Print.
Part One of this book explains "Your Heart and Blood Vessels." All of the sections are complemented by detailed, color and black-and-white illustrations and photographs, including a 16-page color atlas of the heart and circulatory system.

➤ Norris, Maggie, and Donna Rae Siegfried. *Anatomy and Physiology for Dummies.* New York, NY: Wiley, 2011. Print.
Written in plain English and well illustrated, this book offers a basic guide to anatomy and physiology, including that of the heart.

Brochures, Booklets, and Other Short Print Publications

> National Heart, Lung, and Blood Institute (NHLBI). *Your Guide to a Healthy Heart*. NIH Publication No. 06–5269. Washington, DC: U.S. Department of Health and Human Services, 2005. http://www.nhlbi.nih.gov/health/public/heart/other/your_guide/healthyheart.pdf; alternate path: http://www.nhlbi.nih.gov/health/, scroll to "NHLBI Health Publications," click on "List of All Publications," scroll to "Your Guide to Heart Disease Series," and then click on the downloadable booklet titled *Healthy Heart*.
>
> NHLBI is a division of National Institutes of Health from the U.S. Department of Health and Human Services. *Your Guide to a Healthy Heart* is a comprehensive and easy-to-read booklet with stories about heart patients.

Websites

> Cleveland Clinic (Cleveland, OH)—"Your Heart and Blood Vessels." http://my.clevelandclinic.org/heart/heart-blood-vessels/default.aspx; alternate path: http://my.clevelandclinic.org/, search for "heart blood vessels," and then click on the title "Your Heart and Blood Vessels."
>
> The Cleveland Clinic provides comprehensive, patient-friendly information on how the heart and the circulatory system work. Included in this section of associated webpages are excellent detailed drawings of all aspects of the heart.

> The Franklin Institute—"The Human Heart." http://www.fi.edu/learn/heart/; alternate path: http://www.fi.edu/, search for "human heart," and then click on the title "The Human Heart: An Online Exploration."
>
> This explanation of the human heart includes an illustrated overview of heart anatomy; information on the heart and the circulatory, respiratory, and excretory systems; a time line of milestones in cardiology; and a brief glossary.

Online Search Tips

- If you click on a link (e.g., a title) and nothing happens, try this: right-click on that link and then left-click on the option "Open in new window."
- If you experience problems with PDF documents, you can download the latest version of Adobe Reader for free at http://www.adobe.com/products/reader.html or by going to http://www.adobe.com/ and searching for "adobe reader."
- Adobe Flash Player, required to view most short videos, is available as a free download at http://get.adobe.com/flashplayer/; alternate path: http://www.adobe.com/, choose the "Download" tab on the menu bar and select the Adobe Flash Player link.

➢ InnerBody—"Cardiovascular System." http://www.innerbody.com/image/cardov
.html; alternate path: http://www.innerbody.com/, under "Begin by Exploring: A
Body System," click on "Cardiovascular System."
As the user moves a mouse over any graphic of the human body, identifiable
labels appear as well as links to the definitions.

➢ Khan Academy—"Circulatory System and the Heart: Introduction to the Circulatory System and the Heart." http://www.khanacademy.org/video/circulatory
-system-and-the-heart?playlist=Biology; alternate path: http://www.khanacademy
.org/, click on "Search Khan Academy" at the bottom of the screen, and then
search for and click on the title "Circulatory System and the Heart."
Salman Khan, creator of the nonprofit Khan Academy, sketches as he explains
the topic. Khan's mini lessons are all downloadable and free. According to the
website, "With a library of over 3,900 videos covering everything from arithmetic to physics, finance, and history and hundreds of skills to practice, we're on a
mission to help you learn what you want, when you want, at your own pace."
Click on "About" to learn more about this excellent site and maximize its use.
Khan has three degrees from the Massachusetts Institute of Technology and an
MBA from Harvard University.

➢ MayoClinic.com—"Heart Disease: Multimedia." http://www.mayoclinic.com/
health/heart-disease/DS01120/TAB=multimedia; alternate path: http://www
.mayoclinic.com/, search for "heart disease," then click on the table labeled
"Health Information," click on the reference titled "Heart Disease," click on the
tab called "Multimedia," and then scroll down to the "Videos" section where there
is a link to a video titled "Heart and Circulatory System: How They Work."

➢ Medscape Reference—"Heart Anatomy." http://emedicine.medscape.com/article/
905502-overview; alternate path: http://emedicine.medscape.com/, search for and
click on the title "Heart Anatomy."
Medscape is owned and operated by WebMD and is part of the WebMD Network. This comprehensive illustrated explanation of the anatomy of the heart
and cardiovascular system is a useful read. Accessing this webpage will likely
require registration with Medscape, which is free.

➢ MEDtropolis: Home of the Virtual Body—"Human Heart." http://www.medtropolis
.com/VBody.asp; alternate path: http://www.medtropolis.com/, click on the category "Virtual Body," select "English," and then click on "Human Heart."
This site, also available in Spanish, offers an illustration of heart parts and an
animation, as well as a narrated tour of the heart.

➢ *The Merck Manual Home Health Handbook for Patients and Caregivers*—"Biology
of the Heart and Blood Vessels." http://www.merckmanuals.com/home/heart_and
_blood_vessel_disorders/biology_of_the_heart_and_blood_vessels/heart.html;

alternate path: http://www.merckmanuals.com/home/, under "Sections," click on the arrow button to scroll through the options to find the section "Heart and Blood Vessel Disorders," which is divided into the following titles: "Heart," "Blood Vessels," and "Effects of Aging on the Heart and Blood Vessels."
This site, based on the well-known medical textbook by the same title, is provided free of charge as a public service. Also available for purchase through the website are a hardcover Spanish version and several other *Merck Manual* products as downloadable apps for mobile phones.

➤ National Geographic—"Heart." http://science.nationalgeographic.com/science/health-and-human-body/human-body/heart-article.html; alternate path: http://www.nationalgeographic.com/, click on "Science," then click on "Health and Human Body," under "Health and Human Body Topics" click on "Human Body," and under "Human Body Topics" click on "Heart."
From this user-friendly National Geographic website, watch the pumping action of a healthy heart.

➤ National Heart, Lung, and Blood Institute (NHLBI). http://www.nhlbi.nih .gov/.
NHLBI is a division of the National Institutes of Health, part of the U.S. Department of Health and Human Services.
  • "What Is the Heart?" http://www.nhlbi.nih.gov/health/health-topics/topics/hhw/; alternate path: http://www.nhlbi.nih.gov/, search for "how the heart works," and then click on the title "What Is the Heart?" For a brief overview, click on the titles to "Anatomy," "Contraction," "Circulation," "Electrical System," and "Heart Disease."
  • "Your Heart's Electrical System." http://www.nhlbi.nih.gov/health/health-topics/topics/hhw/electrical.html; alternate path: http://www.nhlbi.nih.gov/, search for "heart electrical system," and then click on the title "Your Heart's Electrical System." Click on the "Start" button for an animation demonstrating how the electrical system of the heart works.

➤ NOVA—"Map of the Human Heart." http://www.pbs.org/wgbh/nova/body/map -human-heart.html; alternate path: http://www.pbs.org/wgbh/nova/, search for and then click on the title "Map of the Human Heart."
This is a companion website to the NOVA program *Electric Heart* (http://www .pbs.org/wgbh/nova/eheart/). There is an automatically changing color graphic of a heart in cross-section and amazing heart facts.

➤ Science Museum of Minnesota—"Habits of the Heart." http://www.smm.org/heart/heart/top.html; alternate path: http://www.smm.org/, search for and then click on the title "Human Body Gallery," scroll down to and click on "Habits of the Heart," and then click on the "Heart" tab at top.

This website, from the Science Museum of Minnesota, compiles educational content about how the heart works, including interactive features and animations. It includes animations of heart valves at work and the flow of blood to and from the heart, as well as the options to view images of the heart with interactive labels and to find the heart with a virtual stethoscope.

➤ Texas Heart Institute, Heart Information Center—"Anatomy of the Cardiovascular System." http://www.texasheartinstitute.org/HIC/Anatomy/index.cfm; alternate path: http://www.texasheartinstitute.org/, scroll down under the heading "Heart Information Center," and click on the title "Anatomy."
This short and easy-to-read overview and illustration is labeled with various parts of the heart. The "Anatomy" section allows the user to click on the illustration of the human body for detailed views of the heart and cardiovascular system by clicking links on the heart, torso, head, arm, leg, and blood. A printer-friendly format is available.

➤ University of Minnesota—The Visible Heart Laboratory. http://www.vhlab.umn.edu/. See videos from inside functional human hearts and online tutorials on cardiac anatomy by clicking on such titles as "Atlas of Human Cardiac Anatomy." You can also select an area of the heart to learn more.

Webliography

Children's Hospital of Wisconsin. "The Heart's Electrical System." Accessed February 6, 2013. http://www.chw.org/display/PPF/DocID/24698/router.asp.

Johns Hopkins Medicine (Johns Hopkins University). "Coronary Artery Disease." Accessed February 6, 2013. http://www.hopkinsmedicine.org/healthlibrary/conditions/cardiovascular_diseases/coronary_heart_disease_85,P00207/.

MedlinePlus. "Conduction System of the Heart." Updated June 22, 2012. http://www.nlm.nih.gov/medlineplus/ency/imagepages/18052.htm.

———. "Heart Attack." Updated January 18, 2013. http://www.nlm.nih.gov/medlineplus/heartattack.html.

———. "Heart Valves—Superior View." Updated May 14, 2012. http://www.nlm.nih.gov/medlineplus/ency/imagepages/18093.htm.

National Heart, Lung, and Blood Institute. "Anatomy of the Heart." Updated November 17, 2011. http://www.nhlbi.nih.gov/health/health-topics/topics/hhw/anatomy.html.

———. "What Is the Heart?" Updated November 17, 2011. http://www.nhlbi.nih.gov/health/dci/Diseases/hhw/hhw_whatis.html.

———. "Your Heart's Electrical System." Updated November 17, 2011. http://www.nhlbi.nih.gov/health/health-topics/topics/hhw/electrical.html.

National Library of Medicine. "Cardiovascular Diseases." Accessed January 30, 2013. http://www.nlm.nih.gov/cgi/mesh/2012/MB_cgi?mode=&term=Cardiovascular+Diseases&field=entry#TreeC14.

Resurrection Health Care. "Cardiovascular Diseases." Accessed January 30, 2013. http://www.reshealth.org/yourhealth/healthinfo/default.cfm?pageID=P00225.

Texas Heart Institute, Health Information Center. "The Fetal Heart." Updated August 2012. http://www.texasheartinstitute.org/HIC/Topics/Cond/fetal_ht.cfm.

———. "Heart Anatomy." Updated August 2012. http://www.texasheartinstitute.org/HIC/Anatomy/anatomy2.cfm.

———. "The Heart Valves." Updated August 2012. http://www.texasheartinstitute.org/HIC/Anatomy/valves.cfm.

Chapter 3

Specific Heart and Cardiovascular Diseases and Disorders

This chapter provides information on specific conditions by section in alphabetical order. Each section includes its own Resources for Further Information section. Where available, this chapter also provides information regarding ongoing clinical trials, including those seeking patients who have specific heart conditions. For more information on clinical trials, *see* CHAPTER 5 as above.

Arrhythmias (Including Atrial Fibrillation, Bradycardia, Tachycardia)

An arrhythmia is a condition in which the heart does not beat normally. A healthy heart beats in a pattern in which its chambers are compressed in sequence to move blood through the heart and to the lungs and body. A normal heartbeat will produce an electrical signal (waveform) that has a small hump then a large spike, ending with another small hump over about 0.8 seconds. (To view a normal electrocardiograph and the standard setup for an EKG, go to http://www.nhlbi.nih.gov/health/health-topics/topics/ekg/during.html.) This waveform is often called the QRS waveform, the PQRST waveform, or the complex waveform. It is measured with an electrocardiograph that produces an electrocardiogram (*see also* CHAPTER 5: ELECTROCARDIOGRAPHY). Sometimes a patient may wear a Holter monitor (a small recording electrocardiograph) for 12 or 24 hours to catch irregularities that may infrequently occur.

To learn more, visit the **National Heart, Lung, and Blood Institute** of the National Institutes of Health at http://www.nhlbi.nih.gov/health/health-topics/topics/holt/while.html (alternate path: http://www.nhlbi.nih.gov/, search for "using a holter or event monitor" and then click on the title). The article "What to Expect While Using a Holter or Event Monitor" includes an illustration of a Holter monitor. Part A of the illustration shows how a Holter or event monitor attaches to a patient. In the example, the monitor is clipped to the patient's belt and electrodes are attached to his chest. Part B shows an electrocardiogram strip, which maps the data output from the Holter or event monitor.

The heartbeat waveform reflects the type of arrhythmia. The heart may beat too fast (tachycardia), too slow (bradycardia), or irregularly (two common types of the latter are atrial fibrillation and atrial flutter). Other arrhythmias cause the heart to contract early, late, or out of sequence. The heart may momentarily stop beating, speed up, slow down, or add an extra beat. Many of these irregularities are caused by problems with the nervous (electrical) system of the heart. They can also be brought on by strong emotion or exercise. Many arrhythmias (e.g., fibrillation, increasing tachycardia) can be life threatening.

Palpitations are the feelings of the heart skipping a beat, fluttering, or beating too hard or too fast. Palpitations can be harmless when caused by such factors as strong emotions, caffeine, exercise, or some medicines. However, they may also indicate a possible arrhythmia and should be checked by a physician. *See also* CHAPTER 5: PACEMAKER OR DEFIBRILLATOR IMPLANTATION.

Resources for Further Information on Arrhythmias

Books

➤ Cohen, Todd J. *A Patient's Guide to Heart Rhythm Problems*. Baltimore, MD: Johns Hopkins University Press, 2010. Print.

Written for patients, this book contains sections on heart rhythm problems, sudden cardiac arrest, syncope, tests, procedures and medications for treating heart problems, devices for treating heart problems, the diseased heart, prevention and resuscitation, follow-up, and patient care.

➤ Kastor, John A. *You and Your Arrhythmia: A Guide to Heart Rhythm Problems for Patients and Their Families*. Sudbury, MA: Jones and Bartlett, 2006. Print.

Cardiac arrhythmias are extremely common and range in severity from benign to sudden, life-threatening emergencies. Some patients may be acutely conscious while others may be unaware of the problem. This book includes case histories with simple explanations to provide patients and their families with a better understanding of heart rhythm disorders, diagnosis, treatment, and long-term care.

Brochures, Booklets, and Other Short Print Publications

➤ American Heart Association (AHA)—Educational brochures on arrhythmia. http://www.heart.org/HEARTORG/General/Order-American-Heart-Association-Educational-Brochures_UCM_312777_Article.jsp; alternate path: http://www.heart.org/, search for "educational brochures," then click on the title "Order American Heart Association Educational Brochures," and then click on the topic "Arrhythmia."

Several brochures published by AHA are available, including "Living with Your Pacemaker," "Innocent Heart Murmurs," "Your Child's Abnormal Heart Rhythm," and "Living with Atrial Fibrillation." Individuals can request brochures in English or Spanish. These brochures can be ordered by filling in an online form online. Note that a maximum of one packet and two brochures per household can be ordered at no cost.

➢ Arrhythmia Alliance (AA): The Heart Rhythm Charity (UK)—Arrhythmia patient information booklets in PDF format. http://www.heartrhythmcharity.org .uk/www/649/0/Available_information_booklets/; alternate path: http://www .heartrhythmcharity.org/, click on the menu heading "Patients," and then under the heading "Downloads" click on "Available Information Booklets."
AA, endorsed by the United Kingdom's National Health Service, offers excellent free booklets on various topics on arrhythmia for adults and children. Click on any title listed to view and download. Also in this same "Downloads" section, there are several useful checklists composed of questions for patients to use when they are preparing for a visit to the doctor. Checklists deal with palpitations, blackouts, heart rhythm, and atrial fibrillation.

➢ Atrial Fibrillation Association (AFA) (Australia)—Atrial fibrillation (AF) fact sheets and information booklets. http://www.atrialfibrillation-au.org/publications/ topic-sheets.html; alternate path: http://www.atrialfibrillation-au.org/, scroll to "Publications," click on "Read/Download Fact Sheets," and then click on "Read More" to view any of the fact sheet topics in PDF format.
These fact sheets, published by AFA, summarize key topics related to AF and are quick and easy to download. Topics include AF, amiodarone, aspirin, atrial flutter, beta-blockers, blood thinning, cardioversion, digoxin, ectopic heart beats, medical cardioversion, ongoing trials, treatment, pace and ablate, rate-limiting calcium channel blockers, rate versus rhythm management, warfarin, warfarin and diet, and warfarin and other medications. Also on the homepage (http:// www.atrialfibrillation-au.org/), scroll to "Publications" and click on "Read/ Download Booklets." Click on "Download and Print" to view individual AF booklets in PDF format. AFA produces a range of patient information booklets, AF checklists, and pamphlets. All materials have been approved by an AF medical executive committee and endorsed by the Department of Health.

➢ HeartHub for Patients—"Pacemaker Identification—Wallet Card." http://www .heart.org/idc/groups/heart-public/@wcm/@hcm/documents/downloadable/ ucm_305047.pdf; alternate path: http://www.hearthub.org/, scroll to the section titled "Health Centers," click on the title "Arrhythmia," and then scroll down to click on the topic "Pacemaker ID Card."
HeartHub, a division of the American Heart Association (AHA) and a patient-supported website on cardiac disease and stroke, has a printable pacemaker identification card. Users can print the blank card template, complete the required

information, and carry it with them to help be identified as wearing a pacemaker in case of emergency.

➤ National Prescribing Centre (NPC) (UK)—"Atrial Fibrillation (AF) Patient Decision Aid: Antithrombotic Therapy." http://www.npc.nhs.uk/therapeutics/cardio/atrial/resources/pda_af.pdf; alternate path: http://www.npci.org.uk/, search for "atrial fibrillation patient decision aid AND antithrombotic therapy," click on the title "Atrial Fibrillation Patient Decision Aid," and then click to view and download this article.

NPC is produced by the National Institute for Health and Clinical Excellence (NICE). This 2009 AF decision aid is designed to help patients determine the risk of antithrombotic therapy.

➤ Torpy, Janet M., Cassio Lynm (illus.), and Richard M. Glass (ed.). 2010. "JAMA Patient Page—Atrial Fibrillation," *JAMA* 303(4): 380. http://jama.jamanetwork.com/article.aspx?articleid=185278; alternate path: http://jama.ama-assn.org/, search for "torpy AND jama patient page AND atrial fibrillation AND 2010," and then click on either the title or the PDF option.

Published in the *Journal of the American Medical Association*, Torpy developed a patient education article that explains atrial fibrillation, its symptoms, and its treatment in one straightforward page.

Websites

➤ Aetna InteliHealth. http://www.intelihealth.com/.

Aetna InteliHealth, a subsidiary of Aetna, is reviewed by the faculty of Harvard Medical School and the University College of Dental Medicine. According to its website, "Aetna InteliHealth maintains absolute editorial independence. That means that Aetna InteliHealth makes decisions about the information on our site free of outside influence." Under "Healthy Lifestyle," Aetna InteliHealth also offers free health-related e-mail subscriptions. Also at http://www.intelihealth.com/, search for "bradycardia" to find additional information.

  • "Atrial Fibrillation (AF)." http://www.intelihealth.com/IH/ihtIH/WSIHW000/8059/23693/213152.html?d=dmtHealthAZ; alternate path: http://www.intelihealth.com/, search for and then click on the title "Atrial Fibrillation."

  This webpage provides sections on AF including definitions, symptoms, diagnosis, expected duration, prevention, treatment, when to call a professional, and prognosis.

  • "Cardiac Arrhythmias." http://www.intelihealth.com/IH/ihtIH/WSIHW000/9339/23921.html; alternate path: http://www.intelihealth.com/, search for "arrhythmia," and then click on the title "Cardiac Arrhythmias."

This webpage provides an overview of cardiac arrhythmia including symptoms, diagnosis, expected duration, prevention, treatment, when to call a professional, prognosis, and additional information.

➤ American Heart Association (AHA)—"Arrhythmia." http://www.heart.org/ HEARTORG/Conditions/Arrhythmia/Arrhythmia_UCM_002013_SubHomePage .jsp; alternate path: http://www.heart.org/, search for "arrhythmia," and then click on the title "Visit Our Arrhythmia Website."

AHA provides details on arrhythmia in sections, including information about arrhythmia, why arrhythmia matters, symptoms, diagnosis and monitoring, prevention and treatment, and arrhythmia tools and resources. Scroll to the section titled "Printable Arrhythmia Information Sheets" for downloadable brochures, such as "What Is Arrhythmia?," "What Is Atrial Fibrillation?," and "What Is an Implantable Cardioverter Defibrillator (ICD)?" AHA also offers a free e-mail subscription to *Heart-Health E-News*.

➤ Arrhythmia Alliance (AA): The Heart Rhythm Charity (UK)—"What Is an Arrhythmia?" http://www.heartrhythmcharity.org.uk/www/44/0/Arrhythmia _basics/; alternate path: http://www.heartrhythmcharity.org/, click on the "Patients" menu heading, then under "About Arrhythmias," click on "Arrhythmia Basics" for the main article, or choose another link ("Types of Arrhythmia," "Info for Kids," or "FAQs").

AA, endorsed by UK's National Health Service, offers several topics on arrhythmia written for the patient, including symptoms, diagnosis, and treatment. As noted, the main heading "About Arrhythmias" provides additional links. Additional sections to explore include diagnostic tools, living with arrhythmia, patient groups, patient stories, news and events, and international patient information. Register and sign up for a free monthly e-bulletin and "newsletters and other communications which highlight current topics on cardiac arrhythmias in the national and international forums. Find out about up and coming events and our current projects and campaigns, including information about our affiliate organisations and groups."

➤ Brigham and Women's Hospital (BWH) (Boston, MA). http://www.brigham andwomens.org/.

To possibly participate in a clinical trial at Brigham and Women's Hospital Cardiovascular Center, from the homepage, click on the heading "Research," then on the category "Clinical Trials," and then on the title "Search Open Studies by Therapeutic Area." Scroll down the list to select topics, such as "Heart Disease," "High Blood Pressure," "Stroke," and "Vascular Disorders." Under the heading "Patients and Visitors," click on "Find a Doctor" and select the clinical specialty in the drop-down Search box. Click on the names of physicians or specialists to view their profiles (e.g., specialty, medical board certification, education).

- "Arrhythmias."   http://healthlibrary.brighamandwomens.org/Health Centers/Heart/Conditions/Arrhythmias/; alternate path: http://www.brigham andwomens.org/, scroll under the heading "Health Information" to the category titled "Health Information Center," and click on the title "Heart Information Center." Scroll down and click on the category "Heart Conditions and Diseases," and then click on "Arrhythmias."
BWH's Arrhythmias webpage discusses numerous topics, including definitions, atrial fibrillation, why doctors require EKGs (electrocardiograms), overview of pacemakers and implantable cardioverter defibrillators (ICDs), living with a pacemaker or ICD, and FAQs about pacemakers and ICDs. Excellent videos on cardiac arrhythmia are available.
- "Cardiac Arrhythmia Service: Webcasts and Videos." http://www.brigham andwomens.org/Departments_and_Services/medicine/services/cvcenter/ arrhythmia/arrhythmiawebcasts.aspx?sub=2; alternate path: http://www .brighamandwomens.org/, scroll under the heading "Departments and Services" to the category titled "Centers of Excellence," click on the title "Cardiovascular," under the heading "Cardiovascular Medicine" scroll down and click on the category "Cardiac Arrhythmia Service," and then under the category "For Patients" click on title "Arrhythmia Webcasts and Videos." BWH's website offers numerous webcasts and videos on various arrhythmia topics.

➤ British Heart Foundation (BHF). http://www.bhf.org.uk/.
From the homepage, you can find the following and other related resources through a title search. Also, click on the "Community: Share Experiences with Others" heading to engage with the BHF online community where you can share your own story and read those of others.
- "Abnormal Heart Rhythms." http://www.bhf.org.uk/heart-health/conditions/ abnormal-heart-rhythms.aspx. The BHF website describes abnormal heart rhythms and provides discussion with sections titled "My Heart Rate Sometimes Feels Different. Is This a Problem?" and "My Heart Seems to Beat Differently. What Does This Mean?"
- "Atrial Fibrillation." http://www.bhf.org.uk/heart-health/conditions/atrial -fibrillation.aspx. The BHF website describes AF, its causes and symptoms, how to detect AF, and complications. Scroll down to the section titled "What Should You Do If Your Pulse Is Irregular?" to view a video that demonstrates how to properly check your pulse. In this section, there are also free, downloadable audio examples of both regular pulse rhythm and irregular pulse rhythm.

➤ CardioSmart—"Atrial Fibrillation (AF)." https://www.cardiosmart.org/Heart -Conditions/Atrial-Fibrillation; alternate path: https://www.cardiosmart.org/, search for and then click on the title "Atrial Fibrillation."

CardioSmart's webpage on AF contains an introduction, questions to ask your cardiologist, news, an e-mail sign-up for CardioSmart news updates, a video library (e.g., watch how an echocardiogram is performed), and a link to learn more about AF (with sections such as basic facts, what is AF, causes and risk factors, tests and diagnosis, possible complications, prevention, key facts, by the numbers, symptoms, treatment, living with afib, and AF and stroke). Also, under the heading "Connect with Others" is a link to "Personal Stories." According to the American College of Cardiology (ACC), "CardioSmart is the patient education and support program launched by the [ACC]. Our mission is to engage, inform, and empower patients to better prepare them for participation in their own care."

➢ CenterWatch—Clinical trials listing service. http://www.centerwatch.com/.
This CenterWatch clinical trials listing service lists trials currently looking for volunteers to enroll in medical studies. Click on the "Clinical Trials" heading and search by location, medical condition, or therapeutic area. To search by location, click on your state (or country) and click on a city near you to find information on each available clinical trial. Check back with this website often for new studies. Sign up for a free e-mail service that sends notice of new clinical trials.
  • "Arrhythmia Clinical Trials." http://www.centerwatch.com/clinical-trials/listings/studylist.aspx?CatID=515.
  • "Atrial Fibrillation Clinical Trials." http://www.centerwatch.com/clinical-trials/listings/studylist.aspx?CatID=243.
  • "Atrial Flutter Clinical Trials." http://www.centerwatch.com/clinical-trials/listings/studylist.aspx?CatID=587.
Alternate path: http://www.centerwatch.com/, under the category "Patient Resources" click on "Search Clinical Trials," where you can search by medical condition. Click on the medical condition's first letter (e.g., "A"), and then click on the specific term (e.g., "Arrhythmia"). The "Search Clinical Trials" page also allows searching by location and therapeutic area. Other types of arrhythmia trials might be available, such as those for bradycardia and tachycardia. Search on those medical conditions under the "Search Clinical Trials" page.

➢ Cleveland Clinic (Cleveland, OH)—"Arrhythmias (Abnormal Heart Rhythms)." http://my.clevelandclinic.org/heart/disorders/electric/arrhythmia.aspx; alternate path: http://my.clevelandclinic.org/, under the category "Institutes and Services" click on "Heart and Vascular," then click on "Homepage," then click on the category "Diseases and Conditions," and then click on the title "Abnormal Heart Rhythms."
The Cleveland Clinic provides comprehensive patient-friendly information on abnormal heart rhythms, including definitions, types, causes, heart rhythms on

electrocardiograms, the heart's electrical system, pulse, treatments, diagnostic tests, and finding a doctor who treats arrhythmias. The Cleveland Clinic also offers a link to "Chat Online with a Heart and Vascular Nurse." To participate in a clinical trial, if available in your cardiac condition, at the Cleveland Clinic Heart Center, visit http://my.clevelandclinic.org/heart/research/clinicalresearch.aspx; alternate path: http://my.clevelandclinic.org/, under the category "Institutes and Services" click on "Heart and Vascular," then click on "Homepage," then click on the category "Research and Innovations," and then choose "Clinical Research." Check out Cleveland Clinic's Facebook and Twitter accounts for sharing experiences.

➤ ClinicalTrials.gov. http://clinicaltrials.gov/.
ClinicalTrials.gov, a service of the U.S. National Institutes of Health, lists ongoing and currently enrolling clinical trials. To find clinical trials from the homepage, search for the condition by name (e.g., "arrhythmia"), which will generate a list of possibly hundreds or thousands of studies. To narrow the results, click on "Modify This Search" and select fields to limit your results, such as Recruitment (e.g., "Open Studies"); Locations (e.g., select your state); and Age Group, and then click on the "Search" button. Click on the title of each trial name for additional information, such as purpose of study, study design and type, detailed description, outcome measures, eligibility (age, gender, criteria for participating), study start date, estimated study completion date, and sponsor. Check often for new studies.
  • Arrhythmia clinical trials. http://clinicaltrials.gov/ct2/results/refine?term=Arrhythmia.
  • Atrial fibrillation clinical trials. http://clinicaltrials.gov/ct2/results/refine?term=atrial+fibrillation.
  • Atrial flutter clinical trials. http://clinicaltrials.gov/ct2/results/refine?term=atrial+flutter.
  • Brachycardia clinical trials. http://clinicaltrials.gov/ct2/results/refine?term=brachycardia.
  • Tachycardia clinical trials. http://clinicaltrials.gov/ct2/results/refine?term=tachycardia.
➤ eMedicineHealth—"Atrial Fibrillation (A Fib)." http://www.emedicinehealth.com/atrial_fibrillation/article_em.htm; alternate path: http://www.emedicinehealth.com/, search for and then click on the title "Atrial Fibrillation."
A division of WebMD, eMedicineHealth offers a comprehensive article on AF with discussions on causes, diagnosis, treatment prevention, follow-ups, outlook, and support groups. There are also slides on AF.
➤ Genetics Home Reference—"Familial Atrial Fibrillation." http://ghr.nlm.nih.gov/condition/familial-atrial-fibrillation; alternate path: http://ghr.nlm.nih.gov/, search for and then click on the title "Familial Atrial Fibrillation."

Genetics Home Reference is a division of National Institutes of Health (NIH). This webpage discusses an inherited condition that disrupts the heart's normal rhythm. Links to references and additional information are available.

> Heart Rhythm Society—"Heart Diseases and Disorders." http://www.hrsonline .org/Patient-Resources/Heart-Diseases-Disorders#axzz2bI5O46JQ; alternate path: http://www.hrsonline.org/, click on the title "Patient Resources" and then choose "Heart Diseases and Disorders."
This website provides accurate and clear information about cardiac arrhythmia. Start with links to heart rhythm disorders, symptoms and diagnosis, treatments, risk factors, and prevention. Other sections included are common heart rhythm disorders, atrial fibrillation, heart block, sudden cardiac arrest, long QT syndrome, atrial flutter, sick sinus syndrome, sinus tachycardia, supraventricular tachycardia, ventricular tachycardia, and ventricular fibrillation.

> Hospital of the University of Pennsylvania (HUP) (Philadelphia, PA)—"Cardiac Arrhythmia Program." http://www.pennmedicine.org/heart/patient/clinical -services/cardiac-arrythmia/; alternate path: http://www.pennmedicine.org/, click on the "Departments and Services" icon, then scroll down and click on "Cardiology and Cardiac Surgery," and then scroll down under the heading "Clinical Services" and click on "Cardiac Arrhythmia."
At its Penn Heart and Vascular Center website, HUP offers links in the Cardiac Arrhythmia Program that include an "Overview" (what are arrhythmias and treatment options); the "Team," with links to each physician and specialist (with profiles, e.g., specialty, medical board certification, education); "Clinical Trials"; "The Penn Difference" (program described, patient experiences, unique capabilities and expertise, and hospital highlights); "Physician Interviews" (videos); and "Quality/Outcomes." Click on each treatment option for details and charts. A 54-page *Penn Heart and Vascular 2011 Clinical Activity Report* is available for download; this report is a "summary of surgical, medical and interventional outcomes, as well as clinical research activity and patient volumes." You can also subscribe to the Penn Heart newsletter. To possibly participate in a clinical trial at Penn Cardiovascular Institute, if available, visit http://www.med.upenn.edu/cvi/clinical _trials.shtml (on the homepage, click on the "Clinical Trials" icon [or click the heading "Research"]), and then under the category "Clinical Trials" click on "Penn Cardiovascular Institute." Scroll down the list of "Cardiovascular Clinical Trials."

> Insidermedicine. http://www.insidermedicine.com/.
The physician-led Insidermedicine Project "allows patients, doctors and medical students to keep up on the latest medical information by watching" videos created each weekday by their team of medical experts, allowing anyone to receive daily evidence-based health and medical updates. Previously created videos are available and free to view or download. Under the heading

"Programs," click the category "By Disease or Symptom," scroll through the list of conditions, and click on a heart or cardiovascular topic. Also under the heading "Programs," click on "Universities and Hospitals" for links to "University and Hospital News Segments." From the homepage, you can search for videos by title, or you can search by topic (e.g., atrial fibrillation) to find other related videos.

- "If I Had—Atrial Fibrillation" (AF) (Video). http://www.insidermedicine .com/archives/If_I_Had_Atrial_Fibrillation_Dr_John_L_Sapp_MD_FRCPC _Dalhousie_University_3185.aspx. In this video a cardiologist speaks very clearly, providing demonstrations about what AF is, its symptoms, what kind of doctors to see, what those doctors look for, and treatment options.
- "Low-Risk Lifestyle Reduces Risk of Sudden Cardiac Death in Women" (Video). http://www.insidermedicine.com/archives/Low_Risk_Lifestyle _Reduces_Risk_of_Sudden_Cardiac_Death_in_Women_Video_5368.aspx. In this video, a medical specialist speaks in patient-friendly language and provides demonstrations about recommendations for managing cardiac arrest. Previously created videos on this website are free to view or download. Several other videos on sudden cardiac death are available.

➢ Johns Hopkins Hospital (Baltimore, MD). http://www.hopkinsmedicine.org/. The Johns Hopkins Heart and Vascular Institute webpage (http://www .hopkinsmedicine.org/heart_vascular_institute/) provides detailed information on a variety of conditions, treatments, and services. It also lists links to physicians and specialists (with profiles, e.g., specialty, medical board certification, education). Click on the heading "Clinical Trials" to find links to current trials in various heart and cardiovascular conditions. Alternate path: You can find any of the following resources by returning to the homepage, searching for the topic by name, and then clicking on the corresponding title in the results list.

- "Cardiac Arrhythmias." http://www.hopkinsmedicine.org/heart_vascular _institute/conditions_treatments/conditions/arryhthmias.html and http:// www.hopkinsmedicine.org/healthlibrary/conditions/adult/cardiovascular _diseases/arrhythmias_85,P00195/. This webpage on cardiac arrhythmias discusses what arrhythmia is, types of arrhythmia, when to call an ambulance, symptoms, causes, prevention, diagnosis, and treatment.
- "Electrophysiology and Arrhythmia Service." http://www.hopkinsmedicine.org/ heart_vascular_institute/clinical_services/specialty_areas/electrophysiology .html. This webpage provides patient-friendly, current information on the Johns Hopkins Arrhythmia Services' history and goals, diagnoses, and treatments. Included are links for more details on diagnostic tests. View a video on atrial fibrillation and a free downloadable guide (PDF) on arrhythmia.

➢ KidsHealth.org. http://www.kidshealth.org/.

The Nemours Center for Children's Health Media provides current information on conditions afflicting children, written for both children and parents. Information is available in English and Spanish. Click on the "Listen" button to hear the text read aloud.

- *For Children and Teens:* "Getting an EKG (Electrocardiogram)." http://kidshealth.org/teen/diseases_conditions/heart/video_ekg.html#cat20160; alternate path: http://www.kidshealth.org/, click on "Teens Site," scroll down and click on "Diseases and Conditions," scroll down and click on "Heart and Cardiovascular System," and then click on the title "EKG." To alleviate your child's worries, click on the "Play Video" button and watch this two-minute video demonstration of a child undergoing an EKG.

- *For Parents:* "Arrhythmias." http://kidshealth.org/parent/medical/heart/arrhythmias.html#cat141; alternate path: http://www.kidshealth.org/, click on "Parents Site," then click on "Diseases and Conditions," then scroll down and click on "Heart and Blood Vessels," and then click on the title "Arrhythmias." Topics discussed on this webpage include what arrhythmias are, causes, signs and symptoms, what a normal heart rate is, types of arrhythmias, diagnosis, treatment, and when to call the doctor. Information is available in English and Spanish. Click on the "Listen" button to hear the text read aloud.

- *For Teens:* "Arrhythmias." http://kidshealth.org/teen/diseases_conditions/heart/arrhythmias.html#cat20160; alternate path: http://www.kidshealth.org/, click on "Teens Site," then click on "Diseases and Conditions," then scroll down and click on "Heart and Cardiovascular System," and then click on the title "Arrhythmias." Topics discussed on this webpage include what arrhythmias are, causes, signs and symptoms, what a normal heart rate is, types of arrhythmias, diagnosis, treatment, and when to call the doctor. Information is available in English and Spanish. Click on the "Listen" button to hear the text read aloud.

➢ Massachusetts General Hospital (MGH) (Boston, MA). http://www.massgeneral.org/.

At each of the following MGH webpages are links to comprehensive information in several categories: "Our Approach" includes an overview of the conditions, treatments, and procedures as well as links to each medical expert (with profile, e.g., specialty, medical board certification, education). "About This Program" describes the quality and benefits of the program as well as MGH's commitment. "Conditions and Diseases" offers links to detailed information on specific and related conditions. "Support and Wellness" offers patient guides. "Clinical Trials" links to MGH trials and research studies currently seeking participants. "News and Events" includes the latest information on the conditions. "Multimedia" offers video demonstrations.

- "Atrial Fibrillation." http://www.massgeneral.org/heartcenter/services/ treatmentprograms.aspx?id=1565; alternate path: http://www.massgeneral .org/, click on "Centers and Services," click on "View All Departments and Services," click on "Heart Center," click on the heading "Treatments and Services," and then click on "Atrial Fibrillation Program."
- "Cardiac Arrhythmia Service." http://www.massgeneral.org/heartcenter/ services/treatmentprograms.aspx?id=1001; alternate path: http://www .massgeneral.org/, click on "Centers and Services," click on "View All Departments and Services," click on "Heart Center," click on the heading "Treatments and Services," and then click on "Cardiac Arrhythmia Service."

➤ Mayo Clinic (Rochester, MN)—"Heart Arrhythmias." http://www.mayoclinic.com/ health/heart-arrhythmias/DS00290; alternate path: http://www.mayoclinic.com/, search for "arrhythmia," and then click on the title "Heart Arrhythmias— MayoClinic.com."

Written for patients, the information presented on this webpage includes definitions, symptoms, causes, risk factors, complications, preparing for appointments, tests and diagnosis, treatments and drugs, lifestyle, home remedies, and news. There is also a more comprehensive section titled "In-Depth" on some of these topics. To participate in a clinical trial, if available in your cardiology condition, at the Mayo Clinic Heart, Lung, and Blood Research Center, go to http:// clinicaltrials.mayo.edu/category.cfm?theme_id=6 (or return to the Mayo Clinic homepage, click on the heading "Research," and under the category "Find Clinical Trials" scroll down and click on the title "Heart, Lung, and Blood"). For Patient Services in the various cardiology programs, go to http://www.mayoclinic .org/cardiac-surgery/, http://www.mayoclinic.org/cardiovascular-disease/, or http://www.mayoclinic.org/vascular-and-endovascular-surgery/; alternate path: http://www.mayoclinic.org/, for each topic: search for "cardiac surgery" and click on "Cardiac Surgery at Mayo Clinic," then search for "cardiovascular diseases" and click on "Cardiovascular Diseases at Mayo Clinic," then search for "vascular and endovascular surgery" and click on "Vascular and Endovascular Surgery at Mayo Clinic." For "Cardiac Surgery" and "Cardiovascular Diseases," in the "Overview" section, scroll down, select a state, and then click on the tab "Doctors" to view links to each medical expert (with profile, e.g., specialty, medical board certification, education). For "Vascular and Endovascular Surgery," click on the "Doctors" tab.

➤ MedicineNet. http://www.medicinenet.com/.

MedicineNet.com is owned and operated by WebMD and part of the WebMD Network. According to its website, MedicineNet "provides easy-to-read, in-depth, authoritative medical information for consumers via its user-friendly, interactive website." The medical information is written and edited by a nationally recognized group of more than 70 U.S. board-certified physicians. The website contains a "Symptom Checker" listed in alphabetical order as a guide to "pinpoint your pain." Its homepage links to "Health News of the Week." You can also sign up to receive a health newsletter.

- "Heart Disease and Abnormal Heart Rhythm (Arrhythmia)." http://www .medicinenet.com/arrhythmia_irregular_heartbeat/article.htm; alternate path: http://www.medicinenet.com/, click on the major topic "Diseases and Conditions," click on "Conditions A–Z," then click on "A," and then scroll down to "Arrhythmia (Irregular Heartbeat)." In-depth information on abnormal heart rhythm (arrhythmia) includes causes, types of arrhythmia, diagnosis, treatment options, patient discussions, and finding a local cardiologist.

- "Heart Disease: Treating Arrhythmias with Ablation." http://www .medicinenet.com/ablation_therapy_for_arrhythmias/article.htm; alternate path: http://www.medicinenet.com/, click on the major topic "Diseases and Conditions," click on "Conditions A–Z," then click on "A," and then scroll down to "Arrhythmia Treatment (Ablation Therapy for Arrhythmias)." In-depth information on ablation therapy for arrhythmias is provided, including an introduction to treating arrhythmias with ablation, why ablation therapy might be needed, how to prepare for catheter ablation, what to expect during catheter ablation, what happens after catheter ablation, how to care for the wound site, what to expect during surgical ablation, what happens after nonsurgical catheter ablation, and finding a local cardiologist.

➤ MedlinePlus—"Arrhythmia (Irregular Heartbeat)." http://www.nlm.nih.gov/ medlineplus/arrhythmia.html; alternate path: http://www.nlm.nih.gov/, under "Databases" click on "MedlinePlus," then click on "Health Topics," then click on "A," scroll down and click on "Arrhythmia."
MedlinePlus is a component of the National Institutes of Health (NIH), produced by the National Library of Medicine (NLM), and is updated regularly. The MedlinePlus webpage on arrhythmia offers extensive linked information covering overviews, news, diagnosis/symptoms, treatment, prevention/screening, disease management, specific conditions, related issues, anatomy/physiology, financial issues, clinical trials, genetics, research, journal articles, dictionaries/glossaries, organizations, and specific sections focusing on children, teenagers, and women. Patient handouts are also available. This webpage also includes a multimedia section containing health check tools, tutorials, and videos.

➤ *The Merck Manual Home Health Handbook for Patients and Caregivers*—"Overview of Abnormal Heart Rhythms." http://www.merckmanuals.com/home/heart_and

_blood_vessel_disorders/abnormal_heart_rhythms/overview_of_abnormal_heart
_rhythms.html; alternate path: http://www.merckmanuals.com/home/, at left under
"Sections," click on "All" next to the navigation arrows for a full list, then click on the
section "Heart and Blood Vessel Disorders," and then scroll down to the section
titled "Abnormal Heart Rhythms."

This section on abnormal heart rhythms is divided into several titles, including
"Overview of Abnormal Heart Rhythms," "Atrial Premature Beats," and "Atrial
Fibrillation and Atrial Flutter." This section is based on a well-known medical
textbook titled *The Merck Manual Home Health Handbook for Patients and Caregivers* and extensively covers the topic of abnormal heart rhythms. A hardcover
print version of this textbook in Spanish can be purchased. It is also currently
available for purchase as a downloadable app for smartphones.

➢ National Heart, Lung, and Blood Institute (NHLBI)—"What Is an Arrhythmia?"
http://www.nhlbi.nih.gov/health/dci/Diseases/arr/arr_whatis.html; alternate
path: http://www.nhlbi.nih.gov/, search for "arrhythmia," and then click on the
title "What Is an Arrhythmia?"

NHLBI, a division of the National Institutes of Health from the U.S. Department
of Health and Human Services, provides additional information on arrhythmia,
such as what is arrhythmia, types of arrhythmia, other names, causes, risk factors, signs and symptoms, diagnosis, treatments, living with arrhythmia, clinical
trials, key points, and additional information about arrhythmias.

➢ New York–Presbyterian (NYP) University Hospital of Columbia and Cornell
(New York, NY). http://nyp.org/.

Under the heading "Find a Physician" you can search for physicians and specialists by specialty or name to view their profiles (e.g., specialty, medical board certification, education). Under the heading "Hospital News" are links to detailed
articles explaining recent studies. To possibly participate in a clinical trial at the
Cardiology Center, if one is available, go to the NYP homepage (http://nyp.org/)
and click at the top of the screen on the heading "Research and Clinical Trials,"
then click on the category "Clinical Trials at New York–Presbyterian/Weill Cornell Medical College," and then click on "Heart and Blood Diseases."

    • "Cardiology: Catheter Ablation for Cardiac Arrhythmias." http://nyp.org/
      services/cardiology/catheter-ablation.html; alternate path: http://nyp.org/,
      search for "catheter ablation for cardiac arrhythmias" and then click on the
      title "Ablation Cardiac Procedure, Catheter Ablation, Cardiac." The NYP
      University Hospital of Columbia and Cornell website provides patient-
      friendly information on catheter ablation for cardiac arrhythmias and gives
      an overview on catheter ablation and cardiac arrhythmia. For expanded
      information, there are several links within the text including information
      on CT scans, MRI, and transmission of electrical impulses in the heart,

arrhythmia, congestive heart failure, stroke, and sudden cardiac death. On the homepage (http://nyp.org/), search for "cardiac arrhythmias" and click on the title "Cardiac Arrhythmias: Investigating Mechanisms of Action" for additional descriptions.

- "Cardiology: Implantable Converter Defibrillators and Biventricular Pacing." http://nyp.org/services/cardiology/icd-pacing.html; alternate path: http://nyp.org/, search for and then click on the title "Implantable Converter Defibrillators and Biventricular Pacing." NYP University Hospital of Columbia and Cornell provides patient-friendly information on implantable converter defibrillators (ICDs), biventricular pacing, and cardiac resynchronization therapy. For expanded information, there are several links within the text to ICDs and arrhythmias; discussions on the electrical signals that makes the heart beat; congestive heart failure; and biventricular pacemakers. Under the heading "Find a Specialist" is a link to physicians and specialists (with profiles, e.g., specialty, medical board certification, education) in clinical cardiac electrophysiology at NYP University Hospital of Columbia and Cornell. Under the heading "Related Links" are links to other NYU–Presbyterian cardiology and cardiothoracic surgery services.

- "Interactive Media Library." http://nyp.org/media/index.html; alternate path: http://nyp.org/, click on the icon with the text "Explore the Interactive Media Library." NYP University Hospital of Columbia and Cornell Human Atlas media player includes excellent short videos, text, models, and slides. To view videos, click on "Or Click Here for a Complete Listing of Topics," and then scroll down in and click on "Atrial Fibrillation" or "Bradycardia" or "Ventricular Tachycardia." Also under the heading "Interactive Animations" click on "Atrial Fibrillation" for an audio slide presentation, and then click on "Catheter Ablation."

- "Perelman Heart Institute—Arrhythmias" (Videos). http://nypheart.org/perelman/; alternate path: http://nyp.org/, search for "Ronald O. Perelman Heart Institute," click on the name in the results, scroll down to "Related Links," and then click again on the name. For patients, the Ronald O. Perelman Heart Institute website of the NYP University Hospital of Columbia and Cornell offers links to excellent short videos and audio slide presentations on cardiovascular tests and procedures, such as bradycardia, the conduction system, and ventricular tachycardia. There are also webcasts on atrial fibrillation.

➤ StopAfib.org—"Resources for Atrial Fibrillation Patients and Caregivers." http://www.stopafib.org/resources.cfm; alternate path: http://www.stopafib.org/, click on the heading "Patient and Caregiver Resources" or search for and then click on the title "Patient and Caregiver Resources."
StopAfib.org is part of the American Foundation for Women's Health, which covers general atrial fibrillation (AF) information and provides AF patient

discussion forums and social media, AF guidelines, medications, patient sites, and physician resources. A patient-driven site aiming to help people control AF, it includes patient stories, news and upcoming events, and resource listings.

➢ Texas Heart Institute (Houston, TX)—"Heart Information Center." http://www .texasheartinstitute.org/HIC/; alternate path: http://www.texasheartinstitute.org/, search for the topic by name (e.g., "arrhythmia") and then click on the appropriate title, or on the homepage, click on the heading "Heart Information Center," select "Heart-Health Topics," click "Heart Conditions," and click on the topic by name.

To participate in a clinical trial, if available in your cardiology condition, at the Texas Heart Institute Research Laboratory, visit http://www.texasheartinstitute .org/Research/hfresearch.cfm (or return to the Texas Heart Institute homepage, click on the heading "Research," and on the left side of the page click on the title "Heart Failure Research Laboratory"). Scroll down to the section "Research Projects" and click on the title "FDA-Approved Clinical Trials." Under the heading "About Us" click on "Professional Staff Directory." Click on a category to view a list of physicians and specialists (with profiles, e.g., specialty, medical board certification, education).

- "Arrhythmia." http://www.texasheartinstitute.org/HIC/Topics/Cond/arrhythmia .cfm. The Texas Heart Institute website offers a definition of arrhythmia as well as information on causes, symptoms, diagnosis, and treatment. There is also a link for information on patient care.
- "Heart Surgery Overview." http://www.texasheartinstitute.org/HIC/Topics/ Proced/index.cfm. The Texas Heart Institute website discusses what a heart-lung machine is, what cooling techniques are, who is in the operating room during surgery, and what kinds of heart and blood vessel surgeries there are.
- "Implantable Cardioverter Defibrillator (ICD)." http://www.texasheartinstitute .org/HIC/Topics/Proced/icdtopic.cfm. The Texas Heart Institute website offers a definition of an ICD, why you might need an ICD, how ICDs work, how you feel after you get an ICD, how often you need to be checked, how electric devices could affect your ICD, and using cell phones if you have an ICD.
- "Long Q-T Syndrome (LQTS)." http://www.texasheartinstitute.org/HIC/ Topics/Cond/longqts.cfm. The Texas Heart Institute website offers a definition of LQTS, as well as information on causes, risks, signs and symptoms, diagnosis, and treatment.
- "Maze Surgery." http://www.texasheartinstitute.org/HIC/Topics/Proced/ mazes.cfm. The Texas Heart Institute website offers a definition of Maze surgery, why you might need Maze surgery, and what to expect before the hospital stay, on the day of surgery, and during recovery.

- "Pacemakers." http://www.texasheartinstitute.org/HIC/Topics/Proced/ pacemake.cfm. The Texas Heart Institute website offers a definition of pacemakers, how often they need to be checked, and which electronic devices can affect them.

➤ UCLA Ronald Reagan Medical Center (Los Angeles, CA)—"Arrhythmias." http:// www.uclahealth.org/body.cfm?id=592; scroll down to the "Health Library" under "Diseases and Conditions" and click on the condition (e.g., "arrhythmias"); alternate path: http://www.uclahealth.org/, under the heading "For Patients and Visitors," go to the category "Health Resources," click on "Heart Health Center" to find the "Health Library," and in the list of "Diseases and Conditions," click on "Arrhythmias."

The UCLA Ronald Reagan Medical Center's Heart Health Center provides detailed information on arrhythmias, including definitions, causes, symptoms, exams and tests, treatments, outlook (prognosis), possible complications, when to contact a medical professional, and prevention. The UCLA Heart Health Center (http://www.uclahealth.org/body.cfm?id=592) provides animations related to various conditions. Scroll to the bottom of the page and select "More" under "Animations." To view the animation, you might be asked to allow the installation of a common Internet plug-in called Shockwave Player by Adobe, available for free at http://www.adobe.com/products/shockwaveplayer.html. Also on the Heart Health Center website, under the heading "Health Assessments," you can sign up for "personalized messages to improve your [heart] health and lifestyle" by clicking on one of these categories: "Diet and Nutrition," "Fitness," "Heart Attack," "Stress and Anxiety." For patient services in various cardiology programs, return to the UCLA Health homepage (http://www.uclahealth.org/), under the heading "Medical Departments" scroll down and click on "Medicine," and then scroll and click on "Cardiology." Included is a list of programs and links to physicians and specialists (with profiles, e.g., specialty, medical board certification, education). To possibly participate in a clinical trial at UCLA, if available, visit http://clinicaltrials .ucla.edu/ (or on the homepage type "clinical trials" in the Search box and then click on "Clinical Trials").

➤ WebMD—"Atrial Fibrillation (AF) Health Center." http://www.webmd.com/ heart-disease/atrial-fibrillation/default.htm; alternate path: http://www.webmd .com/, search for and then click on the title "Atrial Fibrillation Health Center."

WebMD website offers the latest information on AF, including articles, slide presentations, videos, FAQs, discussions groups, and expert blogs. Also available is a WebMD heart health e-mail newsletter. According to WebMD, "WebMD News is an independent media service designed to provide news, information, and educational material to consumers and physicians. News content created by WebMD is free from influence by sponsors, partners, or other sources."

Patient Support Groups and Organizations

➢ DailyStrength—"Atrial Fibrillation (AFib) Support Group." http://www .dailystrength.org/c/Atrial-Fibrillation-AFib/support-group; alternate path: http://www.dailystrength.org/, search for "atrial fibrillation" and click on the group name.
DailyStrength website offers online support groups and blogs for those with atrial fibrillation (AF). Free registration is required to participate. According to the website, "DailyStrength is . . . the first truly interactive healthcare eco-system giving consumers the ability to ask, learn and act on the questions of health."

➢ HeartHub for Patients—"Arrhythmia." http://www.hearthub.org/hc-arrhythmia .htm; alternate path: http://www.hearthub.org/, search for "heart hub," click on "HeartHub for Patients," then scroll down to the section titled "Health Centers," and click on the title "Arrhythmia."
From the American Heart Association, HeartHub is a patient support portal for information, tools, and resources on arrhythmia, including information on treat-ments, diagnosis, healthy recipes, how to get help on the phone, how to create a pacemaker identification card, and children with arrhythmia. There is also an e-newsletter on arrhythmia that you can subscribe to by clicking on "eNewsletter Sign Up."

➢ Lone Atrial Fibrillation Bulletin Board—"The Afib Report." http://www.afibbers .org/toboards.htm; alternate path: http://www.afibbers.org/, scroll down and click on "LAF Forum Bulletin Board."
This webpage offers a bulletin board for sharing personal experiences regarding lone atrial fibrillation. No medical advice is offered. Registration is required.

➢ MedHelp—"Arrhythmia." http://www.medhelp.org/search?query=arrhythmia; alternate path: http://www.medhelp.org/, search for "arrhythmia."
According to the website, MedHelp "connects people with the leading medical experts," such as those from Cleveland Clinic, National Jewish Health, Partners Health, and Mount Sinai Hospital, and with those who have similar medical issues. MedHelp's main focus is to enable patients "to take control over their health and find answers to their medical questions" using nontechnical language via an online community through posts, forums and groups, blogs, user journals, as well as recommendations, articles, health pages, and a medical glossary. Free registration is required.

➢ StopAfib Discussion Forum. http://forum.stopafib.org/; alternate path: http:// www.stopafib.org/, scroll down to "Afib Special Interest Topics."
StopAfib.org is part of the American Foundation for Women's Health. These dis-cussion forums are written "for patients by patients."

> Sudden Arrhythmia Death Syndromes (SADS) Foundation. http://www.sads.org/. This website covers long QT syndrome (LQTS), cardiomyopathy (HCM), Brugada syndrome, and other conditions that cause sudden death in young people. The SADS Foundation informs the general public (including families and medical professionals) about the effects of untreated/undiagnosed, inherited cardiac arrhythmias and the methods by which death can be prevented in a detailed section titled "Living with SADS."

> U.S. Hospital Finder. http://www.ushospitalfinder.com/.
Use this site to find the names of hospitals by zip code, city, state, or your address. The search results include a map with directions. You might also want to ask your health care professional, call hospitals in your area, or search for "support groups" on hospital websites to determine if there are any cardiology support groups for people with arrhythmia, atrial fibrillation, bradycardia, tachycardia, and so on, that meet regularly in your area.

> Yahoo! Groups—"AFIBsupport." http://health.groups.yahoo.com/group/AFIB support/; alternate path: http://www.groups.yahoo.com/, search for "atrial fibrillation" in the "Find a Yahoo! Group" Search box and then click on the group "AFIBsupport."
This online Yahoo! group is for patients with atrial fibrillation (AF) and their families and friends. Yahoo! Groups is not a medical site, nor does it provide or endorse medical advice or procedures. The purpose of the website is to share experiences in a kind and caring manner. Free registration is required to participate.

See also the following section, CARDIAC ARREST.

Cardiac Arrest

Cardiac arrest is sometimes incorrectly called a heart attack or sudden cardiac death. Cardiac arrest is actually a condition in which the blood flow is stopped due to such events as arrhythmias (e.g., ventricular fibrillation, bradycardia), stoppage of the heart (e.g., electric shock, trauma), or cardiomyopathy. With cardiac arrest, a patient may be able to be revived with cardiopulmonary resuscitation or defibrillation. Sudden cardiac death is a general term that refers to the stoppage of the heart without the ability to restart it. With sudden cardiac death, the heart has stopped due to one of many causes, most often a myocardial infarction.

Resources for Further Information on Cardiac Arrest
Books
> Cohn, Elizabeth Gross. *Flip and See ECG*. St. Louis, MO: Elsevier-Mosby, 2012.
This easy-to-read, spiral-bound book has lots of pictures, sketches, and cartoons.

Brochures, Booklets, and Other Short Print Publications

➢ American Heart Association (AHA)—"What Is an Automated External Defibrillator (AED)?" (Information Sheet) and "Warning Signs and Actions" (Brochure). http://www.heart.org/idc/groups/heart-public/@wcm/@hcm/documents/downloadable/ucm_300340.pdf and http://www.heart.org/HEARTORG/General/Warning-Signs-and-Actions-Our-Guide-to-Quick-Action_UCM_314705_Article.jsp; alternate path: http://www.heart.org/, search for "cardiac arrest tools," click on the title "Cardiac Arrest Tools and Resources," and then click on the titles "What Is an Automated External Defibrillator (AED)?" and "Order Cardiac Arrest and Other Educational Brochures."

AHA provides printable information on implantable defibrillators and warning signs of cardiac arrest. The *Warning Signs and Actions* brochure is available in both English and Spanish and can be ordered by filling in a form online. (No more than two brochures per household can be ordered at no cost.)

Websites

➢ American Heart Association (AHA)—"Cardiac Arrest." http://www.heart.org/HEARTORG/Conditions/More/CardiacArrest/Cardiac-Arrest_UCM_002081_SubHomePage.jsp; alternate path: http://www.heart.org/, search for and then click on the title "Cardiac Arrest."

AHA provides expanded details on cardiac arrest in several sections about the condition, including warning signs, risk factors, symptoms and emergency treatment, long-term treatment, and tools and resources. You can also sign up for a free heart health e-newsletter.

➢ British Heart Foundation (BHF)—"Cardiac Arrest." http://www.bhf.org.uk/heart-health/conditions/cardiac-arrest.aspx; alternate path: http://www.bhf.org.uk/, search for "cardiac arrest" and then click on the title "British Heart Foundation—Cardiac Arrest."

The BHF website describes cardiac arrest and cardiopulmonary resuscitation (CPR) and provides a link to more information about CPR and how to get training. Also click on the "Community: Share Experiences with Others" heading to engage with the BHF online community where you can share your own story and read those of others.

➢ CardioSmart—"Implantable Cardioverter Defibrillator (ICD)." https://www.cardiosmart.org/HeartDisease/CTT.aspx?id=220; alternate path: https://www.cardiosmart.org/, search for "icd," and then click on the title "Implantable Cardioverter Defibrillator (ICD)."

CardioSmart provides an easy-to-use webpage for understanding ICDs, which are discussed in such sections as basic facts, who might need an ICD, how ICDs work, what to expect during ICD surgery, what to expect after surgery, risk factors of having an ICD, possible complications, and how an ICD affects lifestyle. CardioSmart's ICD webpage states that "[y]our doctor may recommend an ICD if he or she sees signs of an irregular ventricular arrhythmia (or heart damage that would make one likely). He or she also may recommend an ICD if you survive sudden cardiac arrest." According to the American College of Cardiology (ACC), CardioSmart is the patient education and support program launched by the ACC whose mission "is to engage, inform, and empower patients to better prepare them for participation in their own care."

➤ CenterWatch—Clinical trials listing service: Cardiac arrest clinical trials. http://search.centerwatch.com/default.aspx?SearchQuery=cardiac%20arrest; alternate path: http://www.centerwatch.com/, search for "cardiac arrest."
The CenterWatch clinical trials listing service lists trials currently looking for volunteers to enroll in cardiac arrest studies. Click on the "Clinical Trials" heading and search by location, medical condition, or therapeutic area. To search by location, click on your state (or country) and click on a city near you to find information on each available clinical trial. Check back with this website often for new studies. Sign up for a free e-mail service that sends notice of new clinical trials.

➤ ClinicalTrials.gov—Cardiac arrest clinical trials. http://clinicaltrials.gov/ct2/results/refine?term=cardiac+arrest; alternate path: http://clinicaltrials.gov/, search for "cardiac arrest."
To limit your results, click on "Modify This Search" and select specific fields, such as (1) Recruitment (e.g., you might want to select: "Open Studies"); (2) Locations (e.g., select your state); and (3) Age Group, and then click on the "Search" button. Click on the title of each trial name for additional information, such as purpose of the study, study design and type, detailed description, outcome measures, eligibility (age, gender, criteria for participating), study start date, estimated study completion date, and sponsor. Clinical-Trials.gov, developed by the U.S. National Institutes of Health of the National Library of Medicine, lists ongoing and currently enrolling clinical trials. Check often for new studies.

➤ eMedicineHealth—"Sudden Cardiac Arrest." http://www.emedicinehealth.com/sudden_cardiac_arrest/article_em.htm; alternate path: http://www.emedicinehealth.com/, search for "sudden cardiac arrest" and click on the title "Sudden Cardiac Arrest" (Source: Government).
eMedicineHealth, a division of WebMD, offers a comprehensive article on sudden cardiac arrest, including an overview, causes, risk factors, symptoms, diagnosis, treatment, prevention, and viewer comments.

➤ Insidermedicine. http://www.insidermedicine.com/.

The Insidermedicine website offers a variety of heart-health-related videos. For more information on the Insidermedicine Project, see the earlier entry on pp. 33–34. From the homepage, you can search for videos by title, or you can search by topic (e.g., cardiac arrest) to find other related videos.

- "African Americans Who Suffer Cardiac Arrest in Hospital More Likely to Die, Dirty Shower Heads Threaten Health, H1N1 Contagious for Longer Than Previously Thought." http://www.insidermedicine.com/archives/VIDEO_African _Americans_Who_Suffer_Cardiac_Arrest_in_Hospital_More_Likely_to_Die _Dirty_Shower_Heads_Threaten_Health_H1N1_Contagious_For_Longer _than_Previously_Thought_3766.aspx. In this easy-to-understand video, with demonstrations, a medical specialist compares the risk of cardiac arrest in African Americans with Caucasians.
- "In-Hospital Cardiac Arrest Survival Rates Lower during Nights and Weekends" (Video). http://www.insidermedicine.com/archives/In-Hospital _Cardiac_Arrest_Survival_Rates_Lower_During_Nights__Weekends _2198.aspx. In this video, a medical specialist speaking in patient-friendly language, with demonstrations, discusses cardiac arrest occurring during hospitalization.
- "Marathon Runners Are Not at Raised Risk of Cardiac Arrest." http://www .insidermedicine.com/archives/Marathon_Runners_Not_At_Increased _Risk_of_Cardiac_Arrest_Video_5811.aspx. In this video, a medical professional discusses risk factors of marathon runners with cardiovascular disease, guidelines in preparing for a marathon, and published studies on "clinical characteristics of the cardiac arrests that did occur."
- "Overall Incidence of Cardiac Arrests during Marathon Is Very Low." http://www.insidermedicine.com/archives/Overall_Incidence_of_Cardiac _Arrests_During_Marathon_is_Very_Low_Video_5812.aspx. In this video, the medical specialist discusses physical activity recommendations for people who have cardiovascular disease and research out of Massachusetts General Hospital and Harvard Medical School in Boston on the incidence and outcomes of cardiac arrest associated with marathon races in the United States.

➤ Mayo Clinic (Rochester, MN)—"Sudden Cardiac Arrest." http://www.mayoclinic .com/health/sudden-cardiac-arrest/DS00764; alternate path: http://www.mayoclinic .com/, search for "cardiac arrest" and then click on the title "Sudden Cardiac Arrest." Written for patients, this webpage includes definitions, symptoms, causes, risk factors, complications, tests and diagnosis, treatments and drugs, and prevention. There is also a more comprehensive section titled "In-Depth" on some of these topics. For information on clinical trials and patient services, see the Mayo Clinic entry on p. 36.

➢ MedicineNet—"Sudden Cardiac Arrest (Sudden Cardiac Death)." http://www .medicinenet.com/sudden_cardiac_death/article.htm; alternate path: http:// www.medicinenet.com/, under "Diseases and Conditions," click on "Conditions A–Z," then click on "S," and then scroll down to click on "Sudden Cardiac Death." According to its website, MedicineNet "provides easy-to-read, in-depth, authoritative medical information for consumers via its user-friendly, interactive website." In-depth information on sudden cardiac arrest includes definitions, causes, occurrence in a young person, symptoms, risk, diagnosis, treatment, prognosis, and patient discussions.

➢ MedlinePlus—"Cardiac Arrest." http://vsearch.nlm.nih.gov/vivisimo/cgi-bin/ query-meta?v%3Aproject=medlineplus&query=cardiac+arrest&x=0&y=0; alternate path: http://www.nlm.nih.gov/medlineplus/, search for "cardiac arrest." MedlinePlus is a component of the National Institutes of Health (NIH), produced by the National Library of Medicine (NLM), and is updated regularly. This MedlinePlus webpage on cardiac arrest offers extensive linked information covering overviews, news, diagnosis/symptoms, treatment, prevention/screening, related issues, anatomy/physiology, clinical trials, journal articles, dictionaries, directories, organizations, statistics, and separate sections that focus on children and teenagers. This webpage also includes a multimedia section containing health check tools and videos.

➢ Medscape Reference (Drugs, Diseases, and Procedures)—"Sudden Cardiac Arrest." http://emedicine.medscape.com/article/151907-overview; alternate path: http://emedicine.medscape.com/, search for and then click on the title "Sudden Cardiac Arrest." Written for Medscape by Ali A. Sovari, MD, FACP, and associates, this webpage presents a comprehensive report on sudden cardiac arrest. Although written for health care professionals, it might be helpful for interested laypersons. Articles for Medscape Reference are written by medical experts. The webpage states, "Our rigorous literature survey process allows us to rapidly integrate new practice-changing information into the relevant topics by systematically reviewing the major medical and pharmacy journals, news announcements, and important practice guidelines." Free registration is required.

➢ National Heart, Lung, and Blood Institute (NHLBI)—"What Is Sudden Cardiac Arrest?" http://www.nhlbi.nih.gov/health/dci/Diseases/scda/scda_whatis.html; alternate path: http://www.nhlbi.nih.gov/, search for "sudden cardiac arrest," and then click on the title "What Is Sudden Cardiac Arrest?" NHLBI provides information on sudden cardiac arrest including definitions, causes, risk factors, signs and symptoms, diagnosis, treatments, prevention, clinical trials, key points, and additional information.

➤ Texas Heart Institute (Houston, TX)—"Sudden Cardiac Arrest (SCA)." http://
www.texasheartinstitute.org/HIC/Topics/Cond/SCA.cfm; alternate path:
http://www.texasheartinstitute.org/, search for and then click on the title
"Sudden Cardiac Arrest."
The Texas Heart Institute website offers a definition of SCA as well as information on causes, signs and symptoms, diagnosis, and treatment. There is also a
link for information on patient care. An easy-to-print format is available. One
section allows users to "Ask a Texas Heart Institute Doctor" questions. Click on
"Heart Doctor Answers" to explore the questions and answers already published there. For information on clinical trials, see the Texas Heart Institute
entry on p. 40.

➤ WebMD—"Heart Attack and Cardiac Arrest in Men." http://men.webmd.com/
heart-attack-cardiac-arrest; alternate path: http://www.webmd.com/, search for
"cardiac arrest" and then click on the title "Heart Attack and Cardiac Arrest in
Men" (WebMD Medical Reference).
The WebMD website offers up-to-date information on cardiac arrest in men,
using articles, slide presentations, videos, FAQs, discussions groups, and expert
blogs. A WebMD heart health e-mail newsletter is also available. According to
WebMD, "WebMD News is an independent media service designed to provide
news, information, and educational material to consumers and physicians. News
content created by WebMD is free from influence by sponsors, partners, or other
sources."

Patient Support Groups and Organizations

➤ MedHelp—"Cardiac Arrest." http://www.medhelp.org/search?query=cardiac+arrest;
alternate path: http://www.medhelp.org/, search for "cardiac arrest."
According to its website, MedHelp "connects people with the leading medical
experts," such as those from Cleveland Clinic, National Jewish Health, Partners
Health, and Mount Sinai Hospital with those who have similar medical issues.
MedHelp's main focus is to enable patients "to take control over their health and
find answers to their medical questions" using nontechnical language via an
online community through posts, user journals, as well as articles, health pages,
and a medical glossary. Free registration is required.

➤ Sudden Cardiac Arrest Association (SCAA). http://www.suddencardiacarrest
.org/ and http://www.inspire.com/groups/sudden-cardiac-arrest-association/;
alternate path: http://www.inspire.com/, search for "heart," click on the heading
"Groups," scroll down and click on "Heart and Circulation," and then click on
"Sudden Cardiac Arrest."
According to its website, SCAA "is an organization singularly focused on sudden
cardiac arrest. SCAA identifies and unites survivors, those at risk of sudden

cardiac arrest, as well as others who are interested in being advocates on SCAA issues in their communities and beyond."

➤ U.S. Hospital Finder. http://www.ushospitalfinder.com/.
Use this site to find the names of hospitals by zip code, city, state, or your address. The search results include a map with directions. You might also want to ask your health care professional, call hospitals in your area, or search for "support groups" on hospital websites to determine if there are any cardiology support groups for people who have survived cardiac arrest that meet regularly in your area.

➤ Yahoo! Groups—"Cardiac Arrest Support Group." http://health.groups.yahoo.com/group/cardiacarrestmisurvivors/; alternate path: http://www.groups.yahoo.com/, search for "cardiac arrest" in the "Find a Yahoo! Group" Search box and then scroll down and click on the group "Cardiac Arrest MI Survivors."
This online Yahoo! group is for patients with cardiac arrest and their families and friends. Yahoo! Groups is not a medical site, nor does it provide or endorse medical advice or procedures. The purpose of the website is to share experiences in a kind and caring manner. Free registration is required to participate.

Cardiomyopathies

The heart normally pumps blood ceaselessly and steadily for years without problems. Cardiomyopathy is a heart muscle problem that makes it more difficult for the heart to pump properly. Many cardiomyopathies develop over time, others can be inherited, and other types are associated with other diseases or lifestyles. If left untreated or if not discovered in time, cardiomyopathies can cause heart failure and death. There are three main types of cardiomyopathies: dilated cardiomyopathy, hypertrophic cardiomyopathy, and restrictive cardiomyopathy.

Dilated cardiomyopathy, the most common, is a condition in which the heart becomes weak and its chambers enlarge. Consequently, a heart with this disease does not pump efficiently. The condition is often attributed to inheritance (familial dilated cardiomyopathy) where a person's father or mother had cardiomyopathy. Dilated cardiomyopathy can also be caused by coronary artery disease (ischemic cardiomyopathy), diabetes (diabetic cardiomyopathy), viruses, HIV, and some other infections, thyroid disease, pregnancy complications (peripartum cardiomyopathy), toxins (e.g., alcoholic cardiomyopathy), illegal drugs, and some cancer treatment drugs. It is sometimes called idiopathic cardiomyopathy when a clear cause cannot be determined.

A more rare type is hypertrophic cardiomyopathy, in which one ventricle's walls—usually those in the left ventricle—thicken. The thickened walls become stiff and do not contract or relax as easily as normal heart walls. A heart thus affected does not pump effectively. Similar to dilated cardiomyopathy, hypertrophic cardiomyopathy is often inherited (called familial hypertrophic cardiomyopathy) from gene mutation. Long-term high blood pressure can cause hypertrophic cardiomyopathy, as can certain other diseases (e.g., diabetes, thyroid disease). Sometimes a cause is not known (idiopathic hypertrophic cardiomyopathy). In young people, especially athletes, hypertrophic cardiomyopathy is the most common cause of sudden cardiac arrest. The thickened walls sometimes block the outflow from the ventricle, a condition called obstructive hypertrophic cardiomyopathy. If the outflow is not blocked, the disease is called nonobstructive hypertrophic cardiomyopathy. The mitral valve can be affected, causing leakage and reducing pumping efficiency.

With restrictive cardiomyopathy (also called infiltrative cardiomyopathy), a rare type occurring most often in older people, the ventricle walls become stiff and rigid because scar tissue has replaced normal heart muscle. As a result, the ventricle cannot relax to fill with blood, and contraction is weak. This stress over time causes the atria to enlarge, making blood flow to the heart restricted. Restrictive cardiomyopathy is mainly caused by diseases that damage the heart muscle, such as hemochromatosis (i.e., too much iron in the body; the extra iron is toxic). Another cause is sarcoidosis, which triggers inflammation or swelling and which is suspected to be caused from an abnormal immune response triggering the formation of granulomas (small lumps) in the heart and other organs. Cardiomyopathy may also be caused by amyloidosis in which insoluble abnormal proteins accumulate in the heart, weakening or distorting it; or connective tissue disorders in which fibers that hold the body tissues together are attacked by the body (autoimmune diseases)— causing inflammation and edema.

Resources for Further Information on Cardiomyopathies

Books

> Maron, Barry J., and Lisa Salberg. *Hypertrophic Cardiomyopathy: For Patients, Their Families, and Interested Physicians.* Malden, MA: Wiley-Blackwell (Blackwell Futura), 2006. Print.
> Written by the director of Hypertrophic Cardiomyopathy Center of the Minneapolis Heart Institute Foundation, this book for patients discusses such topics as what is hypertrophic cardiomyopathy, origins, causes, symptoms, screenings, diagnostics and tests, treatment, genetics, complications, support groups, and lifestyle changes.

Websites

> Aetna InteliHealth—"Cardiomyopathy." http://www.intelihealth.com/IH/ihtIH/ WSIHW000/8059/11162/213081.html?d=dmtHealthAZ; alternate path: http://www .intelihealth.com/, search for and then click on the title "Cardiomyopathy."

This website provides an overview of cardiomyopathy, including symptoms, diagnosis, expected duration, prevention, treatment, when to call a professional, prognosis, and additional information. Aetna InteliHealth, a subsidiary of Aetna, is reviewed by the faculty of Harvard Medical School and the University College of Dental Medicine. According to Aetna InteliHealth's website, "Aetna InteliHealth maintains absolute editorial independence. That means that Aetna InteliHealth makes decisions about the information on our site free of outside influence." Under "Healthy Lifestyle," Aetna InteliHealth also offers free health-related e-mail subscriptions.

➤ American Heart Association (AHA)—"Pediatric Cardiomyopathies." http://www .heart.org/HEARTORG/Conditions/More/CardiovascularConditionsofChildhood/ Pediatric-Cardiomyopathies_UCM_312219_Article.jsp; alternate path: http://www .heart.org/, search for and then click on the title "Pediatric Cardiomyopathies."
AHA provides expanded details on different types of cardiomyopathies in sections, such as dilated cardiomyopathy, hypertrophic cardiomyopathy, restrictive cardiomyopathy, miscellaneous (rare) cardiomyopathies, and an overview of inheritance for cardiomyopathies.

➤ British Heart Foundation (BHF)—"Cardiomyopathy." http://www.bhf.org.uk/ heart-health/conditions/cardiomyopathy.aspx; alternate path: http://www.bhf .org.uk/, search for "cardiomyopathy" and then click on the title "British Heart Foundation—Cardiomyopathy."
The BHF webpage describes three types of cardiomyopathy. Also click on the "Community: Share Experiences with Others" heading to engage with the BHF online community where you can share your own story and read those of others.

➤ CardioSmart—"Cardiomyopathy." https://www.cardiosmart.org/HeartDisease/ CTT.aspx?id=204; alternate path: https://www.cardiosmart.org/, search for and then click on the title "Cardiomyopathy."
CardioSmart provides an easy-to-use website on understanding the topic of cardiomyopathy, which is discussed in subsections on basic facts, types of cardiomyopathy, causes, risk factors, signs and symptoms, diagnosis, treatment, prevention, and living with cardiomyopathy. According to the American College of Cardiology (ACC), "CardioSmart is the patient education and support program launched by the [ACC]. Our mission is to engage, inform, and empower patients to better prepare them for participation in their own care."

➤ CenterWatch—Clinical trials listing service: "Cardiomyopathy Clinical Trials." http://www.centerwatch.com/clinical-trials/listings/studylist.aspx?CatID=382; alternate path: http://www.centerwatch.com/, under the category "Patient Resources," click on "Search Clinical Trials," then click on "C," and then click on "Cardiomyopathy."

CenterWatch clinical trials listing service lists trials currently looking for volunteers to enroll in cardiomyopathy studies. Click on the "Clinical Trials" heading and search by location, medical condition, or therapeutic area. To search by location, click on your state (or country) and click on a city near you to find information on each available clinical trial. Check back with this website often for new studies. Sign up for a free e-mail service that sends notice of new clinical trials.

➤ Cleveland Clinic (Cleveland, OH)—"What Is Cardiomyopathy?" http://my .clevelandclinic.org/disorders/Cardiomyopathy/hic_What_is_Cardiomyopathy .aspx; alternate path: http://my.clevelandclinic.org/, under the category "Institutes and Services," click on "Heart and Vascular," then click on the category "Diseases and Conditions," and then scroll down to click on the title "Cardiomyopathy."

Cleveland Clinic provides comprehensive patient-friendly information on cardiomyopathy, such as definitions, other names for cardiomyopathy, types, risk, causes, symptoms, diagnostic tests, treatments, lifestyle changes, prevention, and help to find a doctor who treats cardiomyopathy. The Cleveland Clinic also offers a link to "Chat Online with a Heart and Vascular Nurse." For information on clinical trials, see the Cleveland Clinic entry on pp. 31–32.

➤ ClinicalTrials.gov—Cardiomyopathy clinical trials. http://clinicaltrials.gov/ct2/ results/refine?term=cardiomyopathy; alternate path: http://clinicaltrials.gov/, search for "cardiomyopathy."

To limit your results, click on "Modify This Search" and select specific fields, such as (1) Recruitment (e.g., you might want to select "Open Studies"); (2) Locations (e.g., select your state); and (3) Age Group, and then click on the "Search" button. Click on the title of each trial name for additional information, such as purpose of the study, study design and type, detailed description, outcome measures, eligibility (age, gender, criteria for participating), study start date, estimated study completion date, and sponsor. ClinicalTrials.gov, developed by the U.S. National Institutes of Health of the National Library of Medicine, lists ongoing and currently enrolling clinical trials. Check often for new studies.

➤ eMedicineHealth—"Cardiomyopathy." http://www.emedicinehealth.com/cardio myopathy/article_em.htm; alternate path: http://www.emedicinehealth.com/, search for "cardiomyopathy" and then click on the title "Cardiomyopathy" (Medical Reference from Healthwise).

eMedicineHealth, a division of WebMD, offers a comprehensive article on cardiomyopathy including an overview, causes, symptoms, when to seek medical care, diagnosis, treatment, prevention, follow-ups, and outlook.

➤ Genetics Home Reference—"Familial Restrictive Cardiomyopathy." http://ghr
.nlm.nih.gov/condition/familial-restrictive-cardiomyopathy; alternate path:
http://ghr.nlm.nih.gov/, search for and then click on the title "Familial Restrictive Cardiomyopathy."
Genetics Home Reference is a division of National Institutes of Health (NIH).
This webpage discusses an inherited form of cardiomyopathy, familial restrictive
cardiomyopathy, a condition occurring in children and adults.

➤ Hospital of the University of Pennsylvania (HUP) (Philadelphia, PA)—"Familial
Cardiomyopathy Program." http://www.pennmedicine.org/heart/patient/clinical
-services/familial-cardiomyopathy/; alternate path: http://www.pennmedicine.org/,
click on the "Departments and Services" icon (or type "departments and services" in
the Search box at the top of the screen), scroll down and click on the category "Cardiology and Cardiac Surgery," then scroll down under the heading "Clinical Services" and click on "Familial Cardiomyopathy."
At its Penn Heart and Vascular Center website, HUP offers website links in the
Familial Cardiomyopathy Program that include an "Overview" (what familial
cardiomyopathy is, types, signs and symptoms, risks, and what specialists are on
the team); the "Team," which links to each physician and specialist (with profiles,
e.g., specialty, medical board certification, education); "The Penn Difference"
(program described, patient experiences, unique capabilities and expertise, and
hospital highlights); and "Penn–CHOP Partnership" (experts from both hospitals working together). You can also subscribe to the Penn Heart newsletter. For
information on clinical trials, see the HUP entry on p. 33.

➤ Insidermedicine—"If I Had—Shortness of Breath and Was Diagnosed with Cardiomyopathy" (Video). http://www.insidermedicine.com/archives/VIDEO_If_I_Had
_Shortness_of_Breath_and_Was_Diagnosed_With_Cardiomyopathy_Dr_Ann
_Bolger_MD_University_of_California_San_Francisco_3257.aspx; alternate path:
http://www.insidermedicine.com/, search for the video by title.
The Insidermedicine website offers a variety of heart-health-related videos. For more
information on the physician-led Insidermedicine Project, see the earlier entry on
pp. 33–34. This easy-to-understand video, with demonstrations, includes an interview with a cardiologist on having shortness of breath and risks of cardiomyopathy.

➤ Johns Hopkins Hospital (Baltimore, MD). http://www.hopkinsmedicine.org/.
The Johns Hopkins Heart and Vascular Institute webpage (http://www
.hopkinsmedicine.org/heart_vascular_institute/) provides detailed information on a variety of conditions, treatments, and services. It also lists links to
physicians and specialists (with profiles, e.g., specialty, medical board certification, education). Click on the heading "Clinical Trials" to find links to current trials in various heart and cardiovascular conditions. Alternate path: You

can find any of the following resources by returning to the homepage, searching for the topic by name, and then clicking on the corresponding title in the
results list.

- "Cardiomyopathy." http://www.hopkinsmedicine.org/healthlibrary/conditions/
  adult/cardiovascular_diseases/cardiomyopathy_85,P00201/. Johns Hopkins
  Health Library webpage on cardiomyopathy also discusses the disorder in
  similar detail, including causes, types, and how it differs from other types of
  heart conditions.
- "Cardiomyopathy/Heart Failure." http://www.hopkinsmedicine.org/heart
  _vascular_institute/conditions_treatments/conditions/cardiomyopathy.html.
  Johns Hopkins Heart and Vascular Institute webpage on cardiomyopathy
  discusses the disorder, types, when to call an ambulance, when to call your
  doctor, symptoms, causes, prevention, diagnosis, and treatment.
- "Cardiomyopathy and Heart Failure Service." http://www.hopkinsmedicine
  .org/heart_vascular_institute/clinical_services/specialty_areas/cardio
  myopathy.html. The Johns Hopkins Cardiomyopathy and Heart Failure
  Service webpage describes user-friendly, current information on the types
  of services and diagnostic testing provided by this institute.

➤ KidsHealth.org—"For Parents: When Your Child Needs a Heart Transplant."
http://kidshealth.org/parent/medical/heart/heart_transplant.html#cat141; alternate path: http://www.kidshealth.org/, click on "Parents Site," scroll down and click
on "Diseases and Conditions," then scroll down and click on "Heart and Blood
Vessels," and then click on "When Your Child Needs a Heart Transplant."
The Nemours Center for Children's Health Media provides current information,
written for parents, on what happens when a child needs a heart transplant.
Topics discussed include general information about heart transplants, receiving a
donor's healthy heart, preparing for surgery, organ waiting lists, getting "the call,"
recovery, possible complications, and living heart healthy for life. Information is
available in English and Spanish. Click on the "Listen" button to hear the text
read aloud.

➤ Massachusetts General Hospital (MGH) (Boston, MA). http://www.massgeneral
.org/.
On each of the following MGH webpages are links to comprehensive information in several categories: "Our Approach" includes an overview of conditions,
treatments, and procedures, as well as links to each medical expert (with profiles,
e.g., specialty, medical board certification, education). "About This Program"
describes the quality and benefits of the program as well as MGH's commitment.
"Conditions and Diseases" offers links to detailed information on specific and
related conditions. "Support and Wellness" offers patient guides. "Clinical Trials"
links to MGH trials and research studies currently seeking participants. "News

and Events" includes the latest information on conditions. "Multimedia" offers video demonstrations.

- "Cardiac Resynchronization Therapy Program." http://www.massgeneral .org/heartcenter/services/treatmentprograms.aspx?id=1002.
- "Hypertrophic Cardiomyopathy Program." http://www.massgeneral.org/ heartcenter/services/treatmentprograms.aspx?id=1009.

Alternate path: http://www.massgeneral.org/, search for the topic by title using the Search box at the top of the screen or click on "Centers and Services," click on "View All Departments," click on "Heart Center," then click on "Treatments and Services," and then scroll down to find your topic.

➤ Mayo Clinic (Rochester, MN)—"Cardiomyopathy." http://www.mayoclinic.com/ health/cardiomyopathy/DS00519; alternate path: http://www.mayoclinic.com/, search for and then click on the title "Cardiomyopathy."
  Written for patients, this information on cardiomyopathy includes definitions, symptoms, causes, complications, preparing for appointments, tests and diagnosis, treatments and drugs, prevention, lifestyle, home remedies, and news. There is also a more comprehensive section titled "In-Depth" on some of these topics. For information on clinical trials and patient services, see the Mayo Clinic entry on p. 36.

➤ MedicineNet. http://www.medicinenet.com/.
  MedicineNet.com is owned and operated by WebMD and is part of the WebMD Network. According to its website, MedicineNet "provides easy-to-read, in-depth, authoritative medical information for consumers via its user-friendly, interactive website." The medical information is written and edited by a nationally recognized group of more than 70 U.S. board-certified physicians. The website contains a "Symptom Checker" listed in alphabetical order as a guide to "pinpoint your pain." Its homepage links to "Health News of the Week." You can also sign up to receive a health newsletter.

- "Dilated Cardiomyopathy (DCM)." http://www.medicinenet.com/cardio myopathy_dilated/article.htm. In-depth information on DCM includes definitions, symptoms, causes, diagnosis, treatment (surgery and medications), lifestyle changes, and finding a local cardiologist.
- "Hypertrophic Cardiomyopathy (HCM)." http://www.medicinenet.com/ cardiomyopathy_hypertrophic/article.htm. In-depth information on HCM includes definitions, symptoms, causes, diagnosis, treatment (surgery and medications), lifestyle changes, and finding a local cardiologist.
- "Restrictive Cardiomyopathy." http://www.medicinenet.com/cardiomyopathy _restrictive/article.htm. In-depth information on restrictive cardiomyopathy includes definitions, symptoms, causes, diagnosis, treatment (surgery and medications), lifestyle changes, and finding a local cardiologist.

Alternate path: http://www.medicinenet.com/, under on the heading "Diseases and Conditions," click on "Conditions A–Z," click on "C," and then scroll down to "Cardiomyopathy" and click on the corresponding title choice.

➤ MedlinePlus—"Cardiomyopathy." http://www.nlm.nih.gov/medlineplus/cardio myopathy.html; alternate path: http://www.nlm.nih.gov/, under "Databases," click on "MedlinePlus" and then search for "cardiomyopathy."

MedlinePlus website is a component of the National Institutes of Health (NIH), produced by the National Library of Medicine (NLM), and is updated regularly. This MedlinePlus webpage on cardiomyopathy offers extensive linked information covering overviews, news, diagnosis/symptoms, treatment, disease management, specific conditions, related issues, anatomy/physiology, clinical trials, genetics, journal articles, dictionaries/glossaries, organizations, law and policy, and specific sections focusing on children and women. Patient handouts are also available. This website also includes a multimedia section containing videos.

➤ Medscape Reference (Drugs, Diseases, and Procedures)—"Dilated Cardiomyopathy." http://emedicine.medscape.com/article/152696-overview; alternate path: http://emedicine.medscape.com/, search for and then click on the title "Dilated Cardiomyopathy."

Written by Vivek J. Goswami and associates for Medscape, this webpage presents a comprehensive report on dilated cardiomyopathy. Although written for health care professionals, it might be helpful for interested laypersons. There are also articles on restrictive cardiomyopathy and hypertrophic cardiomyopathy; type the name of a condition in the Search box at the top of the screen and click on the appropriate title. Articles for Medscape Reference are written by medical experts. The webpage states, "Our rigorous literature survey process allows us to rapidly integrate new practice-changing information into the relevant topics by systematically reviewing the major medical and pharmacy journals, news announcements, and important practice guidelines." Free registration is required.

➤ *The Merck Manual Home Health Handbook for Patients and Caregivers*— "Cardiomyopathy." http://www.merckmanuals.com/home/heart_and_blood _vessel_disorders/cardiomyopathy/overview_of_cardiomyopathy.html; alternate path: http://www.merckmanuals.com/home/, under "Sections," click on "All" next to the navigation arrows to see a complete list, then click on "Heart and Blood Vessel Disorders," and then scroll down and click on the section "Cardiomyopathy."

This webpage on cardiomyopathy is divided into several titles, including "Overview of Cardiomyopathy," "Dilated Cardiomyopathy," "Hypertrophic Cardiomyopathy," and "Restrictive Cardiomyopathy." This section is based on a well-known medical textbook titled *The Merck Manual Home Health Handbook for Patients and Caregivers* and is "provided free of charge . . . as a public service."

➤ National Heart, Lung, and Blood Institute (NHLBI). http://www.nhlbi.nih.gov/. NHLBI is a division of the National Institutes of Health from the U.S. Department of Health and Human Services. From the homepage, you can find the following resources by searching for the topic or title and clicking on the corresponding link.

- "What Is Cardiomyopathy?" http://www.nhlbi.nih.gov/health/dci/Diseases/ cm/cm_what.html. The NHLBI website provides information on cardiomyopathy, including links to definitions, types of cardiomyopathy, other names, causes, risk factors, signs and symptoms, diagnosis, treatments, prevention, living with cardiomyopathy, clinical trials, and key points about cardiomyopathy.
- "What Is Diabetic Heart Disease?" (DHD). http://www.nhlbi.nih.gov/ health/health-topics/topics/dhd/. This NHLBI website provides information on arrhythmia, including links to definitions, causes, risk factors, signs and symptoms, diagnosis, treatments, prevention, living with DHD, and clinical trials.

➤ Texas Heart Institute (Houston, TX)—"Heart Information Center." http://www .texasheartinstitute.org/.

For information on clinical trials, see the Texas Heart Institute entry on p. 40.

- "Cardiomyopathy." http://www.texasheartinstitute.org/HIC/Topics/Cond/ Cardiomyopathy.cfm. The Texas Heart Institute website offers a definition of cardiomyopathy as well as information on types of cardiomyopathy and prevention. There is also a link for information on patient care. A print-friendly format is available. One section allows users to "Ask a Texas Heart Institute Doctor" questions. Click on "Heart Doctor Answers" to explore the questions and answers already published there.
- "Myocarditis." http://www.texasheartinstitute.org/HIC/Topics/Cond/ myocard.cfm. The Texas Heart Institute website offers a definition of myocarditis as well as information on causes, signs and symptoms, diagnosis, and treatment.

Alternate path: http://www.texasheartinstitute.org/, search for the topic by name (e.g., "cardiomyopathy") and then click on the appropriate title, or under the heading "Heart Information Center," click on "Heart-Health Topics," then "Heart Conditions," and then scroll down and click on the topic of choice.

➤ UCLA Ronald Reagan Medical Center (Los Angeles, CA)—"Cardiomyopathy." http://www.uclahealth.org/body.cfm?id=592; scroll down to the "Health Library" under "Diseases and Conditions" and click on the title "Cardiomyopathy"; alternate path: http://www.uclahealth.org/, under the heading "For Patients and

Visitors," go to the category "Health Resources," click on "Heart Health Center" to find the "Health Library," scroll down to the heading "In-Depth Reports," click on the word "More," and then click on the title "Cardiomyopathy."

The UCLA Ronald Reagan Medical Center's Heart Health Center provides an in-depth report on cardiomyopathy, which includes definition, causes, treatment, and outlook (prognosis). For more information on patient resources and clinical trials, see the UCLA entry on p. 41.

➤ WebMD—"Cardiomyopathy Directory." http://www.webmd.com/heart-disease/cardiomyopathy-directory; alternate path: http://www.webmd.com/, search for "cardiomyopathy," and then click on the title "Cardiomyopathy Directory."

The WebMD website offers the latest information on cardiomyopathy using articles, slide presentations, and videos. Available is a WebMD's heart health e-mail newsletter. According to WebMD, "WebMD News is an independent media service designed to provide news, information, and educational material to consumers and physicians. News content created by WebMD is free from influence by sponsors, partners, or other sources."

Patient Support Groups and Organizations

➤ The Children's Cardiomyopathy Foundation (CCF). http://www.childrenscardiomyopathy.org/.

The CCF website offers several types of support services, including a section that offers help with coping and healing. According to its website, "CCF is a national, non-profit organization focused on pediatric cardiomyopathy, a chronic disease of the heart muscle. CCF is dedicated to accelerating the search for cures while improving diagnosis, treatment, and quality of life for children affected by cardiomyopathy."

➤ DailyStrength—Cardiomyopathy support groups. http://www.dailystrength.org/search?q=cardiomyopathy; alternate path: http://www.dailystrength.org/, search for "cardiomyopathy."

The DailyStrength website offers online support groups and blogs for those with cardiomyopathy. Free registration is required to participate. According to the website, "DailyStrength is a subsidiary of Sharecare. Sharecare, created by WebMD founder and Discovery Communications' Chief of Global Digital Strategy Jeff Arnold, along with America's Doctor, Dr. Mehmet Oz, is the first truly interactive healthcare ecosystem giving consumers the ability to ask, learn and act on the questions of health."

➤ Hypertrophic Cardiomyopathy Association (HCMA). http://www.4hcm.org/forums/forum.php.

According to the website, HCMA "is a not for profit 501(c)(3) organization formed in 1996 to provide information, support and advocacy to patients, their families and medical providers." It offers forums, posts, personal family stories, articles, guidelines, and help finding a doctor. Free registration is required.

➤ MedHelp—"Cardiomyopathy." http://www.medhelp.org/search?query=cardio myopathy; alternate path: http://www.medhelp.org/, search for "cardiomyopathy." According to its website, MedHelp "connects people with the leading medical experts," such as those from Cleveland Clinic, National Jewish Health, Partners Health, and Mount Sinai Hospital, with those who have similar medical issues. MedHelp's main focus is to enable patients "to take control over their health and find answers to their medical questions" using nontechnical language via an online community through posts, forums and groups, blogs, user journals, as well as recommendations, articles, health pages, and a medical glossary. Free registration is required.

➤ U.S. Hospital Finder. http://www.ushospitalfinder.com/.
Use this site to find the names of hospitals by zip code, city, state, or your address. The search results include a map with directions. You might also want to ask your health care professional, call hospitals in your area, or search for "support groups" on hospital websites to determine if there are any cardiology support groups for people with cardiomyopathy that meet regularly in your area.

➤ Yahoo! Groups—"Cardiomyopathy" support group. http://health.dir.groups.yahoo .com/group/cardiomyopathy; alternate path: http://groups.yahoo.com/, search for "cardiomyopathy" in the "Find a Yahoo! Group" Search box and then click on the group "Cardiomyopathy."
This online Yahoo! group is for patients with cardiomyopathy and their families and friends. Yahoo! Groups is not a medical site, nor does it provide or endorse medical advice or procedures. The purpose of the website is to share experiences in a kind and caring manner. Free registration is required to participate.

Coronary Artery Disease

Arteriosclerosis is also called atherosclerosis or hardening of the arteries. Arteriosclerosis has an associated disease, arteriolosclerosis, that affects the small arteries and occurs in any artery in the body; however, when it occurs in the heart's arteries, it is called coronary artery disease.

Normal arteries are elastic and expand or contract as required by the nervous system to help regulate blood pressure. In arteriosclerosis, the large (such as the femoral artery in the upper leg) and major (such as the aorta) arteries become hard and lose their elasticity and are, therefore, unable to expand or contract. They can also become blocked or tortuous, thus slowing the blood flow. In arteriosclerosis and arteriolosclerosis, fat, cholesterol, calcium, and excess fibers toughen the artery wall and reduce its elasticity. If left untreated, these problems can lead to fatigue, short-ness of breath, localized tissue death (necrosis), and death.

When the coronary arteries become clogged, the condition is called coronary heart disease. It is related to high cholesterol, high blood pressure, and high blood sugar. Too much blood sugar alone can cause damage to the coronary arteries. Angina is a symptom of coronary heart disease, as well as some other similar diseases. Angina is pain resulting from poor blood supply to the clogged portion of the heart. It usually radiates from the center of the chest to the left armpit and down the inside of the left arm.

To learn more, visit the **National Heart, Lung, and Blood Institute** of the National Institutes of Health at http://www.nhlbi.nih.gov/health/health-topics/topics/cad/ (alternate path: http://www.nhlbi.nih.gov/, search for "coronary artery disease," and then click on the title "What Is Coronary Artery Disease?—NHLBI, NIH"). This webpage provides illustrations that show the difference between a normal artery and a narrowed one with restricted blood flow. Part B shows a normal artery with normal blood flow. Part C shows an artery with plaque buildup and restricted blood flow.

In coronary microvascular disease (CMVD) or arteriolosclerosis of the heart, the smallest arteries (arterioles) become damaged and limit the blood flow to small portions of the heart. It is a difficult disease to diagnose. Patients with CMVD experience angina, shortness of breath, sleep problems, fatigue, and lack of energy. In women with CMVD, angina pain typically lasts from 10 to 30 minutes but can last longer. CMVD can result from the effects of such problems as high blood cholesterol, high blood pressure, diabetes, being overweight, lack of exercise, and poor diet. CMVD in women has been linked to low estrogen and anemia. Having CMVD increases the risk of heart attack. To see what coronary microvascular disease looks like, go to http://www.nhlbi.nih.gov/health/health-topics/topics/hdw/.

Kawasaki disease (or Kawasaki syndrome) is a disease in children and infants, mostly of Japanese and Korean descent (80 percent are under five years old) that, if left untreated, causes vasculitis (inflammation of blood vessels all through the body), which can then develop into coronary heart disease. Researchers believe an unidentified virus, bacteria, or toxin to be the cause of Kawasaki disease, although this has not been proven, and there is no evidence of it being contagious. Initially, Kawasaki disease begins with a high fever (104°F) that lasts a minimum of five days. According to the National Institutes of Health, other symptoms include swollen lymph nodes in the neck; a rash on the midsection and genital area; red, dry, cracked lips and a red, swollen tongue; red, swollen palms of the hands and soles of the feet; and redness of the eyes.

Resources for Further Information on Coronary Artery Disease

Books

> Granato, Jerome E. *Living with Coronary Heart Disease: A Guide for Patients and Families* (A Johns Hopkins Press Health Book). Baltimore, MD: The Johns Hopkins University Press, 2008. Print.
> This book provides basic information about coronary heart disease and heart attack; it also includes information on causes, symptoms, treatments, surgery, and lifestyle changes.

> Sinatra, Stephen T., and James C. Roberts. *Reverse Heart Disease Now: Stop Deadly Cardiovascular Plaque Before It's Too Late.* Hoboken, NJ: Wiley, 2008. Print.
> This book, written by two cardiologists, provides a basic understanding of cardiovascular disease and "gives you the practical information and strategies you need to stop heart disease in its tracks."

Brochures, Booklets, and Other Short Print Publications

> American Heart Association (AHA). *An Active Partnership for the Health of Your Heart* (Workbook and DVD set). http://www.heart.org/HEARTORG/General/Order-American-Heart-Association-Educational-Brochures_UCM_312777_Article.jsp; alternate path: http://www.heart.org/, search for "educational brochures," click on the title "Order American Heart Association Educational Brochures," click on the topic "Cardiac Rehab," and then click on the title "Active Partnership for the Health of Your Heart Notebook and DVD."
> This AHA brochure includes a workbook and DVD "designed to help patients with coronary artery disease (CAD) recover and improve their health after a cardiac event or surgery." According to the AHA website, "if you are interested in placing an order, receiving print samples or viewing online e-samples, visit our distributor, Krames (https://www.krames.com/AHA). Registration is required to request samples and order online."

> British Heart Foundation (BHF)—"Cardiovascular Disease" (Booklets and DVDs). http://www.bhf.org.uk/heart-health/conditions/cardiovascular-disease.aspx; alternate path: http://www.bhf.org.uk/, search for "cardiovascular disease," and then click on the title "British Heart Foundation—Cardiovascular Disease."
> The BHF website offers free booklets and DVDs to help patients manage and cope with heart failure. Scroll down the screen for the section and click on each title to view and download, such as the following booklets: "Keep Your Heart Healthy" and "Looking After Your Heart" (for South Asian people). You can also

order these free DVDs: *Risking It* (also in booklet form) and *Living to Prevent Heart Disease.*

Websites

➤ Aetna InteliHealth—"Coronary Artery Disease." http://www.intelihealth.com/ IH/ihtIH/WSIHW000/21827/24755/216672.html?d=dmtHealthAZ; alternate path: http://www.intelihealth.com/, search for and then click on the title "Coronary Artery Disease."
This website provides an overview of coronary artery disease including symptoms, diagnosis, expected duration, prevention, treatment, when to call a professional, prognosis, and more. Aetna InteliHealth, a subsidiary of Aetna, is reviewed by the faculty of Harvard Medical School and the University College of Dental Medicine. According to Aetna InteliHealth's website, "Aetna Inteli-Health maintains absolute editorial independence. That means that Aetna InteliHealth makes decisions about the information on our site free of outside influence." Under "Healthy Lifestyle," Aetna InteliHealth also offers free health-related e-mail subscriptions.

➤ American Heart Association (AHA)—"Atherosclerosis." http://www.heart.org/ HEARTORG/Conditions/Cholesterol/WhyCholesterolMatters/Atherosclerosis _UCM_305564_Article.jsp; alternate path: http://www.heart.org/, search for and then click on the title "Atherosclerosis."
AHA discusses atherosclerosis and how it starts. Included on this webpage is a link to "View an Animation of Atherosclerosis."

➤ Brigham and Women's Hospital (BWH) (Boston, MA). http://www.brigham andwomens.org/.
For information on clinical trials, see the BWH entry on p. 29.
  • "Aneurysm Animation." http://healthlibrary.brighamandwomens.org/ interactivetools/animations/94,P08449; alternate path: http://www.brigham andwomens.org/, scroll under "Health Information" to "Interactive Tools and Media," click on "Animations," and then scroll down to click on the topic. BWH offers an easy-to-understand animation on aneurysms that can be accessed by clicking on the "Launch Animation" link. According to its website, an "aneurysm repair can save your life. An aneurysm is an abnormal widening or bulging in the wall of a blood vessel and occurs more often in arteries than in veins. Learn more in this animation."
  • "Animations: Cardiac Catheterization Animation." http://healthlibrary .brighamandwomens.org/interactivetools/animations/94,P08390; alternate path: http://www.brighamandwomens.org/, scroll under "Health Information" to "Interactive Tools and Media," click on "Animations," and then scroll down to click on the topic. BWH offers an easy-to-understand

animation on cardiac catheterization that can be accessed by clicking on the "Launch Animation" link. According to its website, "Often called cardiac cath, this procedure can diagnose certain heart conditions and provide valuable information about your heart function. It may be performed to assess the coronary arteries, heart valves, and function of the heart muscle. A cardiac cath may also help determine the need for future heart surgery or other treatments."

- "Animations: Stent Placement." http://healthlibrary.brighamandwomens .org/InteractiveTools/Animations/94,P08395; alternate path: http://www .brighamandwomens.org/, scroll under the heading "Health Information" to the category "Interactive Tools and Media," click on the title "Animations," and then scroll down and click on the topic. BWH offers an easy-to-understand animation on stent placement that can be accessing by clicking on the "Launch Animation" link. According to its website, "Stents can help keep the heart's arteries open and prevent a heart attack. Coronary artery disease, or CAD, may occur when coronary arteries become obstructed by a buildup of fatty material or plaque. Stents, or small tubes, are placed to help open these vessels."

- "Cardiovascular: Cardiac Catheterization" (Video). http://healthlibrary .brighamandwomens.org/InteractiveTools/Videos/Cardiovascular/ 109,W1706; alternate path: http://www.brighamandwomens.org/, scroll under the heading "Health Information" to the category "Interactive Tools and Media," click on the title "Videos," click on the category "Cardiovascular," and then click on the topic. BWH offers an easy-to-understand short video on cardiac catheterization. According to its website, the "[c]ardiac catheterization procedure can diagnose a variety of heart conditions and determine the health of your coronary arteries, heart valves, and heart muscle. View this video to learn what happens during this procedure and various treatment options."

- "Coronary Artery Disease." http://healthlibrary.brighamandwomens .org/HealthCenters/Heart/Conditions/CAD/; alternate path: http://www .brighamandwomens.org/, scroll under the heading "Health Information" to the category "Health Information Center," click on the title "Heart Information Center," scroll down and click on the category "Heart Diseases and Conditions," and then click on the topic. BWH's coronary artery disease webpage discusses coronary artery disease, atherosclerosis, inflammation, angina pectoris, angina, and six symptoms you should never ignore.

- "Interventional Cardiology: For Patients." http://www.brighamandwomens .org/Departments_and_Services/medicine/services/cvcenter/interventional/ for_patients.aspx; alternate path: http://www.brighamandwomens.org/, scroll under "Departments and Services" to "Centers of Excellence" and click on the title "Cardiovascular," under the heading "Cardiovascular Medicine" scroll down and click on the category "Cardiac Catheterization," and then click on the title "For Patients." BWH offers patient information on cardiac catheterization, such as FAQs and "Patient Educational Material and Procedural Instructions."

➢ British Heart Foundation (BHF)—"Cardiovascular Disease (CVD)." http://www .bhf.org.uk/heart-health/conditions/cardiovascular-disease.aspx; alternate path: http://www.bhf.org.uk/, search for "cardiovascular disease" and then click on the title "British Heart Foundation—Cardiovascular Disease."
The BHF website describes such topics as CVD, what to do if you are worried about developing CVD, prevention, treatment, and risk factors. A video that demonstrates coronary heart disease fat buildup is available. Also click on the "Community: Share Experiences with Others" heading to engage with the BHF online community where you can share your own story and read those of others.

➢ CardioSmart. https://www.cardiosmart.org/.
CardioSmart, produced by the American College of Cardiology (ACC) Foundation, provides an easy-to-use website that offers a variety of information related to heart disease. According to the website, "CardioSmart is the patient education and support program launched by the [ACC]. Our mission is to engage, inform, and empower patients to better prepare them for participation in their own care." You can find the following specific resources, as well as other related pages, from the CardioSmart homepage by using a topic search and clicking on the corresponding titles.

  • "Coronary Artery Disease (CAD)." https://www.cardiosmart.org/HeartDisease/ CTT.aspx?id=604. This webpage discusses understanding CAD through subsections such as overviews, basic facts, detailed explanations, and risk factors. It also includes links to related CAD articles.

  • "Heart Disease Risk Assessment." https://www.cardiosmart.org/CardioSmart/ Default.aspx?id=298. This webpage discusses why and how to use the heart disease risk assessment tool and includes information on entering your data and interpreting the results.

  • "Heart Disease Risk: Should I Have a Coronary Calcium Scan?" https:// www.cardiosmart.org/healthwise/av20/72/av2072. This webpage focuses on understanding what coronary artery calcium scoring is. Discussion includes why this test is important, cost range, risks, benefits, what the amount of blood calcium means, and when coronary artery calcium screening should be used.

➢ CenterWatch—Clinical trials listing service. http://www.centerwatch.com/.
This CenterWatch clinical trials listing service lists trials currently looking for volunteers to enroll in medical studies. Click on the "Clinical Trials" heading and

search by location, medical condition, or therapeutic area. To search by location, click on your state (or country) and click on a city near you to find information on each available clinical trial. Check back with this website often for new studies. Sign up for a free e-mail service that sends notice of new clinical trials.

- "Angina Clinical Trials." http://www.centerwatch.com/clinical-trials/listings/studylist.aspx?CatID=12.
- "Atherosclerosis Clinical Trials." http://www.centerwatch.com/clinical-trials/listings/studylist.aspx?CatID=17.
- "Carotid Artery Disease Clinical Trials." http://www.centerwatch.com/clinical-trials/listings/studylist.aspx?CatID=635.
- "Kawasaki Disease Clinical Trials." http://www.centerwatch.com/clinical-trials/listings/studylist.aspx?CatID=760.
- "Myocardial Ischemia Clinical Trials." http://www.centerwatch.com/clinical-trials/listings/studylist.aspx?CatID=812.
- "Thrombosis Clinical Trials." http://www.centerwatch.com/clinical-trials/listings/studylist.aspx?CatID=147.

Alternate path: http://www.centerwatch.com/, under the category "Patient Resources," click on "Search Clinical Trials" where you can search by medical condition, click on the medical condition's first letter (e.g., "A"), and then click on the specific title (e.g., "Angina"). The "Search Clinical Trials" page also allows searching by location and therapeutic area.

➤ Cleveland Clinic (Cleveland, OH). http://my.clevelandclinic.org/.
For information on clinical trials, see the Cleveland Clinic entry on pp. 31–32.

- "Atherosclerosis." http://my.clevelandclinic.org/disorders/atherosclerosis/vs_overview.aspx. The Cleveland Clinic provides comprehensive patient-friendly information on atherosclerosis, including definition, other names for atherosclerosis, diagnostic tests, treatments, and lifestyle changes and prevention. The Cleveland Clinic also offers a link to "Chat Online with a Heart and Vascular Nurse."
- "Coronary Artery Disease." http://my.clevelandclinic.org/heart/disorders/cad/default.aspx. The Cleveland Clinic provides comprehensive patient-friendly information on coronary artery disease, such as definitions, types, causes and risks, diagnosis, treatments, prevention and disease management, and how to find a doctor who treats coronary artery disease.

Alternate path: http://my.clevelandclinic.org/, under the category "Institutes and Services," click on "Heart and Vascular," then click on "Homepage," then click on the category "Diseases and Conditions," and click on the corresponding title.

➤ ClinicalTrials.gov. http://clinicaltrials.gov/.
ClinicalTrials.gov, developed by the U.S. National Institutes of Health of the National Library of Medicine, lists ongoing and currently enrolling clinical trials.

To find clinical trials from the homepage, search for the condition by name (e.g., "arrhythmia"), which will generate a list of possibly hundreds or thousands of studies. To limit your results, click on "Modify This Search" and select specific fields, such as (1) Recruitment (e.g., you might want to select "Open Studies"); (2) Locations (e.g., select your state); and (3) Age Group, and then click on the "Search" button. Click on the title of each trial name for additional information, such as purpose of the study, study design and type, detailed description, outcome measures, eligibility (age, gender, criteria for participating), study start date, estimated study completion date, and sponsor. Check often for new studies.

- Angina clinical trials. http://clinicaltrials.gov/ct2/results/refine?term=angina.
- Atherosclerosis clinical trials. http://clinicaltrials.gov/ct2/results/refine?term=atherosclerosis.
- Carotid artery disease clinical trials. http://clinicaltrials.gov/ct2/results/refine?term=carotid+artery+disease.
- Coronary artery disease clinical trials. http://clinicaltrials.gov/ct2/results/refine?term=coronary+artery+disease.
- Kawasaki disease clinical trials. http://clinicaltrials.gov/ct2/results/refine?term=kawasaki+disease.
- Myocardial ischemia clinical trials. http://clinicaltrials.gov/ct2/results/refine?term=myocardial+ischemia.
- Thrombosis clinical trials. http://clinicaltrials.gov/ct2/results/refine?term=thrombosis.

➢ eMedicineHealth—"Hardening of the Arteries (Atherosclerosis)." http://www.emedicinehealth.com/hardening_of_the_arteries/article_em.htm; alternate path: http://www.emedicinehealth.com/, search for "atherosclerosis," and then click on the title "Atherosclerosis (Hardening of the Arteries)" (Medical Reference from eMedicineHealth).

eMedicineHealth, a division of WebMD, offers a comprehensive article on atherosclerosis, including an overview, causes, symptoms, when to seek medical care, diagnosis, treatment, prevention, outlook, and follow-up.

➢ Hospital of the University of Pennsylvania (HUP) (Philadelphia, PA)—"Coronary Artery Disease Program." http://www.pennmedicine.org/heart/patient/clinical-services/coronary-artery-disease/; alternate path: http://www.pennmedicine.org/, click on the "Departments and Services" icon (or search for "departments and services"), scroll down and click on the category "Cardiology and Cardiac Surgery," and then scroll down under the heading "Clinical Services" and click on "Coronary Artery Disease."

At its Penn Heart and Vascular Center website, HUP offers website links in the Coronary Artery Disease Program that include an "Overview" (what coronary artery disease is, diagnostic and treatment options); the "Team," which links to each physician and specialist (with profiles, e.g., specialty, medical board certification, education); "Clinical Trials"; "The Penn Difference" (program described, patient experiences, unique capabilities and expertise, and hospital highlights); "Physician Interviews" (videos); and "Quality/Outcomes." Click on each treatment option for details and charts. A 54-page *Penn Heart and Vascular 2011 Clinical Activity Report* is available for download; this report is a "summary of surgical, medical and interventional outcomes, as well as clinical research activity and patient volumes." You can also subscribe to the Penn Heart newsletter. For information on clinical trials, see the HUP entry on p. 33.

➢ Insidermedicine. http://www.insidermedicine.com/.
The Insidermedicine website offers a variety of heart-health-related videos. From the homepage, you can search for videos by title, or you can search by topic (e.g., atrial fibrillation) to find other related videos. For more information on the Insidermedicine Project, see the earlier entry on pp. 33–34.

- "Many Coronary Artery Disease Patients Do Not Receive Optimal Medical Therapy." http://www.insidermedicine.com/archives/Many_Coronary _Artery_Disease_Patients_Do_Not_Receive_Optimal_Medical_Therapy _Video_5223.aspx. In this easy-to-understand video, with demonstrations, a cardiologist speaks about the risks and treatments of coronary artery disease.

- "MRI Best at Diagnosing Coronary Artery Disease; Mediterranean Diet May Prolong Life; Early Salt Exposure Develops Child's Preference for Salty Foods." http://www.insidermedicine.com/archives/MRI_Best_At_Diagnosing _Coronary_Artery_Disease_Mediterranean_Diet_May_Prolong_Life_Early _Salt_Exposure_Develops_Childs_Preference_for_Salty_Foods_Video_5787 .aspx. This video shows an actual MRI scan.

➢ Johns Hopkins Hospital (Baltimore, MD). http://www.hopkinsmedicine.org/.
The Johns Hopkins Heart and Vascular Institute website provides detailed information on a variety of conditions, treatments, and services. It also lists links to physicians and specialists (with profiles, e.g., specialty, medical board certification, education). Click on the heading "Clinical Trials" to find links to current trials in various heart and cardiovascular conditions. You can also access the following and related topics from the homepage through a title or topic search.

- "Coronary Artery Bypass Graft Surgery" (Clinical Services). http://www .hopkinsmedicine.org/heart_vascular_institute/conditions_treatments/ treatments/coronary_artery_bypass_graft_surgery.html and http://www .hopkinsmedicine.org/heart_vascular_institute/clinical_services/specialty _areas/coronary_artery_surgery.html. The Johns Hopkins Cardiomyopathy and Heart Failure Service provides patient-friendly, current information on coronary artery bypass surgery, why it may be necessary, how is it done, what to expect, and what to look for.

- "Coronary Artery Disease" (Conditions and Treatments). http://www .hopkinsmedicine.org/heart_vascular_institute/conditions_treatments/ conditions/coronary_artery.html and http://www.hopkinsmedicine.org/ healthlibrary/conditions/adult/cardiovascular_diseases/coronary_heart _disease_85,P00207. The Johns Hopkins Heart and Vascular Institute webpage on coronary artery disease (ischemic heart disease) discusses this condition, including when to call an ambulance, when to call a doctor, symptoms, causes, prevention, diagnosis, and treatment.

➤ Khan Academy. http://www.khanacademy.org/.
Salman Khan, creator of the nonprofit Khan Academy, sketches as he explains each topic. Khan's mini lessons are all downloadable and free. According to the website, "With a library of over 2,400 videos covering everything from arithmetic to physics, finance, and history and 150 practice exercises, we're on a mission to help you learn what you want, when you want, at your own pace." Click on the heading "About" to get the maximum use of this excellent site. Khan has three degrees from the Massachusetts Institute of Technology and an MBA from Harvard University. You can find the following and other topics from the homepage by performing a title search.

- "Heart Disease and Heart Attacks: Basics of Heart Disease, Heart Attacks, Heart Failure, Angina, Cardiac Arrest." http://www.khanacademy.org/science/ healthcare-and-medicine/heart-disease-and-stroke/v/heart-disease-and-heart -attacks?playlist=Biology.
- "Stenosis, Ischemia, and Heart Failure: Clarifying a Bunch of Medical Terms around Heart Disease." http://www.khanacademy.org/science/healthcare-and -medicine/heart-disease-and-stroke/v/stenosis--ischemia-and-heart-failure.
- "Thrombo-emboli and Thromboembolisms: Clarifying Difference between a Thrombus and an Embolus (and between Thrombosis and Embolism)." http:// www.khanacademy.org/science/healthcare-and-medicine/heart-disease-and -stroke/v/thrombo-emboli-and-thromboembolisms.

➤ KidsHealth.org—"Kawasaki Disease." http://kidshealth.org/parent/medical/heart/ kawasaki.html; alternate path: http://kidshealth.org/, click on "Parents Site," scroll down and click on "Diseases and Conditions," then scroll down and click on "Heart and Blood Vessels," and then click on the title "Kawasaki Disease."
Nemours Foundation's Center for Children's Health provides current information on children with Kawasaki disease, written for parents. Topics include what is Kawasaki disease, signs and symptoms, complications, diagnosis, and treatment. Information is available in English and Spanish. Click on the "Listen" button to hear the information.

➤ Massachusetts General Hospital (MGH) (Boston, MA). http://www.massgeneral
.org/.

At each of the following MGH webpages are links to comprehensive information
in several categories: "Our Approach" includes an overview of conditions, treatments, and procedures as well as links to each medical expert (with profiles, e.g.,
specialty, medical board certification, education); "About This Program" describes
the quality and benefits of the program as well as MGH's commitment; "Conditions and Diseases" offers links to detailed information on specific and related
conditions; "Support and Wellness" offers patient guides; "Clinical Trials" links to
MGH trials and research studies currently seeking participants; "News and
Events" includes the latest information on the conditions; "Multimedia" offers
video demonstrations.

- "Cardiovascular Disease Prevention Center." http://www.massgeneral.org/
  heartcenter/services/treatmentprograms.aspx?id=1012.
- "Cardiovascular Genetics" (Treatments and Services). http://www.massgeneral
  .org/heartcenter/services/treatmentprograms.aspx?id=1234.
- "Coronary Artery Disease Program." http://www.massgeneral.org/heartcenter/
  services/treatmentprograms.aspx?id=1004.
- "Thoracic Aortic Center." http://www.massgeneral.org/heartcenter/services/
  treatmentprograms.aspx?id=1010. This reference is included because aortic
  aneurysms may be caused by atherosclerosis (hardening of the arteries),
  hypertension (high blood pressure), or a congenital abnormality (such as
  Marfan syndrome).

Alternate path: http://www.massgeneral.org/, search for the topic by title or go to
"Centers and Services," click on "View All Departments," then click on "Heart
Center," and then click on the heading "Treatments and Services" and scroll
down to your topic.

➤ Mayo Clinic (Rochester, MN). http://www.mayoclinic.com/.

For information on clinical trials and patient services, see the Mayo Clinic entry
on p. 36.

- "Arteriosclerosis/Atherosclerosis." http://www.mayoclinic.com/health/
  arteriosclerosis-atherosclerosis/DS00525; alternate path: http://www
  .mayoclinic.com/, search for "atherosclerosis," and then click on the title
  "Arteriosclerosis/Atherosclerosis—MayoClinic.com." Written for patients,
  this webpage on atherosclerosis includes definitions, symptoms, causes,
  risk factors, complications, preparing for appointments, tests and diagnosis, treatments and drugs, lifestyle and home remedies, and prevention.
  There is also a more comprehensive section titled "In-Depth" on some of
  these topics.

- "Coronary Artery Disease." http://www.mayoclinic.com/health/coronary -artery-disease/DS00064; alternate path: http://www.mayoclinic.com/, search for and then click on the title "Coronary Artery Disease." Written for patients, this webpage on coronary artery disease includes definitions, symptoms, causes, risk factors, complications, preparing for appointments, tests and diagnosis, treatments and drugs, alternative medicine, lifestyle and home remedies, and prevention. There is also a more comprehensive section titled "In-Depth" on some of these topics and a "Multimedia" section containing videos.

➤ MedicineNet. http://www.medicinenet.com/.
MedicineNet.com is owned and operated by WebMD and part of the WebMD Network. According to its website, MedicineNet "provides easy-to-read, in-depth, authoritative medical information for consumers via its user-friendly, interactive website." The medical information is written and edited by a nationally recognized group of more than 70 U.S. board-certified physicians. The website contains a "Symptom Checker" listed in alphabetical order as a guide to "pinpoint your pain." Its homepage links to "Health News of the Week." You can also sign up to receive a health newsletter.

- "Angina." http://www.medicinenet.com/angina/article.htm. In-depth information on Angina includes symptoms, causes, diagnosis, treatment options, patient discussions, and finding a local cardiologist.
- "Coronary Artery Disease." http://www.medicinenet.com/heart_disease/ article.htm. In-depth information on coronary artery disease includes definitions, risks factors, symptoms, diagnosis, ECG, EKG, CT, heart catheterization, stress testing, echocardiography, prevention, angioplasty, stents, treatment (surgery and medications), pictures, patient discussions, and finding a local cardiologist.
- "Coronary Artery Disease Screening Tests." http://www.medicinenet.com/ coronary_artery_disease_screening_tests_cad/article.htm. In-depth information on coronary artery disease screening tests includes definitions, purpose of screening, common initial screen tests, EKG, various stress tests, coronary angiography, and finding a local cardiologist.

Alternate path: http://www.medicinenet.com/, click on "Diseases and Conditions," click on "Conditions A–Z," then click on the appropriate letter, and then scroll down to click on the specific resource title.

➤ MedlinePlus. http://www.nlm.nih.gov/.
MedlinePlus, a component of the National Institutes of Health, is produced by the National Library of Medicine and is updated regularly.

- "Coronary Artery Disease (Coronary Arteriosclerosis, Coronary Athero-sclerosis)." http://www.nlm.nih.gov/medlineplus/coronaryarterydisease

.html; alternate path: http://www.nlm.nih.gov/, under "Databases," click on "MedlinePlus," and then search for "coronary artery disease" and click on the resource title. This MedlinePlus webpage offers extensive linked information: overviews, news, diagnosis/symptoms, treatment, prevention/screening, alternative therapy, disease management, specific conditions, related issues, anatomy/ physiology, financial issues, clinical trials, genetics, research, journal articles, dictionaries/glossaries, directories, organizations, and a section for women only. Links to patient handouts, related information in *MedlinePlus Magazine*, and multimedia tools, tutorials, and videos are also included.

- "Kawasaki Disease." http://www.nlm.nih.gov/medlineplus/kawasakidisease .html; alternate path: http://www.nlm.nih.gov/, under "Databases," click on "MedlinePlus," and then search for "Kawasaki disease" and click on the title. This MedlinePlus webpage offers a variety of linked information: overviews, diagnosis/symptoms, treatment, clinical trials, genetics, journal articles, organizations, and patient handouts.

➢ Medscape Reference (Drugs, Diseases, and Procedures)—"Coronary Artery Atherosclerosis." http://emedicine.medscape.com/article/153647-overview; alternate path: http://emedicine.medscape.com/, search for and then click on the title "Coronary Artery Atherosclerosis."
Written for Medscape by F. Brian Boudi, MD, and associates, this webpage presents a comprehensive report on coronary artery atherosclerosis. Although written for health care professionals, it might be helpful for interested laypersons. Articles for Medscape Reference are written by medical experts. The webpage states, "Our rigorous literature survey process allows us to rapidly integrate new practice-changing information into the relevant topics by systematically reviewing the major medical and pharmacy journals, news announcements, and important practice guidelines." Free registration is required.

➢ *The Merck Manual Home Health Handbook for Patients and Caregivers*— "Atherosclerosis." http://www.merckmanuals.com/home/sec03/ch030/ch030a.html; alternate path: http://www.merckmanuals.com/home/, under "Sections," click on "All" next to the navigational arrows to view a complete list, then click on "Heart and Blood Vessel Disorders," and then scroll down and click on "Atherosclerosis." This section on atherosclerosis, which includes an overview on causes, risk factors, symptoms, diagnosis, prevention, and treatment, is based on the well-known medical textbook *The Merck Manual Home Health Handbook for Patients and Caregivers* and "is provided free of charge . . . as a public service."

➢ National Heart, Lung, and Blood Institute (NHLBI). http://www.nhlbi.nih.gov/. NHLBI is a division of the National Institutes of Health from the U.S. Department of Health and Human Services. You can find the following resources from the homepage by searching on the title.

- "What Is Coronary Artery Disease?" http://www.nhlbi.nih.gov/health/dci/ Diseases/Cad/CAD_WhatIs.html. This NHLBI website provides additional information on CAD, including what is CAD, other names, causes, risk, signs and symptoms, diagnosis, treatments, prevention, living with CAD, clinical trials, key points, and more. There are also links to podcasts and videos.
- "What Is Diabetic Heart Disease?" http://www.nhlbi.nih.gov/health/health -topics/topics/dhd/. This NHLBI webpage provides information on diabetic heart disease, including definitions, causes, risk factors, signs and symptoms, diagnosis, treatments, prevention, living with DHD, clinical trials, and more.
- "What Is Kawasaki Disease?" http://www.nhlbi.nih.gov/health/health -topics/topics/kd/. This NHLBI webpage provides information on Kawa-saki disease, including what Kawasaki disease is, other names, causes, risk factors, signs and symptoms, diagnosis, treatments, prevention, living with Kawasaki disease, and clinical trials.

➤ New York–Presbyterian (NYP) University Hospital of Columbia and Cornell (New York, NY). http://nyp.org/.
Under the heading "Find a Physician" you can search for physicians and special-ists by specialty or name to view their profiles (e.g., specialty, medical board cer-tification, education). Under the heading "Hospital News" are links to detailed articles explaining recent studies. For clinical trial information, see the NYP entry on p. 38.

- "Angioplasty and Stenting" and "Coronary Artery Disease." http://nyp.org/ services/cardiology/angioplasty.html; alternate path: http://nyp.org/, under the heading "Centers of Excellence," click on the category "Heart," then scroll down to the category "Cardiology," then click on "More Services," and then click on the topic "Angioplasty and Stenting." The NYP University Hospital of Columbia and Cornell website provides patient-friendly information on angioplasty and stenting, which are used to treat blocked coronary arteries. Within the text, click on the title "Blocked Coronary Arteries," which dis-cusses what coronary arteries are, what the different coronary arteries are, their importance, what coronary artery disease is, risk factors, symptoms, diagnosis, and treatment.
- "Interactive Media Library" (Videos). http://nyp.org/media/index.html; alter-nate path: http://nyp.org/, click on the "Explore the Interactive Media Library" icon. The Human Atlas media player contains short videos, text, models, and slides. To view each excellent video, go to "Click Here for a Complete List-ing of Topics" and scroll through the choices, such as "Abdominal Aneurysm," "Angiography," "Angioplasty," "Heart Bypass Surgery," "Heart-Lung Machine," "OPCAB," and "Stress Test/ECG."

➤ ORLive. http://www.orlive.com/.

This website features surgical procedure videos recorded live. If the following links are broken, go to the homepage, on the "Videos" pull-down menu at the top, under "Procedures," click on "Heart Procedures," then click on the topic (e.g., "Coronary Artery Bypass"), and then select the title.

- "Abdominal–Aortic Dissection and Aneurysms." http://www.orlive.com/nyp/videos/abdominal-aortic-dissection-and-aneurysms. Surgical procedure video-recorded live on innovations in minimally invasive and conventional therapies for aortic dissection and aneurysm at the Center for Vascular Surgery at New York–Presbyterian/Weill Cornell Medical Center and New York–Presbyterian (NYP)/Columbia University Medical Center.
- "Minimally Invasive Coronary Artery Bypass Surgery." http://www.orlive.com/medtronic/videos/minimally-invasive-coronary-artery-bypass-surgery. Surgical procedure video-recorded live on minimally invasive coronary artery bypass surgery at the Heart Institute of Staten Island at the Staten Island University Hospital. This surgery is being moderated by Joseph Sabik, Chairman of Thoracic and Cardiovascular Surgery at the Cleveland Clinic.

➤ Texas Heart Institute (Houston, TX)—"Heart Information Center." http://www.texasheartinstitute.org/.

For information on clinical trials, see the Texas Heart Institute entry on p. 40.

- "Aneurysm Repair." http://www.texasheartinstitute.org/HIC/Topics/Proced/asurg.cfm. The Texas Heart Institute website offers a definition of aneurysm repair, as well as information on where it occurs, when surgery is needed, nonsurgical repair of abdominal aortic aneurysms, and what to expect before, during, and after surgery. An easy-to-print format is available.
- "Aneurysms and Dissections." http://www.texasheartinstitute.org/HIC/Topics/Cond/Aneurysm.cfm. The Texas Heart Institute website offers a definition of aneurysms, as well as information on causes, risks, signs and symptoms, detection, nonsurgical procedure for treatment of aneurysms, and other treatment options.
- "Angina." http://www.texasheartinstitute.org/HIC/Topics/Cond/Angina.cfm. The Texas Heart Institute website offers a definition of angina, as well as information on causes, signs and symptoms, types, diagnosis, lifestyle changes, and treatment.
- "Balloon Angioplasty and Stents." http://www.texasheartinstitute.org/HIC/Topics/Proced/angioplasty.cfm. The Texas Heart Institute website offers a definition of balloon angioplasty and stents, as well as information on during and after a balloon angioplasty or stent, procedure, diagnosis, and treatment.

- "Cardiac Syndrome X (not CAD)." http://www.texasheartinstitute.org/HIC/Topics/Cond/CardiacSyndromeX.cfm. The Texas Heart Institute website offers a definition of cardiac syndrome X, as well as information on causes, signs and symptoms, diagnosis, and treatment.
- "Carotid Artery Angioplasty and Stents." http://www.texasheartinstitute.org/HIC/Topics/Proced/carotidangioplasty.cfm. The Texas Heart Institute website offers a definition of carotid artery angioplasty, as well as information on what to expect during and after a carotid angioplasty and stent procedure.
- "Carotid Artery Disease." http://www.texasheartinstitute.org/HIC/Topics/Cond/CarotidArteryDisease.cfm. The Texas Heart Institute website offers a definition of carotid artery disease, as well as information on risk, causes, signs and symptoms, diagnosis, and treatment.
- "Carotid Endarterectomy." http://www.texasheartinstitute.org/HIC/Topics/Proced/carotidendar.cfm. The Texas Heart Institute website offers a definition of carotid endarterectomy, as well as information on what to expect before, during, and after carotid endarterectomy surgery.
- "Coronary Artery Bypass." http://www.texasheartinstitute.org/HIC/Topics/Proced/cab.cfm. The Texas Heart Institute website offers a definition of coronary bypass surgery, as well as information on what to expect before, during, and after coronary bypass surgery.
- "Coronary Artery Disease (CAD)." http://www.texasheartinstitute.org/HIC/Topics/Cond/caa.cfm. The Texas Heart Institute website offers a definition of CAD, as well as information on risks, causes, signs and symptoms, diagnosis, and treatment.
- "Kawasaki Disease." http://www.texasheartinstitute.org/HIC/Topics/Cond/kawasaki_disease.cfm. The Texas Heart Institute website offers a definition of Kawasaki disease, as well as information on risk, signs and symptoms, diagnosis, and treatment.
- "Limited-Access Heart Surgery." http://www.texasheartinstitute.org/HIC/Topics/Proced/limaccess.cfm. The Texas Heart Institute website offers a definition of limited-access heart surgery, as well as information on minimally invasive heart surgery, types of limited-access heart surgery, who are the best candidates for this type of surgery, videoscopic surgery, and robotic-assisted heart surgery.
- "Radial Artery Access." http://www.texasheartinstitute.org/HIC/Topics/Proced/radial_artery_access.cfm. The Texas Heart Institute website offers a definition of radial artery access, as well as information on who are the best candidates for this type of surgery and what to expect during surgery.
- "Transmyocardial Laser Revascularization." http://www.texasheartinstitute.org/HIC/Topics/Proced/tmlrs.cfm. The Texas Heart Institute website offers

a definition of transmyocardial laser revascularization (TMLR), percutaneous transmyocardial revascularization (PTMR), and what to expect before, during, and after TMLR surgery.
- "Vulnerable Plaque." http://www.texasheartinstitute.org/HIC/Topics/Cond/vulplaq.cfm. The Texas Heart Institute website offers a definition of vulnerable plaque, as well as information on causes, detection, prevention, signs and symptoms, diagnosis, and treatment.

Alternate path: go to the homepage, search for the topic by name (e.g., "aneurysm repair"), and then click on the appropriate title; or on the homepage, in the pull-down menu under "Heart Information Center," select "Heart-Health Topics" and then either "Heart Conditions" or "Surgical and Medical Procedures," and click on the topic by name.

➤ UCLA Ronald Reagan Medical Center (Los Angeles, CA)—"Coronary Artery Disease." http://www.uclahealth.org/body.cfm?id=592; scroll down to the heading "In-Depth Reports," and click on the title "Coronary Artery Disease"; alternate path: http://www.uclahealth.org/, under the heading "For Patients and Visitors," scroll down and mouse over the category "Health Resources" and then select "Heart Health Center," scroll down to the heading "In-Depth Reports," and then click on the title "Coronary Artery Disease."

The UCLA Ronald Reagan Medical Center's Heart Health Center provides an in-depth report on coronary artery disease, which includes introductions, risk factors, symptoms, diagnosis, prevention, treatment, medications, surgery, and resources. Under "Tests and Treatments," scroll under the section "Alternative Medicine" for more treatment information, then click on the word "More," and then click on these topics: "Coronary Artery Disease," "Atherosclerosis," and "Arteriosclerosis." For more information on patient resources and clinical trials, see the UCLA entry on p. 41.

➤ WebMD—"Coronary Artery Disease Directory." http://www.webmd.com/heart-disease/coronary-artery-disease-directory; alternate path: http://www.webmd.com/, search for "coronary artery disease" and then click on the title "Coronary Artery Disease Directory" (WebMD Health and Wellness Directory).

The WebMD website offers the linked information on coronary artery disease, including causes, symptoms, risks, treatments, prevention, FAQs, and end-of-life decisions. A WebMD heart health e-mail newsletter is also available. According to WebMD, "WebMD News is an independent media service designed to provide news, information, and educational material to consumers and physicians. News content created by WebMD is free from influence by sponsors, partners, or other sources."

Patient Support Groups and Organizations

➤ DailyStrength—"Coronary Heart Disease Support Group." http://www.dailystrength
.org/c/Coronary-Heart-Disease/support-group; alternate path: http://www
.dailystrength.org/, search for "coronary heart disease," and then click on the title
"Visit the Coronary Heart Disease Support Group."
The DailyStrength website offers online support groups and blogs for those with
coronary heart disease. Free registration is required to participate. According to
the website, "DailyStrength is a subsidiary of Sharecare. Sharecare, created by
WebMD founder and Discovery Communications' Chief of Global Digital Strategy Jeff Arnold, along with America's Doctor, Dr. Mehmet Oz, is the first truly
interactive healthcare ecosystem giving consumers the ability to ask, learn and
act on the questions of health."

➤ Kawasaki Disease Foundation. http://www.kdfoundation.org/.
The Kawasaki Disease Foundation is a support group that offers information on
Kawasaki disease. Available are booklets, videos, newsletters, and support
forums. According to the website, "In October 2000, a group of parents and professionals collaborated to create the Kawasaki Disease Foundation (KDF), the
only non-profit organization dedicated exclusively to addressing issues related to
Kawasaki Disease."

➤ MedHelp. http://www.medhelp.org/.
According to its website, MedHelp "connects people with the leading medical
experts," such as those from Cleveland Clinic, National Jewish Health, Partners
Health, and Mount Sinai Hospital, with those who have similar medical issues.
MedHelp's main focus is to enable patients "to take control over their health and
find answers to their medical questions" using nontechnical language via an
online community through posts, forums and groups, blogs, user journals, as well
as recommendations, articles, health pages, and a medical glossary. Free registration is required. From the homepage, you can find the following and related
groups by searching for the topic.
  • "Atherosclerosis." http://www.medhelp.org/search?query=atherosclerosis.
  • "Coronary Artery Disease." http://www.medhelp.org/search?query=coronary
    +artery+disease.

➤ U.S. Hospital Finder. http://www.ushospitalfinder.com/.
Use this site to find the names of hospitals by zip code, city, state, or your
address. The search results include a map with directions. You might also
want to ask your health care professional, call hospitals in your area, or search
for "support groups" on hospital websites to determine if there are any cardiology support groups for people with coronary artery disease (atherosclerosis) that meet regularly in your area.

> Yahoo! Groups—"Coronary Artery Disease among Indians (CADI) Research Support Group." http://health.groups.yahoo.com/group/cadiresearch/; alternate path: http://www.groups.yahoo.com/, search for "coronary artery disease" in the "Find a Yahoo! Group" Search box and then click on the group "Coronary Artery Disease among Indians."
This online Yahoo! group is for patients with coronary artery disease and their families and friends. Yahoo! Groups is not a medical site, nor does it provide or endorse medical advice or procedures. The purpose of the website is to share experiences in a kind and caring manner. Free registration is required to participate.

Resources for Further Information on Stroke
Books

> Kagan, Jeff. *Life after Stroke: On the Road to Recovery*. Campbell, CA: FastPencil, 2011. Print.
Kagan, a technical analyst, columnist, and consultant who writes for major newspapers and speaks on all the major TV and radio stations, wrote this book seven years after having a stroke. According to the publisher, Kagan's goal was "to help others better understand their new world after stroke and the journey ahead. . . . *Life after Stroke* is written from one stroke survivor to another, and for family and friends. It is full of laughter and tears, ups and downs, and the important lessons learned and the questions answered through the long battle toward recovery."

> Meyer, Maria, Paula Derr, and Jon Casswell. *The Comfort of Home for Stroke: A Guide for Caregivers*. Portland, OR: CareTrust, 2007. Print.
This book, from the Comfort of Home book series, "is committed to providing high-quality, user-friendly information to those who face an illness or the responsibilities of caring for friends, family or clients." This book is divided into three sections, describing stroke, discussing its causes and how to prepare for the task of caring for someone who has had a stroke, and offering guidance for every aspect of daily care for the stroke survivor, and finally providing additional resources and a "list of common medical abbreviations to help you understand the terms many health care professionals use."

> Palmer, Sara, and Jeffery B. Palmer. *When Your Spouse Has a Stroke: Caring for Your Partner, Yourself, and Your Relationship* (A Johns Hopkins Press Health Book). Baltimore, MD: Johns Hopkins University Press, 2011. Print.
Sara Palmer, a rehabilitation psychologist, and Jeffrey Palmer, a physiatrist (a doctor specializing in physical medicine and rehabilitation), who have cared for stroke survivors and their spouses for more than twenty-five years of

clinical experience, wrote this book "specifically [to address] spouse caregivers of stroke survivors . . . [to guide the spouse] how to maintain, improve, [and] rebuild a satisfying marriage after a stroke . . . by discussing and offering solutions for many of the relationship problems you will experience after your spouse's stroke."

➤ Senelick, Richad C. *Living with Stroke: A Guide for Families*. Chicago, IL: Contemporary Publishing, 2010. Print.
Senelick, a neurologist specializing in rehabilitation and brain injury as well as a medical director of HealthSouth Rehabilitation Institute of San Antonio, Texas, describes for the reader (1) types of strokes, risk factors, and warning signs; (2) when stroke occurs, right-hemisphere stroke, left-hemisphere stroke, and diagnostic tools; (3) recovery-meditation, physical therapy, occupational, speech, and recreational therapy; "emotional issues"; and (4) the family's role in coping.

➤ Williams, Olajide. *Stroke Diaries: A Guide for Survivors and Their Families*. New York, NY: Oxford University Press, 2010. Print.
Williams, from the Department of Neurology of the Columbia University Medical Center, wrote this book to tell stoke victims' stories as a way to reduce stroke occurrence. According to the book's introduction, "He uses these [stories] as a springboard to provide helpful facts about prevention, diagnosis, treatment, and recovery of stroke."

Brochures, Booklets, and Other Short Print Publications

➤ American Heart Association (AHA)—Stroke educational brochures. http://www.strokeassociation.org/STROKEORG/General/Patient-Information-Sheets_UCM_310731_Article.jsp; alternate path: http://www.heart.org/, search for "educational brochures," click on the title "Order American Heart Association Educational Brochures," and then click on the topic "Stroke."
Numerous AHA brochures on stroke are available for free download. These brochures can be downloaded or ordered by filling in a form online. (No more than one packet and two brochures per household can be ordered at no cost.)

➤ HeartHub for Patients. "Stroke Fact Sheets." http://www.hearthub.org/hc-stroke.htm; alternate path: http://www.hearthub.org/, scroll down to the section titled "Health Centers" and click on the title "Stroke."
HeartHub is a division of the American Heart Association (AHA). Scroll down to and click on the title "Printable Stroke Fact Sheets," which provides information "about preventing a stroke and living with the effects of a stroke."

➤ National Stroke Association—Brochures and Recovery Fact Sheet series. http://www.stroke.org/site/PageServer?pagename=brochures and http://www.stroke

.org/site/PageServer?pagename=Recov_factsheets; alternate path: http://www
.stroke.org/, click on the main topic "What Is Stroke?," scroll down and click on
the title "Brochures," and then click on the title "Fact Sheets."
The National Stroke Association offers numerous brochures to download for free
in PDF format. (If you click and the PDF does not open, right-click and select
"Open in new window.")

Websites

➢ American Stroke Association. http://www.strokeassociation.org/.
The American Stroke Association has sections on warning signs; about stroke,
which includes sections on risk, diagnosis, treatment, and stroke in children;
life after stroke, which includes regaining independence for family caregivers,
support groups, healthy living, and inspirational stories; power to end stroke,
which includes a variety of lifestyle changes; and advocacy, which includes an
action center, policy resources, and issues and campaigns. In addition, there is
a magazine, *Stroke Connection*, that is available by signing up online. You can
order this magazine in a print version or have it delivered electronically
through e-mail.

➢ BetterMedicine.com—"Stroke." http://www.bettermedicine.com/topic/stroke/;
alternate path: http://www.bettermedicine.com/, scroll down to the section titled
"Common Conditions," and then click the title "Stroke."
The BetterMedicine website offers links to topics such as definitions, stroke
recovery begins with rehabilitation, preventing cardiovascular diseases, signs
and symptoms of stroke, treatment for stroke, and living with stroke. There
are also sections containing expert advice on stroke from Harvard Medical
School and stroke features. According to the Better Medicine website, "all
content is medically reviewed by at least one medical professional. Our content is backed by evidence from sources, such as articles in peer reviewed
journals, government bodies, objective health organizations and medical
groups of specialists. The name and credentials of the medical reviewer(s) are
printed at the end of the article."

➢ Brigham and Women's Hospital (BWH) (Boston, MA)—"Stroke Treatment" (Ani-
mation).   http://healthlibrary.brighamandwomens.org/InteractiveTools/
Animations/94,P08397; alternate path: http://www.brighamandwomens.org/, scroll
under the heading "Health Information" to the category titled "Interactive Tools and
Media," click on the title "Animations," and then scroll down and click on the topic
"Stroke Treatment Animation."
BWH offers an easy-to-understand animation on what is a stroke that can be
accessed by clicking on the "Launch Animation" link. According to its website,

"Once a stroke occurs, what treatment is used? Treatment options vary based on the type, severity, and location of the stroke. Become more aware of these options and the importance of early, life-saving treatment." For information on clinical trials, see the BWH entry on p. 29.

> CardioSmart—"Stroke." https://www.cardiosmart.org/HeartDisease/CTT.aspx?id =686; alternate path: https://www.cardiosmart.org/, search for and then click on the title "Stroke."
CardioSmart provides an easy-to-use website on understanding stroke, including definitions, what is transient ischemic attack, treatment, and prognosis. According to the American College of Cardiology (ACC), "CardioSmart is the patient education and support program launched by the [ACC]. Our mission is to engage, inform, and empower patients to better prepare them for participation in their own care."

> Cleveland Clinic (Cleveland, OH)—"Understanding Stroke." http://my.cleveland clinic.org/disorders/Stroke/hic_Understanding_Stroke.aspx; alternate path: http:// my.clevelandclinic.org/, under the category "Institutes and Services," click on "Heart and Vascular," then click on "Homepage," then click on the category "Diseases and Conditions," and then click on the title "Stroke."
The Cleveland Clinic provides comprehensive patient-friendly information on stroke, including other names for stroke, risk factors, signs and symptoms, transient ischemic attack (TIA), treatments and prevention, rehabilitation, emotional and behavioral changes after stroke, nutrition, and caregiver tips. The Cleveland Clinic also offers a link to "Chat Online with a Heart and Vascular Nurse." For information on clinical trials, see the Cleveland Clinic entry on pp. 31–32.

> eMedicineHealth—"Stroke." http://www.emedicinehealth.com/stroke/article_em .htm and http://www.emedicinehealth.com/stroke-health/article_em.htm; alternate path: http://www.emedicinehealth.com/, search for "stroke" and then click on the title "Stroke" (Medical Reference from eMedicineHealth and also from Healthwise).
eMedicineHealth, a division of WebMD, offers a comprehensive article on stroke, including an overview, causes, symptoms, when to seek medical care, diagnosis, treatment, prevention, outlook, and follow-up. A slide show is also available.

> Insidermedicine—"Calcium Supplements May Raise Risk of Heart Attack, Stroke" (Video). http://www.insidermedicine.com/archives/Calcium_Supplements_May _Raise_Risk_of_Heart_Attack_Stroke_Video_5176.aspx; alternate path: http://www .insidermedicine.com/, search for the video by title.
The Insidermedicine website offers a variety of heart-health-related videos. In this video, a medical specialist speaks in patient-friendly language, with demonstrations, on the use of calcium supplements and calcium-rich food alternatives

for prevention of heart attack and stroke. For information on the Insidermedicine Project, see the earlier entry on pp. 33–34.

➤ Khan Academy—"Strokes: Basics of Strokes." http://www.khanacademy.org/video/strokes?playlist=Biology; alternate path: http://www.khanacademy.org/, search for "stroke."
Salman Khan, creator of the nonprofit Khan Academy, sketches as he explains the topic. Khan's mini lessons are all downloadable and free. According to the website, "With a library of over 2,400 videos covering everything from arithmetic to physics, finance, and history and 150 practice exercises, we're on a mission to help you learn what you want, when you want, at your own pace." Click on the heading "About" to get the maximum use of this excellent site. Khan has three degrees from the Massachusetts Institute of Technology and an MBA from Harvard University.

➤ KidsHealth.org—For Parents: "Strokes." http://kidshealth.org/parent/medical/heart/strokes.html#cat141; alternate path: http://www.kidshealth.org/, click on "Parents Site," scroll down and click on "Diseases and Conditions," scroll down and click on "Heart and Blood Vessels," and then click on the title "Strokes."
The Nemours Center for Children's Health Media provides current information, written for parents, on children who have experienced stroke. Topics discussed include general information about strokes, causes, signs and symptoms, diagnosis, treatment, complications, and outlook. Information is available in English and Spanish. Click on the "Listen" button to hear the text read aloud.

➤ Mayo Clinic (Rochester, MN)—"Stroke." http://www.mayoclinic.com/health/stroke/DS00150; alternate path: http://www.mayoclinic.com/, search for "stroke" and then click on the title "Stroke—MayoClinic.com."
Written for patients, this webpage on coronary artery disease includes definitions, symptoms, causes, risk factors, complications, preparing for appointments, tests and diagnosis, treatments and drugs, coping and support, and prevention. There is also a more comprehensive section titled "In-Depth" on some of these topics and a "Multimedia" section containing videos. For information on clinical trials and patient services, see the Mayo Clinic entry on p. 36.

➤ MedicineNet. http://medicinenet.com/.
MedicineNet.com is owned and operated by WebMD and part of the WebMD Network. According to its website, MedicineNet "provides easy-to-read, in-depth, authoritative medical information for consumers via its user-friendly, interactive website." The medical information is written and edited by a nationally recognized group of more than 70 U.S. board-certified physicians. The website contains a "Symptom Checker" listed in alphabetical order as a guide to

"pinpoint your pain." Its homepage links to "Health News of the Week." You can also sign up to receive a health newsletter.

- "Stroke." http://www.medicinenet.com/stroke/article.htm. In-depth information on stroke includes definitions, causes, risk factors, transient ischemic attack, symptoms, diagnosis, treatment, complications, future treatment, prevention, patient discussions, and finding a local cardiologist.
- "Stroke Prevention." http://www.medicinenet.com/stroke_prevention/article .htm. In-depth information on stroke prevention includes definitions, warning signs, risk factors, treatable risk factors, and knowing your risk.

Alternate path: http://www.medicinenet.com/, click on "Diseases and Conditions," click on "Conditions A–Z," and then click on "S" and scroll down to click on the specific topic.

➤ National Stroke Association. http://www.stroke.org/.

The mission statement of the National Stroke Association is "to reduce the incidence and impact of stroke by developing compelling education and programs focused on prevention, treatment, rehabilitation, and support for all impacted by stroke." There are detailed sections on definitions, prevention, recovery, signs and symptoms, getting involved, and staying informed. There is also a section for caregivers of stroke survivors. Click on these headings: "Life after Stroke," "Effects of Stroke," "Mobility," "Online Education," and "Recurrent Stroke." Each section has several detailed topics. Personal stories are shared and stroke support groups are listed. In addition, you can sign up online for the free *StrokeSmart* magazine.

➤ New York–Presbyterian (NYP) University Hospital of Columbia and Cornell (New York, NY). "Interactive Media Library" (Videos). http://nyp.org/media/index.html; alternate path: http://nyp.org/, click on the "Explore the Interactive Media Library" icon.

The Human Atlas media player presents short videos, text, models, and slides. To view an excellent video on stroke, go to "Click Here for a Complete Listing of Topics" and scroll down to click on "Stroke." For information on clinical trials, see the NYP entry on p. 38.

➤ Texas Heart Institute (Houston, TX). "Stroke." http://www.texasheartinstitute.org/HIC/Topics/Cond/stroke.cfm; alternate path: http://www.texasheartinstitute.org/, search for and then click on the title "Stroke"; or under the heading "Heart Information Center," click on "Heart-Health Topics," then click on "Heart Conditions," and then click on "Stroke."

The Texas Heart Institute's Heart Information Center webpage on stroke presents a description of stroke and its causes. There are numerous topics discussed, including warning signs, risk factors, diagnosis, treatment, and prevention guidelines. An easy-to-print format is available. There is also a link to the National Institutes of Health's eight-minute video on stroke in the "Multimedia" section at http://www.stroke.nih.gov/materials/knowstrokevideo.htm. For information on clinical trials, see the Texas Heart Institute entry on p. 40.

➢ UCLA Ronald Reagan Medical Center (Los Angeles, CA)—"Stroke." http://www .uclahealth.org/body.cfm?id=592; scroll down to the heading "In-Depth Reports," then click on the word "More," and then click on the title "Stroke"; alternate path: http://www.uclahealth.org/, under the heading "For Patients and Visitors," scroll down and mouse over the category "Health Resources," then click on "Heart Health Center," scroll down to the heading "In-Depth Reports," click on the word "More," and then click on the title "Stroke."
The UCLA Ronald Reagan Medical Center's Heart Health Center provides an in-depth report on coronary artery disease, which includes highlights, introductions, risk factors, prognosis, symptoms, diagnosis, treatment, prevention, surgery, and rehabilitation. Also on the Heart Health Center website, under the heading "Tests and Treatments," scroll under the section "Alternative Medicine" for more treatment information. Then click on the word "More" and then click on the title "Stroke—Transient." For more information on patient resources and clinical trials, see the UCLA entry on p. 41.

Patient Support Groups and Organizations

➢ DailyStrength—"Stroke Support Group." http://www.dailystrength.org/c/Stroke/ support-group; alternate path: http://www.dailystrength.org/, search for "stroke," and then click on "Visit the Stroke Support Group."
The DailyStrength website offers online support groups and blogs for those with stroke. Free registration is required to participate. According to the website, "Daily-Strength is a subsidiary of Sharecare. Sharecare, created by WebMD founder and Discovery Communications' Chief of Global Digital Strategy Jeff Arnold, along with America's Doctor, Dr. Mehmet Oz, is the first truly interactive healthcare eco-system giving consumers the ability to ask, learn and act on the questions of health."

➢ HeartHub for Patients—"Stroke." http://www.hearthub.org/hc-stroke.htm; alternate path: http://www.hearthub.org/, scroll down to the section titled "Health Centers," and then click on the title "Stroke."
HeartHub, a division of the American Heart Association (AHA), is a patient support portal for information, tools, and resources on stroke, including definitions, finding a certified primary stroke center near you, TIAs, life after stroke, healthy recipes, how to get help on the phone, personal stories, and a section called "The Power to End Stroke" ("Let the Power to End Stroke Campaign help you get to the root of your family's health and shape your family history"). Sign up for a free subscription to *Stroke Connection Magazine* by scrolling down to and clicking on the magazine's title and completing the online subscription form.

➤ MedHelp—"Stroke." http://www.medhelp.org/search?query=stroke; alternate path: http://www.medhelp.org/, search for "stroke."
According to its website, MedHelp "connects people with the leading medical experts," such as those from Cleveland Clinic, National Jewish Health, Partners Health, and Mount Sinai Hospital, with those who have similar medical issues. MedHelp's main focus is to enable patients "to take control over their health and find answers to their medical questions" using nontechnical language via an online community through posts, forums and groups, blogs, user journals, as well as recommendations, articles, health pages, and a medical glossary. Free registration is required.

➤ WebMD—"WebMD Stroke Community." http://www.webmd.com/stroke; alternate path: http://www.webmd.com/, search for and then click on the title "Stroke Health Center," and then scroll down to "WebMD Stroke Community" (WebMD Community).
Click on the title "Community Experts Support," as well as the links under "Discussions, Expert Blogs, and Community." Join the WebMD stroke community (WebMD moderated), which includes discussions, writing the expert, tips, resources, and support. According to the WebMD stroke community, "Talk with our experts to learn how to prevent stroke as well as treatments and therapy on your road to recovery. Then, stay to share your experiences and get support from other members." To search for other health topic communities, go to http://exchanges.webmd.com/, which is titled "Be a Part of the WebMD Community." Also, scroll down to "Create Your Own Community" for easy instructions on how to start your own group.

➤ U.S. Hospital Finder. http://www.ushospitalfinder.com/.
Use this site to find the names of hospitals by zip code, city, state, or your address. The search results include a map with directions. You might also want to ask your health care professional, call hospitals in your area, or search for "support groups" on hospital websites to determine if there are any cardiology support groups for people who have had a stroke that meet regularly in your area.

➤ Yahoo! Groups—"Heart Attack Support Group." http://health.groups.yahoo.com/group/heartattack/; alternate path: http://www.groups.yahoo.com/, search for "stroke cardiovascular disease" in the "Find a Yahoo! Group" Search box and then click on the group "heartattack."
This online Yahoo! group is for patients with a variety of cardiovascular diseases, including stroke, and their families and friends. Yahoo! Groups is not a medical site, nor does it provide or endorse medical advice or procedures. The purpose of the website is to share experiences in a kind and caring manner. Free registration is required to participate.

Endocarditis

Endocarditis is an infection and inflammation of the lining and valves of the heart. The heart has three layers: the outside or pericardium, the middle or myocardium, and the inside or endocardium. Healthy hearts rarely get endocarditis. The problem can occur if a heart has a roughened endocardium (perhaps from a cardiomyopathy), damaged valves, implanted devices (e.g., replacement valves or pacemaker), an infection elsewhere in the body, or a catheter that has been in place for a long time. These factors allow infectious agents, such as bacteria, fungi, or molds, to enter the bloodstream and attach to damaged areas of the endocardium. Sometimes small colonies of the infection form clumps called vegetation. These colonies can break off and infect other parts of the heart or body.

If the infectious agent can be identified through a blood culture, the infectious endocarditis can be treated with specific drugs. If the infectious agent is not identified, as can happen if the blood culture does not grow the agent, then culture-negative endocarditis would be treated with a broad spectrum of drugs. If the infection is not treated, it can spread to other organs, injure the heart valves, and cause death.

Resources for Further Information on Endocarditis

Brochures, Booklets, and Other Short Print Publications

➤ American Heart Association (AHA)—"Infective (Bacterial) Endocarditis Wallet Card." http://www.heart.org/HEARTORG/General/Infective-Bacterial-Endocarditis-Wallet-Card_UCM_311659_Article.jsp; alternate path: http://www.heart.org/, search for "educational brochures," then click on "Order American Heart Association Educational Brochures," then click on the topic "congenital heart defects," and then click on "Bacterial Endocarditis Wallet Card."
This AHA bacterial endocarditis wallet card is available in English and Spanish, and it can be downloaded as a PDF or ordered by filling in a form online. Also available is an infective endocarditis information packet by completing a product order form. Note that one packet per household can be ordered at no cost. For the patient information sheet titled "What Is Endocarditis?" see the AHA reference in the Websites section that follows.

Websites

➤ Aetna InteliHealth—"Endocarditis." http://www.intelihealth.com/IH/ihtIH/WSIHW000/8059/23696/266755.html?d=dmtHealthAZ; alternate path: http://www.intelihealth.com/, search for and then click on "Endocarditis."

This website provides an overview of endocarditis, including symptoms, diagnosis, expected duration, prevention, treatment, when to call a professional, prognosis, and additional information. Aetna InteliHealth, a subsidiary of Aetna, is reviewed by the faculty of Harvard Medical School and the University College of Dental Medicine. According to Aetna InteliHealth's website, "Aetna InteliHealth maintains absolute editorial independence. That means that Aetna InteliHealth makes decisions about the information on our site free of outside influence." Under "Healthy Lifestyle," Aetna InteliHealth also offers free health-related e-mail subscriptions.

➤ American Heart Association (AHA)—"Infective Endocarditis." http://www.heart
  .org/HEARTORG/Conditions/CongenitalHeartDefects/TheImpactofCongenital
  HeartDefects/Infective-Endocarditis_UCM_307108_Article.jsp; alternate path:
  http://www.heart.org/, search for and then click on the title "Infective
  Endocarditis."
  AHA offers a brief overview of infective endocarditis. Also available is a PDF
  download on bacterial endocarditis.

➤ CardioSmart—"Endocarditis." https://www.cardiosmart.org/HeartDisease/CTT
  .aspx?id=2708; alternate path: https://www.cardiosmart.org/, search for and then
  click on "Endocarditis."
  CardioSmart provides an easy-to-use webpage on understanding endocarditis,
  which is discussed in subsections such as basic facts, background, risk factors,
  complications, signs and symptoms, diagnosis, treatment, prevention, and guidelines and other resources. According to the American College of Cardiology
  (ACC), "CardioSmart is the patient education and support program launched by
  the [ACC]. Our mission is to engage, inform, and empower patients to better
  prepare them for participation in their own care."

➤ Cleveland Clinic (Cleveland, OH)—"Infective Endocarditis." http://my.cleveland
  clinic.org/heart/disorders/valve/sbe.aspx; alternate path: http://my.clevelandclinic
  .org/, under the category "Institutes and Services" click on "Heart and Vascular,"
  then click on "Homepage," then click on the category "Diseases and Conditions,"
  and then scroll down to and click on "Infective Endocarditis."
  Cleveland Clinic provides comprehensive, patient-friendly information on infective endocarditis, including definitions, risks, causes, symptoms, diagnosis, treatments, and prevention. The Cleveland Clinic also offers a link to "Chat Online
  with a Heart and Vascular Nurse." For information on clinical trials, see the
  Cleveland Clinic entry on pp. 31–32.

➤ ClinicalTrials.gov—Endocarditis clinical trials. http://clinicaltrials.gov/ct2/
  results?term=endocarditis; alternate path: http://clinicaltrials.gov/, search for
  "endocarditis" in the Search for Studies box at the top of the screen.

To limit your results, click on "Modify This Search" and select specific fields, such as (1) Recruitment (e.g., you might want to select "Open Studies"); (2) Locations (e.g., select your state); and (3) Age Group, and then click on the "Search" button. Click on the title of each trial name for additional information, such as purpose of the study, study design and type, detailed description, outcome measures, eligibility (age, gender, criteria for participating), study start date, estimated study completion date, and sponsor. ClinicalTrials.gov, developed by the U.S. National Institutes of Health of the National Library of Medicine, lists ongoing and currently enrolling clinical trials. Check often for new studies.

➤ Insidermedicine—"If I Had—Infective Endocarditis" (Video). http://www.insider medicine.com/archives/If_I_Had_Infective_Endocarditis_Dr_Nanette_Wenger_MD _Emory_University_School_of_Medicine_3421.aspx; alternate path: http://www .insidermedicine.com/, search for the video by title.

The Insidermedicine website offers a variety of heart-health-related videos. This easy-to-understand video, with demonstrations, includes an interview with a cardiologist on what this cardiologist would do if she had fever and malaise and had been diagnosed with infective endocarditis. For more information on the physician-led Insidermedicine Project, see the earlier entry on pp. 33–34.

➤ Johns Hopkins Hospital, Heart and Vascular Institute (Baltimore, MD)— "Endocarditis." http://www.hopkinsmedicine.org/heart_vascular_institute/conditions _treatments/conditions/endocarditis.html; alternate path: http://www.hopkins medicine.org/, search for and then click on the title "Endocarditis."

Johns Hopkins Heart and Vascular Institute website on endocarditis discusses what is endocarditis, when to call your doctor, symptoms, causes, prevention, diagnosis, and treatment. It also lists links to physicians and specialists (with profiles, e.g., specialty, medical board certification, education) who treat endocarditis and heart failure. Click on the heading "Clinical Trials" for links to current trials in various heart and cardiovascular conditions.

➤ Mayo Clinic (Rochester, MN)—"Endocarditis." http://www.mayoclinic.com/ health/endocarditis/DS00409; alternate path: http://www.mayoclinic.com/, search for and then click on the title "Endocarditis."

Written for patients, this webpage on endocarditis includes definitions, symptoms, causes, risk factors, complications, preparing for appointments, tests and diagnosis, treatments and drugs, lifestyle, home remedies, and prevention. There is also a more comprehensive section titled "In-Depth" on symptoms. For information on clinical trials and patient services, see the Mayo Clinic entry on p. 36.

➤ MedicineNet—"Endocarditis." http://www.medicinenet.com/endocarditis/article
.htm; alternate path: http://www.medicinenet.com/, under "Diseases and Conditions," click on "Conditions A–Z," then click on "E," and then scroll down to click
on "Endocarditis."
MedicineNet is owned and operated by WebMD and part of the WebMD Network. According to its website, MedicineNet "provides easy-to-read, in-depth,
authoritative medical information for consumers via its user-friendly, interactive
website." In-depth information on endocarditis includes definitions, causes,
symptoms, risks, diagnosis, treatments, and finding a local cardiologist. The
medical information is written and edited by a nationally recognized group of
more than 70 U.S. board-certified physicians. The website contains a "Symptom
Checker" listed in alphabetical order as a guide to "pinpoint your pain." Its
homepage links to "Health News of the Week." You can also sign up to receive a
health newsletter.

➤ MedlinePlus—"Endocarditis." http://www.nlm.nih.gov/medlineplus/endocarditis
.html; alternate path: http://www.nlm.nih.gov/, under "Databases," click on "MedlinePlus" and then search for "endocarditis."
MedlinePlus is a component of the National Institutes of Health (NIH), produced
by the National Library of Medicine (NLM), and is updated regularly. This Medline-
Plus webpage on endocarditis offers extensive linked information covering overviews, diagnosis/symptoms, treatment, prevention/screening, specific conditions,
anatomy/physiology, clinical trials, journal articles, dictionaries/glossaries, organizations, and information specifically about children. Patient handouts are also available. This webpage also includes a multimedia section containing tutorials.

➤ Medscape (Drugs, Diseases, and Procedures)—"Infective Endocarditis." http://
emedicine.medscape.com/article/216650-overview; alternate path: http://
emedicine.medscape.com/, search for and then click on the title "Infective
Endocarditis."
Written for Medscape by John L. Brusch, MD, FACP, and associates, this webpage presents a comprehensive report on infective endocarditis. Although written for health care professionals, it might be helpful for interested laypersons.
Articles for Medscape Reference are written by medical experts. The webpage
states, "Our rigorous literature survey process allows us to rapidly integrate new
practice-changing information into the relevant topics by systematically reviewing the major medical and pharmacy journals, news announcements, and
important practice guidelines." Free registration is required.

➤ *The Merck Manual Home Health Handbook for Patients and Caregivers*—"Infective
Endocarditis." http://www.merckmanuals.com/home/heart_and_blood_vessel
_disorders/infective_endocarditis/infective_endocarditis.html; alternate path:
http://www.merckmanuals.com/home/, under "Sections," click on "All" next to the

navigation arrows to see a complete list, then click on "Heart and Blood Vessel Disorders," and then scroll down to click on "Infective Endocarditis."

This section on infective endocarditis, which discusses causes, symptoms, diagnosis, prognosis, prevention, and treatment, is based on a well-known medical textbook titled *The Merck Manual Home Health Handbook for Patients and Caregivers* and is "provided free of charge . . . as a public service."

➤ National Heart, Lung, and Blood Institute (NHLBI)—"What Is Endocarditis?" http://www.nhlbi.nih.gov/health/dci/Diseases/endo/endo_what.html; alternate path: http://www.nhlbi.nih.gov/, search for "endocarditis," and then click on the title "What Is Endocarditis?"

NHLBI, a division of the National Institutes of Health from the U.S. Department of Health and Human Services, provides information on endocarditis, including definitions, causes, risk factors, signs and symptoms, diagnosis, treatments, prevention, clinical trials, key points, and additional information about endocarditis.

➤ Texas Heart Institute (Houston, TX)—"Infective Endocarditis." http://www.texas heartinstitute.org/HIC/Topics/Cond/endocard.cfm; alternate path: http://www.texas heartinstitute.org/, search for and then click on the title "Infective Endocarditis."

The Texas Heart Institute website offers a definition of infective endocarditis, as well as information on causes, risks, signs and symptoms, diagnosis, and treatment. An easy-to-print format is available. One section allows users to "Ask a Texas Heart Institute Doctor" questions. Click on "Heart Doctor Answers" to explore the questions and answers already published there. For information on clinical trials, see the Texas Heart Institute entry on p. 40.

➤ UCLA Ronald Reagan Medical Center (Los Angeles, CA)—"Infectious Endocarditis." http://www.uclahealth.org/body.cfm?id=477&action=detail&aeproductid =Adam2004_117&aearticleid=000681; alternate path: http://www.uclahealth .org/, search for "infectious endocarditis," and then scroll down to click on the title in the Health Information results list.

UCLA's Health Encyclopedia provides detailed information on infectious endocarditis, including alternate names, causes, symptoms, exams and tests, treatment, outlook (prognosis), and possible complications. Also, on the Heart Health Center website, under the heading "Tests and Treatments," scroll under the section "Alternative Medicine" for more treatment information, then click on the word "More," and then click on the title "Endocarditis." For more information on patient resources and clinical trials, see the UCLA entry on p. 41.

➤ WebMD—"Endocarditis." http://www.webmd.com/heart-disease/tc/endocarditis -topic-overview; alternate path: http://www.webmd.com/, search for "endocarditis" and then click on the title "Endocarditis (WebMD Medical Reference from Healthwise)."

The WebMD website offers the latest information on endocarditis and provides links to a topic overview, symptoms, exams and tests, treatment overview, home treatment, other places to get help, related information, and references. A WebMD heart health e-mail newsletter is also available. According to WebMD, "WebMD News is an independent media service designed to provide news, information, and educational material to consumers and physicians. News content created by WebMD is free from influence by sponsors, partners, or other sources."

Patient Support Groups and Organizations

> MedHelp—"Endocarditis." http://www.medhelp.org/search?query=endocarditis; alternate path: http://www.medhelp.org/, search for "endocarditis" to retrieve a results list from which to choose.
> According to its website, MedHelp "connects people with the leading medical experts," such as those from Cleveland Clinic, National Jewish Health, Partners Health, and Mount Sinai Hospital, with those who have similar medical issues. MedHelp's main focus is to enable patients "to take control over their health and find answers to their medical questions" using nontechnical language via an online community through posts, forums and groups, blogs, and user journals, as well as recommendations, articles, health pages, and a medical glossary. Free registration is required.

> U.S. Hospital Finder. http://www.ushospitalfinder.com/.
> Use this site to find the names of hospitals by zip code, city, state, or your address. The search results include a map with directions. You might also want to ask your health care professional, call hospitals in your area, or search for "support groups" on hospital websites to determine if there are any cardiology support groups for people with endocarditis that meet regularly in your area.

> Yahoo! Groups—"Bacterial Endocarditis Support Group." http://health.groups.yahoo .com/group/Bacterial_Endocarditis/; alternate path: http://www.groups.yahoo.com/, search for "endocarditis" in the "Find a Yahoo! Group" Search box and then click on the group named "Bacterial_Endocarditis."
> This online Yahoo! group is for patients with endocarditis and their families and friends. Yahoo! Groups is not a medical site, nor does it provide or endorse medical advice or procedures. The purpose of the website is to share experiences in a kind and caring manner. Free registration is required to participate.

Heart Attacks (Myocardial Infarctions)

A heart attack, a common term for myocardial infarction, is an interruption or loss of blood flow to a part of the heart with resultant tissue death. Acute myocardial infarction, acute coronary syndrome, coronary thrombosis, and coronary occlusion are all forms of a heart attack.

In a heart attack or myocardial infarction, the blood flow through the cardiac arteries is slowed or blocked, causing chest pain or discomfort, upper body discomfort, shortness of breath, nausea, lightheadedness, and/or cold sweat. Most often preexisting coronary artery disease is present before the heart attack. Plaque inside the artery walls slows the blood flow by narrowing the path of blood to the heart. If the inner wall lining that is filled with plaque bursts, a clot (thrombus) forms at the break, further narrowing the artery. If the clot blocks blood flow, oxygenated blood cannot reach the heart muscle, and that blocked artery starts to die. A clot can break away and while flowing up the artery it can lodge into a narrower artery section. Rapid treatment can break up the clot and restore the blood flow, minimizing heart injury.

A less common heart attack is from a coronary artery spasm, which causes an artery to contract and close off blood flow. Usually coronary artery disease is not present in this case. The actual cause of the spasm is not clear but can be related to several specific stimuli: smoking, exposure to extreme cold, emotional stress, pain, allergic reaction to angiography dye, or illegal drug use.

Cardiogenic shock can occur as a result of a heart attack. In this condition, the weakened heart cannot pump enough blood to supply the body and is therefore similar to heart failure (*see the later section* HEART FAILURE). Signs of impending cardiogenic shock include confusion or lack of alertness; loss of consciousness; a sudden, rapid heartbeat; a weak pulse; sweating; pale skin; rapid breathing, and cool hands and feet. The condition can be fatal if not rapidly treated with emergency life support (e.g., providing oxygen, elevating legs, performing cardiopulmonary resuscitation). Opening the clogged artery causing the heart damage (cardiac catheterization) may be required.

Resources for Further Information on Heart Attacks

Books

➤ Brill, Janet, and Annabelle S. Volgman. *Prevent a Second Heart Attack: 8 Foods, 8 Weeks to Reverse Heart Disease.* New York, NY: Three Rivers Press, 2011. Print.
This book is written for the patient and set up in three sections: How You Got Heart Disease in the First Place; Reversing Heart Disease with Eight Foods and Exercise; and The Prevent a Second Heart Attack Plan in Action. As the book notes, first get approval of your cardiologist before beginning to follow the Mediterranean diet plan.

➤ Rimmerman, Curtis. *The Cleveland Clinic Guide to Heart Attacks* (Cleveland Clinic Guides). New York, NY: Kaplan, 2009. Print.
This book provides basic information about heart disease, heart anatomy, heart attack, risk factors, tests, treatment, intervention, heart health assessment, exercise, prevention, and choosing a physician.

> Wallack, Mark, and Jamie Colby. *Back to Life after a Heart Crisis: A Doctor and His Wife Share Their 8-Step Cardiac Comeback Plan*. New York, NY: Avery, 2010. Print.
> Marc Wallack, who is chief of surgery at Metropolitan Hospital and vice-chair of the Department of Surgery at New York Medical College, describes for the patient a personal story after having a heart attack, offers an eight-step plan, and provides support guidance.

Brochures, Booklets, and Other Short Print Publications

> American Heart Association (AHA)—"Heart Attack" (Patient Information Sheets and Brochures). http://www.heart.org/HEARTORG/Conditions/HeartAttack/HeartAttackToolsResources/Patient-Information-Sheets-Heart-Attack_UCM _303950_Article.jsp and http://www.heart.org/HEARTORG/General/Order -American-Heart-Association-Educational-Brochures_UCM_312777_Article.jsp; alternate path: http://www.heart.org/, search for "heart attack," click on the title "Visit Our Heart Attack Website," and then scroll down to the section called "Tools and Resources" and click on the title "Patient Information Sheets"; or search for "educational brochures," click on the title "Order American Heart Association Educational Brochures," and then scroll down and click on the topic "Heart Attack."
> AHA provides the following printable information sheets: "What Is a Heart Attack?," "How Will I Recover from My Heart Attack?," and "What Are the Warning Signs of Heart Attack?" Numerous additional AHA brochures are available, including the following: "About Your Bypass Surgery," "Coronary Angioplasty and Stenting," "After Your Heart Attack," "Sex and Heart Disease," "Signs of a Heart Attack," "Warning Signs and Actions," "Active Partnership for the Health of Your Heart Notebook and DVD," "Understanding Angina," "Are You at Risk of Heart Attack or Stroke?," and "Women, Heart Disease, and Stroke." Some brochures are also available in Spanish. You can order brochures by filling in a form online. (No more than one packet and two brochures per household can be ordered at no cost.)

> British Heart Foundation (BHF)—"Heart Attack" (Booklets, Poster, and DVDs). http://www.bhf.org.uk/heart-health/conditions/heart-attack.aspx; alternate path: http://www.bhf.org.uk/, search for "heart attack" and then click on the title "British Heart Foundation—Heart Attack."
> The BHF website offers free booklets and DVDs to help patients manage and cope with heart attack. Scroll down the screen for the section titled "Where Can I find More Information?" and click on each title to view and download booklets, such as "Heart Attack," "Keep Your Heart Healthy," "Cardiac Rehabilitation," and "Chest Pain Symptoms" (poster). You can order a free DVD called *Risking It*, which is also available in booklet form.

Websites

➢ Aetna InteliHealth—"Heart Attack (Myocardial Infarction)." http://www.inteli health.com/IH/ihtIH/WSIHW000/8059/8056/213077.html?d=dmtHealthAZ; alternate path: http://www.intelihealth.com/, search for "heart attack," and click on the title "Heart Attack (Myocardial Infarction)."

This webpage provides an overview of heart attack, including definitions, symptoms, diagnosis, expected duration, prevention, treatment, when to call a professional, and prognosis. Aetna InteliHealth, a subsidiary of Aetna, is reviewed by the faculty of Harvard Medical School and University College of Dental Medicine. According to Aetna InteliHealth's website, "Aetna InteliHealth maintains absolute editorial independence. That means that Aetna InteliHealth makes decisions about the information on our site free of outside influence." Under "Healthy Lifestyle," Aetna InteliHealth also offers free health-related e-mail subscriptions.

➢ American Heart Association (AHA)—"Heart Attack." http://www.heart.org/ HEARTORG/Conditions/HeartAttack/Heart-Attack_UCM_001092_SubHomePage .jsp; alternate path: http://www.heart.org/, search for "heart attack," and click on the title "Visit Our Heart Attack Website."

AHA provides details on heart attack, including definitions, warning signs, risk factors, symptoms and diagnosis, prevention and treatment, and tools and resources. Available are printable heart attack information sheets. You can also sign up for a free heart health e-newsletter.

➢ Brigham and Women's Hospital (BWH) (Boston, MA)—"Heart Attack." http:// healthlibrary.brighamandwomens.org/HealthCenters/Heart/Conditions/HeartAttack; alternate path: http://www.brighamandwomens.org/, scroll under the heading "Health Information" to the category titled "Health Information Center" and click on the title "Heart Information Center," then scroll down and click on the category "Heart Diseases and Conditions," and then click on "Heart Attack."

BWH's heart attack webpage discusses heart attack treatment options, thriving after a heart attack, preventing a second heart attack, high-tech help for heart attacks, and six symptoms you should never ignore. For information on clinical trials, see the BWH entry on p. 29.

➢ British Heart Foundation (BHF)—"Heart Attack." http://www.bhf.org.uk/heart -health/conditions/cardiovascular-disease.aspx; alternate path: http://www.bhf .org.uk/, search for "heart attack," and then click on the title "British Heart Foundation—Heart Attack."

The BHF website describes heart attacks, the difference between heart attack and cardiac arrest, symptoms, diagnosis, the value of aspirin, treatment, prevention, loss of a loved one, and bereavement. A video is available that demonstrates a heart attack: "This two-minute film lets you experience what it might be like to have a heart attack firsthand." Also click on the "Community: Share Experiences with Others" heading to engage with the BHF online community where you can share your own story and read those of others.

➤ CardioSmart—"Acute Coronary Syndrome." https://www.cardiosmart.org/Heart -Conditions/Acute-Coronary-Syndrome; alternate path: https://www.cardiosmart .org/, search for and then click on the title "Acute Coronary Syndrome."
CardioSmart provides an easy-to-use website on understanding acute coronary syndrome. CardioSmart's acute coronary syndrome webpage contains an introduction, questions to ask your cardiologist, news, video library (e.g., watch a heart attack survivor and cardiac rehabilitation program), a link to learn more about a heart attack (sections such as basic facts, what is a heart attack, further explanation, risk factors, treatment, sex after heart attack, symptoms, diagnosis, and recovery), and a link to learn more about unstable angina (sections such as basic facts, what unstable angina is, further explanation, risk factors, treatment, differences between stable and unstable angina and heart attack symptoms, diagnosis, and variant angina). At the top of the screen, click on the heading "Connect with Others" for "Community Peer Support," "Patient Stories," and "Discussion Forums." Free sign-up newsletters are available on the CardioSmart homepage. The site is also available in Spanish. According to the American College of Cardiology (ACC), "CardioSmart is the patient education and support program launched by the [ACC]. Our mission is to engage, inform, and empower patients to better prepare them for participation in their own care."

➤ CenterWatch—Clinical trials listing service: "Myocardial Infarction (Heart Attack) Clinical Trials." http://www.centerwatch.com/clinical-trials/listings/ studylist.aspx?CatID=463; alternate path: http://www.centerwatch.com/, under the category "Patient Resources" click on "Search Clinical Trials," then click on "M," and then click on the title "Myocardial Infarction (Heart Attack)."
CenterWatch clinical trials listing service lists trials currently looking for volunteers to enroll in myocardial infarction studies. Click on the "Clinical Trials" heading and search by location, medical condition, or therapeutic area. To search by location, click on your state (or country), and then click on a city near you to find information on each available clinical trial. Check back with this website often for new studies. Sign up for a free e-mail service that sends notice of new clinical trials.

➤ Cleveland Clinic (Cleveland, OH)—"Heart Attack." http://my.clevelandclinic.org/ disorders/Heart_Attack/hic_Heart_Attack.aspx; alternate path: http://my .clevelandclinic.org/, under the category "Institutes and Services" click on "Heart and Vascular," then click on "Homepage," then click on the category "Diseases and Conditions," and then click on the title "Heart Attack."

The Cleveland Clinic provides comprehensive patient-friendly information on heart attack, such as links to definitions, types of heart attack, risk, symptoms, diagnosis, treatment, recovery, and how to find a doctor who treats heart attack. The Cleveland Clinic also offers a link to "Chat Online with a Heart and Vascular Nurse." For information on clinical trials, see the Cleveland Clinic entry on pp. 31–32.

➤ ClinicalTrials.gov. http://clinicaltrials.gov/.
ClinicalTrials.gov, developed by the U.S. National Institutes of Health of the National Library of Medicine, lists ongoing and currently enrolling clinical trials. To find clinical trials from the homepage, search for the condition by name (e.g., "arrhythmia"), which will generate a list of possibly hundreds or thousands of studies. To limit your results, click on "Modify This Search" and select specific fields, such as (1) Recruitment (e.g., you might want to select "Open Studies"); (2) Locations (e.g., select your state); and (3) Age Group, and then click on the "Search" button. Click on the title of each trial name for additional information, such as purpose of the study, study design and type, detailed description, outcome measures, eligibility (age, gender, criteria for participating), study start date, estimated study completion date, and sponsor. Check often for new studies.
- Heart attack clinical trials. http://clinicaltrials.gov/ct2/results/refine?term =heart+attack.
- Myocardial infarction clinical trials. http://clinicaltrials.gov/ct2/results/refine?term=Myocardial+Infarction.

➤ eMedicineHealth—"Heart Attack" and "Heart Attack and Unstable Angina." http://www.emedicinehealth.com/heart_attack/article_em.htm and http://www.emedicinehealth.com/heart_attack_and_unstable_angina-health/article_em.htm; alternate path: http://www.emedicinehealth.com/, search for "heart attack" and click on the title "Heart Attack" (Medical Reference from eMedicineHealth and from Healthwise).
eMedicineHealth, a division of WebMD, offers a comprehensive article on heart attack, including an overview, causes, risk factors, symptoms, when to seek medical care, diagnosis, treatment, prevention, outlook, and follow-up.

➤ Insidermedicine. http://insidermedicine.com/.
The Insidermedicine website offers a variety of heart-health-related videos. From the homepage, you can search for videos by title, or you can search by topic (e.g., "heart attack") to find other related videos. For more information on the Insidermedicine Project, see the earlier entry on pp. 33–34.
- "ECG May Help Predict Risk of Stroke, Heart Attack in Older Adults." http://www.insidermedicine.com/archives/ECG_May_Help_Predict_Risk _of_Stroke_Heart_Attack_in_Older_Adults_Video_6021.aspx. This video

demonstrates how an electrocardiogram works and explains the purpose of understanding the test results from a patient's EKG.

- "Heart Attack Video: Moderate Drinking May Protect Reduce Death in Men with Previous Heart Attack." http://www.insidermedicine.com/archives/Heart_Attack_Video_Moderate_Drinking_May_Protect_Reduce_Death_in_Men_With_Previous_Heart_Attack_5993.aspx. This video demonstrates ways for a patient to remain heart healthy.

- "If I Had—A Heart Attack." http://www.insidermedicine.com/archives/CIHR_Video_If_I_Had_A_Heart_Attack_Dr_Paul_Armstrong_MD_Dr_Robert_Welsh_MD_FRCPC_FACC_University_of_Alberta_5302.aspx. In this easy-to-understand video, with demonstrations, a cardiologist speaks about the importance of calling 911 when suffering a heart attack, symptoms (men versus women), and treatments.

- "New Guidelines Aim to Streamline Care for Severe Heart Attack." http://www.insidermedicine.com/archives/New_guidelines_aim_to_streamline_care_for_severe_heart_attack_6989.aspx. This video discusses new heart attack guidelines aimed at improving recognition and treatment for patients suffering from STEMI (ST elevation myocardial infarction), a severe heart attack.

- "Young Women More Likely to Suffer a Heart Attack without Chest Pain." http://www.insidermedicine.com/archives/Young_Women_Who_Suffer_A_Heart_Attack_Without_Chest_Pain_At_Increased_Risk_of_Death_Video_5912.aspx. This video demonstrates the symptoms other than chest pain that might indicate a woman is experiencing a heart attack.

➤ Johns Hopkins Hospital, Heart and Vascular Institute (Baltimore, MD). "Myocardial Infarction (Heart Attack)." http://www.hopkinsmedicine.org/heart_vascular_institute/conditions_treatments/conditions/myocardial_infarction.html and http://www.hopkinsmedicine.org/healthlibrary/conditions/adult/cardiovascular_diseases/heart_attack_85,P00702/; alternate path: http://www.hopkinsmedicine.org/, search for "myocardial infarction" and click on the title "Myocardial Infarction (Heart Attack)"; for a related resource, click on "Cardiovascular Diseases—Myocardial Infarction (Heart Attack)."
The Johns Hopkins Heart and Vascular Institute website on myocardial infarction (heart attack) discusses definitions, when to call an ambulance, symptoms, causes, prevention, diagnosis, and treatment. Click on the heading "Clinical Trials" for links to current trials in various heart and cardiovascular conditions.

➤ Khan Academy. http://www.khanacademy.org/.
Salman Khan, creator of the nonprofit Khan Academy, sketches as he explains various topics related to heart disease and heart attacks. Khan's mini lessons are all downloadable and free. According to the website, "With a library of over 2,400 videos covering everything from arithmetic to physics, finance, and

history and 150 practice exercises, we're on a mission to help you learn what you want, when you want, at your own pace." Click on the heading "About" to get the maximum use of this excellent site. Khan has three degrees from the Massachusetts Institute of Technology and an MBA from Harvard University. From the homepage, you can find the following resources through a title search.

- "Heart Disease and Heart Attacks: Basics of Heart Disease, Heart Attacks, Heart Failure, Angina, Cardiac Arrest." http://www.khanacademy.org/science/ healthcare-and-medicine/heart-disease-and-stroke/v/heart-disease-and-heart -attacks?playlist=Biology.
- "Stenosis, Ischemia, and Heart Failure: Clarifying a Bunch of Medical Terms around Heart Disease." http://www.khanacademy.org/science/healthcare-and -medicine/heart-disease-and-stroke/v/stenosis--ischemia-and-heart-failure.
- "Thrombo-emboli and Thromboembolisms: Clarifying Difference between a Thrombus and an Embolus (and between Thrombosis and Embolism)." http:// www.khanacademy.org/science/healthcare-and-medicine/heart-disease-and -stroke/v/thrombo-emboli-and-thromboembolisms.

➢ Mayo Clinic (Rochester, MN)—"Heart Attack." http://www.mayoclinic.com/ health/heart-attack/DS00094; alternate path: http://www.mayoclinic.com/, search for "heart attack," and click on the title "Heart Attack—MayoClinic.com." Written for patients, this webpage on heart attack includes definitions, symptoms, causes, risk factors, complications, preparing for appointments, tests and diagnosis, treatments and drugs, lifestyle and home remedies, prevention, and coping and support. There is also a more comprehensive section titled "In-Depth" on some of these topics. For information on clinical trials and patient services, see the Mayo Clinic entry on p. 36.

➢ MedicineNet. http://medicinenet.com/.
MedicineNet.com is owned and operated by WebMD and part of the WebMD Network. According to its website, MedicineNet "provides easy-to-read, in-depth, authoritative medical information for consumers via its user-friendly, interactive website." The medical information is written and edited by a nationally recognized group of more than 70 U.S. board-certified physicians. The website contains a "Symptom Checker" listed in alphabetical order as a guide to "pinpoint your pain." Its homepage links to "Health News of the Week." You can also sign up to receive a health newsletter.

- "Heart Attack (Myocardial Infarction)." http://www.medicinenet.com/heart _attack/article.htm. In-depth information on heart attack includes descriptions, causes, symptoms, complications, risk factors, diagnosis, women and heart attacks, treatment, and patient discussions.
- "Heart Attack—Prevention (Vitamins and Exercise)." http://www.medicinenet .com/vitamins_and_exercise/article.htm. In-depth information on heart

attack prevention using vitamins and exercise includes discussion on folic acid, B vitamins, homocysteine, and antioxidants for heart attack prevention, exercise for heart attack prevention, smoking cessation for heart attack prevention, and recommendations to prevent heart attacks.

- "Heart Attack Treatment." http://www.medicinenet.com/heart_attack _treatment/article.htm. In-depth information on heart attack treatment includes condition description, how heart attacks are treated, antiplatelet agents, aspirin, thienpyridines, glycoprotein IIb/IIIa inhibitors, anticoagulants, clot-dissolving agents, coronary angiography, stents, nitrates, ACE inhibitors, beta-blockers, oxygen, coronary artery bypass, second heart attacks, and finding a local cardiologist.

Alternate path: http://www.medicinenet.com/, click on the major topic "Diseases and Conditions," click on "Conditions A–Z," then click on "H," and then scroll down to click on the resource title.

➤ MedlinePlus—"Heart Attack (MI, Myocardial Infarction)." http://www.nlm.nih .gov/medlineplus/heartattack.html; alternate path: http://www.nlm.nih.gov/, under "Databases," click on "MedlinePlus" and then search for "heart attack."

MedlinePlus is a component of the National Institutes of Health, produced by the National Library of Medicine, and is updated regularly. This MedlinePlus webpage on heart attack offers extensive information covering overviews, news, diagnosis/ symptoms, treatment, prevention/screening, rehabilitation/recovery, disease management, specific conditions, related issues, anatomy/physiology, clinical trials, research, journal articles, dictionaries/glossaries, directories, organizations, statistics, and specific sections focusing on women and seniors. Patient handouts and links to *MedlinePlus Magazine* and related information are also available. This webpage also includes a multimedia section containing health check tools, tutorials, and videos.

➤ Medscape Reference (Drugs, Diseases, and Procedures)—"Myocardial Infarction." http://emedicine.medscape.com/article/155919-overview; alternate path: http://emedicine.medscape.com/, search for and then click on the title "Myocardial Infarction."

Written for Medscape by A. Maziar Zafari, MD, PhD, and associates, this webpage presents a comprehensive report on myocardial infarction. Although written for health care professionals, it might be helpful for interested laypersons. Articles for Medscape Reference are written by medical experts. The webpage states, "Our rigorous literature survey process allows us to rapidly integrate new practice-changing information into the relevant topics by systematically reviewing the major medical and pharmacy journals, news announcements, and important practice guidelines." Free registration is required.

➤ *The Merck Manual Home Health Handbook for Patients and Caregivers*—"Acute Coronary Syndromes (Heart Attack; Myocardial Infarction; Unstable Angina)." http://www.merckmanuals.com/home/sec03/ch031/ch031c.html; alternate path: http://www.merckmanuals.com/home/, under "Sections," click on "All" next to the navigational arrows to view a complete list, then click on the section "Heart and Blood Vessel Disorders," scroll down to the section titled "Coronary Artery Disease," and then click on the title "Acute Coronary Syndromes (Heart Attack, Myocardial Infarction, Unstable Angina)."

This extensively covered section on acute coronary syndromes, which discusses causes, symptoms, complications, diagnosis, prognosis, prevention, and treatment, including rehabilitation, is based on a well-known medical textbook titled *The Merck Manual Home Health Handbook for Patients and Caregivers*, and this topic is part of the extensive section on coronary artery disease. This information is "provided free of charge . . . as a public service."

➤ National Heart, Lung, and Blood Institute (NHLBI)—"Heart Attack." http://www .nhlbi.nih.gov/health/dci/Diseases/HeartAttack/HeartAttack_WhatIs.html; alternate path: http://www.nhlbi.nih.gov/, search for "heart attack," and then click on the title "What Is Heart Attack?"

NHLBI, a division of National Institutes of Health from the U.S. Department of Health and Human Services, provides additional information on heart attack, including links to definitions, other names, causes, risk, signs and symptoms, diagnosis, treatments, prevention, life after a heart attack, clinical trials, and key points.

➤ New York–Presbyterian (NYP) University Hospital of Columbia and Cornell (New York, NY). http://nyp.org/.

Under the heading "Find a Physician" you can search for physicians and specialists by specialty or name to view their profiles (e.g., specialty, medical board certification, education). Under the heading "Hospital News" are links to detailed articles explaining recent studies. For information on clinical trials, see the NYP entry on p. 38.

- "Heart Attack Care." http://nyp.org/services/cardiology/heart-attack.html; alternate path: http://nyp.org/, search for and then click on the title "Heart Attack Care." The NYP University Hospital of Columbia and Cornell website provides patient-friendly information on heart attack, providing an overview to what a heart attack is and links to expanded information on prevention, risk factors, treatment, warning signs, and heart attacks in women. There are also videos discussing symptoms of a heart attack. Under the heading "Related Links" are links to NYP Heart Valve Medical Centers.

- "Interactive Media Library: Myocardial Infarction" (Video). http://nyp.org/ media/index.html; alternate path: http://nyp.org/, click on the icon with the text "Explore the Interactive Media Library." The Human Atlas media player presents short videos, text, models, and slides. To view an excellent video, click on the "Complete Listing of Topics" heading and scroll down to click on "Myocardial Infarction."

- "Perelman Heart Institute—Heart Attack" (Videos). http://nypheart.org/perelman/; alternate path: http://nyp.org/, search for "Ronald O. Perelman Heart Institute," click on the name in the results, scroll down to "Related Links," and then click again on the name. The Perelman Heart Institute website of the NYP University Hospital of Columbia and Cornell offers, for patients, links to a playlist on excellent short videos and audio slide presentations of cardiovascular tests and procedures, such as myocardial infarction (heart attack).

➤ NHS (National Health Service) Choices—"Heart Attack." http://www.nhs.uk/Conditions/Heart-attack/Pages/Introduction.aspx; alternate path: http://www.nhs.uk/, search for "heart block," and click on the reference title "Heart Attack—NHS Choices—Health A–Z."
According to its website, "NHS Choices is the UK's biggest health website. It provides a comprehensive health information service that puts you in control of your healthcare." NHS Choices provides information on heart attack, including an overview of the condition (symptoms, causes, diagnosis, treatment, complications, recovery, and prevention) as well as links to "Clinical Trials" in the United States and worldwide ("provided by WHO International Clinical Trials Registry"), "Real Stories" from people who've experienced a heart attack, and "Community," an online forum where people ask questions and post blog entries.

➤ Texas Heart Institute (Houston, TX). http://www.texasheartinstitute.org/.
For information on clinical trials, see the Texas Heart Institute entry on p. 40.

- "Heart Attack." http://www.texasheartinstitute.org/HIC/Topics/Cond/HeartAttack.cfm. The Texas Heart Institute website offers a definition of heart attack, as well as information on causes, signs and symptoms, diagnosis, outcomes, treatment, and recovery. An easy-to-print format is also available.
- "Silent Ischemia." http://www.texasheartinstitute.org/HIC/Topics/Cond/silent.cfm. The Texas Heart Institute website offers a definition of silent ischemia, as well as information on causes, signs and symptoms, diagnosis, and treatment.

Alternate path: http://www.texasheartinstitute.org/, search for the topic by name (e.g., "heart attack") and then click on the appropriate title; or under "Heart Information Center," select "Heart-Health Topics," then "Heart Conditions," and click on the topic by name.

➤ UCLA Ronald Reagan Medical Center (Los Angeles, CA)—"Heart Attack and Acute Coronary Syndrome." http://www.uclahealth.org/body.cfm?id=592; scroll down to the heading "In-Depth Reports," then click on the word "More," and then click on the title "Heart Attack and Acute Coronary Syndrome"; alternate path: http://www.uclahealth.org/, under the heading "For Patients and Visitors," scroll down and mouse over the category "Health Resources" and then click on "Heart Health Center," then scroll down to the heading "In-Depth Reports," click on the word "More," and then click on the title "Heart Attack and Acute Coronary Syndrome."

The UCLA Ronald Reagan Medical Center's Heart Health Center provides an in-depth report on heart attack and acute coronary syndrome, which includes highlights, introductions, risk factors, prognosis, symptoms, diagnosis, treatment, medications, secondary prevention, and resources. Also on the Heart Health Center website, under the heading "Tests and Treatments," scroll under the section "Alternative Medicine" for more treatment information, click on the word "More," and then click on the title "Heart Attack." For more information on patient resources and clinical trials, see the UCLA entry on p. 41.

➢ WebMD. http://www.webmd.com/.

According to WebMD, "WebMD News is an independent media service designed to provide news, information, and educational material to consumers and physicians. News content created by WebMD is free from influence by sponsors, partners, or other sources."

- "Heart Attack and Unstable Angina." http://www.webmd.com/heart -disease/tc/heart-attack-and-unstable-angina-overview; alternate path: http://www.webmd.com/, search for "heart attack," and then click on the title "Heart Attack and Unstable Angina (WebMD Medical Reference from Healthwise)." The WebMD website offers information on heart attack such as causes, symptoms, risks, treatments, prevention, FAQs, and end-of-life decisions. A WebMD heart health e-mail newsletter is also available.

- "Heart Attack Directory." http://www.webmd.com/heart-disease/heart-attack -directory; alternate path: http://www.webmd.com/, search for "heart attack directory," then click on the title "Heart Attack," go to the section "Heart Attack Home," and then click on the various categories for such information as medical references, videos, and slideshows about heart attack. A WebMD heart health e-mail newsletter is also available.

Patient Support Groups and Organizations

➢ DailyStrength—"Heart Attack Support Group." http://www.dailystrength.org/c/ Heart-Attack/support-group; alternate path: http://www.dailystrength.org/, search for "heart attack" and then click on "Visit the Heart Attack Support Group." The DailyStrength website offers online support groups and blogs for those who had a heart attack. Free registration is required to participate. According to the website, "DailyStrength is a subsidiary of Sharecare. Sharecare, created by WebMD founder and Discovery Communications' Chief of Global Digital Strategy Jeff Arnold, along with America's Doctor, Dr. Mehmet Oz, is the first truly interactive healthcare ecosystem giving consumers the ability to ask, learn and act on the questions of health."

➤ HeartHub for Patients—"Cardiac Rehab." http://www.hearthub.org/hc-cardiac -rehab.htm; alternate path: http://www.hearthub.org/, scroll down to the section titled "Health Centers," and click on the title "Cardiac Rehab."
HeartHub, a division of the American Heart Association (AHA), is a patient-support portal for information, tools, and resources on cardiac rehab, such as coping with feelings, healthy recipes, how to get help on the phone, make the most of appointments, medical contact sheet, cardiac rehab podcast, and finding a local program.

➤ MedHelp. http://www.medhelp.org/.
According to its website, MedHelp "connects people with the leading medical experts," such as those from Cleveland Clinic, National Jewish Health, Partners Health, and Mount Sinai Hospital, with those who have similar medical issues. MedHelp's main focus is to enable patients "to take control over their health and find answers to their medical questions" using nontechnical language via an online community through posts, forums and groups, blogs, user journals, as well as recommendations, articles, health pages, and a medical glossary. Free registration is required. From the homepage, you can find the following and related groups through a topic search.
  • "Heart Attack." http://www.medhelp.org/search?query=heart+attack.
  • "Myocardial Infarction." http://www.medhelp.org/search?query=myocardial +infarction.

➤ U.S. Hospital Finder. http://www.ushospitalfinder.com/.
Use this site to find the names of hospitals by zip code, city, state, or your address. The search results include a map with directions. You might also want to ask your health care professional, call hospitals in your area, or search for "support groups" on hospital websites to determine if there are any cardiology support groups for people who have had a heart attack that meet regularly in your area.

➤ WebMD—"WebMD Heart Health Cardiac Rehabilitation Community." http:// exchanges.webmd.com/heart-health-cardiac-rehabilitation; alternate path: http:// www.webmd.com/, scroll under the category "Home and News" and click on "WebMD Community and Experts," search for "cardiac rehabilitation" in the "Find a Community" Search box, and then click on the title "WebMD Heart Health Cardiac Rehabilitation Community (WebMD Community)."
Join the WebMD heart health cardiac rehabilitation community, which includes discussions, expert blogs, tips, resources, and support. According to the WebMD

heart disease community, "WebMD's heart experts and other knowledgeable members are here to share help and guidance about everything from diagnosis and treatment to getting back on track with a heart-healthy lifestyle." To search for other health-topic communities, click on http://exchanges.webmd.com/, which is titled "Be a Part of the WebMD Community." Scroll down to "Create Your Own Community" for easy instructions.

➤ Yahoo! Groups. http://www.yahoo.com/.
Yahoo! Groups is not a medical site, nor does it provide or endorse medical advice or procedures. The purpose of the website is to share experiences in a kind and caring manner. Free registration is required to participate.
 • "Heart Attack Support Group." http://health.groups.yahoo.com/group/ heartattack/. This online Yahoo! group is for patients with a variety of cardiovascular diseases, including heart attack, and their families and friends.
 • "Heart Smart Recipes Support Group." http://groups.yahoo.com/group/Heart _Smart_Recipes/. This online Yahoo! group is for patients who have had a heart attack and who would like, along with their families and friends, to share heart-healthy recipes.
Alternate path: http://groups.yahoo.com/, type the relevant term (e.g., "heart attack") in the "Find a Yahoo! Group" Search box, and then click on the associated group.

Heart Block

A heart block is a condition in which part of the heart's nervous (electrical) system is damaged, affecting heart rate and rhythm. A heart block can be congenital or acquired. An acquired heart block is caused by diseases, surgery, or medicines. There are also three degrees of heart block: first, second, and third. First-degree block, the least severe, rarely causes serious symptoms. Second-degree block may cause some dizziness or fainting because the heart may skip a few beats. Third-degree block is serious because it limits the ability of the heart to pump effectively. A patient with a third-degree block may feel tired, dizzy, and faint. Third-degree heart block may lead to other arrhythmias, sudden cardiac arrest, or heart failure. Heart blocks are seen on EKG graphs as differences from the normal PQRST wave shape (to view a normal EKG graph and the standard setup for an EKG, go to http://www.nhlbi.nih.gov/health/health-topics/topics/ekg/during.html).

The heart does have special electrical system backups to keep a portion of the heart beating. However, the backups may become out of sync with the rest of the heart, causing poor pumping. First-degree heart block is not usually treated except with watchful waiting. Second-degree and third-degree heart blocks are usually treated with a pacemaker.

Resources for Further Information on Heart Block

Websites

> American Heart Association (AHA)—"Conduction Disorders." http://www.heart
> .org/HEARTORG/Conditions/Arrhythmia/AboutArrhythmia/Conduction
> -Disorders_UCM_302046_Article.jsp; alternate path: http://www.heart.org/, search
> for "conduction disorders" or "heart block," and click on the title "Heart Block and
> Other Conduction Disorders."
> The AHA website discusses conduction disorders and includes such topics as
> bundle branch block, heart block, and long QT syndrome. The AHA also offers a
> free optional registration for *Heart-Health E-News*.

> CardioSmart—"Heart Block." https://www.cardiosmart.org/HeartDisease/CTT
> .aspx?id=152; alternate path: https://www.cardiosmart.org/, search for and then
> click on the title "Heart Block."
> CardioSmart provides an easy-to-use webpage on understanding heart block, which
> is discussed in sections on basic facts, types of heart block, causes, risk factors, signs
> and symptoms, diagnosis, treatment, and living with this condition. According to the
> American College of Cardiology (ACC), "CardioSmart is the patient education and
> support program launched by the [ACC]. Our mission is to engage, inform,
> and empower patients to better prepare them for participation in their own care."

> Children's Hospital of Philadelphia (CHOP) (Philadelphia, PA): The Cardiac
> Center—"Heart Block." http://www.chop.edu/service/cardiac-center/heart
> -conditions/heart-block.html; alternate path: http://www.chop.edu/, click on the
> heading "Specialties and Services," then click on "Cardiac Center," then click on
> "Heart Conditions," and then scroll down and click on the topic "Heart Block."
> CHOP's Cardiac Center offers information on heart block, such as how a normal
> heart works, what heart block is, symptoms, diagnosis, treatment, and follow-up.
> Also available are links to cardiac news, cardiac research at CHOP, videos,
> patient stories, meeting the specialists on the team (with profiles, e.g., specialty,
> medical board certification, education), consultations and second opinions, and
> taking a virtual tour.

> Cleveland Clinic (Cleveland, OH)—"Diseases and Conditions: Heart Block."
> http://my.clevelandclinic.org/heart/disorders/electric/heart_block.aspx; alternate
> path: http://my.clevelandclinic.org/, under the category "Institutes and Services"
> click on "Heart and Vascular," then click on "Homepage," then click on the cate-
> gory "Diseases and Conditions," scroll down to the title "Abnormal Heart
> Rhythms," and click on "Heart Block."
> Cleveland Clinic provides comprehensive patient-friendly information on heart
> block, including its definition, types, risk, causes, symptoms, diagnostic tests,
> treatments, and following up. The Cleveland Clinic also offers a link to "Chat

Online with a Heart and Vascular Nurse." For information on clinical trials, see the Cleveland Clinic entry on pp. 31–32.

➤ ClinicalTrials.gov—Heart block clinical trials. http://clinicaltrials.gov/ct2/results/refine?term=heart+block; alternate path: http://clinicaltrials.gov/, search for "heart block" in the Search for Studies box at the top of the screen.
To limit your results, click on "Modify This Search" and select specific fields, such as (1) Recruitment (e.g., you might want to select "Open Studies"); (2) Locations (e.g., select your state); and (3) Age Group, and then click on the "Search" button. Click on the title of each trial name for additional information, such as purpose of the study, study design and type, detailed description, outcome measures, eligibility (age, gender, criteria for participating), study start date, estimated study completion date, and sponsor. ClinicalTrials.gov, developed by the U.S. National Institutes of Health of the National Library of Medicine, lists ongoing and currently enrolling clinical trials. Check often for new studies.

➤ eMedicineHealth—"Heart Block." http://www.emedicinehealth.com/heart_block -health/article_em.htm; alternate path: http://www.emedicinehealth.com/, search for "heart block," and then click on the title "Heart Block—Source: Healthwise." eMedicineHealth, a division of WebMD, offers an article on heart block with discussions on causes, where it can occur, and types.

➤ Fetal Care Center of Cincinnati, Cincinnati Children's Hospital Medical Center (Cincinnati, OH)—"Complete Heart Block." http://www.cincinnatichildrens.org/service/f/fetal-care/conditions/heart-block/; alternate path: http://www.fetalcarecenter.org/, search for "heart block," and then click on "Complete Heart Block."
The Fetal Care Center of Cincinnati at Cincinnati Children's Hospital Medical Center, which specializes in congenital heart disease/defects, provides comprehensive, patient-friendly information on heart block, including definitions, causes, incidence, diagnosis, and outcomes.

➤ Heart Rhythm Society (HRS)—"Heart Block." http://www.hrsonline.org/Patient Info/HeartRhythmDisorders/HeartBlock/index.cfm; alternate path: http://www .hrsonline.org/, search for and then click on the title "Heart Block."
Written for patients, information on this webpage includes types of heart block, symptoms, risk factors, and treatment options.

➤ Mayo Clinic (Rochester, MN)—"Bradycardia." http://www.mayoclinic.com/ health/bradycardia/DS00947; alternate path: http://www.mayoclinic.com/, search for and then click on the title "Bradycardia."
Bradycardia may occur because of heart block (atrioventricular block). Discussed in an overview are various types of heart blocks that might cause bradycardia (slower than normal heart rate). See also links to definitions, symptoms,

complications, and risk factors. For information on clinical trials and patient services, see the Mayo Clinic entry on p. 36.

➢ Medscape Reference (Drugs, Diseases, and Procedures)—"Atrioventricular Block." http://emedicine.medscape.com/article/151597-overview; alternate path: http://emedicine.medscape.com/, search for and then click on the title "Atrioventricular Block."

Written for Medscape by two medical doctors, Chirag M. Sandesara and Brian Olshansky, this webpage presents a comprehensive report on atrioventricular block. Although written for health care professionals, it might be helpful for interested laypersons. Articles for Medscape Reference are written by medical experts. The webpage states, "Our rigorous literature survey process allows us to rapidly integrate new practice-changing information into the relevant topics by systematically reviewing the major medical and pharmacy journals, news announcements, and important practice guidelines." Free registration is required.

➢ *The Merck Manual Home Health Handbook for Patients and Caregivers*—"Heart Block." http://www.merckmanuals.com/home/sec03/ch025/ch025j.html; alternate path: http://www.merckmanuals.com/home/, at left under "Sections," click on "All" next to the navigation arrows to view a complete list, then click on "Heart and Blood Vessel Disorders," scroll down to the section titled "Abnormal Heart Rhythms," and then click on the title "Heart Block."

This section, which provides an overview on heart block, is based on a well-known medical textbook titled *The Merck Manual Home Health Handbook for Patients and Caregivers*, and this topic is part of an extensive section on abnormal heart rhythms that is "provided free of charge . . . as a public service."

➢ National Heart, Lung, and Blood Institute (NHLBI)—"What Is Heart Block?" http://www.nhlbi.nih.gov/health/dci/Diseases/hb/hb_whatis.html; alternate path: http://www.nhlbi.nih.gov/, search for "heart block," and then click on "What Is Heart Block?"

NHLBI, a division of the National Institutes of Health from the U.S. Department of Health and Human Services, provides information on heart block, including topics such as understanding the heart's electrical system, EKG results, types of heart block, causes, risk factors, signs and symptoms, diagnosis, treatments, living with heart block, clinical trials, and key points.

➢ NHS (National Health Service) Choices—"Heart Block." http://www.nhs.uk/conditions/Heart-block/Pages/Introduction.aspx; alternate path: http://www.nhs.uk, search for "heart block" and click on "Heart Block—NHS Choices—Health A–Z."

According to the website, "NHS Choices is the UK's biggest health website. It provides a comprehensive health information service that puts you in control of your healthcare." NHS Choices provides information on heart block, including an overview of the condition (symptoms, causes, diagnosis, and treatment). This page also features a link to "Clinical Trials," both in the United States and worldwide, "provided by WHO International Clinical Trials Registry."

➤ Texas Heart Institute (Houston, TX)—"Bundle Branch Block" (Heart Information Center). http://www.texasheartinstitute.org/HIC/Topics/Cond/bbblock.cfm; alternate path: http://www.texasheartinstitute.org/, search for and then click on the title "Bundle Branch Block," or under the heading "Heart Information Center" click on "Heart-Health Topics," click on "Heart Conditions," and then click on "Bundle Branch Block."

The Texas Heart Institute website offers a definition of bundle branch block, as well as information on causes, signs and symptoms, diagnosis, and treatment. There is also a link for information on patient care. An easy-to-print format is available. One section allows users to "Ask a Texas Heart Institute Doctor" questions. Click on "Heart Doctor Answers" to explore the questions and answers already published there. For information on clinical trials, see the Texas Heart Institute entry on p. 40.

➤ University of California, San Francisco (UCSF) Benioff Children's Hospital, Department of Surgery—"Heart Block." http://www.ucsfbenioffchildrens.org/conditions/heart_block/; alternate path: http://www.ucsfbenioffchildrens.org/, search for and click on the title "Heart Block," or click on "Conditions and Treatments" and under "H" click on "Heart Block."

Benioff Children's Hospital of UCSF's website provides patient-friendly information on heart block, including sections on signs and symptoms (plus an animated image), diagnosis, and treatment. There are also links to key treatment options, such as electrophysiology study and catheter ablation, implantable cardioverter defibrillators, and pacemaker procedures. Under "Conditions and Treatments," choose "Patient Experiences" to read the personal stories of patients, cataloged by condition. Search for current clinical trials at the link "Clinical Trials and Research."

➤ WebMD—"Heart Block—Topic Overview." http://www.webmd.com/a-to-z-guides/heart-block-topic-overview; alternate path: http://www.webmd.com/, search for "heart block," and then click on "Heart Block—Topic Overview" (WebMD Medical Reference from Healthwise).

This WebMD webpage offers information on causes, where blocks occur, and types of heart block. WebMD's heart health e-mail newsletter is available for subscription. According to WebMD, "WebMD News is an independent media service designed to provide news, information, and educational material to consumers and physicians. News content created by WebMD is free from influence by sponsors, partners, or other sources."

Patient Support Groups and Organizations

> DailyStrength—Heart block discussion groups. http://www.dailystrength.org/search?q=heart+block; alternate path: http://www.dailystrength.org/, search for "heart block."

The DailyStrength website offers online blogs for those with heart conditions; note that at the time of publication, no support group on heart block was yet available. Free registration is required to participate. According to the website, "DailyStrength is a subsidiary of Sharecare. Sharecare, created by WebMD founder and Discovery Communications' Chief of Global Digital Strategy Jeff Arnold, along with America's Doctor, Dr. Mehmet Oz, is the first truly interactive healthcare ecosystem giving consumers the ability to ask, learn and act on the questions of health."

> MedHelp—"Heart Block." http://www.medhelp.org/search?query=heart+block; alternate path: http://www.medhelp.org/, search for and then click on the title "Heart Block."

According to its website, MedHelp "connects people with the leading medical experts," such as those from Cleveland Clinic, National Jewish Health, Partners Health, and Mount Sinai Hospital with those who have similar medical issues. MedHelp's main focus is to enable patients "to take control over their health and find answers to their medical questions" using nontechnical language via an online community through posts, forums and groups, blogs, and user journals, as well as recommendations, articles, health pages, and a medical glossary. Free registration is required.

> U.S. Hospital Finder. http://www.ushospitalfinder.com/.

Use this site to find the names of hospitals by zip code, city, state, or your address. The search results include a map with directions. You might also want to ask your health care professional, call hospitals in your area, or search for "support groups" on hospital websites to determine if there are any cardiology support groups for people with heart block that meet regularly in your area.

> Yahoo! Groups—"Heart Block Kids" support group. http://health.groups.yahoo.com/group/heartblockkids/; alternate path: http://www.groups.yahoo.com/, search for "heart block kids" in the "Find a Yahoo! Group" Search box, and then click on the group "Heart Block Kids."

This online Yahoo! group is for parents who have children with heart block. Yahoo! Groups is not a medical site, nor does it provide or endorse medical advice or procedures. The purpose of the website is to share experiences in a kind and caring manner. Free registration is required to participate.

Heart Failure

Heart failure is the inability of the heart to supply sufficient blood flow to the body, which drastically reduces the amount of oxygen and other nutrients circulating throughout the body. Heart failure takes time to develop. Symptoms, such as fluid that accumulates in parts of the body (e.g., legs, feet, and ankles; lungs, abdomen), occur because the heart is not supplying enough pressure to move the blood through the vascular system, which is called congestive heart failure. Other symptoms include angina, rapid or irregular heartbeat, shortness of breath, dizziness, fatigue, and persistent coughing when lying down.

Heart failure is different from a heart attack in that the heart usually does not stop beating. For example, cardiomyopathy causes the heart to weaken over time and decreases the amount of blood pumped to the lungs and body. If the heart is weakened enough, blood circulation stops or slows to such a degree that the brain is not supplied with sufficient blood, causing heart failure and possibly death.

Other heart diseases that can cause heart failure include valvular diseases, pericarditis, endocarditis, pulmonary hypertension, high blood pressure, heart muscle damaged triggered by a previous heart attack, and diabetes. Also, heart damage from drug and alcohol abuse, cancer chemotherapy, or other diseases, such as AIDS or thyroid disorders, can lead to heart failure.

In children with congenital heart disease, heart failure can be an outcome of the underlying disease (*see* CHAPTER 4). Children do not have the same symptoms as adults. If caught in time, treatment for the underlying disease can usually stave off heart failure. Changes in lifestyle to strengthen and reduce the workload on the heart can extend a heart failure patient's life span. However, heart failure is not curable, except by heart transplant.

Resources for Further Information on Heart Failure

Books

➤ Kasper, Edward K., and Mary Knudson. *Living Well with Heart Failure, the Misnamed, Misunderstood Condition*. Baltimore, MD: The Johns Hopkins University Press, 2010. Print.
This book was written by the director of clinical cardiology at the Johns Hopkins Hospital to help the patient understand topics such as what heart failure is, causes, symptoms, risks, diagnostic tests, and lifestyle changes.

➤ Meyer, Maria M., and Paula Derr. *The Comfort of Home for Chronic Heart Failure: A Guide for Caregivers*. Portland, OR: CareTrust, 2008. Print.
This book was written for caregivers in three sections: the first section is on background knowledge on heart failure, such as what heart failure is, risk factors, diagnosis, treatment, using the health care team effectively, getting in-home care, and planning for end-of-life care. The second section discusses topics such as setting up a plan of care, how to avoid caregiver burnout, activities of daily living, therapies, special challenges, diet, nutrition, and exercise, emergencies,

and hospice care. The final section lists additional resources such as caregiver organizations and common specialists.

> Starling, Randall C. *The Cleveland Clinic Guide to Heart Failure* (Cleveland Clinic Guides). New York, NY: Kaplan, 2009. Print.
This book provides basic information such as definitions, tests, causes, patient stories, and treatments.

Brochures, Booklets, and Other Short Print Publications

> American Heart Association (AHA). http://www.heart.org/.
  • "Order American Heart Association Educational Brochures." http://www.heart .org/HEARTORG/General/Order-American-Heart-Association-Educational -Brochures_UCM_312777_Article.jsp; alternate path: http://www.heart.org/, search for "educational brochures," click on the title "Order American Heart Association Educational Brochures," and then click on the topic "heart failure." Among the AHA brochures available are "Living with Heart Failure" and "About Heart Transplants." Brochures can be ordered online by filling in a form. (Note that no more than one packet and two brochures per household can be ordered at no cost.)
  • "Patient Information Sheets: Heart Failure." http://www.heart.org/HEARTORG/ Conditions/HeartFailure/HeartFailureToolsResources/Patient-Information -Sheets-Heart-Failure_UCM_306377_Article.jsp; alternate path: http:// www.heart.org/, search for "heart failure," click on the title "Visit Our Heart Failure Website," click on the section "Tools and Resources," and then click on "Patient Information Sheets." AHA provides two printable information sheets in PDF format, "What Is Heart Failure?" and "How Can I Live with Heart Failure?"
> British Heart Foundation (BHF)—"Heart Failure" (Booklets and DVDs). http:// www.bhf.org.uk/heart-health/conditions/heart-failure.aspx; alternate path: http:// www.bhf.org.uk/, search for "heart failure," and then click on the title "British Heart Foundation—Heart Failure."
The BHF website offers free booklets and DVDs to help patients manage and cope with heart failure. Scroll down the screen and click on each title to view and download.
  • "'Caring for Someone with a Heart Condition'—Short booklet with practical hints on looking after yourself and someone with a long-term condition."
  • "'Everyday Guide to Living with Heart Failure'—Practical guide to help you to deal with the everyday challenges of life with heart failure."
  • "'Living with Heart Failure Booklet'—Short booklet explaining the diagnosis and treatment of heart failure."
  • "'One Step at a Time—Living with Heart Failure'—A DVD featuring six people telling you how they felt when they were told they had heart

failure. Our health professionals also answer some of the common questions that you may have."

Websites

➢ Aetna InteliHealth—"Heart Failure." http://www.intelihealth.com/IH/ihtIH/ WSIHW000/8059/23704/213151.html?d=dmtHealthAZ; alternate path: http://www.intelihealth.com/, search for "heart failure" and then click on the title "Heart Failure" or the title "Congestive Heart Failure."
This website provides an overview of heart failure, including symptoms, diagnosis, expected duration, prevention, treatment, when to call a professional, prognosis, and additional information. Aetna InteliHealth, a subsidiary of Aetna, is reviewed by the faculty of Harvard Medical School and the University College of Dental Medicine. According to Aetna InteliHealth's website, "Aetna InteliHealth maintains absolute editorial independence. That means that Aetna InteliHealth makes decisions about the information on our site free of outside influence." Under "Healthy Lifestyle," Aetna InteliHealth also offers free health-related e-mail subscriptions.

➢ American Heart Association (AHA)—"Heart Failure." http://www.heart.org/ HEARTORG/Conditions/HeartFailure/Heart-Failure_UCM_002019_SubHome Page.jsp; alternate path: http://www.heart.org/, search for "heart failure" and then click on the title "Visit Our Heart Failure Website."
AHA provides expanded details on heart failure, including such major sections as heart failure facts, about heart failure, warning signs, risk factors, symptoms and diagnosis, prevention and treatment, and tools and resources. You can also sign up for a free heart health e-newsletter.

➢ BetterMedicine.com—"Heart Failure and Congestive Heart Failure." http://www .bettermedicine.com/topic/heart-failure/ and http://www.localhealth.com/ article/congestive-heart-failure; alternate path: http://www.bettermedicine.com/, search for "heart failure" and then click on the titles "Heart Failure" and "Congestive Heart Failure."
The Better Medicine website offers links to heart failure topics, such as learning more about heart failure and treatment: getting the care you need, and living well with congestive heart failure. There are also sections titled "Expert Advice from Harvard Medical School" on heart failure and "Your Guide to Heart Failure," which includes symptoms and causes. According to the Better Medicine website, "[A]ll content is medically reviewed by at least one medical professional. Our content is backed by evidence from sources, such as articles in peer reviewed journals, government bodies, objective health organizations and medical groups of specialists. The name and credentials of the medical reviewer(s) are printed at the end of the article."

➢ Brigham and Women's Hospital (BWH) (Boston, MA)—"Heart Failure." http://health library.brighamandwomens.org/HealthCenters/Heart/Conditions/HeartFailure;

alternate path: http://www.brighamandwomens.org/, scroll under the heading "Health Information" to the category "Health Information Center" and click on the topic "Heart Information Center," then scroll down and click on the category "Heart Diseases and Conditions," and then click on "Heart Failure."
BWH's heart failure webpage discusses numerous linked topics, such as clinical guidelines for good heart care, living well with congestive heart failure, breathing more easily, staying physically active, tracking symptoms, life after hospitalization, and management tips. For information on clinical trials, see the BWH entry on p. 29.

➤ British Heart Foundation (BHF)—"Heart Failure." http://www.bhf.org.uk/heart -health/conditions/heart-failure.aspx; alternate path: http://www.bhf.org.uk/, search for "heart failure," and then click on the title "British Heart Foundation—Heart Failure."
The BHF website describes heart failure, causes, diagnosis, treatment, how heart failure affects you, and support groups. Also click on the "Community: Share Experiences with Others" heading to engage with the BHF online community where you can share your own story and read those of others.

➤ CardioSmart—"Heart Failure." https://www.cardiosmart.org/Heart-Conditions/ Heart-Failure; alternate path: https://www.cardiosmart.org/, search for and then click on the title "Heart Failure."
CardioSmart provides an easy-to-use website on understanding heart failure under the category "Heart Condition." CardioSmart's Heart Failure homepage contains many sections, including an introduction, understanding your condition, questions to ask your cardiologist, patient responsibilities, patient care heart team, getting support and research. Also listed are links to the latest heart failure news and events, videos (top of screen), and an e-mail sign-up for *CardioSmart eNewsletters*. Click on "Overview" to learn more about heart failure (e.g., basic facts, causes and risk factors, tests and diagnosis, heart transplantation, prevention, key facts, by the numbers, symptoms, treatment, and living with heart failure). At the top of the screen, click on the heading "Connect with Others" for "Community Peer Support," "Patient Stories," and "Discussion Forums." This webpage is also available in Spanish. According to the American College of Cardiology (ACC), "CardioSmart is the patient education and support program launched by the [ACC]. Our mission is to engage, inform, and empower patients to better prepare them for participation in their own care."

➤ CenterWatch—Clinical trials listing service. http://www.centerwatch.com/.
This CenterWatch clinical trials listing service lists trials currently looking for volunteers to enroll in medical studies. Click on the "Clinical Trials" heading and search by location, medical condition, or therapeutic area. To search by location, click on your state (or country) and click on a city near you to find information

on each available clinical trial. Check back with this website often for new studies. Sign up for a free e-mail service that sends notice of new clinical trials.

- "Heart Failure Clinical Trials." http://www.centerwatch.com/clinical-trials/listings/studylist.aspx?CatID=281.
- "Heart Transplantation Clinical Trials." http://www.centerwatch.com/clinical-trials/listings/studylist.aspx?CatID=738.

Alternate path: http://www.centerwatch.com/, under the category "Patient Resources" click on "Search Clinical Trials" where you can search by medical condition, then click on the medical condition's first letter (e.g., "H"), and then click on the specific term (e.g., "Heart Failure"). The "Search Clinical Trials" page also allows searching by location and therapeutic area.

➢ Cleveland Clinic (Cleveland, OH)—"What Is Heart Failure?" http://my.clevelandclinic.org/heart/disorders/heartfailure/hfwhatis.aspx; alternate path: http://my.clevelandclinic.org/, under the category "Institutes and Services" click on "Heart and Vascular," then click on "Homepage," then click on the category "Diseases and Conditions," and then click on the title "Heart Failure."
Cleveland Clinic provides comprehensive patient-friendly information on heart failure, such as an overview, symptoms, diagnosis, care and treatment, lifestyle changes, and how to find a doctor who treats heart failure. The Cleveland Clinic also offers a link to "Chat Online with a Heart and Vascular Nurse." For information on clinical trials, see the Cleveland Clinic entry on pp. 31–32.

➢ ClinicalTrials.gov. http://clinicaltrials.gov/.
ClinicalTrials.gov, developed by the U.S. National Institutes of Health of the National Library of Medicine, lists ongoing and currently enrolling clinical trials. To find clinical trials from the homepage, search for the condition by name (e.g., "arrhythmia"), which will generate a list of possibly hundreds or thousands of studies. To limit your results, click on "Modify This Search" and select specific fields, such as (1) Recruitment (e.g., you might want to select "Open Studies"); (2) Locations (e.g., select your state); and (3) Age Group, and then click on the "Search" button. Click on the title of each trial name for additional information, such as purpose of study, study design and type, detailed description, outcome measures, eligibility (age, gender, criteria for participating), study start date, estimated study completion date, and sponsor. Check often for new studies.

- Heart failure clinical trials. http://clinicaltrials.gov/ct2/results/refine?term=heart+failure.
- Heart transplant clinical trials. http://clinicaltrials.gov/ct2/results/refine?term=heart+transplant.

➢ eMedicineHealth—"Congestive Heart Failure" and "Heart Failure." http://www.emedicinehealth.com/congestive_heart_failure/article_em.htm and http://www.emedicinehealth.com/heart_failure-health/article_em.htm; alternate path:

http://www.emedicinehealth.com/, search for and then click on the titles "Congestive Heart Failure" (Medical Reference from eMedicineHealth) and "Heart Failure" (Medical Reference from Healthwise).

eMedicineHealth, a division of WebMD, offers a comprehensive article on congestive heart failure, including an overview, causes, signs and symptoms, when to seek medical care, diagnosis, treatment, prevention, and follow-up.

➤ Heart Failure Society of America (HFSA). http://www.hfsa.org/.

According to its website, HFSA "represents the first organized effort by heart failure experts from the Americas to provide a forum for all those interested in heart function, heart failure, and congestive heart failure (CHF) research and patient care."

➤ Hospital of the University of Pennsylvania (HUP) (Philadelphia, PA)—"Heart Failure Program." http://www.pennmedicine.org/heart/patient/clinical-services/heart-failure/; alternate path: http://www.pennmedicine.org/, click on the "Departments and Services" icon (or type "departments and services" in the Search box at the top of the screen), scroll down and then click on the category "Cardiology and Cardiac Surgery," and then scroll down under the heading "Clinical Services" and click on "Heart Failure."

At its Penn Heart and Vascular Center website, HUP offers links in the Heart Failure Program that include an "Overview" (what are the stages of heart failure and treatment options); the "Team," which links to each physician and specialist (with profiles, e.g., specialty, medical board certification, education); "Clinical Trials"; "The Penn Difference" (program described, patient experiences, unique capabilities and expertise, and hospital highlights); "Physician Interviews" (videos); and "Quality/Outcomes." Click on each treatment option for details and charts. A 54-page *Penn Heart and Vascular 2011 Clinical Activity Report* is available for download; this report is a "summary of surgical, medical and interventional outcomes, as well as clinical research activity and patient volumes." You can also subscribe to the Penn Heart newsletter. For information on clinical trials, see the HUP entry on p. 33.

➤ Insidermedicine. http://www.insidermedicine.com/.

The Insidermedicine website offers a variety of heart-health-related videos. For more information on the Insidermedicine Project, see the earlier entry on pp. 33–34. From the homepage, you can search for videos by title, or you can search by topic (e.g., heart failure) to find other related videos. In the following, a medical specialist discusses recommendations for the self-care of patients with heart failure to decrease the incidence of hospital readmission.

- "Early Follow Up Decreases Readmission Rates of Heart Failure Patients." http://www.insidermedicine.com/archives/IN_DEPTH_DOCTOR_4299.aspx.
- "Men at Raised Risk of Dying from Heart Failure; US Army Suicides Rose Dramatically from 2004–2008; Weight Loss Supplements Ineffective (Week in Review)." http://www.insidermedicine.com/archives/Men_At_Raised_Risk

_of_Dying_From_Heart_Failure_US_Army_Suicides_Rose_Dramatically
_from_20042008_Weight_Loss_Supplements_Ineffective_Week_in_Review
_5957.aspx.

➤ Johns Hopkins Hospital (Baltimore, MD). http://www.hopkinsmedicine.org/.
The Johns Hopkins Heart and Vascular Institute website provides detailed information on a variety of conditions, treatments, and services. It also lists links to physicians and specialists (with profile, e.g., specialty, medical board certification, education). Click on the heading "Clinical Trials" to find links to current trials in various heart and cardiovascular conditions. From the homepage, you can also search for specific resources by title.

- "Cardiomyopathy/Heart Failure." http://www.hopkinsmedicine.org/heart
_vascular_institute/conditions_treatments/conditions/cardiomyopathy
.html and http://www.hopkinsmedicine.org/healthlibrary/conditions/adult/
cardiovascular_diseases/cardiomyopathy_85,P00201/. The Johns Hopkins Heart and Vascular Institute website on cardiomyopathy discusses this condition, its types, when to call an ambulance, when to call a doctor, symptoms, causes, prevention, diagnosis, and treatment.
- "Cardiomyopathy/Heart Failure Service." http://www.hopkinsmedicine.org/
heart_vascular_institute/clinical_services/specialty_areas/cardiomyopathy
.html. The Johns Hopkins Cardiomyopathy and Heart Failure Service describes current information on the type of services they provide and lists and describes associated diagnostic tests.

➤ Khan Academy. http://www.khanacademy.org/.
Salman Khan, creator of the nonprofit Khan Academy, sketches as he explains each topic. Khan's mini lessons are all downloadable and free. According to the website, "With a library of over 2,400 videos covering everything from arithmetic to physics, finance, and history and 150 practice exercises, we're on a mission to help you learn what you want, when you want, at your own pace." Click on the heading "About" to get the maximum use of this excellent site. Khan has three degrees from the Massachusetts Institute of Technology and an MBA from Harvard University. From the homepage, you can also search for specific resources by title.

- "Heart Disease and Heart Attacks: Basics of Heart Disease, Heart Attacks, Heart Failure, Angina, Cardiac Arrest." http://www.khanacademy.org/science/
healthcare-and-medicine/heart-disease-and-stroke/v/heart-disease-and-heart
-attacks?playlist=Biology.
- "Stenosis, Ischemia, and Heart Failure: Clarifying a Bunch of Medical Terms around Heart Disease." http://www.khanacademy.org/science/
healthcare-and-medicine/heart-disease-and-stroke/v/stenosis--ischemia
-and-heart-failure.

➤ KidsHealth.org—"For Parents: When Your Child Needs a Heart Transplant."
http://kidshealth.org/parent/medical/heart/heart_transplant.html#cat141;

alternate path: http://www.kidshealth.org/, click on "Parents Site," scroll down and click on "Diseases and Conditions," and then scroll down and click on "Heart and Blood Vessels" and then click on the title "When Your Child Needs a Heart Transplant."

The Nemours Center for Children's Health Media provides current information, written for parents, on what happens when a child needs a heart transplant. Topics discussed include general information about heart transplants, when a child needs a heart transplant, receiving a donor's healthy heart, preparing for surgery, organ waiting lists, getting "the call," recovery, possible complications, and living heart healthy for life. Information is available in English and Spanish. Click on the "Listen" button to hear the text read aloud.

➤ Massachusetts General Hospital (MGH) (Boston, MA). http://www.massgeneral .org/.

At each of the following MGH webpages are links to comprehensive information in several categories: "Our Approach" includes an overview of conditions, treatments, and procedures as well as links to each medical expert (with profiles, e.g., specialty, medical board certification, education). "About This Program" describes the quality and benefits of the program as well as MGH's commitment. "Conditions and Diseases" offers links to detailed information on specific and related conditions. "Support and Wellness" offers patient guides. "Clinical Trials" links to MGH trials and research studies currently seeking participants. "News and Events" includes the latest information on the conditions. "Multimedia" offers video demonstrations.

- "Cardiac Resynchronization Therapy Program." http://www.massgeneral .org/heartcenter/services/treatmentprograms.aspx?id=1002.
- "Heart Failure and Cardiac Transplant Program." http://www.massgeneral .org/heartcenter/services/treatmentprograms.aspx?id=1006.

Alternate path: http://www.massgeneral.org/, search for topic by title or go to "Centers and Services," click on "View All Departments," then click on "Heart Center," and then click on the heading "Treatments and Services" to find your topic.

➤ Mayo Clinic (Rochester, MN)—"Heart Failure." http://www.mayoclinic.com/ health/heart-failure/DS00061; alternate path: http://www.mayoclinic.com/, search for and then click on the title "Heart Failure."

Written for patients, this webpage on heart failure includes definitions, symptoms, causes, risk factors, complications, preparing for appointments, tests and diagnosis, treatments and drugs, lifestyle and home remedies, and coping and support. There is also a more comprehensive section titled "In-Depth" on some of these topics. For information on clinical trials and patient services, see the Mayo Clinic entry on p. 36.

➤ MedicineNet. http://www.medicinenet.com/.
MedicineNet.com is owned and operated by WebMD and is part of the WebMD Network. According to its website, MedicineNet "provides easy-to-read, in-depth, authoritative medical information for consumers via its user-friendly, interactive website." The medical information is written and edited by a nation-ally recognized group of more than 70 U.S. board-certified physicians. The web-site contains a "Symptom Checker" listed in alphabetical order as a guide to "pinpoint your pain." Its homepage links to "Health News of the Week." You can also sign up to receive a health newsletter.

- "Congestive Heart Failure." http://www.medicinenet.com/congestive_heart _failure/article.htm; alternate path: http://www.medicinenet.com/, click on the major topic "Diseases and Conditions," then click on "Conditions A–Z," then click on "C," and then scroll down to click on "Congestive Heart Fail-ure." In-depth information on congestive heart failure includes definitions, causes, symptoms, diagnosis, treatment (surgery, medications), medications to avoid, stages of heart failure, preventing further damage, quality of life, heart transplant, long-term outlook, and finding a local cardiologist.
- "Heart Disease: Your Guide to Heart Failure." http://www.medicinenet .com/heart_failure/article.htm; alternate path: http://www.medicinenet .com/, click on the major topic "Diseases and Conditions," then click on "Conditions A–Z," then click on "H," and then scroll down to click on "Heart Failure." In-depth information on heart failure includes definitions, causes, symptoms, types of heart failure, diagnosis, treatment, lifestyle changes, heart transplant, long-term outlook, research on heart failure, patient discussions, and finding a local cardiologist.

➤ MedlinePlus—"Heart Failure." http://www.nlm.nih.gov/medlineplus/heartfailure .html; alternate path: http://www.nlm.nih.gov/, under "Databases," click on "Med-linePlus" and then search for "heart failure."
MedlinePlus is a component of the National Institutes of Health (NIH), produced by the National Library of Medicine (NLM), and is updated regularly. This Med-linePlus webpage on heart failure offers extensive linked information covering overviews, news, diagnosis/symptoms, treatment, prevention/screening, alterna-tive therapy, nutrition, coping, disease management, related issues, anatomy/ physiology, clinical trials, research, journal articles, dictionaries/glossaries, direc-tories, organizations, law and policy, statistics, and specific sections that focus on children and women. Patient handouts are also available. This webpage also includes a multimedia section containing tutorials and videos.

➤ Medscape Reference (Drugs, Diseases, and Procedures)—"Heart Failure." http:// emedicine.medscape.com/article/163062-overview; alternate path: http://emedicine .medscape.com/, search for and then click on the title "Heart Failure."

Written for Medscape by Ioana Dumitru, MD, and associates, this webpage presents a comprehensive report on heart failure. Although written for health care professionals, it might be helpful for interested laypersons. Articles for Medscape Reference are written by medical experts. The webpage states, "Our rigorous literature survey process allows us to rapidly integrate new practice-changing information into the relevant topics by systematically reviewing the major medical and pharmacy journals, news announcements, and important practice guidelines." Free registration is required.

➢ *The Merck Manual Home Health Handbook for Patients and Caregivers*—"Heart Failure." http://www.merckmanuals.com/home/heart_and_blood_vessel_disorders/ heart_failure/heart_failure.html; alternate path: http://www.merckmanuals.com/ home/, under "Sections," click on "All" next to the navigation arrows to view a complete list, then click on the section "Heart and Blood Vessel Disorders," and then scroll down to click on "Heart Failure."
Heart failure is covered extensively in this section, which discusses causes, compensatory mechanisms, symptoms, diagnosis, prevention, and treatment, including end-of-life issues. It is based on the well-known medical textbook titled *The Merck Manual Home Health Handbook for Patients and Caregivers* and is "provided free of charge . . . as a public service."

➢ National Heart, Lung, and Blood Institute (NHLBI). http://www.nhlbi.nih.gov/. NHLBI is a division of the National Institutes of Health from the U.S. Department of Health and Human Services. From the homepage, you can also search for specific resources by title.

   • "Heart Transplant." http://www.nhlbi.nih.gov/health/health-topics/topics/ ht/. This NHLBI website provides information on heart failure, including links on what a heart transplant is; who needs one; what to expect before, during, and after surgery; risk factors; and clinical trials.
   • "What Is Diabetic Heart Disease (DHD)?" http://www.nhlbi.nih.gov/ health/health-topics/topics/dhd/. This NHLBI website provides information on diabetic heart disease, including links to what DHD is, causes, risk factors, signs and symptoms, diagnosis, treatments, prevention, living with DHD, clinical trials, and more.
   • "What Is Heart Failure?" http://www.nhlbi.nih.gov/health/dci/Diseases/Hf/ HF_WhatIs.html. This NHLBI webpage provides information on heart failure, including links to what heart failure is, other names, causes, risk factors, signs and symptoms, diagnosis, treatments, prevention, living with heart failure, key points, and more.

➢ New York–Presbyterian (NYP) University Hospital of Columbia and Cornell (New York, NY)—"Interactive Media Library: Congestive Heart Failure" (Video).

http://nyp.org/media/index.html; alternate path: http://nyp.org/, click on the icon with the text "Explore the Interactive Media Library."
The Human Atlas media player presents short videos, text, models, and slides. To view an excellent video, click on the "Complete Listing of Topics" heading and scroll down to click on "Congestive Heart Failure." For information on clinical trials, see the NYP entry on p. 38.

➤ OPTN: Organ Procurement and Transplantation Network. http://optn.transplant .hrsa.gov/.
OPTN, a division of the Health Resources and Services Administration of the U.S. Department of Health and Human Services, is the only national transplant patient waiting list. According to the website, the main goals of this U.S. Congress–enacted network, under the National Organ Transplant Act of 1984, are to "increase the effectiveness and efficiency of organ sharing and equity in the national system of organ allocation, and to increase the supply of donated organs available for transplantation." To find a recommended heart transplant hospital near you, click on "Member Directory," under "Select a Member Type" click on "Transplant Centers by Organ," under "Select Organ Type" click on "Heart," and then under "Select a State" click on your specific state.

➤ Texas Heart Institute (Houston, TX)—"Heart Information Center." http://www .texasheartinstitute.org/HIC/.
For information on clinical trials, see the Texas Heart Institute entry on p. 40.

- "Diastolic Dysfunction." http://www.texasheartinstitute.org/HIC/Topics/ Cond/ddisfunc.cfm. The Texas Heart Institute website offers a description of diastolic dysfunction. An easy-to-print format is available.
- "Heart Failure." http://www.texasheartinstitute.org/HIC/Topics/Cond/CHF .cfm. The Texas Heart Institute website offers a definition of heart failure, as well as information on risks, signs and symptoms, diagnosis, and treatment (medication, surgery).
- "Heart Transplantation." http://www.texasheartinstitute.org/HIC/Topics/ Proced/hearttx.cfm. The Texas Heart Institute website offers a definition of heart transplant, as well as information on reasons for transplant, first steps for transplant, financing, waiting lists, and life after the transplant.
- "Myocarditis." http://www.texasheartinstitute.org/HIC/Topics/Cond/ myocard.cfm. The Texas Heart Institute website offers a definition of myocarditis, as well as information on causes, signs and symptoms, diagnosis, and treatment.
- "Ventricular Assist Devices (VAD)." http://www.texasheartinstitute.org/ HIC/Topics/Proced/vads.cfm. The Texas Heart Institute website offers a definition of VADs, as well as how implantable pumps are placed in the body, how paracorporeal pumps are placed in the body, how paracorporeal

VADs are different, how VADs work, why patients need VADs, and the different kinds of VADs.

Alternate path: http://www.texasheartinstitute.org/, search for the topic by name (e.g., "diastolic dysfunction"), and then click on the appropriate title; or in the pull-down menu under "Heart Information Center," select "Heart-Health Topics" and then "Heart Conditions," and click on the topic by name.

➤ UCLA Ronald Reagan Medical Center (Los Angeles, CA)—"Congestive Heart Failure." http://www.uclahealth.org/body.cfm?id=592; scroll down to the heading "In-Depth Reports," click on the word "More," and then click on the title "Congestive Heart Failure"; alternate path: http://www.uclahealth.org/, under the heading "For Patients and Visitors," scroll down and mouse over the category "Health Resources," then select "Heart Health Center," scroll down to the heading "In-Depth Reports," click on the word "More," and then click on the title "Congestive Heart Failure."

The UCLA Ronald Reagan Medical Center's Heart Health Center provides an in-depth report on congestive heart failure, which includes highlights, introductions, risk factors, complications, symptoms, diagnosis, prevention, treatment, medications, surgery and devices, and lifestyle changes. Also on the Heart Health Center website, under the heading "Tests and Treatments," scroll under the section "Alternative Medicine" for more treatment information. Then click on the word "More" and click on the title "Heart Failure." For more information on patient resources and clinical trials, see the UCLA entry on p. 41.

➤ WebMD—"Heart Failure Health Center." http://www.webmd.com/heart-disease/heart-failure/default.htm; alternate path: http://www.webmd.com/, search for "heart failure," and then click on the title "Heart Failure Health Center (WebMD Health and Wellness Center)."

The WebMD website offers the latest information on heart failure, using articles, slide presentations, videos, FAQs, discussions groups, and expert blogs. A WebMD heart health e-mail newsletter is also available. According to WebMD, "WebMD News is an independent media service designed to provide news, information, and educational material to consumers and physicians. News content created by WebMD is free from influence by sponsors, partners, or other sources."

Patient Support Groups and Organizations

➤ DailyStrength—"Heart Failure Support Group." http://www.dailystrength.org/c/Heart-Failure/support-group; alternate path: http://www.dailystrength.org/, search for "heart failure," and click on "Visit the Heart Failure Support Group."

The DailyStrength website offers online support groups and blogs for those with heart failure. Free registration is required to participate. According to the website, "DailyStrength is a subsidiary of Sharecare. Sharecare, created by WebMD founder and Discovery Communications' Chief of Global Digital Strategy Jeff Arnold, along with America's Doctor, Dr. Mehmet Oz, is the first truly interactive healthcare ecosystem giving consumers the ability to ask, learn and act on the questions of health."

➤ HeartHub for Patients—"Heart Failure." http://www.hearthub.org/hc-heart -failure.htm; alternate path: http://www.hearthub.org/, scroll down to the section titled "Health Centers," and click on the title "Heart Failure."
HeartHub, a division of the American Heart Association (AHA), is a patient-support portal for information, tools, and linked resources on heart failure, including discussions on warning signs, getting help on the phone, living with heart failure, testing knowledge with a quiz, understanding ejection fraction measurement to help doctors know how efficiently a heart is pumping, exercises to do at home, and personal stories.

➤ MedHelp—"Heart Failure." http://www.medhelp.org/search?query=heart+failure; alternate path: http://www.medhelp.org/, search for "heart failure."
According to its website, MedHelp "connects people with the leading medical experts," such as those from Cleveland Clinic, National Jewish Health, Partners Health, and Mount Sinai Hospital, with those who have similar medical issues. MedHelp's main focus is to enable patients "to take control over their health and find answers to their medical questions" using nontechnical language via an online community through posts, forums and groups, blogs, user journals, as well as recommendations, articles, health pages, and a medical glossary. Free registration is required.

➤ Transplant Recipients International Organization (TRIO). http://trioweb.org/.
With local chapters in the United States, TRIO, according to its website, "is a non-profit international organization committed to improving the quality of lives touched by the miracle of transplantation through support, advocacy, education, and awareness." The TRIO Youth Circle support groups are geared directly toward helping the younger transplant community, such as those undergoing heart transplants.

➤ U.S. Hospital Finder. http://www.ushospitalfinder.com/.
Use this site to find the names of hospitals by zip code, city, state, or your address. The search results include a map with directions. You might also want to ask your health care professional, call hospitals in your area, or search for "support groups" on hospital websites to determine if there are any cardiology support groups for people who have experienced heart failure that meet regularly in your area.

➤ Yahoo! Groups. http://www.yahoo.com/.
Yahoo! Groups is not a medical site, nor does it provide or endorse medical advice or procedures. The purpose of the website is to share experiences in a kind and caring manner. Free registration is required to participate. The following groups are for patients and their caregivers, family members, and friends.

- "Heart-Beats: Support for Heart Transplant Patients." http://health.dir.groups .yahoo.com/group/Heart-Beats/?v=1&t=directory&ch=web&pub=groups &sec=dir&slk=4.
- "HeartFailure." http://health.groups.yahoo.com/group/heartfailure/.
- "HeartTransplant." http://health.groups.yahoo.com/group/HeartTransplant/.

Alternate path: http://www.groups.yahoo.com/, search for the name of the support group in the "Find a Yahoo! Group" Search box, and then click on the relevant group name.

Heart Valve Disease

Heart valve disease occurs when one or more of the heart valves are too small or leaking. A valve can become too small when the valve leaflets become stiff or fuse together; this is called valvular stenosis. A valve can become leaky if the leaflets do not seal properly; this is called valvular insufficiency or valvular regurgitation. The disease is identified by the valve and its condition: tricuspid, pulmonic, mitral, and aortic, associated with stenosis or regurgitation. In both cases (too small or leaking valve), the heart must work harder to move blood. Over time, this can lead to other heart diseases such as cardiac insufficiency or heart failure.

A physician using a stethoscope can hear the sounds the blood makes going through the valves. Normally the heart makes a *lub-dub* sound as the valves open and close. A heart murmur indicates a valve problem. Depending on the problem, the sound will be different. A heart murmur has characteristics of loudness, occurrence with the heartbeat cycle, where it is heard around the heart, pitch, length of the sound, and how physical activity (e.g., breathing) or body position affects the sound. These characteristics can tell the physician which problem is present and with which valve.

Some valve diseases are congenital (*see* CHAPTER 4), some are acquired later in life, and others have no known cause. Congenital causes of improper valve development are grouped under the term *dysplasias*. Injury to the heart can scar and deform the valves. Certain infections such as rheumatic fever, strep throat, or endocarditis can damage the valves. Other diseases, such as liver cancer, lupus, and metabolic disorders, can damage the heart valves. Certain medications, such as diet pills, can also damage the valves. Radiation treatments can damage the valves, and the damage may not appear until many years after treatment. As one ages, calcium can deposit in the heart valves and harden them.

Depending on which valve is damaged and how it is damaged, treatments range from protecting the valve from further damage to medication and dietary changes to reduce the symptoms and finally to surgery. Surgery called valvuloplasty is used to open stenosed valves or make hardened valves more flexible. Valvuloplasty involves inflating a balloon catheter in the hardened valve. If the valve is beyond repair, it can be replaced with an animal, cadaverous, or artificial valve.

Resources for Further Information on Heart Valve Disease
Books

> Gassert, Carole A., and Susan G. Burrows. *Going for Heart Surgery: What You Need to Know*. Atlanta, GA: Pritchett and Hull, 2010. Print.
> According to the introduction, "This book can help you get ready for heart surgery. You will not only learn about surgery, but you will also find out how to get your mind and body ready for it . . . it will answer many of your questions and help you think of others to ask your doctor or nurse." The authors also state that "this book can be used for coronary bypass surgery, surgery for congenital defects or surgery for aneurysm of the heart muscles."

> Pai, Ramdas G., and Padmini Varadarajan. *100 Questions and Answers about Valvular Heart Disease*. Sudbury, MA: Jones and Bartlett Learning, 2008. Print.
> In the format of 100 questions, this consumer-oriented book discusses heart basics, causes, symptoms, diagnosis, treatment, surgery, and specific valve problems.

Brochures, Booklets, and Other Short Print Publications

> American Heart Association (AHA). "Your Mitral Valve Prolapse" (Educational Brochure). http://www.heart.org/HEARTORG/General/Your-Mitral -Valve-Prolapse-Brochure_UCM_311617_Article.jsp and http://www.heart .org/HEARTORG/General/Your-Heart-Valve-Surgery_UCM_311655_Article .jsp; alternate path: http://www.heart.org/, search for "educational brochures," then click on the title "Order American Heart Association Educational Brochures," click on the topic "Conditions" to find the brochure "Your Mitral Valve Prolapse," and then click on the topic "Procedures" to find the brochure "Your Heart Valve Surgery."
> The AHA-published brochure "Your Mitral Valve Prolapse" can be ordered by filling in a form online. According to this website, the "Your Heart Valve Surgery" "brochure explains types of valve disorders, replacement options (mechanical and biological), pre-op and post-op procedures, in-hospital and at-home recovery, living with a new heart valve, and more." This brochure can be ordered by filling in a form online. (No more than two brochures per household can be ordered at no cost.)

Websites

> Aetna InteliHealth. http://www.intelihealth.com/.
> Aetna InteliHealth, a subsidiary of Aetna, is reviewed by the faculty of Harvard Medical School and the University College of Dental Medicine. According to its

website, "Aetna InteliHealth maintains absolute editorial independence. That means that Aetna InteliHealth makes decisions about the information on our site free of outside influence." Under "Healthy Lifestyle," Aetna InteliHealth also offers free health-related e-mail subscriptions.

- "Heart Valve Problems." http://www.intelihealth.com/IH/ihtIH/ WSIHW000/8059/23704/266763.html?d=dmtHealthAZ; alternate path: http://www.intelihealth.com/, search for and then click on the title "Heart Valve Problems." This website provides an overview of heart valve problems, including symptoms, diagnosis, expected duration, prevention, treatment, when to call a professional, prognosis, and more.
- "Mitral Valve Prolapse." http://www.intelihealth.com/IH/ihtIH/ WSIHW000/8059/28040/309626.html?d=dmtHealthAZ; alternate path: http://www.intelihealth.com/, search for and then click on the title "Mitral Valve Prolapse." This website provides an overview of mitral valve prolapse, including symptoms, diagnosis, expected duration, prevention, treatment, when to call a professional, prognosis, and more.

➤ Brigham and Women's Hospital (BWH) (Boston, MA). http://www.brigham andwomens.org/.

For information on clinical trials, see the BWH entry on p. 29.

- "Heart Valve Disease." http://healthlibrary.brighamandwomens.org/Health Centers/Heart/Conditions/HVD. BWH's heart valve disease webpage discusses numerous topics, such as heart valve disease, heart murmur, mitral valve prolapse, and managing mitral valve prolapse.
- "Other Heart Conditions: Rheumatic Heart Disease." http://healthlibrary .brighamandwomens.org/HealthCenters/Heart/Conditions/Other/85,P00239. BWH's rheumatic heart disease webpage discusses rheumatic heart disease, its cause, effects from rheumatic fever, symptoms of rheumatic fever, and treatment of rheumatic heart disease.

Alternate path: http://healthlibrary.brighamandwomens.org/, under the heading "Health Information," select "Health Information Center" and then "Heart Information Center," then click on "Heart Conditions and Diseases," and then click on the specific topic.

➤ British Heart Foundation (BHF)—"Heart Valve Disease." http://www.bhf.org.uk/ heart-health/conditions/heart-valve-disease.aspx; alternate path: http://www.bhf .org.uk/, search for "heart valve disease," and then click on the title "British Heart Foundation—Heart Valve Disease."

The BHF website describes heart valve disease, causes, symptoms, diagnosis, treatment, and what happens to heart valves. Also click on the "Community: Share Experiences with Others" heading to engage with the BHF online community where you can share your own story and read those of others.

➤ CenterWatch—Clinical trials listing service. http://www.centerwatch.com/.
  This CenterWatch clinical trials listing service lists trials currently looking for
  volunteers to enroll in medical studies. Click on the "Clinical Trials" heading and
  search by location, medical condition, or therapeutic area. To search by location,
  click on your state (or country) and click on a city near you to find information
  on each available clinical trial. Check back with this website often for new studies. Sign up for a free e-mail service that sends notice of new clinical trials.
  - "Heart Valve Disease Clinical Trials." http://www.centerwatch.com/clinical
    -trials/listings/studylist.aspx?CatID=605.
  - "Mitral Valve Regurgitation Clinical Trials." http://www.centerwatch.com/
    clinical-trials/listings/studylist.aspx?CatID=759.
  Alternate path: http://www.centerwatch.com/, under the category "Patient
  Resources," click on "Search Clinical Trials" where you can search by medical
  condition, click on the medical condition's first letter (e.g., "H"), and then click
  on the specific term (e.g., "Heart Valve Disease"). The "Search Clinical Trials"
  page also allows searching by location and therapeutic area.

➤ Cleveland Clinic (Cleveland, OH)—"Heart Valve Disease." http://my.clevelandclinic
  .org/heart/disorders/valve.aspx; alternate path: http://my.clevelandclinic.org/, under
  the category "Institutes and Services" click on "Heart and Vascular," then click on
  "Homepage," then click on the category "Diseases and Conditions," and click on the
  title "Heart and Vascular."
  Cleveland Clinic provides comprehensive patient-friendly information on heart
  valve disease, with links to definitions, types, symptoms, diagnosis, heart murmur,
  mitral valve prolapse, aortic valve disease, living with valve disease, and finding a
  doctor who treats heart valve disease. The Cleveland Clinic also offers a link to
  "Chat Online with a Heart and Vascular Nurse." For information on clinical trials,
  see the Cleveland Clinic entry on pp. 31–32.

➤ ClinicalTrials.gov. http://clinicaltrials.gov/.
  ClinicalTrials.gov, developed by the U.S. National Institutes of Health of the
  National Library of Medicine, lists ongoing and currently enrolling clinical
  trials. To find clinical trials from the homepage, search for the condition by
  name (e.g., "arrhythmia"), which will generate a list of possibly hundreds or
  thousands of studies. To limit your results, click on "Modify This Search" and
  select specific fields, such as (1) Recruitment (e.g., you might want to select
  "Open Studies"); (2) Locations (e.g., select your state); and (3) Age Group, and
  then click on the "Search" button. Click on the title of each trial name for additional information, such as purpose of study, study design and type, detailed
  description, outcome measures, eligibility (age, gender, criteria for participating), study start date, estimated study completion date, and sponsor. Check
  often for new studies.

- Aortic valve stenosis clinical trials. http://clinicaltrials.gov/ct2/results/refine?term=aortic+valve+stenosis.
- Heart valve defect clinical trials. http://clinicaltrials.gov/ct2/results/refine?term=heart+valve+defect.
- Heart valve disease clinical trials. http://clinicaltrials.gov/ct2/results/refine?term=heart+valve+disease.
- Mitral valve prolapse clinical trials. http://clinicaltrials.gov/ct2/results/refine?term=mitral+valve+prolapse.

➤ eMedicineHealth—"Mitral Valve Prolapse." http://www.emedicinehealth.com/mitral_valve_prolapse/article_em.htm; alternate path: http://www.emedicinehealth.com/, search for and then click on the title "Mitral Valve Prolapse" (Medical Reference from eMedicineHealth).

eMedicineHealth, a division of WebMD, offers a comprehensive article on mitral valve prolapse, including an overview, causes, symptoms, when to seek medical care, diagnosis, treatment, prevention, outlook, and follow-up.

➤ Hospital of the University of Pennsylvania (HUP) (Philadelphia, PA)—"Heart Valve Disease Program." http://www.pennmedicine.org/heart/patient/clinical-services/heart-valve-disease/; alternate path: http://www.pennmedicine.org/, click on the "Departments and Services" icon (or type "departments and services" in the Search box at the top of the screen), and scroll down and click on the category "Cardiology and Cardiac Surgery," and then scroll down under the heading "Clinical Services" and click on "Heart Valve Disease."

At its Penn Heart and Vascular Center website, HUP offers website links in the Heart Valve Disease Program that include an "Overview" (what are possibilities of valve replacement or repair, video of transcatheter aortic valve implantation, and treatment options); the "Team," which links to each physician and specialist (with profiles, e.g., specialty, medical board certification, education); "Clinical Trials"; "The Penn Difference" (program described, patient experiences, unique capabilities and expertise, and hospital highlights); "Physician Interviews" (videos); and "Quality/Outcomes." Click on each treatment option for details and charts. A 54-page *Penn Heart and Vascular 2011 Clinical Activity Report* is available for download; this report is a "summary of surgical, medical and interventional outcomes, as well as clinical research activity and patient volumes." You can also subscribe to the Penn Heart newsletter. For information on clinical trials, see the HUP entry on p. 33.

➤ Insidermedicine. http://www.insidermedicine.com/.

The Insidermedicine website offers a variety of heart-health-related videos. From the homepage, you can search for videos by title, or you can search by topic (e.g., mitral valve prolapse) to find other related videos. For more information on the Insidermedicine Project, see the earlier entry on pp. 33–34.

- "If I Had—Mitral Valve Prolapse (MVP)." http://www.insidermedicine
  .com/archives/VIDEO_If_I_Had_Mitral_Valve_Prolapse_Dr_Vincent
  _Bufalino_MD_Loyola_Stritch_School_of_Medicine_3553.aspx. This
  easy-to-understand video, with demonstrations, presents an interview
  with a cardiologist who describes what he would do if he had mitral valve
  prolapse.
- "In the Clinic—Dr. Paul Malik, MD, on Using the Stethoscope to Detect Aortic
  Valve Stenosis." http://www.insidermedicine.com/archives/In_the_Clinic
  _-_Dr_Paul_Malik_MD_on_Using_the_Stethoscope_to_Detect_Aortic_Valve
  _Stenosis_1733.aspx. In this video, with demonstrations, a cardiologist using
  patient-friendly language discusses how to use stethoscopes to detect aortic
  valve stenosis.

➢ Johns Hopkins Hospital (Baltimore, MD). http://www.hopkinsmedicine.org/.
Johns Hopkins Heart and Vascular Institute website provides detailed information on a variety of conditions, treatments, and services. It also lists links to physicians and specialists (with profiles, e.g., specialty, medical board certification,
education). Click on the heading "Clinical Trials" to find links to current trials in
various heart and cardiovascular conditions. Alternate path: http://www
.hopkinsmedicine.org/, search for the following topics by title.

- "Cardiac Valve Surgery." http://www.hopkinsmedicine.org/heart_vascular
  _institute/clinical_services/specialty_areas/valve_surgery.html. Johns Hopkins Valvular Heart Disease Service provides patient-friendly, current information on such topics as cardiac valve surgery, why it is necessary, how it is
  done, what to expect, and what to watch for.
- "Heart Valve Repair or Replacement Surgery." http://www.hopkinsmedicine
  .org/healthlibrary/test_procedures/cardiovascular/heart_valve_repair_or
  _replacement_surgery_92,P07975/. Johns Hopkins Heart and Vascular Institute website provides patient-friendly, current information on valvular heart
  disease, including a procedure description, reasons for having this surgery,
  risks, and what to expect before, during, and after the procedure.
- "Valvular Heart Disease" (Clinical Services). http://www.hopkinsmedicine
  .org/heart_vascular_institute/clinical_services/specialty_areas/valvular
  _disease.html. On this webpage, the Johns Hopkins Valvular Heart Disease
  Service provides links to current information on minimally invasive valvular heart disease surgeries.
- "Valvular Heart Disease" (Conditions and Treatments). http://www
  .hopkinsmedicine.org/heart_vascular_institute/conditions_treatments/
  conditions/valvular_heart_disease.html. Johns Hopkins Heart and Vascular
  Institute website provides patient-friendly, current information on valvular
  heart disease, including general information on valvular heart disease, types

of valvular heart disease, when to call an ambulance, when to call a doctor, symptoms, causes, prevention, diagnosis, and treatment.

➤ KidsHealth.org. http://www.kidshealth.org/.
The Nemours Center for Children's Health Media provides current information on conditions afflicting children, written for both children and parents. Information is available in English and Spanish. Click on the "Listen" button to hear the text read aloud.
- *For Kids:* "Heart Murmurs." http://kidshealth.org/kid/health_problems/heart/heart_murmurs.html#cat20079. Topics discussed include the heart and how it works, what a heart murmur is, what happens if you have a heart murmur, and what doctors do.
- *For Kids:* "Mitral Valve Prolapse." http://kidshealth.org/kid/health_problems/heart/mvp.html#cat20079. Topics discussed include what the mitral valve is, what mitral valve prolapse is, signs and symptoms, what the doctor will do, infections, and activities for MVP patients.
- *For Parents:* "Heart Murmurs and Your Child." http://kidshealth.org/parent/medical/heart/murmurs.html#cat141. Topics discussed include how the heart works, diagnosing a heart murmur, what an innocent murmur is, congenital heart defects, and common heart defects.
- *For Parents:* "Mitral Valve Prolapse." http://kidshealth.org/parent/medical/heart/mvp.html#cat141. Topics discussed include general information about MVP, what the mitral valve is, where the mitral valve is, signs and symptoms, diagnosis and treatment, and caring for a child with MVP.
Alternate path: http://kidshealth.org/, for information written for children, click on "Kids Site," scroll down and select "Health Problems" and then "Heart and Lungs," and then select the condition; for information for parents, click on "Parents Site," scroll down and select "Diseases and Conditions" and then "Heart and Blood Vessels," and then select the title.

➤ Massachusetts General Hospital (MGH) (Boston, MA).—"Heart Valve Program." http://www.massgeneral.org/heartcenter/services/treatmentprograms.aspx?id=1008; alternate path: http://www.massgeneral.org/, click on "Centers and Services," then click on "View All Departments," then click on "Heart Center," then click on the heading "Treatments and Services," and scroll down to click on the topic "Heart Valve Program."
The Heart Valve Program at the MGH Heart Center website offers links to comprehensive information in several categories. "Our Approach" includes an overview of their team approach, from initial assessment through treatments and procedures, and links to each medical expert (with profiles, e.g., specialty, medical board certification, education). "About This Program" describes the program's benefits and MGH's commitment to, vision and goals for, and "innovative research" at the

program. "Conditions and Diseases" has links to detailed information on "heart conditions and diseases that might be treated within this program," including heart valve disease, mitral valve prolapse (also known as click-murmur syndrome, Barlow's syndrome, balloon mitral valve, or floppy valve syndrome), and rheumatic heart disease. "Support and Wellness" offers patient guides, such as *Understanding and Preparing for a Catheterization Procedure* and *Frequently Asked Questions about Cardiac Anesthesia*. "Clinical Trials" has links to MGH trials and research studies when they are currently seeking participants. "News and Events" includes the latest information on related topics, and "Multimedia" contains video demonstrations.

➢ Mayo Clinic (Rochester, MN). http://www.mayoclinic.com/.
  For information on clinical trials and patient services, see the Mayo Clinic entry on p. 36.

  • "Aortic Valve Stenosis." http://www.mayoclinic.com/health/aortic-valve -stenosis/DS00418; alternate path: http://www.mayoclinic.com/, search for "aortic valve stenosis," and then click on the title "Aortic Valve Stenosis—Mayo Clinic." Written for patients, this webpage on aortic valve stenosis includes definitions, symptoms, causes, risk factors, complications, preparing for appointments, tests and diagnosis, treatments and drugs, and prevention. There is also a more comprehensive section titled "In-Depth" on some of these topics and a "Multimedia" section containing images.

  • "Mitral Valve Stenosis." http://www.mayoclinic.com/health/mitral-valve -stenosis/DS00420; alternate path: http://www.mayoclinic.com/, search for "mitral valve stenosis," and then click on the title "Mitral Valve Stenosis—Mayo Clinic." Written for patients, this webpage on mitral valve stenosis includes definitions, symptoms, causes, risk factors, complications, preparing for appointments, tests and diagnosis, treatments and drugs, prevention, and lifestyle and home remedies. There is also a more comprehensive section titled "In-Depth" on some of these topics and a "Multimedia" section containing images and videos.

➢ MedicineNet. http://www.medicinenet.com/.
  MedicineNet.com is owned and operated by WebMD and part of the WebMD Network. According to its website, MedicineNet "provides easy-to-read, in-depth, authoritative medical information for consumers via its user-friendly, interactive website." The medical information is written and edited by a nationally recognized group of more than 70 U.S. board-certified physicians. The website contains a "Symptom Checker" listed in alphabetical order as a guide to "pinpoint your pain." Its homepage links to "Health News of the Week." You can also sign up to receive a health newsletter.

  • "Heart Valve Disease." http://www.medicinenet.com/heart_valve_disease/ article.htm; alternate path: http://www.medicinenet.com/, click on the major topic "Diseases and Conditions," click on "Conditions A–Z," then click on "H," and then scroll down to "Heart Valve Disease." In-depth information on heart valve disease includes definitions, how heart valves work, types of heart valves, causes, symptoms, diagnosis, treatment, living with valve disease, patient discussions, and finding a local cardiologist.

- "Heart Valve Surgery." http://www.medicinenet.com/heart_valve_disease _treatment/article.htm; alternate path: http://www.medicinenet.com/, click on the major topic "Diseases and Conditions," click on "Conditions A–Z," then click on "H," and then scroll down to "Heart Valve Surgery." In-depth information on heart valve surgery includes definitions, what happens during traditional heart valve surgery, what happens during minimally invasive heart valve surgery, heart valve repair surgery, pros and cons of each type of heart valve surgery, nonsurgical treatments, balloon valvotomy, and finding a local cardiologist.

➤ MedlinePlus—"Heart Valve Diseases (Valvular Heart Disease)." http://www.nlm.nih .gov/medlineplus/heartvalvediseases.html; alternate path: http://www.nlm.nih.gov/, under "Databases," click on MedlinePlus and then search for "heart valve disease." MedlinePlus is a component of the National Institutes of Health (NIH), produced by the National Library of Medicine (NLM), and is updated regularly. Medline-Plus webpage on heart valve diseases offers extensive linked information covering overviews, news, diagnosis/symptoms, treatment, rehabilitation/recovery, disease management, specific conditions, related issues, anatomy/physiology, clinical trials, genetics, research, journal articles, dictionaries/glossaries, directories, organizations, and a specific section focusing on children. Patient handouts are also available. This webpage also includes a multimedia section containing tutorials and videos.

➤ *The Merck Manual Home Health Handbook for Patients and Caregivers*— "Overview of Heart Valve Disorders." http://www.merckmanuals.com/home/heart _and_blood_vessel_disorders/heart_valve_disorders/overview_of_heart_valve _disorders.html; alternate path: http://www.merckmanuals.com/home/, under "Sections," click on "All" next to the navigational arrows to view a complete list, then click on the section "Heart and Blood Vessel Disorders," and then scroll down to click on the section "Heart Valve Disorders."
This website on heart valve disorders is divided into several titles: "Overview of Heart Valve Disorders," "Mitral Regurgitation," "Mitral Valve Prolapse (MVP)," "Mitral Stenosis," "Aortic Regurgitation," "Aortic Stenosis," "Tricuspid Regurgitation," "Tricuspid Stenosis," "Pulmonic Regurgitation," and "Pulmonic Stenosis." This extensively detailed section is based on a well-known medical textbook titled *The Merck Manual Home Health Handbook for Patients and Caregivers* and is "provided free of charge . . . as a public service."

➤ Mount Sinai Hospital (New York, NY)—"Mitral Valve Repair Center." http://www.mitralvalverepair.org/.

The Mitral Valve Repair Center at Mount Sinai Hospital offers comprehensive information on mitral valve repair, including links to definitions, mitral valve disease, diagnosis, treatment, alternative treatment, outcomes, FAQs, team of experts (with professional biographies), and patient stories.

➤ National Heart, Lung, and Blood Institute (NHLBI)—"What Is Heart Valve Disease?" http://www.nhlbi.nih.gov/health/dci/Diseases/hvd/hvd_whatis.html; alternate path: http://www.nhlbi.nih.gov/, search for "heart valve disease," and then click on the title "What Is Heart Valve Disease?"

NHLBI, a division of National Institutes of Health from the U.S. Department of Health and Human Services, provides information on heart valve disease, including definitions, other names, causes, risk factors, signs and symptoms, diagnosis, treatments, living with heart valve disease, clinical trials, key points, and more.

➤ New York–Presbyterian (NYP) University Hospital of Columbia and Cornell (New York, NY). http://nyp.org/.

Under the heading "Find a Physician" you can search for physicians and specialists by specialty or name to view their profiles (e.g., specialty, medical board certification, education). Under the heading "Hospital News" are links to detailed articles explaining recent studies. For information on clinical trials, see the NYP entry on p. 38.

- "Heart Valve Treatments." http://nyp.org/services/cardiology/heart-valve-repair-replacement.html; alternate path: http://nyp.org/, search for "heart valve repair and replacement," and click on the title "Heart Valve Repair and Replacement—New York." The NYP University Hospital of Columbia and Cornell website provides patient-friendly information on heart valve surgical treatments, including several links to expanded information on balloon valvuloplasty, transcatheter aortic valve replacement, and robotic surgery. Under the heading "Health Library" is a link to information on heart valve anatomy and function, and under the heading "Related Links" are links to NYP Heart Valve Medical Centers.

- "Interactive Media Library: Heart Valve Disease" (Videos). http://nyp.org/media/; alternate path: http://nyp.org/, click on the icon with the text "Explore the Interactive Media Library." The Human Atlas media player presents short videos, text, models, and slides. To view each excellent video, click on the "Complete Listing of Topics" heading and scroll down to click on "How the Heart Works," "Mitral Valve Stenosis," and "Valvular Regurgitation."

- "Mitral Valve Stenosis" (Video). http://nypheart.org/perelman/; alternate path: http://nyp.org/, search for "Ronald O. Perelman Heart Institute," click on the name in the results, scroll down to "Related Links," and then click again on the name. The Perelman Heart Institute website of the NYP University Hospital of Columbia and Cornell offers, for patients, links to a selection of excellent short videos and audio slide presentations on cardiovascular tests and procedures, such as mitral valve stenosis.

➢ ORLive. "Early Intervention in the Treatment of Mitral Valve Disease." http://www.orlive.com/davinci/videos/early-intervention-in-the-treatment-of-mitral-valve-disease1; alternate path: http://www.orlive.com/, mouse over the heading "Videos" at the top of the screen to view the list of categories, then click on "Heart Procedures," then click on "Mitral Valve Procedures," and then select the title.

This is a live-recorded video of a surgical procedure used as early intervention in the treatment of mitral valve disease at the Cleveland Clinic Heart and Vascular Institute's Department of Thoracic and Cardiovascular Surgery.

➢ Texas Heart Institute (Houston, TX)—"Heart Information Center." http://www.texasheartinstitute.org/HIC/.

For information on clinical trials, see the Texas Heart Institute entry on p. 40.

- "Heart Murmurs." http://www.texasheartinstitute.org/HIC/Topics/Cond/murmur.cfm. The Texas Heart Institute website offers a definition of heart murmurs as well as information on causes, signs and symptoms, diagnosis, and treatment. There is also a link for information on patient care. An easy-to-print format is available.
- "Limited-Access Heart Surgery." http://www.texasheartinstitute.org/HIC/Topics/Proced/limaccess.cfm. The Texas Heart Institute website offers a definition of limited-access heart surgery as well as information on minimally invasive heart surgery, types of limited-access heart surgery, who can have limited-access heart surgery, videoscopic surgery, and robotic-assisted heart surgery.
- "Mitral Valve Prolapse." http://www.texasheartinstitute.org/HIC/Topics/Cond/mvp.cfm. The Texas Heart Institute website offers a definition of mitral valve prolapse as well as information on causes, risks, and treatment.
- "Rheumatic Fever." http://www.texasheartinstitute.org/HIC/Topics/Cond/rheufev.cfm. The Texas Heart Institute website offers a definition of rheumatic fever as well as information on causes, signs and symptoms, diagnosis, lifestyle changes, and treatment.
- "Valve Disease." http://www.texasheartinstitute.org/HIC/Topics/Cond/valvedis.cfm. The Texas Heart Institute website offers a definition of valve disease as well as information on causes, signs and symptoms, diagnosis, percutaneous interventions, and other treatments.
- "Valve Repair or Replacement." http://www.texasheartinstitute.org/HIC/Topics/Proced/vsurg.cfm. The Texas Heart Institute website offers a

definition of valve repair and valve replacement surgery; information on what to expect before, during, and after surgery; as well as an explanation of minimally invasive valve surgery.

Alternate path: http://www.texasheartinstitute.org/, search for the topic by name (e.g., "heart murmurs"), and then click on the appropriate title; or in the pull-down menu under "Heart Information Center," select "Heart-Health Topics" and then either "Heart Conditions" or "Surgery and Medical Procedures," and click on the topic by name.

➢ UCLA Ronald Reagan Medical Center (Los Angeles, CA). http://www.uclahealth.org/. For more information on patient resources and clinical trials, see the UCLA entry on p. 41.

- "Aortic Valve Stenosis." http://www.uclahealth.org/body.cfm?id=592; scroll down to the heading "Diseases and Conditions" to the end of the list, then click on the word "More," and then click on the title "Aortic Stenosis." The UCLA Ronald Reagan Medical Center's Heart Health Center provides detailed information on aortic stenosis, which includes definitions, alternate names, causes, symptoms, exams and tests, treatment, outlook (prognosis), possible complications, when to contact a medical professional, and prevention.

- "Mitral Regurgitation—Chronic." http://www.uclahealth.org/body.cfm?id =592, scroll down to the heading "Diseases and Conditions" to the end of the list, then click on the word "More," and then click on the title "Mitral Regurgitation—Chronic." The UCLA Ronald Reagan Medical Center's Heart Health Center provides detailed information on chronic mitral regurgitation, which includes definition, alternate names, causes, symptoms, exams and tests, treatment, outlook (prognosis), possible complications, when to contact a medical professional, and prevention. Also click on the title for the topic "Acute Mitral Regurgitation."

- "Mitral Valve Prolapse." http://www.uclahealth.org/body.cfm?id=592, scroll down to the heading "Diseases and Conditions" to the end of the list, then click on the word "More," and then click on the title "Mitral Valve Prolapse." The UCLA Ronald Reagan Medical Center's Heart Health Center provides detailed information on mitral valve prolapse, which includes definitions, alternate names, causes, symptoms, exams and tests, treatment, outlook (prognosis), possible complications, when to contact a medical professional, and prevention.

Alternate path: http://www.uclahealth.org/, under the heading "For Patients and Visitors," go to the category "Health Resources" and then click on "Heart Health Center" to find the "Health Library" topics.

➢ WebMD—"Heart Valve Disease." http://www.webmd.com/heart-disease/guide/heart-valve-disease; alternate path: http://www.webmd.com/, search for "heart valve disease" and then click on the title "Heart Valve Disease" (WebMD Medical Reference from Healthwise).

The WebMD website offers the latest information on heart valve disease, such as definitions, how heart valves work, types of heart valve disease, causes, symptoms, diagnosis, treatment options, living with heart valve disease, and further reading. A WebMD heart health e-mail newsletter is also available. According to WebMD, "WebMD News is an independent media service designed to provide news, information, and educational material to consumers and physicians. News content created by WebMD is free from influence by sponsors, partners, or other sources."

Patient Support Groups and Organizations

➢ DailyStrength. "Mitral Valve Prolapse Syndrome" (Support Group). http://www.dailystrength.org/groups/mitral-valve-prolapse-syndrome; alternate path: http://www.dailystrength.org/, search for "mitral valve prolapse."

The DailyStrength website offers online support groups and blogs for those with mitral valve prolapse. Free registration is required to participate. According to the website, "DailyStrength is a subsidiary of Sharecare. Sharecare, created by WebMD founder and Discovery Communications' Chief of Global Digital Strategy Jeff Arnold, along with America's Doctor, Dr. Mehmet Oz, is the first truly interactive healthcare ecosystem giving consumers the ability to ask, learn and act on the questions of health."

➢ MedHelp. http://www.medhelp.org/.

According to its website, MedHelp "connects people with the leading medical experts," such as those from Cleveland Clinic, National Jewish Health, Partners Health, and Mount Sinai Hospital, with those who have similar medical issues. MedHelp's main focus is to enable patients "to take control over their health and find answers to their medical questions" using nontechnical language via an online community through posts, forums and groups, blogs, user journals, as well as recommendations, articles, health pages, and a medical glossary. Free registration is required. You can search for the following and other groups by going to the homepage and searching by topic.

• "Aortic Valve." http://www.medhelp.org/search?query=aortic+valve.
• "Mitral Valve." http://www.medhelp.org/search?query=mitral+valve.

➢ U.S. Hospital Finder. http://www.ushospitalfinder.com/.

Use this site to find the names of hospitals by zip code, city, state, or your address. The search results include a map with directions. You might also want to ask your health care professional, call hospitals in your area, or search for "support groups" on hospital websites to determine if there are any cardiology support groups for people with heart valve disease that meet regularly in your area.

➤ Yahoo! Groups. http://www.yahoo.com/.
Yahoo! Groups is not a medical site, nor does it provide or endorse medical advice or procedures. The purpose of the website is to share experiences in a kind and caring manner. Free registration is required to participate. You can find the following and related groups by going to the homepage, searching for the condition (e.g., "aortic valve") in the "Find a Yahoo! Group" Search box, and then clicking on the relevant group name.

- "Aortic Valve Support Group." http://groups.yahoo.com/group/AorticValve/. This online Yahoo! group is for patients with aortic valve disease and replacement and their families and friends.
- "Mitral Valve Prolapse Support Group." http://health.groups.yahoo.com/group/mitral_valve/. This online Yahoo! group is for patients with mitral valve prolapse and their families and friends.

High Blood Pressure (Hypertension)

A patient has high blood pressure (HBP), also known as hypertension, when the measured blood pressure in his or her upper arm is above a certain range depending on age, sex, and other factors.

When the heart pumps the blood, it moves the blood forcefully into the aorta and out to the body. The forceful movement is measured as a pressure, like the pressure in a car tire. The pressure is greatest at the heart and lessens as the blood reaches the capillaries (the smallest blood vessels in the body). Normal blood pressure is generally considered to be 120 millimeters of mercury (mm Hg) or less over 80 mm Hg or less. This measurement is often abbreviated as "120 over 80."

There are two blood pressures. As the heart beats (contracts), it creates the higher pressure (systolic pressure). When the heart is at rest between beats, the arterial system maintains a lower blood pressure (diastolic pressure). Blood pressure is considered high if the systolic pressure is above 140 mm Hg or the diastolic pressure is above 90 mm Hg. Commonly, this would be called "140 over 90."

HBP has many causes, such as chronic kidney disease, thyroid disease, sleep apnea, asthma medications and cold-relief medicine, birth control pills, pregnancy, and hormone replacement therapy for menopause.

If blood pressure is too high for too long, many problems can develop in various organs. Such problems include aortic dissection, blood vessel damage (arteriosclerosis), brain damage or stroke, congestive heart failure, kidney damage or failure, heart attack, hypertensive heart disease, and vision loss.

HBP can be controlled by diet (e.g., limiting salt and alcohol, limiting cholesterol-laden foods), maintaining a normal weight, engaging in regular physical exercise, avoiding smoking, and managing stress. In some cases, medication is needed to control blood pressure, which generally works to reduce the fluid load on the heart, slow the heartbeat, or relax the blood vessel muscles. Because the type of medication is selected to reduce or prevent what is causing the HBP, the physician must carefully choose the appropriate prescription from various medication classes, such as diuretics, beta-blockers, ACE inhibitors, angiotensin II receptor blockers, calcium channel blockers, alpha-blockers, alpha-beta-blockers, nervous system inhibitors, and vasodilators.

Resources for Further Information on High Blood Pressure (Hypertension)

Books

➢ Davis, Martha, Elizabeth Robbins Eshelman, Matthew McKay, and Patrick Fanning. *The Relaxation and Stress Reduction Workbook* (New Harbinger Self-Help Workbook). Oakland, CA: New Harbinger, 2008. Print.
  The goal of this book is to help patients reduce stress to lower blood pressure. This workbook teaches topics such as body awareness, breathing techniques, progressive relaxation, meditation, visualization, applied relaxation training, self-hypnosis, autogenics, focusing, refuting irrational ideas, dealing with worry and anxiety, coping skills training for fears, goal setting and time management, assertiveness training, work-stress management, nutrition and stress, exercise, and confronting roadblock. The authors of this book are experts: Martha Davis is a psychologist in the Department of Psychiatry of Kaiser Permanente Medical Center, Santa Clara, California; Elizabeth Robbins Eshelman is a licensed clinical social worker with Kaiser Permanente Online; and Matthew McKay is a clinical director of Haight-Ashbury Psychological Services, San Francisco, California.

➢ Heller, Maria. *The DASH Diet Action Plan: Proven to Lower Blood Pressure and Cholesterol without Medication* New York, NY: Grand Central Life and Style, 2011. Print.
  This registered dietician with an MS in human nutrition and dietetics from the University of Illinois at Chicago has created a user-friendly guide to explain how to create your own personalized DASH (Dietary Approaches to Stop Hypertension) diet, with menu guide, and lifestyle changes to lower high blood pressure.

➢ Khaleghi, Murdoc. *The Everything Guide to Preventing Heart Disease: All You Need to Know to Lower Your Blood Pressure, Beat High Cholesterol, and Stop Heart Disease in Its Tracks* (Everything Series). Avon, MA: Adams Media, 2011. Print.
  Written for the patient, this book contains reliable, science-based information about managing your condition and preventing heart disease.

➢ Manger, William M., and Norman M. Kaplan. *101 Questions and Answers about Hypertension*. Alameda, CA: Hunter House, 2012. Print.

Two medical specialists created this consumer-friendly, easy-to-use book on high blood pressure and how to manage and prevent complications.

➤ Moore, Thomas, and Mark Jenkins. *The DASH Diet for Hypertension*. New York, NY: Free Press, 2011. Print.

According to the introduction, "A world-class team of hypertension and nutrition experts from the medical schools of Harvard, Duke, Johns Hopkins, and Louisiana State University have joined together to produce *The DASH Diet for Hypertension*—a medication-free program to lower blood pressure."

➤ Rubin, Alan J. *High Blood Pressure for Dummies*. Indianapolis, IN: For Dummies, 2012. Print.

This easy-to-understand consumer-oriented book explains topics such as understanding high blood pressure, considering medical consequences, treatment, prevention, and taking care of special populations.

➤ Zuzman, Randall M., and Kathleen Cahill Allison. *Harvard Medical School Hypertension: Controlling the "Silent Killer."* Boston, MA: Harvard Health, 2010. Print, Kindle editions.

This book helps patients to understand hypertension, types, risk factors, monitoring, diagnosing, treatment, and lifestyle changes.

Brochures, Booklets, and Other Short Print Publications

➤ American Heart Association (AHA). http://www.heart.org/.
  • "High Blood Pressure" (Educational Brochures). http://www.heart.org/HEARTORG/General/Order-American-Heart-Association-Educational-Brochures_UCM_312777_Article.jsp; alternate path: http://www.heart.org/, search for "educational brochures," click on the title "Order American Heart Association Educational Brochures," and then click on the topic "High Blood Pressure." Several AHA brochures are available, including "High Blood Pressure," "High Blood Pressure in African Americans," "Shaking Your Salt Habit," and "Understanding and Controlling High Blood Pressure." These brochures can be ordered by filling in a form online. (No more than one packet and two brochures per household can be ordered at no cost.)
  • "High Blood Pressure Resources in Print." http://www.heart.org/HEARTORG/Conditions/HighBloodPressure/HighBloodPressureToolsResources/High-Blood-Pressure-Resources-in-Print_UCM_303470_Article.jsp; alternate path: http://www.heart.org/, search for "high blood pressure resources in print." AHA provides numerous printable patient information sheets and brochures on high blood pressure.

➤ American Society of Hypertension—"Blood Pressure and Your Health." http://www.ash-us.org/For-Patients/Patient-Education-Information.aspx; alternate path: http://www.ash-us.org/, under the heading "Patients," click on "Patient Education Information."

This free booklet for patients, titled "Blood Pressure and Your Health," is available in English and Spanish.

> British Heart Foundation (BHF)—"Blood Pressure" (Booklet). http://www.bhf .org.uk/publications/view-publication.aspx?ps=1000948; alternate path: http:// www.bhf.org.uk/, search for "blood pressure," click on the title "British Heart Foundation—Blood Pressure," scroll down to the section called "Related Links," and then click on the title "Blood Pressure Booklet."

The BHF website offers this free booklet on blood pressure, which, according to the website, "explains what high blood pressure is, why it is so important to bring your blood pressure down to a normal level, what you can do to help lower your blood pressure. It also describes the medicines that your doctor may give you to help lower your blood pressure."

Websites

> Aetna InteliHealth—"High Blood Pressure (Hypertension)." http://www.intelihealth .com/IH/ihtIH/WSIHW000/21827/24755/195803.html?d=dmtHealthAZ; alternate path: http://www.intelihealth.com/, search for "high blood pressure," and then click on the title "High Blood Pressure (Hypertension)."

This website provides sections on high blood pressure, such as definitions, symptoms, diagnosis, expected duration, prevention, treatment, when to call a professional, and prognosis. Aetna InteliHealth, a subsidiary of Aetna, is reviewed by the faculty of Harvard Medical School and University College of Dental Medicine. According to Aetna InteliHealth's website, "Aetna InteliHealth maintains absolute editorial independence. That means that Aetna InteliHealth makes decisions about the information on our site free of outside influence." Under "Healthy Lifestyle," Aetna InteliHealth also offers free health-related e-mail subscriptions.

> American Heart Association (AHA)—"High Blood Pressure (HBP)." http://www .heart.org/HEARTORG/Conditions/HighBloodPressure/High-Blood-Pressure _UCM_002020_SubHomePage.jsp; alternate path: http://www.heart.org/, search for "high blood pressure" and then click on the title "Visit Our High Blood Pressure Website."

AHA provides details on HBP in such sections as about HBP, why HBP matters, risk factors, symptoms, diagnosis and monitoring of HBP, and prevention and treatment of HBP. The website also provides tools, including the HBP risk calculator and HBP trackers. You can also sign up for a free heart health e-newsletter.

> American Society of Hypertension (ASH). http://www.ash-us.org/.

ASH offers information for patients, videos for viewing, directories of hypertension specialists, designated hypertension centers, a support community, and a blog.

➢ Brigham and Women's Hospital (BWH) (Boston, MA)—"High Blood Pressure (HBP)." http://healthlibrary.brighamandwomens.org/HealthCenters/Heart/Conditions/BloodPressure/; alternate path: http://www.brighamandwomens.org/, scroll under the heading "Health Information" to the category titled "Health Information Center" and click on the title "Heart Information Center," then scroll down and click on the category "Heart Diseases and Conditions," and then click on "High Blood Pressure."

The BWH's HBP website discusses numerous linked topics, such as what blood pressure numbers mean, what HBP is, understanding prehypertension, heeding the warning of prehypertension, and how HBP can damage kidneys. For information on clinical trials, see the BWH entry on p. 29.

➢ British Heart Foundation (BHF)—"High Blood Pressure." http://www.bhf.org.uk/heart-health/conditions/high-blood-pressure.aspx; alternate path: http://www.bhf.org.uk/, search for "high blood pressure" and then click on the title "British Heart Foundation—High Blood Pressure."

The BHF website discusses blood pressure, what the numbers mean, what HBP is, and what can be done to reduce blood pressure. Click on the "Community: Share Experiences with Others" heading to engage with the BHF online community where you can share your own story and read those of others.

➢ CardioSmart—"High Blood Pressure." https://www.cardiosmart.org/healthwise/hw62/787/hw62787; alternate path: https://www.cardiosmart.org/, search for and then click on the title "High Blood Pressure."

CardioSmart provides an easy-to-use website on understanding high blood pressure (hypertension). CardioSmart's high blood pressure webpage contains an introduction, questions to ask your cardiologist, news, an e-mail subscription option to receive CardioSmart news updates, a video library (e.g., high blood pressure and what can be done to manage your risk factors for this condition), and a link to learn more about hypertension (basic facts, what hypertension is, a more detailed explanation, risk factors, diagnosis, treatment, prevention, key facts, causes, symptoms, tests, medicine, and track your blood pressure). According to the American College of Cardiology (ACC), "CardioSmart is the patient education and support program launched by the [ACC]. Our mission is to engage, inform, and empower patients to better prepare them for participation in their own care."

➢ CenterWatch—Clinical trials listing service: "High Blood Pressure (Hypertension) Clinical Trials." http://www.centerwatch.com/clinical-trials/listings/studylist.aspx?CatID=85; alternate path: http://www.centerwatch.com/, under the category "Patient Resources," click on "Search Clinical Trials," then click on "H," and then click on the title "High Blood Pressure (Hypertension)."

This CenterWatch clinical trials listing service lists trials currently looking for volunteers to enroll in hypertension studies. Click on the "Clinical Trials" heading and search by location, medical condition, or therapeutic area. To search by location, click on your state (or country) and click on a city near you to find information on each available clinical trial. Check back with this website often for new studies. Sign up for a free e-mail service that sends notice of new clinical trials.

➢ Cleveland Clinic (Cleveland, OH)—"Hypertension (High Blood Pressure)." http://my.clevelandclinic.org/disorders/Hypertension_High_Blood_Pressure/hic_Hypertension_High_Blood_Pressure.aspx; alternate path: http://my.clevelandclinic.org/, under the category "Institutes and Services," click on "Heart and Vascular," click on "Homepage," click on the category "Diseases and Conditions," and then click on the title "Hypertension."
The Cleveland Clinic provides comprehensive patient-friendly information on hypertension, such as links to definitions, other names for hypertension, frequently asked questions, blood pressure, prevention, myths, when to call the doctor, treatments, checking blood pressure at home, nutrition, and finding a doctor who treats hypertension. The Cleveland Clinic also offers a link to "Chat Online with a Heart and Vascular Nurse." For information on clinical trials, see the Cleveland Clinic entry on pp. 31–32.

➢ ClinicalTrials.gov. http://clinicaltrials.gov/.
ClinicalTrials.gov, developed by the U.S. National Institutes of Health of the National Library of Medicine, lists ongoing and currently enrolling clinical trials. To find clinical trials from the homepage, search for the condition by name (e.g., "hypertension"), which will generate a list of possibly hundreds or thousands of studies. To limit your results, click on "Modify This Search" and select specific fields, such as (1) Recruitment (e.g., you might want to select "Open Studies"); (2) Locations (e.g., select your state); and (3) Age Group, and then click on the "Search" button. Click on the title of each trial name for additional information, such as purpose of the study, study design and type, detailed description, outcome measures, eligibility (age, gender, criteria for participating), study start date, estimated study completion date, and sponsor. Check often for new studies.
  • High blood pressure clinical trials. http://clinicaltrials.gov/ct2/results/refine?term=high+blood+pressure.
  • Hypertension clinical trials. http://clinicaltrials.gov/ct2/results/refine?term=hypertension.

➢ eMedicineHealth—"High Blood Pressure." http://www.emedicinehealth.com/high_blood_pressure/article_em.htm and http://www.emedicinehealth.com/high_blood_pressure-health/article_em.htm; alternate path: http://www.emedicinehealth.com/, search for and then click on the title "High Blood Pressure" (from Medical Reference from eMedicineHealth and from Medical Reference from Healthwise).

eMedicineHealth, a division of WebMD, offers a comprehensive article on high blood pressure, including an overview, causes, symptoms, when to seek medical care, diagnosis, treatment, medications, other therapy, prevention, outlook, and follow-up.

➤ Insidermedicine. http://www.insidermedicine.com/.
The Insidermedicine website offers a variety of heart-health-related videos. From the homepage, you can search for videos by title, or you can search by topic (e.g., hypertension) to find other related videos. For more information on the Insider-medicine Project, see the earlier entry on pp. 33–34.

- "Behavioral Interventions Improve Adherence to Hypertension Medical Therapy" (Video). http://www.insidermedicine.com/archives/Behavioral _Interventions_Improves_Adherence_to_Hypertension_Medical_Therapy _Video_5840.aspx. This video offers suggestions on how to increase patients' success with self-managing their daily regimen for treating high blood pressure.

- "Decreased Risk of Hypertension with Upwards Social Mobility" (Video). http://www.insidermedicine.com/archives/Decreased_Risk_of_Hypertension _with_Upwards_Social_Mobility_Video_5395.aspx. According to research published online in the *Journal of Epidemiology and Community Health*, "Increased risk for hypertension associated with being born into a low socioeconomic status can be modified by improving that status later in life." In this video, a medical specialist discusses in user-friendly language, with demonstrations, recommendations on treatment of hypertension.

- "Diagnosing High Blood Pressure Best Done with Ambulatory Blood Pres-sure Monitor" (Video). http://www.insidermedicine.com/archives/Diagnosing _High_Blood_Pressure_Best_Done_with_Ambulatory_Blood_Pressure _Monitor_Video_5475.aspx. In this consumer-focused video, with demon-strations, a medical specialist speaks on the benefits of using an ambulatory blood-pressure monitoring device.

➤ Johns Hopkins Hospital, Heart and Vascular Institute (Baltimore, MD)— "Hypertension (High Blood Pressure)." http://www.hopkinsmedicine.org/heart _vascular_institute/conditions_treatments/conditions/hypertension.html and http:// www.hopkinsmedicine.org/healthlibrary/conditions/adult/cardiovascular_diseases/ high_blood_pressure_hypertension_85,P00224/; alternate path: http://www.hopkins medicine.org/, search for "hypertension (high blood pressure)," and then click on the title "Hypertension (High Blood Pressure)"; for a related resource, click on the title "High Blood Pressure/Hypertension."
The Johns Hopkins Heart and Vascular Institute webpage on hypertension dis-cusses HBP, when to call a doctor, symptoms, causes, prevention, diagnosis, and treatment. It also lists links to physicians and specialists (with profiles, e.g.,

specialty, medical board certification, education) who treat HBP. Click on the heading "Clinical Trials" for links to current trials in various heart and cardiovascular conditions.

> KidsHealth.org. http://www.kidshealth.org/.
The Nemours Center for Children's Health Media provides current information on conditions afflicting children, written for both children and parents. Information is available in English and Spanish. Click on the "Listen" button to hear the text read aloud.

- *For Parents:* "High Blood Pressure (HBP) (Hypertension)." http://kidshealth .org/parent/medical/heart/hypertension.html#cat141. This webpage, written for parents, provides information on children with HBP. Topics discussed include HBP in kids, understanding BP, long-term consequences of HBP, measuring blood pressure, causes, diagnosis, and treatment.
- *For Teens:* "Hypertension (High Blood Pressure)." http://kidshealth.org/ teen/diseases_conditions/heart/hypertension.html#cat20160. This webpage, written for teens, provides information on HBP. Topics discussed include understanding high blood pressure, what hypertension is, causes, how HBP affects the body, diagnosis of HBP, treatment, and prevention.

Alternate path: http://kidshealth.org/, for information for teens, click on "Teens Site," scroll down and select "Diseases and Conditions" and then "Heart and Cardiovascular System," and then select the condition; for information for parents, click on "Parents Site," scroll down and select "Diseases and Conditions" and then "Heart and Blood Vessels," and then select the title.

> Massachusetts General Hospital (MGH) (Boston, MA). http://www.massgeneral .org/.
At each of the following MGH webpages are links to comprehensive information in several categories: "Our Approach" includes an overview of conditions, treatments, and procedures as well as links to each medical expert (with profiles, e.g., specialty, medical board certification, education). "About This Program" describes the quality and benefits of the program as well as MGH's commitment. "Conditions and Diseases" offers links to detailed information on specific and related conditions. "Support and Wellness" offers patient guides. "Clinical Trials" links to MGH trials and research studies currently seeking participants. "News and Events" includes the latest information on the conditions. "Multimedia" offers video demonstrations.

- "Hypertension Treatment" (Treatment Programs). http://www.massgeneral .org/heartcenter/services/treatmentprograms.aspx?id=1228. Hypertension specialists work as a team to help each patient manage and control high blood pressure through a treatment regimen (e.g., antihypertensive drug therapy and lifestyle modifications).

- "Thoracic Aortic Center." http://www.massgeneral.org/heartcenter/services/ treatmentprograms.aspx?id=1010. This reference is included because aortic aneurysms may be caused by atherosclerosis (hardening of the arteries), hypertension (high blood pressure), or a congenital abnormality (such as Marfan syndrome).

Alternate path: http://www.massgeneral.org/, search for the topic by title or go to "Centers and Services," click on "View All Departments," then click on "Heart Center," and then click on the heading "Treatments and Services" to find your topic.

➤ Mayo Clinic (Rochester, MN)—"High Blood Pressure (HBP) (Hypertension)." http://www.mayoclinic.com/health/high-blood-pressure/DS00100 and http:// www.mayoclinic.com/health/high-blood-pressure-in-children/DS01102; alternate path: http://www.mayoclinic.com/, search for "high blood pressure," and click on the titles "High Blood Pressure (Hypertension)—MayoClinic.com" and "High Blood Pressure (Hypertension) in Children—MayoClinic.com."

Written for patients, this webpage on HBP includes definitions, symptoms, causes, risk factors, complications, preparing for appointments, tests and diagnosis, treatments and drugs, lifestyle and home remedies, alternative medicine, coping and support, and news. There is also a more comprehensive section titled "In-Depth" on some of these topics. In the "See Also" section, there are titles such as "White-Coat Hypertension," which discusses the condition that occurs when blood pressure rises at the doctor's office, and "Isolated Systolic Hypertension," which is another health concern, as well as "Secondary Hypertension," "Prehypertension," and "High Blood Pressure in Children." For information on clinical trials and patient services, see the Mayo Clinic entry on p. 36.

➤ MedicineNet. http://www.medicinenet.com/.

MedicineNet.com is owned and operated by WebMD and is a part of the WebMD Network. According to its website, MedicineNet "provides easy-to-read, in-depth, authoritative medical information for consumers via its user-friendly, interactive website." The medical information is written and edited by a nationally recognized group of more than 70 U.S. board-certified physicians. The website contains a "Symptom Checker" listed in alphabetical order as a guide to "pinpoint your pain." Its homepage links to "Health News of the Week." You can also sign up to receive a health newsletter.

  - "High Blood Pressure (HBP) (Hypertension)." http://www.medicinenet .com/high_blood_pressure/article.htm. In-depth information includes definitions, how HBP is measured, causes, symptoms, treatment, patient discussions, and finding a local internist.
  - "High Blood Pressure (HBP) Treatment." http://www.medicinenet.com/ high_blood_pressure_treatment/article.htm. In-depth information includes

various drug treatments, lifestyle changes, emergency treatment, patient discussions, and finding a local internist.

- "Preeclampsia (Pregnancy Induced Hypertension)." http://www.medicinenet .com/pregnancy_induced_hypertension/article.htm. In-depth information includes definitions, causes, symptoms, treatment, patient discussions, and finding a local obstetrician-gynecologist.

Alternate path: http://www.medicinenet.com/, click on the major topic "Diseases and Conditions," click on "Conditions A–Z," then click on the first letter of the topic ("H" or "P"), and then scroll down to click on the resource title.

➤ MedlinePlus—"High Blood Pressure (HBP/Hypertension)." http://www.nlm.nih .gov/medlineplus/highbloodpressure.html; alternate path: http://www.nlm.nih .gov/, under "Databases," click on "MedlinePlus," and then search for "high blood pressure."

MedlinePlus is a component of the National Institutes of Health (NIH), produced by the National Library of Medicine (NLM), and is updated regularly. This MedlinePlus webpage on high blood pressure offers extensive linked information covering overviews, news, diagnosis/symptoms, treatment, nutrition, disease management, specific conditions, related issues, clinical trials, research, journal articles, dictionaries/glossaries, organizations, statistics, and specific sections focusing on children, teenagers, women, and seniors. There are also patient handouts and a link to *MedlinePlus Magazine* for related information. This website also includes a multimedia section containing pictures, health check tools, tutorials, and videos.

➤ Medscape Reference (Drugs, Diseases, and Procedures)—"Hypertension." http:// emedicine.medscape.com/article/241381-overview; alternate path: http://emedicine .medscape.com/, search for and then click on the title "Hypertension."

Written for Medscape by Kamran Riaz, MD, FACP, FCCP, FCCM, and associates, this webpage presents a comprehensive report on hypertension. Although written for health care professionals, it might be helpful for interested laypersons. Articles for Medscape Reference are written by medical experts. The webpage states, "Our rigorous literature survey process allows us to rapidly integrate new practice-changing information into the relevant topics by systematically reviewing the major medical and pharmacy journals, news announcements, and important practice guidelines." Free registration is required.

➤ *The Merck Manual Home Health Handbook for Patients and Caregivers*—"High Blood Pressure." http://www.merckmanuals.com/home/sec03/ch020/ch020a .html; alternate path: http://www.merckmanuals.com/home/, under "Sections," click on "All" to view a complete list, then click on the section "Heart and Blood Vessel Disorders," and then scroll down to the section "High Blood Pressure."

This section on high blood pressure, which includes information on the body's control of blood pressure, causes, symptoms, diagnosis, treatment, and prognosis, is based on a well-known medical textbook titled *The Merck Manual Home Health Handbook for Patients and Caregivers* and is "provided free of charge . . . as a public service."

> National Heart, Lung, and Blood Institute (NHLBI)—"What Is High Blood Pressure? (HBP) (Hypertension)." http://www.nhlbi.nih.gov/health/dci/Diseases/Hbp/HBP_WhatIs.html; alternate path: http://www.nhlbi.nih.gov/, search for "high blood pressure," and then click on the title "What Is High Blood Pressure?"

NHLBI, a division of the National Institutes of Health from the U.S. Department of Health and Human Services, provides information on HBP, including definitions, causes, risk factors, signs and symptoms, diagnosis, treatments, prevention, living with HBP, clinical trials, and key points. There are also links to podcasts and videos on high blood pressure.

> Texas Heart Institute (Houston, TX)—"High Blood Pressure (Hypertension)." http://www.texasheartinstitute.org/HIC/Topics/Cond/hbp.cfm; alternate path: http://www.texasheartinstitute.org/, search for and then click on the title "High Blood Pressure (Hypertension)"; or under the heading "Heart Information Center," click on "Heart-Health Topics," then click on "Heart Conditions," and then click on "High Blood Pressure (Hypertension)."

The Texas Heart Institute website offers a definition of high blood pressure, as well as information on causes, signs and symptoms, diagnosis, blood pressure readings, and treatment. One section allows users to "Ask a Texas Heart Institute Doctor" questions. Click on "Heart Doctor Answers" to explore the questions and answers already published there. For information on clinical trials, see the Texas Heart Institute entry on p. 40.

> UCLA Ronald Reagan Medical Center (Los Angeles, CA)—"High Blood Pressure (Hypertension)." http://www.uclahealth.org/body.cfm?id=592; scroll down to the heading "In-Depth Reports," then click on the word "More," and then click on the title "High Blood Pressure"; alternate path: http://www.uclahealth.org/, under the heading "For Patients and Visitors," scroll down and mouse over the category "Health Resources" and then click on "Heart Health Center," scroll down to the heading "In-Depth Reports," click on the word "More," and then click on the title "High Blood Pressure."

The UCLA Ronald Reagan Medical Center's Heart Health Center provides an in-depth report on high blood pressure (hypertension), which includes highlights, introduction, causes, risk factors, symptoms, diagnosis, complications, treatment, lifestyle changes, and medications. Also on the Heart Health Center website, under the heading "Tests and Treatments," scroll under the section

"Alternative Medicine" for more treatment information, then click on the word "More," and then click on the title "Hypertension." Scroll down to the heading "Care Guides," then click on the word "More," and then click on the title "High Blood Pressure (Hypertension) Guide." For more information on patient resources and clinical trials, see the UCLA entry on p. 41.

➤ WebMD—"Hypertension/High Blood Pressure Health." http://www.webmd.com/ hypertension-high-blood-pressure/default.htm; alternate path: http://www.webmd .com/, search for "hypertension health center" and then click on the title "Hypertension/High Blood Pressure Health" (WebMD Health and Wellness Center).
The WebMD website offers the latest information on heart disease, using articles, slide presentations, videos, FAQs, discussions groups, and expert blogs. WebMD's heart health e-mail newsletter is also available. According to WebMD, "WebMD News is an independent media service designed to provide news, information, and educational material to consumers and physicians. News content created by WebMD is free from influence by sponsors, partners, or other sources."

Patient Support Groups and Organizations

➤ American Society of Hypertension (ASH)—"Hypertension Outreach Program." http://www.ash-us.org/HTN-Community-Outreach.aspx and http://www.ash outreach.blogspot.com/; alternate path: http://www.ash-us.org/, search for and then click on the title "HTN Community Outreach," or scroll down and click on the heading "HTN Community Outreach."
ASH offers a support community and a blog, as well as information for patients, videos, a directory of hypertension specialists, and a list of designated hypertension centers. Scroll over the heading "HTN Community Outreach," and click on the topic "BP Without Borders" (Blog).

➤ DailyStrength—"High Blood Pressure Support Group." http://www.dailystrength .org/c/High-Blood-Pressure/support-group; alternate path: http://www.dailystrength .org/, search for "high blood pressure," and then click on "Visit the High Blood Pressure Support Group."
The DailyStrength website offers online support groups and blogs for those with high blood pressure. Free registration is required to participate. According to the website, "DailyStrength is a subsidiary of Sharecare. Sharecare, created by WebMD founder and Discovery Communications' Chief of Global Digital Strategy Jeff Arnold, along with America's Doctor, Dr. Mehmet Oz, is the first truly interactive healthcare ecosystem giving consumers the ability to ask, learn and act on the questions of health."

➤ HeartHub for Patients—"High Blood Pressure (HBP)." http://www.hearthub.org/ hc-high-blood-pressure.htm; alternate path: http://www.hearthub.org/, scroll down to the section titled "Health Centers," and then click on the title "High Blood Pressure."

HeartHub, a division of the American Heart Association (AHA), is a patient-support portal for information, tools, and resources on HBP, including how to manage blood pressure, how to calculate HBP-related risks, low sodium recipes, how to get help on the phone, how stress affects blood pressure, and monitoring blood pressure at home. Blood pressure tracking applications are also available.

➤ Inspire—"Blood Pressure Support Group." http://www.inspire.com/groups/blood -pressure/; alternate path: http://www.inspire.com/, search for "heart," click on the heading "Groups," scroll down and click on "Heart and Circulation," and then click on "High Blood Pressure."

According to the website, "Inspire was created with the belief that patients and caregivers need a safe and secure place to support and connect with one another."

➤ MedHelp. http://www.medhelp.org/.

According to its website, MedHelp "connects people with the leading medical experts," such as those from Cleveland Clinic, National Jewish Health, Partners Health, and Mount Sinai Hospital, with those who have similar medical issues. MedHelp's main focus is to enable patients "to take control over their health and find answers to their medical questions" using nontechnical language via an online community through posts, forums and groups, blogs, user journals, as well as recommendations, articles, health pages, and a medical glossary. Free registration is required. From the homepage, you can find the following resources through a topic search.

- "High Blood Pressure." http://www.medhelp.org/search?query=high+blood +pressure.
- "Hypertension." http://www.medhelp.org/search?query=hypertension.

➤ U.S. Hospital Finder. http://www.ushospitalfinder.com/.

Use this site to find the names of hospitals by zip code, city, state, or your address. The search results include a map with directions. You might also want to ask your health care professional, call hospitals in your area, or search for "support groups" on hospital websites to determine if there are any cardiology support groups for people with high blood pressure that meet regularly in your area.

➤ WebMD—"WebMD Hypertension and High Blood Pressure Community." http:// www.webmd.com/hypertension-high-blood-pressure/; alternate path: http://www .webmd.com/, search for "hypertension health center," click on the title "Hyper-tension/High Blood Pressure Health Center," and then scroll down to the "WebMD Hypertension Community."

Click on the link "Community. Experts. Support.," as well as the links under "Discussions and Expert Blogs." Join the WebMD hypertension community

(WebMD moderated), which includes reading and writing questions, tips, resources, and support. According to the WebMD hypertension community, "Are you struggling with how to best manage and treat your high blood pressure? Share your tips and experiences with other members striving to overcome their hypertension and seek guidance from our knowledgeable experts." To search for other health-topic communities, go to http://exchanges.webmd.com/, which is titled "Be a Part of the WebMD Community." You can also scroll down to "Create Your Own Community" for easy instructions on how to start your own support group/community.

➤ Yahoo! Groups. http://www.yahoo.com/.
Yahoo! Groups is not a medical site, nor does it provide or endorse medical advice or procedures. The purpose of the website is to share experiences in a kind and caring manner. Free registration is required to participate.
  • "DASH Diet Support Group." http://health.groups.yahoo.com/group/dashdiet/. This online Yahoo! group is for patients with high blood pressure and their families and friends. This support group focuses on managing high blood pressure by following the DASH (Dietary Approaches to Stop Hypertension) diet and other lifestyle changes, such as exercise.
  • "Hypertension (High Blood Pressure) (HBP) Support Group." http://health.groups.yahoo.com/group/hypertension/. This online Yahoo! group is for patients with HBP and their families and friends.
Alternate path: http://health.yahoo.com/, search for "high blood pressure" in the "Find a Yahoo! Group" Search box, and then click on the relevant group.

High Cholesterol

High cholesterol is the term for too much cholesterol (a waxy fatty substance) in the blood. It is also called hypercholesterolemia or hyperlipidemia. Cholesterol is used by the body to make hormones, vitamin D, and chemicals that help digest food. Many foods contain cholesterol. Cholesterol is carried in the bloodstream in small globules of lipoprotein that surround the cholesterol and allow it to mix in with the blood.

There are two types of lipoproteins: low density and high density. Both are needed for the body to function properly. Low-density lipoprotein (LDL) is often called "bad cholesterol," because too much LDL causes a buildup of cholesterol in the arteries (a building block for plaque). High-density lipoprotein (HDL) is called "good cholesterol," because it carries cholesterol to the liver where the substance is broken down. High LDL is bad; high HDL is good. High levels of LDL can lead to heart disease; high levels of HDL decrease the chance of getting heart disease.

High LDL can lead to arteriosclerosis, coronary artery disease, and heart attack. High LDL can be caused by family history, diabetes mellitus, and other metabolic syndromes, kidney disease, hypothyroidism, Cushing's syndrome, anorexia nervosa, certain drugs, sleep deprivation, diet, body weight, and physical activity. However, there are no outward signs of high LDL; it must be determined by a blood test. Total cholesterol should be less than 200 milligrams per deciliter of blood (mg/dL); above 240 mg/dL is considered a high cholesterol blood level. LDL levels should be below 100 mg/dL; above 160 mg/dL is considered high. HDL levels should be above 60 mg/dL to protect against heart disease; levels below 40 mg/dL present a risk of heart disease.

A portion of LDL is called very-low-density lipoprotein, which is mostly triglycerides. Four risk factors can cause an increase in triglycerides: too much fat, too much sugar, and too much alcohol, along with family-inherited genes. Triglycerides can also raise the risk for heart disease, especially if a person is overweight, physically inactive, smokes, uses alcohol excessively, has a very high carbohydrate diet, has certain diseases, takes certain drugs, or has some genetic disorders. Triglyceride levels are also measured by a blood test. Levels above 150 mg/dL should be treated. Studies have shown that when triglycerides are above 150 mg/dL, LDL particles become smaller and denser (compacting) and therefore more harmful and easier to form into plaque; in addition, the level of HDL (the "good cholesterol") decreases.

Resources for Further Information on High Cholesterol
Books

➤ American Heart Association. *American Heart Association Low-Fat, Low-Cholesterol Cookbook: Delicious Recipes to Help Lower Your Cholesterol*, 4th ed. New York, NY: Clarkson Potter, 2010. Print.
Experts present the effects of fats and cholesterol on heart health, the value of healthy food for a healthy heart, an extensive listing of recipes from appetizers to main meals to desserts, and an appendix with how-to strategies on healthy shopping, cooking, and eating out, as well as information on risk factors and the "science behind the recommendations."

➤ Freeman, Mason W. *What to Do about High Cholesterol* (A Harvard Medical School Special Report). Boston, MA: Harvard Medical School Press, 2012. Print. Freeman, Chief of the Lipid Metabolism Unit at Massachusetts General Hospital, and the editors of Harvard Health Publications describe what cholesterol test results mean, types of tests, treatment options, and the effect of family history.

➤ Khaleghi, Murdoc. *The Everything Guide to Preventing Heart Disease: All You Need to Know to Lower Your Blood Pressure, Beat High Cholesterol, and Stop Heart Disease in Its Tracks* (Everything Series). Avon, MA: Adams Media, 2011. Print. Written for the patient, this book contains reliable, science-based information about managing your condition and preventing heart disease.

➤ Rinzler, Carol Ann. *Controlling Cholesterol for Dummies* (For Dummies: Health and Fitness). Indianapolis, IN: For Dummies, 2008. Print.
This easy-to-understand, consumer-oriented book explains topics such as what cholesterol is, diet, lifestyle changes, and treatment.

Brochures, Booklets, and Other Short Print Publications

➤ American Heart Association (AHA). http://www.heart.org/.
   • "Downloadable Documents for Cholesterol" (Information Sheets). http://www
     .heart.org/HEARTORG/Conditions/Cholesterol/CholesterolToolsResources/
     Downloadable-Documents-for-Cholesterol_UCM_305648_Article.jsp; alter-
     nate path: http://www.heart.org/, search for "cholesterol," click on the title
     "Tools and Resources," and then click on "Downloadable Documents." AHA
     provides several printable information sheets on lowering cholesterol, such
     as "Cholesterol Tracker," "Cholesterol Questions to Ask Your Doctor," "What
     Do My Cholesterol Levels Mean?," "How Can I Lower High Cholesterol?," and
     "How Can I Monitor My Cholesterol, Blood Pressure, and Weight?" (No more
     than one packet and two brochures per household can be ordered at no cost.)
   • "Order American Heart Association Educational Brochures: Cholesterol."
     http://www.heart.org/HEARTORG/General/Order-American-Heart
     -Association-Educational-Brochures_UCM_312777_Article.jsp; alternate
     path: http://www.heart.org/, search for "educational brochures," click on the
     title "Order American Heart Association Educational Brochures," and then
     click on the topic "cholesterol." Several AHA-published brochures are avail-
     able, such as "Understanding and Controlling Cholesterol," "Your Guide to
     Lowering Your Cholesterol w/TLC," "About Your Bypass Surgery," "Coronary
     Angioplasty and Stenting," and "Your Cardiac Catheterization." These bro-
     chures can be ordered by filling in a form online. Also available is a choles-
     terol information packet that contains a cholesterol brochure. (No more than
     one packet and two brochures per household can be ordered at no cost.)

➤ British Heart Foundation (BHF)—"Reducing Your Blood Cholesterol" (Booklet).
   http://www.bhf.org.uk/publications/view-publication.aspx?ps=1000139; alternate path: http://www.bhf.org.uk/, search for "blood cholesterol," and then click
   on the title "British Heart Foundation—Blood Pressure." Scroll down to the section called "Related Links," and then click on "Reducing Your Blood Cholesterol
   Booklet."
   The BHF website offers a free booklet on reducing your blood cholesterol.
   According to the website: "Designed for people with high blood cholesterol, their
   family and friends, this booklet explains what cholesterol is, how it is measured,
   its role in coronary heart disease, how physical activity and healthy eating can
   help, and medications available."

Websites

➢ Aetna InteliHealth—"High Cholesterol (Hypercholesterolemia)." http://www .intelihealth.com/IH/ihtIH/WSIHW000/8775/24049/201972.html?d=dmtHealthAZ; alternate path: http://www.intelihealth.com/, search for "high cholesterol," and then click on the title "High Cholesterol (Hypercholesterolemia)."
This website provides sections on high cholesterol, including definitions, symptoms, diagnosis, expected duration, prevention, treatment, when to call a professional, and prognosis. Aetna InteliHealth, a subsidiary of Aetna, is reviewed by the faculty of Harvard Medical School and University College of Dental Medicine. According to Aetna InteliHealth's website, "Aetna InteliHealth maintains absolute editorial independence. That means that Aetna InteliHealth makes decisions about the information on our site free of outside influence." Under "Healthy Lifestyle," Aetna InteliHealth also offers free health-related e-mail subscriptions.

➢ American Heart Association (AHA)—"Cholesterol." http://www.heart.org/ HEARTORG/Conditions/Cholesterol/Cholesterol_UCM_001089_SubHomePage .jsp; alternate path: http://www.heart.org/, search for "cholesterol," and then click on the title "Visit Our Cholesterol Website."
AHA provides details in sections about cholesterol, why cholesterol matters, risk factors, symptoms, diagnosis and monitoring of cholesterol, prevention and treatment, and cholesterol tools and resources. You can also sign up for a free heart health e-newsletter.

➢ BetterMedicine.com—"Cholesterol." http://www.bettermedicine.com/topic/ cholesterol/; alternate path: http://www.bettermedicine.com/, scroll down to the section titled "Common Conditions," and then click on the title "Cholesterol."
The Better Medicine website offers links to cholesterol topics, such as cholesterol facts, symptoms, treatment, and living with high cholesterol. There is also a section titled "Expert Advice from Harvard Medical School." According to its website, "All content is medically reviewed by at least one medical professional. Our content is backed by evidence from sources, such as articles in peer reviewed journals, government bodies, objective health organizations and medical groups of specialists. The name and credentials of the medical reviewer(s) are printed at the end of the article."

➢ Brigham and Women's Hospital (BWH) (Boston, MA)—"Cholesterol" (Animation). http://healthlibrary.brighamandwomens.org/InteractiveTools/Animations/ 94,P09428; alternate path: http://www.brighamandwomens.org/, scroll under the heading "Health Information" to the category titled "Interactive Tools and Media," click on the title "Animations," and then scroll down and click on the topic "Cholesterol."

BWH offers an easy-to-understand animation on cholesterol that can be accessed by clicking on the "Launch Animation" link. According to its website, "Cholesterol is essential to life. But too much cholesterol in the blood is linked [to] heart disease and stroke. Watch this Cholesterol animation to learn how cholesterol works in the body and what steps you can take to make healthy lifestyle changes." For information on clinical trials, see the BWH entry on p. 29.

> British Heart Foundation (BHF)—"High Cholesterol." http://www.bhf.org.uk/ heart-health/conditions/high-cholesterol.aspx; alternate path: http://www.bhf .org.uk/, search for "high cholesterol," and then click on the title "British Heart Foundation—High Cholesterol."

The BHF website describes LDL cholesterol and HDL cholesterol, triglycerides, causes, how to reduce cholesterol levels, how sterol-enriched foods affects cholesterol levels, and information on eating eggs. There is also a link to a podcast titled "Five Things You Can Do to Lower Your Cholesterol." You can also click on the "Community: Share Experiences with Others" heading to engage with the BHF online community where you can share your own story and read those of others.

> CardioSmart. https://www.cardiosmart.org/.

CardioSmart provides easy-to-use webpages on various heart-health topics. From the homepage, you can find the following resources by searching for the condition and then clicking on the corresponding title. According to the American College of Cardiology (ACC), "CardioSmart is the patient education and support program launched by the [ACC]. Our mission is to engage, inform, and empower patients to better prepare them for participation in their own care."

- "High Cholesterol." https://www.cardiosmart.org/conditioncenters/ctt .aspx?id=3136. CardioSmart's Cholesterol Condition Center's webpage contains an introduction, five questions to ask your cardiologist, news, an e-newsletter sign-up for CardioSmart news updates, a video library (e.g., HDL, LDL, triglycerides), and a link to learn more about cholesterol (basic facts, what high blood cholesterol is, what cholesterol is, symptoms, treatment, causes, and diagnosis). This information is also available in Spanish.
- "High Cholesterol: Raising Your HDL Level." https://www.cardiosmart.org/ Healthwise/aba5/690/aba5690. CardioSmart provides an easy-to-use webpage on understanding HDL (high-density lipoprotein) cholesterol.
- "LDL: 'Bad' Cholesterol." (Video with Transcript). https://www.cardiosmart .org/News-and-Events/2013/01/Video-LDL. This CardioSmart video, with transcript, provides information on understanding LDL (low-density lipoprotein) cholesterol.
- "Triglycerides" (Video with Transcript). https://www.cardiosmart.org/ CardioSmart/AmIAtRisk.aspx?id=294. This CardioSmart video, with transcript, provides information on understanding triglycerides.

➢ Centers for Disease Control and Prevention (CDC). "Cholesterol." http://www
.cdc.gov/cholesterol/index.htm; alternate path: http://www.cdc.gov/, search for
"cholesterol," and then click on "CDC—Cholesterol—DHDSP."
The CDC, part of the U.S. Department of Health and Human Services, offers a
website dedicated to heart-health issues. This webpage features links to several
topics, including what cholesterol is, facts and statistics, risk factors, publications,
educational materials for both patients and professionals, FAQs, and guidelines
and recommendations. Also available is a sign-up for free e-mail updates.

➢ CenterWatch—Clinical trials listing service. http://www.centerwatch.com/.
This CenterWatch clinical trials listing service lists trials currently looking for
volunteers to enroll in medical studies. Click on the "Clinical Trials" heading,
and search by location, medical condition, or therapeutic area. To search by location, click on your state (or country) and click on a city near you to find information on each available clinical trial. Check back with this website often for new
studies. Sign up for a free e-mail service that sends notice of new clinical trials.
  • "Dyslipidemia Clinical Trials." http://www.centerwatch.com/clinical-trials/
    listings/studylist.aspx?CatID=676.
  • "High Cholesterol (Hyperlipidemia) Clinical Trials." http://www.centerwatch
    .com/clinical-trials/listings/studylist.aspx?CatID=170.
  • "Hypertriglyceridemia Clinical Trials." http://www.centerwatch.com/
    clinical-trials/listings/studylist.aspx?CatID=410.
Alternate path: http://www.centerwatch.com/, under the category "Patient
Resources," click on "Search Clinical Trials" where you can search by medical con-
dition, then click on the medical condition's first letter (e.g., "D"), and then click
on the specific term (e.g., "Dyslipidemia"). The "Search Clinical Trials" page also
allows searching by location and therapeutic area.

➢ Cleveland Clinic (Cleveland, OH)—"Cholesterol." http://my.clevelandclinic.org/
healthy_living/cholesterol/hic_cholesterol.aspx; alternate path: http://my
.clevelandclinic.org/, scroll down to "Health Information—By All Topics (A–Z),"
click on the letter "C," and then scroll down and click on the topic "Cholesterol."
Cleveland Clinic provides comprehensive patient-friendly information on cholesterol, including definitions, other names, risk factors, why high cholesterol is
dangerous, and how it travels through the bloodstream. Also featured are numerous links for expanded information on cholesterol test result scores, facts and
fiction, diseases linked to high cholesterol, eating out, beneficial exercises, drug
treatments, alternative therapy, lipid disorders, children with high cholesterol,
and finding a doctor who treats high cholesterol. The Cleveland Clinic also offers
a link to "Chat Online with a Health Information Search Specialist." Sign up for
free e-mails with the "latest health and wellness information." For information
on clinical trials, see the Cleveland Clinic entry on pp. 31–32.

➤ ClinicalTrials.gov. http://clinicaltrials.gov/.

ClinicalTrials.gov, developed by the U.S. National Institutes of Health of the National Library of Medicine, lists ongoing and currently enrolling clinical trials. To find clinical trials from the homepage, search for the condition by name (e.g., "arrhythmia"), which will generate a list of possibly hundreds or thousands of studies. To limit your results, click on "Modify This Search" and select specific fields, such as (1) Recruitment (e.g., you might want to select "Open Studies"); (2) Locations (e.g., select your state); and (3) Age Group, and then click on the "Search" button. Click on the title of each trial name for additional information, such as purpose of the study, study design and type, detailed description, outcome measures, eligibility (age, gender, criteria for participating), study start date, estimated study completion date, and sponsor. Check often for new studies.

- Dyslipidemia clinical trials. http://clinicaltrials.gov/ct2/results/refine?term =dyslipidemia.
- High cholesterol clinical trials. http://clinicaltrials.gov/ct2/results/refine ?term=high+cholesterol.
- Hyperlipidemia clinical trials. http://clinicaltrials.gov/ct2/results/refine?term =hyperlipidemia.
- Hypertriglyceridemia clinical trials. http://clinicaltrials.gov/ct2/results/ refine?term=hypertriglyceridemia.

➤ eMedicineHealth. http://www.emedicinehealth.com/.

eMedicineHealth, a division of WebMD, offers comprehensive articles related to cholesterol. From the homepage, you can find the following and related topics by searching for the condition and clicking on the appropriate title.

- "High Cholesterol." http://www.emedicinehealth.com/high_cholesterol/ article_em.htm and http://www.emedicinehealth.com/high_cholesterol -health/article_em.htm. This article includes an overview and information on causes, risk factors, symptoms, diagnosis, treatment, medications, prevention, outlook, and follow-up. A slide show is also available.
- "Lowering High Cholesterol in Children." http://www.emedicinehealth .com/cholesterol_and_children/article_em.htm. This article includes an overview and information on screening, research results, treatment, medications, dietary guidelines, and exercise. A slide show is also available.

➤ EverydayHealth.com—"High Cholesterol." http://www.everydayhealth.com/heart -disease/cholesterol/index.aspx; alternate path: http://www.everydayhealth.com/, under "Health A–Z," click on "High Cholesterol."

The EverydayHealth website offers current information for the consumer on risk factors, prevention, treatment, management, high cholesterol–related conditions, and expert Q&As ("questions and answers from our board-certified experts at top-tier institutions such as Harvard Medical School, Memorial Sloan-Kettering Cancer Center, Mount Sinai Medical Center, and more").

➢ Genetics Home Reference—"Hypercholesterolemia." http://ghr.nlm.nih.gov/condition/hypercholesterolemia; alternate path: http://ghr.nlm.nih.gov/, search for "hypercholesterolemia."

Genetics Home Reference is a division of the National Institutes of Health (NIH). This webpage discusses hypercholesterolemia, an inherited condition causing high levels of blood cholesterol, which create a high risk for developing coronary artery disease.

➢ Hospital of the University of Pennsylvania (HUP) (Philadelphia, PA)—"Lipid Disorders Program." http://www.pennmedicine.org/heart/patient/clinical-services/lipid-disorders/penn-difference.html; alternate path: http://www.pennmedicine.org/, click on the "Departments and Services" icon (or search for "departments and services"), scroll down and click on the category "Cardiology and Cardiac Surgery," and then scroll down under the heading "Clinical Services" and click on "View All Clinical Services" and then "Lipid Disorders."

At its Penn Heart and Vascular Center website, HUP offers website links in the Lipid Disorders Program that include an "Overview" (what lipid disorders are and treatment options); the "Team," which links to each physician and specialist (with profiles, e.g., specialty, medical board certification, education); "The Penn Difference" (program described, patient experiences, unique capabilities and expertise, and hospital highlights); and "Physician Interviews" (videos). You can also subscribe to the Penn Heart newsletter. For information on clinical trials, see the HUP entry on p. 33.

➢ Insidermedicine. http://www.insidermedicine.com/.

The Insidermedicine website offers a variety of heart-health-related videos. From the homepage, you can search for videos by title, or you can search by topic (e.g., atrial fibrillation) to find other related videos. For more information on the Insidermedicine Project, see the earlier entry on pp. 33–34.

- "Physical Activity Improves Cholesterol, Blood Pressure, and Waist Size in Children." http://www.insidermedicine.com/archives/Physical_Activity _Improves_Cholesterol_Blood_Pressure_and_Waist_Size_in_Children_Video _5898.aspx. This video offers suggestions for helping children become aware of age-appropriate ways to be proactive in lowering their cardiovascular risk factors, such as through vigorous physical activity.
- "Reducing Saturated Fats and Increasing Cholesterol Lowering Foods Best Approach to Improving Hyperlipidemia." http://www.insidermedicine.com/archives/Reducing_Saturated_Fats_and_Increasing_Cholesterol_Lowering _Foods_Best_Approach_to_Improving_Hyperlipidemia_Video_5468.aspx.

In these easy-to-understand videos with demonstrations, a medical special-ist discusses recommendations for lifestyle changes for lipid management.

➤ Johns Hopkins Hospital, Heart and Vascular Institute (Baltimore, MD)—"High Cholesterol (Hypercholesterolemia)." http://www.hopkinsmedicine.org/ heart_vascular_institute/conditions_treatments/conditions/high_cholesterol .html and http://www.hopkinsmedicine.org/healthlibrary/conditions/adult/ cardiovascular_diseases/cholesterol_in_the_blood_85,P00220/; alternate path: http://www.hopkinsmedicine.org/, search for "high cholesterol hypercholester-olemia," and then click on the title "High Cholesterol (Hypercholesterolemia)"; for a related resource, also click on "Cardiovascular Diseases—Cholesterol in the Blood."

The Johns Hopkins Heart and Vascular Institute webpage on high cholesterol (hypercholesterolemia) discusses what high cholesterol is, when to call a doctor, symptoms, causes, prevention, diagnosis, and treatment. It also lists links to phy-sicians and specialists (with profiles, e.g., specialty, medical board certification, education) who treat high cholesterol. You can also click on the heading "Clinical Trials" for links to current trials in various heart and cardiovascular conditions.

➤ KidsHealth.org. http://www.kidshealth.org/.

The Nemours Center for Children's Health Media provides current information on conditions afflicting children, written for both children and parents. Informa-tion is available in English and Spanish. Click on the "Listen" button to hear the text read aloud.

- "Cholesterol and Your Child." http://kidshealth.org/parent/medical/heart/ cholesterol.html#cat141. Written for parents, this article provides current information on children with high cholesterol. Topics discussed include general information about cholesterol, good versus bad cholesterol, moni-toring and treatment, and ways to lower cholesterol.

- "Parents of Children with Metabolic Syndrome." http://kidshealth.org/ parent/medical/heart/metabolic_syndrome.html#cat141. Written for parents, this article provides current information on children with meta-bolic syndrome. Topics discussed include general information about metabolic syndrome, causes, effects, diagnosis, treating risk factors, and changing course.

Alternate path: http://kidshealth.org/, click on "Parents Site," scroll down and select "Diseases and Conditions" and then "Heart and Blood Vessels," and then select the title.

➤ Massachusetts General Hospital (MGH) (Boston, MA)—"Lipid Management." http://www.massgeneral.org/heartcenter/services/treatmentprograms.aspx?id =1235; alternate path: http://www.massgeneral.org/, search for and then click on the title "Lipid Management"; or click on "Centers and Services," click on "View

All Departments," click on "Heart Center," click on the heading "Treatments and Services," scroll down, and then click on the topic "Lipid Management."

At this lipid management webpage from the MGH Heart Center are links to comprehensive information in several categories: "Our Approach" includes an overview of their team approach to "provide specialized care for patients who have disorders of lipid metabolism, which includes high cholesterol levels, high blood triglyceride levels, low HDL cholesterol levels or a combination of these conditions," treatment plans, and links to each medical expert (with profiles, e.g., specialty, medical board certification, education); "Conditions and Diseases" has a link to detailed information on coronary heart disease; "Support and Wellness" offers a series of classes at MGH Heart Center each on nutrition and relaxation; "Heart Smart" contains "various topics related to improving and maintaining cardiovascular health, including exercise, coronary artery disease and secondary prevention, symptom recognition and management, cardiac medications and managing stress"; and "Clinical Trials" offers links to MGH trials and research studies when they are currently seeking participants.

➤ Mayo Clinic (Rochester, MN)—"High Cholesterol." http://www.mayoclinic.com/ health/high-blood-cholesterol/DS00178; alternate path: http://www.mayoclinic .com/, search for "high cholesterol" and then click on the title "High Cholesterol— MayoClinic.com."

Written for patients, this webpage on high cholesterol includes definitions, symptoms, causes, risk factors, complications, preparing for appointments, tests and diagnosis, treatments and drugs, lifestyle and home remedies, alternative medicine, prevention, and what's new. There is also a more comprehensive section titled "In-Depth" on some of these topics, as well as links to other related topics such as very-low-density lipoprotein cholesterol, triglycerides, and cholesterol levels. For information on clinical trials and patient services, see the Mayo Clinic entry on p. 36.

➤ MedicineNet. http://www.medicinenet.com/.

MedicineNet.com is owned and operated by WebMD and is a part of the WebMD Network. According to its website, MedicineNet "provides easy-to-read, in-depth, authoritative medical information for consumers via its user-friendly, interactive website." The medical information is written and edited by a nationally recognized group of more than 70 U.S. board-certified physicians. The website contains a "Symptom Checker" listed in alphabetical order as a guide to "pinpoint your pain." Its homepage links to "Health News of the Week." There is also a health newsletter that you can subscribe to by e-mail.

• "Cholesterol." http://www.medicinenet.com/cholesterol/article.htm. In-depth information on high cholesterol includes discussions on what cholesterol is, what HDL and LDL are, why HDL is good, what triglycerides and very-low-density lipoproteins are, treatment, current cholesterol treatment guidelines, patient discussions, and finding a local cardiologist.

- "High Cholesterol: Frequently Asked Questions." http://www.medicinenet .com/high_cholesterol_frequently_asked_questions/article.htm. In-depth information on high cholesterol includes discussions on what cholesterol is, what the difference between good and bad cholesterol is, what makes cholesterol increase or decrease, and treatment.

Alternate path: http://www.medicinenet.com/, click on the major topic "Diseases and Conditions," click on "Conditions A–Z," then click on the letter of the topic ("C" or "H"), and then scroll down to click on the corresponding title.

➤ MedlinePlus—"Cholesterol (HDL, Hypercholesterolemia, Hyperlipidemia, Hyperlipoproteinemia, LDL)." http://www.nlm.nih.gov/medlineplus/cholesterol .html; alternate path: http://www.nlm.nih.gov/, under "Databases," click on "MedlinePlus," and then search for "cholesterol."

MedlinePlus is a component of the National Institutes of Health (NIH), produced by the National Library of Medicine (NLM), and is updated regularly. This MedlinePlus webpage on cholesterol offers extensive linked information covering overviews, news, diagnosis/symptoms, treatment, prevention/screening, alternative therapy, nutrition, disease management, specific conditions, related issues, anatomy/physiology, clinical trials, genetics, research, journal articles, organizations, statistics, and specific sections focusing on children, teenagers, women, and seniors. Patient handouts are also available. This webpage also includes a multimedia section containing health check tools, tutorials, and videos.

➤ *The Merck Manual Home Health Handbook for Patients and Caregivers*— "Cholesterol Disorders." http://www.merckmanuals.com/home/sec14/ch169/ ch169a.html; alternate path: http://www.merckmanuals.com/home/, under "Sections," click on "All" to view a complete list, then click on the section "Hormonal and Metabolic Disorders," and then scroll down to the section "Cholesterol Disorders."

This section on cholesterol disorders is divided into three titles: "Overview of Cholesterol and Lipid Disorders," "Dyslipidemia," and "Hypolipoproteinemia." Information includes symptoms, diagnosis, treatment, and hereditary conditions. This section is based on a well-known medical textbook titled *The Merck Manual Home Health Handbook for Patients and Caregivers* and is "provided free of charge . . . as a public service."

➤ National Heart, Lung, and Blood Institute (NHLBI). http://www.nhlbi.nih.gov/. NHLBI is a division of the National Institutes of Health from the U.S. Department of Health and Human Services. From the homepage, you can find the following resources through a title search.

- "High Blood Cholesterol." http://www.nhlbi.nih.gov/health/dci/Diseases/ Hbc/HBC_WhatIs.html. This NHLBI webpage provides information on high cholesterol, including links to definitions, other names, causes, signs and symptoms, diagnosis, treatments, clinical trials, and key points.
- "National Cholesterol Education Program (NCEP)." http://www.nhlbi.nih .gov/about/ncep/. This NHLBI webpage presents such information as a NCEP program description, health and related information to patients/ general public, and clinical guidelines for cholesterol management in adults. The goal of the NCEP is to "contribute to reducing illness and death from coronary heart disease (CHD) in the United States by reducing the percent of Americans with high blood cholesterol. Through educational efforts directed at health professionals and the public, the NCEP aims to raise awareness and understanding about high blood cholesterol as a risk factor for CHD and the benefits of lowering cholesterol levels as a means of preventing CHD."

➤ Texas Heart Institute (Houston, TX). http://www.texasheartinstitute.org/.
  For information on clinical trials, see the Texas Heart Institute entry on p. 40.
- "Cholesterol." http://www.texasheartinstitute.org/HIC/Topics/HSmart/ choleste.cfm. The Texas Heart Institute website offers a definition of cholesterol, as well as information on low-density lipoprotein, high-density lipoprotein, triglycerides, total cholesterol, and cholesterol testing. One section allows users to "Ask a Texas Heart Institute Doctor" questions. Click on "Heart Doctor Answers" to explore the questions and answers already published there. An easy-to-print format is available.
- "Metabolic Syndrome." http://www.texasheartinstitute.org/HIC/Topics/ Cond/metabolic.cfm. The Texas Heart Institute website offers a definition of metabolic syndrome as well as information on causes, signs and symptoms, diagnosis, and treatment.

Alternate path: http://www.texasheartinstitute.org/, search for the topic by name (e.g., "cholesterol"), and then click on the appropriate title; or in the pull-down menu under "Heart Information Center," select "Heart-Health Topics" and then "Heart Conditions," and then click on the topic by name.

➤ UCLA Ronald Reagan Medical Center (Los Angeles, CA)—"Cholesterol." http:// www.uclahealth.org/body.cfm?id=592; scroll down to the heading "In-Depth Reports" and click on the title "Cholesterol"; alternate path: http://www.uclahealth .org/, under the heading "For Patients and Visitors," scroll down and mouse over the category "Health Resources" and then click on "Heart Health Center," scroll down to the heading "In-Depth Reports," then click on the word "More," and then click on the title "Cholesterol."

The UCLA Ronald Reagan Medical Center's Heart Health Center provides an in-depth report on cholesterol, which includes highlights, introductions, risk factors, complications, symptoms, diagnosis, treatment, medications, and lifestyle changes. Also on the Heart Health Center website, under the heading "Tests and Treatments," scroll under the section "Alternative Medicine" for more treatment information. Then click on the word "More," and then click on the title "Cholesterol—High." For more information on patient resources and clinical trials, see the UCLA entry on p. 41.

> WebMD—"Cholesterol Management Health Center." http://www.webmd.com/cholesterol-management/default.htm; alternate path: http://www.webmd.com/, search for "cholesterol management health center," and then click on the title "Cholesterol Management Health Center" (WebMD Health and Wellness Center).

The WebMD website offers the latest information on cholesterol management using articles, slide presentations, videos, FAQs, discussions groups, and expert blogs. Available is a WebMD's heart health e-mail newsletter. According to WebMD, "WebMD News is an independent media service designed to provide news, information, and educational material to consumers and physicians. News content created by WebMD is free from influence by sponsors, partners, or other sources."

Patient Support Groups and Organizations

> DailyStrength—"High Cholesterol Support Group." http://www.dailystrength.org/c/High-Cholesterol/support-group; alternate path: http://www.dailystrength.org/, search for "high cholesterol," and then click on "Visit the High Cholesterol Support Group."

The DailyStrength website offers online support groups and blogs for those with high cholesterol. Free registration is required to participate. According to the website, "DailyStrength is a subsidiary of Sharecare. Sharecare, created by WebMD founder and Discovery Communications' Chief of Global Digital Strategy Jeff Arnold, along with America's Doctor, Dr. Mehmet Oz, is the first truly interactive healthcare ecosystem giving consumers the ability to ask, learn and act on the questions of health."

> HeartHub for Patients—"Cholesterol." http://www.hearthub.org/hc-cholesterol.htm; alternate path: http://www.hearthub.org/, scroll down to the section titled "Health Centers," and then click on the title "Cholesterol."

HeartHub, a division of the American Heart Association (AHA), is a patient-support portal for information, tools, and resources on cholesterol, including a tool to help you find out if you meet the recommended guidelines to qualify for cholesterol-lowering drug therapy, learning what treatment options are best for you, healthy recipes, getting help on the phone, common misconceptions, and take a quiz to test your knowledge. Also available is a "Track Your Medications Chart" for free download to allow you to view and plan your weekly medication schedule.

➤ MedHelp—"Cholesterol." http://www.medhelp.org/search?query=cholesterol; alternate path: http://www.medhelp.org/, search for "cholesterol." According to its website, MedHelp "connects people with the leading medical experts," such as those from Cleveland Clinic, National Jewish Health, Partners Health, and Mount Sinai Hospital, with those who have similar medical issues. MedHelp's main focus is to enable patients "to take control over their health and find answers to their medical questions" using nontechnical language via an online community through posts, forums and groups, blogs, user journals, as well as recommendations, articles, health pages, and a medical glossary. Free registration is required.

➤ U.S. Hospital Finder. http://www.ushospitalfinder.com/. Use this site to find the names of hospitals by zip code, city, state, or your address. The search results include a map with directions. You might also want to ask your health care professional, call hospitals in your area, or search for "support groups" on hospital websites to determine if there are any cardiology support groups for people with high cholesterol that meet regularly in your area.

➤ WebMD—"Cholesterol Management Community." http://www.webmd.com/ cholesterol-management/; alternate path: http://www.webmd.com/, search for "cholesterol management community," click on the title "Cholesterol Management Health Center," and then scroll down to "WebMD Cholesterol Management Community" (WebMD Community).
Click on the title "Community Experts Support" as well as the links under "Discussions," "Expert Blogs," and "Community." Join the cholesterol management community at WebMD (WebMD moderated) that includes discussions, expert blogs, tips, and resources. As stated on the WebMD Cholesterol Management Community page, "Join this group to find out if you're at risk, and get information on medications, their effects, and ways to lower your cholesterol naturally from our experts and other members like you." To search for other health-topic communities, go to http://exchanges.webmd.com/, which is titled "Be a Part of the WebMD Community." You can also scroll down to "Create Your Own Community" for easy instructions on starting your own support group/community.

➤ Yahoo! Groups—"Cholesterol Management Support Group." http://health.groups .yahoo.com/group/cholesterol_management/; alternate path: http://www.groups .yahoo.com/, search for "cholesterol management" in the "Find a Yahoo! Group" Search box and then click on the group "Cholesterol Management."
This online Yahoo! group is for patients with high cholesterol and their families and friends. Yahoo! Groups is not a medical site, nor does it provide or endorse medical advice or procedures. The purpose of the website is to share experiences in a kind and caring manner. Free registration is required to participate.

Low Blood Pressure (Hypotension)

Hypotension or low blood pressure (LBP) is the opposite of hypertension. Blood pressures lower than 90 mm Hg over 60 mm Hg (measured in millimeters of mercury) are considered hypotensive. Hypotension is not usually a problem unless there is some underlying heart disease. People with hypotension may experience dizziness, fainting, cold and clammy skin, tiredness, blurred vision, or nausea. Very low blood pressure can cause shock, a serious health problem.

There are three types of hypotension: orthostatic, neurally mediated, and severe. Orthostatic hypertension can be caused by dehydration, eating a large meal, or pregnancy. These issues are not generally serious and can be addressed by proper hydration, diet, and prenatal care. However, some diseases can cause hypotension, such as bradycardia, heart valve disease, heart attack or heart failure, severe infections, pulmonary embolisms, anemia, or central nervous system disorders. Tilt table testing can indicate hypotension. Some medications will lower blood pressure or cause dehydration. Good doctor–patient communication can minimize the risks presented by orthostatic hypotension.

In neurally mediated hypotension, the brain and heart are not communicating properly. For example, soldiers standing at attention for long periods sometimes pass out. This occurs because blood pools in the legs, causing a blood pressure drop. Then, because of neurally mediated hypotension, the brain mistakenly thinks the blood pressure is too high and slows the heart rate. This leads to dizziness and fainting. By recognizing the symptoms and avoiding the conditions that lead to the symptoms, a person can avoid neurally mediated hypotension.

Severe hypotension often leads to shock, an emergency condition. The blood pressure drops very low and does not return to normal. Severe hypotension can be caused by hypovolemia, which occurs with major blood loss, severe diarrhea, and other low blood volume affects. Cardiogenic shock occurs if the heart cannot pump enough blood, which triggers a blood pressure drop. Vasodilatory shock occurs when the arteries become generally relaxed, causing blood pressure to fall. Vasodilatory shock is caused by head injuries, liver failure, poisoning, allergic reactions, or medication reactions.

A person experiencing hypotension should be treated for shock by restoring blood flow to the brain and heart to reverse the cause of the shock. For example, a person in a car accident may be severely bleeding. Making the person lie down, raising his or her legs, and stopping the bleeding can minimize the risk of shock. Other measures can be taken at the hospital, such as replenishing some of the blood volume by intravenous therapy.

Resources for Further Information on Low Blood Pressure (Hypotension)

Books

➤ U.S. Government. *Hypotension (Low Blood Pressure) Toolkit—Comprehensive Medical Encyclopedia with Treatment Options, Clinical Data, and Practical Information.* Carson City, NV: Progressive Management, 2009. CD-ROM.
This toolkit contains a comprehensive set of current documents collected from U.S. databases on hypotension as a reference guide for patients and health care professionals.

Websites

➤ American Heart Association (AHA)—"Low Blood Pressure." http://www.heart.org/HEARTORG/Conditions/..re_UCM_301785_Article.jsp; alternate path: http://www.heart.org/, search for and then click on the title "Low Blood Pressure."
AHA provides details on what to do if blood pressure stays around 85/55, how to know if LBP is a health problem, what other conditions slow blood pressure can occur with, what if there is a sudden decline in blood pressure, and when to see a health care professional. You can also sign up for a free heart health e-newsletter.

➤ CenterWatch—Clinical trials listing service: "Hypotension (Low Blood Pressure) Clinical Trials." http://www.centerwatch.com/clinical-trials/listings/studylist.aspx?CatID=824; alternate path: http://www.centerwatch.com/, under the category "Patient Resources," click on "Search Clinical Trials," then click on "H," and then click on the title "Hypotension (Low Blood Pressure)."
This CenterWatch clinical trials listing service lists trials currently looking for volunteers to enroll in hypotension studies. Click on the "Clinical Trials" heading and search by location, medical condition, or therapeutic area. To search by location, click on your state (or country) and click on a city near you to find information on each available clinical trial. Check back with this website often for new studies. Sign up for a free e-mail service that sends notice of new clinical trials.

➤ ClinicalTrials.gov. http://clinicaltrials.gov/.
ClinicalTrials.gov, developed by the U.S. National Institutes of Health of the National Library of Medicine, lists ongoing and currently enrolling clinical trials. To find clinical trials from the homepage, search for the condition by name (e.g., "arrhythmia"), which will generate a list of possibly hundreds or thousands of studies. To limit your results, click on "Modify This Search" and select specific fields, such as (1) Recruitment (e.g., you might want to select "Open Studies"); (2) Locations (e.g., select your state); and (3) Age Group, and then click on the "Search" button. Click on the title of each trial name for additional information,

such as purpose of the study, study design and type, detailed description, outcome measures, eligibility (age, gender, criteria for participating), study start date, estimated study completion date, and sponsor. Check often for new studies.

- Hypotension clinical trials. http://clinicaltrials.gov/ct2/results/refine?term =hypotension.
- Low blood pressure clinical trials. http://clinicaltrials.gov/ct2/results/refine ?term=low+blood+pressure.

➤ eMedicineHealth—"Low Blood Pressure (Hypotension)." http://www.emedicine health.com/low_blood_pressure/article_em.htm and http://www.emedicinehealth .com/low_blood_pressure_hypotension-health/article_em.htm; alternate path: http://www.emedicinehealth.com/, search for and then click on the title "Low Blood Pressure" (Medical Reference from eMedicineHealth and from Healthwise).

eMedicineHealth, a division of WebMD, offers a comprehensive article on low blood pressure, including an overview, causes, risk factors, symptoms, when to seek medical care, diagnosis, treatment, medications, and complications.

➤ Mayo Clinic (Rochester, MN)—"Low Blood Pressure (Hypotension)." http://www .mayoclinic.com/health/low-blood-pressure/DS00590; alternate path: http://www .mayoclinic.com/, search for "low blood pressure (hypotension)," and then click on the title "Low Blood Pressure (Hypotension)—MayoClinic.com."

Written for patients, this webpage on low blood pressure includes definitions, symptoms, causes, risk factors, complications, preparing for appointments, tests and diagnosis, treatments and drugs, and lifestyle and home remedies. There is also a more comprehensive section titled "In-Depth" on some of these topics and another useful article titled "Orthostatic Hypotension (Postural Hypotension)." For information on clinical trials and patient services, see the Mayo Clinic entry on p. 36.

➤ MedicineNet—"Low Blood Pressure (Hypotension)." http://www.medicinenet .com/low_blood_pressure/article.htm; alternate path: http://www.medicinenet .com/, click on the major topic "Diseases and Conditions," click on "Conditions A–Z," then click on "H," and then scroll down to "Hypotension."

MedicineNet is owned and operated by WebMD and is a part of the WebMD Network. According to its website, MedicineNet "provides easy-to-read, in-depth, authoritative medical information for consumers via its user-friendly, interactive website." In-depth information on hypotension includes definitions, causes, symptoms, diagnosis, treatment, living with LBP, and patient discussions. The medical information is written and edited by a nationally recognized group of more than 70 U.S. board-certified physicians. The website contains a "Symptom Checker" listed in alphabetical order as a guide to "pinpoint your pain." Its homepage links to "Health News of the Week." You can also sign up to receive a health newsletter.

➤ MedlinePlus—"Low Blood Pressure (Hypotension/LBP)." http://www.nlm.nih
.gov/medlineplus/lowbloodpressure.html; alternate path: http://www.nlm.nih
.gov/, under "Databases," click on MedlinePlus, and then search for "low blood
pressure."
MedlinePlus is a component of the National Institutes of Health, produced by
the National Library of Medicine, and is updated regularly. This MedlinePlus
webpage on low blood pressure offers extensive linked information covering
overviews, news, diagnosis/symptoms, treatment, disease management, specific
conditions, clinical trials, journal articles, organizations, and one section focusing on seniors. Patient handouts are also available. This webpage also includes a
multimedia section containing videos.

➤ *The Merck Manual Home Health Handbook for Patients and Caregivers*—"Low
Blood Pressure." http://www.merckmanuals.com/home/sec03/ch021/ch021a
.html; alternate path: http://www.merckmanuals.com/home/, under "Sections,"
click on "All" to view a complete list, then click on the section "Heart and Blood
Vessel Disorders," and then scroll down to the section "Low Blood Pressure."
This section on low blood pressure is divided into several titles: "Overview of
Low Blood Pressure," "Fainting," "Orthostatic Hypotension," and "Postprandial
Hypotension." Subsections include additional information on causes, symptoms,
diagnosis, treatment, and prognosis and are based on a well-known medical textbook titled *The Merck Manual Home Health Handbook for Patients and Caregiv-
ers*. The site is "provided free of charge . . . as a public service."

➤ National Heart, Lung, and Blood Institute (NHLBI)—"What Is Hypotension?"
http://www.nhlbi.nih.gov/health/dci/Diseases/hyp/hyp_whatis.html; alternate
path: http://www.nhlbi.nih.gov/, search for "hypotension" and then click on the
title "What Is Hypotension?"
NHLBI, a division of the National Institutes of Health from the U.S. Department
of Health and Human Services, provides information on low blood pressure
(hypotension), including links to definitions, types of hypotension, other names,
causes, risk factors, signs and symptoms, diagnosis, treatments, living with hypotension, clinical trials, and key points.

➤ WebMD—"Low Blood Pressure Directory." http://www.webmd.com/hypertension
-high-blood-pressure/low-blood-pressure-directory; alternate path: http://www
.webmd.com/, search for and then click on the title "Low Blood Pressure" (WebMD
Health and Wellness Directory).
The WebMD website offers the latest information on low blood pressure using
articles, medical references, videos, and expert commentary. Under the topic
"Medical References" are discussions on causes, symptoms, treatments, risks,
and more. A WebMD heart health e-mail newsletter is also available. According
to WebMD, "WebMD News is an independent media service designed to

provide news, information, and educational material to consumers and physicians. News content created by WebMD is free from influence by sponsors, partners, or other sources."

Patient Support Groups and Organizations

➤ MedHelp. http://www.medhelp.org/.

According to its website, MedHelp "connects people with the leading medical experts," such as those from Cleveland Clinic, National Jewish Health, Partners Health, and Mount Sinai Hospital, with those who have similar medical issues. MedHelp's main focus is to enable patients "to take control over their health and find answers to their medical questions" using nontechnical language via an online community through posts, forums and groups, blogs, user journals, as well as recommendations, articles, health pages, and a medical glossary. Free registration is required. From the homepage, you can find the following resources through a topic search.

- "Hypotension." http://www.medhelp.org/search?query=hypotension.
- "Low Blood Pressure." http://www.medhelp.org/search?query=low+blood+pressure.

➤ U.S. Hospital Finder. http://www.ushospitalfinder.com/.

Use this site to find the names of hospitals by zip code, city, state, or your address. The search results include a map with directions. You might also want to ask your health care professional, call hospitals in your area, or search for "support groups" on hospital websites to determine if there are any cardiology support groups for people with low blood pressure that meet regularly in your area.

Metabolic Syndrome

Metabolic syndrome (also called dysmetabolic syndrome, insulin resistance syndrome, obesity syndrome, and hypertriglyceridemic waist) is a condition composed of inherited traits (family history) and lifestyle habits that increase risk for developing heart and cardiovascular disease, as well as stroke and diabetes. A person with metabolic syndrome has two times the risk factor of developing heart disease. Metabolic syndrome is also more common in some ethic and racial groups, such as South Asians and Mexican Americans; also, African American women and Mexican American women are more likely to have metabolic syndrome than their male counterparts.

There are five metabolic risk factors: (1) abdominal obesity, or having a large waistline (known as "apple-shaped") composed of too much fat surrounding the stomach; (2) high triglyceride blood level (type of fat); (3) low blood level of high-density lipoprotein (HDL) cholesterol; HDL, also known as good cholesterol, aids in getting rid of bad cholesterol low-density lipoprotein (LDL) from the arteries to reduce the accumulation of plaque; (4) high blood pressure; when the heart pumps the blood, it moves the blood forcefully into the aorta and out to the body, and over a long time heart damage or plaque will build up; and (5) high fasting blood sugar. Insulin resistance is when the insulin hormone does not work properly to break down blood sugar efficiently; this might be a signal for diabetes.

Lifestyle habits have a major impact on those with metabolic syndrome, which include being overweight or obese and remaining inactive (little physical exercise, such as walking, jogging, bicycling, aerobics, swimming, sporting activity). Although you cannot control your genetic traits, lifestyle changes may make the difference between preventing and delaying heart and cardiovascular disease.

Metabolic syndrome (formally known as metabolic syndrome X) can be confused with the condition known as cardiac syndrome X. Metabolic syndrome is composed of a group of risk factors that can cause cardiovascular disease. However, cardiac syndrome X (also known as microvascular angina) is when a patient (70 percent are women) feels sudden chest pain similar to angina but does not have the blocked or narrowed arteries that usually cause angina (and are a major risk factor of a heart attack). The cause of cardiac syndrome X is not known but is also not a risk factor for heart disease. Since studies have indicated that cardiac syndrome X occurs most often after menopause, one suggested cause is a drop in estrogen levels. Another suspected cause is having small blood vessels (known as microvascular dysfunction), which reduces oxygen flow, particularly during exercise.

Resources for Further Information on Metabolic Syndrome

Websites

➤ Aetna InteliHealth—"Metabolic Syndrome—Lifestyle Changes Are Key." http://www .intelihealth.com/IH/ihtIH/WSIHW000/35320/35327/1333050.html?d=dmtHMS Content; alternate path: http://www.intelihealth.com/, search for "metabolic syndrome" and click on the title "Metabolic Syndrome—Lifestyle Changes Are Key." This webpage provides an overview of metabolic syndrome, including definitions, who gets metabolic syndrome, who is at risk, and how symptoms are treated. Aetna InteliHealth, a subsidiary of Aetna, is reviewed by the faculty of Harvard Medical School and the University College of Dental Medicine. According to Aetna InteliHealth's website, "Aetna InteliHealth maintains absolute editorial independence. That means that Aetna InteliHealth makes decisions about the information on our site free of outside influence." Under "Healthy Lifestyle," Aetna InteliHealth also offers free health-related e-mail subscriptions.

➤ American Heart Association (AHA)—"Metabolic Syndrome." http://www.heart .org/HEARTORG/Conditions/More/MetabolicSyndrome/Metabolic-Syndrome

_UCM_002080_SubHomePage.jsp; alternate path: http://www.heart.org/, search for "metabolic syndrome," and then click on the title "Visit Our Metabolic Syndrome Website."

AHA provides expanded details on metabolic syndrome in such sections as an overview, why metabolic syndrome matters, risk factors, symptoms and diagnosis, and prevention and treatment. You can also sign up for a free heart health e-newsletter.

➢ CardioSmart—"Metabolic Syndrome." https://www.cardiosmart.org/Heart-Conditions/Metabolic-Syndrome; alternate path: https://www.cardiosmart.org/, search for "metabolic syndrome," and then click on the title "CardioSmart: Metabolic Syndrome."

CardioSmart provides an easy-to-use website on understanding metabolic syndrome. Topics of discussion include what metabolic syndrome is (causes, symptoms, risks, and diagnosis), "Questions to Ask Your Doctor," "Your Responsibilities," "Your Care Team," support groups, and current research. According to the American College of Cardiology (ACC), "CardioSmart is the patient education and support program launched by the [ACC]. Our mission is to engage, inform, and empower patients to better prepare them for participation in their own care."

➢ CenterWatch—Clinical trials listing service: "Metabolic Syndrome Clinical Trials." http://www.centerwatch.com/clinical-trials/listings/condition/556/metabolic-syndrome; alternate path: http://www.centerwatch.com/, under the category "Patient Resources," click on "Search Clinical Trials," click on "M," and then click on the title "Metabolic Syndrome."

This CenterWatch clinical trials listing service lists trials currently looking for volunteers to enroll in metabolic syndrome studies. Click on the "Clinical Trials" heading and search by location, medical condition, or therapeutic area. To search by location, click on your state (or country) and click on a city near you to find information on each available clinical trial. Check back with this website often for new studies. Sign up for a free e-mail service that sends notice of new clinical trials.

➢ Cleveland Clinic (Cleveland, OH)—"Metabolic Syndrome." http://my.clevelandclinic.org/disorders/Metabolic_Syndrome/hic_Metabolic_Syndrome.aspx; alternate path: http://my.clevelandclinic.org/, under the category "Institutes and Services," click on "Heart and Vascular," then click on "Homepage," then click on the category "Diseases and Conditions," and then click on the title "Metabolic Syndrome."

The Cleveland Clinic provides comprehensive patient-friendly information on metabolic syndrome, such as links to definitions, health risks, who has metabolic syndrome, symptoms, causes, what health problems might develop, and prevention.

The website also offers a link to "Chat Online with a Heart and Vascular Nurse." For information on clinical trials, see the Cleveland Clinic entry on pp. 31–32.

➤ ClinicalTrials.gov—Metabolic syndrome clinical trials. http://clinicaltrials.gov/ ct2/results/refine?term=metabolic+ syndrome; alternate path: http://clinicaltrials .gov/, search for "metabolic syndrome" in the Search for Studies box at the top of the screen.

To limit your results, click on "Modify This Search" and select specific fields, such as (1) Recruitment (e.g., you might want to select "Open Studies"); (2) Locations (e.g., select your state); and (3) Age Group, and then click on the "Search" button. Click on the title of each trial name for additional information, such as purpose of the study, study design and type, detailed description, outcome measures, eligibility (age, gender, criteria for participating), study start date, estimated study completion date, and sponsor. ClinicalTrials.gov, developed by the U.S. National Institutes of Health of the National Library of Medicine, lists ongoing and currently enrolling clinical trials. Check often for new studies.

➤ eMedicineHealth—"Metabolic Syndrome." http://www.emedicinehealth.com/ metabolic_syndrome/article_em.htm and http://www.emedicinehealth.com/ metabolic_syndrome-health/article_em.htm; alternate path: http://www .emedicinehealth.com/, search for and then click on the title "Metabolic Syndrome" (Medical Reference from eMedicineHealth and Healthwise).

eMedicineHealth, a division of WebMD, offers a comprehensive article on metabolic syndrome, including an overview, causes, when to seek medical care, symptoms, diagnosis, treatment, medications, prevention, next steps, and follow-up.

➤ HeartHealthyWomen.org—"Cardiac Syndrome X—Diagnosis, Treatment, Prognosis." http://www.hearthealthywomen.org/cardiovascular-disease/cardiac-syndrome -x/cardiac-syndrome-x.html; alternate path: http://www.hearthealthywomen.org/, search for "cardiac syndrome," and then click on the related article title.

HearthealthyWomen.org offers a consumer-friendly explanation of what cardiac syndrome X is as well as information on diagnosis, treatment, prevention, and prognosis. Scroll to the bottom of the screen and click on the link "Cardiac Syndrome X" for additional information, including causes. According to its website, "HeartHealthyWomen.org is a joint project of the Cardiovascular Research Foundation, the Office on Women's Health of the Department of Health and Human Services, and WomenHeart: the National Coalition for Women with Heart Disease."

➤ Insidermedicine—"Mediterranean Diet Plus Mixed Nuts Helps Combat Metabolic Syndrome" (Video). http://www.insidermedicine.com/archives/Mediterranean_Diet _Plus_Mixed_Nuts_Helps_Combat_Metabolic_Syndrome_3098.aspx; alternate path: http://www.insidermedicine.com/, search for the video by title.

The Insidermedicine website offers a variety of heart-health-related videos. According to the website, "a traditional Mediterranean diet enhanced with mixed nuts may help stave off metabolic syndrome in those at high risk for heart disease." In this easy-to-understand video, a medical specialist speaks about metabolic syndrome. You can also search for "metabolic syndrome" to find this and related videos. For more information on the Insidermedicine Project, see the earlier entry on pp. 33–34.

➢ Johns Hopkins Hospital (Baltimore, MD)—"Metabolic Syndrome." http://www
.hopkinsmedicine.org/digestive_weight_loss_center/conditions/metabolic_syndrome
.html and http://www.hopkinsmedicine.org/healthlibrary/conditions/adult/
cardiovascular_diseases/metabolic_syndrome_85,P08342/; alternate path: http://
www.hopkinsmedicine.org/, search for and then click on the title "Metabolic Syndrome"; for a related resource, also click on "Cardiovascular Diseases—Metabolic Syndrome."

The Johns Hopkins Heart and Vascular Institute webpage on metabolic syndrome discusses definitions, when to call a doctor, symptoms, causes, risks, prevention, diagnosis, and treatment. It also lists links to physicians and specialists (with profiles, e.g., specialty, medical board certification, education) who treat metabolic syndrome. Also, you can click on the heading "Clinical Trials" for links to current trials in various heart and cardiovascular conditions.

➢ KidsHealth.org—"Parents of Children with Metabolic Syndrome." http://
kidshealth.org/parent/medical/heart/metabolic_syndrome.html#cat141; alternate
path: http://www.kidshealth.org/, click on "Parents Site," scroll down and click on
"Diseases and Conditions," then scroll down and click on "Heart and Blood Vessels," and then click on the title "Metabolic Syndrome."

The Nemours Center for Children's Health Media provides current information on children with metabolic syndrome, written for parents. Topics discussed include general information about metabolic syndrome, causes, effects, diagnosis, treating risk factors, and changing course. Information is available in English and Spanish. Click on the "Listen" button to hear the text read aloud.

➢ Massachusetts General Hospital (MGH) (Boston, MA)—"Metabolic Syndrome"
(Conditions and Treatments). http://www.massgeneral.org/conditions/condition
.aspx?id=303; alternate path: http://www.massgeneral.org/, search for "metabolic
syndrome," and then click on the titles "Metabolic Syndrome—Massachusetts
General Hospital" and "Cardiovascular Disease Prevention Center—Metabolic
Syndrome."

Under the heading "Conditions and Treatment" is a section on metabolic syndrome that describes metabolic syndrome, its causes, symptoms, risk factors, diagnosis, treatment, and treatment programs. The Cardiovascular Disease Prevention Center at the MGH Heart Center website offers links to comprehensive information in several categories: "Our Approach" includes an overview of their team approach to "provide a unique, prevention-as-treatment approach for patients who have heart disease or who are at risk for developing heart disease"; "Treatments and Procedures Available through the Center"; "Support and Wellness" offers a series of classes at MGH Heart Center each on nutrition and relaxation; "Heart Smart" contains "various topics related to improving and maintaining cardiovascular health, including exercise, coronary artery disease and secondary prevention, symptom recognition and management, cardiac medications and managing stress"; and "Clinical Trials" has links to MGH trials and research studies when they are currently seeking participants.

➤ Mayo Clinic (Rochester, MN)—"Metabolic Syndrome." http://www.mayoclinic .com/health/metabolic%20syndrome/DS00522; alternate path: http://www .mayoclinic.com/, search for "metabolic syndrome," and then click on the title "Metabolic Syndrome—MayoClinic.com."
Written for patients, this webpage on peripheral artery disease includes definitions, symptoms, causes, risk factors, complications, preparing for appointments, tests and diagnosis, treatments and drugs, lifestyle and home remedies, coping and support, and prevention. There is also a more comprehensive section titled "In-Depth" on some of these topics. For information on clinical trials and patient services, see the Mayo Clinic entry on p. 36.

➤ MedicineNet—"Metabolic Syndrome." http://www.medicinenet.com/metabolic _syndrome/article.htm; alternate path: http://www.medicinenet.com/, click on the major topic "Diseases and Conditions," click on "Conditions A–Z," then click on "M," and then scroll down to "Metabolic Syndrome."
MedicineNet is owned and operated by WebMD and is a part of the WebMD Network. According to its website, MedicineNet "provides easy-to-read, in-depth, authoritative medical information for consumers via its user-friendly, interactive website." In-depth information on metabolic syndrome includes what metabolic syndrome is, how metabolic syndrome is defined, causes, risks, treatments, diagnosis, treatment, patient discussions, and finding a local cardiologist. The medical information is written and edited by a nationally recognized group of more than 70 U.S. board-certified physicians. The website contains a "Symptom Checker" listed in alphabetical order as a guide to "pinpoint your pain." Its homepage links to "Health News of the Week." You can also sign up to receive a health newsletter.

➤ MedlinePlus—"Metabolic Syndrome." http://www.nlm.nih.gov/medlineplus/ metabolicsyndrome.html; alternate path: http://www.nlm.nih.gov/, under "Databases," click on "MedlinePlus" and then search for "metabolic syndrome."
MedlinePlus is a component of the National Institutes of Health (NIH), produced by the National Library of Medicine (NLM), and is updated regularly. This MedlinePlus webpage on metabolic syndrome offers extensive linked information

covering overviews, news, diagnosis/symptoms, treatment, prevention/screening, related issues, videos, clinical trials, research, journal articles, directories, organizations, and sections that focus on women and seniors. There are also patient handouts available, as well as related information in the linked *MedlinePlus Magazine*. This website also includes a multimedia section containing health check tools and tutorials.

➢ Medscape Reference (Drugs, Diseases, and Procedures)—"Metabolic Syndrome." http://emedicine.medscape.com/article/165124-overview; alternate path: http://emedicine.medscape.com/, search for and then click on the title "Metabolic Syndrome."
Written for Medscape by Stanley S. Wang, MD, JD, MPH, and associates, this webpage presents a comprehensive report on metabolic syndrome. Although written for health care professionals, it might be helpful for interested laypersons. Articles for Medscape Reference are written by medical experts. The webpage states, "Our rigorous literature survey process allows us to rapidly integrate new practice-changing information into the relevant topics by systematically reviewing the major medical and pharmacy journals, news announcements, and important practice guidelines." Free registration is required.

➢ National Heart, Lung, and Blood Institute (NHLBI)—"What Is Metabolic Syndrome?" http://www.nhlbi.nih.gov/health/health-topics/topics/ms/; alternate path: http://www.nhlbi.nih.gov/, search for "metabolic syndrome," and then click on the title "What Is Metabolic Syndrome?"
NHLBI, a division of the National Institutes of Health from the U.S. Department of Health and Human Services, provides additional information on metabolic syndrome, including links to definitions, other names, causes, risk factors, signs and symptoms, diagnosis, treatments, prevention, living with metabolic syndrome, clinical trials, and key points.

➢ New York–Presbyterian (NYP) University Hospital of Columbia and Cornell (New York, NY)—"Metabolic Syndrome." http://nyp.org/health/diabetes-metabolic .html; alternate path: search for "metabolic syndrome," and then click on the title "Metabolic Syndrome—New York–Presbyterian Hospital."
NYP University Hospital of Columbia and Cornell provides patient-friendly information on metabolic syndrome topics, such as definitions, causes, risk factors, symptoms, and treatment. For information on clinical trials, see the NYP entry on p. 38.

➢ Texas Heart Institute (Houston, TX)—"Metabolic Syndrome." http://www .texasheartinstitute.org/HIC/Topics/Cond/metabolic.cfm; alternate path: http://www.texasheartinstitute.org/, search for "metabolic syndrome," and then click on the title "Metabolic Syndrome"; or under the heading "Heart Information

Center," click on "Heart-Health Topics," click on "Heart Conditions," and then click on "Metabolic Syndrome."

Texas Heart Institute website offers a definition of metabolic syndrome, causes, signs, diagnosis, and treatment. For information on clinical trials, see the Texas Heart Institute entry on p. 40.

➢ WebMD—"Metabolic Syndrome Health Center." http://www.webmd.com/heart/metabolic-syndrome/default.htm; alternate path: http://www.webmd.com/, search for "metabolic syndrome," and then click on the title "Metabolic Syndrome Health Center" (WebMD Health and Wellness Center).

The WebMD website offers information on metabolic syndrome such as definitions, who is at risk, health problems, treatment, preventions, questions to ask your doctor, and news. Also available is the WebMD heart health e-mail newsletter. According to WebMD, "WebMD News is an independent media service designed to provide news, information, and educational material to consumers and physicians. News content created by WebMD is free from influence by sponsors, partners, or other sources."

Patient Support Groups and Organizations

➢ MedHelp—"Metabolic Syndrome." http://www.medhelp.org/search?utf8=%26%23x2713%3B&query=metabolic+syndrome&camp=top_nav_search; alternate path: http://www.medhelp.org/, search for "metabolic syndrome."

According to its website, MedHelp "connects people with the leading medical experts," such as those from Cleveland Clinic, National Jewish Health, Partners Health, and Mount Sinai Hospital, with those who have similar medical issues. MedHelp's main focus is to enable patients "to take control over their health and find answers to their medical questions" using nontechnical language via an online community through posts, forums and groups, blogs, user journals, as well as recommendations, articles, health pages, and a medical glossary. Free registration is required.

➢ U.S. Hospital Finder. http://www.ushospitalfinder.com/.
Use this site to find the names of hospitals by zip code, city, state, or your address. The search results include a map with directions. You might also want to ask your health care professional, call hospitals in your area, or search for "support groups" on hospital websites to determine if there are any cardiology support groups for people with metabolic syndrome that meet regularly in your area.

➢ Yahoo! Groups—"Metabolic Syndrome Support Group." http://health.groups.yahoo.com/group/Metabolic_Syndrome/; alternate path: http://www.groups.yahoo.com/, search for "metabolic syndrome" in the "Find a Yahoo! Group" Search box and then click on the group "Metabolic Syndrome."

This online Yahoo! support group is for patients with metabolic syndrome and their families and friends. Yahoo! Groups is not a medical site, nor does it provide or endorse medical advice or procedures. The purpose of the website is to share experiences in a kind and caring manner. Free membership is required to participate.

Pericarditis

The pericardium is a three-layered sac that surrounds the heart. The inner layer, called the visceral pericardium, is in contact with the heart. The outer layer, called the parietal pericardium, is a fibrous sac that protects the heart from the rubbing of the lungs during the process of breathing. Between these two layers is a layer of fluid that allows the inner and outer layers to move smoothly over each other without friction. When the pericardium becomes irritated, inflamed, or infected, that condition is called pericarditis.

Pericarditis has many causes, usually a bacterial, fungal, or viral infection. However, pericarditis is associated with many other causes, such as heart surgery or other trauma, heart attack, tumors in or rubbing against the pericardium, cancer, radiation therapy, some autoimmune diseases, and some other diseases (e.g., tuberculosis, kidney disease). In some cases no cause may be identified, which is called idiopathic pericarditis. Pericarditis can occur suddenly (acute) or be long-standing (chronic).

Pericarditis can feel like a heart attack, with a sharp pain in the center of the chest. The pain is usually worse when the patient swallows, coughs, or reclines. Leaning forward usually eases the pain. When acute, a fever is often present, along with weakness, breathing troubles, coughing, and feeling the heart skipping beats (palpitations). When chronic, chest pain may be absent, but tiredness, coughing, and shortness of breath are present. Pericarditis can be further diagnosed by heart sounds (pericardial rub) and imaging techniques (excess fluid around heart). Certain electrocardiogram (EKG) diagnostic results may suggest pericarditis (*see* CHAPTER 5 *for information on EKG*).

Depending on its type, pericarditis can lead to serious complications. Arrhythmias can result from rubbing or pressure. If there is too much fluid in the middle layer (e.g., from infection or trauma), cardiac tamponade may result, causing compression of the heart and preventing the heart ventricle from expanding normally. The blood pressure drops as the heart tries to overcome the pressure. If the pressure is quickly relieved, the heart may recover; if not, it can be fatal. With chronic pericarditis, the pericardium becomes scarred and stiff over time. This is a condition called constrictive pericarditis. The heart has difficulty working against the stiff pericardium, and this can lead to heart failure.

Resources for Further Information on Pericarditis
Websites

> Aetna InteliHealth—"Pericarditis." http://www.intelihealth.com/IH/ihtIH/
WSIHW000/8059/23696/284782.html?d=dmtHealthAZ; alternate path: http://
www.intelihealth.com/, search for and then click on the title "Pericarditis."
The InteliHealth website provides an overview of pericarditis, including definitions, symptoms, diagnosis, expected duration, prevention, treatment, when to call
a professional, and prognosis. Aetna InteliHealth, a subsidiary of Aetna, is reviewed
by the faculty of Harvard Medical School and the University College of Dental
Medicine. According to Aetna InteliHealth's website, "Aetna InteliHealth maintains
absolute editorial independence. That means that Aetna InteliHealth makes decisions about the information on our site free of outside influence." Under "Healthy
Lifestyle," Aetna InteliHealth also offers free health-related e-mail subscriptions.

> American Association of Retired People (AARP)—"Pericarditis Learning
Center." http://healthtools.aarp.org/learning-center/pericarditis; alternate path:
http://aarp.org/, search for "pericarditis," and then click on the title "Learn about
Pericarditis."
AARP's health section on pericarditis offers a consumer-friendly wealth of information, such as definitions, causes, incidence, risk factors, symptoms and signs,
tests, treatment, expectations (prognosis), complications, prevention, and heart
research news. With membership, you will receive a magazine that includes current health information focusing on patients age 50 and older.

> CardioSmart—"Acute Pericarditis." https://www.cardiosmart.org/HeartDisease/
CTT.aspx?id=92; alternate path: https://www.cardiosmart.org/, search for and
then click on the title "Acute Pericarditis."
CardioSmart provides an easy-to-use website on understanding acute pericarditis, which is discussed in such subsections as definitions, basic facts, causes, risk
factors, signs and symptoms, complications, diagnosis, tests, treatment, and prevention. According to the American College of Cardiology (ACC), "CardioSmart
is the patient education and support program launched by the [ACC]. Our mission is to engage, inform, and empower patients to better prepare them for participation in their own care."

> Cleveland Clinic (Cleveland, OH)—"Pericarditis." http://my.clevelandclinic.org/
heart/disorders/other/pericarditis.aspx; alternate path: http://my.clevelandclinic
.org/, under the category "Institutes and Services," click on "Heart and Vascular"
and then click on "Homepage," click on the category "Diseases and Conditions," and
then click on the title "Pericarditis."
The Cleveland Clinic provides comprehensive patient-friendly information on
pericarditis, such as definitions of pericardium and pericarditis, risk factors,

causes, symptoms, diagnosis, diagnostic tests, treatments, and possible complications, outlook, and help finding a doctor who treats pericarditis. The Cleveland Clinic also offers a link to "Chat Online with a Heart and Vascular Nurse." For information on clinical trials, see the Cleveland Clinic entry on pp. 31–32.

➤ ClinicalTrials.gov—Pericarditis clinical trials. http://clinicaltrials.gov/ct2/ results?term=pericarditis; alternate path: http://clinicaltrials.gov/, type "pericarditis" in the Search for Studies box at the top of the screen.

To limit your results, click on "Modify This Search" and select specific fields, such as (1) Recruitment (e.g., you might want to select "Open Studies"); (2) Locations (e.g., select your state); and (3) Age Group, and then click on the "Search" button. Click on the title of each trial name for additional information, such as purpose of the study, study design and type, detailed description, outcome measures, eligibility (age, gender, criteria for participating), study start date, estimated study completion date, and sponsor. ClinicalTrials.gov, developed by the U.S. National Institutes of Health of the National Library of Medicine, lists ongoing and currently enrolling clinical trials. Check often for new studies.

➤ eMedicineHealth—"Pericarditis." http://www.emedicinehealth.com/pericarditis/ article_em.htm and http://www.emedicinehealth.com/pericarditis-health/article _em.htm; alternate path: http://www.emedicinehealth.com/, search for and then click on the title "Pericarditis" (Medical Reference from eMedicineHealth and from Healthwise).

eMedicineHealth, a division of WebMD, offers a comprehensive article on pericarditis, including an overview, causes, symptoms, when to seek medical care, diagnosis, treatment, medication, prevention, outlook, and follow-up.

➤ Johns Hopkins Hospital, Heart and Vascular Institute (Baltimore, MD). "Pericardial Disease" (Conditions and Treatments). http://www.hopkinsmedicine .org/heart_vascular_institute/conditions_treatments/conditions/pericardial _disease.html and http://www.hopkinsmedicine.org/healthlibrary/conditions/ adult/cardiovascular_diseases/pericarditis_85,P00235/; alternate path: http:// www.hopkinsmedicine.org/, search for and then click on the title "Pericardial Disease"; for a related resource, also click on "Cardiovascular Diseases— Pericardial Disease."

The Johns Hopkins Heart and Vascular Institute website on pericardial disease discusses definitions, types of pericardial disease, when to call an ambulance, symptoms, causes, prevention, diagnosis, and treatment. It also lists links to physicians and specialists (with profiles, e.g., specialty, medical board certification, education) who treat pericardial disease. Also click on the heading "Clinical Trials" for links to current trials in various heart and cardiovascular conditions.

➤ Mayo Clinic (Rochester, MN)—"Pericarditis." http://www.mayoclinic.com/
health/pericarditis/DS00505; alternate path: http://www.mayoclinic.com/, search
for "pericarditis," and then click on the title "Pericarditis—MayoClinic.com."
Written for patients, this webpage on pericarditis includes definitions, symptoms, causes, complications, preparing for your appointment, tests and diagnosis, and treatments and drugs. There is also a more comprehensive section titled
"In-Depth" on some of these topics. For information on clinical trials and patient
services, see the Mayo Clinic entry on p. 36.

➤ MedicineNet—"Pericarditis." http://www.medicinenet.com/pericarditis/article
.htm; alternate path: http://www.medicinenet.com/, click on the major topic "Diseases and Conditions," click on "Conditions A–Z," then click on "P," and then
scroll down to "Pericarditis."
MedicineNet is owned and operated by WebMD and is part of the WebMD Network. According to its website, MedicineNet "provides easy-to-read, in-depth,
authoritative medical information for consumers via its user-friendly, interactive
website." In-depth information on pericarditis includes definitions, causes,
symptoms, diagnosis, treatment, complications, patient discussions, and finding
a local cardiologist. The medical information is written and edited by a nationally recognized group of more than 70 U.S. board-certified physicians. The website contains a "Symptom Checker" listed in alphabetical order as a guide to
"pinpoint your pain." Its homepage links to "Health News of the Week." You can
also sign up to receive a health newsletter.

➤ MedlinePlus. http://www.nlm.nih.gov/.
MedlinePlus is a component of the National Institutes of Health (NIH), produced by the National Library of Medicine (NLM), and is updated regularly. You
can find the following and related resources from the homepage; under "Databases," click on "MedlinePlus" and then search for the resource by title.

- "Pericardial Disorders." http://www.nlm.nih.gov/medlineplus/pericardial
disorders.html. This MedlinePlus website on pericardial disorders offers
linked information covering overviews, diagnosis/symptoms, treatment,
specific conditions, related issues, clinical trials, journal articles, organizations, and a specific section focusing on children. Patient handouts are also
available.

- "Pericarditis." http://www.nlm.nih.gov/medlineplus/ency/article/000182
.htm. This MedlinePlus webpage on pericarditis offers an overview on
causes, symptoms, exams and tests, treatment, outlook (prognosis), possible
complications, when to contact a medical professional, and prevention. For
more information, under the heading "Read More," click on "Pericarditis—
After Heart Attack."

> Medscape Reference (Drugs, Diseases, and Procedures)—"Acute Pericarditis." http://emedicine.medscape.com/article/156951-overview; alternate path: http://emedicine.medscape.com/, search for and then click on the title "Acute Pericarditis."
>
> Written for Medscape by Sean Spangler, MD, and associates, this webpage presents a comprehensive report on acute pericarditis. Although written for health care professionals, it might be helpful for interested laypersons. Articles for Medscape Reference are written by medical experts. The webpage states, "Our rigorous literature survey process allows us to rapidly integrate new practice-changing information into the relevant topics by systematically reviewing the major medical and pharmacy journals, news announcements, and important practice guidelines." Free registration is required.

> *The Merck Manual Home Health Handbook for Patients and Caregivers*—"Pericardial Disease." http://www.nlm.nih.gov/medlineplus/ency/article/000182.htm; alternate path: http://www.merckmanuals.com/home/, under "Sections," click on "All" next to the navigational arrows to view a complete list, then click on the section "Heart and Blood Vessel Disorders," and then scroll down to the section titled "Pericardial Disease."
>
> This webpage on pericardial disease is divided into three sections, "Overview of Pericardial Disease," "Acute Pericarditis," and "Chronic Pericarditis," including information on causes, symptoms, diagnosis, prognosis, and treatment, and is based on a well-known medical textbook titled *The Merck Manual Home Health Handbook for Patients and Caregivers*. It is "provided free of charge . . . as a public service."

> National Heart, Lung, and Blood Institute (NHLBI)—"Pericarditis." http://www.nhlbi.nih.gov/health/dci/Diseases/peri/peri_whatis.html; alternate path: http://www.nhlbi.nih.gov/, search for "pericarditis," and then click on the title "What Is Pericarditis?"
>
> NHLBI, a division of National Institutes of Health from the U.S. Department of Health and Human Services, provides additional information on pericarditis, including links to definitions, causes, risk factors, signs and symptoms, diagnosis, treatments, living with pericarditis, clinical trials, and key points.

> Texas Heart Institute (Houston, TX)—"Pericarditis." http://www.texasheartinstitute.org/HIC/Topics/Cond/pericard.cfm; alternate path: http://www.texasheartinstitute.org/, search for and then click on the title "Pericarditis"; or under the heading "Heart Information Center," click on "Heart-Health Topics," then click on "Heart Conditions," and then click on "Pericarditis."
>
> The Texas Heart Institute website offers a definition of pericarditis, as well as information on causes, signs and symptoms, diagnosis, and treatment. One section allows users to "Ask a Texas Heart Institute Doctor" questions. Click on

"Heart Doctor Answers" to explore the questions and answers already published there. An easy-to-print format is available. For information on clinical trials, see the Texas Heart Institute entry on p. 40.

➢ UCLA Ronald Reagan Medical Center (Los Angeles, CA)—"Pericarditis." http://www .uclahealth.org/body.cfm?id=592; scroll down to the heading "Diseases and Conditions," and click on the title "Pericarditis"; alternate path: http://www.uclahealth .org/, under the heading "For Patients and Visitors," scroll down and mouse over the category "Health Resources" and then click on "Heart Health Center," then scroll down to the heading "Diseases and Conditions," and click on the title "Pericarditis." The UCLA Ronald Reagan Medical Center's Heart Health Center provides detailed information on pericarditis, which includes definition, causes, symptoms, exams and tests, treatment, outlook (prognosis), possible complications, when to contact a medical professional, and prevention. Also click on the title to the related disease "Bacterial Pericarditis." On the Heart Health Center website, under the heading "Tests and Treatments," scroll under the section "Alternative Medicine" for more treatment information, then click on the word "More," and then click on the title "Pericarditis." For more information on patient resources and clinical trials, see the UCLA entry on p. 41.

➢ WebMD. http://www.webmd.com/.
According to WebMD, "WebMD News is an independent media service designed to provide news, information, and educational material to consumers and physicians. News content created by WebMD is free from influence by sponsors, partners, or other sources." Available is a WebMD's heart health e-mail newsletter. You can find the following resources from the homepage through a title search.
  • "Heart Disease and Pericarditis." http://www.webmd.com/heart-disease/ pericarditis-directory. The WebMD website offers the latest information on pericarditis topics such as causes, symptoms, diagnosis, treatment, what constrictive pericarditis is, symptoms of constrictive pericarditis, diagnosis of constrictive pericarditis, and treatment of constrictive pericarditis.
  • "Pericarditis Directory." http://www.webmd.com/heart-disease/pericarditis -directory. This WebMD webpage on pericarditis offers an extensive directory divided by categories: medical reference, features, videos, slide shows, and images and health tools.

Patient Support Groups and Organizations

➢ MedHelp—"Pericarditis." http://www.medhelp.org/search?query=pericarditis; alternate path: http://www.medhelp.org/, search for "pericarditis."
According to its website, MedHelp "connects people with the leading medical experts," such as those from Cleveland Clinic, National Jewish Health, Partners Health, and Mount Sinai Hospital, with those who have similar medical issues.

MedHelp's main focus is to enable patients "to take control over their health and find answers to their medical questions" using nontechnical language via an online community through posts, forums and groups, blogs, user journals, as well as recommendations, articles, health pages, and a medical glossary. Free registration is required.

➤ U.S. Hospital Finder. http://www.ushospitalfinder.com/.
Use this site to find the names of hospitals by zip code, city, state, or your address. The search results include a map with directions. You might also want to ask your health care professional, call hospitals in your area, or search for "support groups" on hospital websites to determine if there are any cardiology support groups for people with pericarditis that meet regularly in your area.

➤ Yahoo! Groups—"Pericarditis1 Support Group." http://health.groups.yahoo.com/group/pericarditis1/; alternate path: http://www.groups.yahoo.com/, search for "pericarditis" in the "Find a Yahoo! Group" Search box and then click on the group "Pericarditis1."
This online Yahoo! group is for patients with pericarditis and their families and friends. Yahoo! Groups is not a medical site, nor does it provide or endorse medical advice or procedures. The purpose of the website is to share experiences in a kind and caring manner. Free registration is required to participate.

Peripheral Arterial Disease

Peripheral arterial disease (PAD) is a hardening of the large arteries in the arms and legs. It is similar to and is caused by arteriosclerosis (*see earlier section* CORONARY ARTERY DISEASE). The root causes of arteriosclerosis are unknown. However, it is known that certain factors can damage the lining of arteries and lead to PAD. These factors include smoking, high fats and cholesterol in the blood, high blood pressure, and high blood sugar (related to insulin resistance or diabetes).

In PAD, the peripheral arteries become damaged and a plaque (of calcium, fats, cholesterol, and excess fibers) forms in the injured area, narrowing the blood vessel. The narrowed artery slows the amount of blood reaching the affected limb, initially causing intermittent claudication. Claudication is pain, numbness, aching, or heaviness in a limb during physical activity that goes away when resting. During physical activity, muscles need more blood flow because they are working. The decreased flow through the narrowed artery causes the symptoms. When resting, the muscles do not need as much blood and the symptoms are relieved.

PAD is also indicated by weak or absent pulses in the legs or feet, sores or wounds on the toes, feet, or legs that heal slowly, poorly, or not at all; a pale, bluish color or bruised appearance to the skin of the affected limb; a lower temperature in one limb compared to the other limb; poor nail growth on the toes or fingers; and decreased hair growth on the limbs.

To learn more, visit the **National Heart, Lung, and Blood Institute** of the National Institutes of Health at http://www.nhlbi.nih.gov/health/health-topics/topics/cad and http://www.nhlbi.nih.gov/health/health-topics/topics/pad (alternate path: http://www.nhlbi.nih.gov/, search for "coronary artery disease," and then click on the title "What Is Coronary Artery Disease?—NHLBI, NIH"; search for "peripheral arterial disease," and then click on the title "What Is Peripheral Arterial Disease?— NHLBI, NIH"). On these webpages are illustrations showing, respectively, narrowing of an artery and the difference between a normal and an atherosclerotic artery filled with plaque caused by PAD.

If, as in coronary artery disease (*see earlier section* CORONARY ARTERY DISEASE), the plaque breaks, a clot may form at the break and completely block the artery. In this case, the limb may die (necrose), become gangrenous (a disease caused by loss of blood and infection in the injured area), and may need to be amputated.

Resources for Further Information on Peripheral Arterial Disease

Brochures, Booklets, and Other Short Print Publications

➢ American Heart Association (AHA). http://www.heart.org/.
  • "Peripheral Artery Disease" (Educational Brochures). http://www.heart.org/ HEARTORG/General/About-Your-Peripheral-Artery-Disease_UCM_313197 _Article.jsp; alternate path: http://www.heart.org/, search for "educational brochures," click on the title "Order American Heart Association Educational Brochures," and then click on the topic "Peripheral Artery Disease." A brochure titled "About Your Peripheral Artery Disease" is available. This brochure can be ordered by filling in a form online. (No more than one packet and two brochures per household can be ordered at no cost.)
  • "Peripheral Artery Disease" (Information Sheets). http://www.heart.org/ HEARTORG/Conditions/More/PeripheralArteryDisease/Peripheral-Artery -Disease_UCM_002082_SubHomePage.jsp; alternate path: http://www .heart.org/, search for "peripheral artery disease," click on the title "Visit Our Peripheral Artery Disease Website," scroll down to the section called "Tools," and then click on the title "Printable PAD Information Sheet."

Websites

➢ Aetna InteliHealth—"Peripheral Artery Disease." http://www.intelihealth.com/ IH/ihtIH/WSIHW000/35072/35115/266764.html?d=dmtHealthAZ; alternate path: http://www.intelihealth.com/, search for and then click on the title "Peripheral Artery Disease."

This webpage provides an overview of peripheral artery disease, including what PAD is, who gets PAD, symptoms, diagnosing PAD, treatment, and the bottom line. Aetna InteliHealth, a subsidiary of Aetna, is reviewed by the faculty of Harvard Medical School and the University College of Dental Medicine. According to Aetna InteliHealth's website, "Aetna InteliHealth maintains absolute editorial independence. That means that Aetna InteliHealth makes decisions about the information on our site free of outside influence." Under "Healthy Lifestyle," Aetna InteliHealth also offers free health-related e-mail subscriptions.

➢ American Heart Association (AHA)—"Peripheral Artery Disease (PAD)." http://www.heart.org/HEARTORG/Conditions/More/PeripheralArteryDisease/Peripheral-Artery-Disease_UCM_002082_SubHomePage.jsp; alternate path: http://www.heart.org/, search for "peripheral artery disease," and then click on the title "Visit our Peripheral Artery Disease Website."
AHA provides details such as descriptions, why PAD matters, risk factors, symptoms and diagnosis, and prevention and treatment. You can also sign up for a free heart health e-newsletter.

➢ Brigham and Women's Hospital (BWH) (Boston, MA)—"Peripheral Vascular Disease" (Animation). http://healthlibrary.brighamandwomens.org/InteractiveTools/Animations/94,P08450; alternate path: http://www.brighamandwomens.org/, scroll under the heading "Health Information" to the category titled "Interactive Tools and Media," click on the title "Animations," and then scroll down and click on the topic "Peripheral Vascular Disease."
BWH offers an easy-to-understand animation on what is peripheral vascular disease that can be accessed by clicking on the "Launch Animation" link. According to its website, "Peripheral vascular disease or PVD is a slow, progressive circulation disorder that may affect any of the veins, arteries, or lymph vessels. By viewing this animation, you can learn more about what you can do to prevent this disease." For information on clinical trials, see the BWH entry on p. 29.

➢ CardioSmart—"Peripheral Arterial Disease (PAD)." https://www.cardiosmart.org/HeartDisease/CTT.aspx?id=134; alternate path: https://www.cardiosmart.org/, search for and then click on the title "Peripheral Arterial Disease."
CardioSmart provides an easy-to-use website on understanding PAD, which is discussed in subsections such as what PAD is, basic facts, causes, risk factors, signs and symptoms, diagnosis, treatment, prevention, and living with PAD. According to the American College of Cardiology (ACC), "CardioSmart is the patient education and support program launched by the [ACC]. Our mission is to engage, inform, and empower patients to better prepare them for participation in their own care."

➤ CenterWatch—Clinical trials listing service. http://www.centerwatch.com/.
This CenterWatch clinical trials listing service lists trials currently looking for
volunteers to enroll in medical studies. Click on the "Clinical Trials" heading
and search by location, medical condition, or therapeutic area. To search by
location, click on your state (or country) and click on a city near you to find
information on each available clinical trial. Check back with this website often
for new studies. Sign up for a free e-mail service that sends notice of new
clinical trials.

- "Peripheral Arterial Disease (PAD) Clinical Trials." http://www.centerwatch
  .com/clinical-trials/listings/studylist.aspx?CatID=698.
- "Peripheral Arterial Occlusive Disease Clinical Trials." http://www.centerwatch
  .com/clinical-trials/listings/studylist.aspx?CatID=204.
- "Peripheral Vascular Disease Clinical Trials." http://www.centerwatch.com/
  clinical-trials/listings/studylist.aspx?CatID=208.

Alternate path: http://www.centerwatch.com/, under the category "Patient
Resources," click on "Search Clinical Trials" where you can search by medical
condition, click on the medical condition's first letter (e.g., "P"), and then click
on the specific term (e.g., "Peripheral Arterial Disease"). The "Search Clinical
Trials" page also allows searching by location and therapeutic area.

➤ Cleveland Clinic (Cleveland, OH)—"Peripheral Arterial Disease (PAD)." http://my
.clevelandclinic.org/heart/disorders/vascular/pad.aspx; alternate path: http://
my.clevelandclinic.org/, under the category "Institutes and Services," click on
"Heart and Vascular," then click on "Homepage," then click on the category "Diseases
and Conditions," and then click on the title "Peripheral Arterial Disease (PAD)."
The Cleveland Clinic provides comprehensive patient-friendly information on
PAD, such as links to definitions, symptoms and risk factors, peripheral artery
disease, circulation in the legs, warning signs, causes, symptoms, lower extremity
ulcers, and intestinal ischemic syndrome. The Cleveland Clinic also offers a link
to "Chat Online with a Heart and Vascular Nurse." For information on clinical
trials, see the Cleveland Clinic entry on pp. 31–32.

➤ ClinicalTrials.gov. http://clinicaltrials.gov/.
ClinicalTrials.gov, developed by the U.S. National Institutes of Health of the
National Library of Medicine, lists ongoing and currently enrolling clinical trials.
To find clinical trials from the homepage, search for the condition by name (e.g.,
"arrhythmia"), which will generate a list of possibly hundreds or thousands of
studies. To limit your results, click on "Modify This Search" and select specific
fields, such as (1) Recruitment (e.g., you might want to select "Open Studies");
(2) Locations (e.g., select your state); and (3) Age Group, and then click on the
"Search" button. Click on the title of each trial name for additional information,
such as purpose of the study, study design and type, detailed description, outcome

measures, eligibility (age, gender, criteria for participating), study start date, estimated study completion date, and sponsor. Check often for new studies.

- Peripheral arterial disease clinical trials. http://clinicaltrials.gov/ct2/results/refine?term=peripheral+arterial+disease.
- Peripheral artery disease clinical trials. http://clinicaltrials.gov/ct2/results/refine?term=peripheral+artery+disease.
- Peripheral vascular disease clinical trials. http://clinicaltrials.gov/ct2/results/refine?term=peripheral+vascular+disease.

➢ eMedicineHealth. http://www.emedicinehealth.com/.
From the homepage, you can find the following resources by searching for the condition by name and then clicking on the appropriate title.

- "Blood Clots" and "Blood Clots: Differences in Vein Clots and Artery Clots." http://www.emedicinehealth.com/blood_clots/article_em.htm and http://www.emedicinehealth.com/blood_clots_differences_in_vein_clots _and_artery_clots-health/article_em.htm. eMedicineHealth, a division of WebMD, offers a comprehensive article on blood clots, including an overview, causes, when to seek medical care, symptoms, diagnosis, treatment, medications, prevention, next steps, and follow-up.
- "Peripheral Vascular Disease" and "Peripheral Arterial Disease of the Legs." http://www.emedicinehealth.com/peripheral_vascular_disease/article_em .htm and http://www.emedicinehealth.com/peripheral_arterial_disease_of _the_legs-health/article_em.htm. eMedicineHealth, a division of WebMD, offers a comprehensive article on peripheral vascular disease, including an overview, causes, when to seek medical care, symptoms, diagnosis, treatment, medications, prevention, follow-up, and support groups.

➢ Harvard Medical School, *Harvard Women's Health Watch*—"Peripheral Artery Disease (PAD)." http://www.health.harvard.edu/newsletters/Harvard_Womens _Health_Watch/2012/April/peripheral-artery-disease; alternate path: http:// www.health.harvard.edu/, search for and then click on the title "Peripheral Artery Disease—Harvard Health Publications."
Harvard Women's Health Watch is part of a series of consumer-friendly newsletters from Harvard Health Publications. Some information is free, such as who gets PAD, symptoms, diagnosis, and risk factors. Full reports can be purchased for a nominal fee. Also available from Harvard Health Publications are free weekly *HEALTHbeat* e-newsletters.

➢ Hospital of the University of Pennsylvania (HUP) (Philadelphia, PA)—"Vascular Surgery and Endovascular Therapy Program." http://www.pennmedicine.org/ heart/patient/clinical-services/vascular-surgery/; alternate path: http://www .pennmedicine.org/, click on the "Departments and Services" icon (or search for "departments and services"), scroll down and click on the category "Cardiology and Cardiac Surgery," and then scroll down under the heading "Clinical Services" and click on "Vascular Surgery and Endovascular Therapy."

At its Penn Heart and Vascular Center website, HUP offers website links in the Vascular Surgery and Endovascular Therapy Program that include an "Overview" (what blood vessel repair is and reconstruction and treatment options); the "Team," which links to each physician and specialist (with profiles, e.g., specialty, medical board certification, education); "Clinical Trials"; "The Penn Difference" (program described, patient experiences, unique capabilities and expertise, and hospital highlights); "Featured Video"; and "Quality/Outcomes." Click on each treatment option for details and charts. A 54-page *Penn Heart and Vascular 2011 Clinical Activity Report* is available for download; this report is a "summary of surgical, medical and interventional outcomes, as well as clinical research activity and patient volumes." You can also subscribe to the Penn Heart newsletter. For information on clinical trials, see the HUP entry on p. 33.

> Insidermedicine. http://www.insidermedicine.com/.

The Insidermedicine website offers a variety of heart-health-related videos. From the homepage, you can search for videos by title, or you can search by topic (e.g., peripheral artery disease) to find other related videos. For more information on the Insidermedicine Project, see the earlier entry on pp. 33–34.

- "Standard Test for Peripheral Artery Disease (PAD) Fails to Identify Who Would Benefit from Aspirin Therapy." http://www.insidermedicine.com/archives/ASPIRIN_VIDEO_Standard_Test_for_Peripheral_Artery_Disease_Fails_to_Identify_Who_Would_Benefit_From_Aspirin_Therapy_4135.aspx. According to the website, a "standard test for [PAD] fails to identify those without cardiovascular disease who might benefit from aspirin therapy." In this video, a medical specialist speaks about what PAD is and the beneficial use of aspirin therapy for PAD.

- "Treadmill Exercise Program Improves Quality of Life in Patients with Peripheral Artery Disease" (Interview with Dr. Mary McDermott, MD, Northwestern University). http://www.insidermedicine.com/archives/Treadmill_Exercise_Program_Improves_Quality_of_Life_in_Patients_with_Peripheral_Artery_Disease_Interview_with_Dr_Mary_McDermott_MD_Northwestern_University_3187.aspx. In this video, the medical specialist explains in easy-to-understand language the results of a six-month study comparing "supervised treadmill exercise or lower extremity resistance training" with no exercise by patients with PAD.

> Johns Hopkins Hospital (Baltimore, MD). http://www.hopkinsmedicine.org/.

The Johns Hopkins Heart and Vascular Institute website provides detailed information on a variety of conditions, treatments, and services. It also lists links to physicians and specialists (with profiles, e.g., specialty, medical board certification, education). Click on the heading "Clinical Trials" to find links to current trials in various heart and cardiovascular conditions. From the homepage, you can find the following resources by searching for the topic by title.

- "Peripheral Arterial Disease." http://www.hopkinsmedicine.org/heart_vascular _institute/conditions_treatments/conditions/peripheral_arterial_disease .html and http://www.hopkinsmedicine.org/healthlibrary/conditions/adult/ cardiovascular_diseases/peripheral_vascular_disease_85,P00236/. This website on peripheral arterial disease (PAD) discusses what PAD is, when to call a doctor, symptoms, causes, risks, prevention, diagnosis, and treatment.
- "Vascular Surgery and Endovascular Therapy." http://www.hopkinsmedicine .org/surgery/div/Vascular.html. The Johns Hopkins Cardiomyopathy and Heart Failure Service provides patient-friendly information on vascular surgery and endovascular therapy, which is a treatment option for peripheral arterial occlusive disease. Also described are other cardiovascular uses for vascular surgery.

➢ Khan Academy. http://www.khanacademy.org/.
Salman Khan, creator of the nonprofit Khan Academy, sketches as he explains each topic. Khan's mini lessons are all downloadable and free. According to the website, "With a library of over 2,400 videos covering everything from arithmetic to physics, finance, and history and 150 practice exercises, we're on a mission to help you learn what you want, when you want, at your own pace." Click on the heading "About" to get the maximum use of this excellent site. Khan has three degrees from the Massachusetts Institute of Technology and an MBA from Harvard University. From the homepage, you can find the following resources by searching for the topic by title.

- "Heart Failure, Angina, Cardiac Arrest." http://www.khanacademy.org/science/ healthcare-and-medicine/heart-disease-and-stroke/v/heart-disease-and -heart-attacks?playlist=Biology.
- "Stenosis, Ischemia, and Heart Failure: Clarifying a Bunch of Medical Terms around Heart Disease." http://www.khanacademy.org/science/ healthcare-and-medicine/heart-disease-and-stroke/v/stenosis--ischemia -and-heart-failure.
- "Thrombo-emboli and Thromboembolisms: Clarifying Difference between a Thrombus and an Embolus (and between Thrombosis and Embolism)." http://www.khanacademy.org/science/healthcare-and-medicine/heart -disease-and-stroke/v/thrombo-emboli-and-thromboembolisms.

➢ Mayo Clinic (Rochester, MN)—"Peripheral Artery Disease (PAD)." http://www .mayoclinic.com/health/peripheral-arterial-disease/DS00537; alternate path: http://www.mayoclinic.com/, search for "peripheral artery disease," and click on the title "Peripheral Artery Disease (PAD)—MayoClinic.com."
Written for patients, this webpage on peripheral artery disease includes definitions, symptoms, causes, risk factors, complications, preparing for appointments,

tests and diagnosis, treatments and drugs, lifestyle and home remedies, coping and support, and prevention. There is also a more comprehensive section titled "In-Depth" on some of these topics. For information on clinical trials and patient services, see the Mayo Clinic entry on p. 36.

➢ MedicineNet—"Peripheral Vascular Disease (PVD, Peripheral Artery Disease, Peripheral Arterial Disease, PAD)." http://www.medicinenet.com/peripheral _vascular_disease/article.htm; alternate path: http://www.medicinenet.com/, click on the major topic "Diseases and Conditions," click on "Conditions A–Z," then click on "P," and then scroll down to "Peripheral Vascular Disease."
MedicineNet is owned and operated by WebMD and is a part of the WebMD Network. According to its website, MedicineNet "provides easy-to-read, in-depth, authoritative medical information for consumers via its user-friendly, interactive website." In-depth information on peripheral vascular disease includes discussion of what peripheral vascular disease is, how atherosclerosis causes disease, risks, complications, causes, symptoms, diagnosis, treatment, lifestyle changes, patient discussions, and finding a local cardiologist. The medical information is written and edited by a nationally recognized group of more than 70 U.S. board-certified physicians. The website contains a "Symptom Checker" listed in alphabetical order as a guide to "pinpoint your pain." Its homepage links to "Health News of the Week." You can also sign up to receive a health newsletter.

➢ MedlinePlus—"Peripheral Arterial Disease." http://www.nlm.nih.gov/medlineplus/ peripheralarterialdisease.html; alternate path: http://www.nlm.nih.gov/, under "Databases," click on "MedlinePlus" and then search for "peripheral arterial disease."
MedlinePlus is a component of the National Institutes of Health (NIH), produced by the National Library of Medicine (NLM), and is updated regularly. This MedlinePlus webpage on peripheral arterial disease offers extensive linked information covering overviews, news, diagnosis/symptoms, treatment, prevention/ screening, specific conditions, related issues, clinical trials, research, journal articles, directories, organizations, and sections that focus on women and seniors. Plus there are patient handouts available, as well as related information in the linked *MedlinePlus Magazine*. This webpage also includes a multimedia section containing health check tools and tutorials.

➢ *The Merck Manual Home Health Handbook for Patients and Caregivers*— "Peripheral Arterial Disease (PAD)." http://www.merckmanuals.com/home/sec03/ ch032/ch032a.html; alternate path: http://www.merckmanuals.com/home/, under "Sections," click on "All" by the navigational arrows to see a complete list, then click on the section "Heart and Blood Vessel Disorders," and then scroll down to the section "Peripheral Arterial Disease."

This website is divided into three titles: "Overview of PAD," "Occlusive PAD," and "Functional PAD." Occlusive PAD includes additional information on symptoms, diagnosis, prevention, and treatment. Functional PAD discusses Raynaud's syndrome, acrocyanosis, and erythromelalgia. These sections are based on a well-known medical textbook titled *The Merck Manual Home Health Handbook for Patients and Caregivers* and is "provided free of charge . . . as a public service."

➢ National Heart, Lung, and Blood Institute (NHLBI)—"What Is Peripheral Arterial Disease (PAD)?" http://www.nhlbi.nih.gov/health/dci/Diseases/pad/pad_what.html; alternate path: http://www.nhlbi.nih.gov/, search for "peripheral arterial disease," and then click on the title "What Is Peripheral Arterial Disease?"
NHLBI, a division of the National Institutes of Health from the U.S. Department of Health and Human Services, provides information on PAD, including links to what PAD is, other names, causes, risk factors, signs and symptoms, diagnosis, treatments, prevention, living with PAD, clinical trials, and key points.

➢ New York–Presbyterian (NYP) University Hospital of Columbia and Cornell (New York, NY)—"Lower Extremity Arterial Disease." http://nyp.org/services/lower -extremity-arterial-disease.html; alternate path: http://nyp.org/, search for and then click on the title "Lower Extremity Arterial Disease—New York-Presbyterian."
NYP University Hospital of Columbia and Cornell provides patient-friendly information on treatment, risks, and symptoms of lower extremity arterial disease. Under the heading "Clinical Services" is expanded information on "unusual vascular conditions" and "vascular disease screening and prevention," and under the heading "Health Library," click on "Vascular" and then "Peripheral Vascular Disease" for more information in this condition. Under the heading "Related Links" are links to various NYU–Presbyterian medical centers for vascular surgery. For information on clinical trials, see the NYP entry on p. 38.

➢ Texas Heart Institute (Houston, TX). http://www.texasheartinstitute.org/.
For information on clinical trials, see the Texas Heart Institute entry on p. 40.
  • "Peripheral Vascular Disease (PVD)." http://www.texasheartinstitute.org/ HIC/Topics/Cond/pvd.cfm. The Texas Heart Institute website offers definitions of PVD, as well as information on (1) arterial blockage, its causes, symptoms, diagnosis, and treatment; (2) aortic aneurysm, its causes, symptoms, detection, and treatment; (3) venous blood clots, its causes, symptoms, diagnosis, and treatment; (4) pulmonary embolism, its symptoms, diagnosis, and treatment; and (5) how to avoid deep vein thrombosis.
  • "Vulnerable Plaque." http://www.texasheartinstitute.org/HIC/Topics/Cond/ vulplaq.cfm. The Texas Heart Institute website offers a definition of vulnerable plaque as well as information on causes, detection, and prevention.
Alternate path: http://www.texasheartinstitute.org/, search for the topic by name (e.g., "peripheral vascular disease"), and then click on the appropriate title; or in

the pull-down menu under "Heart Information Center," select "Heart-Health Topics" and then "Heart Conditions," and then click on the topic by name.

➢ UCLA Ronald Reagan Medical Center (Los Angeles, CA)—"Peripheral Arterial Disease." http://www.uclahealth.org/body.cfm?id=592; scroll down to the heading "In-Depth Reports," then click on the word "More," and then click on the title "Peripheral Arterial Disease"; alternate path: http://www.uclahealth.org/, under the heading "For Patients and Visitors," scroll down and mouse over the category "Health Resources" and then click on "Heart Health Center," scroll down to the heading "In-Depth Reports," click on the word "More," and then click on the title "Peripheral Arterial Disease."

The UCLA Ronald Reagan Medical Center's Heart Health Center provides several in-depth reports on lifestyle changes to lower risk of heart disease. They include such sections as highlights, introductions, symptoms, risk factors, diagnosis, complications, treatment, lifestyle changes, medications, and surgery. For more information on patient resources and clinical trials, see the UCLA entry on p. 41.

➢ WebMD. http://www.webmd.com/.

According to WebMD, "WebMD News is an independent media service designed to provide news, information, and educational material to consumers and physicians. News content created by WebMD is free from influence by sponsors, partners, or other sources." From the homepage, you can find the following resources through a title search.

- "Peripheral Arterial Disease Directory." http://www.webmd.com/heart -disease/peripheral-arterial-disease-pad-directory. This WebMD webpage offers additional information on PAD in sections such as medical references and videos.
- "Peripheral Arterial Disease of the Legs." http://www.webmd.com/heart -disease/tc/peripheral-arterial-disease-of-the-legs-overview. The WebMD website offers the latest information on PAD of the legs, including an overview, causes, symptoms of PAD of the legs, diagnosing PAD of the legs, treatment, living with PAD, and further reading. Also available is WebMD's heart health e-mail newsletter.

Patient Support Groups and Organizations

➢ HeartHub for Patients—"Peripheral Artery Disease (PAD)." http://www.hearthub .org/hc-peripheral.htm; alternate path: http://www.hearthub.org/, scroll down to the section titled "Health Centers," and then click on the title "Peripheral Artery Disease." HeartHub, a division of the American Heart Association (AHA), is a patient-support portal for information, tools, and resources on PAD, including discussions of such aspects as risk factors, healthy recipes, getting help on the phone, and exercises for use at home. You can view the ankle-brachial index exam video, and there is also a free Heart360 tool available to "track your blood pressure, physical activity, and much more." You can also download for free a chart to keep track of prescription medications, over-the-counter, and herbal drugs being taken. Also available is a sign-up for a free PAD e-newsletter.

➤ MedHelp—"Peripheral Artery Disease." http://www.medhelp.org/search?query =peripheral+artery+disease; alternate path: http://www.medhelp.org/, search for "peripheral artery disease."
According to its website, MedHelp "connects people with the leading medical experts," such as those from Cleveland Clinic, National Jewish Health, Partners Health, and Mount Sinai Hospital, with those who have similar medical issues. MedHelp's main focus is to enable patients "to take control over their health and find answers to their medical questions" using nontechnical language via an online community through posts, forums and groups, blogs, user journals, as well as recommendations, articles, health pages, and a medical glossary. Free registration is required.

➤ U.S. Hospital Finder. http://www.ushospitalfinder.com/.
Use this site to find the names of hospitals by zip code, city, state, or your address. The search results include a map with directions. You might also want to ask your health care professional, call hospitals in your area, or search for "support groups" on hospital websites to determine if there are any cardiology support groups for people with peripheral artery disease that meet regularly in your area.

➤ Vascular Disease Foundation—"Online Support Community." http://vasculardisease .org/resources-support/online-support-community/; alternate path: http://vascular disease.org/padcoalition/, under "Resources and Support," click on "Online Support Community."
The Vascular Disease Foundation partners with the PAD (Peripheral Artery Disease) Coalition (http://vasculardisease.org/padcoalition/) in providing this online support network, with the goal of improving "the prevention, early detection, treatment, and rehabilitation of people with, or at risk for, PAD."

➤ Yahoo! Groups—"Peripheral Arterial Disease (PAD) Support Group." http:// health.groups.yahoo.com/group/PADSupport/; alternate path: http://www.groups .yahoo.com/, search for "peripheral arterial disease" in the "Find a Yahoo! Group" Search box and then click on the group "PADSupport."
This online Yahoo! group is for patients with peripheral artery disease and their families and friends. Yahoo! Groups is not a medical site, nor does it provide or endorse medical advice or procedures. The purpose of the website is to share experiences in a kind and caring manner. Free registration is required to participate.

Pulmonary Hypertension

Pulmonary hypertension (PH) is a condition in which blood pressure in the lung arteries is elevated. The right ventricle pumps blood through the pulmonary artery and into the arteries in the lungs. The lungs oxygenate the blood and return it to the left ventricle of the heart through the pulmonary vein. The blood pressure in the lungs can become elevated when the arteries tighten or close up, when the arteries are stiff at birth, when they become stiff from an overgrowth of cells, or when blood clots block off some arteries.

The mean pulmonary artery pressure should be 12 to 16 mm Hg (millimeters of mercury). A pressure of 25 mm Hg indicates PH. Pulmonary artery pressure can be estimated by echocardiography; however, it is best measured through right cardiac catheterization (*see* CHAPTER 5).

There are five types of PH, grouped by their causes. Group 1 has no known cause, is inherited, and is related to congenital heart disease, HIV infection, thyroid diseases, certain diet drugs, or illegal drug use—it is sometimes called idiopathic PH. Group 2 includes PH with left heart disease, such as mitral valve disease or long-term high blood pressure. Group 3 is related to lung diseases and breathing problems such as chronic obstructive pulmonary disease (COPD), diseases that scar the lungs, or sleep apnea. Group 4 PH is caused by blood clots in the lungs or blood-clotting disorders, such as sickle-cell anemia. Group 5 is a catchall for other diseases and conditions that can cause PH, such as sarcoidosis (granulomas in the lung), Langerhans cell histiocytosis (an autoimmune disease that causes swelling of the bronchioles and arterioles in the lungs), lymphangioleiomyomatosis (a disorder that causes proliferation of smooth muscle in the lungs), or an object or tumor pressing on the pulmonary blood vessels. Secondary PH is another name for PH that occurs along with another disease or condition.

Patients with PH are subject to shortness of breath, dizziness, and fainting, which are made worse by physical exertion. Over time these symptoms get worse. A cough may develop along with edema of the lungs or swelling in the legs. Without treatment, the right side of the heart weakens because of the difficulty of pumping blood through the lungs. Eventually heart failure occurs.

Resources for Further Information on Pulmonary Hypertension

Books

➤ Handler, Clive, and Gerry Coghlan. *Pulmonary Arterial Hypertension (The Facts)*. New York, NY: Oxford University Press, 2010. Print.
   This book was written by pulmonary hypertension experts from the Royal Free Hospital in London to aid patients and their families in understanding what pulmonary arterial hypertension is and how to manage and live with their illness.

There is a detailed section on the difference between pulmonary hypertension and pulmonary arterial hypertension.

Websites

➤ American Heart Association (AHA)—"Pulmonary Hypertension (PH)." http:// www.heart.org/HEARTORG/Conditions/CongenitalHeartDefects/TheImpactof CongenitalHeartDefects/Pulmonary-Hypertension_UCM_307044_Article.jsp; alternate path: http://www.heart.org/, search for "pulmonary hypertension" and then click on the title "Pulmonary Hypertension (PH)."
AHA provides expanded details on arrhythmia on sections, such as causes and repairs, pulmonary hypertension in children, cyanosis due to PH with congenital heart disease, treatment, physical activity, medications, pregnancy and contraception, and additional precautions.

➤ Cleveland Clinic (Cleveland, OH)—"Pulmonary Hypertension." http://my .clevelandclinic.org/disorders/Pulmonary_Hypertension/hic_Pulmonary_ Hypertension_Causes_Symptoms_Diagnosis_Treatment.aspx; alternate path: http://my.clevelandclinic.org/, under the category "Institutes and Services," click on "Heart and Vascular," then click on "Homepage," then click on the category "Diseases and Conditions," and then click on the title "Pulmonary Hypertension."
The Cleveland Clinic provides comprehensive patient-friendly information on pulmonary hypertension, such as definitions, other names for pulmonary hypertension, causes, symptoms, diagnosis, treatments, lifestyle changes, and finding a doctor who treats pulmonary hypertension. The Cleveland Clinic also offers a link to "Chat Online with a Heart and Vascular Nurse." For information on clinical trials, see the Cleveland Clinic entry on pp. 31–32.

➤ ClinicalTrials.gov—Pulmonary hypertension clinical trials. http://clinicaltrials.gov/ ct2/results?term=Pulmonary+Hypertension; alternate path: http://clinicaltrials.gov/, type "pulmonary hypertension" in "Search for Studies" at the top of the screen.
To limit your results, click on "Modify This Search" and select specific fields, such as (1) Recruitment (e.g., you might want to select "Open Studies"); (2) Locations (e.g., select your state); and (3) Age Group, and then click on the "Search" button. Click on the title of each trial name for additional information, such as purpose of the study, study design and type, detailed description, outcome measures, eligibility (age, gender, criteria for participating), study start date, estimated study completion date, and sponsor. ClinicalTrials.gov, developed by the U.S. National Institutes of Health of the National Library of Medicine, lists ongoing and currently enrolling clinical trials. Check often for new studies.

➤ eMedicineHealth—"Pulmonary Hypertension" and "Pulmonary Hypertension, Primary." http://www.emedicinehealth.com/pulmonary_hypertension/article_em.htm

and http://www.emedicinehealth.com/pulmonary_hypertension_primary-health/ article_em.htm; alternate path: http://www.emedicinehealth.com/, search for "pulmonary hypertension," and then click on the titles "Pulmonary Hypertension" (Medical Reference from eMedicineHealth) and "Pulmonary Hypertension, Primary" (Medical Reference from Healthwise).
eMedicineHealth, a division of WebMD, offers a comprehensive article on pulmonary hypertension, including an overview, causes, risk factors, symptoms, when to seek medical care, diagnosis, treatment, prevention, outlook, and follow-up.

➢ Genetics Home Reference—"Pulmonary Arterial Hypertension." http://ghr.nlm .nih.gov/condition/pulmonary-arterial-hypertension; alternate path: http://ghr .nlm.nih.gov/, search for "pulmonary arterial hypertension."
Genetics Home Reference is a division of the National Institutes of Health (NIH). This website discusses an inherited form of pulmonary arterial hypertension.

➢ Hospital of the University of Pennsylvania (HUP) (Philadelphia, PA)—"Pulmonary Hypertension Program." http://www.pennmedicine.org/heart/patient/clinical -services/pulmonary-hypertension/; alternate path: http://www.pennmedicine .org/, click on the "Departments and Services" icon (or search for "departments and services"), scroll down and click on the category "Cardiology and Cardiac Surgery," then scroll down under the heading "Clinical Services," and then click on "Pulmonary Hypertension."
At its Penn Heart and Vascular Center website, HUP offers website links in the Pulmonary Hypertension Program that include an "Overview" (what pulmonary hypertension is and improving quality of life); the "Team," which links to each physician and specialist (with profiles, e.g., specialty, medical board certification, education); and "The Penn Difference" (program described, patient experiences, unique capabilities and expertise, and hospital highlights). You can also subscribe to the Penn Heart newsletter. For information on clinical trials, see the HUP entry on p. 33.

➢ Johns Hopkins Hospital, Heart and Vascular Institute (Baltimore, MD)— "Pulmonary Hypertension." http://www.hopkinsmedicine.org/heart_vascular _institute/conditions_treatments/conditions/pulmonary_hypertension.html; alternate path: http://www.hopkinsmedicine.org/, type "pulmonary hypertension conditions treatment" in the Search box and click on the title "Pulmonary Hypertension."
The Johns Hopkins Heart and Vascular Institute website on pulmonary hypertension (PHT) discusses what PHT is, valve repair surgery for PHT, when to call your doctor, symptoms, causes, prevention, diagnosis, and treatment. Also, click on the heading "Clinical Trials" for links to current trials in various heart and cardiovascular conditions.

➤ Mayo Clinic (Rochester, MN)—"Pulmonary Hypertension." http://www.mayoclinic .com/health/pulmonary-hypertension/DS00430; alternate path: http://www .mayoclinic.com/, search for "pulmonary hypertension," and then click on the title "Pulmonary Hypertension—MayoClinic.com."
Written for patients, this webpage on pulmonary hypertension includes definitions, symptoms, causes, risk factors, complications, preparing for appointments, tests and diagnosis, treatments and drugs, and lifestyles and home remedies. For information on clinical trials and patient services, see the Mayo Clinic entry on p. 36.

➤ MedicineNet—"Pulmonary Hypertension." http://www.medicinenet.com/ pulmonary_hypertension/article.htm; alternate path: http://www.medicinenet.com/, click on the major topic "Diseases and Conditions," click on "Conditions A–Z," click on "P," and then scroll down to "Pulmonary Hypertension (PH)."
MedicineNet is owned and operated by WebMD and is part of the WebMD Network. According to its website, MedicineNet "provides easy-to-read, in-depth, authoritative medical information for consumers via its user-friendly, interactive website." The webpage provides in-depth information on tension PH, primary and secondary PH, causes, symptoms, diagnosis, treatment, life expectancy, patient discussions, and finding a local cardiologist. The medical information is written and edited by a nationally recognized group of more than 70 U.S. board-certified physicians. The website contains a "Symptom Checker" listed in alphabetical order as a guide to "pinpoint your pain." Its homepage links to "Health News of the Week." You can also sign up to receive a health newsletter.

➤ MedlinePlus—"Pulmonary Hypertension." http://www.nlm.nih.gov/medlineplus/ pulmonaryhypertension.html; alternate path: http://www.nlm.nih.gov/, under "Databases," click on "MedlinePlus," and then search for "pulmonary hypertension."
MedlinePlus is a component of the National Institutes of Health (NIH), produced by the National Library of Medicine (NLM), and is updated regularly. This MedlinePlus webpage on pulmonary hypertension offers extensive information covering overviews, news, diagnosis/symptoms, treatment, nutrition, disease management, specific conditions, clinical trials, genetics, journal articles, directories, organizations, statistics, and specific sections focusing on children. Patient handouts are available. This webpage also includes a multimedia section containing tutorials.

➤ Medscape Reference (Drugs, Diseases, and Procedures)—"Secondary Pulmonary Hypertension." http://emedicine.medscape.com/article/303098-overview; alternate path: http://emedicine.medscape.com/, search for and then click on the title "Secondary Pulmonary Hypertension."
Written for Medscape by Nader Kamangar, MD, FACP, FCCP, FCCM, and associates, this webpage presents a comprehensive report on secondary pulmonary

hypertension. Although written for health care professionals, it might be helpful for interested laypersons. Articles for Medscape Reference are written by medical experts. The webpage states, "Our rigorous literature survey process allows us to rapidly integrate new practice-changing information into the relevant topics by systematically reviewing the major medical and pharmacy journals, news announcements, and important practice guidelines." Free registration is required.

➢ *The Merck Manual Home Health Handbook for Patients and Caregivers*— "Pulmonary Hypertension." http://www.merckmanuals.com/home/lung_and _airway_disorders/pulmonary_hypertension/pulmonary_hypertension.html?qt =pulmonary%20hypertension&alt=sh; alternate path: http://www.merckmanuals .com/home/, under "Sections," click on "All" to view a complete list, then click on the section "Lung and Airway Disorders," and then scroll down to the section "Pulmonary Hypertension."
This webpage on pulmonary hypertension gives an overview on causes, symptoms, diagnosis, and treatment of pulmonary hypertension. This section is based on a well-known medical textbook titled *The Merck Manual Home Health Handbook for Patients and Caregivers* and is "provided free of charge . . . as a public service."

➢ National Heart, Lung, and Blood Institute (NHLBI)—"What Is Pulmonary Hypertension (PH)?" http://www.nhlbi.nih.gov/health/dci/Diseases/pah/pah_what.html; alternate path: http://www.nhlbi.nih.gov/, search for "pulmonary hypertension," and then click on the title "What Is Pulmonary Hypertension?"
NHLBI, a division of the National Institutes of Health from the U.S. Department of Health and Human Services, provides additional information on PH, including links to definitions, types of PH, other names, causes, who is at risk, signs and symptoms, diagnosis, treatments, living with PH, clinical trials, and key points.

➢ New York–Presbyterian (NYP) University Hospital of Columbia and Cornell (New York, NY)—"Interactive Media Library: Pulmonary Hypertension" (Video). http://nyp.org/media/index.html; alternate path: http://nyp.org/, click on the "Explore the Interactive Media Library" icon, then click to reveal a complete list of topics, and then scroll down to the topic "Pulmonary Hypertension."
The Human Atlas media player presents short videos, text, models, and slides. To view an excellent video, click on the "Complete Listing of Topics" heading and scroll down to click on "Pulmonary Hypertension." For information on clinical trials, see the NYP entry on p. 38.

➢ Pulmonary Hypertension Association (PHA). https://www.phassociation.org/.
PHA offers information for patients, caregivers, and medical professionals. Click on the heading "Patients" for categories: newly diagnosed, about PH, find a

doctor, living with PH, PH kids, young adults with PH, associated diseases, insurance resources, educational programs, research and clinical trials, and resources. Under "Community" are links to local support groups and other online connections (e.g., Facebook at https://www.facebook.com/PulmonaryHypertensionAssociation). Available on the homepage is a sign-up for PHA's newsletter, *PHA Daily Beat.*

➤ UCLA Ronald Reagan Medical Center (Los Angeles, CA)—"Pulmonary Hypertension." http://www.uclahealth.org/body.cfm?id=592; scroll down to the heading "Tests and Treatments," under the section "Alternative Medicine" click on the word "More," and then click on the title "Pulmonary Hypertension"; alternate path: http://www.uclahealth.org/, under the heading "For Patients and Visitors," scroll down and mouse over the category "Health Resources" and then click on "Heart Health Center," then scroll down to the heading "Tests and Treatments," scroll under the section "Alternative Medicine," click on the word "More," and then click on the title "Pulmonary Hypertension."

The UCLA Ronald Reagan Medical Center's Heart Health Center provides detailed information on pulmonary hypertension, which includes introductions, signs and symptoms, causes, what to expect at your provider's office, treatment options, including alternative medicine, follow-up, and special considerations. For more information on patient resources and clinical trials, see the UCLA entry on p. 41.

➤ WebMD. http://www.webmd.com/.

According to WebMD, "WebMD News is an independent media service designed to provide news, information, and educational material to consumers and physicians. News content created by WebMD is free from influence by sponsors, partners, or other sources." From the homepage, you can find the following and related resources by searching for the topic by name.

• "Pulmonary Hypertension." http://www.webmd.com/lung/pulmonary-hypertension-1. The WebMD website offers the latest information on pulmonary hypertension, symptoms, causes, diagnosis, and treatment.

• "Pulmonary Hypertension Directory." http://www.webmd.com/lung/pulmonary-hypertension-directory. This WebMD directory offers information on pulmonary hypertension including news, medical references, and videos.

Patient Support Groups and Organizations

➤ DailyStrength—"Pulmonary Hypertension Support Group." http://www.dailystrength.org/c/Pulmonary-Hypertension/support-group; alternate path: http://www.dailystrength.org/, search for "pulmonary hypertension," and then click on "Visit the Pulmonary Hypertension Support Group."

The DailyStrength website offers online support groups and blogs for those with pulmonary hypertension. Free registration is required to participate. According to the website, "DailyStrength is a subsidiary of Sharecare. Sharecare, created by WebMD founder and Discovery Communications' Chief of Global Digital Strategy Jeff Arnold, along with America's Doctor, Dr. Mehmet Oz, is the first truly interactive healthcare ecosystem giving consumers the ability to ask, learn and act on the questions of health."

➤ MedHelp—"Pulmonary Hypertension." http://www.medhelp.org/search?query =pulmonary+hypertension; alternate path: http://www.medhelp.org/, search for "pulmonary hypertension."
According to the website, MedHelp "connects people with the leading medical experts," such as those from Cleveland Clinic, National Jewish Health, Partners Health, and Mount Sinai Hospital, and with those who have similar medical issues. MedHelp's main focus is to enable patients "to take control over their health and find answers to their medical questions" using nontechnical language via an online community through posts, forums and groups, blogs, user journals, as well as recommendations, articles, health pages, and a medical glossary. Free registration is required.

➤ Pulmonary Hypertension Association. http://www.phassociation.org/.
The Pulmonary Hypertension Association has support groups and an online community. According to its website, PHA's "mission is to find ways to prevent and cure pulmonary hypertension, and to provide hope for the pulmonary hypertension community through support, education, advocacy and awareness."

➤ U.S. Hospital Finder. http://www.ushospitalfinder.com/.
Use this site to find the names of hospitals by zip code, city, state, or your address. The search results include a map with directions. You might also want to ask your health care professional, call hospitals in your area, or search for "support groups" on hospital websites to determine if there are any cardiology support groups for people with pulmonary hypertension that meet regularly in your area.

➤ Yahoo! Groups—"PH International Support Group." http://health.groups.yahoo .com/group/PHinternational/; alternate path: http://www.groups.yahoo.com/, search for "pulmonary hypertension" in the "Find a Yahoo! Group" Search box, and then click on the group "PH International."
This online Yahoo! group is for patients with pulmonary hypertension and their families and friends and is "provided by the Pulmonary Hypertension Association [http://www.phassociation.org/] of the United States as a resource for all PH patients, family members and medical professionals around the world." Yahoo! Groups is not a medical site, nor does it provide or endorse medical advice or procedures. The purpose of the website is to share experiences in a kind and caring manner. Free registration is required to participate.

Webliography

Aetna InteliHealth. "Endocarditis." May 11, 2011. http://www.intelihealth.com/IH/
    ihtIH/WSIHW000/21827/24755/216672.html?d=dmtHealthAZ.
American Heart Association. "Metabolic Syndrome." Accessed April 11, 2013.
    http://www.heart.org/HEARTORG/Conditions/More/MetabolicSyndrome/
    Metabolic-Syndrome_UCM_002080_SubHomePage.jsp.
British Heart Foundation. "Cardiomyopathy." Accessed April 10, 2013. http://www
    .bhf.org.uk/heart-health/conditions/cardiomyopathy.aspx.
CardioSmart (American College of Cardiology). "Acute Coronary Syndrome."
    Accessed April 10, 2013. https://www.cardiosmart.org/Heart-Conditions/Acute
    -Coronary-Syndrome.
———. "Heart Attack." Accessed April 24, 2013. https://www.cardiosmart.org/Heart
    -Conditions/Heart-Attack.
———. "Metabolic Syndrome." Accessed April 10, 2013. https://www.cardiosmart
    .org/Heart-Conditions/Metabolic-Syndrome.
Centers for Disease Control and Prevention. "Cholesterol." Updated July 10, 2012.
    http://www.cdc.gov/cholesterol/.
eMedicineHealth. "Congestive Heart Failure." Revised July 26, 2011. http://www
    .emedicinehealth.com/congestive_heart_failure/article_em.htm.
HealthyChildren.org (American Academy of Pediatrics). "Kawasaki Disease."
    Updated February 28, 2013. http://www.healthychildren.org/english/health
    -issues/conditions/heart/pages/kawasaki-disease.aspx.
HeartHealthyWomen.org. "Cardiac Syndrome X." Accessed April 25, 2013. http://
    www.hearthealthywomen.org/cardiovascular-disease/cardiac-syndrome-x/
    cardiac-syndrome-x.html.
HeartValveSurgery.com. "Diagram of the Human Heart Valves." Accessed April 11,
    2013. http://www.heart-valve-surgery.com/human-heart-diagram.php.
KidsHealth (Nemours). "Kawasaki Disease." Reviewed September 2011. http://
    kidshealth.org/parent/medical/heart/kawasaki.html.
MedlinePlus. "Angina." Updated March 20, 2013. http://www.nlm.nih.gov/medlineplus/
    angina.html.
———. "Arrhythmia." Updated December 2012. http://www.nlm.nih.gov/medlineplus/
    arrhythmia.html.
———. "Cardiac Arrest." Updated March 26, 2013. http://www.nlm.nih.gov/medlineplus/
    cardiacarrest.html.
———. "Cardiomyopathy." Updated March 26, 2013. http://www.nlm.nih.gov/
    medlineplus/cardiomyopathy.html.
———. "Endocarditis." Updated April 10, 2013. http://www.nlm.nih.gov/medlineplus/
    endocarditis.html.

———. "Heart Attack." Updated April 9, 2013. http://www.nlm.nih.gov/medlineplus/heartattack.html.

———. "Heart Disease in Women." Updated April 10, 2013. http://www.nlm.nih.gov/medlineplus/heartdiseaseinwomen.html.

———. "Heart Diseases." Updated April 10, 2013. http://www.nlm.nih.gov/medlineplus/heartdiseases.html.

———. "Heart Failure." Updated April 10, 2013. http://www.nlm.nih.gov/medlineplus/heartfailure.html.

———. "Heart Surgery." Updated April 10, 2013. http://www.nlm.nih.gov/medlineplus/heartsurgery.html.

———. "Heart Valve Diseases." Updated April 10, 2013. http://www.nlm.nih.gov/medlineplus/heartvalvediseases.html.

———. "High Blood Pressure." Updated April 5, 2013. http://www.nlm.nih.gov/medlineplus/highbloodpressure.html.

———. "Kawasaki Disease." Updated December 5, 2012. http://www.nlm.nih.gov/medlineplus/kawasakidisease.html.

———. "Pericardial Disorders." Updated March 12, 2013. http://www.nlm.nih.gov/medlineplus/pericardialdisorders.html.

Medscape Reference (WebMD). "Coronary Artery Anomalies." Updated October 18, 2012. http://emedicine.medscape.com/article/895854-overview.

National Heart, Lung, and Blood Institute. "What Are Holter and Event Monitors?" March 16, 2012. http://www.nhlbi.nih.gov/health/dci/Diseases/holt/holt_what.html.

———. "What Are Overweight and Obesity?" July 13, 2012. http://www.nhlbi.nih.gov/health/dci/Diseases/obe/obe_whatare.html.

———. "What Are Palpitations?" July 1, 2011. http://www.nhlbi.nih.gov/health/dci/Diseases/hpl/hpl_what.html.

———. "What Is a Heart Attack?" March 1, 2011. http://www.nhlbi.nih.gov/health/dci/Diseases/HeartAttack/HeartAttack_WhatIs.html.

———. "What Is a Heart Murmur?" September 20, 2012. http://www.nhlbi.nih.gov/health/dci/Diseases/heartmurmur/hmurmur_what.html.

———. "What Is a Heart Transplant?" January 3, 2012. http://www.nhlbi.nih.gov/health/dci/Diseases/ht/ht_whatis.html.

———. "What Is a Pacemaker?" February 28, 2012. http://www.nhlbi.nih.gov/health/dci/Diseases/pace/pace_whatis.html.

———. "What Is an Arrhythmia?" July 1, 2011. http://www.nhlbi.nih.gov/health/dci/Diseases/arr/arr_whatis.html.

———. "What Is an Electrocardiogram?" October 1, 2010. http://www.nhlbi.nih.gov/health/dci/Diseases/ekg/ekg_what.html.

———. "What Is an Implantable Cardioverter Defibrillator?" November 9, 2011. http://www.nhlbi.nih.gov/health/dci/Diseases/icd/icd_whatis.html.

———. "What Is Angina?" June 1, 2011. http://www.nhlbi.nih.gov/health/dci/Diseases/Angina/Angina_WhatIs.html.

———. "What Is Atherosclerosis?" July 1, 2011. http://www.nhlbi.nih.gov/health/dci/Diseases/Atherosclerosis/Atherosclerosis_WhatIs.html.

———. "What Is Atrial Fibrillation?" July 1, 2011. http://www.nhlbi.nih.gov/health/dci/Diseases/af/af_what.html.

———. "What Is Cardiac Catheterization?" January 30, 2012. http://www.nhlbi.nih.gov/health/dci/Diseases/cath/cath_keypoints.html.

———. "What Is Cardiogenic Shock?" July 1, 2011. http://www.nhlbi.nih.gov/health/dci/Diseases/shock/shock_what.html.

———. "What Is Cardiomyopathy?" January 1, 2011. http://www.nhlbi.nih.gov/health/dci/Diseases/cm/cm_what.html.

———. "What Is Cholesterol?" September 19, 2012. http://www.nhlbi.nih.gov/health/dci/Diseases/Hbc/HBC_WhatIs.html.

———. "What Is Coronary Heart Disease?" August 23, 2012. http://www.nhlbi.nih.gov/health/dci/Diseases/Cad/CAD_WhatIs.html.

———. "What Is Coronary Microvascular Disease?" November 2, 2011. http://www.nhlbi.nih.gov/health/dci/Diseases/cmd/cmd_whatis.html.

———. "What Is Heart Block?" July 9, 2012. http://www.nhlbi.nih.gov/health/dci/Diseases/hb/hb_whatis.html.

———. "What Is Heart Failure?" July 9, 2012. http://www.nhlbi.nih.gov/health/dci/Diseases/Hf/HF_WhatIs.html.

———. "What Is Heart Surgery?" March 23, 2012. http://www.nhlbi.nih.gov/health/dci/Diseases/hs/hs_whatis.html.

———. "What Is Heart Valve Disease?" November 16, 2011. http://www.nhlbi.nih.gov/health/dci/Diseases/hvd/hvd_whatis.html.

———. "What Is High Blood Pressure?" August 2, 2012. http://www.nhlbi.nih.gov/health/dci/Diseases/Hbp/HBP_WhatIs.html.

———. "What Is Hypotension?" November 1, 2010. http://www.nhlbi.nih.gov/health/dci/Diseases/hyp/hyp_whatis.html.

———. "What Is Kawasaki Disease?" September 20, 2011. http://www.nhlbi.nih.gov/health/health-topics/topics/kd/.

———. "What Is Long QT Syndrome?" September 21, 2011. http://www.nhlbi.nih.gov/health/dci/Diseases/qt/qt_whatis.html.

———. "What Is Metabolic Syndrome?" November 3, 2011. http://www.nhlbi.nih.gov/health/health-topics/topics/ms/.

———. "What Is Mitral Valve Prolapse?" July 1, 2011. http://www.nhlbi.nih.gov/health/dci/Diseases/mvp/mvp_whatis.html.

———. "What Is Pericarditis?" September 26, 2012. http://www.nhlbi.nih.gov/health/dci/Diseases/peri/peri_whatis.html.

———. "What Is Peripheral Arterial Disease?" April 1, 2011. http://www.nhlbi.nih .gov/health/dci/Diseases/pad/pad_what.html.

———. "What Is Sudden Cardiac Arrest?" April 1, 2011. http://www.nhlbi.nih.gov/ health/dci/Diseases/scda/scda_whatis.html.

NHS (National Health Service) Choices. "Heart Block." Reviewed May 30, 2012. http://www.nhs.uk/conditions/Heart-block/Pages/Introduction.aspx

Patient.co.uk. "Cardiac Syndrome X." Reviewed February 20, 2012. http://www .patient.co.uk/doctor/Cardiac-Syndrome-X.htm.

PubMed Health (National Center for Biotechnology Information, U.S. National Library of Medicine). "Cardiac Tamponade." Reviewed May 14, 2012. http:// www.ncbi.nlm.nih.gov/pubmedhealth/PMH0001245/.

Resurrection Health Care. "Cardiovascular Diseases." Accessed April 11, 2013. http://www.reshealth.org/yourhealth/healthinfo/default.cfm?pageID=P00225.

Sudden Cardiac Arrest Association. "Learn about Sudden Cardiac Arrest." Accessed April 10, 2013. http://www.suddencardiacarrest.org/aws/SCAA/pt/sp/edmaterials.

U.S. National Library of Medicine (National Institutes of Health). "Cardiovascular Diseases." Accessed April 11, 2013. http://www.nlm.nih.gov/cgi/mesh/2012/MB _cgi?mode=&term=Cardiovascular+Diseases&field=entry.

Vascular Disease Foundation. "Peripheral Artery Disease." Modified April 27, 2012. http://vasculardisease.org/peripheral-artery-disease/.

WebMD, Atrial Fibrillation Health Center. "Atrial Fibrillation—Overview." Updated February 18, 2011. http://www.webmd.com/heart-disease/atrial-fibrillation/ atrial-fibrillation-overview.

WebMD, Heart Disease Health Center. "What Is Heart Disease—Overview." Accessed April 11, 2013. http://www.webmd.com/heart-disease/guide/heart -disease-overview-facts.

WebMD, Lung Disease and Respiratory Health Center. "Pulmonary Hypertension." May 14, 2012. http://www.webmd.com/lung/pulmonary-hypertension-1.

Chapter 4

Congenital Heart Diseases

Some people are born with problems that occurred during fetal development as a result of genetics, chromosomal anomalies, or exposure to certain chemicals, such as alcohol, cocaine, or certain medications (e.g., thalidomide). However, most causes of congenital heart diseases are unknown. And although there are numerous types, congenital heart diseases can be classified in four categories:

- *Defects in heart valves* (stenosis or narrowing) cause constriction of blood flow, allowing insufficient blood (and therefore oxygen) to the lungs. Common types of heart valve defects resulting in constricted blood flow are tricuspid atresia, pulmonary atresia, transposition of the great arteries, double outlet right ventricle, and truncus arteriosus.
- *Defects in heart walls* (septal defects) allow too much blood flow through the lungs, causing stress to the lungs. Common types of septal defects resulting in too much blood flow are atrial septal defect, ventricular defect, and patent ductus arteriosus.
- *Abnormalities of the heart* are obstructions that cause insufficient blood to reach the rest of the body from blood vessel blockages or from underdeveloped atria or ventricles. Conditions that stem from abnormalities of the heart are coarctation of the aorta, aortic stenosis, and total anomalous pulmonary venous connection (TAPVC), the latter of which is also known as total anomalous pulmonary venous return (TAPVR).
- *DNA abnormalities or genetic disorders* can develop into a disease or defect such as congenital heart malformations (e.g., when certain genes mutate after exposure to a hostile environment, such as tobacco smoke). Genetic disorders can also be caused by inheriting a mutated gene, such as Marfan syndrome. Other congenital heart problems caused by genetic disorders or DNA abnormalities include Down syndrome, trisomy 13 (also known as Patau syndrome), and Turner syndrome.

While the majority of these defects occur alone, an infant may be born with more than one defect. In addition, other types of congenital heart disease, such as atrioventricular canal defect (atrioventricular septal defect), hypoplastic left heart syndrome, and tetralogy of Fallot (*see* GLOSSARY), are a combination of multiple heart defects.

With most of these defects, surgery is needed to correct the problem. In many cases, multiple surgeries are required. For some individuals, a patent hole, or a small hole in the heart that never closed through natural growth processes, is located; this condition is often resolved by using a catheter to place a mesh plug in the hole. The mesh provides a structure over which tissue can then grow and eventually close the hole. Some defects will resolve without intervention or are so small that no intervention is needed. Drugs can help alleviate symptoms in some cases and improve the surgical outcome. Depending on the problem, surgery may not be required, may be delayed, or may be immediately necessary at or prior to birth.

The risks of treatment depend on the severity of the problem. The risks include the possibility of perforation of the heart wall or damage to heart valves, inability to restructure the heart, or death. For newborn babies who have life-threatening fetal defects (e.g., congenital heart diseases) and need immediate surgery and other specialized treatment, pediatric hospitals, such as the Children's Hospital of Philadelphia (since June 2008; the first hospital to develop a special treatment center for congenital heart diseases in newborns), have a special delivery unit for mothers. (*See* RESOURCES FOR FURTHER INFORMATION ON CONGENITAL HEART DISEASE *at the end of this chapter.*)

Abnormalities of the Heart (Obstructions; Insufficient Blood to the Rest of the Body)

Abnormalities can be described as parts of the heart that are positioned incorrectly (e.g., transposition of the great arteries), blockages, such as heart muscles or walls (septum) that are too thick or become too thick, abnormally developed heart blood vessels or heart valves (e.g., aortic, pulmonary, mitral, and tricuspid), or lack of a

Online Search Tips

- If you click on a link (e.g., a title) and nothing happens, try this: right-click on the link and then left-click on the option "Open in new window."
- If you experience problems with PDF documents, you can download the latest version of Adobe Reader for free at http://www.adobe.com/products/reader .html or by going to http://www.adobe.com/ and searching for "adobe reader."
- To view an animation, you might be asked to allow the installation of a common Internet plug-in called Shockwave Player by Adobe (http://www.adobe.com/ products/shockwaveplayer/).
- Adobe Flash Player, required to view most short videos, is available as a free download at http://get.adobe.com/flashplayer/; alternate path: http://www .adobe.com/, choose the "Download" tab on the menu bar, and select the Adobe Flash Player link.

valve (atrioventricular canal between the two chambers). Other examples are right ventricular hypertrophy, in which the muscle of the right ventricle is too thick, causing it to overwork; and coarctation of the aorta, where a portion of the aorta (main artery) is constricted enough to obstruct the flow of oxygenated blood from the heart to the lungs to reach the rest of the body. Aortic stenosis and pulmonary stenosis are conditions that range in severity from the narrowing of the aortic valve to obstruction. Severe forms of stenosis obstruct the flow of blood from, as in aortic stenosis, the left lower heart chamber to the aorta, where the blood flows out from the heart, and as in pulmonary stenosis obstructs, where the blood flows from the right ventricle to the lungs.

Resources for Further Information on Heart Abnormalities

See also RESOURCES FOR FURTHER INFORMATION ON CONGENITAL HEART DISEASE at the end of this chapter for a more comprehensive list of resources.

➤ Lucile Packard Children's Hospital at Stanford (Palo Alto, CA)—"Heart Defects Causing Obstructions to Blood Flow." http://www.lpch.org/DiseaseHealthInfo/ HealthLibrary/cardiac/obfhub.html; alternate path: http://www.lpch.org/, search for "heart defects causing obstruction," and then click on the title "Heart Defects Causing Obstructions to Blood Flow."
The Lucile Packard Children's Hospital at Stanford (of Stanford University School of Medicine) website provides information on heart defects causing extra blood flow through the lungs and links to such conditions as coarctation of the aorta, aortic stenosis, and pulmonary stenosis. Each topic further discusses the defect, including illustrations, causes, symptoms, diagnosis, treatments, postoperative care, follow-up, and long-term outlook. Under the heading "For Patients and Families" are links to many services.

Aortic Stenosis

➤ Cincinnati Children's Hospital Medical Center (Cincinnati, OH)—"Aortic Stenosis." http://www.cincinnatichildrens.org/health/a/avs/; alternate path: http://www .cincinnatichildrens.org/, search for and then click on the title "Aortic Stenosis." Cincinnati Children's Hospital provides patient-friendly information on aortic stenosis. Click on such topics as signs and symptoms, diagnosis, and treatment. Under the heading "Patients and Families," click on "Clinical Trials" to search for any current studies.

Coarctation of the Aorta

➤ Children's Hospital of Philadelphia (CHOP) (Philadelphia, PA)—"Coarctation of the Aorta." http://www.chop.edu/service/cardiac-center/heart-conditions/coarctation-of -the-aorta.html; alternate path: http://www.chop.edu/, click on the heading

"Specialties and Services," then click on the category "Cardiac Center," and then click on "Heart Conditions" and scroll down to click on the topic.

CHOP's Cardiac Center offers information on coarctation of the aorta such as how a normal heart works, what coarctation of the aorta is, including an illustration, symptoms, diagnosis, treatment, and follow-up. Also available are links to cardiac news, cardiac research at CHOP, videos, patient stories, meeting the specialists in the team (with profile, e.g., specialty, medical board certification, education), consultations and second opinions, and taking a virtual tour.

➤ Cleveland Clinic (Cleveland, OH)—"Coarctation of the Aorta." http://my.cleveland clinic.org/heart/disorders/congenital/coarctation_of_the_aorta.aspx; alternate path: http://my.clevelandclinic.org/, under the category "Institutes and Services," click on "Heart Vascular," then click on the category "Diseases and Conditions," scroll down to the title "Congenital Heart Disease," and then click "Coarctation of the Aorta."

Cleveland Clinic provides comprehensive patient-friendly information on coarctation of the aorta such as definitions, including illustrations, who is affected, long-term effects, symptoms, diagnosis, treatments, follow-up care, and how to find a doctor who treats congenital heart disease. The Cleveland Clinic also offers a link to "Chat Online with a Heart and Vascular Nurse." To participate in a clinical trial, if available for your cardiac condition, at the Cleveland Clinic Heart Center, visit http://clevelandclinic.trialx.com/findatrial/; alternate path: http://my.clevelandclinic.org/, under the category "Institutes and Services," click on "Heart and Vascular" and then on the category "Research and Innovations," then click on the title "Clinical Research," click on "Search for a Clinical Trial," and then click on "Search for Clinical Trials at Cleveland Clinic and across the Country" to browse for research studies by condition. Also check out Cleveland Clinic's Facebook and Twitter accounts for sharing experiences.

➤ KidsHealth.org. http://kidshealth.org/.

The Nemours Center for Children's Health Media provides current information on conditions afflicting children, written for both children and parents. Information is available in English and Spanish. Some webpages contain a "Listen" button that you can click on to hear the text read aloud.

- *For Parents:* "Coarctation of the Aorta." http://kidshealth.org/parent/medical/ heart/coa.html#cat141; alternate path: http://www.kidshealth.org/, click on "Parents Site," scroll down and click on "Medical Problems," scroll down and click on "Heart and Blood Vessels," and then click on the title. For parents, this webpage includes discussion of definitions, causes, signs and symptoms, diagnosis and treatment, and home care.
- *For Teens:* "Coarctation of the Aorta." http://kidshealth.org/teen/diseases _conditions/heart/coa.html#; alternate path: http://www.kidshealth.org/,

click on "Teens Site," scroll down and click on "Diseases and Conditions," scroll down and click on "Heart and Cardiovascular System," and then click on the title. For teens, this webpage features such topics as definitions, causes, signs and symptoms, diagnosis and treatment, and self-care.

➤ Mayo Clinic (Rochester, MN)—"Coarctation of the Aorta." http://www.mayoclinic .com/health/coarctation-of-the-aorta/DS00616; alternate path: http://www .mayoclinic.com/, search for and then click on the title "Coarctation of the Aorta." Written for patients, this information on coarctation of the aorta includes links to definitions, symptoms, causes, risk factors, complications, preparing for appointments, tests and diagnosis, treatments and drugs, lifestyles and home remedies, and prevention. There is also a more comprehensive section titled "In-Depth" on some of these topics. To participate in a clinical trial, if available for your cardiology condition, at the Mayo Clinic Heart, Lung, and Blood Research Center, go to http://clinicaltrials.mayo.edu/dspSubthemes.cfm?theme_id=6; alternate path: return to the Mayo Clinic homepage, click on the heading "Research," and under the category "Find Clinical Trials" scroll down and click "Browse Studies," then click "See All Categories," and finally click on the title "Heart, Lung, and Blood." For patient services in the various cardiology programs, go to http://www .mayoclinic.org/cardiac-surgery/ or http://www.mayoclinic.org/cardiovascular -disease/ or http://www.mayoclinic.org/vascular-and-endovascular-surgery/; alternate path: http://www.mayoclinic.org/, for each topic, search for "cardiac surgery," "cardiovascular diseases," or "vascular and endovascular surgery," and then click on the relevant title: "Cardiac Surgery at Mayo Clinic," "Cardiovascular Diseases at Mayo Clinic," or "Vascular and Endovascular Surgery at Mayo Clinic." For "Cardiac Surgery" and "Cardiovascular Diseases," in the "Overview" section, scroll down, select a state, and then click on the tab "Doctors" to view links to each medical expert's profile (e.g., specialty, medical board certification, education). For "Vascular and Endovascular Surgery," click on the "Doctors" tab.

➤ Medscape Reference (Drugs, Diseases, and Procedures)—"Coarctation of the Aorta." http://emedicine.medscape.com/article/895502-overview; alternate path: http://emedicine.medscape.com/, search for and then click on the title "Coarctation of the Aorta."
Written for Medscape by two medical doctors, P. Syamasundar Rao and Paul M. Seib, this webpage presents a comprehensive report on coarctation of the aorta. Although written for health care professionals, it might be helpful for interested laypersons. Articles for Medscape Reference are written by medical experts. The website states, "Our rigorous literature survey process allows us to rapidly integrate new practice-changing information into the relevant topics by systematically reviewing the major medical and pharmacy journals, news announcements, and important practice guidelines." Free registration is required.

Total Anomalous Pulmonary Venous Connection (Anomalous Pulmonary Venous Return)

➤ American Heart Association (AHA)—"Total Anomalous Pulmonary Venous Connection (TAPVC)." http://www.heart.org/HEARTORG/Conditions/ CongenitalHeartDefects/AboutCongenitalHeartDefects/Total-Anomalous -Pulmonary-Venous-Connection-TAPVC_UCM_307039_Article.jsp; alternate path: http://www.heart.org/, search for and then click on the title "Total Anomalous Pulmonary Venous Connection."

AHA provides expanded details on definitions of the condition, causes, how it affects the heart, treatment, and ongoing care. The AHA also offers a free sign-up for its newsletter, *Heart-Health E-News*.

➤ Children's Hospital of Philadelphia (CHOP) (Philadelphia, PA)—"Total Anomalous Pulmonary Venous Return (TAPVR)." http://www.chop.edu/service/cardiac -center/heart-conditions/total-anomalous-pulmonary-venous-return.html; alternate path: http://www.chop.edu/, click on the heading "Specialties and Services" and then on the category "Cardiac Center," click on "Heart Conditions," and then scroll down and click on the topic.

CHOP's Cardiac Center offers information on TAPVR, such as how a normal heart works, what TAPVR is, including an illustration and an animation, symptoms, diagnosis, treatment, and follow-up. Also available are links to cardiac news, cardiac research at CHOP, videos, patient stories, meeting the specialists in the team (with profile, e.g., specialty, medical board certification, education), consultations and second opinions, and taking a virtual tour.

➤ Cincinnati Children's Hospital Medical Center (Cincinnati, OH)—"Total Anomalous Pulmonary Venous Return (TAPVR)." http://www.cincinnatichildrens.org/ health/t/tapvr/; alternate path: http://www.cincinnatichildrens.org/, search for and then click on the title "Total Anomalous Pulmonary Venous Return."

Cincinnati Children's Hospital provides patient-friendly information on TAPVR. Click on such topics as types, associated problems, signs and symptoms, diagnosis, treatment, and outcomes. Under the heading "Patients and Families" click on "Clinical Trials" to search for any current studies.

➤ MedlinePlus—"Total Anomalous Pulmonary Venous Return (TAPVR)." http:// www.nlm.nih.gov/medlineplus/ency/article/001115.htm; alternate path: http://www .nlm.nih.gov/, under "Databases," click on "MedlinePlus," and then search for "total anomalous pulmonary venous return."

MedlinePlus, a component of the National Institutes of Health (NIH) and produced by the National Library of Medicine (NLM), is updated regularly. This MedlinePlus webpage on TAPVR offers extensive linked information covering overviews, causes, symptoms, exams and tests, treatment, outlook, and prevention. This webpage also includes a multimedia section containing tutorials.

➤ Medscape Reference (Drugs, Diseases, and Procedures)—"Total Anomalous Pulmonary Venous Connection (TAPVC)." http://emedicine.medscape.com/article/899491-overview; alternate path: http://emedicine.medscape.com/, search for "total anomalous pulmonary venous connection," and then click on the resource title.
Written by for Medscape by medical doctor Allen D. Wilson, this webpage presents a comprehensive report on total anomalous pulmonary venous connection. Although written for health care professionals, it might be helpful for interested laypersons. Articles for Medscape Reference are written by medical experts. The website states, "Our rigorous literature survey process allows us to rapidly integrate new practice-changing information into the relevant topics by systematically reviewing the major medical and pharmacy journals, news announcements, and important practice guidelines." Free registration is required.

Transposition of the Great Arteries

➤ Centers for Disease Control and Prevention (CDC)—"Transposition of the Great Arteries." http://www.cdc.gov/ncbddd/heartdefects/TGA.html; alternate path: http://www.cdc.gov/, search for and then click on the title "Transposition of the Great Arteries."
At the CDC, there are several linkable topics, such as facts, how does it occur, symptoms, treatments, causes, and prevention.

➤ Children's Hospital of Philadelphia (CHOP) (Philadelphia, PA)—"Transposition of the Great Arteries." http://www.chop.edu/service/cardiac-center/heart-conditions/transposition-of-the-great-arteries.html; alternate path: http://www.chop.edu/, click on the heading "Specialties and Services" and then on the category "Cardiac Center," click on "Heart Conditions," and then scroll down and click on the topic.
CHOP's Cardiac Center offers information on transposition of the great arteries (TGA), such as how a normal heart works, what TGA is, including an illustration and an animation, symptoms, diagnosis, treatment, and follow-up. Also available are links to cardiac news, cardiac research at CHOP, videos, patient stories, meeting the specialists in the team (with profile, e.g., specialty, medical board certification, education), consultations and second opinions, and taking a virtual tour.

➤ Cincinnati Children's Hospital Medical Center (Cincinnati, OH)—"Transposition of the Great Arteries." http://www.cincinnatichildrens.org/patients/child/encyclopedia/defects/transposition/; alternate path: http://www.cincinnatichildrens.org/, search for and then click on the title "Transposition of the Great Arteries."

Cincinnati Children's Hospital provides patient-friendly information on transposition of the great arteries (TGA). Click on such topics as what TGA is, including an illustration and animation, signs and symptoms, diagnosis, treatment, and outcomes. Under the heading "Patients and Families" click on "Clinical Trials" to search for any current studies.

➤ Mayo Clinic (Rochester, MN)—"Transposition of the Great Arteries (TGA)." http://www.mayoclinic.com/health/transposition-of-the-great-arteries/DS00733; alternate path: http://www.mayoclinic.com/, search for "transposition of the great arteries," and then click on the resource title.
Written for patients, this information on TGA includes links to definitions, symptoms, causes, risk factors, complications, preparing for appointments, tests and diagnosis, treatments and drugs, coping and support, and prevention. There is also a more comprehensive section titled "In-Depth" on some of these topics. For information on clinical trials and patient services, see the Mayo Clinic entry on p. 207.

➤ Medscape Reference (Drugs, Diseases, and Procedures)—"Transposition of the Great Arteries." http://emedicine.medscape.com/article/900574-overview; alternate path: http://emedicine.medscape.com/, search for and then click on the title "Transposition of the Great Arteries."
Written for Medscape by two medical doctors, John R. Charpie and Kevin O. Maher, this webpage presents a comprehensive report on transposition of the great arteries. Although written for health care professionals, it might be helpful for interested laypersons. Articles for Medscape Reference are written by medical experts. The website states, "Our rigorous literature survey process allows us to rapidly integrate new practice-changing information into the relevant topics by systematically reviewing the major medical and pharmacy journals, news announcements, and important practice guidelines." Free registration is required.

Patient Support Groups and Organizations

For additional related patient support groups, *see* RESOURCES FOR FURTHER INFORMATION ON CONGENITAL HEART DISEASE at the end of this chapter.

➤ MedHelp—"Aortic Valve Stenosis." http://www.medhelp.org/search?query=Aortic+Valve+Stenosis; alternate path: http://www.medhelp.org/, search for "aortic valve stenosis."
According to its website, MedHelp "connects people with the leading medical experts," such as those from Cleveland Clinic, National Jewish Health, Partners Health, and Mount Sinai Hospital, with those who have similar medical issues. MedHelp's main focus is to enable patients "to take control over their health and find answers to their medical questions" using nontechnical language via an online community through posts and articles on aortic valve stenosis. Free registration is required.

> U.S. Hospital Finder. http://www.ushospitalfinder.com/.
> Use this site to find the names of hospitals by zip code, city, state, or your
> address. The search results include a map with directions. You might also want
> to ask your health care professional, call hospitals in your area, or search for
> "support groups" on hospital websites to determine if there are any cardiology
> support groups for people with congenital heart disease that meet regularly in
> your area.

Long QT Syndrome (Rare Congenital Heart Defect)

Long QT syndrome (referring to the cardiac waveform; *see* CHAPTER 5: ELECTRO-
CARDIOGRAPHY) is a rare congenital heart defect in which the heart cells are unable
to process ions (such as calcium, sodium, and potassium) properly. There are seven
types based on the particular ion processing problem a patient has. It can also be
caused by certain medications such as antihistamines, diuretics, antibiotics, antide-
pressants, and cholesterol-lowering drugs. Patients with long QT syndrome may
develop an arrhythmia and/or cardiac arrest. These patients need to avoid triggers
to the syndrome such as strenuous exercise and some medicines. Patients may benefit from beta-blockers or implantable pacemakers or defibrillators.

Resources for Further Information on Long QT Syndrome

See also RESOURCES FOR FURTHER INFORMATION ON CONGENITAL HEART DISEASE at
the end of this chapter for a more comprehensive list of resources.

> Children's Hospital of Philadelphia (CHOP) (Philadelphia, PA)—"Long QT Syn-
> drome." http://www.chop.edu/service/cardiac-center/heart-conditions/long-qt
> -syndrome.html; alternate path: http://www.chop.edu/, under the heading "Spe-
> cialties and Services," click on the title "Cardiac Center," scroll down the topics
> and click on "Heart Conditions," and then click on "Long QT Syndrome."
> CHOP's Cardiac Center offers information on long QT syndrome such as how a
> normal heart works, what long QT syndrome is, including an animation, symp-
> toms, diagnosis, treatment, and follow-up. Also available are links to cardiac
> news, cardiac research at CHOP, videos, patient stories, meeting the specialists in
> the team (with profile, e.g., specialty, medical board certification, education),
> consultations and second opinions, and taking a virtual tour.

> Mayo Clinic (Rochester, MN)—"Long QT Syndrome." http://www.mayoclinic
> .com/health/long-qt-syndrome/DS00434; alternate path: http://www.mayoclinic
> .com/, search for and then click on the title "Long QT Syndrome."
> Written for patients, this information on long QT syndrome includes links to
> definitions, symptoms, causes, risk factors, complications, tests and diagnosis,
> treatments and drugs, prevention, and coping and support. There is also a more

comprehensive section titled "In-Depth" on some of these topics. For information on clinical trials and patient services, see the Mayo Clinic entry on p. 207.

> National Heart, Lung, and Blood Institute (NHLBI)—"What Is Long QT Syn-
> drome?" http://www.nhlbi.nih.gov/health/health-topics/topics/qt/; alternate
> path: http://www.nhlbi.nih.gov/health/, search for "long QT syndrome," and
> then click on "What Is Long QT Syndrome?"
> NHLBI, a division of National Institutes of Health from the U.S. Department of
> Health and Human Services, provides additional information on long QT syn-
> drome, including links to definitions, other names, causes, signs and symptoms,
> diagnosis, treatments, living with long QT syndrome, and clinical trials.

Patient Support Groups and Organizations

For additional related patient support groups, *see* RESOURCES FOR FURTHER INFOR-
MATION ON CONGENITAL HEART DISEASE at the end of this chapter.

> MedHelp—"Long QT Syndrome." http://www.medhelp.org/search?query=Long
> +QT+Syndrome; alternate path: http://www.medhelp.org/, search for and then
> click on the title "Long QT Syndrome."
> According to its website, MedHelp "connects people with the leading medical
> experts," such as those from Cleveland Clinic, National Jewish Health, Partners
> Health, and Mount Sinai Hospital, and with those who have similar medical
> issues. MedHelp's main focus is to enable patients "to take control over their
> health and find answers to their medical questions" using nontechnical language
> via an online community. Free registration is required.

> U.S. Hospital Finder. http://www.ushospitalfinder.com/.
> Use this site to find the names of hospitals by zip code, city, state, or your address.
> The search results include a map with directions. You might also want to ask your
> health care professional, call hospitals in your area, or search for "support groups"
> on hospital websites to determine if there are any cardiology support groups for
> people with congenital heart disease that meet regularly in your area.

> Yahoo! Groups—"Cardiac Rhythm Disorders" (Long QT Syndrome). http://
> health.groups.yahoo.com/group/cardiacrhythmdisorders/; alternate path:
> http://www.groups.yahoo.com/, search for "long QT syndrome" in the "Find a
> Yahoo! Group" Search box at the top of the screen, and then click on the title
> "CardiacRhythmDisorders."
> This online Yahoo! support group is for patients who are afflicted with long QT
> syndrome and their families and friends. Yahoo! Groups is not a medical site,
> nor does it provide or endorse medical advice or procedures. The purpose of the
> website is to share experiences in a kind and caring manner. Free membership
> sign-up is required to participate.

Marfan Syndrome (DNA Abnormality or Genetic Disorder)

Each specific set of DNA molecules within a living cell contains the instructions for how that cell will develop, such as a heart cell or a brain cell. Each cell has a precise function. Highly specific groups of DNA molecules assemble together to create genes; however, the arrangement of those molecules is vital. These genes become the genetic code, or a how-to guidebook, for creating specific proteins.

Thousands of different but precisely designated proteins must team up and work together to create precisely designated cells as well as give directions to those cells about how to execute specific functions and instruct those cells on how to work with other cells to develop into hearts, livers, bladders, brains, etc. A genetic disorder can develop into a disease or defect, such as a congenital heart malformation, when a gene, or more than one gene, mutates while being exposed to a hostile environment, such as tobacco smoke, alcohol abuse, drug abuse, smog, pesticides, formaldehyde, paradichlorobenzene, and perchloroethylene; the last three in this list are in many common cleaning, beauty, and personal hygiene products. Also, a genetic disorder can be caused by inheriting a mutated gene, such as Down syndrome, trisomy 13, Turner syndrome, Marfan syndrome, Huntington's disease, cystic fibrosis, and Tay-Sachs disease. Most genetic disorders, such as heart disease, high blood pressure, arthritis, and diabetes, are caused by more than one genetic mutation; many disorders are caused by combinations of both inherited abnormal DNA (also called chromosome abnormality) and environmental mutations.

For example, red blood cells contain the protein hemoglobin, which bonds to oxygen to transport oxygen throughout the body. If a sequence (specific arrangement) of DNA molecules develops out of order, this action alters the instructions (mutation occurs). For example, if the genetic code for producing hemoglobin protein is altered (a DNA abnormality), a genetic disorder that can occur is sickle cell anemia, an inherited genetic disorder.

An example of an inherited genetic disorder is Marfan syndrome. Marfan syndrome is a genetic connective tissue disorder that affects many parts of the body, including the heart. Connective tissue supports and holds together all parts of the body. Not every patient with Marfan syndrome will have the same difficulties despite having the same defective gene. (The syndrome was first identified in a five-year-old-girl in 1896 by Antoine Marfan, a French pediatrician. It was not until 1991 that the problem gene was identified by Francesco Ramirez at Mount Sinai Medical Center in New York City.)

People with Marfan syndrome are typically tall and thin with long limbs and long fingers. This connective tissue disorder can cause problems, such as an indented chest, vision problems, crowded teeth, spontaneous lung collapse (pneumothorax), curvature of the spine (scoliosis), flat feet, and spinal cord problems (due to loss of its protective myelin sheath). The condition is incurable. Some of its symptoms may be addressed in childhood, while others may only manifest later in life.

In a Marfan patient, heart palpitations, angina, valve murmur and prolapse, dilated aorta, and aortic dissection are possible outcomes. Of these, in aortic dissection, a serious and possibly deadly situation, the layers of the aorta separate and peel apart due to high blood pressure. Eventually the blood vessel bursts, causing the patient to rapidly bleed to death internally. If such a condition goes undetected, it can cause death. However, if the condition is found soon enough, immediate surgery can sometimes save the patient. It can be detected by a bulging of the aorta near the heart, which can be seen on a radiograph. A preventive treatment is to replace that part of the aorta and its adjacent valve. A regimen of medicines can reduce the stress on the aorta and valves and mitigate the palpitations and angina.

Resources for Further Information on Marfan Syndrome

Books

> Parker, James N., and Philip M. Parker, eds. *The Official Patient's Sourcebook on Marfan Syndrome*. San Diego, CA: ICON Health, 2002. Print.
> This book, which offers patients a comprehensive background on Marfan syndrome, is divided into three sections: Section 1 describes "guidelines on diagnosis, treatments, and prognosis . . . organizations, associations, and networks." Section 2 describes advanced research and medical professional guidelines. Section 3 contains appendixes on types of medications, contraindications and drug interactions, alternative medications, nutritional advice, glossaries of terms, and patient responsibilities.

Brochures, Booklets, and Other Short Print Publications

> Cleveland Clinic (Cleveland, OH). *Marfan Syndrome Treatment Guide*. http://my .clevelandclinic.org/ccforms/heart_marfan_syndrome_guide.aspx; alternate path: http://my.clevelandclinic.org/, under the category "Institutes and Services," click on "Heart and Vascular" and then on the category "Diseases and Conditions," then scroll down to the title "Marfan Syndrome," and click on the title "Download a Free Guide on Marfan Syndrome Disease and Treatment."
> The Cleveland Clinic provides a comprehensive, patient-friendly, free guide on Marfan syndrome that includes an overview on Marfan syndrome, how Marfan syndrome affects you and your heart, and treatment options. For information on clinical trials, see the Cleveland Clinic entry on p. 206.

Websites

> Aetna InteliHealth—"Marfan's Syndrome." http://www.intelihealth.com/IH/ ihtIH/WSIHW000/8059/21403/221656.html?d=dmtHealthAZ; alternate path:

http://www.intelihealth.com/, search for "marfan syndrome," and then click on the title "Marfan's Syndrome."

This website provides an overview of Marfan syndrome, including symptoms, diagnosis, expected duration, prevention, treatment, when to call a professional, prognosis, and additional information. Aetna InteliHealth, a subsidiary of Aetna, is reviewed by the faculty of Harvard Medical School and University College of Dental Medicine. According to Aetna InteliHealth's website, "Aetna InteliHealth maintains absolute editorial independence. That means that Aetna InteliHealth makes decisions about the information on our site free of outside influence." Under "Healthy Lifestyle," Aetna InteliHealth also offers free health-related e-mail subscriptions.

➤ Brigham and Women's Hospital (Boston, MA)—"Marfan and Related Disease Clinic." http://www.brighamandwomens.org/Departments_and_Services/ medicine/services/cvcenter/genetics/marfan.aspx; alternate path: http://www .brighamandwomens.org/, scroll under the heading "Departments and Services" to the category titled "Centers of Excellence," click on the title "Cardiovascular," then under the heading "Cardiovascular Medicine" scroll down and click on the category "Cardiovascular Genetics Program," and then scroll down to click on "Marfan Syndrome/Connective Tissue Disorders."

Brigham and Women's Hospital offers "the only comprehensive adult Marfan clinic in the Northeast, including the entire New England region and New York [S]tate." This website discusses symptoms, diagnosis, and treatment. To possibly participate in a clinical trial at Brigham and Women's Hospital Cardiovascular Center, go to the website homepage, http://www.brighamandwomens.org/, click on the heading "Research," then on the category "Clinical Trials," and then on the title "Search Open Studies by Therapeutic Area." Scroll down the list to select topics, such as heart disease, high blood pressure, stroke, and vascular disorders. Under the heading "Patients and Visitors" click on "Find a Doctor" and select clinical specialty by drop-down Search box. Click on the name of the physician or specialist to view profile (e.g., specialty, medical board certification, education).

➤ Cleveland Clinic (Cleveland, OH)—"Marfan Syndrome." http://my.cleveland clinic.org/heart/disorders/aorta_marfan/marfan.aspx; alternate path: http://my .clevelandclinic.org/, under the category "Institutes and Services," click on "Heart and Vascular" and then on the category "Diseases and Conditions," and then scroll down to click on the title "Marfan Syndrome."

Cleveland Clinic provides comprehensive, patient-friendly information on Marfan syndrome, such as definitions, causes, symptoms, who is affected, diagnosis, genetic testing, treatments and lifestyle changes, prevention, and how to find a doctor who treats Marfan syndrome. The Cleveland Clinic also offers a link to "Chat Online with a Heart and Vascular Nurse." For information on clinical trials, see the Cleveland Clinic entry on p. 206.

➤ ClinicalTrials.gov—Marfan syndrome clinical trials. http://clinicaltrials.gov/ct2/ results?term=marfan+syndrome; alternate path: http://clinicaltrials.gov/, search for "marfan syndrome," click on "Modify This Search," select fields to limit your results (e.g., Recruitment—you might want to select "Open Studies"; Locations—select your state; and Age Group), click on the "Search" button, and then click on the title of each trial name for additional information, such as purpose of the study, study design and type, detailed description, outcome measures, eligibility (e.g., age, gender, criteria for participating), study start date, estimated study completion date, and sponsor. ClinicalTrials.gov, a service of the U.S. National Institutes of Health, lists ongoing and currently enrolling clinical trials. Check often for new studies.

➤ Johns Hopkins Hospital, Heart and Vascular Institute (Baltimore, MD)—"Marfan Syndrome." http://www.hopkinsmedicine.org/heart_vascular_institute/conditions _treatments/conditions/marfan_syndrome.html; alternate path: http://www .hopkinsmedicine.org/, search for and then click on the title "Marfan Syndrome." This webpage on Marfan syndrome discusses what Marfan syndrome is, what medical problems are associated with Marfan syndrome, symptoms, causes, diagnosis, and treatment. It also lists links to physicians and specialists (with profile, e.g., specialty, medical board certification, education) who treat Marfan syndrome. The Johns Hopkins Comprehensive Marfan Center (http://www .hopkinsmedicine.org/heart_vascular_institute/clinical_services/centers_excellence/ marfan_center.html) lists links to several centers throughout Johns Hopkins Medicine that provide diagnostic, treatment, and counseling services for Marfan patients. Categories of medical centers include diagnosis and medical management of Marfan syndrome, advanced genetics studies related to Marfan syndrome, individuals with the Marfan syndrome who need evaluation of aortic and heart disease for possible surgical intervention, evaluation and management of Marfan ocular problems, and evaluation and management of Marfan orthopedic problems. Click on the heading "Clinical Trials" for links to current trials in various heart and cardiovascular conditions.

➤ KidsHealth.org. http://kidshealth.org/.
The Nemours Center for Children's Health Media provides current information on conditions afflicting children, written for both children and parents. Information is available in English and Spanish. Some webpages contain a "Listen" button that you can click on to hear the text read aloud.

- *For Kids:* "Marfan Syndrome." http://kidshealth.org/kid/health_problems/ birth_defect/marfan.html; alternate path: http://www.kidshealth.org/, click on "Kids Site," scroll down and click on "Birth Defects and Genetic Problems," scroll down again and click on "Heart and Lungs," and then click on "Marfan Syndrome." For kids, this webpage includes such topics as definitions, how children get the condition, how doctors diagnose the condition, what doctors do, what a child with Marfan syndrome can do, and what life is like for children with Marfan syndrome.

- *For Parents:* "Marfan Syndrome" http://kidshealth.org/parent/medical/ heart/marfan.html#cat141; alternate path: http://www.kidshealth.org/, click on "Parents Site," scroll down and click on "Heart and Blood Vessels," scroll down again, click on "Heart and Blood Vessels," and then click on the title "Marfan Syndrome." For parents, this webpage includes discussion of definitions, causes, signs and symptoms, complications, skeletal problems, diagnosing, diagnostic criteria, monitoring and treatment, keeping active, caring for your child, finding safe activities, and when to call the doctor.
- *For Teens:* "Getting an EKG" (Video). http://kidshealth.org/teen/diseases _conditions/heart/video_ekg.html#cat20160; alternate path: http://www .kidshealth.org/, click on "Teens Site," scroll down and click on "Diseases and Conditions," then scroll down again, click on "Heart and Cardiovascular System," and then click on the title "EKG." To alleviate worries for your child, click on the "Listen" button and watch this two-minute video demonstration of a child getting an EKG.

➤ Massachusetts General Hospital (MGH) (Boston, MA)—"Thoracic Aortic Center." http://www.massgeneral.org/heartcenter/services/treatmentprograms.aspx?id=1010; alternate path: http://www.massgeneral.org/, search for and then click on the title "Thoracic Aortic Center"; or click on "Centers and Services," click on "View All Departments," click on "Heart Center," click on the heading "Treatments and Services," scroll down, and then click on the topic "Thoracic Aortic Center."

Because aortic aneurysms may be caused by atherosclerosis (hardening of the arteries), hypertension (high blood pressure), or a congenital abnormality (such as Marfan syndrome), this reference was included. The Thoracic Aortic Center at the MGH Heart Center website offers links to comprehensive information in several categories. "Our Approach" includes an overview of their team approach to multidisciplinary "care for patients with conditions of the thoracic aorta, including acute and chronic aortic dissections, thoracic and thoracoabdominal aortic aneurysms, Marfan syndrome and coarctation of the aorta," diagnosing thoracic aortic disease, imaging techniques, treatments, lifelong care, and links to each medical expert (with profile, e.g., specialty, medical board certification, education). "About This Program" describes the benefits, commitment, vision, and goal of the Thoracic Aortic Center at MGH and commitment to education. "Conditions and Diseases" has links to detailed information on "heart conditions and diseases that might be treated within this program": aortic anatomy, abdominal aortic aneurysm, and thoracic aortic aneurysm. "Support and Wellness" offers patient guides, such as *Understanding and Preparing for a Catheterization Procedure* and *Frequently Asked Questions about Cardiac Anesthesia.* "Clinical

Trials" has links to MGH trials and research studies when they are currently seeking participants. "News and Events" includes the latest information on related topics, and "Multimedia" contains video demonstrations.

> Mayo Clinic (Rochester, MN)—"Marfan Syndrome." http://www.mayoclinic.com/
> health/marfan-syndrome/DS00540; alternate path: http://www.mayoclinic.com/,
> search for and then click on the title "Marfan Syndrome."
> Written for patients, this information on Marfan syndrome includes links to definitions, symptoms, causes, risk factors, complications, preparing for appointments, tests and diagnosis, treatments and drugs, lifestyle and home remedies, and what's new. For information on clinical trials and patient services, see the Mayo Clinic entry on p. 207.

> MedicineNet—"Marfan Syndrome." http://www.medicinenet.com/marfan
> _syndrome/article.htm; alternate path: http://www.medicinenet.com/, click on
> the major topic "Diseases and Conditions," click on "Conditions A–Z," then
> click "M," and then scroll down to "Marfan Syndrome."
> Owned and operated by WebMD and part of the WebMD Network, according to its website MedicineNet "provides easy-to-read, in-depth, authoritative medical information for consumers via its robust user-friendly, interactive website." In-depth information on Marfan syndrome includes definitions, causes, symptoms, diagnosis, treatment, type of doctors who treat Marfan syndrome, what research is being conducted, patient discussions, and finding a local cardiologist. The medical information is written and edited by a nationally recognized group of more than 70 U.S. board-certified physicians. The website contains a "Symptom Checker" listed in alphabetical order as a guide to pinpoint pain. MedicineNet's homepage lists links to articles in a section titled "Health News of the Week." Also available is a health newsletter sign-up.

> MedlinePlus—"Marfan Syndrome." http://www.nlm.nih.gov/medlineplus/marfan
> syndrome.html; alternate path: http://www.nlm.nih.gov/, under "Databases," click
> on "MedlinePlus," and then search for "marfan syndrome."
> MedlinePlus, a component of the National Institutes of Health (NIH) and produced by the National Library of Medicine (NLM), is updated regularly. This MedlinePlus webpage on Marfan syndrome offers extensive linked information covering overviews, diagnosis/symptoms, treatment, disease, related issues, clinical trials, genetics, journal articles, directories, organizations, and specific sections that focus on children, teenagers, and women, plus patient handouts. This website also includes a multimedia section containing tutorials.

> National Heart, Lung, and Blood Institute (NHLBI)—"What Is Marfan Syndrome?" http://www.nhlbi.nih.gov/health/dci/Diseases/mar/mar_whatis.html;

alternate path: http://www.nhlbi.nih.gov/, search for "marfan syndrome," and then click on the title "What Is Marfan Syndrome?"
NHLBI, a division of National Institutes of Health (NIH) from the U.S. Department of Health and Human Services, provides additional information on Marfan syndrome, including links to what Marfan syndrome is, causes, risk factors, signs and symptoms, diagnosis, treatments, living with Marfan syndrome, clinical trials, key points, and additional information about Marfan syndrome.

➤ National Marfan Foundation (NMF). http://www.marfan.org/.
The NMF has family- and patient-friendly information on living with Marfan syndrome, research, diagnosis, treatments, asking a question, finding a doctor, an online children's book, lists of conferences and events, related disorders, and an NMF newsletter.

➤ Texas Heart Institute (Houston, TX)—"Marfan Syndrome" (Heart Information Center). http://www.texasheartinstitute.org/HIC/Topics/Cond/marfans.cfm; alternate path: http://www.texasheartinstitute.org/, search for and then click on the title "Marfan Syndrome"; or scroll down to the heading "Heart Information Center" to click on "Heart-Health Topics," click on "Heart Conditions," and then click on "Marfan Syndrome."
The Texas Heart Institute website offers a definition of marfan syndrome, as well as information on causes, signs and symptoms, diagnosis, and treatment. An easy-to-print format is available. To participate in a clinical trial, if available in your cardiology condition, at the Texas Heart Institute Research Laboratory, visit http://www .texasheartinstitute.org/Research/hfresearch.cfm (or return to the Texas Heart Institute homepage, click on the heading "Research," under the category "Departments," click on the title "Heart Failure Research Laboratory"). Scroll down to the section "Research Projects," and click on the title "FDA-Approved Clinical Trials." Under the heading "About Us," click on "Professional Staff Directory." Click on category to view a list of physicians and specialists (with profile, e.g., specialty, medical board certification, education).

➤ WebMD—"Heart Disease and Marfan Syndrome." http://www.webmd.com/ heart-disease/guide/marfan-syndrome; alternate path: http://www.webmd.com/, search for "marfan syndrome," and then click on the resource title.
The WebMD website offers information on Marfan syndrome such as causes, diagnosis, treatment options, medications and surgery, and outlook for people with Marfan syndrome. Available is a WebMD heart health e-mail newsletter. According to WebMD, "WebMD News is an independent media service designed to provide news, information, and educational material to consumers and physicians. News content created by WebMD is free from influence by sponsors, partners, or other sources."

Patient Support Groups and Organizations

➤ Canadian Marfan Association (CMA). http://www.marfan.ca/.
CMA, a member of the International Federation of Marfan Syndrome Organizations, is a nonprofit organization that provides an education and support network to patients and their families, including youth support groups, to help improve quality of life.

➤ Children's Hospital of Philadelphia (CHOP) (Philadelphia, PA)—"Marfan Syndrome Support Group." http://www.chop.edu/visitors/family-support-and-resources/support -groups.html; alternate path: http://www.chop.edu/, click on the heading "For Patients and Visitors," click on the category "Family Support and Resources," and then click on the category "Support Groups."
CHOP "hosts" support groups, including one designated to Marfan syndrome, at the hospital. According to its support group website, "Through these groups, parents and caregivers meet others facing similar issues, exchange helpful, practical information and learn new skills to help in caring for their child, while managing his or her healthcare and any stress that family members may be experiencing as a result of their child's diagnosis or medical condition."

➤ DailyStrength—"Marfan Syndrome Support Group." http://www.dailystrength.org/ c/Marfan-Syndrome/support-group; alternate path: http://www.dailystrength.org/, search for "marfan syndrome," and then click on the group name.
The DailyStrength website offers online support groups and blogs for those with Marfan syndrome. Free registration sign-up is required to participate. According to the website, "DailyStrength is a subsidiary of Sharecare. Sharecare, created by WebMD founder and Discovery Communications Chief of Global Digital Strategy Jeff Arnold, along with America's Doctor, Dr. Mehmet Oz, is the first truly interactive healthcare ecosystem giving consumers the ability to ask, learn and act on the questions of health."

➤ MedHelp—"Marfan Syndrome." http://www.medhelp.org/search?query=Marfan +Syndrome; alternate path: http://www.medhelp.org/, search for "marfan syndrome," and then click on the group name.
According to its website, MedHelp "connects people with the leading medical experts," such as those from Cleveland Clinic, National Jewish Health, Partners Health, and Mount Sinai Hospital, and with those who have similar medical issues. MedHelp's main focus is to enable patients "to take control over their health and find answers to their medical questions" using nontechnical language via an online community through posts, forums and groups, blogs, user journals, as well as recommendations, articles, health pages, and a medical glossary. Free registration is required

➤ U.S. Hospital Finder. http://www.ushospitalfinder.com/.
Use this site to find the names of hospitals by zip code, city, state, or your address. The search results include a map with directions. You might also want to ask your

health care professional, call hospitals in your area, or search for "support groups" on hospital websites to determine if there are any cardiology support groups for people with Marfan syndrome that meet regularly in your area.

➤ Yahoo! Groups—"Marfans Syndrome Support and Chat." http://health.groups .yahoo.com/group/marfans_support_and_chat/; alternate path: http://www.groups .yahoo.com/, search for "marfan syndrome" in the "Find a Yahoo! Group" Search box and then click on "marfans_support_and_chat."

This online Yahoo! support group is for patients who are afflicted with Marfan syndrome and their families and friends. Yahoo! Groups is not a medical website, nor does it provide or endorse medical advice or procedures. The purpose of the website is to share experiences in a kind and caring manner. Free membership sign-up is required to participate. There are several Yahoo! Groups support groups on Marfan syndrome.

Multiple Congenital Heart Defects

Other types of congenital heart disease are a combination of multiple heart defects, such as atrioventricular canal defect (atrioventricular septal defect), hypoplastic left heart syndrome, and tetralogy of Fallot, the latter of which has four defects: pulmonary valve stenosis, an enlarged ventricular septal defect, an aorta that is not positioned properly, and right ventricular hypertrophy (muscle too thick).

To learn more, visit the **National Heart, Lung, and Blood Institute** of the National Institutes of Health at http://www.nhlbi.nih.gov/health/health-topics/topics/chd/types.html; alternate path: http://www.nhlbi.nih.gov/, search for and then click on the title "Types of Congenital Heart Defects." This webpage includes an illustration of a cross-section comparison of a normal heart versus one with the four defects of tetralogy of Fallot.

Resources for Further Information on Multiple Congenital Heart Defects

See also RESOURCES FOR FURTHER INFORMATION ON CONGENITAL HEART DISEASE at the end of this chapter for a more comprehensive list of resources.

➤ Children's Hospital Colorado (Aurora, CO)—"Complex Congenital Heart Disease and Development Clinic." http://www.childrenscolorado.org/conditions/ heart/services/treatments-programs/complex-congenital-heart-disease-and -development-clinic/complex-congenital.aspx; alternate path: http://www .childrenscolorado.org/, search for "complex congenital heart disease," and then scroll down to click on the title "Complex Congenital Heart Disease and Development Clinic."

The Children's Hospital Colorado (of University of Colorado School of Medicine) website discusses topics such as follow-up care after heart surgery and throughout childhood and the types of complex congenital heart diseases that CCHDD treats.

Atrioventricular Septal Defects—AV Canal

➢ Cincinnati Children's Hospital Medical Center (Cincinnati, OH)—"Atrioventricular Septal Defects—AV Canal." http://www.cincinnatichildrens.org/patients/child/encyclopedia/defects/avsd/; alternate path: http://www.cincinnatichildrens.org/, search for "atrioventricular septal defects," and then click on the resource title.

Cincinnati Children's Hospital provides patient-friendly information on atrioventricular septal defects (AVSD). Click on such topics as categories, problems with AVSD, signs and symptoms, diagnosis, and treatment. Under the heading "Patients and Families" click on "Clinical Services" to search for any current studies.

➢ Lucile Packard Children's Hospital at Stanford (Palo Alto, CA)—"Atrioventricular Canal (AV Canal or AVC)." http://www.lpch.org/DiseaseHealthInfo/HealthLibrary/cardiac/avc.html; alternate path: http://www.lpch.org/, search for "atrioventricular canal," and then click on the resource title.

The Lucile Packard Children's Hospital at Stanford (of Stanford University School of Medicine) website provides such information as what atrioventricular canal (AVC) is, including illustrations, causes, why it is a concern, symptoms, diagnosis, treatments, postoperative care, follow-up, and long-term outlook. Under the heading "For Patients and Families" are links to many services.

➢ Mayo Clinic (Rochester, MN)—"Atrioventricular Canal Defect." http://www.mayoclinic.com/health/atrioventricular-canal-defect/DS00745; alternate path: http://www.mayoclinic.com/, search for and then click on the title "Atrioventricular Canal Defect."

Written for patients, this information on atrioventricular canal defect includes links definitions, symptoms, causes, risk factors, complications, preparing for appointments, tests and diagnosis, treatments and drugs, coping and support, and prevention. There is also a more comprehensive section titled "In-Depth" on some of these topics. For information on clinical trials and patient services, see the Mayo Clinic entry on p. 207.

Hypoplastic Left Heart Syndrome

➢ Centers for Disease Control and Prevention (CDC)—"Facts about Hypoplastic Left Heart Syndrome." http://www.cdc.gov/ncbddd/heartdefects/HLHS.html; alternate path: http://www.cdc.gov/, search for "hypoplastic left heart syndrome," and then click on the resource title.

At the CDC website, there are several topics to click on, such as facts, causes and risks, diagnosis, and treatments.

➤ Children's Hospital of Philadelphia (CHOP) (Philadelphia, PA)—"Hypoplastic Left Heart Syndrome (HLHS)." http://www.chop.edu/service/cardiac-center/heart-conditions/hypoplastic-left-heart-syndrome-hlhs.html; alternate path: http://www.chop.edu/, click on the heading "Specialties and Services" and then on "Cardiac Center," click on the category "Heart Conditions," and then scroll down to click on the topic.

CHOP's Cardiac Center offers information on HLHS, such as how a normal heart works, what HLHS is, including an illustration and an animation, symptoms, diagnosis, treatment, and follow-up. Also available are links to cardiac news, cardiac research at CHOP, videos, patient stories, meeting the specialists in the team (with profile, e.g., specialty, medical board certification, education), consultations and second opinions, and taking a virtual tour.

➤ Mayo Clinic (Rochester, MN)—"Hypoplastic Left Heart Syndrome." http://www.mayoclinic.com/health/hypoplastic-left-heart-syndrome/DS00744; alternate path: http://www.mayoclinic.com/, search for and then click on the title "Hypoplastic Left Heart Syndrome."

Written for patients, this information on hypoplastic left heart syndrome includes links to definitions, symptoms, causes, risk factors, complications, tests and diagnosis, treatments and drugs, prevention, and coping and support. There is also a more comprehensive section titled "In-Depth" on some of these topics. For information on clinical trials and patient services, see the Mayo Clinic entry on p. 207.

➤ Medscape Reference (Drugs, Diseases, and Procedures)—"Pediatric Hypoplastic Left Heart Syndrome." http://emedicine.medscape.com/article/890196-overview; alternate path: http://emedicine.medscape.com/, search for and then click on the title "Pediatric Hypoplastic Left Heart Syndrome."

Written for Medscape by medical doctor P. Syamasundar Rao and colleagues, this webpage presents a comprehensive report on pediatric hypoplastic left heart syndrome. Although written for health care professionals, it might be helpful for interested laypersons. Articles for Medscape Reference are written by medical experts. The website states, "Our rigorous literature survey process allows us to rapidly integrate new practice-changing information into the relevant topics by systematically reviewing the major medical and pharmacy journals, news announcements, and important practice guidelines." Free registration is required.

Tetralogy of Fallot

➤ Children's Hospital of Philadelphia (CHOP) (Philadelphia, PA)—"Tetralogy of Fallot." http://www.chop.edu/service/cardiac-center/heart-conditions/tetralogy

-of-fallot.html; alternate path: http://www.chop.edu/, click on the heading "Specialties and Services" and then on the category "Cardiac Center," click on "Heart Conditions," and then scroll down to click on the topic.

CHOP's Cardiac Center offers information on tetralogy of Fallot such as how a normal heart works, what tetralogy of Fallot is, including an animation, symptoms, diagnosis, treatment, and follow-up. Also available are links to cardiac news, cardiac research at CHOP, videos, patient stories, meeting the specialists in the team (with profile, e.g., specialty, medical board certification, education), consultations and second opinions, and taking a virtual tour.

> Cleveland Clinic (Cleveland, OH)—"Tetralogy of Fallot in Adults." http://my .clevelandclinic.org/heart/disorders/congenital/tetralogy_of_fallot_in_adults.aspx; alternate path: http://my.clevelandclinic.org/, under the category "Institutes and Services," click on "Heart and Vascular," then click on the category "Diseases and Conditions," then scroll down to "Congenital Heart Disease," and click on "Tetralogy of Fallot in Adults."

Cleveland Clinic provides comprehensive patient-friendly information on tetralogy of Fallot, such as definitions, including illustrations, cause, diagnosis, treatments, potential complications, and how to find a doctor who treats congenital heart disease. The Cleveland Clinic also offers a link to "Chat Online with a Heart and Vascular Nurse." For information on clinical trials, see the Cleveland Clinic entry on p. 206.

> eMedicineHealth (from Healthwise). "Tetralogy of Fallot." http://www.emedicine health.com/tetralogy_of_fallot/article_em.htm and http://www.emedicinehealth .com/tetralogy_of_fallot-health/article_em.htm; alternate path: http://www .emedicinehealth.com/, search for and then click on the title "Tetralogy of Fallot" (Medical Reference from eMedicineHealth and Healthwise).

A division of WebMD, eMedicineHealth offers a comprehensive article on tetralogy of Fallot with such information as overviews, causes, symptoms, diagnosis, treatment, self-care at home, follow-ups, outlook, and when to seek medical care.

> Mayo Clinic (Rochester, MN)—"Tetralogy of Fallot." http://www.mayoclinic .com/health/tetralogy-of-fallot/DS00615; alternate path: http://www.mayoclinic .com/, search for and then click on the title "Tetralogy of Fallot."

Written for patients, this information on tetralogy of Fallot includes links to definitions, symptoms, causes, risk factors, complications, preparing for appointments, tests and diagnosis, treatments and drugs, lifestyle and home remedies, and coping and support. There is also a more comprehensive section titled "In-Depth" on some of these topics. For information on clinical trials and patient services, see the Mayo Clinic entry on p. 207.

> Medscape Reference (Drugs, Diseases, and Procedures)—"Tetralogy of Fallot." http://emedicine.medscape.com/article/2035949-overview; alternate path:

http://emedicine.medscape.com/, search for and then click on the title "Tetralogy of Fallot."
Written for Medscape by two medical doctors, Shabir Bhimji and Gary Setnik, this webpage presents a comprehensive report on tetralogy of Fallot. Although written for health care professionals, it might be helpful for interested laypersons. Articles for Medscape Reference are written by medical experts. The website states, "Our rigorous literature survey process allows us to rapidly integrate new practice-changing information into the relevant topics by systematically reviewing the major medical and pharmacy journals, news announcements, and important practice guidelines." Free registration is required.

➤ National Heart, Lung, and Blood Institute (NHLBI)—"What Is Tetralogy of Fallot?" http://www.nhlbi.nih.gov/health/health-topics/topics/tof/; alternate path: http://www.nhlbi.nih.gov/, search for "tetralogy of Fallot," and then click on the title "What Is Tetralogy of Fallot?"
NHLBI, a division of National Institutes of Health (NIH) from the U.S. Department of Health and Human Services, provides additional information on tetralogy of Fallot, including links to definitions, other names, causes, signs and symptoms, diagnosis, treatments, living with tetralogy of Fallot, and clinical trials.

➤ WebMD—"Tetralogy of Fallot." http://www.webmd.com/heart-disease/tetralogy-fallot; alternate path: http://www.webmd.com/, search for and then click on the title "Tetralogy of Fallot."
WebMD website offers information such as definitions, causes, symptoms, when to seek medical care, exams and tests, treatments, follow-up, and outlook. WebMD's heart health e-mail newsletter is also available. According to the website, "WebMD News is an independent media service designed to provide news, information, and educational material to consumers and physicians. News content created by WebMD is free from influence by sponsors, partners, or other sources."

Patient Support Groups and Organizations

For additional related patient support groups, *see* RESOURCES FOR FURTHER INFORMATION ON CONGENITAL HEART DISEASE at the end of this chapter.

➤ MedHelp. http://www.medhelp.org/.
According to its website, MedHelp "connects people with the leading medical experts," such as those from Cleveland Clinic, National Jewish Health, Partners Health, and Mount Sinai Hospital, and with those who have similar medical issues. MedHelp's main focus is to enable patients "to take control over their health and find answers to their medical questions" using nontechnical language via an online community. Free registration is required. From the homepage, you

can find the following and other related groups by searching for the name of the condition.

- "Hypoplastic Left Heart Syndrome." http://www.medhelp.org/search?query =hypoplastic+left+heart+syndrome.
- "Tetralogy of Fallot." http://www.medhelp.org/search?query=Tetralogy +of+Fallot.

➤ U.S. Hospital Finder. http://www.ushospitalfinder.com/.
Use this site to find the names of hospitals by zip code, city, state, or your address. The search results include a map with directions. You might also want to ask your health care professional, call hospitals in your area, or search for "support groups" on hospital websites to determine if there are any cardiology support groups for people with congenital heart disease that meet regularly in your area.

➤ Yahoo! Groups. http://www.groups.yahoo.com/.
Yahoo! Groups is not a medical site, nor does it provide or endorse medical advice or procedures. The purpose of the website is to share experiences in a kind and caring manner. Free membership sign-up is required to participate. From the homepage, you can find the following and related groups by searching for the name of the condition in the "Find a Yahoo! Group" Search box.

- "Hope for Children with HLHS." http://www.groups.yahoo.com/group/ Atrial_Septal_Defects/. This online Yahoo! support group is for patients who are afflicted with HLHS and their families and friends.
- "Tetralogy of Fallot." http://health.groups.yahoo.com/group/tetralogy_of _fallot/. This online Yahoo! support group is for patients who are afflicted with tetralogy of Fallot and their families and friends.

Narrowed Heart Valves

Blood flows through the heart from the atria to the ventricles into its two arteries known as the aorta and pulmonary arteries. If any of these valves is narrowed, blood cannot flow through quickly enough. Cyanotic defects cause poor circulation to the lungs, preventing the blood from being fully oxygenated. The result is a bluish appearance of the infant's skin at birth and until the defect is repaired. There are three types of narrowed valve defects: stenosis, which causes the heart to pump harder because the valve is not able to fully open; atresia, which is an incompletely formed heart valve that blocks blood flow; and regurgitation, where some blood leaks backward because the valves do not close fully. The most common valve defect is pulmonary valve stenosis. Other types include aortic valve stenosis, transposition of the great vessels, tricuspid atresia, total anomalous pulmonary venous return, truncus arteriosus, some forms of total anomalous pulmonary venous return, and Ebstein's anomaly (*see* GLOSSARY).

Resources for Further Information on Narrowed Heart Valves

See also RESOURCES FOR FURTHER INFORMATION ON CONGENITAL HEART DISEASE at the end of this chapter for a more comprehensive list of resources.

➤ Lucile Packard Children's Hospital at Stanford (Palo Alto, CA)—"Heart Defects Causing Too Little Blood Flow through the Lungs." http://www.lpch.org/DiseaseHealthInfo/HealthLibrary/cardiac/toolitle.html; alternate path: http://www.lpch.org/, search for "heart defects causing too little blood flow," and then click on the title "Heart Defects Causing Too Little Blood Flow through the Lungs."
The Lucile Packard Children's Hospital of Stanford (of Stanford University School of Medicine) website provides information on heart defects causing too little blood flow through the lungs, links to such topics as tricuspid atresia, pulmonary atresia, transposition of the great arteries, and tetralogy of Fallot. Each topic further discusses definitions, including illustrations, causes, symptoms, diagnosis, treatments, postoperative care, follow-up, and long-term outlook. Under the heading "For Patients and Families" are links to many services.

Aortic Valve Stenosis

➤ Cincinnati Children's Hospital Medical Center (Cincinnati, OH)—"Aortic Stenosis." http://www.cincinnatichildrens.org/health/a/avs/; alternate path: http://www.cincinnatichildrens.org/, search for and then click on the title "Aortic Valve Stenosis."
Cincinnati Children's Hospital provides patient-friendly information on ventricular septal defect, including an illustration and an animation. Click on such topics as descriptions, signs and symptoms, diagnosis, treatment, and long-term outlook. Under the heading "Patients and Families," click on "Clinical Trials" to search for current studies.

➤ eMedicineHealth (from Healthwise)—"Aortic Valve Stenosis." http://www.emedicinehealth.com/aortic_valve_stenosis-health/article_em.htm; alternate path: http://www.emedicinehealth.com/, search for and then click on the title "Aortic Valve Stenosis."
A division of WebMD, eMedicineHealth offers a comprehensive article on aortic valve stenosis with such discussion areas as overviews, FAQs, causes, diagnosis, treatment, ongoing concerns, follow-ups, outlook, and when to seek medical care.

➤ Mayo Clinic (Rochester, MN)—"Aortic Valve Stenosis." http://www.mayoclinic.com/health/aortic-valve-stenosis/DS00418; alternate path: http://www.mayoclinic.com/, search for and then click on the title "Aortic Valve Stenosis."
Written for patients, this information on aortic valve stenosis includes links to definitions, symptoms, causes, risk factors, complications, preparing for appointments, tests and diagnosis, treatments and drugs, and prevention. There is also a

more comprehensive section titled "In-Depth" on some of these topics. For information on clinical trials and patient services, see the Mayo Clinic entry on p. 207.

➤ MedicineNet—"Aortic Valve Stenosis." http://www.medicinenet.com/aortic _stenosis/article.htm; alternate path: http://www.medicinenet.com/, click on the major topic "Diseases and Conditions," click on "Conditions A–Z," then click "A," and then scroll down to "Aortic Valve Stenosis."
MedicineNet is owned and operated by WebMD and is part of the WebMD Network. According to its website, it "provides easy-to-read, in-depth, authoritative medical information for consumers via its robust user-friendly, interactive website." In-depth information on aortic valve stenosis includes definitions, how the heart works, causes, symptoms, diagnosis, treatment, patient discussions, and finding a local cardiologist. There is also a section titled "Suggested Reading on Aortic Stenosis by Our Doctors." The medical information is written and edited by a nationally recognized group of more than 70 U.S. board-certified physicians. The website contains a "Symptom Checker" listed in alphabetical order as a "guide to pinpoint your pain." MedicineNet's homepage lists links to articles in a section titled "Health News of the Week." Also available is a health newsletter sign-up.

➤ Medscape Reference (Drugs, Diseases, and Procedures)—"Pediatric Valvar Aortic Stenosis." http://emedicine.medscape.com/article/894095-overview; alternate path: http://emedicine.medscape.com/, search for "aortic valve stenosis," and then click on the resource title.
Written for Medscape by two medical doctors, Howard S. Weber and Paul M. Seib, this webpage presents a comprehensive report on aortic valve stenosis. Although written for the health care professional, it might be helpful for interested laypersons. Articles on Medscape Reference are written by medical experts. The website states, "Our rigorous literature survey process allows us to rapidly integrate new practice-changing information into the relevant topics by systematically reviewing the major medical and pharmacy journals, news announcements, and important practice guidelines." Free registration is required.

➤ WebMD—"Aortic Valve Stenosis." http://www.webmd.com/heart-disease/tc/ aortic-valve-stenosis-overview; alternate path: http://www.webmd.com/, search for and then click on the title "Aortic Valve Stenosis."
The WebMD website offers such information as a definition of aortic valve stenosis, causes, symptoms, diagnosis, treatments, and more information. WebMD's heart health e-mail newsletter is also available. According to its website, "WebMD News is an independent media service designed to provide news, information, and educational material to consumers and physicians. News content created by WebMD is free from influence by sponsors, partners, or other sources."

Pulmonary Atresia

➢ Children's Hospital of Philadelphia (CHOP) (Philadelphia, PA)—"Pulmonary Atresia." http://www.chop.edu/service/cardiac-center/heart-conditions/pulmonary -atresia.html; alternate path: http://www.chop.edu/, click on the heading "Specialties and Services" and then on the category "Cardiac Center," click on the category "Heart Conditions," and then scroll down to click on the topic "Pulmonary Atresia."

CHOP's Cardiac Center offers information on pulmonary atresia, such as how a normal heart works, what patent pulmonary atresia is, symptoms, diagnosis, treatment, and follow-up. Also available are links to cardiac news, cardiac research at CHOP, videos, patient stories, meet the specialists in the team (with profile, e.g., specialty, medical board certification, education), consultations and second opinions, and taking a virtual tour.

➢ Cincinnati Children's Hospital Medical Center (Cincinnati, OH)—"Pulmonary Atresia (PA)." http://www.cincinnatichildrens.org/patients/child/encyclopedia/ defects/pa/; alternate path: http://www.cincinnatichildrens.org/, search for "pulmonary atresia," and then click on the resource title.

Cincinnati Children's Hospital provides patient-friendly information on pulmonary atresia. Click on such topics as signs and symptoms, diagnosis, and treatment. Under the heading "Patients and Families," click on "Clinical Trials" to search for any current studies.

➢ Lucile Packard Children's Hospital at Stanford (Palo Alto, CA)—"Pulmonary Atresia (PA)." http://www.lpch.org/DiseaseHealthInfo/HealthLibrary/cardiac/pa .html; alternate path: http://www.lpch.org/, search for "pulmonary atresia," and then click on the resource title.

The Lucile Packard Children's Hospital at Stanford (of Stanford University School of Medicine) website provides information on topics such as definitions, including illustrations, causes, symptoms, diagnosis, treatments, postoperative care, follow-up, and long-term outlook. Under the heading "For Patients and Families" are links to many services.

➢ Mayo Clinic (Rochester, MN). "Pulmonary Atresia." http://www.mayoclinic .com/health/pulmonary-atresia/DS01204; alternate path: http://www.mayoclinic .com/; search for and then click on the title "Pulmonary Atresia."

Written for patients, this webpage on pulmonary atresia includes links to definitions, symptoms, causes, risk factors, complications, preparing for appointments, tests and diagnosis, treatments and drugs, coping and support, and prevention. Some of these topics also include a more comprehensive section titled "In-Depth." For information on clinical trials and patient services, see the Mayo Clinic entry on p. 207.

Pulmonary Valve Stenosis

➤ American Heart Association (AHA)—"Pulmonary Valve Stenosis." http://www
.heart.org/HEARTORG/Conditions/CongenitalHeartDefects/AboutCongenital
HeartDefects/Pulmonary-Valve-Stenosis_UCM_307034_Article.jsp; alternate
path: http://www.heart.org/, search for and then click on the title "Pulmonary
Valve Stenosis."
Click on such topics as "Parents of Children with Pulmonary Valve Stenosis" and
"Adults with Pulmonary Valve Stenosis."

➤ Children's Hospital of Philadelphia (CHOP) (Philadelphia, PA)—"Pulmonary Stenosis." http://www.chop.edu/service/cardiac-center/heart-conditions/pulmonary
-stenosis.html; alternate path: http://www.chop.edu/, click on the heading "Specialties and Services" and then on the category "Cardiac Center," click on the category "Heart Conditions," and then scroll down to click on the topic "Pulmonary
Stenosis."
CHOP's Cardiac Center offers information on pulmonary stenosis, such as how
a normal heart works, what pulmonary stenosis is, symptoms, diagnosis, treatment, and follow-up. Also available are links to cardiac news, cardiac research at
CHOP, videos, patient stories, meet the specialists in the team (with profile, e.g.,
specialty, medical board certification, education), consultations and second
opinions, and take a virtual tour.

➤ Cincinnati Children's Hospital Medical Center (Cincinnati, OH)—"Pulmonary
Valvar Stenosis." http://www.cincinnatichildrens.org/patients/child/encyclopedia/
defects/pvs/; alternate path: http://www.cincinnatichildrens.org/, search for "pulmonary stenosis," and then click on the resource title.
Cincinnati Children's Hospital provides patient-friendly information on pulmonary valvar stenosis. Click on such topics as signs and symptoms, diagnosis, and
treatment. Under the heading "Patients and Families," click on "Clinical Trials"
to search for any current studies.

➤ Cleveland Clinic (Cleveland, OH)—"Pulmonary Artery Stenosis." http://my
.clevelandclinic.org/disorders/pulmonary_artery_stenosis/hic_Pulmonary_Artery
_Stenosis.aspx; alternate path: http://my.clevelandclinic.org/, under the category
"Institutes and Services," click on "Heart Vascular," then click on the category "Diseases and Conditions," and then scroll down to the title "Congenital Heart Disease"
and click on "Pulmonary Artery Stenosis."
Cleveland Clinic provides comprehensive patient-friendly information on pulmonary artery stenosis, such as definitions, including illustrations, symptoms,
causes, diagnosis, treatments, and how to find a doctor who treats congenital
heart disease. For information on clinical trials, see the Cleveland Clinic entry
on p. 206.

➤ Lucile Packard Children's Hospital at Stanford (Palo Alto, CA)—"Pulmonary Stenosis." http://www.lpch.org/DiseaseHealthInfo/HealthLibrary/cardiac/ps .html; alternate path: http://www.lpch.org/, search for and then click on the title "Pulmonary Stenosis."

The Lucile Packard Children's Hospital at Stanford (of Stanford University School of Medicine) website provides information on such topics as what pulmonary stenosis is, including illustrations, types, causes, symptoms, diagnosis, treatments, postoperative care, follow-up, and long-term outlook. Under the heading "For Patients and Families" are links to many services.

➤ Mayo Clinic (Rochester, MN)—"Pulmonary Valve Stenosis." http://www.mayoclinic .com/health/pulmonary-valve-stenosis/DS00610; alternate path: http://www .mayoclinic.com/, search for and then click on the title "Pulmonary Valve Stenosis." Written for patients, this information on pulmonary valve stenosis includes links to definitions, symptoms, causes, risk factors, complications, preparing for appointments, tests and diagnosis, treatments and drugs, and prevention. There is also a more comprehensive section titled "In-Depth" on some of these topics. For information on clinical trials and patient services, see the Mayo Clinic entry on p. 207.

➤ Medscape Reference (Drugs, Diseases, and Procedures)—"Valvar Pulmonary Stenosis." http://emedicine.medscape.com/article/891729-overview; alternate path: http://emedicine.medscape.com/, search for and then click on the title "Valvar Pulmonary Stenosis."

Written for Medscape by medical doctor P. Syamasundar Rao and colleagues, this webpage presents a comprehensive report on pulmonary valve stenosis. Although written for health care professionals, it might be helpful for interested laypersons. The articles for Medscape Reference are written by medical experts. The website states, "Our rigorous literature survey process allows us to rapidly integrate new practice-changing information into the relevant topics by systematically reviewing the major medical and pharmacy journals, news announcements, and important practice guidelines." Free registration is required.

Tricuspid Atresia

➤ Children's Hospital of Philadelphia (CHOP) (Philadelphia, PA)—"Tricuspid Atresia." http://www.chop.edu/service/cardiac-center/heart-conditions/tricuspid -atresia.html; alternate path: http://www.chop.edu/, click on the heading "Specialties and Services" and then on the category "Cardiac Center," click on the category "Heart Conditions," and then scroll down to click on the topic "Tricuspid Atresia."

CHOP's Cardiac Center offers information on tricuspid atresia, such as how a normal heart works, what tricuspid atresia is, symptoms, diagnosis, treatment, and follow-up. Also available are links to cardiac news, cardiac research at CHOP, videos, patient stories, meeting the specialists in the team (with profile, e.g., specialty, medical board certification, education), consultations and second opinions, and taking a virtual tour.

➢ Cleveland Clinic (Cleveland, OH)—"Tricuspid Atresia." http://my.clevelandclinic .org/disorders/pediatric/congenital-heart-defects/hic-tricuspid-atresia.aspx; alternate path: http://my.clevelandclinic.org/, under the category "Institutes and Services," click on "Heart Vascular," then click on the category "Diseases and Conditions," and then scroll down to the title "Congenital Heart Disease" and click on "Tricuspid Atresia."
Cleveland Clinic provides comprehensive patient-friendly information on tricuspid atresia, such as definitions, diagnosis, risk factors, causes, symptoms, treatments, outlook, and how to find a doctor who treats congenital heart disease. For information on clinical trials, see the Cleveland Clinic entry on p. 206.

➢ Mayo Clinic (Rochester, MN)—"Tricuspid Atresia." http://www.mayoclinic.com/ health/tricuspid-atresia/DS00796; alternate path: http://www.mayoclinic.com/, search for and then click on the title "Tricuspid Atresia."
Written for patients, this information on tricuspid atresia includes links to definitions, symptoms, causes, risk factors, complications, preparing for appointments, tests and diagnosis, treatments and drugs, lifestyle changes, coping and support, and prevention. There is also a more comprehensive section titled "In-Depth" on some of these topics. For information on clinical trials and patient services, see the Mayo Clinic entry on p. 207.

➢ Medscape Reference (Drugs, Diseases, and Procedures)—"Tricuspid Atresia." http:// emedicine.medscape.com/article/158359-overview; alternate path: http://emedicine .medscape.com/, search for and then click on the title "Tricuspid Atresia."
Written for Medscape by medical doctor Mary C. Mancini, this webpage presents a comprehensive report on tricuspid atresia. Although written for health care professionals, it might be helpful for interested laypersons. The articles for Medscape Reference are written by medical experts. The website states, "Our rigorous literature survey process allows us to rapidly integrate new practice-changing information into the relevant topics by systematically reviewing the major medical and pharmacy journals, news announcements, and important practice guidelines." Free registration is required.

➢ New York–Presbyterian (NYP) Morgan Stanley Children's Hospital of the University Hospital of Columbia and Cornell (New York, NY)—"Tricuspid Atresia." http:// childrensnyp.org/mschony/cardiac-ta.html; alternate path: http://childrensnyp.org/, click on "Morgan Stanley Children's Hospital," and then search for and click on the title "Tricuspid Atresia."

NYP University Hospital of Columbia and Cornell website provides patient-friendly information on tricuspid atresia, such as its definition, why it is a concern, symptoms, diagnosis, treatment, postoperative care, follow-up, and long-term outlook. To possibly participate in a clinical trial at NYP University Hospital Cardiology Center, if one is available, go to the homepage (http://nyp.org/), click on the heading "Research and Clinical Trials," then click on the category "Clinical Trials at New York–Presbyterian/Weill Cornell Medical Center," then scroll down and click on "Diseases and Abnormalities at or before Birth," and then scroll down and select relevant trials: "Heart Defects, Congenital," "Cardiovascular Abnormalities," "Congenital Abnormalities," or "Aortic Coarctation." For additional trials, return to "Research and Clinical Trials," click on "Clinical Trials at New York–Presbyterian Hospital/Columbia University Medical Center," scroll down and click on "www.clinicaltrials.gov," and then in the "Search for Studies" box, type "congenital heart" and "Columbia University Medical Center."

Truncus Arteriosus

> Children's Hospital of Philadelphia (CHOP) (Philadelphia, PA)—"Truncus Arteriosus." http://www.chop.edu/service/cardiac-center/heart-conditions/truncus-arteriosus.html; alternate path: http://www.chop.edu/, click on the heading "Specialties and Services" and then on the category "Cardiac Center," click on the category "Heart Conditions," and then scroll down to click on the topic.
CHOP's Cardiac Center offers information on truncus arteriosus, such as how a normal heart works, what truncus arteriosus is, symptoms, diagnosis, treatment, and follow-up. Also available are links to cardiac news, cardiac research at CHOP, videos, patient stories, meeting the specialists in the team (with profile, e.g., specialty, medical board certification, education), consultations and second opinions, and taking a virtual tour.

> Cincinnati Children's Hospital Medical Center (Cincinnati, OH)—"Truncus Arteriosus." http://www.cincinnatichildrens.org/patients/child/encyclopedia/defects/truncus/; alternate path: http://www.cincinnatichildrens.org/, search for and then click on the title "Truncus Arteriosus."
Cincinnati Children's Hospital provides patient-friendly information on truncus arteriosus, including an illustration and an animation. Click on such topics as descriptions, signs and symptoms, diagnosis, treatment, and selection of delayed sternal closure. Under the heading "Patients and Families," click on "Clinical Trials" to search for any current studies.

> Mayo Clinic (Rochester, MN)—"Truncus Arteriosus." http://www.mayoclinic.com/health/truncus-arteriosus/DS00746; alternate path: http://www.mayoclinic.com/, search for and then click on the title "Truncus Arteriosus."

Written for patients, this information on truncus arteriosus includes links to definitions, symptoms, causes, risk factors, complications, preparing for appointments, tests and diagnosis, treatments and drugs, coping and support, and prevention. There is also a more comprehensive section titled "In-Depth" on some of these topics. For information on clinical trials and patient services, see the Mayo Clinic entry on p. 207.

➤ Medscape Reference (Drugs, Diseases, and Procedures)—"Truncus Arteriosus." http://emedicine.medscape.com/article/892489-overview; alternate path: http://emedicine.medscape.com/, search for and then click on the title "Truncus Arteriosus."

Written for Medscape by two medical doctors, Doff B. McElhinney and Gil Wernovsky, this webpage presents a comprehensive report on truncus arteriosus. Although written for health care professionals, it might be helpful to interested laypersons. Articles for Medscape Reference are written by medical experts. The website states, "Our rigorous literature survey process allows us to rapidly integrate new practice-changing information into the relevant topics by systematically reviewing the major medical and pharmacy journals, news announcements, and important practice guidelines." Free registration is required.

Patient Support Groups and Organizations

For additional related patient support groups, *see* RESOURCES FOR FURTHER INFORMATION ON CONGENITAL HEART DISEASE at the end of this chapter.

➤ MedHelp. http://www.medhelp.org/.

According to its website, MedHelp "connects people with the leading medical experts," such as those from Cleveland Clinic, National Jewish Health, Partners Health, and Mount Sinai Hospital, with those who have similar medical issues. MedHelp's main focus is to enable patients "to take control over their health and find answers to their medical questions" using nontechnical language via an online community through posts and articles. Free registration is required. From the homepage, you can find the following and related groups by searching for the condition.

- "Aortic Valve Stenosis." http://www.medhelp.org/search?query=Aortic+Valve+Stenosis.
- "Pulmonary Valve Stenosis." http://www.medhelp.org/search?query=Pulmonary+Valve+Stenosis.

➤ U.S. Hospital Finder. http://www.ushospitalfinder.com/.

Use this site to find the names of hospitals by zip code, city, state, or your address. The search results include a map with directions. You might also want to ask your health care professional, call hospitals in your area, or search for "support groups" on hospital websites to determine if there are any cardiology support groups for people with congenital heart disease that meet regularly in your area.

Septal Defects

A septal defect is a hole in the heart. There is a muscular wall (septum) between the right side and left side of the heart so the oxygen-rich blood will not mix together with the oxygen-depleted blood. Atrial septal defect is a hole in the wall between the upper chambers (atria) of the heart. Ventricular septal defect is a hole in the wall between the lower chambers (ventricles) of the heart. Septal defects occur in the wall between chambers of the heart and cause the blood to flow in the heart too quickly. These defects include atrial septum, ventricular septum, and patent ductus arteriosus. Depending on the size of the hole, the heart's pumping efficiency can be affected and cyanosis may be present. Hypoplasia is incomplete formation of one of the ventricles. If patent ductus arteriosus (a hole between the aorta and the pulmonary artery) is present, the infant may survive until surgery can correct the defects. (*See* GLOSSARY.)

To learn more, visit the **National Heart, Lung, and Blood Institute** of the National Institutes of Health at http://www.nhlbi.nih.gov/health/health-topics/topics/chd/types.html (alternate path: http://www.nhlbi.nih.gov/, search for and then click on the title "Types of Congenital Heart Defects"). This webpage provides illustrations of cross-section comparisons of a normal heart versus one with an atrial septal defect and one with a ventricular septal defect. In a heart with an atrial septal defect, the hole allows oxygen-rich blood from the left atrium to mix with oxygen-poor blood from the right atrium. In a heart with a ventricular septal defect, the defect allows oxygen-rich blood from the left ventricle to mix with oxygen-poor blood in the right ventricle. Holes with similar effects can occur between the aorta and the pulmonary artery.

Resources for Further Information on Septal Defects

See also RESOURCES FOR FURTHER INFORMATION ON CONGENITAL HEART DISEASE at the end of this chapter for a more comprehensive list of resources.

➤ Lucile Packard Children's Hospital at Stanford (Palo Alto, CA)—"Heart Defects Causing Extra Blood Flow through the Lungs." http://www.lpch.org/Disease HealthInfo/HealthLibrary/cardiac/hdcebftl.html; alternate path: http://www.lpch .org/, search for "heart defects causing extra blood flow," and then click on the title "Heart Defects Causing Extra Blood Flow through the Lungs."
The Lucile Packard Children's Hospital at Stanford (of Stanford University School of Medicine) website provides information on heart defects causing extra blood flow through the lungs, with linkable topics such as atrial septal defects, patent ductus arteriosus, ventricular septal defect, and atrioventricular canal. Each topic further discusses what each defect is, including illustrations, causes,

symptoms, diagnosis, treatments, postoperative care, follow-up, and long-term outlook. Under the menu heading "For Patients and Families" are links to many services.

Atrial Septal Defect

➤ Children's Hospital of Philadelphia (CHOP) (Philadelphia, PA)—"Atrial Septal Defect (ASD) in Children." http://www.chop.edu/service/cardiac-center/heart -conditions/atrial-septal-defect-asd.html; alternate path: http://www.chop.edu/, under the heading "Specialties and Services," click on the category "Cardiac Center" and then on the category "Heart Conditions," and then scroll down to click on the topic "Atrial Septal Defect."

CHOP's Cardiac Center offers information on atrial septal defects in children: definitions with illustrations, symptoms, diagnosis, treatment, and follow-up. Also available are links to the latest cardiac news, cardiac research at CHOP, videos, patient stories, information on the specialists in the team (with profile, e.g., specialty, medical board certification, education), consultations and second opinions, and a virtual tour.

➤ Johns Hopkins Hospital, Heart and Vascular Institute (Baltimore, MD)— "Minimally-Invasive Atrial Septal Defect Closure." http://www.hopkinsmedicine .org/heart_vascular_institute/conditions_treatments/treatments/minimally _invasive_atrial_septal_defect_closure.html; alternate path: http://www.hopkins medicine.org/; search for and then click on the title "Minimally-Invasive Atrial Septal Defect Closure."

This webpage offers information on minimally invasive atrial septal defect (ASD), such as definitions, treatment, and repair, with illustrations. It also provides links to physicians and specialists (with profile, e.g., specialty, medical board certification, education) who treat ASD.

➤ KidsHealth.org. http://kidshealth.org/.

The Nemours Center for Children's Health Media provides current information on conditions afflicting children, written for both children and parents. Information is available in English and Spanish. Some webpages contain a "Listen" button that you can click on to hear the text read aloud.

• *For Parents:* "Atrial Septal Defect." http://kidshealth.org/parent/medical/ heart/asd.html#cat141; alternate path: http://kidshealth.org/, click on "Parents Site," scroll down and select "Diseases and Conditions," then "Heart and Blood Vessels," and then click on the title. For parents, this webpage includes discussion of causes, signs and symptoms, diagnosis, treatment, and self-care.

• *For Teens:* "Atrial Septal Defect." http://kidshealth.org/teen/diseases_conditions/ heart/asd.html#cat20160; alternate path: http://www.kidshealth.org/, click on

"Teens Site," scroll down and click on "Diseases and Conditions," then scroll down and click on "Heart and Cardiovascular System," and then click on the title. For teens, this webpage includes such topics as heart basics, causes, signs and symptoms, diagnosis, treatment, and self-care.

➢ Mayo Clinic (Rochester, MN)—"Atrial Septal Defect (ASD)." http://www.mayoclinic .com/health/atrial-septal-defect/DS00628; alternate path: http://www.mayoclinic .com/, search for "atrial septal defect," and then click on the resource title.
Written for patients, online information on ASD includes links to definitions, symptoms, causes, risk factors, complications, preparing for appointments, tests and diagnosis, treatments and drugs, lifestyle and home remedies, and prevention. There is also a more comprehensive section titled "In-Depth" on some of these topics. For information on clinical trials and patient services, see the Mayo Clinic entry on p. 207.

➢ Medscape Reference (Drugs, Diseases, and Procedures)—"Atrial Septal Defect." http://emedicine.medscape.com/article/162914-overview; alternate path: http:// emedicine.medscape.com, search for and then click on the title "Atrial Septal Defect."
Written for Medscape by two medical doctors, Larry W. Markham and Marc G. Cribbs, this webpage presents a comprehensive report on atrial septal defect. Although written for health care professionals, it might be helpful for interested laypersons. Articles for Medscape Reference are written by medical experts. The webpage states, "Our rigorous literature survey process allows us to rapidly integrate new practice-changing information into the relevant topics by systematically reviewing the major medical and pharmacy journals, news announcements, and important practice guidelines." Free registration is required.

➢ National Heart, Lung, and Blood Institute (NHLBI)—"What Are Holes in the Heart?" http://www.nhlbi.nih.gov/health/health-topics/topics/holes/; alternate path: http://www.nhlbi.nih.gov/, search for "what are holes in the heart," and then click on the resource title.
NHLBI, a division of National Institutes of Health from the U.S. Department of Health and Human Services, provides additional information, including articles on types of atrial septal defects, signs and symptoms, diagnosis, living with this condition, clinical trials, and other related topics.

➢ New York–Presbyterian (NYP) University Hospital of Columbia and Cornell (New York, NY)—"Interactive Media Library" (Videos). http://nyp.org/media/ index.html, click on "Or Click Here for a Complete Listing of Topics," and scroll down to the title "Congenital Heart Disease"; alternate path: http://nyp.org/, click on the "Explore the Interactive Media Library" icon, and then select the video title from the drop-down list of topics.

NYP University Hospital of Columbia and Cornell provides the Human Atlas media player that contains short videos, text, models, and slides. Among the list of topics is a video on congenital heart disease that covers both aortic and ventricular septal defects. To find information on a specific doctor, return to the homepage (http://nyp.org/), click on "Find a Physician," under "By Specialty, Disease, or Expertise," click on "Find a Doctor," and then scroll down to and click on "Congenital Heart Disease." This produces a clickable list of physicians and specialists by specialty; click on a name to view the physician's profile (e.g., specialty, medical board certification, education). For information on clinical trials, see the NYP entry on pp. 232-233.

Patent Ductus Arteriosus

> Children's Hospital of Philadelphia (CHOP) (Philadelphia, PA)—"Patent Ductus Arteriosus (PDA)." http://www.chop.edu/service/cardiac-center/heart-conditions/patent-ductus-arteriosus-pda.html; alternate path: http://www.chop.edu/, click on the heading "Specialties and Services" and then on the category "Cardiac Center," click on the category "Heart Conditions," and then scroll down to click on the topic "Patent Ductus Arteriosus (PDA)."
> CHOP's Cardiac Center offers information on patent ductus arteriosus, such as how a normal heart works, what patent ductus arteriosus is, symptoms, diagnosis, treatment, and follow-up. Also available are links to cardiac news, cardiac research at CHOP, videos, patient stories, information on the specialists in the team (with profile, e.g., specialty, medical board certification, education), consultations and second opinions, and taking a virtual tour.

> Cincinnati Children's Hospital Medical Center (Cincinnati, OH)—"Patent Ductus Arteriosus." http://www.cincinnatichildrens.org/health/p/pda/; alternate path: http://www.cincinnatichildrens.org/, search for and then click on the title "Patent Ductus Arteriosus."
> Cincinnati Children's Hospital provides patient-friendly information on patent ductus arteriosus. Click on topics such as signs and symptoms, diagnosis, and treatment. Under the heading "Patients and Families," click on "Clinical Studies" to search for any current studies.

> Cleveland Clinic (Cleveland, OH)—"Patent Ductus Arteriosus." http://my.clevelandclinic.org/heart/disorders/patent-ductus-arteriousis-adults.aspx; alternate path: http://my.clevelandclinic.org/, under the category "Institutes and Services," click on "Heart and Vascular," then click on the category "Diseases and Conditions," then scroll down to the title "Congenital Heart Disease," and then click "Patent Ductus Arteriosus."
> Cleveland Clinic provides comprehensive patient-friendly information on patent ductus arteriosus such as definitions, including illustrations, who is affected,

symptoms, causes, diagnosis, treatments, prognosis, and how to find a doctor who treats congenital heart disease. The Cleveland Clinic also offers a link and other contact information to "Chat Online with a Heart and Vascular Nurse." For information on clinical trials, see the Cleveland Clinic entry on p. 206.

➢ Mayo Clinic (Rochester, MN)—"Patent Ductus Arteriosus." http://www .mayoclinic.com/health/patent-ductus-arteriosus/DS00631; alternate path: http:// www.mayoclinic.com/, search for "patent ductus arteriosus," and then click on the resource title.

Written for patients, online information on PDA includes links to definitions, symptoms, causes, risk factors, complications, preparing for your appointment, tests and diagnosis, treatments and drugs, prevention, lifestyle, and home reme-dies. There is also a more comprehensive section titled "In-Depth" on some of these topics. For information on clinical trials and patient services, see the Mayo Clinic entry on p. 207.

➢ MedlinePlus—"Patent Ductus Arteriosus (PDA)." http://www.nlm.nih.gov/ medlineplus/ency/article/001560.htm; alternate path: http://www.nlm.nih.gov/, under "Databases," click on "MedlinePlus," search for "patent ductus arteriosus," and then click on the resource title.

MedlinePlus is a component of the National Institutes of Health and produced by the National Library of Medicine and is updated regularly. The MedlinePlus webpage on patent ductus arteriosus offers information covering overview, causes, symptoms, exams and tests, treatment, outlook (prognosis), when to con-tact a medical professional, and illustrations.

➢ Medscape Reference (Drugs, Diseases, and Procedures)—"Patent Ductus Arte-riosus." http://emedicine.medscape.com/article/891096-overview; alternate path: http://emedicine.medscape.com/, search for and then click on the title "Patent Ductus Arteriosus."

Written for Medscape by two medical doctors, Luke K. Kim and Jeffrey C. Mil-liken, this webpage contains a comprehensive report on patent ductus arteriosus. Although written for health care professionals, it might be helpful for interested laypersons. Articles for Medscape Reference are written by medical experts. The webpage states, "Our rigorous literature survey process allows us to rapidly inte-grate new practice-changing information into the relevant topics by systemati-cally reviewing the major medical and pharmacy journals, news announcements, and important practice guidelines." Free registration is required.

➢ National Heart, Lung, and Blood Institute (NHLBI)—"Patent Ductus Arterio-sus." http://www.nhlbi.nih.gov/health/health-topics/topics/pda/; alternate path: http://www.nhlbi.nih.gov/, search for "patent ductus arteriosus," and then click on the title "What Is Patent Ductus Arteriosus?"

NHLBI, a division of National Institutes of Health from the U.S. Department of Health and Human Services, provides additional information on patent ductus arteriosus, including definitions, how the heart works, causes, risks, signs and symptoms, diagnosis, treatments, living with patent ductus arteriosus, and clinical trials.

Ventricular Septal Defect

➤ Cincinnati Children's Hospital Medical Center (Cincinnati, OH)—"Ventricular Septal Defect." http://www.cincinnatichildrens.org/patients/child/encyclopedia/defects/vsd/; alternate path: http://www.cincinnatichildrens.org/, search for and then click on the title "Ventricular Septal Defect."
Cincinnati Children's Hospital provides patient-friendly information on ventricular septal defect, including an illustration and an animation. Click on such topics as description, signs and symptoms, diagnosis and treatment, and long-term outlook. Under the heading "Patients and Families," click on "Clinical Studies" to search for any current studies.

➤ eMedicineHealth—"Ventricular Septal Defect." http://www.emedicinehealth.com/ventricular_septal_defect/article_em.htm; alternate path: http://www.emedicinehealth.com/, search for and then click on the title "Ventricular Septal Defect."
eMedicineHealth, a division of WebMD, offers a comprehensive article on ventricular septal defect, including an overview, causes, symptoms, diagnosis, treatment, prevention, follow-ups, outlook, and when to seek medical care.

➤ KidsHealth.org. http://kidshealth.org/.
The Nemours Center for Children's Health Media provides current information on conditions afflicting children, written for both children and parents. Information is available in English and Spanish. Some webpages contain a "Listen" button that you can click on to hear the text read aloud.
- *For Parents:* "Ventricular Septal Defect." http://kidshealth.org/parent/medical/heart/vsd.html#cat141; alternate path: http://kidshealth.org/, click on "Parents Site," scroll down and click on "Diseases and Conditions," then scroll down and click on "Heart and Blood Vessels," and then click on the title "Ventricular Septal Defect." Topics discussed include definitions, causes, signs and symptoms, normal heart rate, diagnosis, treatment, and caring for a child with ventricular septal defect.
- *For Teens:* "Ventricular Septal Defect." http://kidshealth.org/teen/diseases_conditions/heart/vsd.html#cat20160; alternate path: http://www.kidshealth.org/, click on "Teens Site," scroll down and click on "Diseases and Conditions," then scroll down and click on "Heart and Cardiovascular System," and then click on the title "Ventricular Septal Defect." Topics discussed include

definitions, causes, signs and symptoms, normal heart rate, diagnosis, treatment, and taking care of yourself.

➢ Mayo Clinic (Rochester, MN)—"Ventricular Septal Defect (VSD)." http://www
.mayoclinic.com/health/ventricular-septal-defect/DS00614; alternate path:
http://www.mayoclinic.com/, search for and then click on the title "Ventricular
Septal Defect."
Written for patients, this information on VSD includes definitions, symptoms,
causes, risk factors, complications, preparing for appointments, tests and diagnosis, treatments and drugs, coping and support, and prevention. There is also a
more comprehensive section titled "In-Depth" on some of these topics. For information on clinical trials and patient services, see the Mayo Clinic entry on p. 207.

➢ MedicineNet—"Ventricular Septal Defect (VSD)." http://www.medicinenet.com/
ventricular_septal_defect/article.htm; alternate path: http://www.medicinenet
.com/, click on the major topic "Diseases and Conditions," click on "Conditions
A–Z," then click "V," and then scroll down to click on "Ventricular Septal Defect."
MedicineNet is owned and operated by WebMD and part of the WebMD Network. According to its website, it "provides easy-to-read, in-depth, authoritative
medical information for consumers via its robust user-friendly, interactive website." In-depth information on VSD includes information on what VSD is, how
common VSD is, normal design of the heart, causes, treatment, outlook, precautions, complications from surgery, patient discussions, and finding a local cardiologist. The medical information is written and edited by a nationally recognized
group of more than 70 U.S. board-certified physicians. The website contains a
"Symptom Checker" listed in alphabetical order as a guide to "pinpoint your
pain." MedicineNet's homepage lists links to articles in a section titled "Health
News of the Week." Also available is a health newsletter sign-up.

➢ Medscape Reference (Drugs, Diseases, and Procedures)—"Ventricular Septal
Defect." http://emedicine.medscape.com/article/892980-overview; alternate
path: http://emedicine.medscape.com/, search for and then click on the title
"Ventricular Septal Defect."
Written for Medscape by two medical doctors, Prema Ramaswamy and Kuruchi
Srinivasan, this webpage presents a comprehensive report on ventricular septal
defect. Although written for health care professionals, it might be helpful for
interested laypersons. Free registration is required.

➢ WebMD—"Ventricular Septal Defect." http://www.webmd.com/heart-disease/
ventricular-septal-defect; alternate path: http://www.webmd.com/, search for
and then click on the title "Ventricular Septal Defect."
The WebMD website offers definitions, causes, symptoms, tests, treatments, follow-up, and outlook. WebMD's heart health e-mail newsletter is also available.

According to the website, "WebMD News is an independent media service designed to provide news, information, and educational material to consumers and physicians. News content created by WebMD is free from influence by sponsors, partners, or other sources."

Patient Support Groups and Organizations

For additional related patient support groups, *see* RESOURCES FOR FURTHER INFORMATION ON CONGENITAL HEART DISEASE at the end of this chapter.

➢ MedHelp. http://www.medhelp.org/.
According to its website, MedHelp "connects people with the leading medical experts," such as those from Cleveland Clinic, National Jewish Health, Partners Health, and Mount Sinai Hospital, with those who have similar medical issues. MedHelp's main focus is to enable patients "to take control over their health and find answers to their medical questions" using nontechnical language via an online community through posts, forums and groups, blogs, and user journals, as well as recommendations, articles, health pages, and a medical glossary. Free registration is required. From the homepage, you can find the following and related groups by searching for the condition.
  - "Atrial Septal Defect." http://www.medhelp.org/search?query=atrial+septal +defect.
  - "Patent Ductus Arteriosus." http://www.medhelp.org/search?query=Patent +ductus+arteriosus.
  - "Ventricular Septal Defect." http://www.medhelp.org/search?query=ventricular +septal+defect.

➢ U.S. Hospital Finder. http://www.ushospitalfinder.com/.
Use this site to find the names of hospitals by zip code, city, state, or your address. The search results include a map with directions. You might also want to ask your health care professional, call hospitals in your area, or search for "support groups" on hospital websites to determine if there are any cardiology support groups for people with septal defects that meet regularly in your area.

➢ Yahoo! Groups. http://www.groups.yahoo.com/.
Yahoo! Groups is not a medical site, nor does it provide or endorse medical advice or procedures. The purpose of the website is to share experiences in a kind and caring manner. Free membership sign-up is required to participate. Note that there are usually several Yahoo! Groups dedicated to any particular condition. From the homepage, you can find the following and related groups by searching for the condition in the "Find a Yahoo! Group" Search box.
  - "Atrial Septal Defects." http://groups.yahoo.com/group/Atrial_Septal _Defects/. This online Yahoo! support group is for patients who are afflicted with atrial septal defect and their families and friends.

- "Children with VSD." http://health.groups.yahoo.com/group/Childrenwith VSD/. This online Yahoo! support group is for patients who are afflicted with ventricular septal defect and their families and friends.

Resources for Further Information on Congenital Heart Disease

Books

➢ Everett, Allen D., Scott D. Lim, and Jasper Burns, eds. *Illustrated Field Guide to Congenital Heart Disease and Repair*. Charlottesville, VA: Scientific Software Solutions, 2011. Print.
Now in its third edition, this book, according to its introduction, "was created to provide a pocket-sized visual resource for pediatric cardiologists to assist their discussions with staff, students, patients and their families."

Brochures, Booklets, and Other Short Print Publications

➢ American Heart Association (AHA). http://www.heart.org/.
- "Congenital Heart Defects" (Educational Brochures). http://www .heart.org/HEARTORG/General/Order-American-Heart-Association -Educational-Brochures_UCM_312777_Article.jsp; alternate path: http://www.heart.org/, search for "educational brochures," click on the title "Order American Heart Association Educational Brochures," and then click on the topic "Congenital Heart Defects." Some AHA brochures that are available include "If Your Child Has a Congenital Heart Defect" and "Bacterial Endocarditis Wallet Card." These brochures can be ordered by completing an online form. Also available by completing a product order form is an infective endocarditis information packet. Note that a maximum of one packet and two brochures per household can be ordered at no cost.
- "Congenital Heart Defects" (Web Booklets). http://www.heart.org/ HEARTORG/Conditions/More/CardiovascularConditionsofChildhood/ Commonly-Asked-Questions-About-Children-and-Heart-Disease_UCM _311917_Article.jsp; alternate path: http://www.heart.org/, search for "booklets congenital heart defects," and then click on the two web booklet titles in the right-hand sidebar: "Adults with Congenital Heart Defects" and "If Your Child Has a Congenital Heart Defect." AHA provides a large series of free online booklets that can also be viewed and downloaded in PDF format.

➢ British Heart Foundation (BHF)—"Congenital Heart Disease" (booklets and DVDs). http://www.bhf.org.uk/heart-health/conditions/congenital-heart-disease

.aspx; alternate path: http://www.bhf.org.uk/, search for "congenital heart disease," and then click on the title "British Heart Foundation—Congenital Heart Disease." The BHF website offers free publications—some written for parents and others specifically for children. Scroll down the screen and click on each title to view and download. The first section of resources covers organizations (children's helplines and funding), followed by resources for parents and for children. Publications for parents include a DVD that aids parents in coming to terms with their child's condition; information sheets on helplines for children, heart hospitals, and endocarditis; and a series of booklets titled "Understanding Your Child's Heart." Publications for children and young people include a DVD for teenagers about growing up with heart disease, a book that prepares children aged 7–11 for hospital visits, and Heart.net/meet, a website specifically for young people with heart conditions.

Websites

➢ American Association of Retired People (AARP)—"Congenital Heart Defects: Learning Center." http://healthtools.aarp.org/adamcontent/congenital-heart -defect-corrective-surgeries; alternate path: http://aarp.org/, search for "congenital heart defects," and then click on the title "Congenital Heart Defect Corrective Surgeries." Subscription.
AARP's health section on congenital heart defects offers a consumer-friendly wealth of information, including definitions, alternative names, and descriptions of surgeries on various types of congenital heart defects. This reference, with interactive tools, is for member subscribers only. With membership, you will receive a magazine that includes current health information focusing on those 50 years and older. For nonsubscribers, AARP has basic information on congenital heart defect topics at http://healthtools.aarp.org/health/congenital-heart-disease; alternate path: http://aarp.org/, search for and then click on the title "Congenital Heart Disease."

➢ American Heart Association (AHA)—"Congenital Heart Defects." http://www .heart.org/HEARTORG/Conditions/CongenitalHeartDefects/Congenital-Heart -Defects_UCM_001090_SubHomePage.jsp; alternate path: http://www.heart .org/, search for "congenital heart defects," and then scroll down to click on the title "Congenital Heart Defects."
AHA provides expanded details on congenital heart defects in linkable sections such as about congenital heart defects, impact of congenital heart defects, risk factors, symptoms and diagnosis, care and treatment, and tools and resources.

➢ British Heart Foundation (BHF)—"Congenital Heart Disease." http://www.bhf .org.uk/heart-health/conditions/congenital-heart-disease.asp; alternate path:

http://www.bhf.org.uk/, search for "congenital heart disease," and then click on the title "British Heart Foundation—Congenital Heart Disease."

The BHF website describes what congenital heart disease is, causes, how congenital heart disease is discovered, treatment, and support for patient and families. Also available is a section called "Community—A Place to Share Experiences."

> CardioSmart—"Congenital Heart Disease." https://www.cardiosmart.org/Heart Disease/CTT.aspx?id=994; alternate path: https://www.cardiosmart.org/, search for "congenital heart disease," and then click on the title "CardioSmart: Congenital Heart Disease."

CardioSmart provides an easy-to-use website on understanding congenital heart disease, which is discussed in subsections such as basic facts, normal heart, and normal blood flow through the heart. There are also links to atrial septal defects, ventricular septal defects, and coarctation of the aorta. According to the American College of Cardiology (ACC), "CardioSmart is the patient education and support program launched by the [ACC]. Our mission is to engage, inform, and empower patients to better prepare them for participation in their own care."

> Centers for Disease Control and Prevention (CDC)—"Congenital Heart Defects." http://www.cdc.gov/ncbddd/heartdefects/index.html; alternate path: http://www.cdc.gov/, search for "congenital heart defects" and then click on the title "CDC—Congenital Heart Defects, Home."

At the CDC, there are several linkable topics, including facts, screenings, living with heart defects, data and statistics, tracking and research, and articles. Under "Specific Heart Defects," there is expanded information, with illustrations related to specific conditions: atrial septal defect, hypoplastic left heart syndrome, tetralogy of Fallot, transposition of the great arteries, and ventricular septal defect.

> CenterWatch—Clinical trials listing service: "Congenital Heart Disease Clinical Trials." http://www.centerwatch.com/clinical-trials/listings/studylist.aspx?CatID =48; alternate path: http://www.centerwatch.com/, under the category "Resources for Patients and Families," click on "Find Clinical Trials," click on "C," and then click on the title.

The CenterWatch clinical trials listing service website lists trials currently looking for volunteers to enroll in congenital heart disease studies. Scroll down by state and click on a city near you to find additional information available on each clinical trial. To view all trials in your state, at the bottom of your selected state click "View More." Check often for new studies. Available is a free sign-up for e-mails about new clinical trials.

> Children's Hospital of Philadelphia (CHOP) (Philadelphia, PA). http://www.chop .edu/.

From the homepage, you can find the following resources under the heading "Specialties and Services."

- "Cardiac Center." http://www.chop.edu/service/cardiac-center. CHOP's Cardiac Center offers links to news, cardiac research at CHOP, videos, patient stories, meeting the specialists in the team (with profile, e.g., specialty, medical board certification, education); pediatric heart conditions, consultations and second opinions, and taking a virtual tour.
- "Fetal Diagnosis and Treatment." http://www.chop.edu/service/fetal-diagnosis -and-treatment/home.html. CHOP's Center for Fetal Diagnosis and Treatment offers links to services (e.g., Specialty Delivery Unit), fetal conditions treated (e.g., congenital heart diseases), fetal discussion forums, and related specialties and services.

➢ Cleveland Clinic (Cleveland, OH)—"Congenital Heart Disease." http://my .clevelandclinic.org/heart/disorders/congenital.aspx; alternate path: http://my .clevelandclinic.org/, under the category "Institutes and Services," click on "Heart and Vascular," then click on the category "Diseases and Conditions," and then scroll down to click on the title "Congenital Heart Disease."
Cleveland Clinic provides comprehensive patient-friendly information on congenital heart disease, such as definitions, links to various types of congenital heart disorders, symptoms, diagnosis, treatments, and how to find a doctor who treats congenital heart disease. The Cleveland Clinic also offers a link to "Chat Online with a Heart and Vascular Nurse." For information on clinical trials, see the Cleveland Clinic entry on p. 206.

➢ ClinicalTrials.gov—Congenital heart disease clinical trials. http://clinicaltrials .gov/ct2/results?term=congenital+heart+disease; alternate path: http:// clinicaltrials.gov/, search for "congenital heart disease," click on "Modify This Search," select fields to limit your results (e.g., Recruitment—you might want to select "Open Studies"; Locations—select your state; and Age Group), click on the "Search" button, and then click on the title of each trial name for additional information, such as purpose of the study, study design and type, detailed description, outcome measures, eligibility (age, gender, criteria, for participating), study start date, estimated study completion date, and sponsor. ClinicalTrials.gov, a service of the U.S. National Institutes of Health, lists ongoing and currently enrolling clinical trials. Check often for new studies.

➢ Fetal Care Center of Cincinnati—Cincinnati Children's Hospital Medical Center (Cincinnati, OH)—"Fetal Heart Program." http://www.fetalcarecenter.org/ services/heart.htm; alternate path: http://www.fetalcarecenter.org/, click on the category "Services," and then click on the topic "Fetal Heart Program."
The Fetal Care Center of Cincinnati at Cincinnati Children's Hospital Medical Center specializes in congenital heart disease/defects. Its goal is to provide

exemplary care to the fetus diagnosed with structural or functional heart disease. Also provided is comprehensive, patient-friendly information, described under the category "Fetal Conditions," such as aortic stenosis, complete heart block, and hypoplastic left heart syndrome. The category "For Patients" includes family-focused support, patient stories, patient process, questions and answers, information, and resources (e.g., research studies and findings and educational materials).

➤ Genetics Home Reference—"Familial Atrial Fibrillation." http://ghr.nlm.nih.gov/condition/familial-atrial-fibrillation; alternate path: http://ghr.nlm.nih.gov/, search for and then click on the title "Familial Atrial Fibrillation."
Genetics Home Reference is a division of National Institutes of Health (NIH). This particular link discusses familial atrial fibrillation, an inherited condition that disrupts the heart's normal rhythm, and provides links to references and additional information.

➤ Hospital of the University of Pennsylvania (HUP) (Philadelphia, PA)—"Adult Congenital Heart Disease Program." http://www.pennmedicine.org/heart/patient/clinical-services/adult-congenital-heart-disease/; alternate path: http://www.pennmedicine.org/, click on the "Departments and Services" icon (or search for "departments and services"), scroll down to click on the category "Cardiology and Cardiac Surgery," and then scroll down under the heading "Clinical Services" to click on "Adult Congenital Heart Disease."
HUP offers at its Penn Heart and Vascular Center website links in the Adult Congenital Heart Disease Program that include an "Overview" (what adult congenital heart disease is and what specialists are on the team); the "Team," which links to each physician and specialist (with profile, e.g., specialty, medical board certification, education); "The Penn Difference" (program described, patient experiences, unique capabilities and expertise, and hospital highlights); "Physician Interviews" (videos); and "Quality/Outcomes" (plus click on each treatment option for details and charts). In addition, a 54-page *Penn Heart and Vascular 2011 Clinical Activity Report* is available for download. It is a "summary of surgical, medical and interventional outcomes, as well as clinical research activity and patient volumes." To possibly participate in a clinical trial at Penn Cardiovascular Institute, if available, visit http://www.med.upenn.edu/cvi/clinical_trials.shtml (on the homepage, click on the "Clinical Trials" icon [or click the heading "Research"]), and then under the category "Clinical Trials" click on "Penn Cardiovascular Institute." Scroll down the list of "Cardiovascular Clinical Trials."

➤ Insidermedicine. http://www.insidermedicine.com/.
The physician-led Insidermedicine Project "allows patients, doctors and medical students to keep up on the latest medical information by watching" videos created each weekday by their team of medical experts, allowing anyone to receive

daily "evidence-based" health and medical updates. Previously created videos on its website are free to view or download. In addition to the following, there are several other videos related to congenital heart defects. From the homepage, you can find the following and other related videos by searching for "congenital heart defect" and then clicking on specific video titles.

- "Folic Acid May Reduce Rate of Congenital Heart Defects" (Video). http://www.Insidermedicine.com/archives/VIDEO_Folic_Acid_May_Reduce_Rate_of_Congenital_Heart_Defects_Interview_with_Raluca_IonescuIttu_McGill_University_3509.aspx. This easy-to-understand video includes an interview with a medical specialist discussing fortified folic acid foods and supplements use during pregnancy to lower risk for congenital heart defects.
- "Risk of Congenital Heart Abnormalities Raised When Mother Is Overweight and Smokes during Pregnancy" (Video). http://www.insidermedicine.com/archives/Risk_of_Congenital_Heart_Abnormalities_Raised_When_Mother_is_Overweight_and_Smokes_During_Pregnancy_Video_5857.aspx. Smoking and obesity together increases risk of congenital heart abnormalities. Using research published in the journal *Heart*, this video offers recommendations for quitting smoking and losing weight during pregnancy to reduce that risk.

➢ Johns Hopkins Hospital (Baltimore, MD). http://www.hopkinsmedicine.org/. The Johns Hopkins Heart and Vascular Institute website provides links to patient-friendly, current information on numerous surgical procedures for congenital heart diseases in adults. Most linked topics include an animation to help explain the surgical procedure. This website also lists links to physicians and specialists (with profile, e.g., specialty, medical board certification, education) who treat pediatric congenital heart disease. Click on the heading "Clinical Trials" for links to current studies in various heart and cardiovascular conditions. From the homepage, you can find the following resources through a title search.

- "Adult Congenital Heart Disease" (Clinical Services). http://www.hopkinsmedicine.org/heart_vascular_institute/conditions_treatments/conditions/adult_congenital_heart_disease.html.
- "Congenital Heart Defects." http://www.hopkinsmedicine.org/healthlibrary/conditions/adult/cardiovascular_diseases/congenital_heart_defects_85,P00205/.
- "Congenital Heart Treatment Procedures." http://www.hopkinsmedicine.org/heart_vascular_institute/conditions_treatments/conditions/adult_congenital_heart_disease.htm.
- "Pediatric Congenital Heart Disease." http://www.hopkinsmedicine.org/heart_vascular_institute/conditions_treatments/conditions/pediatric_congenital_heart_disease.html.

➤ Kids with Heart—National Association for Children's Heart Disorders. http://www.kidswithheart.org/.
Kids with Heart is a nonprofit organization whose mission is "[p]roviding support, education, and resources to those affected by congenital heart defects since 1985."

➤ KidsHealth.org. http://kidshealth.org/.
The Nemours Center for Children's Health Media provides current information on conditions afflicting children, written for both children and parents. Information is available in English and Spanish. Some webpages contain a "Listen" button that you can click on to hear the text read aloud. The following resources are for parents.

- "Congenital Heart Defects." http://kidshealth.org/parent/medical/heart/congenital_heart_defects.html#cat141. Topics discussed include how a healthy heart works, common heart defects, signs and symptoms, diagnosis, and if you suspect a problem.
- "When Your Child Needs a Heart Transplant." http://kidshealth.org/parent/medical/heart/heart_transplant.html#cat141. Topics discussed include information about heart transplants, when a heart transplant is needed, getting a healthy heart, preparing for surgery, organ waiting lists, getting the call, recovery, possible complications, and living heart healthy for life.

Alternate path: http://www.kidshealth.org/, click on "Parents Site," scroll down and click on "Medical Problems," scroll down again and click on "Heart and Blood Vessels," and then click on the specific title.

➤ Little Hearts. http://www.littlehearts.org/.
Little Hearts is a "national organization providing support, education, resources, networking, and hope to families affected by congenital heart defects. Membership consists of families nationwide who have or are expecting a child with a congenital heart defect. Our mission is to offer support, education, and hope to families affected by congenital heart defects through our support services, and to promote public awareness for this #1 birth defect."

➤ Massachusetts General Hospital (MGH) (Boston, MA)—"Adult Congenital Heart Disease Program." http://www.massgeneral.org/heartcenter/services/treatmentprograms.aspx?id=1003; alternate path: http://www.massgeneral.org/, click on "Centers and Services" and then on "View All Departments," click on "Heart Center" and then on the heading "Treatments and Services," and then scroll down to click on the topic "Adult Congenital Heart Disease Program."
The Adult Congenital Heart Disease Program at the MGH Heart Center website offers links to comprehensive information in several categories. "Our Approach" includes an overview of types of adult congenital heart disease, team approach, diagnosing, treatment, and links to each medical expert (with profile, e.g.,

specialty, medical board certification, education). "About This" describes the benefits and commitment of this program at MGH. "Conditions and Diseases" has a link to detailed information on types of adult congenital heart disease. "Support and Wellness" offers patient guides. "Clinical Trials" has links to MGH trials and research studies when they are currently seeking participants. "News and Events" includes the latest information on adult congenital heart disease, and "Multimedia" contains video demonstrations.

➤ Mayo Clinic (Rochester, MN). http://www.mayoclinic.com/.
Written for patients, this information on congenital heart defects includes links to definitions, symptoms, causes, risk factors, complications, preparing for appointments, tests and diagnosis, treatments and drugs, coping and support, and prevention. Scroll down to the section called "See Also" for links to specific congenital heart defects, such as tetralogy of Fallot, tricuspid atresia, atrial septal defect, Epstein's anomaly, hypoplastic left heart syndrome, and atrioventricular canal defect. There is also a more comprehensive section titled "In-Depth" on some of these topics. This website also includes a multimedia section containing images of congenital heart defects and a video. For information on clinical trials and patient services, see the Mayo Clinic entry on p. 207. From the homepage, you can find the following and related resources by searching for "congenital heart defects."

- "Congenital Heart Defects in Children." http://www.mayoclinic.com/health/congenital-heart-defects/DS01117.
- "Congenital Heart Disease in Adults." http://www.mayoclinic.com/health/congenital-heart-disease/DS01140.

➤ MedicineNet—"Congenital Heart Defects." http://www.medicinenet.com/congenital_heart_disease/article.htm; alternate path: http://www.medicinenet.com/, click on the major topic "Diseases and Conditions," click on "Conditions A–Z," then click "C," and then scroll down to "Congenital Heart Defects."
MedicineNet is owned and operated by WebMD and part of the WebMD Network and, according to its website, "provides easy-to-read, in-depth, authoritative medical information for consumers via its robust user-friendly, interactive website." In-depth information on congenital heart defects includes definitions of congenital heart defects, how the heart works, types, other names of congenital heart defects, causes, symptoms, diagnosis, treatment, lifestyle changes, and finding a local cardiologist. The medical information is written and edited by a nationally recognized group of more than 70 U.S. board-certified physicians. The website contains a "Symptom Checker" listed in alphabetical order as a guide to "pinpoint your pain." MedicineNet's homepage lists links to articles in a section titled "Health News of the Week." Also available is a health newsletter sign-up.

➢ MedlinePlus. http://www.nlm.nih.gov/.

MedlinePlus, a component of the National Institutes of Health, is produced by the National Library of Medicine and updated regularly. From the homepage, you can find the following resources by clicking on "MedlinePlus" under "Databases" and then searching for the topic by title.

- "Congenital Heart Defects." http://www.nlm.nih.gov/medlineplus/congenital heartdefects.html. This webpage offers extensive linked information, covering overviews, latest news, diagnosis/symptoms, treatment, nutrition, disease management, specific conditions, related issues, anatomy/physiology, financial issues, clinical trials, genetics, research, journal articles, dictionaries/glossaries, directories, and organizations. It includes specific sections that focus on children, teenagers, women, and adults as well as patient handouts and a multimedia section containing videos.

- "Heart Murmurs and Other Sounds." http://www.nlm.nih.gov/medlineplus/ency/article/003266.htm. This webpage offers information on heart murmurs and other sounds through sections providing an overview as well as specific information on causes, tests, and what to expect during a physician exam. Also available is a video on the heart with audio of the heartbeat.

➢ *The Merck Manual Home Health Handbook for Patients and Caregivers*—"Heart Defects." http://www.merckmanuals.com/home/sec03/ch025/ch025j.html; alternate path: http://www.merckmanuals.com/home/, under "Sections," click on "All" to view a complete list, then click on the section "Children's Health Issues," click on "Birth Defects," and then click on "Heart Defects."

This section, which provides an overview on heart defects, is based on a well-known medical textbook titled *The Merck Manual Home Health Handbook for Patients and Caregivers*, and this topic is part of the extensive section on abnormal heart rhythms and is "provided free of charge . . . as a public service."

➢ National Heart, Lung, and Blood Institute (NHLBI)—"Congenital Heart Defects." http://www.nhlbi.nih.gov/health/dci/Diseases/chd/chd_what.html; alternate path: http://www.nhlbi.nih.gov/, search for "congenital heart defects," and then click on the title "What Are Congenital Heart Defects?"

NHLBI, a division of National Institutes of Health (NIH) from the U.S. Department of Health and Human Services, provides additional information on congenital heart defects, including links to definitions, how the heart works, types of congenital heart defects, other names, causes, signs and symptoms, diagnosis, treatments, living with congenital heart defects, clinical trials, key points, and additional information about congenital heart defects.

➢ New York–Presbyterian (NYP) University Hospital of Columbia and Cornell (New York, NY)—"Adult Congenital Heart Disease." http://nyp.org/services/cardiology/adult-congenital.html; alternate path: http://nyp.org/, under the heading "Centers of Excellence" click on the category "Heart," scroll down and click on the category "Cardiology," click on "More Services," and then click on the topic "Adult Congenital Heart Disease."

The NYP University Hospital of Columbia and Cornell website provides patient-friendly information on adult congenital heart disease, such as its definition and treatment. Under the heading "Health Library" are links to detailed information on related conditions, including abdominal aortic aneurysm, aneurysm overview, and rheumatic heart disease. For information on clinical trials, see the NYP entry on pp. 232–233.

➤ NHS (National Health Service) Choices—"Congenital Heart Disease—Treatment." http://www.nhs.uk/Conditions/Congenital-heart-disease/Pages/Treatment.aspx; alternate path: http://www.nhs.uk/, search for "congenital heart disease," and then click on the title "Congenital Heart Disease—NHS Choices—Health A–Z."

This section from the NHS website from the United Kingdom describes congenital heart disease. Click on each linked tab at the top of the screen for sections that deal with overview (introduction), symptoms, causes, diagnosis, treatment, complications, and prevention. Some of these sections include videos. There is also a section on clinical trials that is provided by the World Health Organization (WHO) International Clinical Trials Registry. These clinical trials can be searched by country.

➤ Texas Heart Institute (Houston, TX). http://www.texasheartinstitute.org/.

Texas Heart Institute website offers links to numerous types of congenital heart diseases and definitions of conditions as well as information on causes, risks, signs and symptoms, diagnosis, and treatment. Easy-to-print formats are available. For information on clinical trials, see the Texas Heart Institute entry on p. 219.

- "Congenital Heart Disease" (Heart Information Center). http://www.texasheartinstitute.org/HIC/Topics/Cond/CongenitalHeartDisease.cfm.
- "Coronary Artery Anomalies" (Heart Information Center). http://www.texasheartinstitute.org/HIC/Topics/Cond/caa.cfm.

  Alternate path: http://www.texasheartinstitute.org/, search for the topic by title, and then click on the corresponding title; or from the pull-down menu under the heading "Heart Information Center," select "Heart-Health Topics" and then "Heart Conditions," and then click on the title.

➤ UCLA Ronald Reagan Medical Center (Los Angeles, CA)—"Congenital Heart Disease." http://www.uclahealth.org/body.cfm?id=592, scroll down to the heading "Diseases and Conditions," and click on the title "Congenital Heart Disease"; alternate path: http://www.uclahealth.org/, under the heading "For Patients and Visitors," scroll down and mouse over the category "Health Resources" to click on "Heart Health Center," scroll down to the heading "Diseases and Conditions," and then click on the title "Congenital Heart Disease."

UCLA Ronald Reagan Medical Center's Heart Health Center provides detailed information on coronary artery disease that includes definition, causes, symptoms, exams and tests, treatment, outlook (prognosis), possible complications, when to contact a medical professional, and prevention. The UCLA Heart Health Center (http://www.uclahealth.org/body.cfm?id=592) also provides animations related to various conditions. Scroll to the bottom of the page and select "More" under "Animations." (Note that, to view the animations, you might be asked to allow the installation of a common Internet plug-in called Shockwave Player by Adobe, available for free at http://www.adobe.com/products/shockwaveplayer.html.) Also on the Heart Health Center website, under the heading "Health Assessment," you can sign up for "personalized messages to improve your [heart] health and lifestyle" by clicking on one of these categories "Diet and Nutrition," "Fitness," "Heart Attack," or "Stress and Anxiety." For patient services in various cardiology programs, return to the UCLA Health System homepage, http://www.uclahealth.org/, scroll down under the heading "Medical Departments," then scroll down and click on "Medicine," and then scroll down and click on the category "Cardiology." Included is a list of programs and links to physicians and specialists (with profile, e.g., specialty, medical board certification, education). To possibly participate in a clinical trial at UCLA, if available, visit http://clinicaltrials.ucla.edu/ (or on the homepage type "clinical trials" in the Search box, and then click on the title "Clinical Trials").

> WebMD—"Congenital Heart Disease." http://www.webmd.com/heart-disease/guide/congenital-heart-disease; alternate path: http://www.webmd.com/, search for and then click on the title "Congenital Heart Disease."

This section of the WebMD website offers the latest information on congenital heart disease, using articles, slide presentations, videos, FAQs, discussion groups, and expert blogs. Also available is WebMD's heart health e-mail newsletter. According to WebMD, "WebMD News is an independent media service designed to provide news, information, and educational material to consumers and physicians. News content created by WebMD is free from influence by sponsors, partners, or other sources."

Patient Support Groups and Organizations

> Adult Congenital Heart Association (ACHA). http://www.achaheart.org/.
According to its website, the ACHA is a national nonprofit support group that "seeks to improve the quality of life and extend the lives of adults with congenital heart defects. Through education, outreach, advocacy, and promotion of research, ACHA serves and supports the more than one million adults with congenital heart defects, their families and the medical community."

➤ Children's Hospital of Philadelphia (CHOP) (Philadelphia, PA)—"Fetal Discussion Forum" (from the Center for Fetal Diagnosis and Treatment). http://www.chop.edu/forum/forums/list.page?referer=Fetal; alternate path: http://www.chop.edu/, click on the heading "Specialties and Service," click on the category "Center for Fetal Diagnosis and Treatment," and then scroll down to click on "Fetal Discussion Forum."
CHOP's Center for Fetal Diagnosis and Treatment offers a link to a fetal discussion forum to "talk with other families about fetal diagnoses," such as congenital heart diseases. Free registration is required.

➤ Congenital Heart Information Network (CHIN). http://www.tchin.org/.
According to the CHIN website, "the Congenital Heart Information Network, a 501(c)(3) organization created by the mother of a child with complex heart defects, provides reliable information, support services, and resources to families of children with congenital defects and acquired heart disease, adults with congenital heart defects, and the professionals who work with them."

➤ DailyStrength—"Congenital Heart Defect Support Group." http://www.dailystrength.org/c/Congenital-Heart-Disease/support-group; alternate path: http://www.dailystrength.org/, search for "congenital heart defect," and then click on the title "Visit the Congenital Heart Disease Support Group."
The DailyStrength website offers online support groups and blogs for those with congenital heart defects. Free registration sign-up is required to participate. According to the website, "DailyStrength is a subsidiary of Sharecare. Sharecare, created by WebMD founder and Discovery Communications Chief of Global Digital Strategy Jeff Arnold, along with America's Doctor, Dr. Mehmet Oz, is the first truly interactive healthcare ecosystem giving consumers the ability to ask, learn and act on the questions of health."

➤ Dr.Greene.com—"Congenital Heart Disease." http://www.drgreene.com/azguide/congenital-heart-disease; alternate path: http://www.drgreene.com/, search for "congenital-heart-disease," and then click on the resource title.
Dr. Alan Greene is a clinical professor of pediatrics at Stanford University School of Medicine. He is part of a "team of pediatric and health experts offer[ing] medical expertise, parental experience and a focus on healthy living in a searchable, interactive library of resources to make raising healthy families easier." Also, after clicking on the section titled "Ask Answer and Learn," you can write your personal medical question to Dr. Greene. Questions are posted to the Dr. Greene Facebook page online community.

➤ Hearts of Hope (SE Michigan). http://www.heartsofhopemi.org/.
According to its website, "Hearts of Hope SE Michigan is a 501(c)(3) non-profit organization founded in 2005 by a group of mothers whose children all share a

complex heart defect. We are dedicated to providing hope and support to families affected by congenital heart defects, as well as creating awareness for this number one birth defect. . . . Membership is free and is not limited to Michigan residents."

➤ Kids with Heart National Association for Children's Heart Disorders. http://www .kidswithheart.org/.

According to its website, "Providing support, education and resources to those affected by congenital heart defects since 1985. . . . The intention of this information is to give parents of children with congenital heart disorders a place to find information about specific disorders and other support resources."

➤ Little Hearts. http://www.littlehearts.org/.

Little Hearts is a "national organization providing support, education, resources, networking, and hope to families affected by congenital heart defects. Membership consists of families nationwide who have or are expecting a child with a congenital heart defect. Our mission is to offer support, education, and hope to families affected by congenital heart defects through our support services, and to promote public awareness for this #1 birth defect."

➤ SADS (Sudden Arrhythmia Death Syndromes) Foundation. http://www.sads.org/.

This website covers long QT syndrome, cardiomyopathy, Brugada syndrome, and other conditions that cause sudden death in young people. The SADS Foundation informs the general public (and families and medical professionals) about the effects of untreated/undiagnosed, inherited cardiac arrhythmias and the methods by which death can be prevented with a detailed support section titled "Living with SADS."

➤ U.S. Hospital Finder. http://www.ushospitalfinder.com/.

Use this site to find the names of hospitals by zip code, city, state, or your address. The search results include a map with directions. You might also want to ask your health care professional, call hospitals in your area, or search for "support groups" on hospital websites to determine if there are any cardiology support groups for people with congenital heart disease that meet regularly in your area.

➤ Yahoo! Groups. "Congenital Heart Defect Support." http://health.groups.yahoo .com/group/CHDFamilies/; alternate path: http://www.groups.yahoo.com/, search for "congenital heart defect" in the "Find a Yahoo! Group" Search box, and then click on CongenitalHeartDefectSupport.

This online Yahoo! support group is for patients who are afflicted with congenital heart defects and their families and friends. The Yahoo! Groups support group is one of several congenital heart defects support groups that have a large number of members. Yahoo! Groups is not a medical site, nor does it provide or endorse medical advice or procedures. The purpose of the website is to share experiences in a kind and caring manner. Free membership sign-up is required to participate.

Webliography

Children's Hospital of Philadelphia. "Cardiac Center: Coarctation of the Aorta." Reviewed April 2009. http://www.chop.edu/service/cardiac-center/heart-conditions/coarctation-of-the-aorta.html.

————. "Cardiac Center: Long QT Syndrome." Reviewed March 2010. http://www.chop.edu/service/cardiac-center/heart-conditions/long-qt-syndrome.html.

————. "Center for Fetal Diagnosis and Treatment: Special Delivery Unit." June 2012. http://www.chop.edu/service/fetal-diagnosis-and-treatment/special-delivery-unit/.

————. "Health Information: Overview of Congenital Heart Disease." Accessed August 20, 2013. http://www.chop.edu/healthinfo/congenital-heart-disease.html

Genetic Science Learning Center. "What Are Genetic Disorders?" *Learn.Genetics.* Accessed February 28, 2013. http://learn.genetics.utah.edu/content/disorders/whataregd/.

Gesundheit! Project Foundation. "Genetic Abnormalities and Cancer." 2009. http://www.gpfoundation.com/genetic-abnormalities-and-cancer.htm.

InteliHealth. "Health A–Z: Heart Valve Problems." Updated December 19, 2011. http://www.intelihealth.com/IH/ihtIH/WSIHW000/9339/23659.html.

Lucile Packard Children's Hospital at Stanford. "Overview of Congenital Heart Disease." Accessed February 28, 2013. http://www.lpch.org/DiseaseHealthInfo/HealthLibrary/cardiac/chd.html.

Mayo Clinic. "Aortic Valve Stenosis." July 13, 2012. http://www.mayoclinic.com/health/aortic-valve-stenosis/DS00418/DSECTION=causes l.

MedlinePlus. "Cardiomyopathy." Updated January 18, 2013. http://www.nlm.nih.gov/medlineplus/cardiomyopathy.html.

————. "Congenital Heart Defects." Accessed February 28, 2013. http://vsearch.nlm.nih.gov/vivisimo/cgi-bin/query-meta?v%3Aproject=medlineplus&query=congenital+heart+defects.

————. "Heart Surgery." Updated February 22, 2013. http://www.nlm.nih.gov/medlineplus/heartsurgery.html.

National Heart, Lung, and Blood Institute. "How Is Heart Valve Disease Diagnosed?" Updated November 16, 2011. http://www.nhlbi.nih.gov/health/health-topics/topics/hvd/diagnosis.html.

————. "Types of Congenital Heart Defects." Updated July 1, 2011. http://www.nhlbi.nih.gov/health/health-topics/topics/chd/types.html.

————. "What Are Congenital Heart Defects?" Updated July 1, 2011. http://www.nhlbi.nih.gov/health/health-topics/topics/chd/.

————. "What Are Holes in the Heart?" Updated July 1, 2011.http://www.nhlbi.nih.gov/health/health-topics/topics/holes/.

———. "What Is a Heart Murmur?" Updated September 20, 2012. http://www.nhlbi .nih.gov/health/dci/Diseases/heartmurmur/hmurmur_what.html.

———. "What Is Heart Valve Disease?" Updated November 16, 2011. http://www .nhlbi.nih.gov/health/health-topics/topics/hvd/.

———. "What Is Long QT Syndrome?" Updated September 21, 2011. http://www .nhlbi.nih.gov/health/health-topics/topics/qt/.

———. "What Is Marfan Syndrome?" Updated October 1, 2010. http://www.nhlbi .nih.gov/health/dci/Diseases/mar/mar_whatis.html.

———. "What Is Mitral Valve Prolapse?" Updated July 1, 2011. http://www.nhlbi .nih.gov/health/dci/Diseases/mvp/mvp_whatis.html.

National Human Genome Research Initiative. "Frequently Asked Questions about Genetic Disorders." Updated February 27, 2012. http://www.genome.gov/19016930.

National Library of Medicine, Medical Subheadings. "Heart Defects, Congenital." Accessed February 28, 2013. http://www.nlm.nih.gov/cgi/mesh/2012/MB _cgi?mode=&term=Heart+Defects,+Congenital&field=entry#TreeC14.240.400.

Office of Rare Diseases Research. "Genetic and Rare Diseases Information Center." Accessed February 28, 2013. http://rarediseases.info.nih.gov/GARD/Default .aspx.

WebMD. "Heart Disease Health Center: Ventricular Septal Defects." Updated May 16, 2012. http://www.webmd.com/heart-disease/ventricular-septal-defects.

Chapter 5

Diagnostic Tests, Treatments, and Therapies

Heart and cardiovascular problems can be discovered or addressed during diagnostic testing and can be treated with drugs and/or surgery, along with lifestyle changes. The earlier these discoveries occur, the more positive impact diagnostic tests, treatments, and therapies will have on the patient's life.

Most diagnostic procedures take place on an outpatient basis and require only a few hours at the hospital or diagnostic center. Surgical procedures may require hospital stays of a few hours, a few days, or a few weeks, depending on the procedure. For example, placement of a stent may require only a few hours or a day or two in a hospital and may be done during an exploratory angiography. Heart transplant surgery requires several weeks of hospital care and continued drug therapy.

Hospitalized patients are often placed in a monitored area of a hospital such as a monitoring wing or an intensive care unit (ICU). Each patient in these areas is connected to a monitoring device that watches such factors as heart rate and rhythm (e.g., using an electrocardiogram machine), blood pressure, and blood oxygenation (e.g., by using a pulse oximeter). Each patient's monitor is connected to a central monitoring station, which is constantly attended by a nurse. If a monitor detects a problem, it sounds an alarm at the patient's monitor and at the central monitor, enabling staff to quickly respond to the problem.

In more serious cases, such as bypass surgery or transplant surgery, the patient may be placed in an ICU. This is intended to allow the patient's organs to rest and recover from major surgery or severe injury or to maintain the patient until surgery can be performed. Most ICU patients are not conscious. These areas provide considerably more attention to the patients because of the seriousness of their cases. Patients may be unconscious for some time, may be connected to a ventilator to help breathing, may have an external heart assist device, and will be monitored and observed.

Basically, cardiac diagnostics and testing are composed of six categories: electrocardiographic (e.g., EKG, stress test, tilt test), nuclear imaging (e.g., PET, nuclear stress test), radiographic (e.g., cardiac CT, calcium scan, MRI), ultrasound (e.g., echocardiogram, arterial and venous mapping), autonomic reflex, invasive (e.g., catheterization, myocardial biopsy, angiography, carotid stenting), and blood lab analysis. Although an extensive list of test procedures and treatments is described in this chapter, not every possible option is included. See RESOURCES FOR FURTHER INFORMATION for links to websites that offer the latest medical inventions and techniques on these topics.

If you are not sure what hospital or heart specialist would be best for your situation, numerous hospital rating websites are considered reliable and comprehensive enough to help you decide. *U.S. News and World Report* rankings of top doctors and hospitals, overall or by specialty (e.g., cardiology), is probably the most well-known. Although these groups basically have access to all the same medical databases, each ranking service decides the weighted values of individual criteria (its rating methodology), which, when all criteria listed are totaled, generate diverse ranking values for the national hospitals listed. Hospital ratings can change year to year if improvements were made or quality has slipped. Ratings criteria include but are not limited to mortality (number of patient deaths), number of patients who had to be readmitted to the hospital, number of patients who contracted infections in the hospital, patient customer satisfaction surveys, surgical safety practices, treatment and surgical complications, and Medicare records. Some rating agencies charge a licensing fee for the use of their ranking symbols if used in advertising; however, such groups claim this fee has no influence on ranking. There are three types of national hospital-ranking websites: government (Medicare's Hospital Compare, http://www.medicare.gov/hospitalcompare), nonprofit organizations (e.g., *Consumer Reports*, http://www.consumerreports.org/health/doctors-hospitals/hospital-ratings.htm [users of this website may need to subscribe]; the Joint Commission, http://www.qualitycheck.org/; and Leapfrog Group Hospital Safety Score, http://www.hospitalsafetyscore.org/), and private companies (e.g., Healthgrades, http://www.healthgrades.com/quality/top-hospitals-2013; Truven Health Analytics 100 Top Hospitals, http://www.100tophospitals.com/; and *U.S. News and World Report*, http://health.usnews.com/best-hospitals). A March 18, 2013, report from the Kaiser Health News website, a nonprofit health care news organization associated with the Kaiser Family Foundation, explained that because there might be consumer confusion with so many hospital rating groups with different results, patients should consult the Informed Patient Institute (http://www.informedpatientinstitute.org/), which, according to its website, is "an independent nonprofit organization that provides credible online information about health care quality and patient safety for consumers . . . [and] provide[s] performance information about health care providers and professionals" (*see also* TOP-RANKED U.S. HOSPITALS AND DOCTORS FOR CARDIOLOGY AND HEART SURGERY FROM *U.S. NEWS AND WORLD REPORT*).

All Resources for Further Information on Diagnostic Tests, Treatments, and Therapies are combined in the final section of this chapter.

Automated External Defibrillator

An automated external defibrillator (AED) is a small, lightweight, mobile, battery-operated, medical device used when someone appears to be having a sudden cardiac

Online Search Tips

- If you click on a link (e.g., a title) and nothing happens, try this: right-click on the link and then left-click on the option "Open in new window."
- If you experience problems with PDF documents, you can download the latest version of Adobe Reader for free at http://www.adobe.com/products/reader .html or by going to http://www.adobe.com/ and searching for "adobe reader."
- To view an animation, you might be asked to allow the installation of a common Internet plug-in called Shockwave Player by Adobe (http://www.adobe.com/ products/shockwaveplayer/).
- Adobe Flash Player, required to view most short videos, is available as a free download at http://get.adobe.com/flashplayer/; alternate path: http://www .adobe.com/, choose the "Download" tab on the menu bar, and select the Adobe Flash Player link.

arrest (i.e., heart suddenly stops beating). An AED measures arrhythmia (or abnormal rhythm of the heartbeat). If the heart stops beating, oxygen can no longer flow to the brain and the rest of the body, and there is a very short window of time before death occurs—a few minutes. Every minute that passes during sudden cardiac arrest diminishes survival rate by 10 percent. An AED can be used to jump-start the heart's electrical system by sending an electrical shock in an effort to get the heart beating again.

Because AEDs are designed with voice-activated instructions, even nonprofessionals can use these devices to provide assistance; however, taking a class in their use, along with learning cardiopulmonary resuscitation (CPR), would be beneficial. Most public places have AEDs available, such as shopping malls, convention centers, schools, sports stadiums, airports, airplanes, work buildings, and schools.

Cardiac Blood Tests

Blood tests (e.g., measuring blood cholesterol) range from assessing whether there is a risk for cardiovascular disease event to determining whether damage has occurred (e.g., from heart attack or stroke) and, if present, how severe the damage is.

Risk assessment tests that help prevent or manage heart disease include the lipid profile, which measures cholesterol, triglycerides, high-density lipoprotein cholesterol (HDL-C), low-density lipoprotein cholesterol (LDL-C), and triglycerides; high-sensitivity C-reactive protein (hs-CRP); and Lp(a), or lipoprotein A, as an increase in LDL-associated PLA2 (PLAC) levels is linked to heart attack, and fibrinogen (aids in blood clotting, but high levels indicate risk of cardiovascular disease and heart attack). *See* CHAPTER 3: HIGH CHOLESTEROL *and* CHAPTER 6: RISK FACTORS for more information.

As cardiovascular muscle cells become injured, as in a heart attack, specific blood proteins increase. Blood tests can measure these proteins (cardiac biomarkers) to assess whether there is any amount of damage. Such tests measure troponin (determines heart muscle injury and heart attack), CK-MB (type of creatine kinase, also indicates heart muscle damage), hs-CRP (indicates risk of heart attack, stroke, or peripheral vascular disease), and BNP or NT-pro-BNP (increase in this enzyme indicates congestive heart failure),

Cardiac Catheterization and Myocardial Biopsy

Cardiac catheterization (five types) is a diagnostic procedure for examining the heart and its components. The first, *angiography*, identifies blocked arteries and problems with heart valves. Sometimes a biopsy device routed through the catheter is used to take a tissue sample. The second, *angioplasty*, is used to treat blocked arteries. Angiography and angioplasty are often done one after the other if narrowed or blocked arteries are found. The third type of cardiac catheterization is used to examine and treat the heart's nervous system (*see also the later section* ELECTROPHYSIOLOGIC STUDIES). The fourth type is used to measure pressures in the heart chambers, and the fifth type uses catheters for minimally invasive surgery to repair valves, close holes, and perform other treatments.

Myocardial biopsy, also known as heart biopsy or cardiac biopsy, is a sample of heart muscle extracted using a small catheter that has a grabbing device on one end (called a bioptome) to be analyzed in a lab to determine whether the heart has an infection, myocarditis, cardiomyopathy, cardiac amyloidosis, heart transplant rejection, or other cardiac disorders. Biopsy may be used if less invasive diagnostic tests cannot determine the cause of heart disease, especially if the disease is worsening.

During cardiac catheterizations, patients may be awake or sedated. All types of cardiac catheterization require a several-step procedure performed in a special operating room equipped to allow examination and treatment.

In all five procedures types, a long, narrow tube called a catheter is inserted through a port. The port is a device that provides a seal around the catheter, a seal against the blood vessel, and the ability to change catheters. Patients receive local anesthesia during the procedure when the port is placed. There are no pain receptors in the blood vessels or heart, so no anesthetic is needed. The femoral vein is used for examination of the right side of the heart. The femoral artery is used for examination of the left side of the heart. Sometimes the brachial artery or subclavian vein is used as the point of entry. Once the catheter is inserted, its tip is moved to the heart to allow examination and treatment.

Angiography

In angiography, the catheters have springy J-shaped tips so they can be hooked into the entrance of the coronary arteries just above the aortic valve. Once the tip is placed at an entrance to an artery, a small amount of radiopaque cardiac dye is injected through the catheter. A radiography machine called a fluoroscope is used to record a movie of the dye as it passes through the artery. The dye shows the shape of the artery and any blockage. If no stenoses (narrowed sections) are seen, the other artery is examined. Sometimes the catheter is advanced into a coronary artery for improved imaging.

Cardiac catheterization is also used to examine the heart valves. The tip of the dye catheter is placed so dye is injected into the catheter, travels through the catheter, and is released upstream from a valve. As the dye travels through the heart, it shows the shape of the heart chambers, how the blood moves through the valves and chambers, the amount of blood ejected from a chamber during contraction, the amount of backflow, and if the valves are leaking. As with angiography, the dye disperses in the body and is later excreted.

Depending on which valves are being examined, the dye catheter would be inserted into the femoral vein or clavicular vein and into the heart to examine the right atrial and tricuspid valves and then through the femoral artery to the heart to examine the left atrial and mitral valves. During this examination, the physician can also determine whether there is a hole in the heart wall, such as a patent foramen ovale, between the right and left atria (*see* GLOSSARY).

Angioplasty (and Use of a Stent)

After angiography, narrowed or blocked arteries often are treated with angioplasty procedures to restore blood flow through the arteries. This involves expanding a small balloon catheter in a narrowed coronary vessel to open the channel. Other procedures use a cutting head (atherectomy) or laser (laser angioplasty) to bore through the plaque and open the artery. Similarly, some problem valves may be repaired by inflating a valvuloplasty balloon in the valve to open it or to break up plaque or calcification of the valve. Some valve disease requires more specialized surgery (*see* CHAPTER 3: HEART VALVE DISEASE).

If an artery is narrowed, the physician will determine whether a stent is needed to hold the artery open. If the artery is blocked, the physician will determine if the artery can be opened. The physician may place a guide wire to the problem section so that subsequent catheters can easily reach the section.

A stent is an intricately formed metal tube that is expanded by a balloon to hold a section of artery open. Stents are a few millimeters in diameter and several centimeters long to conform to the size and shape of the artery. Some stents are coated with drugs (drug-eluting stents) to prevent tissue growth that would reblock the artery. Small radioactive pellets can also be inserted near the problem section to retard tissue growth; this is known as brachytherapy. Recently, some doctors have backed away from implanting drug-eluting stents and stent implantation altogether and instead use more time-tested techniques.

In placing a stent, the physician passes a special catheter through the femoral artery into the narrowed coronary artery. A stent is on a balloon near the tip of the catheter. The balloon looks a bit like a hot dog in a metallic bun but is the size of the ink tube in a pen. The stent is placed so it bridges the narrowed section of artery. Then the balloon is inflated to several atmospheres (about 150 pounds per square inch or five times the pressure in a car tire) to expand the stent against the inside wall of the narrowed artery and hold it open. (When inflated, the balloon is about the size of a Brazil nut.) Several stents may be placed along a long narrowed section of artery. Stents have also been used in other organs that have stenosed arteries or ducts.

If the artery is severely narrowed or completely blocked, cutting devices can be used to remove the material blocking the artery. A guide wire may be pushed through the blockage to allow placement of a stent. If the blockage is too hard or twisted, a special angioplasty catheter is placed to cut through the blockage. The cutting may be done by a small clipper, a small rotating burr, or a laser. This procedure is a bit like opening a clogged sink drain in that most of the problematic tissue is cut away to open the artery. With rotational arterectomy, a catheter with a very small cutting burr at its tip is used to drill or cut through the blockage (which is a bit like the process used in clearing out a clogged sewer pipe). The catheter also has irrigation and suction to cool the burr and remove the cut material so it does not cause a blockage further down the artery. Alternately, in laser arterectomy, a laser is used with a wavelength that is preferentially absorbed by the blocking material. A laser typically vaporizes the blocking material. As with the burr, irrigation and suction are used to cool the area being irradiated by the laser and to remove the dislodged material. Once the blockage is opened, a stent is usually placed to hold it open.

Electrophysiological Studies

The third type of catheterization is for electrophysiological studies, which are used to examine how the heart contracts. In this examination, a special catheter with electrical pickups is placed into the right atrium and ventricle. This electrophysiological catheter can read the nerve impulses as they proceed through the heart. If the impulses are not proceeding properly, the physician can destroy the problem parts of the nerve pathways or determine where pacemaker leads should be implanted in a subsequent surgery.

Fractional Flow Reserve

To determine whether arteries are clogged enough to need a stent or if medication would be sufficient to help resolve the problem, the fractional flow reserve (FFR) procedure (which takes a minimum of 30 minutes) can precisely measure blood flow by insertion of a wire with a sensor through a catheter in the constricted artery (and can be performed when a patient is already prepped and having an angiogram). A drug is added to optimize blood flow in the artery. Then blood pressure is measured on opposite sides of the constricted area to determine how much the blockage is actually obstructing blood flow. If the FFR threshold value is high enough, studies have shown medication can be used instead of a stent or an angioplasty.

Minimally Invasive Cardiac Surgery

Minimally invasive cardiac surgery or percutaneous (through the skin) coronary interventions use small instruments and endoscopes inserted through small skin incisions to treat some heart problems. Many surgical instruments have been miniaturized or developed that now allow surgeons to do minimally invasive surgeries that would previously have required open-chest surgery.

In some types of heart disease, the arteries become narrowed or blocked by deposits of cholesterol, fat, calcium, or plaque in sections of the coronary arteries. When this happens, the blood supply to sections of the heart is diminished, and the heart muscle may not work as effectively as it should, or it may even die (necrose). For additional information, *see the entire section* CARDIAC CATHETERIZATION AND MYOCARDIAL BIOPSY. Usually more than one of these procedures is done to open the artery and prevent its reclosing.

Depending on the disease process, the patient may have recurring narrowing or blockage that can be treated in the same manner as the first narrowing or blockage. If the blockage is more severe, coronary artery bypass grafting may be done by an open procedure (*see the section* CORONARY ARTERY BYPASS GRAFTING) or endoscopically (using small flexible telescopes and instruments) through a small incision in the chest wall. In some cases the heart is stopped to allow the delicate surgery. Some physicians have learned how to do the bypass procedure without stopping the heart.

If the heart has an open duct, such as a patent ductus arteriosis (*see* CHAPTER 4: SEPTAL DEFECTS) or a patent foramen ovale, a percutaneous catheter can be used to insert a special plug into the hole to seal it. The mesh plug is inserted through the hole and then expanded on both sides to seal over the hole. Tissue grows into the mesh to hold the plug in place.

Percutaneous (also known as endovascular) procedures are considered much safer than surgical procedures because they use very small incisions and are thus minimally invasive. Still, some rare problems might occur, such as perforation of an artery, inability to deflate a balloon, getting a catheter stuck in the artery, or severe bleeding.

Pressure Measurement

Sometimes the pressures in the heart need to be measured to determine the pumping ability of the heart and to assess other problems. A pressure catheter (also called a Swan-Ganz catheter) can be used to measure the pressures in the right side of the heart and estimate pressures in the left. This catheter can also determine the type of shock, diagnose the causes of respiratory and cardiac failure, and diagnose and manage other conditions in critically ill patients. For example, inspection of the pressure waveforms can detect cardiac tamponade, cardiomyopathy, mitral valvular leakage, tricuspid valvular leakage, intracardiac holes, and how a particular therapy is working (*see also* CHAPTER 3: PULMONARY HYPERTENSION).

The catheter is inserted into a large vein, such as the femoral, subclavian, or jugular. From there the tip of the multilumened catheter is moved into the right side of the heart and into the pulmonary artery and its branches, if needed. The several lumens or channels in the catheter allow the pressure measurements and injection of saline for testing or sampling of blood. A monitor attached to the catheter measures and records the data from the heart.

Risks of Cardiac Catheterization

As with any interventional procedure, various problems can occur during cardiac catheterizations, such as a catheter perforating or tearing a blood vessel, a patient's allergic reaction to cardiac dye, being unable to deflate the stenting balloon, getting the catheter stuck in a blood vessel, valve injury, severe bleeding, or death. Most of these problems can be avoided by a careful and knowledgeable surgeon. Indeed, thousands of cardiac catheterizations each year are performed with no adverse outcomes.

Cardioversion

Cardioversion is an external (noninvasive) heart procedure that is performed to correct a form of arrhythmia, an irregular or rapid heartbeat. Arrhythmias alter the efficiency of the heart's ability to pump blood throughout the body, which can lead to a heart attack, sudden cardiac arrest, and stroke. Two types of treatment are medication and an electrical procedure (not defibrillation, which uses a higher electrical shock; defibrillation can cause burns or fires and ultimately may not be successful, depending on the patient's condition). Medications can be used to affect the heart's pumping effectiveness by such means as regulating heart rate, muscle contractibility, and blood pressure. Using two soft-padded electrodes, a cardioversion machine sends one or more low-energy electrical shocks to the heart, while the machine records the patient's heart rhythm. First, electric shocks are delivered to briefly stop the heart rhythm, and then the low energy is sent again to restart the heart's electric activity. *See also the section* PACEMAKER OR DEFIBRILLATOR IMPLANTATION, which discusses the implantable cardioverter-defibrillator (ICD), an internal device used to treat recurring arrhythmia.

Carotid Endarterectomy (Carotid Artery Surgery)

Carotid endarterectomy, also known as carotid artery surgery, is used to remove plaque narrowing the carotid artery; if this artery becomes blocked, it prevents oxygenated blood from reaching the brain and thus will cause a stroke (*see* CHAPTER 3 for expanded information on stroke). There are two carotid arteries, one on each side of the neck. During an approximately two-hour surgery, usually the blocked portion of the carotid artery will be cut open and plaque will be removed, along with the inner lining surrounding the plaque. Then the incision will be closed with stitches.

Carotid Ultrasound

A carotid ultrasound, also known as Doppler ultrasound and carotid duplex ultrasound, creates an image of the carotid arteries with the use of high-frequency sound waves to determine whether plaque is building up and narrowing the carotid arteries. This is a safe and pain-free diagnostic test to determine whether preventive treatment is needed for carotid artery disease.

Clinical Trials

Clinical trials involve testing a new drug therapy, a new device, or a new surgical procedure to determine if it works or is better than existing therapies; just because something is new does not mean it is better. A clinical trial is a study intended to benefit society and future patients. So some patients participating in a trial may not receive the treatment being tried. For example, in a clinical trial a patient might receive a placebo treatment (e.g., a pill that does nothing or another type of treatment that has no medical effect) so that the placebo patient is a control or point of comparison for patients who do receive the new treatment. Usually the physicians conducting the trial do not know which patients are getting the treatment and which are getting the placebo. If the new treatment trial proves that the treatment is successful, the control patients may eventually be offered the new treatment as well.

Because clinical trials work on testing new drugs and new treatments, everything may not be known about the treatment to be tested. There are often risks in receiving the new treatment. However, the physicians running the trial carefully monitor each patient and intervene should some life-threatening problem arise.

Those who decide to participate in a clinical trial should discuss it with their doctor and with the physician running the trial. Patients should understand the risks and benefits, how the trial came to be, the duration of the trial, costs, and all the details of how the patients and their family members can interact with the clinical trial.

One current experimental surgical procedure is cardiomyoplasty. In this procedure, muscles from the back or abdomen are wrapped around a damaged heart. A pacemaker-like device is implanted to stimulate the muscle wrap. The intent is to increase the pumping ability of the heart. Another clinical trial injects the patient's own stem cells into damaged but viable portions of the heart wall in an attempt to build new heart muscle.

Complementary and Alternative Therapies

Complementary and alternative therapy refers to products, techniques, theories, or practices that fall outside conventional medicine. Complementary therapy is used together with conventional medicine. Alternative therapy is used instead of, or as a replacement for, conventional medicine.

There are many complementary and alternative therapies for heart disease. These involve products, techniques, theories, or practices that have debatable or unproven effectiveness. However, some complementary therapies that have been shown to help the heart are those that reduce stress and anxiety, encourage exercise, and improve diet. These include meditation, tai chi, yoga, biofeedback, and diet and nutrition improvement and supplements.

Some alternative therapies, such as acupressure, sound therapy, flower therapy, massage therapy, and aromatherapy, may provide some relaxation and stress relief, which could help a diseased heart. Many providers of alternative therapies recommend using such treatments in conjunction with conventional medicine. These alternative therapies should not be solely relied on to improve, treat, or cure heart disease. Patients should be wary of scams, unproven therapies, and cure-alls. It is important for those with heart disease to check with their doctors and other reputable sources about the proposed treatment before trying the alternative therapy.

Most vitamins have not been shown to decrease any heart disease risk. However, omega-3 fatty acids (mainly from fish) have been shown to lower triglyceride levels and are helpful in treating high blood pressure. They also reportedly have a beneficial effect on depression.

Enhanced external counterpulsation (EECP) is a complementary therapy that uses an air pump to inflate and deflate cuffs around the legs, causing blood to be

Understanding Clinical Trials—Recommended Resources

➢ CardioSmart—"Clinical Trials: Treatment Overview." https://www.cardiosmart.org/ healthwise/tv70/19/tv7019; alternate path: https://www.cardiosmart.org/, search for "clinical trials," and then click on the resource title. CardioSmart provides an easy-to-use webpage on understanding clinical trials, including definitions, the phases of a clinical trial, finding out about clinical trials, what to expect after treatment, why clinical trials are important, how clinical trials work, what happens when a trial finishes, risks, and safety. According to the American College of Cardiology, "CardioSmart is the patient education and empowerment initiative brought to you by the American College of Cardiology. Our mission is to help individuals prevent, treat and manage cardiovascular disease."

➢ National Heart, Lung, and Blood Institute (NHLBI)—"Children and Clinical Studies." http://www.nhlbi.nih.gov/childrenandclinicalstudies/; alternate path: http://www.nhlbi.nih.gov/; search for "children and clinical studies home," and then click on the title "Home, Children and Clinical Studies, NHLBI, NIH." NHLBI, a division of National Institutes of Health from the U.S. Department of Health and Human Services, provides information on children and clinical studies, including why they are important, participant considerations, getting started, once in a study, resources (e.g., how to find reliable information and searching for clinical trials), and news. Videos are featured to help parents understand the importance of "enrolling their child in a clinical study." Also under "Resources," click on "Related Materials" for a link to the "Children and Clinical Studies Campaign" support group (http://www.nhlbi.nih.gov/ childrenandclinicalstudies/relatedmaterials.php).

➢ PubMed Health—"About Clinical Effectiveness Research." http://www.ncbi.nlm .nih.gov/pubmedhealth/aboutcer/; alternate path: http://www.ncbi.nlm.nih.gov/ pubmedhealth/, click on the heading "Understand Clinical Effectiveness," and then click on the title "What Is Clinical Effectiveness?" PubMed Health provides links to explanations on patient-relevant outcomes, clinical trials, systematic reviews, and informed decision making. According to its website, "PubMed Health specializes in reviews of clinical effectiveness research, with easy-to-read summaries for consumers as well as full technical reports. Clinical effectiveness research finds answers to the question 'What works?' in medical and health care. PubMed Health is a service provided by the National Center for Biotechnology Information (NCBI) at the U.S. National Library of Medicine (NLM)."

➢ PubMed Health—"Understanding Research Results." http://www.ncbi.nlm.nih .gov/pubmedhealth/understanding-research-results/; alternate path: http:// www.ncbi.nlm.nih.gov/pubmedhealth/, click on the heading "Understand Clinical Effectiveness," and then click on the resource title. PubMed Health provides links to explanations on understanding the basics of clinical trials and why randomization is important.

pushed into the heart. In various studies, it has relieved angina, reduced the need for nitrates, and possibly caused beneficial changes in the heart. It is sometimes recommended for patients with angina who do not respond to standard therapies. Patients with three-vessel coronary artery disease, heart failure, or blood clots in the legs should not have this therapy.

Chelation using disodium ethylenediaminetetraacetic acid (EDTA, an amino acid) to flush out heavy metals or minerals, such as lead and iron (by bonding to EDTA), throughout the bloodstream by infusion is a complementary or alternative therapy that might reduce hardening of the arteries. The Trial to Assess Chelation Therapy (TACT), a 10-year, multicenter, randomized, double-blind, efficacy clinical trial compared chelation therapy using EDTA (along with "high doses of vitamin C and B-vitamins, electrolytes, a local anesthetic and heparin, an anti-clotting drug") to a placebo (infusion contained "salt water and a little bit of sugar") on 1,708 patients who were age 50 and over and had previously had a heart attack. Published March 27, 2013, in the *Journal of the Medical Association* (*JAMA*), trial results indicated reduced cardiovascular events by 18 percent (death, another heart attack, "stroke, coronary revascularization or hospitalization for angina"). During the trial, most participants continued their physician-prescribed therapy of aspirin, beta-blockers, and statins. The Food and Drugs Administration (FDA) has not given approval for chelation for treatment of heart disease; peer-review researchers, including cardiologist Steven Nissen of the Cleveland Clinic, want additional studies to prove its effectiveness due to missing data and high placebo dropout rate. However, many researchers agree to this study's importance. This study was approved for grants by the National Institutes of Health (NIH), the National Heart, Lung, and Blood Institute (NHLBI), and the NIH's National Center for Complementary and Alternative Medicine.

Coronary Artery Bypass Grafting

The heart receives blood from the main arteries that branch from the aorta just above the aortic valve. These arteries are the right coronary artery, the left coronary artery, and its major branch, the circumflex branch of the left coronary artery. Sometimes a section of one of these arteries is blocked with clots, plaque, calcification, or fat deposits. If the artery cannot be opened and stented, it must be bypassed to deliver blood to sections of the heart that are affected by the blockage. Otherwise the section of heart without good blood flow will die and the heart will not pump properly.

In coronary artery bypass grafting a vein is taken from the patient's leg or an artery is taken from inside the chest wall and is grafted across the blocked section of the coronary artery. Coronary artery bypass grafting is often abbreviated to CABG (or "cabbage"). This is usually an open procedure in which the chest is cut open to access the heart and one or both legs are cut open to access veins.

To learn more, visit the **National Heart, Lung, and Blood Institute** of the National Institutes of Health at http://www.nhlbi.nih.gov/health/health-topics/topics/cabg/ (alternate path: http://www.nhlbi.nih.gov/, search for "cabg," and then click on the title "What Is Coronary Artery Bypass Grafting?"). This webpage includes an illustration of coronary artery bypass grafting. Part A shows the location of the heart. Part B shows how vein and artery bypass grafts are attached to the heart.

In some cases the heart is stopped to more easily graft the blood vessel across the blocked artery. In this case, the patient is put on a heart–lung bypass (cardiopulmonary bypass) machine, which bypasses the heart, removes blood from the body, removes carbon dioxide, and adds oxygen and pumps the oxygenated blood back into the body. This machine uses special pumps to act like the heart and special chambers to exchange oxygen for carbon dioxide in the blood. Cannulae or tubes are placed into the heart or major vessels to connect the patient to the machine. Once connected, the patient's heart is stopped with drugs, and the surgery proceeds. When the surgery is completed, the cannulae are removed, their holes are repaired, and the heart is restarted.

To learn more, visit the **National Heart, Lung, and Blood Institute** of the National Institutes of Health at http://www.nhlbi.nih.gov/health/health-topics/topics/hs/ during.html (alternate path: http://www.nhlbi.nih.gov/, search for "during heart surgery," and then click on the title "What to Expect during Heart Surgery"). This webpage includes an illustration of how a heart–lung bypass machine works during surgery.

Recently, bypass procedure have begun to take place through ports cut through the chest wall to allow surgical access with endoscopic or robotic instruments. In some cases this port surgery is done with the heart still beating. Robotic surgery allows the surgeon more precise and controlled surgery than could otherwise be had by hand. These surgeries are often called by their acronyms: CABG (cardiac artery bypass grafting), PACAB or PortCAB (port-access coronary artery bypass), and MIDCAB (minimally invasive direct coronary artery bypass surgery).

CABG is a well-known and long-practiced surgery. However, as with all open procedures, CABG has risks. For example, care must be taken to ensure that a harvested vein is properly oriented to allow proper blood flow and not cause a blockage by the valves normally occurring in a vein. Arteries do not have valves. Also, infection, severe blood cell damage from pumping, bleeding, nonfusion of the sternum, and death can occur as a result of CABG. As with other procedures, most of these risks can be avoided by a careful and knowledgeable surgeon.

Coronary Calcium Scan

A coronary calcium scan, also known as a calcium scan test or cardiac CT for calcium scoring, is used to view any calcium particles within the coronary artery walls. These particles will eventually combine with cholesterol and other debris to form plaque (a waxy material in and on the vessel wall), which narrows coronary arteries. The amount of calcium measured, known as an Agatston score, can determine the risk for narrowing or hardening of the arteries and determine whether preventive treatment would be effective.

> To learn more, visit the **National Heart, Lung, and Blood Institute** of the National Institutes of Health at http://www.nhlbi.nih.gov/health/health-topics/topics/cscan/ (alternate path: http://www.nhlbi.nih.gov/, search for "coronary calcium scan," and then click on the title "What Is a Coronary Calcium Scan?"). This webpage on coronary calcium scans includes an illustration of what these scans can reveal. Part A shows the position of the heart in the body and the location and angle of the coronary calcium scan image. Part B is the coronary calcium scan image, which shows calcification in a coronary artery.

The two X-ray machines that take coronary artery images are called electron beam computed tomography (EBCT) or electron beam tomography (EBT) and multidetector computed tomography (MDCT).

Diagnosing Congenital Heart Disease

See also CHAPTER 4.

Sometimes heart problems begin during fetal development. A fetal heart is different from a child's or an adult's heart in that the openings are needed in the heart to route the blood quickly from the placenta to the growing fetal body. If these ducts do not close at birth or if the heart and its blood vessels do not properly form, the infant will have a congenital heart disease.

Congenital heart disease is typically diagnosed by the signs of poor blood circulation, such as cyanosis (blue baby); shortness of breath; or buildup of blood and fluid in lungs, feet, ankles, and legs. Ultrasonography can detect some fetal abnormalities in the womb. An infant with a congenital heart disease may also experience respiratory infections, underdevelopment of limbs and muscles, poor feeding, and poor growth. Observing the infant can detect most defects. Some congenital heart defects cause a heart murmur that can vary depending on the defect. Most defects will present early in life, but some can go undetected throughout the patient's life. The defects can be imaged through various methods like computed tomography (CT) or ultrasound scans. Processes for repairing defects range from simple catheter insertion of a hole-closing device into the heart to major surgery to move vessels and reorient the heart (*see the section* MAJOR VESSEL REPAIR). Other major surgeries are usually rare, long, and complicated and are not covered in this guide.

Drug Therapies

There is a wide variety of heart drugs, many targeted for specific problems, and many with multiple uses. For example, Cozaar (losartan potassium) is prescribed for lowering blood pressure, as well as to treat some heart failure problems (e.g., it helps the pumping action of the left ventricle heart chamber).

Many drugs have similar-sounding names, which can lead to confusion. For example, Amicar (aminocaproic acid) and Omacor (omega-3-acid ethyl esters) sound alike but have very different purposes. Omacor is for lowering high triglyceride blood levels, while Amicar is used to control severe bleeding due to blood-clotting problems.

Medications are usually prescribed by their brand names rather than their generic names until a pharmaceutical manufacturer's patent runs out. For example, Zocor originally was patented and sold exclusively by Merck. Since Zocor's patent ended, it is now sold by its generic name, simvastatin, by U.S. FDA-approved manufacturers at a much cheaper price. In the United States, a drug patent lasts 20 years; however, because pharmaceutical companies file their patents before they begin clinical trials, the average time after manufacturing begins is 8 to 10 years, except when patent extensions are granted for new uses.

There are different drugs that have the same basic effect on specific heart conditions. Most drugs, however, can treat more than one type of heart condition, although not all medications are as effective for every patient or have the same side effects. Most common side effects diminish after a few weeks. Some of these drugs can have serious or life-threatening side effects, such as warfarin and its effect on reducing blood clotting, and they require close collaboration between the patient and doctor to monitor dosage and side effects. Following is a list of drug classes that are commonly prescribed for various heart and cardiovascular conditions; nevertheless, just as the American Heart Association states, the authors of this book are "not recommending or endorsing any" medications.

- *For angina:* beta-blockers, calcium channel blockers (CCBs), and nitrates (nitroglycerin)
- *For blood clot disorders:* anticoagulants

- *For heart disease:* anticoagulants, antiplatelets, and warfarin
- *For heart failure:* ACE inhibitors, beta-blockers, digoxin, diuretics, and aldosterone antagonists (eplerenone or spironolactone)
- *For heart rhythm disorders:* antiarrhythmic, calcium channel blockers, beta-blockers, digitalis, and anticoagulants
- *For high blood pressure:* angiotensin-converting enzyme (ACE) inhibitors, angiotensin-II receptor blockers (ARBs), alpha-agonists and -blockers, beta-blockers, calcium channel blockers, centrally acting drugs, peripheral adrenergic antagonists, vasodilators, and diuretics
- *For low-density lipoprotein (LDL) cholesterol lowering:* cholesterol absorption inhibitors (ezetimibe), fibrates, niacin, bile-acid resins, and statins
- *For treatment after a heart attack:* anticoagulants, antiplatelet agents, thrombolytics, angiotensin-converting enzyme (ACE) inhibitors, angiotensin II receptor blockers (ARBs), beta-blockers, calcium channel blockers, diuretics, vasodilators, digitalis preparations, and statins
- *For treatment after heart valve replacement:* anticoagulants

A patient's local pharmacy can provide information on the prescribed drugs, usually when they are dispensed. However, more detail is available from the patient's doctor, the drug's package insert, and the drug's Internet site.

In the final section of this chapter, Resources for Further Information, there is a separate section titled Websites on General Drug Information for Treatment and Prevention of Heart Diseases. At these websites, including the Food and Drug Administration (FDA) for consumers, you can find the latest information on medications, including daily updates.

Common Types of Heart and Cardiovascular Disease Medications

Aldosterone Antagonists

Aldosterone antagonists, also known as aldosterone receptor antagonists, are used to treat high blood pressure and heart failure. They are a type of diuretic (known as a "water pill") that works by blocking the hormone aldosterone, which causes the buildup of salt and water in the blood and raises blood pressure, increasing stress on heart function. Aldosterone antagonists also help prevent the loss of potassium, which is why these drugs are also known as potassium-sparing diuretics. These medications are commonly taken in combination with other drugs, such as angiotensin-converting enzyme (ACE) inhibitors, other diuretics, digoxin, and beta-blockers. Two examples are eplerenone (Inspra) or spironolactone (Aldactone). According to the Cleveland Clinic, common side effects include extreme tiredness, increased urination, upset stomach, rash or itching, shortness of breath, confusion, irregular heartbeat, nervousness, and numbness or tingling in the hands, feet, or lips (http://my.clevelandclinic.org/drugs/diuretics/hic_diuretics.aspx).

Alpha-Blockers

Alpha-blockers, also called alpha-adrenergic antagonists, aid in keeping small blood vessels open to increase blood flow and reduce blood pressure, as well as reducing stress on the heart. They also act as a muscle relaxant. Some alpha-blockers are longer lasting than others. Short-acting drugs act more quickly, but their effects last only a few hours; long-acting alpha-blockers work in the system for a longer period of time, but their effects do not kick in as quickly. Some alpha-blockers are alfuzosin (Uroxatral), doxazosin (Cardura), prazosin (Minipress), terazosin (Hytrin), and tamsulosin (Flomax). When patients initially begin taking alpha-blockers, they sometimes experience a sudden drop in blood pressure, commonly known as first-dose effect, which can usually be remedied by sitting or lying down until blood pressure increases. Alpha-blockers may interfere with the effectiveness of other medications. Additional side effects include nausea, dizziness, headache, weakness, rapid heartbeat, and weight gain.

Angiotensin-Converting Enzyme Inhibitors

Angiotensin-converting enzyme (ACE) inhibitors expand blood vessels and decrease blood flow resistance by lowering the blood level of the peptide angiotensin II. This allows the blood to flow more easily and reduces the workload on the heart. It is usually prescribed for patients with high blood pressure, heart failure, and other cardiovascular conditions.

Common ACE inhibitors include (generic name followed by brand name in parentheses) benazepril (Lotensin), captopril (Capoten), enalapril (Vasotec), fosinopril (Monopril), lisinopril (Prinivil, Zestril), moexipril (Univasc), perindopril (Aceon), quinapril (Accupril), ramipril (Altace), and trandolapril (Mavik). Common side effects of these drugs include skin rash, loss of taste, or chronic dry, hacking cough. A rare side effect is kidney damage. Women should not become pregnant while taking these drugs because of the dangerous effects that can occur to the mother and the fetus.

Angiotensin II Receptor Blockers

Angiotensin II receptor blockers (also called ARBs, or angiotensin-2 receptor antagonists, AT-2s) block angiotensin II from having any effect on the blood vessels and heart and thus prevents blood pressure from rising. It is normally used to treat high blood pressure and heart failure.

Common angiotensin II receptor blockers include (generic name followed by brand name in parentheses) candesartan (Atacand), eprosartan (Teveten), irbesartan

(Avapro), losartan potassium (Cozaar), telmisartan (Micardis), and valsartan (Diovan). A common side effect of these drugs is occasional dizziness. These drugs should not be used during pregnancy because these drugs can injure or kill the fetus.

Antiarrhythmics

Antiarrhythmics are drugs used to control but not cure arrhythmia (abnormal heart rhythm) by lowering heart rate, which in turn lowers stress on the heart. According to the American Heart Association's "Medications for Arrhythmia" webpage, these drugs "suppress the abnormal firing of pacemaker tissue or depress the transmission of impulses in tissues that either conduct too rapidly or participate in reentry."

Antiarrhythmic drugs reduce electrical system impulses by inhibiting potassium channels. Examples are amiodarone (Cordarone, Pacerone), bepridil hydrochloride (Vascor), disopyramide (Norpace), dofetilide (Tikosyn), dronedarone (Multaq), flecainide (Tambocor), ibutilide (Corvert), lidocaine (Xylocaine), procainamide (Procan, Procanbid), propafenone (Rythmol), propranolol (Inderal), quinidine (many trade names), sotalol (Betapace), and tocainide (Tonocarid). According to WebMD, common side effects can include fast or slow heartbeat, dizziness or fainting, lower extremity swelling, cough, loss of appetite, metallic taste, shortness of breath, diarrhea or constipation, blurred vision, chest pain, and sensitivity to sunlight.

Other types of drugs that slow down heart rate are calcium channel blockers, digoxin, and beta-blockers.

Anticoagulants

Anticoagulants (or blood thinners) are used to minimize blood clotting, prevent strokes, minimize the growth of existing clots, and prevent new clots from forming. The most common blood thinner is warfarin (Coumadin). Other anticoagulant drugs may be used when a patient is hospitalized or for short-term use. There are three newer anticoagulants in which daily monitoring is not needed: dabigatran (Pradaxa), rivaroxaban (Xarelto), and apixaban (Eliquis). With these three newer drugs, there is currently no known corrective method to stop severe bleeding should it occur; there are such safety measures in place with warfarin.

Anticoagulants are often prescribed for patients at risk of stroke, heart attack, atrial fibrillation, or other cardiovascular diseases. Common anticoagulants include (generic name followed by brand name in parentheses) dalteparin (Fragmin), danaparoid (Orgaran), enoxaparin (Lovenox), heparin (many trade names), and tinzaparin (Innohep). Common side effects of these drugs include bloating and gas. Less common side effects include bleeding and bruising in many body areas. A doctor should be contacted if nausea, vomiting, diarrhea, stomach pain, or cramps is experienced while using any of these drugs.

Antiplatelet Agents

Antiplatelet agents are another type of anticlotting medication that prevents blood platelets from sticking together and starting a clot. These agents are prescribed for patients with plaques that have not fully blocked an artery, for patients who have had ischemic strokes, for those who have had a heart attack, and for those with other types of cardiovascular disease.

These drugs have been on the market for a long time and are mostly generic, such as aspirin, ticlopidine, clopidogrel, and dipyridamole. Common side effects of these drugs include bloating and gas. Less common side effects include bleeding and bruising. A doctor should be contacted if nausea, vomiting, diarrhea, stomach pain, or cramps is experienced.

Beta-Blockers

Beta-blockers or beta-adrenergic blocking agents reduce the effectiveness of stress hormones and thereby decrease heart rate and cardiac output. The drugs' effects lower blood pressure and make the heart beat more slowly and less forcefully. In other words, beta-blockers make the heart work less hard. Beta-blockers are used to treat high blood pressure, cardiac arrhythmias, and angina and as a preventive of additional heart attacks for those who have already had a heart attack.

Common beta-blockers include (generic name followed by brand name in parentheses) acebutolol (Sectral), atenolol (Tenormin), betaxolol (Kerlone), bisoprolol/hydrochlorothiazide (Ziac), bisoprolol (Zebeta), carteolol (Cartrol), metoprolol (Lopressor, Toprol XL), nadolol (Corgard), propranolol (Inderal), sotalol (Betapace), and timolol (Blocadren). Common side effects of these drugs include insomnia, cold hands and feet, tiredness, depression, slow heartbeat, asthma symptoms, and impotence. Diabetics taking these drugs should be closely monitored by a doctor. Women who are or could become pregnant should consult a doctor about taking these drugs.

Calcium Channel Blockers

Calcium channel blockers (also called calcium antagonists or calcium blockers) disrupt the movement of calcium into the body's cells. Calcium helps the muscles contract and the nerves work. Because these blockers work on the heart and blood vessels, it is thought that they decrease the heart's pumping strength and relax blood vessels. Patients with high blood pressure, angina, and some arrhythmias may be prescribed this type of drug.

Common calcium channel blockers include (generic name followed by brand name in parentheses) amlodipine (Norvasc, Lotrel), bepridil (Vascor), diltiazem (Cardizem, Tiazac), felodipine (Plendil), nifedipine (Adalat, Procardia), nimodipine (Nimotop), nisoldipine (Sular), and verapamil (Calan, Isoptin, Verelan). Possible side effects of these drugs include palpitations, swollen ankles, constipation, headache, and dizziness.

Centrally Acting Drugs

Centrally acting drugs, also known as central adrenergic inhibitors, central alpha-agonists, and central agonists, inhibit the brain from sending electrical signals, which slows down the heart rate and aids in preventing blood vessels from narrowing. This process reduces stress on the heart, allows easier blood flow, and reduces high blood pressure. Some centrally acting drugs are clonidine (Catapres), guanfacine (Tenex), and methyldopa (Aldomet). According to WebMD, common side effects include difficulty breathing, hives, headache, dizziness, increased or irregular heartbeat, and swelling of the face, lips, tongue, or throat.

Cholesterol-Lowering Drugs

Cholesterol-lowering drugs do just that but in various ways. They help lower low-density lipoprotein (LDL, or bad) cholesterol, raise high-density lipoprotein (HDL, or good) cholesterol, and lower triglyceride levels in the blood. Some cholesterol-lowering drugs work in the liver to inhibit formation of cholesterol, in the intestines to prevent absorption of cholesterol, or in the circulatory system. Patients with high cholesterol are often prescribed these drugs. Common cholesterol-lowering drugs include statins, resins, nicotinic acid (niacin, B12), gemfibrozil, and clofibrate. Common side effects of these drugs include muscle and joint aches, nausea, diarrhea, and constipation. More serious side effects such as liver damage and muscle problems should be discussed with a doctor.

Clot Busters (Thrombolytic Drugs)

Clot busters, also known as thrombolytic drugs, are very potent drugs administered intravenously in a hospital during life-threatening situations. They are used to prevent additional heart damage during or after a heart attack or stroke by breaking up any clots throughout the body.

Since clot busters can cause bleeding to become much worse, it is important for patients to inform their physician about any anticoagulants (or blood thinners) they have taken, such as warfarin (Coumadin) or anti-inflammatory medications or pain relievers, such as ibuprofen or aspirin.

Some clot busters are tissue plasminogen activator (TPA), tenecteplase, urokinase, alteplase, reteplase, and streptokinase. The two most serious side effects are bleeding and stroke.

Digitalis

Digitalis preparations increase the forcefulness of a heart's contractions. This is helpful in heart failure because more blood is forced into the coronary arteries. Digitalis can also slow some irregular heartbeat conditions, such as that which occurs in atrial fibrillation. Patients with heart failure and certain arrhythmias are prescribed digitalis preparations. These preparations can be a pill that dissolves in the mouth, a chewable pill, or a cream. Digitalis preparations are sometimes used to replace ACE inhibitors and diuretics if the patient is not responding to those drugs.

Common digitalis preparations include (generic name followed by brand name in parentheses) digoxin and digitoxin (Lanoxin, Digitek, Lanoxicaps). These drugs can have serious interactions with other drugs and should be prescribed only if the interactions are known and can be controlled.

Common side effects include erectile dysfunction and breast enlargement in men. Serious side effects that require a doctor's consultation include irregular heartbeat, dizziness, palpitations, shortness of breath, sweating, fainting, hallucinations, confusion, mental changes (e.g., depression), unusual tiredness or weakness, loss of appetite, nausea, blurry eyesight, double vision, and seeing yellow, green, or white halos around objects.

Digoxin

Digoxin is used to efficiently treat heart failure, atrial fibrillation, and heart function that deteriorated or has been damaged. Digoxin reinforces contractions of heart muscle, reduces heart rate, and allows blood to flow more easily. According to MedlinePlus, common side effects include dizziness, drowsiness, blurred or yellow vision, rash, irregular heartbeat, stomachache, vomiting or diarrhea, difficulty breathing, swelling of hands or feet, loss of appetite, and unusual weight gain.

Digoxin is commonly prescribed with other heart medications, including diuretics, ACE inhibitors, angiotensin receptor blockers, and beta-blockers.

Diuretics

Diuretics or water pills cause the body to excrete excess water and sodium. Diuretics are used to lower blood pressure and reduce edema or swelling. Basically these drugs cause a patient to urinate more often. With less fluid in the circulatory system, the heart's workload is lightened. Diuretics also help relieve edema in the lungs, limbs, and other parts of the body. While all diuretics cause these things to happen, different diuretics have different rates and methods of action.

Common diuretics include (generic name followed by brand name in parentheses) amiloride (Midamor), bumetanide (Bumex), chlorothiazide (Diuril), chlorthalidone (Hygroton), furosemide (Lasix), hydrochlorothiazide (Esidrix, Hydrodiuril), indapamide (Lozol), and spironolactone (Aldactone). Common side effects of these drugs include weakness, leg cramps or tiredness (from potassium loss), gout (from prolonged use), and impotence. Diabetics may experience increased blood glucose levels, which can be adjusted by diet or change in medication.

Inotropic Therapy

Involving a class of powerful, heart-pumping drugs, inotropic therapy is used to treat end-stage congestive heart failure to ease and manage symptoms by energizing the damaged heart muscle to increase contractions. These heart-pump drugs may also increase the heart rhythm. There are two types: positive inotropic agents (to increase the force of the heartbeat contractions to allow more blood to pump through with fewer heartbeats) and negative inotropic agents (to decrease the force of heartbeat contractions that pump blood to slow heart rate and reduce stress on heart).

Two common heart pump medications are dobutamine (Dobutrex) and milrinone (Primacor), both taken intravenously through a catheter line or from an infusion pump installed at the hospital to be worn continuously. Positive inotropic agents include digoxin, dopamine, dobutamine, eicosanoids, epinephrine, inamrinone, isoprenaline, milrinone, norepinephrine, phosphodiesterase inhibitors, and theophylline. Negative inotropic agents include beta-blockers, calcium channel blockers, disopyramide, flecainide, procainamide, and quinidine.

Low-Dose Aspirin

Low-dose aspirin (between 80 and 160 mg per day) has long been used to help prevent and manage heart disease and stroke. Aspirin relieves pain and inflammation and inhibits formation of blood clots. Aspirin administered during a heart attack can reduce heart damage. However, aspirin can have serious side effects; patients should consult their doctors before starting an aspirin regimen.

Nitrates

Nitrates are used to treat angina and relieve chest pain. Nitrates act as vasodilators by quickly expanding arteries, which increases oxygenated blood flow to the heart so that the left ventricle will not have to work as hard to pump blood. Nitrates also expand veins, allowing more blood to flow quickly through them throughout the body, which also allows the heart muscle not to work as hard and therefore need less blood and oxygen. Common sides effects include dizziness caused by sudden drop in blood pressure, nausea or stomach upset, reddening of face and neck, headache, pulsating-type headache, and a burning feeling when the medication is placed under the tongue.

Some common nitrates are nitroglycerin (Nitrostat, Nitroquick, Nitrolingual, Nitro-Dur, Minitran, Nitro-Bid), isosorbide dinitrate (Dilatrate, Isordil), and isosorbide mononitrate (ISMO).

Peripheral Adrenergic Antagonists

Peripheral adrenergic antagonists inhibit the release of the hormone adrenaline or block the effects of adrenaline in response to stress. These drugs cause blood vessels to relax and expand so that blood can flow easier, which lowers blood pressure and reduces heart rate.

Peripheral adrenergic antagonists are commonly used with diuretics for lowering high blood pressure. One such peripheral adrenergic antagonist is reserpine (Serpasil). Common side effects include dizziness, nausea, tiredness, vomiting, diarrhea, slow heartbeat, and a congested nose; rare is an allergic reaction causing breathing difficulties and swelling of the neck, face, and mouth.

Vasodilators

Vasodilators (sometimes called nitrates or nitroglycerin tablets) relax blood vessels, which allows more blood to move to the heart muscles. This decreases the heart's workload. Patients with angina are sometimes prescribed vasodilators.

Common vasodilators include (generic name followed by brand name in parentheses) isosorbide dinitrate (Isordil), nesiritide (Natrecor), hydralazine (Apresoline), nitrates, and minoxidil. Some side effects that usually subside after a few weeks of vasodilator treatment are headaches, swelling around the eyes, heart palpitations, or aches and pains in the joints. Minoxidil may cause fluid retention, weight increase, or excessive hair growth.

Echocardiography

Echocardiography uses ultrasonic sound waves to produce an image of the heart. A technician places a probe coated with coupling gel on the patient's chest and moves the probe around to get the desired image of the heart. The probe sends out sound waves and receives reflected waves from a patient's internal structures. A computer is used to convert the reflected sound waves into an image of the internal structures. The gel helps get the sound waves into and out of the body and the sensor. The procedure is noninvasive and only a bit messy because of the gel.

During echocardiography, the technician measures such things as heart wall thickness, motion of the heart valves, heart rate, the sound of the valves opening and closing, and the amount of blood pumped by the various chambers. Of particular interest is ejection fraction or the amount of the blood volume that the left ventricle pumps into the left atrium. This indicates the effectiveness of the heart in moving blood through the body. Usually an ejection fraction higher than 50 percent is considered good and below 50 percent indicates a problem. Echocardiography is widely used, from small doctors' offices to large hospitals, and has no known risks.

Transesophageal echocardiography (TEE) uses a probe that is placed down the esophagus to image the heart, similar to an echocardiograph. The images are improved over regular external echocardiography because the probe in the esophagus is close to and behind the heart. Other than minor throat irritation, TEE has few risks.

Transthoracic echocardiogram (TTE) includes using a transducer to move around the chest or abdominal wall and record sound waves to create a video of the heart. There are no known risks with TTE.

Electrocardiography

In Chapter 2, the section Electrical System of the Heart explained how the heart's nerves send electrical signals in sequence to sections of the heart causing the heart to contract in such a way to cause the blood to be pumped through the heart. So over the 0.8 seconds or so during which the heart sequentially contracts, electrical nerve signals can actually be measured.

The electrocardiograph or electrocardiogram is a graph of the heart's electrical or nerve activity. ECG and EKG are the common abbreviations for this procedure. (EKG is based on the German word *Elektrokardiogramm*. EKG is sometimes used in English-speaking countries to avoid confusion with EEG, which sounds similar to ECG. An EEG is an electroencephalogram or study of the brain's electrical activity.) The graph of the nerve impulses has particular shapes for normal and abnormal conditions. A normal graph is called a PQRST wave. Each letter defines a portion of the wave, with P and T being small humps and QRS being a large spike (*see* CHAPTER 2: ELECTRICAL SYSTEM OF THE HEART). Deviation from the normal wave shape points to abnormalities within certain sections of the heart.

In electrocardiography, a measuring device reads the electrical activity of the heart through wires attached to a patient's chest. Usually three wires are used, but as many as 12 can be used to get a more complete picture of how the heart is contracting. The device typically prints out a graph of several heartbeats. Some devices will identify and note on the graphs any abnormality that is measured. Electrocardiographs are taken in doctors' offices, during stress tests, in response to a cardiac emergency, and during surgery. Many defibrillators and automatic external defibrillators have built-in electrocardiographs to help determine the best time, or if, to deliver a lifesaving shock to the patient.

To learn more, visit the **National Heart, Lung, and Blood Institute** of the National Institutes of Health at http://www.nhlbi.nih.gov/health/health-topics/topics/ekg/during.html (alternate path: http://www.nhlbi.nih.gov/, search for "during an electrocardiogram," and then click on the title "What to Expect during an Electrocardiogram"). This webpage includes an illustration of the standard setup for an EKG. In Part A, a heart rhythm recording shows the electrical pattern of a normal heartbeat. In Part B, a patient lies in a bed with EKG electrodes attached to his chest, upper arms, and legs, while a nurse oversees the painless procedure.

Body hair can prevent the electrical leads from making good electrical contact with the skin. Without good contact, a proper waveform may not be seen. Therefore, some patients are shaved or otherwise have body hair removed to allow good electrical contact of the leads. The leads are small wires connected to the conductive and adhesive patches that are placed on the patient.

Electrocardiography measures only the heart's electrical activity; it is a passive procedure with little to no risk.

Electrophysiologic Studies

Electrophysiologic studies tell us about the heart's nervous system. The heart contains a special nervous system to ensure that the heart contracts properly to move the blood through the heart, body, and lungs. With some diseases, the heart's nervous system is injured or otherwise imperfect, and the heart contracts abnormally. Such abnormalities include tachycardia (fast heartbeat), bradycardia (slow heartbeat, sometimes associated with fainting), and other arrhythmias (abnormal heartbeats).

Unlike electrocardiography (*see* ELECTROCARDIOGRAPHY), which measures the heart's electrical activity from the outside of the body, electrophysiologic studies measure the heart's electrical activity directly in the heart. To do this, a catheter is placed through a port in the femoral vein in the groin, up to the inferior vena cava (large vein just below the right side of the heart), and then into the right atrium and the right ventricle of the heart. Sometimes the catheter is inserted through the subclavian vein in the upper chest (*see* CARDIAC CATHETERIZATION). Electrical pickups or leads on the catheter are placed near the major nerve areas, the sinoatrial node at the top of the right atrium, the atrioventricular node at the bottom of the right atrium next to the atrial septum (wall), and the nerve bundle branches in the ventricular septum.

Depending on the electrical signals (usually output as graphs) found at these points, certain diseases can be diagnosed and treated. For example, some types of tachycardia can be treated by destroying (ablating) the nerve that is causing the heart to beat too fast. In some cases, pacemakers must be implanted to replace a heart's abnormal nervous system. Electrophysiologic studies are sometimes used to determine the placement of pacemaker leads in the heart. In other cases, drugs can be used to control heart rate.

As with any interventional procedure, various problems can occur, such as perforation of the heart wall, getting the catheter stuck in the heart, or valve injury. Most of these problems can be avoided by a careful and knowledgeable surgeon.

Heart Augmentation and Replacement

If the heart is significantly and irreparably damaged, it is sometimes replaced with a donor heart matched to the patient or, more rarely, a prosthetic or artificial heart. Until a replacement heart can be obtained, a transitional procedure is sometimes used to augment or assist the damaged heart. In some cases, the heart's workload is lessened by use of a left ventricular assist device attached to the ventricle. In other cases, a large (about the size of a hot dog when inflated) balloon catheter is placed in the aorta and paced to the heart's rhythm to act as an aortic pump. The patient is usually kept in the hospital's intensive care unit before and after the surgery until he or she is stable enough to have the surgery and leave the hospital.

Several types of total artificial hearts have been made. Only two are approved for use by the FDA. They are complex to implant and can cause complications. A total artificial heart is often a transition aid until a donor heart can be found. The patient's heart is surgically removed while he or she is connected to a heart–lung bypass machine. The donor heart is then implanted in the patient and connected to the various blood vessels and nerves. A pacemaker may be needed transitionally until the new heart nerves grow.

Risks: As with any major surgery, heart surgery has many risks. Some of the general risks include excessive bleeding, infection, tissue rejection, memory loss, damage to other organs, and death. The longer the surgery, the greater the risks are. The risks also increase for older patients, patients with previous surgeries, and patients with other diseases like high blood pressure, peripheral artery disease, diabetes, kidney disease, and lung disease. Clot formation, caused by the surgery or the heart–lung bypass machine, can present a risk of stroke or other tissue damage.

Imaging Tests (X-rays, Computed Tomography, Magnetic Resonance Imaging, Positron Emission Tomography, etc.)

To get a picture of the heart and how it is working can be difficult because of the location of the heart in the body. The heart is found in the central part of the thorax or rib cage between the lungs, above the diaphragm (which separates the lungs from the abdomen), in front of the spine, and behind the sternum (to which most ribs are attached). Several large structures connect to and are near the heart, such as the aorta, the pulmonary vein, the bronchus (windpipe), and esophagus. The heart is covered with a protective and lubricating sack called the pericardium.

Imaging tests include radiography (e.g., X-ray, angiography, fluoroscopy), computed tomography (CT), calcium scan, magnetic resonance imaging (MRI), positron emission tomography (PET), and echocardiography (ultrasonography). Most of these imaging devices are large, have moving or very noisy parts, require a computer to create the images, may require an injection of a radioisotope (which emits particles that can be imaged), and are generally safe. However, numerous or long exposures to some imaging techniques (e.g., X-ray, CT, PET) can cause patient radiation injuries.

Imaging risks: X-rays are known to cause cellular injury, and such radiation damage is cumulative. Long exposures during a cardiac catheterization have been known to cause burns. The amount of X-ray exposure in CT is high. Some physicians take the number of CT scans a patient has had under consideration of the need for future CT scans because of the radiation risk.

A contrast medium is sometimes used to better differentiate the various organs and provide greater detail than can be had using an imaging technique alone. The media vary depending on the imaging technique and are injected into a patient shortly before the imaging procedure. Some patients are allergic to the contrast medium.

The size and strength of MRI units are growing. Patients with any iron (ferrous metal, such as a pacemaker, tattoos, surgical implants, or iron from an injury) in their bodies may not be able to have an MRI because the metal may become displaced, move in the body, or heat up (due to the wiggler magnet) and cause internal burns. In some cases, patients with tattoos containing iron oxide have been burned in MRI machines. The bore of the magnet can be claustrophobic to some patients. The amount of noise the magnet makes can be temporarily deafening or disorienting, although patients are often offered earplugs or headphones that play music. While an MRI scan does cause slight heating of tissue (a kind of warming feeling), it is not known to cause any bodily harm.

With PET, the radioactive drug rapidly decays and does not remain in the body or do it significant harm. However, the number of times PET can be used on a patient is a consideration because radiation damage is cumulative. And if CT is used with PET, the additional radiation must be considered against the need for that type of imaging.

Computed Tomography

Computed tomography (CT) uses X-rays to create a three-dimensional image of the heart. The CT machine is shaped like a large donut (2.5 m [8.2 ft] diameter by 1 m [3.28 ft] thick torus) with the patient placed at the center hole. An X-ray tube and detector rotate about the patient very quickly and spiral along the patient's body. The moving X-ray emitter and detector create a loud whirring noise. A computer puts the many images taken of the body during this motion together to create the three-dimensional image of the patient's insides. Using computers, only the organs of interest can be shown, with very great detail (down to very small blood vessels), in modern CT units. The computerized images can be rotated, sliced, angled, and manipulated to enable the physician to see the areas of interest. CT scans will also show any calcium deposits as may be found in the coronary arteries, the heart valves, and the aorta (see, e.g., the illustration at http://www.nhlbi.nih.gov/health/health-topics/topics/cscan/).

Magnetic Resonance Imaging

Magnetic resonance imaging (MRI) uses a very large and strong magnet to produce an image of the body. As with CT, the patient is placed at the center hole of a large (2 m [6.56 ft] diameter by 2 m [6.56 ft] long) magnet. The strong magnet causes the atoms of the body to align with the magnet's magnetic field. A wiggler magnet, which is a second magnet built into the large magnet, causes the atoms to be momentarily misaligned with the large field. (This also strains the magnet and its frame, creating a very loud noise.) When these atoms return to the orientation of the large field, they give off a radiofrequency signal that is measured. Different tissues produce different signals and the source of the signals can be located, and so the patient's insides can be imaged. As with CT, a computer is used to put the various signals together into a three-dimensional image. The amount of detail can be very precise, even down to the blood vessels in an organ.

Positron Emission Tomography

In positron emission tomography (PET), emission of positrons during radioactive decay of a radioactive-isotope-tagged chemical (e.g., glucose) is used to image the heart. The short-lived radioactive drug is injected into the patient, and the drug is used by the heart. Depending on the activity of the portions of the heart, more or less radiation (positron emission) occurs. A radiation detector and a computer system are used to build the image of the heart from the varying amounts of positron radiation coming from the active heart. Healthy areas have high emissions because they are using the tagged chemical. Unhealthy areas have low emissions because they are not using the chemical. CT and MRI are sometimes used with PET to enhance the final image. If areas of the heart have been injured (e.g., by myocardial infarction, arteriosclerosis), PET can identify injured areas, which can then be targeted for treatment. The radioisotope quickly decays into a harmless element that is soon excreted by the body (*see also* RADIONUCLIDE IMAGING).

Radiography

Radiography is an imaging technique that uses an emission of X-ray radiation to image the interior of the body. Hard structures trap more radiation than do softer structures. In cardiology, a simple X-ray may be taken to determine if the heart is enlarged, displaced, or has other imageable problems. X-ray images or radiographs are usually still and two-dimensional. Other imaging techniques that use X-rays are fluoroscopy and computed tomography.

Radionuclide Imaging or Nuclear Heart Scan

Radionuclide imaging, also known as radionuclide ventriculography and nuclear heart scan, uses a radioactive isotope to image the heart. The heart, like other muscles, uses certain chemicals in the blood to provide energy for muscle contraction. These chemicals can be detected by adding a radioactive isotope (an atom that emits radiation) to these chemicals. These modified chemicals are used in the same way by the muscles as the unmodified chemicals (usually glucose). The muscles that are the most active use the most of these chemicals and are therefore the most radioactive. Thus the distribution of radioactivity in the muscles can be seen by special detectors that produce a three-dimensional image of how the heart is using the chemical energy. Sometimes CT scans or MRIs are done at the same time to get an even more precise picture of what parts of the heart are active and what parts are not. This information can then be used to determine the best treatment for any problems that are uncovered.

The radioactive isotope decays when it emits radiation and turns (transmutes) into a safe chemical that is excreted by the body. The radioactive isotope must be short lived (meaning it emits radiation for only a short time, such as a few minutes, hours, or days) to minimize the patient's exposure to the radioactivity, which can be dangerous in large or repeated exposures. Positron emission tomography is one type of radionuclide imaging.

X-ray Fluoroscopy

In viewing the beating heart, X-ray fluoroscopy is used in cardiac catheterization to present a moving image (a quick series of still, two-dimensional images). It shows a shadow of the heart that is better defined when a special radiopaque dye is injected into the area of interest. The amount of detail is not as good as can be had with other methods but is sufficient to identify the parts of the heart that are being examined. It enables the physician to see the catheter, its position in the heart or blood vessels, and how the dye moves in the heart and arteries.

Major Vessel Repair

Major vessel repair for serious congenital defects or aortic aneurysms involves removing or reconfiguring the damaged portion of the vena cava or aorta. The vessel may be replaced with harvested tissue from the patient, processed cadaver tissue, or biocompatible synthetic replacement vessel segments. This is usually open chest surgery that uses a heart–lung bypass machine.

Nerve Ablation

When the heart is not contracting properly nerve ablation can, in some cases, allow the heart to resume a normal rhythm. To replace the destroyed nerve, a pacemaker can be used to regulate the heartbeat. A pacemaker is implanted in the patient's upper chest wall and connected to the heart with electrical leads. The leads are routed either through a blood vessel or directly through tissue to the heart. The pacemaker periodically delivers a small electric shock to the heart to cause it to contract in a normal rhythm. A pacemaker can stop working when in or near magnetic fields, such as antitheft portals in stores. Patients with these implanted pacemakers should keep at least 2 meters (6.56 feet) away from electromagnetic-field-generating devices such as antitheft portals, transmitters, two way radios.

Pacemaker or Defibrillator Implantation

To correct certain arrhythmias, a pacemaker or a defibrillator can be implanted. A pacemaker emits low-energy electrical pulses to help regulate milder forms of arrhythmia; an implantable cardioverter defibrillator (ICD) in addition offers higher energy current to defibrillate (i.e., provide an electric shock to) the heart rhythm. For most arrhythmias, leads or wires are connected to the heart in the proper places to detect and correct the abnormal heartbeat by applying a properly timed small electrical pulse into the heart. For defibrillation, leads are connected to the heart to stop the arrhythmia and start a normal heartbeat with a large electrical pulse. The leads are connected to a small metal box that is placed in a pocket made in the chest or abdomen. To avoid the risks of a wire breaking or an infection occurring, a newer, less-invasive version, called subcutaneous implantable cardioverter defibrillator (S-ICD), that has its electrodes implanted near the surface of the chest was approved by the FDA in September 2012. No wires are directly connected to the heart; its drawback is that is cannot be used as a pacemaker to regulate slow heartbeat.

These devices run on batteries that must be replaced every few years, and they may be adversely affected by exposure to electromagnetic fields, such as antitheft portals in stores. Patients with these implanted devices should keep at least 2 meters (6.56 feet) away from electromagnetic-field-generating devices such as antitheft portals, transmitters, and two-way radios. An alternative to implanted defibrillators is a defibrillator vest that monitors the heart and delivers a shock should the heart go into fibrillation.

Renal Denervation

For those who have hypertension that cannot be lowered with medication, renal denervation is a new procedure in which radio-frequency waves are sent through a catheter into the kidney artery walls to overheat and scar them and strike the nerves within. This action prevents these nerves from releasing vessel-constricting enzymes that normally would increase blood pressure as a response to stress or excitement.

Stents

A stent is an intricately formed metal tube that is expanded by a balloon to hold a section of artery open. Stents are a few millimeters in diameter and several centimeters long to conform to the size and shape of the artery. Some stents are coated with drugs (i.e., drug-eluting stents) to prevent tissue growth that would reblock the artery. Small radioactive pellets can also be inserted near the problem section to retard tissue growth; this is known as brachytherapy. Recently, some doctors have backed away from implanting drug-eluting stents and stent implantation altogether and instead use more time-tested techniques (*see* ANGIOPLASTY for more information on the use of stents).

Stress Testing

In a stress test, the heart is made to beat faster so its effectiveness can be measured by electrocardiography (ECG or EKG) and sometimes PET. When a person exercises, the heart beats faster to pump more blood to the muscles. The more efficient the heart is, the slower it needs to pump in response to the exercise.

Most stress tests require the patient to walk or run on a treadmill while heart function is measured through leads attached to the EKG machine (*see* ELECTRO-CARDIOGRAPHY). With patients who cannot walk or run on a treadmill, a drug is administered to accelerate the heartbeat to simulate exercise. If PET is used, a radioactive isotope is administered before the test. Images are taken before the test and after the test to determine how much of the heart was active during the test (*see* IMAGING TESTS: POSITRON EMISSION TOMOGRAPHY).

Stress tests do stress the patient and have brought on heart attacks and cardiac arrests in some people, which is why stress tests are typically given in a hospital or outpatient care facility where emergency care can be quickly provided.

Therapeutic Hypothermia

A relatively new treatment for heart attack patients is therapeutic hypothermia. The patient is wrapped in cooling blankets to lower the body temperature to 92°F/33.3°C. This slows body functions, especially brain functions, which reduces tissue death, allowing more time to treat the heart attack.

Tilt Table Testing

A tilt table test mimics body motions that can induce a heart problem. As the body moves, the heart adjusts its function to the position of the body. Sometimes the adjustment is not sufficient and fainting may occur when moving from sitting to standing. In this case, not enough blood gets to the head during the transition, and the patient loses consciousness.

Tilt table testing identifies problems such as dysautonomia (failure of the autonomic nervous system to compensate for the change in body position) or syncope (fainting due to a drop in blood pressure or failure of the heart to beat faster). The patient is placed flat on the table and is connected to an EKG and a blood pressure monitor. The table is then quickly tilted upright (i.e., to mimic a standing position). The onset of dizziness, lightheadedness, fainting, a drop in blood pressure, or cardiac arrhythmia indicates a problem with the autonomic nervous system or the heart's nervous system.

The risks of this procedure are that patients may fall off of the table, they may lose consciousness, or their heart may stop. When the procedure is conducted, there are usually medical personnel nearby to be of immediate assistance.

Transmyocardial Revascularization

A relatively new process called transmyocardial revascularization uses a laser to bore holes through the heart wall into the blood-filled spaces. It is believed that these holes will develop into arteries to replace or supplement damaged cardiac arteries. However, this procedure does have some serious and life-threatening complications, and it may not significantly improve the patient's quality of life.

Valvuloplasty

Heart valves can be repaired by removing plaque or calcifications. Sometimes a balloon catheter is used to break up the calcification and make the valve more flexible so it can open more fully and close without leaking. If the valve is beyond repair, it can be replaced with a prosthetic valve, a cadaverous donor valve, or an animal valve. With some mechanical replacement valves, the patient may be able to hear a clicking sound as the valve opens and shuts.

Resources for Further Information on Diagnostic Tests, Treatments, and Therapies

Books

➤ American Medical Association, Martin S. Lipsky, Marla Mendelson, Stephen Havas, and Michael Miller. *American Medical Association Guide to Preventing and Treating Heart Disease: Essential Information You and Your Family Need to Know about Having a Healthy Heart.* Hoboken, NJ: John Wiley and Sons, 2008. Print.

From the experts associated with the American Medical Association, this comprehensive resource includes diagnosis and treatment of heart and cardiovascular disease.

➤ Cannon, Christopher P., and Elizabeth Vierck. *The New Heart Disease Handbook: Everything You Need to Know to Effectively Reverse and Manage Heart Disease.* Beverly, MA: Fair Winds Press, 2009. Print.

Cannon, a medical doctor who is also an associate professor of medicine at Harvard Medical School in the Cardiovascular Division at Brigham and Women's Hospital in Boston, and Vierck, who is a health writer, together wrote a user-friendly highly detailed handbook on the heart that focuses on treatment and maintaining a healthy heart.

➤ DeVane, Matthew S. *Heart Smart: A Cardiologist's 5-Step Plan for Detecting, Preventing, and Even Reversing Heart Disease.* Hoboken, NJ: Wiley, 2006. Print.

This cardiologist explains diagnostic tests in easy-to-understand detail. Interactive quizzes help the consumer identify risk factors and health issues.

➤ Everett, Allen D., Scott D. Lim, Jasper Burns, eds., and Paul Burns, illus. *Illustrated Field Guide to Congenital Heart Disease and Repair.* 3rd ed. Charlottesville, VA: Scientific Software Solutions, 2011. Print.

According to its introduction, this book "was created to provide a pocket-sized visual resource for pediatric cardiologists to assist their discussions with staff, students, patients and their families."

➤ Granato, Jerome. *Living with Coronary Heart Disease: A Guide for Patients and Families* (A Johns Hopkins Press Health Book). Baltimore, MD: Johns Hopkins University Press, 2008. Print.

Granato, MD, FACC, is the medical director of the coronary care unit at Allegheny General Hospital (Pittsburgh, PA) and a fellow of the American College of Cardiology (American Heart Association). Granato's goal is make the patient an "active participant" in deciding treatment by explaining diagnostic tests, medications, and various treatments. According to the introduction, "The book takes you on a journey, as seen through the eyes of a typical patient, addressing important questions as they might arise during the course of an illness."

> Griffith, H. Winter. *Complete Guide to Symptoms, Illness, and Surgery.* 5th ed. Revised and updated by Stephen Moore and Kenneth Yoder. New York, NY: Perigee, 2006. Print.
This is a general resource for diagnosing, understanding, and seeking treatment for health problems.

> Komaroff, Anthony L. ed. *Harvard Medical School Family Health Guide.* New York, NY: Simon and Schuster, 2004. Print.
This family health guide for the age of managed care, filled with accessible information, was compiled by the world's most esteemed doctors and researchers. This book includes more than 900 illustrations, original full-color slides showing the latest diagnostic imaging tests, and online updates keyed to the book.

> Labus, Diane. *Cardiovascular Care Made Incredibly Easy!* (Incredibly Easy! Series). Philadelphia, PA: Lippincott Williams and Wilkins, 2008. Print.
Although this book is written for nurses, the easy-to-understand-format might offer additional understanding in cardiovascular diagnostic tests and procedures and treatments. To test your comprehension, there is a Practice Makes Perfect test with answers provided.

> Margolis, Simeon. *The Johns Hopkins Consumer Guide to Medical Tests: What You Can Expect, How You Should Prepare, What Your Results Mean* [Illustrated]. New York, NY: Rebus, 2001. Print.
This consumer-oriented book, which includes medical tests for heart diseases, is divided into topics: laboratory testing, diagnostic imaging, screening for disease, home testing, and genetic testing and screening.

> McPhee, Stephen, Maxine Papadakis, and Michael W. Rabow. *Current Medical Diagnosis and Treatment 2012* (Lange Current Series). New York, NY: McGraw-Hill, 2012 (Annual). Print.
This book lists relevant journal articles after discussions of diseases, updated and published annually.

> Skidmore-Roth, Linda. *Mosby's 2013 Nursing Drug Reference.* 26th ed. Philadelphia, PA: Elsevier-Mosby, 2012. Print.
Although this book is written for nurses, the easy-to-understand format might offer additional understanding of drugs, their uses, side effects, and interactions. Remember that using this book is not a substitute for consulting with your physician.

> Stein, Richard. *Outliving Heart Disease: The 10 New Rules for Prevention and Treatment.* New York, NY: Newmarket Press, 2006. Print.
Stein, who is the director of preventive cardiology at Beth Israel Hospital, professor of clinical medicine at the Albert Einstein College of Medicine in New York,

and professor of medicine and director of the Urban Community Cardiology Program of New York University School of Medicine (NYC), writes an easy-to-understand and simple-to-follow guidebook that has 10 rules to follow for preventing and treating heart disease, with each rule described extensively in its own chapter.

Brochures, Booklets, and Other Short Print Publications

➤ American Heart Association (AHA)—http://www.heart.org/.
Choose from AHA's PDFs offering patient information on numerous tests and treatments for cardiovascular conditions and tips on disease management, recovery, and taking medication by clicking on any title to view and download.
  • "Answers by Heart Fact Sheets: Treatments and Tests." http://www.heart.org/ HEARTORG/Conditions/Answers-by-Heart-Fact-Sheets-Treatments-and -Tests_UCM_300573_Article.jsp; alternate path: http://www.heart.org/, search for "heart fact sheets treatments tests," and then click on the topic "Answers by Heart Fact Sheets: Treatments and Tests."
  • "Congenital Heart Defects Tools and Resources" (Patient Information Sheets and Brochures). http://www.heart.org/HEARTORG/Conditions/ CongenitalHeartDefects/CongenitalHeartDefectsToolsResources/Congenital -Heart-Defects-Tools-and-Resources_UCM_002031_Article.jsp; alternate path: http://www.heart.org/, search for "congenital heart defects tools resources"; or click on "Congenital Defects in Children and Adults," and then click on "Tools and Resources."

➤ British Heart Foundation (BHF)—*Heart Matters* (Magazine). http://www.bhf.org .uk/heart-health/how-we-help/information/heart-matters.aspx?sc_id=FP-00249; alternate path: http://www.bhf.org.uk/, search for "heart matters" and then click on the title "British Heart Foundation—Heart Matters."
The BHF offers a free magazine on women and heart disease. According to the website, "Many women aren't aware that they are three times as likely to die from heart and circulatory disease than from breast cancer." Free registration is required.

➤ *New York Times*—"Congenital Heart Disease." http://health.nytimes.com/health/ guides/disease/congenital-heart-disease/overview.html; alternate path: http:// health.nytimes.com/, click on the heading "Health Guide," then click on the letter "C," scroll down the topic list, and click on the title "Congenital Heart Disease."
Read this article from the *New York Times* for clear and comprehensive information on several congenital heart diseases.

Websites on Diagnosis and Treatment of Heart Diseases

For websites with a main focus on medications, *see the section* WEBSITES ON GENERAL DRUG INFORMATION FOR TREATMENT AND PREVENTION OF HEART DISEASES.

For websites with a main focus on congenital heart disease, *see the section* WEBSITES DEDICATED TO DIAGNOSIS AND TREATMENT OF CONGENITAL HEART DISEASE. (*See also* CHAPTER 4.) For websites on top-ranked doctors and hospitals in the United States, *see the section* TOP-RANKED U.S. HOSPITALS AND DOCTORS FOR CARDIOLOGY AND HEART SURGERY FROM *U.S. NEWS AND WORLD REPORT.*

> American Heart Association—"AHA/ASA Newsroom." http://www.newsroom .heart.org/.
> This AHA (American Heart Association)/ASA (American Stroke Association) Newsroom website offers the latest heart and cardiovascular disease news.

Guidelines on Diagnosis and Treatment of Heart Diseases

The **National Guideline Clearinghouse** (NGC), created by the Agency for Healthcare Research and Quality of the U.S. Department of Health and Human Services, is a comprehensive database of evidence-based clinical practice guidelines. NGC's mission is to provide physicians and other health professionals, health care providers, health plans, integrated delivery systems, purchasers, and others an accessible mechanism for obtaining objective, detailed information on clinical practice guidelines and to further their dissemination, implementation, and use. Although these guidelines are written for health care professionals, they might offer patients valuable information to discuss with their physicians.

The NGC website (http://www.guideline.gov/ or http://www.ngc.gov/) offers free access to numerous summaries of guidelines published by national heart and cardiovascular disease organizations, such as the American Heart Association, American College of Cardiology, American Stroke Association, and Heart Failure Society of America. Many of the summary webpages at NGC contain links to the complete guidelines on the publishing organizations' websites, where many of those guidelines are free to view and download. Some organizations require online registration; some charge a fee.

On the homepage, under the "Find" heading, click on "Organizations," which will open a webpage of linkable organization names; scroll down to select the organization of choice, which will produce a results list; if the number of retrieved references is too large, under "Filter results by" select one year at a time (e.g., 2012) to retrieve a shorter list, and then click on any appropriate title. Once on the article page, under the tab "Related Content" is a link to the full-text article, if available. (If you click on the full-text article link, the next screen will read "You are leaving the National Guideline Clearinghouse." Click on the "Continue" button. If the full-text article does not appear, it may help to click the Refresh icon at the top of your screen.)

This website also provides access to other heart and cardiovascular disease organizations, for example, the European Society of Cardiology, Heart and Stroke Foundation of Canada, and Australia's National Stroke Foundation. Scroll through the "Organizations" list to see the variety of organizations represented.

Newsroom topics are searchable. This website contains heart disease information describing research announcements, published studies, and guidelines and is aided by multimedia (audio, images, podcasts, and video and animation).

➢ Angioplasty.Org—"Fractional Flow Reserve (FFR)." http://www.ptca.org/ivus/FFR .html; alternate path: http://www.ptca.org/, search for "fractional flow reserve," and then click on the title "Fractional Flow Reserve (FFR)—Angioplasty.org." The Angioplasty.Org website offers an explanation of what FFR is, how it affects future treatments, and how FFR works.

➢ Brigham and Women's Hospital (Boston, MA)—"Cardiac Tests and Procedures." http://healthlibrary.brighamandwomens.org/HealthCenters/Heart/Cardiac; alternate path: http://www.brighamandwomens.org/, scroll under the heading "Health Information" to click on the title "Health Information Center," then click on "Heart Information Center," and then click on the category "Cardiac Tests and Procedures." Brigham and Women's Hospital's Heart Information Center's website offers numerous links to cardiac tests and procedures.

➢ CardioSmart.org. https://www.cardiosmart.org/. CardioSmart, produced by the American College of Cardiology (ACC) Foundation, provides information on heart disease topics. It is also available in Spanish. Under the heading "Browse by Subject" click on different categories, including "Tests," "Treatments," and "Medications." According to ACC, "CardioSmart is the patient education and empowerment initiative brought to you by the American College of Cardiology. Our mission is to help individuals prevent, treat and manage cardiovascular disease." Sign up for CardioSmart news updates by e-mail. A video section is available.

  • "Clinical Trial Finder." https://www.cardiosmart.org/Heart-Conditions/ Heart-Attack/The-Research/Clinical-Trial-Finder; alternate path: https:// www.cardiosmart.org/, search for and then click on the title "Clinical Trial Finder." CardioSmart provides an easy-to-use website on clinical trials, including definitions, the phases of a clinical trial, finding out about clinical trials, what to expect after treatment, why clinical trials are important, how clinical trials work, what happens when it is finished, risks, and safety.

➢ Cleveland Clinic. http://myclevelandclinic.org/. The following three Cleveland Clinic webpages explain various blood tests that help evaluate the risk and/or damage due to cardiovascular disease and aids doctors in providing heart disease management. Patient blood test preparation and test results are explained. Other blood lab tests are described. From the homepage, you can find the following and related resources by searching for the name of the blood test.

- "Blood Tests to Determine Risk of Coronary Artery Disease." http://my .clevelandclinic.org/heart/services/tests/labtests/testscad.aspx.
- "B-type Natriuretic Peptide (BNP) Blood Test." http://my.clevelandclinic .org/heart/services/tests/labtests/bnp.aspx.
- "Lipid Blood Tests." http://my.clevelandclinic.org/heart/services/tests/ labtests/lipid.aspx.

➢ Cleveland Clinic, Heart and Vascular Institute (Cleveland, OH)—"Treatments and Procedures." http://my.clevelandclinic.org/heart/disorders/services.aspx; alternate path: http://my.clevelandclinic.org/, search for "heart vascular insti- tute," click on "Miller Family Heart and Vascular Institute," and then scroll down to the link "Treatments and Procedures."
The Cleveland Clinic provides a comprehensive patient-friendly list of links to numerous heart and cardiovascular treatments and procedures. Included is help to find a doctor who manages heart diseases. The Cleveland Clinic also offers a link to "Chat Online with a Heart and Vascular Nurse" where you can speak by phone or submit a question online. Also on the "Heart and Vascular" main page (http://my.clevelandclinic.org/heart) is a section titled "Free Online Chats" that lists several current topics with their designated dates; click to reg- ister. To participate in a clinical trial at the Cleveland Clinic Heart Center, go to http://my.clevelandclinic.org/heart/research/clinicalresearch.aspx; or click on the category "Research and Innovations," and under the category "For Patients" click on the title "Clinical Research," and then click on "Search for a Clinical Trial."

➢ EverydayHealth.com. http://www.everydayhealth.com/.
EverydayHealth offers current information on diagnosing and treating heart dis- ease. According to EverydayHealth, the website has "helpful questions and answers from our board-certified experts at top-tier institutions such as Harvard Medical School, Memorial Sloan-Kettering Cancer Center, Mount Sinai Medical Center, and more."
- "Diagnosing Heart Disease." http://www.everydayhealth.com/heart-health/ diagnosis.aspx.
- "Heart Disease Tests." http://www.everydayhealth.com/heart-health/heart -disease-tests.aspx.
- "Heart Disease Treatment." http://www.everydayhealth.com/heart-health/ treatment.aspx.
Alternate path: http://www.everydayhealth.com/, under the heading "Health A–Z," click on the topic "Heart Health," then scroll down to the heading "Heart Health Center," and then scroll down to click on the topic of choice.

➢ Johns Hopkins Hospital, Heart and Vascular Institute (Baltimore, MD)—"Treatments/ Procedures." http://www.hopkinsmedicine.org/heart_vascular_institute/conditions

_treatments/treatments/; alternate path: http://www.hopkinsmedicine.org/, search for "treatments procedures endovascular therapy," and then scroll down to click on the resource title.

Johns Hopkins Heart and Vascular Institute provides patient-friendly, comprehensive, current information on heart and cardiovascular treatments and procedures. Included are links for detailed information on diagnostic tests. Also click on the heading "Clinical Trials" for links to current trials for various heart and cardiovascular conditions.

➤ Massachusetts General Hospital (MGH), Heart Center (Boston, MA)—"Treatments and Services." http://www.massgeneral.org/heartcenter/services/; alternate path: http://www.massgeneral.org/, search for "heart center services," click on the title "Massachusetts General Hospital Heart Center Home," and then click on the heading "Treatments and Services"; or click on "Centers and Services," click "View All Departments and Services," then click "Heart Center," and then click on the heading "Treatments and Services."

MGH offers at its Heart Center website links to comprehensive information for numerous treatment programs and tests and procedures. Some of the treatment programs are on atrial fibrillation, cardiac arrhythmia, cardiovascular disease prevention, heart failure and cardiac transplant, and lipid management. Some of the tests and procedures described include cardiac catheterization, cardiac imaging, cardiac surgery, and cardiac resynchronization therapy. Several topics include video demonstrations and patient guides. Also, click on the heading "Research and Clinical Trials" and then on the tab "Clinical Trials and Studies" for links to current trials for various heart and cardiovascular conditions.

➤ Mayo Clinic (Rochester, MN). http://www.mayoclinic.com/.

To participate in a clinical trial, if available in your cardiology condition, at the Mayo Clinic Heart, Lung, and Blood Research Center, go to http://clinicaltrials.mayo.edu/dspSubthemes.cfm?theme_id=6; alternate path: http://www.mayo.edu/, under the heading "Research" click on the category "Find Clinical Trials," scroll down and click on "Browse Studies," then click on "See All Categories," and finally click on the title "Heart, Lung, and Blood Clinical Trials." For patient services in the various cardiology programs, go to http://www.mayoclinic.org/cardiac-surgery/ for "Cardiac Surgery" or http://www.mayoclinic.org/cardiovascular-disease/ for "Cardiovascular Diseases" or http://www.mayoclinic.org/vascular-and-endovascular-surgery/ for "Vascular and Endovascular Surgery"; alternate path: http://www.mayoclinic.org/, for each topic, search for the topic by name, and then click on the associated title. On the webpages for "Cardiac Surgery" and "Cardiovascular Diseases," in the "Overview" section scroll down, select a state, and then click on the tab "Doctors" to view links to each medical expert (with profiles, e.g., specialty, medical board certification, education). On the "Vascular and Endovascular Surgery" webpage, click on the "Doctors" tab.

- "Complementary and Alternative Medicine," http://www.mayoclinic.com/health/alternative-medicine/PN00001; "Complementary and Alternative Medicine: Evaluate Treatment Claims," http://www.mayoclinic.com/health/alternative-medicine/SA00078; alternate path: http://www.mayoclinic.com/, search for "complementary and alternative medicine," and then click on each resource title. The Mayo Clinic offers links to expanded information on numerous alternative and complementary treatments for a variety of health conditions; some might help reduce stress and be relevant for heart disease, for example, to lower blood pressure.

- "Heart Disease: Tests and Diagnoses." http://www.mayoclinic.com/health/heart-disease/DS01120/DSECTION=tests-and-diagnosis; alternate path: http://www.mayoclinic.com/, search for "heart disease tests diagnosis" and then click on the title "Heart Disease—Tests and Diagnosis—MayoClinic.com." This section of the Mayo Clinic's website covers blood tests, including cholesterol and triglyceride levels, blood cell counts, and other blood tests that might show damage to the heart; chest X-rays; electrocardiogram (ECG); Holter monitoring; echocardiogram; cardiac catheterization; heart biopsy; cardiac computerized tomography (CT) scans; and cardiac magnetic resonance imaging (MRI). If you scroll down, you will find links under the "See Also" heading that offer more detailed information, such as on blood tests for heart disease, C-reactive protein test, chest X-rays, cholesterol test, cardiac catheterization, acute coronary syndrome, and Kawasaki disease. Note that for each of these topics there is a tab for "Basic" information and one for more "In-Depth" descriptions.

- "Preparing for Your Appointment." http://www.mayoclinic.com/health/heart-disease/DS01120/DSECTION=preparing-for-your-appointment; alternate path: http://www.mayoclinic.com/, search for "heart disease," click on the title "Heart Disease—MayoClinic.com," and then scroll down to the section titled "Preparing for Your Appointment." This section of the Mayo Clinic's website covers what to do to prepare, what to expect from your doctor, and what you can do in the meantime.

- "Treatments and Drugs." http://www.mayoclinic.com/health/heart-disease/DS01120/DSECTION=treatments-and-drugs; alternate path: http://www.mayoclinic.com/, search for "heart disease treatments drugs" and then click on the title "Heart Disease—Treatments and Drugs—MayoClinic.com." This section of the Mayo Clinic's website covers cardiovascular disease treatments (i.e., lifestyle changes, medications, medical procedures, surgery), heart arrhythmia treatments (i.e., vagal maneuvers, medications, medical procedures, pacemakers, implantable cardioverter-defibrillators [ICDs], surgery), heart defect treatments (i.e., medications, special procedures using catheters, open-heart surgery, heart transplant), treatments for cardiomyopathy (i.e., medications, medical devices, heart transplant), heart infection treatment (i.e., antibiotics, medications to regulate your heartbeat), valvular heart disease treatments (i.e., medications, balloon valvuloplasty, valve repair, valve replacement). If you scroll down, you will find links under "See Also" that offer more detailed information, including information on the polypill, daily aspirin therapy, cardioversion, gene therapy, heart attack, coronary artery disease, angina treatment, small vessel disease, acute coronary syndrome, and Kawasaki disease.

➢ *The Merck Manual Home Health Handbook for Patients and Caregivers.* http://www.merckmanuals.com/home/.
This website, based on the well-known medical textbook *The Merck Manual Home Health Handbook for Patients and Caregivers*, provides extremely detailed information. A hardcover copy of *The Merck Manual of Medical Information: Home Edition* (Spanish Version) can be purchased. It is also currently available for purchase as a downloadable app for smartphones.

- "Diagnosis of Heart and Blood Vessel Disorders." http://www.merckmanuals .com/home/heart_and_blood_vessel_disorders.html. This section on diagnosis of heart and blood vessel disorders is divided into several linked topics, including "Medical History and Physical Examination" and "Other Tests for Heart and Blood Vessel Disorders." Information includes how to read an ECG strip, along with illustrations. It covers electrocardiography, exercise stress testing, continuous ambulatory electrocardiography, continuous ambulatory blood pressure monitoring, electrophysiologic testing, tilt table testing, radiologic procedures, computed tomography, fluoroscopy, echocardiography and other ultrasound procedures, magnetic resonance imaging (MRI), radionuclide imaging, positron emission tomography (PET), cardiac catheterization (including angiography, valvuloplasty, and angioplasty) and coronary angiography (including cineangiography, valvuloplasty, and angioplasty), pulmonary artery catheterization, central venous catheterization, and angiography of peripheral blood vessels (including aortography and digital subtraction angiography).

- "Symptoms of Heart and Blood Vessel Disorders." http://www.merckmanuals .com/home/sec03/ch018/ch018a.html. This section includes such linked topics as an overview of heart and blood vessel symptoms, chest pain, palpitations, limitations of physical activity, light-headedness and fainting, swelling, and pain in the limbs.

Alternate path: http://www.merckmanuals.com/home/, under "Sections," click on "All" next to the navigational arrows to view a complete list, scroll down to click on the section "Heart and Blood Vessel Disorders," and then scroll down to click on the section title corresponding to the resource title.

➢ National Center for Complementary and Alternative Medicine (NCCAM)— "Cardiovascular Disease." http://nccam.nih.gov/health/heart-disease; alternate path: http://nccam.nih.gov/, search for "cardiovascular diseases" and then click on the title "Cardiovascular Disease | NCCAM."
NCCAM is a division of the National Institutes of Health, part of the U.S. Department of Health and Human Services. This website offers information on complementary and alternative medicine for cardiovascular disease with separate links for the consumer and the health professional. Included are general information on treatments (e.g., flaxseed, garlic, cinnamon, omega-3 fatty acids, yoga, meditation), research articles on treatments, ongoing medical studies, and safety information. Also included for the health professional are clinical practice guidelines and scientific literature. Click on the heading "Home" at the top of the screen and then click on "Subscribe to Our e-Newsletters" to start receiving "e-newsletters to keep up with complementary health practices."

➢ National Heart, Lung, and Blood Institute (NHLBI). http://www.nhlbi.nih.gov/.
NHLBI is a division of the National Institutes of Health from the U.S. Department of Health and Human Services. Some topics are also available in Spanish, indicated by a separate link titled "en Espanol."

- "A–Z Index." http://www.nhlbi.nih.gov/health/health-topics/by-alpha/; alternate path: http://www.nhlbi.nih.gov/, search for "A Z index," and then click on the title "Health Topics AZ Index—NHLBI, NIH." This alphabetical index has links to easy-to-understand information alphabetized by topic. Each section covers what the condition is, what to expect before, what to expect during, what to expect after, what the risks are, key points, and links to additional information.

- "Tests and Procedures." http://www.nhlbi.nih.gov/health/health-topics/by-category/, scroll down to the heading "Tests and Procedures"; alternate path: http://www.nhlbi.nih.gov/, search for "test by category," click on the title "Health Topics Index by Category—NHLBI, NIH," and then scroll down to click on the heading "Tests and Procedures." This section of the NHLBI website covers angiogram (coronary angiography), angioplasty (balloon angioplasty, coronary angioplasty), cardiac catheterization, cardiac CT scan, cardiac MRI, carotid ultrasound (carotid Doppler ultrasound), catheter ablation, chest CT scan, chest MRI, coronary angiography (angiogram), coronary calcium scan, echocardiography, electrocardiogram

(ECG), Holter monitor and event monitors, nuclear heart scan, stress testing, and transesophageal echocardiography.

➤ National Institute of Child Health and Development (NICHD). http://www.nichd.nih.gov/health.
The NICHD, a division of National Institutes of Health (NIH) from the U.S. Department of Health and Human Services, conducts research on the health of children and their families. The website presents information based on that research. It covers a wide range of topics. There are links to consumer-level information on more than 100 health topics, as well as valuable information about participation in clinical research and NICHD public health campaigns.

➤ New York–Presbyterian (NYP) University Hospital of Columbia and Cornell (New York, NY). http://nyp.org/.
Under the heading "Find a Physician" are links to physicians and specialists with profiles (e.g., specialty, medical board certification, education). Under "By Specialty, Disease, or Expertise," click on "Find a Doctor" and scroll down to select a condition. Also on the homepage, under the heading "Hospital News," are links to detailed articles explaining recent studies. To possibly participate in a clinical trial at NYP University Hospital Cardiology Center, if one is available, go to http://nyp.org/, click at the top of the screen on the heading "Research and Clinical Trials," click on the category "Clinical Trials at New York–Presbyterian/Weill Cornell Medical Center," and then scroll down and click on "Heart and Blood Disease."

- "Cardiology: Diagnostic Techniques." http://nyp.org/services/cardiology/diagnostic-techniques.html; alternate path: http://nyp.org/, search for "cardiology diagnostic techniques," and then click on the title "Diagnostic Techniques—New York Presbyterian Hospital." The NYP University Hospital of Columbia and Cornell website provides patient-friendly information on advanced cardiac diagnostic tests, including cardiac catheterization, electrocardiographic tests, electrophysiological studies, and tilt table testing.

- Interactive Media Library—"Podcasts: Tests and Procedures (Cardiovascular)." http://nyp.org/media/index.html; alternate path: http://nyp.org/, click on the "Explore the Interactive Media Library" icon, then click on the subject heading "Audio Podcasts: Tests and Procedures," and then click on or download each podcast topic, including cardiac catheterization, coronary artery bypass graft surgery (CABG), echocardiogram, heart valve repair or replacement surgery, and implantable cardioverter defibrillator (ICD) Insertion. There are at least 26 topics.

➤ Texas Heart Institute (Houston, TX). http://www.texasheartinstitute.org/.
Texas Heart Institute's Heart Information Center provides a wealth of information on selected cardiovascular topics. To participate in a clinical trial, if available in your cardiology condition, at the Texas Heart Institute Research Laboratory,

go to http://www.texasheartinstitute.org/Research/hfresearch.cfm (or return to the Texas Heart Institute homepage, click on the heading "Research," then click on the title "Heart Failure Research Laboratory"). Scroll down to the section "Research Projects," and click on the title "FDA-Approved Clinical Trials." Under the heading "About Us," click on "Professional Staff Directory" to view a list of physicians and specialists (with profiles, e.g., specialty, medical board certification, education).

- "Diagnostic Tests and Procedures." http://www.texasheartinstitute.org/HIC/Topics/Diag/index.cfm. This section provides numerous titles on diagnostic tests and procedures for the heart and cardiovascular system, including angiography, blood tests, cardiac catheterization, computed tomography (CT scan), electron beam computed tomography (EBCT), Ultrafast CT, multidetector computed tomography (MDCT), echocardiography, intravascular ultrasound (IVUS)/intravascular echocardiography, stress echocardiography, transesophageal echocardiography (TEE), electrocardiogram (ECG or EKG), electrophysiology studies (EPS), exercise stress test, gated blood pool scan (MUGA), Holter monitoring, magnetic resonance angiography (MRA), cardiac magnetic resonance imaging (cardiac MRI), nuclear (thallium) stress test, and positron emission tomography (PET). An easy-to-print format is available. One section allows users to "Ask a Texas Heart Institute Doctor" questions. Click on the current question to explore the questions and answers already published there.

- "Medical and Surgical Procedures." http://www.texasheartinstitute.org/HIC/Topics/index.cfm. This section provides numerous titles on medical and surgical procedures for the heart and cardiovascular system, including heart surgery overview, aneurysm repair, balloon angioplasty and stents, carotid artery angioplasty and stents, carotid endarterectomy, coronary bypass surgery, heart transplant, implantable cardioverter defibrillator (ICD), limited-access heart surgery, Maze surgery, pacemakers, radial artery access, transmyocardial laser revascularization, and ventricular assist devices.

Alternate path: http://www.texasheartinstitute.org/, search for the resource title; or click on the heading "Heart Information Center," click on "Heart-Health Topics," and then scroll down to click on the corresponding title.

➢ UCLA Ronald Reagan Medical Center (Los Angeles, CA)—"Tests and Treatments for Heart Disease." http://www.uclahealth.org/body.cfm?id=592, scroll down to the heading "Tests and Treatments"; alternate path: http://www.uclahealth.org/, under the heading "For Patients and Visitors," scroll down and mouse over the category "Health Resources" to click on "Heart Health Center," and then scroll down to click on the heading "Tests and Treatments."

The UCLA Ronald Reagan Medical Center's Heart Health Center provides consumer-friendly, detailed information on numerous tests and treatments for heart disease. To view each topic, scroll down to the heading "Tests and Treatments," then click on the word "More" for each category "Tests," "Surgeries," and "Alternative Medicine." The UCLA Heart Health Center (http://www.uclahealth .org/body.cfm?id=592) provides animations related to various conditions. Scroll to the bottom of the page and select "More" under "Animations." Also on the Heart Health Center website, under the heading "Health Assessment," you can sign up for "personalized messages to improve your [heart] health and lifestyle" by clicking on one of these categories: "Diet and Nutrition," "Fitness," "Heart Attack," or "Stress and Anxiety." For patient services in various cardiology programs, return to the UCLA Health System homepage (http://www.uclahealth.org/), scroll down under the heading "Medical Departments," then scroll down and click on "Medicine," and then scroll down and click on "Cardiology." Included is a list of programs and links to physicians and specialists (with profiles, e.g., specialty, medical board certification, education). To possibly participate in a clinical trial at UCLA, if available, visit http://clinicaltrials.ucla.edu/ (or on the homepage type "clinical trials" in the Search box and then click on "Clinical Trials").

➤ WebMD—"New Procedure May Aid Stubborn High Blood Pressure." http://www .webmd.com/hypertension-high-blood-pressure/news/20121213/new-procedure -high-blood-pressure; alternate path: http://www.webmd.com/, search for "renal denervation," and then click on the title "New Procedure May Aid Stubborn High Blood Pressure."

The WebMD website offers a patient-friendly explanation of renal denervation as an alternative to medication-resistant high blood pressure. According to WebMD, "WebMD News is an independent media service designed to provide news, information, and educational material to consumers and physicians. News content created by WebMD is free from influence by sponsors, partners, or other sources."

Websites on General Drug Information for Treatment and Prevention of Heart Diseases

➤ DailyMed—Drug information. http://dailymed.nlm.nih.gov/dailymed, type in the name of the heart medication in the Search box, and click "Go."

According to DailyMed, it "provides high quality information about marketed drugs," describing FDA labels (package inserts). It offers consumers detailed, current drug information including descriptions, indications and usage, contraindications, warnings, precautions, adverse reactions, dosage and administration, patient counseling information, and labeling. According to the website, "The National Library of Medicine (NLM) provides this as a public service and does not accept advertisements."

➤ Food and Drug Administration (FDA). http://www.fda.gov/ForConsumers/; alternate path: http://www.fda.gov/, scroll down to click on the section titled "Consumers."

The FDA, a division of the U.S. Department of Health and Human Services, is responsible for protecting the public health by assuring the safety, efficacy, and security of pharmaceuticals, medical devices, and food. The consumer section offers information including updates, how to protect yourself, information for various age groups (e.g., seniors, women, children, caregivers), recalls and alerts, and up-to-the-minute health articles. Included on the professional website of the FDA are more drug details, science and research, regulatory information, and public health issues.

➤ National Library of Medicine (NLM) Drug Information Portal. http://druginfo .nlm.nih.gov/drugportal/drugportal.jsp.

The NLM Drug Information Portal, a division of the National Institutes of Health (NIH) from the U.S. Department of Health and Human Services, offers a quick access database to reliable information on prescription and nonprescription drugs, including vitamins and supplements. Users may search by category or specific drug (generic or brand name). Sources for drug information are NLM databases, the Food and Drugs Administration (FDA), the Drug Enforcement Agency (DEA), the Centers for Disease Control and Prevention (CDC), the National Guideline Clearinghouse (NGC), and the U.S. government search engine (http://www.USA.gov/).

➤ Needy Meds. http://www.needymeds.org/.

For those who cannot afford their heart medications, NeedyMeds is a "501(c)(3) nonprofit information resource devoted to helping people in need find assistance programs to help them afford their medications and costs related to health care." It offers coupons for medicine as well as other patient assistance programs and information about government-sponsored programs.

➤ PDRHealth (*Physicians' Desk Reference*). http://www.pdrhealth.com/, type in the name of "your prescription drug, nonprescription drug, herbal medicine, or supplement," in the *Physicians' Desk Reference* Search box.

At this consumer's website, you can also search for diseases and conditions, surgery, and clinical trials. Included near the top of the screen are links to popular articles and information on how to prepare for surgery.

➤ RxList: The Internet Drug Index. http://www.rxlist.com/.

RxList, owned and operated by WebMD and part of the WebMD network, according to its website, "is an online medical resource dedicated to offering detailed and current pharmaceutical information on brand and generic drugs," which includes such topics as prescription drugs, nonprescription drugs, herbs, and supplements. You can also click on menu headings for a useful pill identifier tool, slideshows about diseases, image collections, diseases and conditions, and a medical dictionary.

Websites Dedicated to Diagnosis and Treatment of Congenital Heart Disease

➤ American Heart Association (AHA). http://www.heart.org/.
From the homepage, you can find the following resources by searching for the topic by title.

- "Care and Treatment for Congenital Heart Defects." http://www.heart .org/HEARTORG/Conditions/CongenitalHeartDefects/CareTreatmentfor CongenitalHeartDefects/Care-and-Treatment-for-Congenital-Heart-Defects _UCM_002030_Article.jsp. AHA offers information describing various treatments and care options (for those who need to be monitored but may not need treatment).

- "Symptoms and Diagnosis of Congenital Heart Defects." http://www.heart .org/HEARTORG/Conditions/CongenitalHeartDefects/SymptomsDiagnosis ofCongenitalHeartDefects/Symptoms-Diagnosis-of-Congenital-Heart-Defects _UCM_002029_Article.jsp. This AHA guide provides an overview linked

Guidelines on Diagnosis and Treatment of Congenital Heart Disease

The **National Guideline Clearinghouse** (NGC) offers access to a variety of guidelines on congenital heart disease (http://www.ngc.gov/). Here you can view and download for free numerous summaries of guidelines on congenital heart disease published by national heart and cardiovascular disease organizations such as the American Heart Association (AHA), the American College of Cardiology (ACC), the American Stroke Association (ASA), and the Heart Failure Society of America (HFSA). Many of the summary website pages at NGC contain links to the complete guidelines on the publishing organizations' websites, where many of those guidelines are also free to view and download. Some organizations require online registration and/or charge a fee. These guidelines are written primarily for health care professionals; however, consumers might also find the information valuable.

To find guidelines specific to congenital heart disease, type "congenital heart disease" in the Search box at the top of the screen. If the number of retrieved references is too large, under "Filter Results By" select one year at a time, such as "2012." Click on any appropriate titles. Under the tab "Related Content" is a link to the full-text article, if available. (If you click on the full-text article link, the next screen will read "You are leaving the National Guideline Clearinghouse." Click on the "Continue" button. If the full-text article does not appear, it may help to click the Refresh icon at the top of your screen.)

to more detailed information on the common types of tests associated with heart defects.

➤ British Heart Foundation (BHF)—"Heart Treatments." http://www.bhf.org.uk/heart-health/treatment.aspx; alternate path: http://www.bhf.org.uk/, search for "heart treatments," and then click on the title "British Heart Foundation—Treatment."
The BHF webpage on treatment of heart disease provides information on developing new treatments, living with a heart condition, ablation, cardioversion, coronary angioplasty and stents, coronary bypass surgery, heart transplant, implantable cardioverter defibrillator, heart medications, pacemakers, statins, valve heart surgery, and types of health care professionals. There is also a link to a podcast; click on "Podcast—Heart Drugs and You."

➤ Children's Hospital of Wisconsin—"Congenital Heart Disease and Defects." http://www.chw.org/display/PPF/DocID/34305/Nav/1/router.asp; alternate path: http://www.chw.org/, search for and then click on the title "Congenital Heart Disease Defects."
This webpage covers such topics as prenatal diagnosis and neonatal treatment, septal defects, obstructive cardiac anomalies, and cyanotic defects. Return to the homepage and click on the heading "Programs and Clinics" to access these topics: "Cardiology/Cardiovascular Surgery" and "Heart." On each of those pages, click on the section "Treatments" for links to treatments and diagnostic tests. Also under "Programs and Clinics" are other cardiovascular topics including fetal cardiac, heart transplant, and Marfan syndrome. On the homepage, you can search for and then click on the topic "Fetal Concerns Center of Wisconsin" to learn about this cooperative joint effort between the Children's Hospital of Wisconsin and Froedtert and the Medical College of Wisconsin.

➤ Insidermedicine. "If I Had—A Newborn with a Heart Murmur" (Video). http://www.insidermedicine.com/archives/VIDEO_If_I_Had_A_Newborn_With_A_Heart_Murmur_Dr_Dianne_Atkins_MD_University_of_Iowa_Childrens_Hospital_3323.aspx; alternate path: http://www.insidermedicine.com/, search for "congenital heart disease" in the Search News box and then scroll down to click on the video title.
This video includes an interview with a cardiologist, who speaks in patient-friendly language about newborn babies with heart murmurs, the difference between a functional and a pathological murmur, causes, management, recommendations, and prevention. The physician-led Insidermedicine Project (http://www.insidermedicine.com/) "allows patients, doctors and medical students to keep up on the latest medical information by watching" videos created each weekday by their team of medical experts, allowing anyone to receive daily evidence-based health and medical updates. Previously created videos are available and free to view or download. Under the heading "Programs," click the

category "By Disease or Symptom," scroll through the list of conditions, and click on a heart or cardiovascular topic. Also under the heading "Programs," click on "Universities and Hospitals" for links to "University and Hospital News Segments."

➢ Johns Hopkins Hospital (Baltimore, MD)—"Pediatric Cardiology" (Clinical Services). http://www.hopkinsmedicine.org/heart_vascular_institute/clinical_services/specialty_areas/pediatric_cardiology.html and http://www.hopkinschildrens.org/cardiology; alternate path: http://www.hopkinsmedicine.org/, search for "pediatric cardiology," click on the title "Pediatric Cardiology.""

The Helen B. Taussig Congenital Heart Center provides a list of services available for pediatric cardiology, including a list of pediatric procedures performed. One available section is titled "Meet the Kids at the Johns Hopkins Children's Center." It also lists links to physicians and specialists (with profiles, e.g., specialty, medical board certification, education) who treat pediatric cardiology, including their published research. Click on the heading "Clinical Trials" for links to current trials in various heart and cardiovascular conditions.

➢ Mayo Clinic (Rochester, MN). http://www.mayoclinic.com/.
For information on clinical trials and patient services, see the Mayo Clinic entry on pp. 297–298.

- "Congenital Heart Disease in Children: Tests and Diagnosis." http://www.mayoclinic.com/health/congenital-heart-defects/DS01117/DSECTION=tests-and-diagnosis; alternate path: http://www.mayoclinic.com/, search for "congenital heart defects," and then scroll down to click on the title "Tests and Diagnosis." This webpage offers a guide to a variety of diagnostic procedures. There is also a more comprehensive section titled "In-Depth" for expanded information on diagnostic tests. A section titled "Multimedia" contains images of congenital heart defects and a video.

- "Congenital Heart Disease in Children: Treatments and Drugs." http://www.mayoclinic.com/health/congenital-heart-defects/DS01117/DSECTION=treatments-and-drugs; alternate path: http://www.mayoclinic.com/, search for "congenital heart defects in children," then scroll down to click on the title "Treatments and Drugs," then click on the tab "Multimedia," and then scroll down to click on the title "Slideshow: Common Types of Congenital Heart Defects." A guide to a variety of treatment options is presented. There is also a more comprehensive section titled "In-Depth" for additional information on heart transplantation. This color slideshow from the Mayo Clinic's website illustrates and explains a variety of defects.

➢ NHS (National Health Service) Choices. http://www.nhs.uk/.
Information on clinical trials, provided by the World Health Organization (WHO) International Clinical Trials Registry, can be found by clicking on the

"Clinical Trials" tab at the top of the specific resource page, if available. These clinical trials can be searched by country.

- "Diagnosing Congenital Heart Disease." http://www.nhs.uk/Conditions/ Congenital-heart-disease/Pages/Diagnosis.aspx; alternate path: http://www .nhs.uk/, search for "congenital heart disease," click on the title "Congenital Heart Disease—NHS Choices—Health A–Z," and then click on the section "Diagnosis." This webpage describes tests and procedures used to diagnose problems in fetuses and infants.

- "Treatment of Congenital Heart Disease." http://www.nhs.uk/Conditions/ Congenital-heart-disease/Pages/Treatment.aspx; alternate path: http://www .nhs.uk/, search for "congenital heart disease," click on the title "Congenital Heart Disease—NHS Choices—Health A–Z," and then click on the section "Treatment." This webpage describes specific treatments for the most common types of congenital heart disease.

➤ Texas Heart Institute (Houston, TX)—"Plain Radiographic Diagnosis of Congenital Heart Disease." http://www.bcm.edu/radiology/cases/pediatric/index .htm; alternate path: http://www.bcm.edu/, search for and then click on the title "Plain Radiographic Diagnosis of Congenital Heart Disease."

The Edward B. Singleton Diagnostic Imaging Service of Texas Children's Hospital offers this webpage with links to radiographs of a variety of conditions for diagnosing congenital heart disease, including a normal chest radiograph image as well as radiographic images of conditions with increased pulmonary vascularity, decreased pulmonary vascularity, normal pulmonary vascularity, aortic arch anomalies/vascular rings, malposition cardiac lesions, miscellaneous cardiac lesions, postoperative conditions, and postinterventional radiography. For information on clinical trials, see the Texas Heart Institute entry on pp. 301–302.

➤ WebMD. http://www.webmd.com/.

According to its website, "WebMD News is an independent media service designed to provide news, information, and educational material to consumers and physicians. News content created by WebMD is free from influence by sponsors, partners, or other sources."

- "Heart Disease Health Center: Congenital Heart Disease—Exams and Tests." http://www.webmd.com/heart-disease/tc/congenital-heart-defects -exams-and-tests; alternate path: http://www.webmd.com/, search for "congenital heart defects," and then click on the title "Congenital Heart Defects—Exams and Tests." This webpage offers one-sentence descriptions with links to expanded explanations on diagnostic heart tests for these categories: tests during pregnancy, tests after the baby is born, tests for children and adults, and early detection. Also on this webpage are links to other topics under the heading "Congenital Heart Defects."

- "Heart Disease Health Center: Diagnosis and Tests." http://www.webmd .com/heart-disease/guide/heart-disease-diagnosis-tests; alternate path: http://www.webmd.com/, search for "heart disease health center," click on the title "Heart Disease Health Center Guide," and then scroll down to click on the heading "Diagnosis and Tests." WebMD's heart disease guide offers one-sentence descriptions with links to expanded explanations. There are several videos, slideshows, and images on congenital heart disease.
- "Heart Disease Health Center: Heart Disease—Treatment and Care." http:// www.webmd.com/heart-disease/guide/heart-disease-treatment-care; alternate path: http://www.webmd.com/, search for "congenital heart disease," click on the title "Congenital Heart Disease" (from WebMD Medical Reference), and then scroll down and click on the topic "Treatment and Care." This heart disease guide offers one-sentence descriptions with links to expanded explanations of treatment options.

Top-Ranked U.S. Hospitals and Doctors for Cardiology and Heart Surgery from *U.S. News and World Report*

➤ "Best Hospitals 2012–2013 (Top-Ranked) for Cardiology and Heart Surgery." http:// health.usnews.com/best-hospitals/rankings/cardiology-and-heart-surgery; alternate path: http://www.usnews.com/, click on the main category "Health," click on the title "Best Hospitals," click on the title "Rankings by Specialty," and then click on the title "Cardiology and Heart Surgery." These links go to the most recent rankings.
Use this website to search for the best-ranked U.S. hospitals in cardiology and heart disease. Type in your choice of location (e.g., city) and use the drop-down menu to indicate a specific number of miles within which to search (e.g., 25 miles). According to the U.S. News Health website, "More than 700 hospitals are listed in Cardiology and Heart Surgery. All are experienced in treating difficult cases—a hospital is listed only if at least 1,308 inpatients in need of a high level of expertise in this specialty were treated there in 2008, 2009, and 2010. The top 50 hospitals are ranked, based on score. The rest are listed alphabetically." Additional valuable searching options are available. Under the webpage "Best Hospitals," also check out the link to the hospital honor roll rankings. Under the heading "Related Articles" click on related titles such as "How the Best Hospitals Were Ranked."

➤ "Best Hospitals 2012–2013: The Honor Roll." http://health.usnews.com/health -news/best-hospitals/articles/2011/07/18/best-hospitals-2011–12-the-honor-roll; alternate path: http://www.usnews.com/, click on the main category "Health," click on the title "Best Hospitals," click on the title "Rankings by Specialty," and then click on the title "Honor Roll." These links go to the most recent rankings. Click on the title to the best-ranked honor roll for U.S. hospitals. Type in your choice of location (e.g., city) and use the drop-down menu to indicate a specific number of miles within which to search (e.g., 25 miles). According to the U.S. News Health website, the "medical centers in the Best Hospitals Honor Roll are members of an unusually exclusive club, one that makes up less than 0.4 percent of the nearly 5,000 hospitals nationwide that U.S. News evaluated for the 2012–13 rankings. The 17 hospitals on the list, most of them household names, excel across a broad spectrum of patient care, scoring at or near the top this year in at least six of the 16 Best Hospitals medical specialties."

➤ "Methodology: *U.S. News and World Report* Best Hospitals 2012–2013." http://www .usnews.com/pubfiles/BHmethodAugust.pdf?s_cid=related-links:TOP; alternate path: http://static.usnews.com/documents/health/best-hospitals-methodology.pdf. This report provides a detailed description of the rating criteria for ranking top hospitals. There are additional types of hospital rankings on the webpage titled "Best Hospitals." The top 15 ranked hospitals are listed in the following section in ranking order (*U.S. News and World Report,* Best Hospitals 2013 Guidebook).

➤ "Top Doctors for Cardiology and Heart Surgery." http://health.usnews.com/top -doctors/directory/best-cardiologists; alternate path: http://www.usnews.com/, click on the main category "Health," click on the title "Top Doctors," scroll down to the category "Common Types of Specialists," and then click on the title "Cardiologists." These links go to the most recent rankings.
Search for the best-ranked U.S. cardiologists. You can narrow your search by typing your choice of location (e.g., city, state, or ZIP code), and use the drop-down menu to indicate a specific number of miles within which to search (e.g., 25 miles) or type in the name of a cardiologist at a specific hospital. Click on the doctor's name to view contact information, medical practice location (using Google Maps), type of specialist, special expertise, admitting hospital(s), board certification(s), and detailed education. According to the U.S. News Health website, "There are 2,254 top cardiologists on the list of U.S. News Top Doctors. These physicians were selected based on a peer nomination process. Within this list of the best cardiologists, 330 have been named to a highly selective list of America's Top Doctors (ATD) by achieving national recognition for outstanding work." Additional valuable searching options are available, such as extended information on this ranking methodology of the doctors, at http://health.usnews .com/top-doctors/articles/2011/07/18/peer-nominations-and-the-process -behind-top-doctors.

List of Top 15 Ranked U.S. Hospitals in Cardiology and Heart Surgery

➤ Cleveland Clinic (Cleveland, OH)—"Heart and Vascular." http://my.clevelandclinic .org/heart/; alternate path: http://my.clevelandclinic.org/, under the category "Institutes and Services," click on "Heart and Vascular."

The Cleveland Clinic, ranked #1 in cardiology and heart surgery, offers a link to "Chat Online with a Heart and Vascular Nurse." Click on the category "Online Services" for a medical second opinion. According to its website, "MyConsult online medical second opinion service connects you to the specialty physician expertise you need when you are faced with a serious diagnosis. Following a thorough review of your medical records and diagnostic tests, Cleveland Clinic experts render a medical second opinion that includes treatment options or alternatives, as well as recommendations regarding your future therapeutic considerations." There are also free online clinic chats on different heart conditions and a blog. For information on clinical trials, see the Cleveland Clinic entry on p. 296.

➤ Mayo Clinic (Rochester, MN)—"Cardiovascular Diseases." http://www.mayoclinic .org/cardiovascular-disease/; alternate path: http://www.mayoclinic.com/, search for "cardiovascular diseases," and then click on the title "Cardiovascular Diseases at Mayo Clinic in Minnesota."

The Mayo Clinic, ranked #2 in cardiology and heart surgery, offers at its cardiovascular diseases department links to categories such as patient care, health information (e.g., diseases and treatment), doctors and departments (e.g., cardiovascular disease), patient and visitor guide, and online services. To participate in a clinical trial at the Mayo Clinic Heart, Lung, and Blood Research Center, if available in your cardiology condition, go to http://clinicaltrials.mayo.edu/ dspSubthemes.cfm?theme_id=6; or go to http://www.mayoclinic.org/, click on the heading "Research," and under the category "Find Clinical Trials" scroll down to click on the title "Heart, Lung, and Blood." For patient services in the various cardiology programs, go to http://www.mayoclinic.org/cardiac-surgery/; or http://www.mayoclinic.org/cardiovascular-disease/ or http://www.mayoclinic .org/vascular-and-endovascular-surgery/; or return to the Mayo Clinic homepage at http://www.mayoclinic.org/, click on the heading "Doctors and Departments," select the state location under "Department," and scroll down to select "Cardiac Surgery," "Cardiovascular Diseases," or "Vascular and Endovascular Surgery." In the "Overview" section, scroll down to select a state, and then click on the tab "Doctors" to view links to each medical expert, with profiles (e.g., specialty, medical board certification, education).

➤ Johns Hopkins Hospital (Baltimore, MD)—"Heart and Vascular Institute." http:// www.hopkinsmedicine.org/heart_vascular_institute/; alternate path: http://www .hopkinsmedicine.org/, search for "heart and vascular institute," and then click on the title "Johns Hopkins Heart and Vascular Institute."

Johns Hopkins Hospital, ranked #3 in cardiology and heart surgery, offers at its Heart and Vascular Institute links to "See All Centers of Excellence and Specialty Areas," including specialized women's cardiovascular care, a list of all medical doctors at "Our Experts," patient stories, current clinical trials, news, and other recently published medical reports in cardiology. Click on the heading "Clinical Trials" for links to current trials in various heart and cardiovascular conditions.

➤ New York–Presbyterian (NYP) University Hospital of Columbia and Cornell (New York, NY). http://nyp.org/heart/; alternate path: http://nyp.org/, under the category "Clinical Services," click on "Heart."
NYP University Hospital of Columbia and Cornell, ranked #4 in cardiology and heart surgery, offers at its heart department links to categories, such as a video playlist of heart topics, webcasts of several heart procedures; and for patients and visitors, the NYP YouTube channel; view the heart playlist (excellent short videos) and audio slide presentations of cardiovascular tests and procedures, descriptions of different heart tests and procedures and "Learn about [NYP] operating rooms featuring the state-of-the-art Siemens Artis zeego imaging system. . . . Take a 360° tour." Also, click on the "Explore the Interactive Media Library" icon for access to the Human Atlas media player, which contains short videos, text, models, and slides. For information on clinical trials, see the NYP entry on p. 301.

➤ Massachusetts General Hospital (MGH) (Boston, MA)—"Heart Center." http://www.massgeneral.org/heartcenter/; alternate path: http://www.massgeneral.org/, search for and click on the title "Heart Center"; or click on "Centers and Services," scroll to "Care Centers," and then click on "Massachusetts General Hospital Heart Center Home."
MGH, ranked #5 in cardiology and heart surgery, offers at its heart center department links to categories such as patient experiences, treatments and services, research and clinical trials, news, and patient guides to procedures. Under the heading "Patient Experience" click on the topic "Explore the Heart Center" to take a virtual tour. Under the heading "Research and Clinical Trials," there are also links to current research and the latest news in cardiovascular care.

➤ Texas Heart Institute at St. Luke's Episcopal Hospital (Houston, TX). http://www.texasheartinstitute.org/; Texas Heart Institute at St. Luke's Episcopal Hospital, ranked #6 in cardiology and heart surgery, offers an excellent link to the category "Heart Information Center," which includes heart anatomy, how the heart works, and heart disease topics. Under the "About Us" category is a description of its museum, which demonstrates the advances in technology achieved over the years, including interactive computers, videos, and other multimedia and a "walk-in" heart. Under the heading "Research" are links to published and current ongoing heart studies at the Texas Heart Institute. To participate in a clinical trial at the Texas Heart Institute Research Laboratory, if available in your cardiology condition, go to http://www.texasheartinstitute.org/Research/hfresearch.cfm; or return to the Texas Heart Institute homepage at http://www.texasheartinstitute/, click on the heading "Research," then under the category "Departments" click on the title "Heart Failure Research Laboratory," then scroll down to the section

"Research Projects," and click on the title "FDA-Approved Clinical Trials." Under the heading "About Us," click on "Professional Staff Directory." Click on category to view a list of physicians and specialists (with profiles, e.g., specialty, medical board certification, education).

➤ Duke University Medical Center (Durham, NC)—"Duke Heart Center." http://www.dukehealth.org/heart_center; alternate path: http://www.dukehealth.org/, click the category titled "Services," click on "H," and then scroll down to click on "Heart Services."

Duke University Medical Center, ranked #7 in cardiology and heart surgery, offers at its Duke Heart Center links to categories such as "Programs" (e.g., numerous treatment services), "Patient Care," "Health Library" (e.g., patient care guides, videos, health articles), and "About Us" (descriptions of cardiovascular medical doctors, including their specialty, board certification, and education), research and education, and under the heading "On Other Websites" click on the section titled "Duke Cardiovascular and Thoracic Surgery Department" for information on research. To possibly participate in a clinical trial at its Cardiology Center, if one is available, click on the title "Clinical Trial" for "those currently seeking people to participate."

➤ UCLA Ronald Reagan Medical Center (Los Angeles, CA)—"Cardiology" (Department of Medicine). http://www.uclahealth.org/body.cfm?xyzpdqabc =0&id=453&action=detail&limit_department=15&limit_division=1003; alternate path: http://www.uclahealth.org/, under the heading "Hospitals and Medical Offices," scroll down to click on "Ronald Reagan UCLA Medical Center," and then under the heading "Departments and Services," scroll down to "Medicine" and click on the category "Cardiology."

The UCLA Ronald Reagan Medical Center, ranked #8 in cardiology and heart surgery, offers at its cardiology website links to categories such as "Programs" (links to types of cardiology laboratories and cardiovascular centers) and "Physicians and Specialists" (with profiles, e.g., specialty, medical board certification, education). Under the category "Contact Information" click on the other UCLA cardiology websites where there are links to additional program information and cardiology research at UCLA. To possibly participate in a clinical trial at UCLA, if available, go to http://clinicaltrials.ucla.edu/; or on the homepage, search for "clinical trial" (in quotes) and then click on title "Clinical Trial."

➤ UCLA Ronald Reagan Medical Center (Los Angeles, CA)—"Cardiac and Thoracic Surgery and Vascular Surgery" (both from Department of Surgery). http://www.uclahealth.org/body.cfm?id=453&action=detail&limit_department =28&limit_division=1002 and http://www.uclahealth.org/body.cfm?id=453& action=detail&limit_department=28&limit_division=1106; alternate path: http://www.uclahealth.org/, under the heading "Hospitals and Medical Offices," scroll down to click on "Ronald Reagan UCLA Medical Center," and then under the heading "Departments and Services," scroll down and click on the section link "Surgery," and then click on the topic "Cardiac and Thoracic Surgery" or "Vascular Surgery."

The UCLA Ronald Reagan Medical Center, ranked #8 in cardiology and heart surgery, offers at its Cardiac and Thoracic Surgery webpage links to categories such as video demonstrations about cardiac surgery, various surgical programs, and information on physicians and specialists.

➤ Brigham and Women's Hospital (BWH) (Boston, MA)—"Cardiovascular Center." http://www.brighamandwomens.org/Departments_and_Services/excellence/cardiovascular.aspx; alternate path: http://www.brighamandwomens.org/, scroll under the heading "Departments and Services" to the category titled "Centers of Excellence," and then click on the title "Cardiovascular Center."

Brigham and Women's Hospital, ranked #9 in cardiology and heart surgery, offers at its Cardiovascular Center website links to categories such as "Ask the Cardiologist," as well as individual topics on cardiac surgeries, vascular surgeries, and cardiac medicine. Click on each topic link, such as "Brigham Cardiac Valve Center" for a description of types of surgery, patient guides (includes a list of staff physicians with profiles, including specialty, medical board certification, education), research at BWH, an overview of the types of valve surgeries performed at BWH, and a section for patients (e.g., publications on valve surgeries, video demonstrations, and other interactive tools and media). To possibly participate in a clinical trial at the BWH Cardiovascular Center, click at the top of the screen on the heading "Research" and then click on the category "Clinical Trials," then click on the title "Search Open Studies by Therapeutic Area," and then scroll down the list to select topics, such as heart disease, high blood pressure, stroke, and vascular disorders.

➤ Mount Sinai Medical Center (New York, NY)—"Mount Sinai Cardiac Services." http://www.mountsinai.org/patient-care/service-areas/heart; alternate path: http://www.mountsinai.org/, under the heading "Patient Care," click on "Service Areas," and then click on "Heart Disease."

Mount Sinai Medical Center, ranked #10 in cardiology and heart surgery, offers at its Mount Sinai Cardiac Services website links to categories such as "Areas of Care" (e.g., "Arrhythmia—Heart Rhythm Disorder"), "Doctors" (click on each cardiology program for a list of its physicians with their profiles, e.g., specialty, medical board certification, education), "Patient Stories," "Procedures and Services" (e.g., "Cardiac Catheterization Labs"), "Diseases and Conditions," and under the heading "Research" click on the title "Institutes" and then click on "Cardiovascular Research Institute." Also under the heading "Research" click on the title "Centers," and then click on "Cardiovascular Research Center" and "Center for Molecular Cardiology."

➤ St. Francis Hospital—The Heart Center (Roslyn, NY). http://www.stfrancis heartcenter.com/.

St. Francis Hospital—The Heart Center, ranked #11 in cardiology and heart surgery, offers at its St. Francis Heart Center website links to categories such as "Patient Center," where you can find a St. Francis physician or request an appointment. Under "Patient Center Dropbox" you can select expanded information on such areas as "Cardiac Diagnostic Imaging," "Cardiac Fitness and Rehabilitation," "Cardiac Outreach Program," "Cardiology," and "Cardiothoracic Surgery" with further details on diagnostic procedures, treatments, and programs. Under "Find a Doctor in the Department" are links to additional information about each cardiologist or cardiothoracic surgeon. Under the category "Research" is a link to current "Clinical Trials" for possible recruitment. The "Video Center" offers animated explanations of numerous cardiovascular topics. A free subscription to a newsletter for medical updates is available.

➤ Methodist Hospital (Houston, TX)—"Methodist DeBakey Heart and Vascular Center." http://www.methodisthealth.com/basic.cfm?id=36166 and http://www.methodisthealth.com/basic.cfm?id=36164; alternate path: http://www.methodisthealth.com/, under the heading "Services and Specialties," click on "View All Services and Specialties," and then click on "Cardiology" or "Cardiovascular Surgery."

Methodist Hospital, ranked #12 in cardiology and heart surgery, offers at its Methodist Hospital Cardiac Services website links, for example, under "Find a Doctor" click on the department (e.g., cardiology, cardiovascular surgeon) for a list of its physicians with their profiles, e.g., specialty, special procedures, education, language). Under the category "Research" is a link to current "Clinical Trials" for possible recruitment. Click on the heading "Methodist DeBakey Heart and Vascular Center" for additional links to patient stories, visiting the heart center, registering for a heart scan, and patient resources (e.g., free web-based educational programs and free downloadable heart and cardiovascular brochures and publications).

➤ Barnes-Jewish Hospital/Washington University (Saint Louis, MO)—"Heart and Vascular Center." http://www.barnesjewish.org/heart-vascular; alternate path: http://www.barnesjewish.org/, under the heading "Centers of Excellence," click on "Heart and Vascular."

Barnes-Jewish Hospital/Washington University, ranked #13 in cardiology and heart surgery, offers at its Heart and Vascular Center website links to a variety of cardiovascular conditions and related latest news and events. Under "Find a Doctor" click on the department (e.g., cardiothoracic surgery, cardiovascular disease) for a list of its physicians with their profiles (e.g., specialty, medical board certification, education). Getting a second opinion is available. Click on the heading "Find Health Info" to access interactive tools and multimedia. A free subscription to an e-newsletter for medical updates is also available.

➤ NYU Langone Medical Center (New York, NY)—"Cardiology, Cardiac Surgery, and Vascular Surgery." http://www.med.nyu.edu/clinical-services/cardiology -cardiac-surgery-and-vascular-surgery; alternate path: http://www.med.nyu.edu/, scroll down under "Patients and Visitors," click on the heading "Clinical Services," and then select the category "Cardiology, Cardiac Surgery, and Vascular Surgery." NYU Langone Medical Center, ranked #14 in cardiology and heart surgery, offers at its Cardiology, Cardiac Surgery, and Vascular Surgery website links to categories such as cardiology, cardiac cauterization laboratory, cardiac electrophysiology (Heart Rhythm Center), cardiac surgery, cardiac rehabilitation and prevention, interventional radiology, pediatric cardiology (includes links to other cardiac intensive care services and vascular surgery). Expanded information at these categories include details on the medical team (expertise and education), clinical services, research overview, faculty publications, types of labs, treatments (heart valve disease), insurance information, and asking a cardiac surgeon a question by e-mail or phone.

➤ Hospital of the University of Pennsylvania (HUP) (Philadelphia, PA)—"Penn Heart and Vascular." http://www.pennmedicine.org/heart/; alternate path: http://www .pennmedicine.org/hup/, under "Featured Services at HUP," click on "Cardiac." HUP, ranked #15 in cardiology and heart surgery, offers at its Penn Heart and Vascular Center website links to categories such as clinical services (e.g., coronary artery disease), news (up-to-the-minute reports, such as "Next Big Drug Against Cholesterol Takes Shape" or "Bad Batteries in AEDs Tied to Cardiac Deaths"), and upcoming events (patient classes and events, e.g., peripheral arterial disease). Click on "Learn More about Penn Heart and Vascular Care" for detailed overview of the Penn Heart and Vascular Center, Quality, and Outcomes (Penn clinical research), patient testimonials, and videos. You can also subscribe to the Penn Heart newsletter. To possibly participate in a clinical trial at Penn Cardiovascular Institute, if available, go to http://www.med.upenn.edu/cvi/ clinical_trials.shtml; or click on the category "Search Clinical Trials," and then scroll down the list of cardiac clinical trial categories.

Webliography

Acurian. "Clinical Trial Patient Recruiter." Accessed April 2, 2013. http://www.acurian .com/.

American Heart Association. "Cardiac Medications." Updated September 12, 2012. http:// www.heart.org/HEARTORG/Conditions/HeartAttack/PreventionTreatmentofHeart Attack/Cardiac-Medications_UCM_303937_Article.jsp.

———. "Cardiac Procedures and Surgeries." Updated March 22, 2013. http://www.heart
.org/HEARTORG/Conditions/HeartAttack/PreventionTreatmentofHeartAttack/
Cardiac-Procedures-and-Surgeries_UCM_303939_Article.jsp.

———. "Medications for Arrhythmia." Updated December 11, 2012. http://www.heart
.org/HEARTORG/Conditions/Arrhythmia/PreventionTreatmentofArrhythmia/
Medications-for-Arrhythmia_UCM_301990_Article.jsp.

———. "Types of Blood Pressure Medications." Updated August 14, 2012. http://www
.heart.org/HEARTORG/Conditions/HighBloodPressure/PreventionTreatmentof
HighBloodPressure/Types-of-Blood-Pressure-Medications_UCM_303247
_Article.jsp.

American Heart Association Newsroom. "Latest Heart Disease News." Accessed
April 2, 2013. http://www.newsroom.heart.org/.

Angioplasty.Org. "Fractional Flow Reserve (FFR)." Reviewed February 2013. http://
www.ptca.org/ivus/FFR.html.

AnswerBag. "What Are the Side Effects of Anticoagulant and Antiplatelet Drugs?"
November 7, 2007. http://www.answerbag.com/q_view/453070#ixzz1AAxJaMs.

CenterWatch. "Helping People Connect with Clinical Trials." Accessed April 2,
2013. http://centerwatch.com/.

Cleveland Clinic. "Aldosterone Inhibitors." Reviewed September 1, 2010. http://my
.clevelandclinic.org/drugs/aldosterone_inhibitors/hic_aldosterone_inhibitors.aspx.

———. "Blood Tests to Determine Risk of Coronary Artery Disease." Reviewed
January 2013. http://my.clevelandclinic.org/heart/services/tests/labtests/testscad
.aspx.

———. "B-Type Natriuretic Peptide (BNP) Blood Test." Reviewed September 2011.
http://my.clevelandclinic.org/heart/services/tests/labtests/bnp.aspx.

———. "Lipid Blood Tests." Reviewed February 2011. http://my.clevelandclinic.org/
heart/services/tests/labtests/lipid.aspx.

———. "Percutaneous and Endoscopic Interventions." Accessed May 9, 2013. http://
my.clevelandclinic.org/heart/percutaneous/default.aspx.

ClinicalTrials.gov. Clinical trial database. Accessed April 2, 2013. http://clinicaltrials.gov/.

———. Clinical trials in heart disease. Accessed April 2, 2013. http://www
.clinicaltrials.gov/ct2/results?term=heart+disease.

———. Clinical trials in heart disease categories. Accessed April 2, 2013. http://www
.clinicaltrials.gov/ct2/search/browse?brwse=cond_cat_BC14.

EverydayHealth.com. "High Blood Pressure Treatment; Receptor Blockers." Updated
July 8, 2010. http://www.everydayhealth.com/hypertension/treating/receptor
-blockers-fooling-the-body.aspx.

Heart and Stroke Foundation. "Antiarrhythmics." Modified July 2011. http://www
.heartandstroke.on.ca/site/c.pvI3IeNWJwE/b.3581859/k.1844/Heart_Disease
__Antiarrhythmics.htm.

————. "Nitrates (Nitroglycerin)." Modified July 2011. http://www.heartandstroke .com/site/c.ikIQLcMWJtE/b.3484117/k.9876/Heart_disease__Nitrates _Nitroglycerin.htm.

Holisticonline.com. "Heart Remedies." Accessed April 2, 2013. http://www.holistic online.com/remedies/heart/heart_home.htm.

Huffington Post. "Pradaxa and Xarelto: Top Heart Doctors Concerned over New Blood Thinners." June 14, 2012. http://www.huffingtonpost.com/2012/06/14/ pradaxa-xarelto-blood-thinner-doctors-heart_n_1595971.html.

Lab Tests Online. "Heart Disease." Modified September 24, 2012. http://www .labtestsonline.org/understanding/conditions/heart-4.html.

Lamas, G. A., et al. "Effect of Disodium EDTA Chelation Regimen on Cardiovascular Events in Patients with Previous Myocardial Infarction: The TACT Randomized Trial." *JAMA*, 309, no. 12 (2013): 1241–1250. http://jama.jamanetwork.com/ article.aspx?articleid=1672238.

Mayo Clinic. "Alpha Blockers." December 16, 2010. http://www.mayoclinic.com/ health/alpha-blockers/HI00055.

————. "Blood Tests for Heart Disease" June 1, 2011. http://www.mayoclinic.com/ health/heart-disease/HB00016.

————. "Cardiac Ablation." June 22, 2011. http://www.mayoclinic.com/health/ cardiac-ablation/MY00706.

————. "Cardiac Catheterization." November 19, 2010. http://www.mayoclinic.com/ health/cardiac-catheterization/MY00218.

————. "Complementary and Alternative Medicine: Evaluate Treatment Claims." October 22, 2011. http://www.mayoclinic.com/health/alternative-medicine/SA00078.

————. "Herbs, Supplements, and Vitamins." Accessed April 2, 2013. http://www .mayoclinic.com/health/drug-information/DrugHerbIndex.

————. "High Blood Pressure Medications: Central-Acting Agents." December 16, 2010. http://www.mayoclinic.com/health/high-blood-pressure-medication/ HI00056.

MedicineNet.com. "Nitroglycerin, Nitro-Bid, Nitro-Dur, Nitrostat, Transderm-Nitro, Minitran, Deponit, Nitrol." Accessed April 2, 2013. http://www.medicinenet .com/nitroglycerin/article.htm.

————. "Reserpine—Oral." Accessed April 2, 2013. http://www.medicinenet.com/ reserpine-oral/article.htm.

MedlinePlus. "Angina." Updated March 20, 2013. http://www.nlm.nih.gov/medlineplus/ angina.html.

————. "Arrhythmia." Updated March 26, 2013. http://www.nlm.nih.gov/medlineplus/ arrhythmia.html.

————. "Aspirin and Heart Disease." Updated August 28, 2012. http://www.nlm.nih .gov/medlineplus/ency/patientinstructions/000092.htm.

———. "Complementary and Alternative Medicine (CAM)." Updated March 18, 2013. http://www.nlm.nih.gov/medlineplus/complementaryandalternativemedicine.html.

———. "Coronary Angiography and Possible Angioplasty—Tutorial." Accessed April 2, 2013. http://www.nlm.nih.gov/medlineplus/tutorials/coronaryangiographyand possibleangioplasty/htm/index.htm.

———. "Digoxin." Revised August 1, 2010. http://www.nlm.nih.gov/medlineplus/ druginfo/meds/a682301.html.

———. "Echocardiogram—Tutorial." Accessed April 2, 2013. http://www.nlm.nih .gov/medlineplus/tutorials/echocardiogram/htm/index.htm.

———. "Echocardiography—Diagnostics—Tutorial." Accessed April 2, 2013. http:// www.diagnosticimagingclinic.com/tutorials/echocardiogram/htm/.

———. "Heart Attack." Updated March 26, 2013. http://www.nlm.nih.gov/medlineplus/ heartattack.html.

———. "Heart Failure." Updated March 29, 2013. http://www.nlm.nih.gov/medlineplus/ heartfailure.html.

———. "Heart Surgery." Updated March 21, 2013. http://www.nlm.nih.gov/medlineplus/ heartsurgery.html.

———. "Stroke." Updated March 31, 2013. http://www.nlm.nih.gov/medlineplus/ stroke.html.

Medscape Reference. "Pulmonary Artery Catheterization." Updated March 27, 2013. http://emedicine.medscape.com/article/1824547-overview.

Medscape Today: Medscape Cardiology. "Renal Denervation: Is Reality Meeting Expectations?" January 7, 2013. http://www.medscape.com/viewarticle/776985.

National Caregivers Library. "Common Heart Disease Medications." Accessed April 2, 2013. http://www.caregiverslibrary.org/caregivers-resources/grp-diseases/hsgrp -heart-disease/common-heart-disease-medications-article.aspx.

National Heart, Lung, and Blood Institute. "Children and Clinical Studies." July 1, 2011. http://www.nhlbi.nih.gov/childrenandclinicalstudies/index.php.

———. "What Are Blood Tests?" January 6, 2012. http://www.nhlbi.nih.gov/health/ health-topics/topics/bdt/.

———. "What Are Holes in the Heart?" July 1, 2011. http://www.nhlbi.nih.gov/ health/dci/Diseases/holes/holes_whatare.html.

———. "What Is a Heart Attack?" March 1, 2011. http://www.nhlbi.nih.gov/health/ dci/Diseases/HeartAttack/HeartAttack_WhatIs.html.

———. "What Is a Heart Murmur?" September 20, 2012. http://www.nhlbi.nih.gov/ health/dci/Diseases/heartmurmur/hmurmur_what.html.

———. "What Is a Heart Transplant?" January 3, 2012. http://www.nhlbi.nih.gov/ health/dci/Diseases/ht/ht_whatis.html.

———. "What Is a Nuclear Heart Scan?" March 9, 2012. http://www.nhlbi.nih.gov/ health/dci/Diseases/nscan/nscan_whatis.html.

———. "What Is a Pacemaker?" February 28, 2012. http://www.nhlbi.nih.gov/health/dci/Diseases/pace/pace_whatis.html.

———. "What Is a Stent?" November 8, 2011. http://www.nhlbi.nih.gov/health/dci/Diseases/stents/stents_whatis.html.

———. "What Is a Stress Test?" December 14, 2011. http://www.nhlbi.nih.gov/health/dci/Diseases/stress/stress_whatis.html.

———. "What Is a Total Artificial Heart?" July 6, 2012. http://www.nhlbi.nih.gov/health/health-topics/topics/tah/.

———. "What Is an Arrhythmia?" July 1, 2011. http://www.nhlbi.nih.gov/health/dci/Diseases/arr/arr_whatis.html.

———. "What Is an Automated External Defibrillator?" December 2, 2011. http://www.nhlbi.nih.gov/health/health-topics/topics/aed/.

———. "What Is an Electrocardiogram?" October 1, 2010. http://www.nhlbi.nih.gov/health/dci/Diseases/ekg/ekg_what.html.

———. "What Is an Implantable Cardioverter Defibrillator?" November 9, 2011. http://www.nhlbi.nih.gov/health/dci/Diseases/icd/icd_whatis.html.

———. "What Is Angina?" June 1, 2011. http://www.nhlbi.nih.gov/health/dci/Diseases/Angina/Angina_WhatIs.html.

———. "What Is Atrial Fibrillation?" July 1, 2011. http://www.nhlbi.nih.gov/health/dci/Diseases/af/af_what.html.

———. "What Is Cardiac Catheterization?" January 30, 2012. http://www.nhlbi.nih.gov/health/dci/Diseases/cath/cath_keypoints.html.

———. "What Is Cardiac Computed Tomography?" February 29, 2012. http://www.nhlbi.nih.gov/health/dci/Diseases/ct/ct_whatis.html.

———. "What Is Cardioversion?" May 25, 2012. http://www.nhlbi.nih.gov/health/health-topics/topics/crv/.

———. "What Is Carotid Endarterectomy?" December 1, 2010. http://www.nhlbi.nih.gov/health/health-topics/topics/carend/.

———. "What Is Carotid Ultrasound?" February 3, 2012. http://www.nhlbi.nih.gov/health/health-topics/topics/cu/.

———. "What Is Cholesterol?" September 19, 2012. http://www.nhlbi.nih.gov/health/health-topics/topics/hbc/.

———. "What Is Congenital Heart Defects?" July 1, 2011. http://www.nhlbi.nih.gov/health/dci/Diseases/chd/chd_what.html.

———. "What Is Coronary Angiography?" March 2, 2012. http://www.nhlbi.nih.gov/health/dci/Diseases/ca/ca_whatis.html.

———. "What Is Coronary Angioplasty?" February 1, 2012. http://www.nhlbi.nih.gov/health/dci/Diseases/Angioplasty/Angioplasty_WhatIs.html.

———. "What Is Coronary Artery Bypass Grafting (CABG)?" February 23, 2012. http://www.nhlbi.nih.gov/health/dci/Diseases/cabg/cabg_whatis.html.

————. "What Is Coronary Calcium Scan?" March 30, 2012. http://www.nhlbi.nih .gov/health/dci/Diseases/cscan/cscan_whatis.html.

————. "What Is Echocardiography?" October 31, 2011. http://www.nhlbi.nih.gov/ health/dci/Diseases/echo/echo_whatis.html.

————. "What Is Heart Failure?" January 9, 2012. http://www.nhlbi.nih.gov/health/ dci/Diseases/Hf/HF_WhatIs.html.

————. "What Is Heart Surgery?" March 23, 2012. http://www.nhlbi.nih.gov/health/ dci/Diseases/hs/hs_types.html.

————. "What Is Heart Valve Disease?" November 16, 2011. http://www.nhlbi.nih .gov/health/dci/Diseases/hvd/hvd_whatis.html.

————. "What Is High Blood Pressure?" August 2, 2012. http://www.nhlbi.nih.gov/ health/dci/Diseases/Hbp/HBP_WhatIs.html.

————. "What Is Transesophageal Echocardiography?" March 7, 2012. http://www .nhlbi.nih.gov/health/dci/Diseases/tee/tee_whatis.html.

National Institutes of Health. "News and Events: EDTA Chelation Therapy Modestly Reduces Cardiovascular Events." March 27, 2013. http://www.nih.gov/news/ health/mar2013/nhlbi-26.htm.

National Institutes of Health, National Center for Complementary and Alternative Medicine. (NCCAM). "Chelation for Coronary Heart Disease." March 27, 2013. http://nccam.nih.gov/health/chelation.

Nissen, S. E. "Concerns about Reliability in the Trial to Assess Chelation Therapy (TACT)." *JAMA*, 309, no. 12 (2013): 1293–1294. http://jama.jamanetwork.com/ article.aspx?articleid=1672219.

Texas Heart Institute. "Inotropic Agents." Updated August 2012. http://www .texasheartinstitute.org/HIC/Topics/Meds/inotropic.cfm.

————. "Nitrate." Updated August 2012. http://www.texasheartinstitute.org/HIC/ Topics/Meds/nitrmeds.cfm.

WebMD, Heart Disease Health Center. "Coronary Artery Disease Directory." Accessed April 2, 2013. http://www.webmd.com/heart-disease/coronary-artery -disease-directory.

————. "Diagnoses and Tests." Accessed March 17, 2013. http://www.webmd.com/ heart-disease/guide/heart-disease-diagnosis-tests.

————. "Heart Disease and Antiarrhythmics." February 22, 2012. http://www .webmd.com/heart-disease/medicine-antiarrhythmics.

————. "Heart Disease and Aspirin Therapy." February 15, 2012. http://www .Webmd.com/heart-disease/aspirin-therapy.

————. "Heart Disease and Clot Buster Drugs." February 22, 2012. http://www .webmd.com/heart-disease/medicine-clot-busters.

————. "Heart Disease and MRI Testing." May 15, 2012. http://www.webmd.com/ heart-disease/guide/heart-mri.

———. "Heart Disease and the Heart Biopsy." Reviewed February 28, 2012. http://www.webmd.com/heart-disease/guide/myocardial-biopsy.

———. "Heart Disease and Treatment with Digoxin." February 22, 2012. http://www.webmd.com/heart-disease/treatment-digoxin.

———. "Heart Disease, Electrocardiogram, and Specialized EKGs." February 15, 2012. http://www.webmd.com/heart-disease/guide/electrocardiogram-specialized-ekgs.

———. "How the Heart Works." February 16, 2012. http://www.webmd.com/heart-disease/guide/how-heart-works.

———. "New Test Helps Decide if Heart Patient Needs Stent." August 28, 2012. http://www.webmd.com/heart/news/20120828/new-test-helps-decide-if-heart-patient-needs-stent.

———. "Nitrates for Coronary Artery Disease." May 10, 2010. http://www.webmd.com/heart-disease/nitrates-for-coronary-artery-disease.

———. "Warfarin and Other Blood Thinners for Heart Disease." February 22, 2012. http://www.webmd.com/heart-disease/warfarin-other-blood-thinners.

WebMD, Heart Failure Health Center. "Aldosterone Receptor Antagonists: Diuretics for Heart Failure." April 15, 2011. http://www.webmd.com/heart-disease/heart-failure/aldosterone-receptor-antagonists-diuretics-for-heart-failure.

———. "Treating Severe Heart Failure." May 16, 2012. http://www.webmd.com/heart-disease/heart-failure/treating-severe-failure.

WebMD, Hypertension/High Blood Pressure Health Center. "New Procedure May Aid Stubborn High Blood Pressure." December 18, 2012. http://www.webmd.com/hypertension-high-blood-pressure/news/20121213/new-procedure-high-blood-pressure.

———. "Other Medicines for High Blood Pressure." Updated April 4, 2011. http://www.webmd.com/hypertension-high-blood-pressure/vasodilators-for-high-blood-pressure.

Wolters Kluwer: Health. "Pulmonary Artery Catheterization: Interpretation of Tracings." September 14, 2012. http://www.uptodate.com/patients/content/topic.do?topicKey=~c..mmz2B/GSttJ.

Chapter 6

Risk Factors and Prevention

M ost types of heart disease can be prevented or delayed by lifestyle changes. Understanding heart disease risks and what to do about them can help patients proactively maximize their efforts to reduce or prevent heart or cardiovascular disease. Patients should consult with their physician about their personal prevention program. *See the final section of this chapter,* RESOURCES FOR FURTHER INFORMATION ON RISKS AND PREVENTION, *for all related references.*

Risk Factors

Many factors in life can lead to heart disease. Some are unavoidable. For example, males, people of advanced age, persons with a family history of heart disease, postmenopausal women, and certain races are more likely to develop a heart disease. However, for most people, even those with a high risk, heart disease can be mitigated by health care monitoring and changes in lifestyle.

Changes in lifestyle that can help reduce the risks for heart disease include stopping smoking; controlling diet; managing cholesterol, C-reactive protein, triglycerides, blood pressure, and weight; avoiding or controlling diabetes; participating in physical activity; and reducing stress.

Many of these risk factors are interrelated. Having one factor can increase the risk of developing other risk factors and the risk of heart disease. Obviously, controlling some of these factors requires a doctor's monitoring to measure factors and guide the patient toward good health practices.

Abnormal Blood Pressure

Blood pressure is the measure of the heart's blood-pumping ability. The measure has two values, the systolic or beating pressure and the diastolic or resting pressure. Normal blood pressure is 120/80 mm Hg (millimeters of mercury), read with the systolic pressure over the diastolic pressure. However, normal blood pressure varies with age, gender, and height.

Blood pressure is measured by placing a pressure cuff around the arm. Inflating the cuff stops blood flow and, as the cuff pressure is reduced, a heartbeat will be heard at the systolic pressure and then will not be heard at the diastolic pressure. A physician or nurse will typically use a blood pressure cuff and a stethoscope to determine blood pressure, but other similar devices can be used.

High blood pressure can damage the heart and arteries and may lead to plaque buildup. Any pressure above normal (systolic, diastolic, or both) increases heart disease risk (*see* CHAPTER 3: HIGH BLOOD PRESSURE). Low blood pressure presents risks of fainting and shock, especially if there is underlying heart disease (*see* CHAPTER 3: LOW BLOOD PRESSURE).

Aging and Gender

Men are at risk of heart disease at a younger age than women are. After age 45 for men and after age 55 for women, heart disease risk increases. With people of advanced age, heart disease risk increases because plaque narrows the coronary arteries slowly, over time. Because these changes to the arteries take time to develop, they can often be delayed by reducing risk factors through lifestyle changes.

In women, estrogen helps protect the heart from disease. After menopause, estrogen levels significantly decrease; consequently, heart disease risk increases. Once menopause occurs, men and women have similar risk for heart disease. However, some risk factors, such as diabetes, increase heart disease risk more for women than for men (*see* CHAPTER 8).

Alcohol Consumption

Although a glass of red wine each day might be beneficial for the heart and may even reduce stress, drinking too much alcohol increases blood pressure, blood cholesterol levels, and risk of stroke, heart failure, and irregular heartbeat. Studies suggest that the flavonoids and other antioxidants in red wine reduce risk of cardiovascular disease by increasing the body's "good cholesterol," high-density lipoprotein (HDL). HDL possesses anticlotting factors and protects the heart and vessels from body-produced free oxygen radicals that aid in forming plaque in arteries, which is particularly damaging to diabetics. Because the source of these antioxidants is the skin of the grape, red grapes and red grape juice might be an appropriate substitute for red wine.

C-reactive Protein Blood Level

C-reactive protein is released by the liver when certain chemicals are released from fat cells in response to inflammation. When an artery or the heart is damaged, it becomes inflamed, and thus the C-reactive protein blood level increases. However, other disease processes also increase C-reactive protein levels. Directly relating C-reactive protein levels to heart disease can be difficult; some studies indicate that the more C-reactive protein in the blood, the higher the risk of developing diabetes, high blood pressure, and heart disease. So if elevated C-reactive protein levels are present in a patient, it may indicate increased risk or presence of heart disease. C-reactive protein can be measured by a blood test.

Diabetes

Diabetes is a disease in which the blood sugar levels are too high. Too much blood sugar can damage blood vessels. Diabetes is related to how the body makes and uses insulin. Insulin is a hormone that regulates carbohydrate and fat metabolism in the body. If the body is not metabolizing fat properly, plaque can build up in the damaged arteries and lead to heart disease.

Diet

Food choices affect heart disease risk. Those foods that increase cholesterol in the body should be limited—a list which includes foods with saturated fats, trans fats, and cholesterol. Specifically, meats, dairy products, eggs, high-fat sweets, processed foods (e.g., fried foods, baked goods), and certain shellfish can raise cholesterol. In addition, too much salt increases the risk of high blood pressure. Too much sugar in the diet can cause weight gain; obesity is a heart disease risk. Similarly, drinking too much alcohol will raise blood pressure and can also increase a patient's weight. Healthy levels of HDL and low-density lipoprotein (LDL; "bad cholesterol") can prevent plaque formation in the arteries. However, in addition to diet, other factors such as age and gender affect cholesterol levels.

As noted, two types of cholesterol are found in the body, HDL and LDL. HDL cholesterol is called good cholesterol because it helps remove cholesterol from the arteries. Too little HDL in the blood increases the risk of heart disease. LDL cholesterol is called bad cholesterol because it carries cholesterol to the tissues. The more LDL there is in the blood, the greater the risk of heart disease. The amount of HDL and LDL in the blood can be measured by blood tests. At-risk patients should have their blood tested regularly for cholesterol, both HDL and LDL, levels (*see* CHAPTER 3 *and* CHAPTER 5: CARDIAC BLOOD TESTS).

Also, Lp(a), or lipoprotein A, is a combination of LDL and apolipoprotein (a). The level of Lp(a) appears to be determined by a patient's genetic makeup and often cannot be lowered through the use of lipid-lowering medications, diet, and exercise. Therefore, a high blood level of Lp(a) may indicate a cardiovascular risk in which additional treatment and testing is needed.

Erectile Dysfunction (Risk Marker)

Erectile dysfunction (ED) may be an indication of atherosclerosis. Plaque can cause narrowing of the vessels of the penis thereby limiting blood flow, which produces ED. Due to the narrowness of these vessels, ED can be a major sign that cardiovascular disease (CVD) is developing before more commonly known heart disease symptoms appear. According to a major prospective cohort study by Banks and colleagues, which included questionnaire data from 2006 to 2009, followed by 2.2 years for CVD hospitalization data and 2.8 years for mortality data due to CVD, involving 95,038 males, age 45 and over, with and without CVD, "compared to men without erectile dysfunction, there is an increasing risk of ischemic heart disease, peripheral vascular disease, and death from all causes in those with increasing degrees of severity of erectile dysfunction. The authors emphasize that erectile dysfunction is a risk marker for cardiovascular disease, not a risk factor that causes cardiovascular disease. These findings add to previous studies. . . . Men with erectile dysfunction, even at mild or moderate levels, should be screened and treated for cardiovascular disease accordingly."

Genetics

Genetic makeup (or family history) affects a person's risk of heart disease. An individual's risk is greater if a family member has heart disease. However, adjusting lifestyles and habits, as described in later sections, can help minimize some genetic risks. Individuals who are aware of a family history of CVD should inform their doctors so that an optimal medical plan can be developed to reduce their known risks of heart disease.

Inactivity or Lack of Exercise

After stopping smoking, participating in physical activity produces the most important impact in reducing heart disease risk. Physical activity helps strengthen the heart and vascular system and protects these systems against disease processes. A lack of physical activity can worsen other heart disease risk factors, such as high blood cholesterol and high triglyceride levels, high blood pressure, diabetes, and being overweight or obese. Even low-impact exercises, such as walking, can reduce the risk. As the amount of exercise increases, the level of risk decreases. Exercise is important for everyone, from children to adults, to help prevent heart disease.

Obesity, Being Overweight, and Anorexia

Body weight depends on the body's basic structure and how much extra fat is present. The measure used to determine whether a person is overweight is the body mass index (BMI). Using a person's height and weight in a mathematical formula gives the BMI. A BMI below 25 is considered normal weight; above 25 but below 30 is considered overweight; and above 30 is considered obese. Because being overweight or obese is related to high blood cholesterol, high triglycerides, high blood pressure, and diabetes, either condition raises the risk of heart disease and heart attack. Websites such as the Centers for Disease Control and Prevention have useful BMI calculators, usually one for adults and one for children and teens. *See the final section of this chapter,* RESOURCES FOR FURTHER INFORMATION ON RISKS AND PREVENTION, *for specific BMI calculator website addresses.*

Conversely, chronic anorexia can lead to mitral valve prolapse, low blood pressure, and heart failure, commonly from bradycardia (slow heartbeat), which leads to heart muscle death. The lack of water and food in the body causes an electrolyte imbalance of calcium and potassium, two elements that are required to sustain the electric current that allows the heart to beat. Heart disease is the primary cause of death for individuals with severe anorexia.

Racial Designation

Certain races are more likely to develop heart disease, typically because of high rates of other conditions that lead to heart disease. For example, African Americans have more severe high blood pressure disease than Caucasians and are, therefore, at a higher risk of heart disease. Heart disease risk is also higher among Mexican Americans, American Indians, native Hawaiians, and some Asian Americans than for Caucasians mainly because of the higher rate of diabetes and obesity in these populations. Studies suggest some Mediterranean peoples have lower rates of heart disease than Americans, probably because of their dietary habits.

Smoking

Stopping smoking is the single most important step to reduce the risk of heart attack. This includes use of cigarettes, cigars, and pipe tobacco. Smoking tobacco causes plaque to form in arteries, increases the risk of blood clots in arteries, and lowers the level of high-density lipoprotein (HDL), the good cholesterol. Each of these changes can lead to arterial disease, cardiomyopathy, and heart attack. Because of smoking's interaction with other risk factors (e.g., high cholesterol, high blood pressure), stopping smoking aids in reducing the other risks. In addition, smoking cessation reduces the risk of other health problems such as cancer, lung disease, and cerebrovascular disease.

The more a patient smokes, the higher the risk is of these problems occurring. However, stopping smoking can significantly decrease the risk, even for longtime smokers. Of course, never smoking is ideal, and youth should be discouraged from smoking. In addition, secondhand smoke can cause adverse effects in children and adults, and in some cases has caused heart attacks. Secondhand smoke should be avoided whenever possible.

Stress

Stress and its cousins, anger and anxiety, have considerable effects on the body. The longer they last, the higher their likelihood of contributing to heart disease. When under stress, a person's arteries tighten and constrict blood flow, which increases blood pressure. When stressed or anxious, people tend to overeat and to smoke, both of which increase heart disease risk. Many heart attacks occur during or shortly after emotionally upsetting events like a fight, a dangerous situation, or finding out about the loss of a loved one.

Triglyceride Blood Level

Triglycerides are a type of fat found in the blood. Some clinical studies suggest that high triglyceride blood levels may increase heart disease risk. Particularly, women with high triglycerides levels are believed to have an increased risk of heart diseases.

Four risk factors can cause an increase in triglycerides: fat in the diet, sugar in the diet, alcohol consumption, and inherited genes for high triglyceride blood levels. Triglycerides can raise the risk for heart disease, especially if a person is overweight, is physically inactive, is a smoker, uses alcohol excessively, has a very high carbohydrate diet, takes certain drugs, has some genetic disorders, or has certain diseases.

Triglyceride blood level can be measured by a blood test. Levels above 150 mg/dL should be treated. Clinical studies have shown that high levels of triglycerides have a negative effect on the composition of cholesterol. When triglycerides are above 150 mg/dL, LDL (the bad cholesterol) particles become smaller and denser (compacted) and therefore are more harmful because they more easily form into plaque; in addition, this high level of triglycerides is known to cause a decrease in the level of HDL (the good cholesterol).

Prevention

Prevention starts with knowing what a patient's risks are and making changes to reduce or eliminate those risks. If the patient has genetic risks, then watchful medical care and elimination of exacerbating risks will help increase a patient's life span and reduce complications. Regular health checkups can detect a potential problem early enough to minimize its effect. Stopping smoking, maintaining a healthy weight, eating heart-healthy foods, exercising regularly, and reducing stress are the main preventive measures for most people. These preventive measures can decrease the load of toxins the heart may face, reduce cholesterol, help strengthen the heart, and reduce work that the heart must do. It is never too late to start changing things to improve the quality of life (*see* CHAPTER 7). Many medications are useful in addressing cholesterol, high blood pressure, diabetes, stress, and anger (*see* DRUG THERAPIES IN CHAPTER 5). A low dose of aspirin daily has been shown to reduce the risk of heart attack and stroke (*see* DRUG THERAPIES: LOW-DOSE ASPIRIN IN CHAPTER 5).

Healthy Diet and Weight

Maintaining a healthy weight reduces the workload of the heart and helps reduce high cholesterol and other heart risks. Like stopping smoking, reaching and maintaining a healthy weight requires willingness, a plan, and in some cases a doctor's help. To maintain a healthy weight requires first getting to a healthy weight. This may require losing weight. Reducing caloric intake, adding or increasing regular exercise, and giving it time can get a person to his or her healthy weight. To maintain a healthy weight, a person's diet should be mainly vegetables, fruits, whole grains, and fat-free or low-fat milk and milk products. It should include some lean meats, poultry, fish, beans, eggs, and nuts. It is important to keep such a diet low in saturated fats, trans fats, cholesterol, salt (sodium), and sugar. Most important, the diet should stay within the person's daily calorie needs. Individuals should consult a doctor to help design optimal programs of healthy diet to promote weight loss or weight maintenance, especially if disease processes are already present.

Limited Alcohol Consumption

As described in the Risk Factors section, too much alcohol consumption increases the risk of cardiovascular disease and stroke. Other foods, such as red grapes and red grape juice, contain antioxidants that are similar to those in red wine and are a healthier choice. According to the American Heart Association ("Alcohol and Heart Disease"), recommended limits are "one to two drinks per day for men and one drink per day for women. (A drink is one 12 oz. beer, 4 oz. of wine, 1.5 oz. of 80-proof spirits, or 1 oz. of 100-proof spirits.)"

Regular Exercise

Like any muscle, the heart needs regular exercise to keep it fit. Exercising regularly also helps achieve the goal of getting to and maintaining a healthy weight. Activities can range from doing yard work to walking, to taking part in fitness classes, to running, bicycling, swimming, or rollerblading. Whatever the exercise, it needs to be worked into a person's weekly schedule and be of sufficient duration to be of benefit. A weekly mix of moderate-intensity aerobic activity and vigorous-intensity aerobic activity is often recommended. For example, a 30-minute walk plus 15 minutes of lap swimming each weekday would be a good plan. A doctor should be consulted before beginning any exercise program, especially if disease processes are already present.

Smoking Cessation

Stopping smoking is the single most important step people can take to reduce the risk of heart attack, regardless of how long or how much they have smoked. To stop smoking requires willingness to stop, a plan to stop, and in some cases a doctor's help. Diagnosis of a heart disease may provide the impetus to stop smoking. Support from family and friends can help a person be successful in stopping smoking. A simple plan involves reducing smoking in small steps over time and replacing the urge to smoke with healthy alternatives. A doctor can prescribe nicotine patches or other medications that provide the addictive nicotine to the patient in decreasing doses.

Stress Reduction

Stress is a major part of modern daily life. It can lead to a variety of diseases (such as heart disease and stroke) and other problems if not properly handled. Stress can be caused by physical, chemical, or emotional factors. Stress causes the body to release adrenaline, which increases heart rate and blood pressure. If stress continues for long periods, cardiovascular damage may result. Compounding the risk, to cope with stress a person may overeat, smoke, or develop other bad habits that can also affect the heart.

Stress reduction involves many facets of life. Some of the stress reduction methods are also known to help improve heart health, including talking with family and friends, exercising regularly, laughing, pacing life so time is not an issue, getting enough good sleep, and prioritizing to focus on important issues. Yoga, breathing exercises, and meditation are known to reduce stress. Whatever method is used, it must become a lifelong habit to be most effective.

Resources for Further Information on Risks and Prevention

Books

➢ American Medical Association, Martin S. Lipsky, Marla Mendelson, Stephen Havas, and Michael Miller. *American Medical Association Guide to Preventing and Treating Heart Disease: Essential Information You and Your Family Need to Know about Having a Healthy Heart.* Hoboken, NJ: John Wiley, 2008. Print.
From the experts associated with the American Medical Association, this comprehensive resource includes prevention and risk factors of heart and cardiovascular disease.

➢ Brill, Janet B. *Prevent a Second Heart Attack: 8 Foods, 8 Weeks to Reverse Heart Disease.* New York, NY: Three Rivers Press, 2011. Print.
Written for the patient in three sections: How You Got Heart Disease in the First Place; Reversing Heart Disease with Eight Foods and Exercise; and The Prevent a Second Heart Attack Plan in Action. As with most legitimate self-help manuals, this book states that readers should first get the approval of their cardiologist before beginning to follow the Mediterranean-style diet advocated within.

➢ Esselstyn, Caldwell B. *Prevent and Reverse Heart Disease: The Revolutionary, Scientifically Proven, Nutrition-Based Cure.* New York, NY: Avery, 2008. Print.
For 35 years Esselstyn, MD, FACS, has, according to his biography, performed research and was trained as a surgeon at the Cleveland Clinic. Esselstyn has personally "followed a plant-based diet for more than 26 years." The book offers a heart-healthy vegetarian lifestyle guide to prevent and reverse heart disease.

> Khaleghi, Murdoc. *The Everything Guide to Preventing Heart Disease: All You Need to Know to Lower Your Blood Pressure, Beat High Cholesterol, and Stop Heart Disease in Its Tracks* (Everything Series). Avon, MA: Adams Media, 2011. Print.
> Written for the patient, this book contains reliable, science-based information about managing conditions and preventing heart disease. Author Khaleghi is "an emergency physician attending in Massachusetts. After studying biomedical engineering and medicine at the University of California, San Diego, he trained in emergency medicine through Tufts University."

> Labus, Diane. *Cardiovascular Care Made Incredibly Easy!* (Incredibly Easy! Series). Philadelphia, PA: Lippincott Williams and Wilkins, 2008. Print.
> Although this book is written for nurses, the easy-to-understand-format might offer additional understanding for laypersons in cardiovascular assessment, prevention, and risk reduction. To test reading comprehension, a Practice Makes Perfect test is included, with the answers following the test.

> Lippincott. *Cardiovascular Care Made Incredibly Visual!* (Incredibly Easy! Series). Philadelphia, PA: Lippincott Williams and Wilkins, 2011. Print.
> Although this book is written for nurses, the easy-to-understand-visual format might offer additional understanding for laypersons in cardiovascular assessment, prevention, and risk reduction.

> Stein, Richard. *Outliving Heart Disease: The 10 New Rules for Prevention and Treatment*. New York, NY: Newmarket Press, 2008. Print.
> Stein, who is the director of preventive cardiology at Beth Israel Hospital; professor of clinical medicine at the Albert Einstein College of Medicine in New York; and professor of medicine and director of the Urban Community Cardiology Program of New York University School of Medicine (NYC), writes an easy-to-understand and follow 10-rule guidebook in preventing and treating heart disease, with each rule described extensively in separate chapters.

Brochures, Booklets, and Other Short Print Publications

> American Heart Association (AHA). http://www.heart.org/.
> The following brochures can be ordered by filling in a form online. Also available are risk factor information packets that contain these brochures. If interested, complete the product information form online. No more than one packet per household can be ordered at no cost.
>   • "Heart-Health Screenings" (Reference Chart). http://www.heart.org/ HEARTORG/Conditions/Heart-Health-Screenings_UCM_428687_Article .jsp; alternate path: http://www.heart.org/, search for and then click on the title "Heart Health Screenings." Download and print this patient-friendly

AHA PDF two-page quick reference chart titled Recommended Screenings and Risk Factors.

- Risk factors educational brochures. http://www.heart.org/HEARTORG/ General/Order-American-Heart-Association-Educational-Brochures _UCM_312777_Article.jsp; alternate path: http://www.heart.org/, search for "educational brochures," click on the title "Order American Heart Association Educational Brochures," and then click on the topic "risk factors." Available brochures include "Controlling Your Risk Factors," "Life's Simple 7: Seven Simple Steps to a Healthier Heart," and "My Personal Health Tracker."

➤ CardioSmart—"CardioSmart Patient Fact Sheets (PDFs)." https://www.cardiosmart .org/Heart-Conditions/Fact-Sheets; alternate path: https://www.cardiosmart.org/, search for "fact sheet" and then click on the title "CardioSmart Patient Fact Sheets."

CardioSmart provides a comprehensive list of easy-to-use consumer-friendly patient fact sheets in PDF form for free download. Scroll down to choose from multiple categories, including "Major Risk Factors," "Exercise," "Healthy Eating and Weight Management," and "Your Health." Click on any relevant category to see the fact sheets available on that topic. Also, check out the homepage at https://www.cardiosmart.org/ for news. According to the American College of Cardiology (ACC), "CardioSmart is the patient education and support program launched by the [ACC]. Our mission is to engage, inform, and empower patients to better prepare them for participation in their own care."

➤ National Stroke Association—*Hope: A Stroke Recovery Guide* (Chapter 3). http:// www.stroke.org/site/DocServer/hope3.pdf?docID=523; alternate path: http://www .stroke.org/, under the menu heading "Recovery," scroll down to click on the title "HOPE Guide," and then scroll down to click on "Chapter Three" to view and download this section as a PDF.

The National Stroke Association provides an excellent comprehensive stroke recovery guide in PDF format on preventing another stroke. The guide is divided into four chapters, each of which can be downloaded individually. You can also download the full guide in PDF format at no cost.

Websites

➤ American Heart Association (AHA). http://www.heart.org/.

From the homepage, you can find the following resources by searching for the topic by title.

- "Alcohol and Heart Disease." http://www.heart.org/HEARTORG/Conditions/ More/MyHeartandStrokeNews/Alcohol-and-Heart-Disease_UCM_305173 _Article.jsp. This AHA webpage describes AHA recommended daily alcohol

Online Search Tips

- If you click on a link (e.g., a title) and nothing happens, try this: right-click on that link and then left-click on the option "Open in new window."
- If you experience problems with PDF documents, you can download the latest version of Adobe Reader for free at http://www.adobe.com/products/reader .html or by going to http://www.adobe.com/ and searching for "adobe reader."
- Adobe Flash Player, required to view most short videos, is available as a free download at http://get.adobe.com/flashplayer/; alternate path: http://www .adobe.com/, choose the "Download" tab on the menu bar and select the Adobe Flash Player link.

consumption, cardiovascular risks associated with drinking alcohol, red wine and heart disease, potential benefits of drinking wine or other alcoholic beverages, alcohol and aspirin, and alcohol and pregnancy. AHA also offers a free e-mail sign-up for "Hearth-Health E-news."

- "Cardiac Medications." http://www.heart.org/HEARTORG/Conditions/ HeartAttack/PreventionTreatmentofHeartAttack/Cardiac-Medications_UCM _303937_Article.jsp. This AHA webpage offers a list of common medications and their specific cardiac purpose. A free downloadable PDF chart titled "Cardiac Medications At-A-Glance" is available on this list, which includes name of medication, what the medication does, and reason for medication. AHA also offers a free e-mail sign-up for "Hearth-Health E-news."
- "Heart Disease—The Top 10 Reasons Men Put Off Doctor Visits." http://www .heart.org/HEARTORG/Conditions/More/MyHeartandStrokeNews/Heart -Disease—-The-Top-10-Reasons-Men-Put-Off-Doctor-Visits_UCM_433365 _Article.jsp. This AHA webpage offers a list of reasons men put off doctor check-ups, which can be crucial in prevention of heart and cardiovascular disease. AHA also offers a free e-mail sign-up for "Hearth-Health E-news."
- "Heart-Health Screenings." http://www.heart.org/HEARTORG/Conditions/ Heart-Health-Screenings_UCM_428687_Article.jsp. This AHA webpage describes "screening tests recommended for optimal cardiovascular health," including blood pressure, fasting lipoprotein (cholesterol and triglycerides), body weight, blood glucose, smoking, physical activity, and diet.

➢ Brigham and Women's Hospital (BWH) (Boston, MA)—"Preventing Heart Disease." http://healthlibrary.brighamandwomens.org/HealthCenters/Heart/ Preventing/; alternate path: http://www.brighamandwomens.org/, under the heading "Health Information," click on "Health Information Center," then click on "Heart Information Center," and then scroll down to click on the resource title.

This BWH webpage includes these sections: "Self Care," "Risk Factors," "Smoking," "Blood Pressure," "Diet and Nutrition," "High Blood Cholesterol," "Overweight and Obesity," "Physical Inactivity," "Stress," and "Other Factors." Under the heading "Patients and Visitors" at the top of the screen, click on "Find a Doctor" to search for doctors by name, clinical department, or location. Click on the name of the physician or specialist to view a profile (e.g., specialty, medical board certification, education).

➢ British Heart Foundation (BHF)—"Preventing Heart Disease" and "Risk Factors." https://www.bhf.org.uk/heart-health/prevention.aspx and http://www.bhf.org.uk/research/statistics/risk-factors.aspx; alternate path: http://www.bhf.org.uk/, search for "heart prevention" and "risk factors," and then click on the titles "British Heart Foundation—Preventing Heart Disease" and "British Heart Foundation—Risk Factors."
The BHF webpage on prevention of heart disease describes use of alcohol, family history, healthy eating, risk factors, staying active, smoking, stress, tips for parents, and weight. Also available is a section called "Community: Share Experiences with Others."

➢ CardioSmart. https://www.cardiosmart.org/.
CardioSmart is an easy-to-use consumer-friendly website that provides information on heart disease, including understanding and assessing risk factors. Check out the homepage for news. According to the American College of Cardiology (ACC), "CardioSmart is the patient education and support program launched by the [ACC]. Our mission is to engage, inform, and empower patients to better prepare them for participation in their own care."

- "Heart Disease Risk Assessment." https://www.cardiosmart.org/CardioSmart/Default.aspx?id=298; alternate path: https://www.cardiosmart.org/, search for "risk assessment," and then click on the title "Heart Disease Risk Assessment."
- "Risk Factors for Coronary Artery Disease." https://www.cardiosmart.org/healthwise/te74/49/te7449; alternate path: https://www.cardiosmart.org/, search for and then click on the title "Risk Factors for Coronary Artery Disease." Also, search for and click on the title "Risk Factors" to view the webpage "Ask an Expert—Risk Factors," which includes a vast number of specific heart disease risk factor questions with answers. You can also submit new questions that, according to its website, "are answered by more than two dozen members of the American College of Cardiology who volunteer their time with CardioSmart."

➢ Centers for Disease Control and Prevention (CDC). http://www.cdc.gov/.
The CDC, part of the U.S. Department of Health and Human Service, is a website devoted to the control and prevention of disease. The site offers various

pages dedicated to heart health issues, offering a broad range of information aimed at both consumers and health professionals.

- "Body Mass Index (BMI)." http://www.cdc.gov/healthyweight/assessing/ bmi/index.html; alternate path: http://www.cdc.gov/, search for "BMI," click on "Healthy Weight: Assessing Your Weight: Body Mass Index," and then scroll down to click on "Adult BMI Calculator" (or "Child and Teen BMI Calculator"). These pages offer detailed information on BMI.

- "Division for Heart Disease and Stroke Prevention." http://www.cdc.gov/ dhdsp/; alternate path: http://www.cdc.gov/, search for "heart disease and stroke prevention," and then click on "CDC—Division for Heart Disease and Stroke Prevention." This page links to articles on heart disease topics ranging from facts and statistics to educational materials. Click on the title "Heart Disease" for additional detailed links on risk factors, prevention, symptoms, FAQs, guidelines and recommendations, new articles, and publications and products. Articles written for easy reading are identified. Also available is a sign-up for free e-mail updates.

- "Heart Disease Risk Factors." http://www.cdc.gov/heartdisease/risk_factors .htm; alternate path: http://www.cdc.gov/, search for "heart disease risk factors" and then click on "CDC—DHDSP—Heart Disease Risk Factors." This page offers links to risk factor topics, including conditions (e.g., cholesterol levels, high blood pressure), behavior (e.g., smoking, drinking alcohol, diet, lack of exercise, obesity), and heredity (family history).

- "Men's Health—Heart Disease and Stroke (Cardiovascular Disease)." http:// www.cdc.gov/men/az/heart.htm; alternate path: http://www.cdc.gov/, search for "men's health," click on "CDC—Men's Health—Home," click on "Topics A–Z," scroll down to click on "Diseases and Conditions," and then click on the topic "Heart Disease." This page is dedicated to men's health issues and provides numerous links to articles related to heart disease. Articles written for easy reading are identified. Scrolling down, there are articles on the latest information in risk factors, symptoms, and prevention.

➢ Cleveland Clinic (Cleveland, OH)—"Heart and Vascular Health and Prevention." http://my.clevelandclinic.org/heart/prevention; alternate path: http://my .clevelandclinic.org/, search for "heart disease prevention," and then click on the title "Prevention."

The Cleveland Clinic provides comprehensive patient-friendly information on heart disease and vascular disease prevention. Included is help to find a doctor who manages heart diseases. The Cleveland Clinic also offers a link to "Chat Online with a Heart and Vascular Nurse" where you can speak by phone or submit a question online, along with a section (scroll down to "Web Chats") with links to transcripts on previous prevention chat questions.

➤ EverydayHealth.com—"Preventing Heart Disease." http://www.everydayhealth.com/ heart-health/prevention.aspx; alternate path: http://www.everydayhealth.com/, scroll down to the heading "Heart Health Center," and then scroll down and click on the topic "Preventing Heart Disease."

The EverydayHealth website offers current information on heart disease prevention for the consumer. According to EverydayHealth, the website provides "helpful questions and answers from our board-certified experts at top-tier institutions such as Harvard Medical School, Memorial Sloan-Kettering Cancer Center, Mount Sinai Medical Center, and more."

➤ HeartHub—"HeartHub for Patients." http://www.hearthub.org/.

HeartHub is the American Heart Association's (AHA) portal for information, tools, and resources about cardiovascular disease. Use online tools to understand risks and treatment options. Go to the Search box at the top of the screen to search for your area of interest; the table of contents and index to this book may help you with search terms and their spelling. Go to the blue box titled "Health Centers" for information on arrhythmia, cardiac rehab, cholesterol, heart attack, heart failure, and high blood pressure, among other topics. Below "Health Centers," click on the title for "Video Library" to find videos on conditions, prevention and treatment, getting healthy, and emergency care. Look under the blue box for "Health Centers on the Video Library" page to find a list of "Helpful Tools," such as the "Blood Pressure Tool" on the bottom left-hand side of the page screen per link to see the list of podcasts that you can listen to on your computer or download for use on your iPod or MP3 player. This site provides patient information on healthy living and dealing with various heart conditions. The site has many links to take the user to videos, articles, and tools on such topics as healthy eating, how to do CPR, and warning signs. The American Heart Association's *Heartwire* newsletter has the gateway http://www.theheart.org/ to news and current information on heart issues. It includes sections on acute coronary syndromes, arrhythmias, clinical cardiology, heart failure, hypertension, imaging, interventional surgery, prevention, thrombosis risk, and many other issues.

➤ Hospital of the University of Pennsylvania (HUP) (Philadelphia, PA)— "Preventive Cardiovascular Program." http://www.pennmedicine.org/heart/ patient/clinical-services/preventive-cardiology/; alternate path: http://www .pennmedicine.org/, click on the "Departments and Services" icon (or search for "departments and services"), scroll down to click on the category "Cardiology and Cardiac Surgery," and then scroll down to the heading "Preventive Cardiovascular Medicine."

HUP offers at its Penn Heart and Vascular Center website a wide range of areas of information, including educational programs and events. Their prevention specialist team approach links physicians, nurses, and dieticians for a personalized preventive care program. You can also subscribe to the Penn Heart newsletter.

➤ Johns Hopkins Hospital (Baltimore, MD)—"Ciccarone Preventive Cardiology Center." http://www.hopkinsmedicine.org/heart_vascular_institute/clinical _services/specialty_areas/preventive_cardiology_center.html and http://www .hopkinsmedicine.org/heart_vascular_institute/clinical_services/centers_excellence/ ciccarone_center.html; alternate path: http://www.hopkinsmedicine.org/, search for and then click on "Ciccarone Preventive Cardiology Center," and then click on the title "Ciccarone Center for the Prevention of Heart Disease."
The Ciccarone Center for the Prevention of Heart Disease offers a program to help prevent coronary heart disease events. This webpage offers three areas of interest: history of the center, clinical and research activities at the center, and patient services at the center. Also, click on the heading "Clinical Trials" for links to current trials in various heart and cardiovascular conditions.

➤ Massachusetts General Hospital (MGH) (Boston, MA)—"Cardiovascular Disease Prevention Center." http://www.massgeneral.org/heartcenter/treatmentprograms .aspx?id=1012; alternate path: http://www.massgeneral.org/heartcenter/, search for "heart prevention," and click on the title "Cardiovascular Disease Prevention Center."
The Cardiovascular Disease Prevention Program at the MGH Heart Center website offers links to four prevention programs with a team approach to personalize a prevention program for each patient. There are links to each medical expert (with profiles, e.g., specialty, medical board certification, education). The "About This Program" section describes benefits and commitment of this program at MGH. The "Support and Wellness" section offers patient guides.

➤ Mayo Clinic (Rochester, MN). http://www.mayoclinic.com/.
The Mayo Clinic website offers a variety of resources related to the prevention of heart disease and the risk factors that cause it. To participate in a clinical trial, if available for your cardiology condition, at the Mayo Clinic Heart, Lung, and Blood Research Center, go to http://clinicaltrials.mayo.edu/dspSubthemes .cfm?theme_id=6; alternate path: http://www.mayoclinic.com/, under the heading "Research," click on "Find Clinical Trials," then scroll down and click on "Browse Studies," then click "See All Categories," and finally click on the title "Heart, Lung, and Blood Clinical Trials." For patient services in the various cardiology programs, visit the "Cardiac Surgery" webpage at http://www.mayoclinic .org/cardiac-surgery/ or the "Cardiovascular Diseases" webpage at http://www .mayoclinic.org/cardiovascular-disease/ or the "Vascular and Endovascular Surgery" webpage at http://www.mayoclinic.org/vascular-and-endovascular -surgery/; alternate path: for each topic, http://www.mayoclinic.org/, search for the topic title (e.g., "cardiac surgery") and then click on the corresponding title

(e.g., "Cardiac Surgery at Mayo Clinic"). On the "Cardiac Surgery" and "Cardio-vascular Diseases" webpages, in the "Overview" section, click on "Doctors" to view links to each medical expert (with profiles, e.g., specialty, medical board certification, education). For "Vascular and Endovascular Surgery," click on the "Doctors" tab.

- "Heart Disease: Prevention." http://www.mayoclinic.com/health/heart -disease/DS01120/DSECTION=prevention; alternate path: http://www .mayoclinic.com/, search for "heart disease," click on the title "Heart Disease—Mayo Clinic," and then scroll down to the section titled "Prevention." This section of the Mayo Clinic's website covers age, sex, family history, smoking, diet, blood pressure, blood cholesterol levels, diabetes, obesity, physical activity, stress, and hygiene. Scroll down to the section titled "See Also" for additional topics related to preventing heart disease. Note that there is a tab for "Basic" information and one for more "In-depth" description. Scroll down the "In-Depth" webpage to the section on prevention for several important topics, including "5 Medication-Free Strategies to Help Prevent Heart Disease."

- "Heart Disease: Risk Factors." http://www.mayoclinic.com/health/heart -disease/DS01120/DSECTION=risk-factors; alternate path: http://www .mayoclinic.com/, search for "heart disease," click on the title "Heart Disease—Mayo Clinic," and then scroll down to the section titled "Risk Factors." This section of the Mayo Clinic's website covers heart disease risk factors related to age, sex, family history, smoking, diet, blood pressure, blood cholesterol levels, diabetes, obesity, physical activity, stress, and hygiene. Scroll down to the section titled "See Also" for additional tools and articles related to heart disease risk factors, including a risk calculator, stress symptoms, metabolic syndrome, heart attack, coronary heart disease, small vessel disease, acute coronary syndrome, and Kawasaki disease. Note that there is a tab for "Basic" information and one for more "In-depth" description. Scroll down the "In-Depth" webpage to the section on "Risk Factors" for several relevant topics, including obesity, metabolic syndrome, heart disease in women, a risk calculator, and stress symptoms.

➢ Medicare.gov—"Preventive and Screening Services." http://www.medicare.gov/. From the homepage, you can find the following resources by searching for "preventive services," clicking on "Preventive Services," and then clicking on the specific resource title.

- "Cardiovascular Disease (Behavioral Therapy)." http://www.medicare.gov/ coverage/cardiovascular-disease-behavioral-therapy.html. Here you will find information on how often behavioral therapy is covered, costs, who is eligible, and other resources.

- "Cardiovascular Disease Screenings." http://www.medicare.gov/coverage/cardiovascular-disease-screenings.html. Here you will find information on how often screenings are covered, costs, who is eligible, and other resources. Click also on the headings, including "Manage Your Health," "Medicare Basics," and "Resource Locator." Click on the heading "Home" for links to other consumer-friendly Medicare services and plan comparisons.

➤ MedlinePlus—"Heart Diseases—Prevention." http://www.nlm.nih.gov/medlineplus/heartdiseasesprevention.html; alternate path: http://www.nlm.nih.gov/, under "Databases," click on "MedlinePlus," search for "heart diseases prevention," and then click on the resource title.
MedlinePlus is a component of the National Institutes of Health (NIH) and produced by the National Library of Medicine (NLM) and is updated regularly. This MedlinePlus webpage on prevention of heart diseases offers information via links covering overviews, news, prevention, risk factors, related issues, journal articles, and a specific section focusing on children, teenagers, and women. Printer-friendly patient handouts are available. This website also includes a multimedia section containing health check tools, tutorials, and videos.

➤ National Heart, Lung, and Blood Institute (NHLBI)—"How Does Smoking Affect the Heart and Blood Vessels?" and "What Is Diabetic Heart Disease?" http://www.nhlbi.nih.gov/health/health-topics/topics/smo/ and http://www.nhlbi.nih.gov/health/health-topics/topics/dhd/; alternate path: http://www.nhlbi.nih.gov/, search for "does smoking affect the heart," and then click on the title. Also, search for "diabetic heart disease," and click on the title "What Is Diabetic Heart Disease?—NHLBI, NIH."
NHLBI, a division of National Institutes of Health from the U.S. Department of Health and Human Services, provides additional information on how smoking affects heart and blood vessels, its risks, and the benefits of quitting smoking. The webpage on diabetic heart disease includes definitions, risk factors, and prevention.

➤ National Stroke Association—"Stroke Prevention." http://www.stroke.org/site/PageServer?pagename=prevent; alternate path: http://www.stroke.org/, click on the menu heading "Prevention."
The National Stroke Association provides excellent comprehensive information on the prevention of stroke in three sections: controllable risks, uncontrollable risks, and transient ischemic attack (TIA); there is also a section on recurrent stroke. Sign up for news from the NSA via their "Stay Informed" e-mails.

➤ New York–Presbyterian (NYP) University Hospital of Columbia and Cornell (New York, NY). http://nyp.org/.

The NYP University Hospital of Columbia and Cornell website provides patient-friendly information on preventive cardiology that, according to its website, "supports patient care, education, research, and community and corporate outreach to reduce the burden of cardiovascular disease and to promote heart health. An active working group of more than 40 faculty and staff from New York–Presbyterian/Columbia and New York–Presbyterian/Weill Cornell meets regularly to design, implement, and monitor preventive services at New York–Presbyterian Hospital and in the community."

- "Cardiology: Prevention." http://nyp.org/services/cardiology/; alternate path: http://nyp.org/, search for "preventive cardiology program," click on the title "Cardiology—New York Presbyterian Hospital," and then scroll down to the topic "Prevention." Described at this webpage are the purpose of this program and the types of individualized prevention plans.
- "Cardiology: Risk Factors for Heart Attacks." http://nyp.org/services/cardiology/heart-attack-risk.html; alternate path: http://nyp.org/, search for and click on the title "Risk Factors for Heart Attacks." Discussed on this webpage are the risk factors for heart attacks, who is at risk due to inherited (genetic) or acquired (genetic) factors, and how to manage heart attack risk factors. Click on the link titled "Prevention," and then click on the topic "Learn More about Preventing Cardiovascular Disease."

➢ NHS (National Health Service) Choices—"Cardiovascular Disease—Risk Factors" and "Cardiovascular Disease—Prevention—Adults." http://www.nhs.uk/Conditions/cardiovascular-disease/Pages/Risk-factors.aspx and http://www.nhs.uk/Conditions/cardiovascular-disease/Pages/Prevention-adults.aspx; alternate path: http://www.nhs.uk/, search for "cardiovascular risk factors," and then click on the title "Cardiovascular Risk Factors—NHS Choices—Health A–Z."
NHS Choices provides information on risk factors for cardiovascular disease. Click on the other headings, including "Prevention—Children." The webpage includes helpful videos and health news. According to its website, "NHS Choices is the UK's biggest health website. It provides a comprehensive health information service that puts you in control of your healthcare."

➢ Texas Heart Institute (Houston, TX). http://www.texasheartinstitute.org/.
From the homepage, you can find the following resources by searching for the topic by title; or go to the Heart Information Center, click on "Heart-Health Topics," and then scroll down to select the resource title. To participate in a clinical trial, if available for your cardiology condition, at the Texas Heart Institute Research Laboratory, visit the "Heart Failure Research Laboratory" webpage at http://www.texasheartinstitute.org/Research/hfresearch.cfm (or return to the Texas Heart Institute homepage, click on the heading "Research," and then scroll down and click on the title "Heart Failure Research Laboratory"). Scroll down to

the section "Research Projects," and click on the title "FDA-Approved Clinical Trials." Under the heading "About Us," click on "Professional Staff Directory" to view a list of physicians and specialists (with profiles, e.g., specialty, medical board certification, education).

- "Heart Disease Risk Factors." http://www.texasheartinstitute.org/HIC/ Topics/HSmart/riskfact.cfm. The Texas Heart Institute's Heart Information Center website discusses major risk factors, such as high blood pressure, high blood cholesterol, diabetes, smoking, body mass index, gender, heredity, age, stress, alcohol, and hormones.
- "Heart Disease Risk Factors for Children and Teenagers." http://www .texasheartinstitute.org/HIC/Topics/HSmart/children_risk_factors.cfm. The Texas Heart Institute's Heart Information Center website discusses major risk factors, including high blood pressure, cholesterol, smoking, obesity, body mass index, and physical activity.

➢ WebMD. http://www.webmd.com/.

According to WebMD, "WebMD News is an independent media service designed to provide news, information, and educational material to consumers and physicians. News content created by WebMD is free from influence by sponsors, partners, or other sources." Available is a WebMD's heart health e-mail newsletter.

- "Common Drugs and Medications to Treat Primary Prevention of Coronary Heart Disease." http://www.webmd.com/drugs/condition-8595-Primary +Prevention+of+Coronary+Heart+Disease.aspx?diseaseid=8595; alternate path: http://www.webmd.com/, search for "primary prevention heart disease," and then click on the title "Drug Results for Heart Disease Primary Prevention" (WebMD Drug Information from First DataBank). The WebMD website offers the latest information on commonly prescribed drugs for primary prevention of heart disease. Each listed medication has a link to detailed, user-friendly information, including uses, side effects, precautions, interactions, and overdose.
- "Heart Disease: Prevention Myths—Topic Overview." http://www.webmd .com/heart-disease/tc/heart-disease-prevention-myths-topic-overview; alternate path: http://www.webmd.com/, search for "heart disease prevention myths," and then click on the title "Heart Disease: Prevention Myths— Topic Overview" (WebMD Medical Reference from Healthwise). The WebMD website offers the latest information on myths that are not effective in prevention of heart disease.
- "Risk Factors for Heart Disease," http://www.webmd.com/heart-disease/ risk-factors-heart-disease, and "Erectile Dysfunction May Signal Heart Disease," http://www.webmd.com/erectile-dysfunction/news/20130129/ erectile-dysfunction-may-signal-hidden-heart-disease; alternate path:

http://www.webmd.com/, search for "risk factors heart disease," and then scroll down to click on the title "Risk Factors for Heart Disease" (WebMD Medical Reference). WebMD website describes the latest information on risk factors for heart disease and offers ways to reduce your risk.

See also CHAPTER 5 *for general drug information websites.*

Webliography

American Heart Association. "Alcohol and Heart Disease." Updated September 20, 2012. http://www.heart.org/HEARTORG/Conditions/More/MyHeartandStrokeNews/Alcohol-and-Heart-Disease_UCM_305173_Article.jsp.

———. "Heart Attack Risk Assessment." Updated September 24, 2012. http://www.heart.org/HEARTORG/Conditions/HeartAttack/HeartAttackToolsResources/Heart-Attack-Risk-Assessment_UCM_303944_Article.jsp.

———. "Lifestyle Changes." Updated January 23, 2013. http://www.heart.org/HEARTORG/Conditions/HeartAttack/PreventionTreatmentofHeartAttack/Lifestyle-Changes_UCM_303934_Article.jsp.

———. "Stress Management." Updated April 4, 2013. http://www.heart.org/HEARTORG/GettingHealthy/StressManagement/Stress-Management_UCM_001082_SubHomePage.jsp.

———. "Understand Your Risk of Heart Attack." Updated January 23, 2013. http://www.heart.org/HEARTORG/Conditions/HeartAttack/UnderstandYourRiskofHeartAttack/Understand-Your-Risk-of-Heart-Attack_UCM_002040_Article.jsp.

Banks, E., G. Joshy, W. P. Abhayaratna, L. Kritharides, P. S. Macdonald, R. J. Korda, and J. P. Chalmers. "Erectile Dysfunction Severity as a Risk Marker for Cardiovascular Disease Hospitalisation and All-Cause Mortality: A Prospective Cohort Study." *PLoS Medicine*, 10, no. 1 (2013): 1–13. http://www.plosmedicine.org/article/info%3Adoi%2F10.1371%2Fjournal.pmed.1001372.

Boston Children's Hospital. "Anorexia Nervosa." Accessed May 19, 2013. http://www.childrenshospital.org/az/Site3172/mainpageS3172P1.html.

Centers for Disease Control and Prevention. "Body Mass Index." Reviewed September 13, 2011. http://www.cdc.gov/healthyweight/assessing/bmi/index.html.

———. "Genomics and Health: Heart Disease and Family History." Reviewed February 13, 2013. http://www.cdc.gov/genomics/resources/diseases/heart.htm.

———. "Healthy Eating for a Healthy Weight." Reviewed September 27, 2012. http://www.cdc.gov/healthyweight/healthy_eating/index.html.

———. "Heart Disease Risk Factors." Reviewed October 26, 2009. http://www.cdc.gov/HeartDisease/risk_factors.htm.

———. "Losing Weight." Reviewed August 17, 2011. http://www.cdc.gov/healthyweight/losing_weight/index.html.

———. "Occupational Heart Disease." Updated August 4, 2010. http://www.cdc.gov/niosh/topics/heartdisease/.

———. "Physical Activity for a Healthy Weight." Updated September 13, 2011. http://www.cdc.gov/healthyweight/physical_activity/index.html.

———. "Stress at Work." Reviewed January 13, 2012. http://www.cdc.gov/niosh/topics/stress/.

Cleveland Clinic. "Heart and Vascular Health and Prevention." Accessed April 4, 2013 (updated daily). http://my.clevelandclinic.org/heart/prevention/smoking/smoking_hrtds.aspx.

eMedicineHealth. "Smoking and Coronary Artery Disease." Revised May 10, 2010. http://www.emedicinehealth.com/smoking_and_coronary_artery_disease-health/article_em.htm.

Health Magazine. "10 Risk Factors for Heart Disease." Updated May 12, 2008. http://www.health.com/health/condition-article/0,,20188499,00.html.

Johns Hopkins Medicine. "The New Blood Lipid Tests—Sizing Up LDL Cholesterol." June 13, 2008. http://www.johnshopkinshealthalerts.com/reports/heart_health/1886–1.html.

Lab Tests Online. "Lp(a)." Modified July 11, 2011. http://labtestsonline.org/understanding/analytes/lp-a/tab/test.

Mayo Clinic. "C-Reactive Protein Test." December 16, 2011. http://www.mayoclinic.com/health/c-reactive-protein/MY01018.

———. "5 Medication-Free Strategies to Help Prevent Heart Disease." January 12, 2011. http://www.mayoclinic.com/health/heart-disease-prevention/WO00041.

———. "Heart Attack: Risk Factors." May 15, 2013. http://www.mayoclinic.com/health/heart-attack/DS00094/DSECTION=risk-factors.

MedicalNewsToday (MNT). "Erectile Dysfunction Linked to Heart Disease." January 30, 2013. http://www.medicalnewstoday.com/articles/255638.php.

MedlinePlus. "Aging Changes in the Heart and Blood Vessels." Updated March 22, 2013. http://www.nlm.nih.gov/medlineplus/ency/article/004006.htm.

———. "Aspirin and Heart Disease." Updated August 28, 2012. http://www.nlm.nih.gov/medlineplus/ency/patientinstructions/000092.htm.

———. "Cardiomyopathy." Updated March 26, 2013. http://www.nlm.nih.gov/medlineplus/cardiomyopathy.html.

———. "C-reactive Protein." Updated March 22, 2013. http://www.nlm.nih.gov/medlineplus/ency/article/003356.htm.

———. "Heart Attack." Updated May 16, 2013. http://www.nlm.nih.gov/medlineplus/heartattack.html.

———. "Heart Disease in Women." Updated May 15, 2013. http://www.nlm.nih.gov/medlineplus/heartdiseaseinwomen.html.

———. "Heart Diseases—Prevention." Updated May 17, 2013. http://www.nlm.nih.gov/medlineplus/heartdiseasesprevention.html.

————. "High Blood Pressure." Updated May 16, 2013. http://www.nlm.nih.gov/medlineplus/highbloodpressure.html.

Medscape Today: Medscape Cardiology. "Assessing the Risk for Development of Heart Disease—The Role of Genetics: An Expert Interview with John P. Kane, MS, MD, PhD." Accessed April 4, 2013. http://www.medscape.org/viewarticle/707881. (Free registration is required.)

Mimić-Oka, Jasmina, Dragan V. Simić, and Tatjana P. Simić. "Free Radicals in Cardiovascular Diseases." *Facta Universitatis—Medicine and Biology*, 6, no. 1 (1999): 11–22. http://facta.junis.ni.ac.rs/mab/mab99/mab99–02.pdf.

National Diabetes Information Clearinghouse. "Diabetes, Heart Disease, and Stroke." Updated December 7, 2012. http://diabetes.niddk.nih.gov/dm/pubs/stroke/.

National Heart, Lung, and Blood Institute. "Calculate Your Body Mass Index." Accessed April 4, 2013. http://www.nhlbisupport.com/bmi/.

————. "Expert Panel on Integrated Guidelines for Cardiovascular Health and Risk Reduction in Children and Adolescents: Summary Report." Accessed April 4, 2013. http://www.nhlbi.nih.gov/guidelines/cvd_ped/summary.htm#chap1.

————. "The Heart Truth for African American Women: An Action Plan." Revised July 2009. http://www.nhlbi.nih.gov/educational/hearttruth/downloads/pdf/factsheet-actionplan-aa.pdf.

————. "What Are Coronary Heart Disease Risk Factors?" Revised February 1, 2011. http://www.nhlbi.nih.gov/health/dci/Diseases/hd/hd_whatare.html.

————. "What Are Overweight and Obesity?" Revised July 13, 2012. http://www.nhlbi.nih.gov/health/dci/Diseases/obe/obe_whatare.html.

————. "What Is a Heart Attack?" Revised March 1, 2011. http://www.nhlbi.nih.gov/health/dci/Diseases/HeartAttack/HeartAttack_WhatIs.html.

————. "What Is Cardiomyopathy?" Revised January 1, 2011. http://www.nhlbi.nih.gov/health/dci/Diseases/cm/cm_what.html.

————. "What Is Cholesterol?" Revised September 19, 2012. http://www.nhlbi.nih.gov/health/dci/Diseases/Hbc/HBC_WhatIs.html.

————. "What Is Diabetic Heart Disease?" Revised September 20, 2011. http://www.nhlbi.nih.gov/health/health-topics/topics/dhd/.

————. "What Is High Blood Pressure?" Revised August 2, 2012. http://www.nhlbi.nih.gov/health/dci/Diseases/Hbp/HBP_WhatIs.html.

University of Maryland Medical Center. "Eating Disorders—Complications of Anorexia." Reviewed January 22, 2009. http://www.umm.edu/patiented/articles/how_serious_anorexia_nervosa_000049_5.htm.

U.S. News and World Report, Health. "Best Diets." August 2012. http://health.usnews.com/best-diet.

WebMD, Erectile Dysfunction Health Center. "Erectile Dysfunction May Signal Hidden Heart Disease." Reviewed January 29, 2013. http://www.webmd.com/

erectile-dysfunction/news/20130129/erectile-dysfunction-may-signal-hidden -heart-disease.

WebMD, Heart Disease Health Center. "Exercises to Control Your Cholesterol." Updated June 15, 2012. http://www.webmd.com/cholesterol-management/ features/exercises-to-control-your-cholesterol.

———. "Heart Disease and High Blood Pressure." Reviewed February 22, 2012. http://www.webmd.com/heart-disease/guide/heart-disease-prevent.

———. "Heart Disease and Lowering Cholesterol." Reviewed October 10, 2011. http://www.webmd.com/heart-disease/guide/heart-disease-lower-cholesterol-risk.

———. "Heart Disease and Stress." Reviewed August 23, 2012. http://www.webmd .com/heart-disease/guide/stress-heart-attack-risk.

———. "Heart Disease: Exercise for a Healthy Heart." Reviewed September 21, 2012. http://www.webmd.com/heart-disease/guide/exercise-healthy-heart.

———. "Silent Risk: Women and Heart Disease." Reviewed January 28, 2005. http://www.webmd.com/heart-disease/guide/women-more-afraid-of-breast-cancer -than-heart-disease.

———. "Smoking and Heart Disease." Reviewed May 12, 2012. http://www.webmd .com/heart-disease/guide/smoking-heart-disease.

———. "Tips for Reducing Heart Disease Risk." Reviewed May 12, 2012. http://www .webmd.com/heart-disease/guide/heart-disease-risk-factors.

WebMD, Heart Health Center. "New Genetic Links to Heart Disease." March 8, 2011. http://www.webmd.com/heart/news/20110308/new-genetic-links-to-heart -disease.

WebMD, Stress Management Health Center. Homepage. Accessed April 4, 2013. http://www.webmd.com/balance/stress-management/default.htm.

———. "Stress Management—Ways to Relieve Stress." Updated April 20, 2011. http://www.webmd.com/balance/stress-management/stress-management -relieving-stress.

Chapter 7

Quality of Life with Heart Disease

When a person learns that he or she has a heart disease, life changes for that person. To improve heart health, a new patient may have to break old habits and develop new ones; some of the topics presented in Chapter 6 on heart disease prevention may need to become part of a heart disease patient's routine. There is an adjustment period for significant changes in the patient's life. For example, if he or she receives an implanted heart device, it may take getting used to having the implant periodically checked or to hearing a prosthetic valve's click as the heart beats. There is a learning phase in which the new patient finds out the particulars of heart disease, there may be surgery and a rehabilitation period, and it is hoped that there may again be a return to a normal life—but a healthier life. It takes effort and time, but it is worth it for the patient and his or her family.

Most of this book contains resources for patients and their families to help them understand particular conditions. Patients might benefit from this book as a prelude to discussions with their doctor; patients who know about their own type of heart disease will be able to speak the same language during clinical visits and reduce the risk of misunderstandings and miscommunication. However, as with all diseases, patients should first consult their doctor before trying anything recommended in this book or in the cited references. Heart disease can be especially trying for patients, physically and emotionally, and they should take all necessary steps to reduce these stressors. *See* RESOURCES FOR FURTHER INFORMATION ON QUALITY OF LIFE WITH HEART DISEASE; *see also* CHAPTER 6: PREVENTION.

Caregivers, whether family members or professionals, have a responsibility to their patients and to themselves. Finding needed devices, training, supplies, and help can be difficult. Stress and depression are other issues faced by caregivers. It is equally important for caregivers to take time to care for themselves; well-equipped, well-rested, and unstressed caregivers are better able to provide good care for their patients. For example, having a patient-lift device allows the caregiver to lift and move the patient with ease. The resources section of this chapter includes some sources for caregiver information. (*See, for instance,* RESOURCES FOR PATIENTS AND CAREGIVERS *in the* BROCHURES, BOOKLETS, AND OTHER SHORT PRINT PUBLICATIONS *section.*) The Websites section includes numerous links to caregiver resources, for example, the American Heart Association's "AgingCare.com—Connecting People Caring for Elderly Parents," the American Geriatrics Society's Foundation for Health in Aging, the Family Caregiver Alliance, HeartHub for Patients, and USA.gov's section

"Senior Citizens' Resources: Caregivers' Resources." *See also* CHAPTER 6: PREVENTION for caregiver issues.

All references on quality of life with heart disease are at the end of this chapter in Resources for Patients; Resources for Caregivers; and Resources for Further Information on Quality of Life.

Diet, Nutrition, and Weight Management

Eating heart-healthy foods, including vegetables, fruits, whole grains, nuts, seeds, beans, low-fat dairy, and fish, as well as other foods that are low in saturated fat, cholesterol, and sodium, can help patients manage their blood pressure, cholesterol levels, and weight.

Limiting or eliminating red meat might be beneficial, because it might not be only the fat in red meat that is detrimental. Eating red meat releases the enzyme L-carnitine into the gut. The gut's intestinal bacteria can break L-carnitine down into TMAO (trimethylamine-N-oxide). L-carnitine is also a naturally produced amino acid that helps break down fatty acids in mitochondria to release energy as well as break down fat. In addition, L-carnitine is added as a protein supplement to many energy drinks that claim to boost energy; however, the body usually makes all it needs. Consequently, increasing L-carnitine intake causes the gut bacteria to flourish and to continue to break down the enzyme and thus produce even more TMAO. In a study, lab tests showed that vegans and vegetarians had fewer of these microbes and less TMAO than did red meat eaters. Results published in *Nature Medicine* from this study comparing red meat eaters to vegans and vegetarians revealed that high blood levels of TMAO affect how blood cholesterol metabolizes, which might lead to clogging and hardening of the arteries (atherosclerosis) in those who often eat red meat, as reported by lead researcher, Stanley Hazan, section head of preventive cardiology and rehabilitation in the Miller Family Heart and Vascular Institute at Cleveland Clinic (Koeth et al., 2013). In this cohort study of 2,595 volunteers, each participant underwent a cardiovascular evaluation, and analysis of the data indicated those with high blood levels of TMAO were associated with an increased risk for heart attack, stroke, or death. Hazan concluded from this study, which also included comparing meat-fed and non-meat-fed mice, that a "byproduct that the microbes make gets released and converted in our bodies and then detected in the blood into a compound that actually helps promote clogging of the arteries or cholesterol deposition in the artery wall. . . . It actually works through cholesterol. It changes how our body senses cholesterol and metabolizes cholesterol at the artery wall, in the liver and in the intestines."

U.S. News and World Report has ranked the top four heart-healthy diets for 2013: the Ornish diet; the TLC (Therapeutic Lifestyle Changes) and DASH (Dietary

Approaches to Stop Hypertension) diets, both developed by the National Institutes of Health; and the Mediterranean Diet. The DASH and TLC diets were rated the top two overall diets for maintaining a healthy lifestyle (*see* WEBLIOGRAPHY *for details*). Maintaining a healthy weight range lowers a person's risk for heart disease in general, and peer-reviewed studies have indicated that limiting alcohol intake to one serving per day for women and two servings per day for men can help individuals stay heart healthy. While limiting alcohol intake lowers blood pressure by two to four points and increases high-density lipoprotein (HDL—the "good cholesterol"), excessive alcohol drinking raises blood pressure, damages heart muscles (progressing to heart failure), and increases the risk of a stroke or heart attack (*see also* CHAPTER 6: PREVENTION: LIMIT ALCOHOL CONSUMPTION).

Following the Mediterranean diet may help reduce the risk of heart attack, stroke, and death from heart disease by approximately 30 percent, according to the first randomized, controlled trial to measure those outcomes by meticulously comparing patients following a Mediterranean diet versus those following a low-fat diet. This major trial, which ran from October 2003 to June 2009, included 7,447 people (age range 55 to 80) who had at least three major cardiovascular disease (CVD) risk factors. The results were so remarkable and pronounced that the authors did not want to prevent those in the study who were not on the Mediterranean diet from benefiting from it, so they ended the trial early (4.8 years) (Estruch et al., 2013).

In addition, another cohort study, which contained a random selection of 43,000 Swedish women (aged 30 to 49 years) who were followed for an average of 15.7 years, concluded that using a long-term (e.g., numerous years) high-protein/low-carbohydrate diet increases the risk of cardiovascular disease by 28 percent (Lagiou et al., 2012). Although the risk is low, many heart specialists, such as Dr. Gregg Fornarow, chairman of cardiovascular medicine and science at the University of California, Los Angeles, are not convinced. Fornalow commented: "This study raises concerns about the long-term effects on cardiovascular health of low-carbohydrate, high-protein diets—particularly if there is not careful consideration given to whether plant versus animal proteins are consumed."

A customized food plan that complements a patient's lifestyle and food preferences might be helpful. According to the article titled "How to Eat Well: What You'd Learn If You Had Your Own Nutrition Pro" (*Educational Blog*), a registered dietician (RD) works with clients to devise a practical food strategy that fits their lifestyles and family situations, including family members with and without heart disease, while keeping the menu heart healthy to benefit the person who has been diagnosed with CVD.

An RD is a title certified by the Commission on Dietetic Registration, the credentialing agency for the Academy of Nutrition and Dietetics (http://cdrnet.org/). An RD must also take continuing education classes to maintain certification. Note that someone claiming to be a certified "nutritionist" might not be a certified RD. "Nutritionist" is a title that is not nationally regulated. Other dietitian nutritionist certifications that are licensed in some states are certified nutrition specialist (certified by the Certification Board for Nutrition Specialists, http://cbns.org/), certified clinical nutritionist (certified by the Clinical Nutrition Certification Board, http://www.cncb.org/), and diplomate of the American Clinical Board of Nutrition (accredited by the American Clinical Board of Nutrition, http://www.acbn.org/). However, some states, such as Illinois (as of January 28, 2013), do not license dietitian nutritionists, certified nutrition consultants, certified nutritionists, certified health coaches, or holistic nutritionists.

Before creating a plan of food choices and menus, an RD reviews a client's food likes and dislikes, food allergies, weight issues, personal health history, family medical history, lifestyle (e.g., single, have children, travel for work), "current lab results . . . and nutritional concerns." The *ShopSmart* article "How to Eat Well" also recommends that, before meeting with an RD, it would be beneficial to create a daily food log for a week or two of what the client regularly eats, how much, and how often, including at restaurants. An alternative is to use a cell phone to create a photo diary or log of what the patient eats during that time period. Current smartphone apps that might be useful for this task include MyFitnessPal (http://www.myfitnesspal.com/) and SparkPeople (http://www.sparkpeople.com/).

To find a locally based RD, visit the Academy of Nutrition and Dietetics website for consumers at http://www.eatright.org/ (for details, *see* RESOURCES FOR FURTHER INFORMATION: WEBSITES).

Cardiac Rehabilitation

Cardiac rehabilitation brings together all the elements of obtaining and maintaining a healthy heart with the support of nurses and physicians to educate, encourage, and establish lifestyle changes that can minimize, if not prevent, future heart problems. The program usually is started in the hospital after a patient has had a heart attack or heart surgery and continues on an outpatient basis. A long-term program is developed for the patient that includes medical evaluation, prescribed exercise, cardiac risk factors modification, education, and counseling. The clinical team involved includes the patient's doctors (such as a family doctor, a heart specialist, and a surgeon), nurses, exercise specialists, physical and occupational therapists, dietitians or nutritionists, and psychologists or other mental health specialists. A case manager usually is involved to track the patient's care and coordinate the program. The success of a regimen such as this depends on long-term commitments by the patient and the clinical team to make and maintain the needed changes. While most programs last three months, they can vary from six weeks to several years. By the time the program is complete, it should have become part of the patient's lifestyle, and the patient is expected to be willing and able to continue with it independently.

Preventive cardiac care is an evolving therapy intended to head off or delay cardiac disease. Preventive cardiac care includes nutritional therapies, weight loss programs, management of lipid abnormalities with diet and medication, blood pressure control, diabetes management, and stress management. As with cardiac rehabilitation, preventive cardiac care should be done under a doctor's supervision and requires the patient to commit to the care program.

Emotional Support and Stress

Managing stress lowers blood pressure and reduces risks for recurring heart attacks and atherosclerosis, as well as other heart disease complications, according to a report by Guliksson and colleagues (2011). Anger alone may initiate a heart attack. Patients who learn relaxation, yoga, or breathing techniques and those who participate in stress-management programs may be able to reduce their stress levels. And though it may seem a simple idea, patients should be aware that talking with someone—a family member, a friend, a counselor, or a health care professional—about problems or concerns has been shown to help lift the burden of stress.

Exercise

The heart, like any other muscle, grows stronger as it is exercised. With many heart problems and their treatments, a regular, doctor-supervised exercise program is recommended to keep the heart healthy or to improve its health. Such programs can vary widely—from taking short walks, pushing a grocery cart, or gardening to engaging in more vigorous activities such as swimming, running, biking, and doing other aerobic exercises. (An aerobic exercise is one that works the lungs and heart.) Most programs start new patients at a low rate or low stress set of exercises and work up to more strenuous exercise, depending on the condition of the heart and other health conditions. The goal is to get the heart as healthy as it can be and improve the patient's quality of life.

A healthy heart exercise program should be part of every person's life, even for those people who do not have heart conditions. Studies have found that 30 minutes of exercise five days each week can lower blood pressure, lower cholesterol, and help maintain weight. Lower levels of exercise also provide some benefit. People who exercise are less likely to die an early death than are people who do not exercise at all.

For patients who need encouragement, regularly scheduled cardio workout parties, which combine exercise and fun with friends, are becoming increasingly popular at "local gyms and exercise studios," as described in the article written by Dimity McDowell titled "Move Over Book Club, Fitness Parties Are Hot." A gym's personal trainer may be able to "customize a workout for you and your friends" that will fit a heart-healthy lifestyle safely.

When a heart has been damaged, part of the recovery process involves exercise. Like moving an injured limb after it has healed, working the heart back to health requires exercise that slowly improves the heart's function. Eventually, an exercise program becomes part of a patient's life to help maintain quality of life and extend life as long as possible.

Health Coaching

Health coaching "can be defined as helping patients gain the knowledge, skills, tools and confidence to become active participants in their care so that they can reach their self-identified health goals" (Bennett et al., 2012). A study published in the *Annals of Family Medicine* (Margolius et al., 2012) involved 237 patients with tension who were regularly guided by a personal health coach. They significantly lowered their blood pressure (by an average of 22 mm Hg systolic) and lowered the number of health checks needed with their primary care physician. Many health insurance companies and Medicare now agree that health coaching improves patient quality of life, can lower health risks, and can improve patient health care satisfaction, while also reducing overall health care costs by decreasing hospital readmissions and doctor visits. Patients must check with their health insurance provider to determine whether their plan covers a personal health coach—particularly if patients have a chronic condition (e.g., cardiovascular disease).

Home Health Care (Caregivers)

Home health care for a cardiac patient is possible but requires time, money, patience, and determination. Home health care may be taken on in the short term, for example, to assist a patient until recovery is sufficient to allow him or her to function without help; in other situations, such care may be especially difficult for the caregiver, such as when caring for a patient who will likely die soon. Home health care for heart disease patients may require simple or complex skills, depending on an individual patient's condition. For example, a patient with high blood pressure may need help monitoring blood pressure, taking medications, eating a healthy diet, being encouraged or assisted to exercise, and controlling stress. In addition to those needs, a patient with the potential for heart failure may also need special monitoring, emergency treatment devices, help getting dressed and bathing, and round-the-clock care. Some families and close friends learn to provide such care; caregivers can also be hired to provide simple to specialized home care. Some hospices or nursing homes can provide a home-like setting with specialized care.

Home health care for the cardiac patient may require a variety of special devices. These devices can be simple, including grabbing sticks, shower seats, walkers, grab bars, oxygen supplies, and scooters, and their presence and proper use can help make the patient more mobile and independent. More complex devices may be needed, such as a heart monitor, a patient lift, an automatic external defibrillator, or a hospital bed for a patient with a more serious condition. Some of these devices can present serious hazards if improperly used. For example, oxygen supplies present hazards of frostbite, fire, and explosion. If used improperly a patient can fall from a lift, walker, or wheelchair.

No matter who the chosen caregivers are, all caregivers should know how to take basic vital signs like heart rate and blood pressure, perform cardiopulmonary resuscitation (CPR), use an automated external defibrillator (AED), use heart monitoring devices, understand the patient's medications and their uses and effects, and know when to call the patient's doctor or get the patient to a hospital. A caregiver might need to be strong enough to lift a patient during dressing, bathing, or ambulating. Caregivers need considerable amounts of patience in dealing with common issues of home health care, such as patients who are resistant to care, worried families, helping with grocery shopping or house cleaning, and dealing with various other kinds of requests for help. Caregivers also provide emotional help to families and patients to help them get through the issues of the patient's disease. Alternatives to home health care include adult day care, assisted living housing, and hospices that provide skilled nursing and physician care. These can be costly but are sometimes covered by governmental and private health care plans.

Regular Heart Health Screenings

Blood pressure, cholesterol levels, and blood sugar levels (especially in diabetics) should be routinely checked to make sure measurements are within recommended ranges. A physician or other health care professional can determine how often these tests are needed.

Smoking Cessation

As discussed in previous chapters, stopping smoking has the largest impact in reducing a patient's risk for getting heart disease or complications from heart disease. *See* CHAPTER 6: SMOKING AND PREVENTION: STOP SMOKING.

Staying Healthy

For those who already have heart disease, viral and bacterial infections can place added stress on the heart. Patients should wash their hands regularly and stay away from people who have infectious diseases, including cold or flu. They should be encouraged to have a flu shot; doing so has been shown to reduce heart attack risk in CVD patients. On a related note, germs from a patient's mouth can travel toward the heart and embed into plaque, exacerbating CVD. Patients should floss and brush their teeth at least twice a day to help counteract this process.

Resources for Further Information on Quality of Life with Heart Disease

Books

Resources Specifically on Speaking to Your Doctor

> Korsch, Barbara M., and Caroline Harding. *The Intelligent Patient's Guide to the Doctor–Patient Relationship: Learning How to Talk So Your Doctor Will Listen.* London: Oxford University Press, 1998. Print.
> For those who are concerned about their health and who want to take control of their medical care, this book discusses and gives examples of asking the right questions and provides advice on finding a doctor who will listen to you. This book gives you the tools and the confidence to talk meaningfully with your health care team.

> Rimmerman, Curtis. *The Cleveland Clinic Guide to Speaking with Your Cardiologist* (Cleveland Clinic Guides). New York, NY: Kaplan, 2009. Print.
> Written for the patient on topics such as choosing a cardiologist, the first meeting with a new doctor, maximizing the usefulness of an appointment, and continuing the information exchange with health care professionals. Chapters discuss diagnostic tests, treatments, medications, and managing heart health. Included in the appendix is a section on preparing for a doctor's appointment.

Resources for Patients and Caregivers

> American Heart Association (AHA). *American Heart Association Low-Fat, Low-Cholesterol Cookbook: Delicious Recipes to Help Lower Your Cholesterol,* 4th ed. New York, NY: Clarkson Potter, 2010. Print.
> Experts explain the effects of fats and cholesterol on heart health; the value of healthy food for a healthy heart; an extensive listing of recipes, from appetizers to main meals to desserts; and an appendix with how-to strategies on healthy

shopping, cooking, and eating out. There is additional information on risk factors and the "science behind the recommendations." AHA has several other heart-healthy cookbooks available in print: *The New American Heart Association Cookbook*, 8th ed., New York, NY: Clarkson Potter, 2010; *American Heart Association Healthy Family Meals: 150 Recipes Everyone Will Love*, New York, NY: Clarkson Potter, 2011; *American Heart Association Low-Salt Cookbook: A Complete Guide to Reducing Sodium and Fat in Your Diet*, 4th ed. New York, NY: Clarkson Potter, 2011; *American Heart Association Quick and Easy Cookbook: More Than 200 Healthful Recipes You Can Make in Minutes*, New York, NY: Clarkson Potter, 2001; *Eat Less Salt: An Easy Action Plan for Finding and Reducing the Sodium Hidden in Your Diet*, New York, NY: Clarkson Potter, 2013.

➤ Casey, Aggie, and Herbert Benson. *Harvard Medical School Guide to Lowering Your Blood Pressure* (Harvard Medical School Guides). New York, NY: McGraw-Hill, 2006. Print.
Casey, an associate in medicine at Harvard Medical School, and Benson, an associate professor of medicine at Harvard Medical School, cowrote this patient-friendly guide to lowering blood pressure through relaxation techniques and exercise.

➤ Cleveland Clinic, Bonnie Sanders Polin, and Frances Towner Giedt. *Cleveland Clinic Healthy Heart Lifestyle Guide and Cookbook: Featuring More Than 150 Tempting Recipes*. New York, NY: Clarkson Potter, 2007. Print.
Using the expertise of the Cleveland Clinic, heart specialists created an easy-to-use consumer-oriented how-to-book to be proactive in lowering risk; this book includes a lifestyle guide that stresses maintaining a healthy body weight and learning to love heart-healthy recipes.

➤ Franklin, Barry, and Joseph Piscatella. *Prevent, Halt, and Reverse Heart Disease: 109 Things You Can Do*. New York, NY: Workman, 2011. Print.
Franklin, who is the director of the Cardiac Rehabilitation and Exercise Laboratories in Royal Oak, Michigan, as well as professor at Wayne State University School of Medicine and the University of Michigan Medical School, helps the patient with a practical plan of action by assessing risk, managing daily stress, setting up an exercise plan, and managing diet.

➤ Gillinov, Marc, and Steven Nissen. *Heart 411: The Only Guide to Heart Health You'll Need*. New York, NY: Three Rivers Press, 2012. Print.
In this book Nissen, who is chairman of the Department of Cardiovascular Medicine, and Gillinov, who is a staff cardiac surgeon, both at Cleveland Clinic, have written a patient-friendly comprehensive 560-page book on managing lifestyle changes for those with heart or cardiovascular disease.

➤ Griffith, Winter H. *Griffith's Instructions for Patients*, 8th ed. Philadelphia, PA: W. B. Saunders, 2010. Online and Print.

This collection of one-page fact sheets and summaries includes explanations of diseases, special diets, exercise regimens, and illustrations.

➤ Heller, Maria. *The DASH Diet Action Plan: Proven to Lower Blood Pressure and Cholesterol without Medication.* New York, NY: Grand Central Life and Style, 2011. Print.

Heller, a registered dietician with a master of science in human nutrition and dietetics from the University of Illinois at Chicago, provides a user-friendly guide on how to create an individualized "personal DASH diet design" and menu guide, as well as ways to incorporate lifestyle changes to lower high blood pressure.

➤ Lester, Meera, Murdoc Khaleghi, Susan Reynolds, and Brett Aved. *Healthiest You Ever: 365 Ways to Lose Weight, Build Strength, Boost Your BMI, Lower Your Blood Pressure, Increase Your Stamina, Improve Your Cholesterol Levels, and Energize from Head to Toe!* Avon, MA: Adams Media, 2012. Print.

Written for the patient, this book offers a day-by-day guide in food choices, exercise plans, relieving stress, and overall healthy living. One of the coauthors, Khaleghi, is "an emergency physician attending in Massachusetts. After studying biomedical engineering and medicine at the University of California, San Diego, he trained in emergency medicine through Tufts University."

➤ Magee, Elaine. *If I Suffer from Heart Disease: Nutrition You Can Live with (Tell Me What to Eat).* Franklin Lakes, NJ: Career Press, 2010. Print.

Magee, MPH, RD, who is a national columnist and on WebMD.com as "The Recipe Doctor," explains in six sections how to manage what you eat to maintain a healthier heart; the who, what, where, why, and how of heart disease; why it's important to "know your numbers"; 10 steps to slow and possibly reverse heart disease; heart-smart versions of favorite recipes; heart-smart supermarket shopping; and how heart patients can eat healthy when dining out.

➤ Mayo Clinic, Martha Grogan, ed. *Mayo Clinic Healthy Heart for Life! The Mayo Clinic Plan for Preventing and Conquering Heart Disease.* New York, NY: Oxmoor House, 2012. Print.

According to the publisher, this Mayo Clinic book "provides a comprehensive, step by-step plan to reduce the risks and life-changing effects of heart disease . . . [and] provides up-to-date, clinically proven information that addresses the key causes of heart disease and provides clear, actionable advice in an easy-to follow format."

➤ Meyer, Maria M., and Paula Derr. *The Comfort of Home for Chronic Heart Failure: A Guide for Caregivers.* Portland, OR: CareTrust, 2008. Print.

Written for caregivers in three sections, the first section focuses on background knowledge of heart failure, such as definitions, risk factors, diagnosis, treatments, using the health care team effectively, in-home care, and planning for end-of-life care. The second section discusses setting up a plan of care; how to avoid caregiver burnout; activities of daily living; therapies; special challenges; diet, nutrition, and exercise; emergencies; and hospice care. The final section lists additional resources, such as caregiver organizations and specialists that are commonly consulted by heart disease patients and their families.

➤ Mieres, Jennifer H., and Terri Ann Parnell. *Heart Smart for Black Women and Latinas: A 5-Week Program for Living a Heart-Healthy Lifestyle.* New York, NY: St. Martin's Press, 2008. Print.
Mieres, a board-certified cardiologist in New York, discusses heart disease in minorities and focuses on risks, signs and symptoms, treatment, and lifestyle changes to allow readers to take control of their heart health.

➤ Moore, Thomas, and Mark Jenkins. *The DASH Diet for Hypertension.* New York, NY: Free Press, 2011. Print.
According to the introduction, "A world-class team of hypertension and nutrition experts from the medical schools of Harvard, Duke, Johns Hopkins, and Louisiana State University have joined together to produce *The DASH Diet for Hypertension*—a medication-free program to lower blood pressure."

➤ National Heart, Lung, and Blood Institute/National Institutes of Health, U.S. Department of Health and Human Services. *Keep the Beat: Heart Healthy Recipes.* Washington, DC: National Institutes of Health, 2011. Print.
According to the book, "The recipes in this collection grew out of research and education projects supported by the National Heart, Lung, and Blood Institute. The studies and projects dealt with ways to help Americans keep their hearts strong by reducing their intake of calories, fat, especially saturated fat, cholesterol, and sodium." It includes the DASH clinical study and the Stay Young at Heart nutrition education program. The 156-page PDF of this book is free to download and print; visit the NHLBI website at http://www.nhlbi.nih.gov/health/public/heart/other/ktb_recipebk/ktb_recipebk.pdf; alternate path: http://www.nhlbi.nih.gov/health/, click on "Heart and Vascular Diseases," then scroll down to click on "Recipes," and then click on "*Keep the Beat: Heart Healthy Recipes from the National Heart, Lung, and Blood Institute* PDF." From the "Recipes" link you can select from an additional group of heart-healthy, free, downloadable cookbooks. There is also a link to more webpages containing healthy recipes; a "My Recipes" feature that allows users to bookmark and save their favorites; videos on recipe preparation; and an online toolbox.

➤ Piscatella, Joseph, and Barry A. Franklin. *Prevent, Halt, and Reverse Heart Disease: 109 Things You Can Do.* New York, NY: Workman, 2011. Print.
Written for patients, this book offers ways to take control in helping manage heart disease. This book is divided into three sections: how to look for cardiac

markers (risk factors) and know to ask your doctor; life skills—what you can do to lower your risks; and cardiac basics—understanding tests and treatments.

➢ Sinatra, Stephen T., James C. Roberts, with Martin Zucker. *Reverse Heart Disease Now: Stop Deadly Cardiovascular Plaque Before It's Too Late.* Somerset, NJ: Wiley, 2008. Print.
From inside of the book cover, "While most books focus solely on the role of cholesterol in heart disease, *Reverse Heart Disease Now* draws on new research that points to the surprising other causes. Leading cardiologists Dr. Stephen Sinatra and Dr. James Roberts draw on their collective fifty years of clinical cardiology research to show you how to combine the benefits of modern medicine, over-the-counter vitamins and supplements, and simple lifestyle changes to have a healthy heart—whether you have acute or chronic disease or just want to prevent cardiovascular disease from developing."

➢ Wood, Malissa. *Smart at Heart: A Holistic 10-Step Approach to Preventing and Healing Heart Disease for Women.* Berkeley, CA: Celestial Arts, 2011. Print.
Wood, a Harvard-trained cardiologist who is the co-director of the Corrigan Women's Heart Health Program at Massachusetts General Hospital (MGH) and sits on the board of the Northeast Affiliate of the American Heart Association, presents a mind–body program to teach patients strategies to build a stronger and healthier heart.

➢ Zaret, Barry L., and Genell Subak-Sharpe. *Heart Care for Life.* New Haven, CT: Yale University Press, 2006. Print.
This guide to heart care offers specific directions for designing a lifelong heart care program. It is filled with practical advice, instructional case histories, self-tests to assess risk, and questions to ask your doctor.

Brochures, Booklets, and Other Short Print Publications

➢ American Heart Association (AHA). http://www.heart.org/.
  • "Answers by Heart Fact Sheets: Lifestyle and Risk Reduction." http://www.heart .org/HEARTORG/Conditions/More/ToolsForYourHeartHealth/Answers-by -Heart-Fact-Sheets-Lifestyle-and-Risk-Reduction_UCM_300611_Article.jsp; alternate path: http://www.heart.org/, search for "heart fact sheets," and then click on "Answers by Heart Fact Sheets: Lifestyle and Risk Reduction."
  • "Order American Heart Association Educational Brochures." http://www .heart.org/HEARTORG/Conditions/More/ToolsForYourHeartHealth/ Order-American-Heart-Association-Educational-Brochures_UCM_312777 _Article.jsp; alternate path: http://www.heart.org/, search for "educational brochures," click on the title "Order American Heart Association Educational Brochures," and then click on each of the following topics: "Caregiver,"

"Nutrition," "Physical Activity," "Smoking," and "Weight Management." Choose from an extensive list of PDFs offering patient information on lifestyle choices, including the categories mentioned. Each category offers several AHA brochures that can be viewed and downloaded by clicking on the linked titles. Some categories offer information packets as well, which require the completion of an online order form. Note that a maximum of one packet and two brochures per household can be ordered at no cost.

➤ CardioSmart. "CardioSmart Patient Fact Sheets." https://www.cardiosmart.org/Heart-Conditions/Fact-Sheets; alternate path: https://www.cardiosmart.org/, search for "patient fact sheets," and then click on the title.
CardioSmart provides a comprehensive list of easy-to-use consumer-friendly patient fact sheets in PDF form for free download. Scroll down to choose from categories that include "Exercise" and "Healthy Eating and Weight Management." Also, check out the homepage at https://www.cardiosmart.org/ for heart news. According to the American College of Cardiology (ACC), "CardioSmart is the patient education and support program launched by the [ACC]. Our mission is to engage, inform, and empower patients to better prepare them for participation in their own care."

➤ HeartHub for Patients. "Take Control—Medication Chart (for Caregivers)." http://www.heart.org/idc/groups/heart-public/@wcm/@hcm/documents/downloadable/ucm_307467.pdf; alternate path: http://www.hearthub.org/, scroll down to the section "Health Centers" and click on the title "Caregiver," and then scroll down to click on "Medication Chart."
HeartHub is a division of the American Heart Association (AHA). As the accompanying text on its webpage link notes, "Print this handy chart to keep track of the prescription, over-the-counter and herbal drugs being taken."

➤ National Heart, Lung, and Blood Institute (NHLBI). http://www.nhlbi.nih.gov/.
NHLBI, a division of National Institutes of Health from the U.S. Department of Health and Human Services, published the following guidelines, which are available for download. *U.S. News and World Report* news magazine ranked for 2012 the DASH (Dietary Approaches to Stop Hypertension) and the TLC (Therapeutic Lifestyle Changes) diets, both developed by the National institutes of Health, as the top two overall diets to maintain a healthy lifestyle.

  • *Your Guide to Lowering Your Blood Pressure with DASH: The DASH Eating Plan* (Guideline) (PDF). http://www.nhlbi.nih.gov/health/public/heart/hbp/dash/new_dash.pdf; alternate path: http://www.nhlbi.nih.gov/, search for "dash," click on the title "What Is the DASH Eating Plan?," and then scroll down to the link to the PDF guideline title.

  • *Your Guide to Lowering Your Cholesterol with TLC: Therapeutic Lifestyle Changes* (Guideline) (PDF). http://www.nhlbi.nih.gov/health/public/heart/

chol/chol_tlc.pdf; alternate path: http://www.nhlbi.nih.gov/, search for "tlc," and then click on the title "Your Guide to Lowering Your Cholesterol with TLC."

➤ National Stroke Association—*Hope: A Stroke Recovery Guide* (PDF). http://www .stroke.org/site/PageServer?pagename=HOPE; alternate path: http://www.stroke .org/, search for "stroke guide," and then click on the title "HOPE: A Stroke Recovery Guide—National Stroke Association."

The National Stroke Association, which states that "recovery from stroke is a life-long process," provides this excellent stroke recovery guide, which can be viewed and downloaded for free. The guide is divided into four parts: (1) helpful information: a collection of important after-stroke issues and suggestions for how to address these concerns; (2) opportunity through self-advocacy: finding out how to be an active participant in recovery and why it is so important; (3) preventing another stroke: lifesaving information about stroke awareness, symptom recognition, and how to decrease the chances of having another stroke; and (4) exercises and recommendations: two illustrated exercise programs to help the patient improve strength and range of motion.

Health-Oriented Magazines and Journals

Many consumer-oriented magazines and journals whose main focus is to provide information on maintaining a healthy lifestyle are available, and their intended audiences are those with and those without chronic diseases, including cardiovascular disease. While every related magazine cannot be listed, a sampling of well-respected journals was selected, all of which are composed of articles written by authors who have advanced degrees in health and science, including cardiologists. (Note: The authors of this book did not receive any money or other benefits for endorsing these journals.)

➤ American Heart Association (AHA). http://www.heart.org/.

From the homepage, you can find the following and related resources by searching for "patient/caregiver magazines," clicking on "Free Patient/Caregiver Magazines," and then clicking on the title of choice.

• *Heart Insight Magazine* (quarterly). http://www.heart.org/HEARTORG/ Conditions/Free-PatientCaregiver-Magazines_UCM_308720_Article.jsp or http://journals.lww.com/heartinsight/pages/default.aspx. According to the AHA website, this is a "quarterly online magazine to help patients, their families and caregivers manage and prevent cardiovascular disease and related conditions. Access *Heart Insight* online for free."

• *Stroke Connection Magazine* (bimonthly). http://www.strokeassociation.org/ STROKEORG/StrokeConnectionMagazine/InStroke-Connection-Magazine _UCM_308575_SubHomePage.jsp. According to the AHA website, "Our bimonthly magazine is a must-have for stroke survivors and their caregivers. Get your first six issues free with no obligation to purchase future issues."

➤ *Clean Eating.* http://www.cleaneatingmag.com/.
Clean Eating, published eight times per year by Robert Kennedy Publishing (Mississauga, ON, CAN), is a consumer magazine with the motto "Improving your life one meal at a time." The main goal of the magazine is to take "you beyond the food you eat, exploring the multitude of health and nutritional benefits that can be yours when you subscribe to a clean lifestyle," including exercise. The online version includes "Ask the Doctor" (Jonny Bowden, PhD, CNS, a board-certified nutrition specialist) and "Ask the Dietician" (Susan Kleiner, PhD, RD, FACN, CNS, FISSN) sections. Also available is a free online *Clean Eating* newsletter. For customer service: (800) 728–2729.

➤ *Consumer Reports* Health Organization Consumers Union—E-mail newsletters. http://web.consumerreports.org/newsletter/email-newsletters-step1.html; alternate path: http://www.consumerreports.org/cro/health/index.htm/ or http://www.consumerreports.org/, click on "Health," scroll down to "E-Mail Newsletters," and click on "Sign Up Now."
Free registration is required. Select the e-newsletter topic "Heart"; several more health newsletter topics are available. According to its website, "Our trusted research, testing, and reporting on health topics [is] always free of advertising and commercial or government influence. . . . For more than 70 years, Consumers Union, the nation's expert, independent, nonprofit consumer organization, has been working for a fair, just, and safe marketplace for all consumers and empowering consumers to protect themselves. We're a leading advocate for patient safety, health-care quality and effectiveness, and affordable health coverage for all. Consumers Union's rich array of research and recommendations about health care and healthy living [are] on one continuously updated Web site. Our goal is to answer your pressing questions—from which diet plan is rated the best to cost-effective alternatives to your prescription drugs—and to help you make better health-care decisions. For customer service: (800) 274–7596 (on health)."

➤ *Cooking Light Magazine.* http://www.cookinglight.com/.
Cooking Light is a monthly consumer magazine, published by Time, Lifestyle Group, a division of Time-Warner (Birmingham, AL), with the motto "Making healthy taste great." Each issue contains a blend of healthy recipes, easy-to-understand nutrition articles, "healthy living," and "healthy habits." There is also an excellent community support section online and a free online *Cooking Light* newsletter. According to its website, *Cooking Light* is a "long-established health, nutrition and fitness authority that inspires readers to eat smart and live a healthier lifestyle. As a leader in translating cutting-edge nutrition research into

recipes and guidance for the home cook, we offer the tools you need to make better choices for everyday healthy living. Each recipe is tested by our staff of Test Kitchens professionals and registered dietitians to meet stringent nutritional requirements and high flavor standards; each story is vetted by our advisory board of leading physicians, nutrition experts, and research specialists." For customer service: (800) 336–0125.

> *EatingWell.* http://www.eatingwell.com/.

Published by EatingWell Media Group (Charlotte, VT), *EatingWell* is a bimonthly consumer magazine written by experts in their field with its main focus being to maintain a healthier lifestyle. The magazine and website are composed of articles on healthy cooking; recipes and menus; diet, nutrition, and health; food news and origins; and an online community support forum. Their nutrition and advisory board members are Philip Ade, MD, director, cardiac rehabilitation and preventive cardiology, University of Vermont College of Medicine, Burlington, Vermont; Rachel K. Johnson, PhD, MPH, RD, professor of nutrition and food sciences, University of Vermont, Burlington, Vermont; Alice H. Lichtenstein, DSc, senior scientist, director of the Cardiovascular Nutrition Laboratory, Jean Mayer USDA Human Nutrition Research Center on Aging, Tufts University, Boston, Massachusetts; Richard Mattes, PhD, MPH, RD, professor of foods and nutrition, Purdue University, West Lafayette, Indiana; Miriam E. Nelson, PhD, director, John Hancock Center for Physical Activity and Nutrition, Tufts University, Boston, Massachusetts; Marion Nestle, PhD, MPH, Paulette Goddard professor of nutrition, food studies, and public health, New York University, New York, New York; and Brian Wansink, PhD, John S. Dyson professor of marketing, College of Agricultural and Life Sciences, Cornell University, Ithaca, New York. Also available is a free online *EatingWell* newsletter. For customer service: (800) 337–0402.

> *Health Magazine.* http://www.health.com/health/.

Health Magazine is published 10 times per year by Time, a division of Time-Warner (New York, NY). According to its website, the magazine "is produced by editors and journalists dedicated to delivering accurate, trusted, up-to-date health and medical information, for consumers. We focus on problem-solving content to help you make decisions during complicated, stressful times. We write in plain English, using real-life examples. For additional medical and diagnostic information, we partner with medically accredited sources 'Healthwise' (http://www.healthwise.org/), 'HealthDay' (http://www.healthday.com/), and 'Healthline' (http://www.healthline.com/)." For information on these references, scroll down to the bottom of their screen, and click on the title "About Us." Also, a free online newsletter is available by signing up. For customer service: (800) 274–2522.

➤ *Vegetarian Times Magazine.* http://www.vegetariantimes.com/.
Eating more vegetables is heart healthy, and this magazine offers a vast variety of delicious ways to prepare them in a healthy style, plus the background information on vegetables is educational and interesting. *Vegetarian Times*, which is published by Cruz Bay Publishing (San Francisco, CA) nine times per year, is a consumer magazine that, according to its website, "for over 30 years . . . has been at the forefront of the healthy living movement, providing delicious recipes, expert wellness information and environmentally sound lifestyle solutions to a wide variety of individuals. Our goal is to remain a trusted resource for our faithful readers and to reach out to the new generation of full-time vegetarians and flexitarians who find themselves increasingly drawn to the health-conscious, eco-friendly, 'green' lifestyle we have always promoted." Also, several free online newsletters are available by signing up online. For customer service: (877) 717–8923.

➤ *WebMD Magazine.* http://www.webmd.com/magazine/.
This is a monthly consumer magazine produced by the WebMD website. Its mission is "to bring you objective, trustworthy, and timely health information." WebMD also "provides valuable health information, tools for managing your health, and support to those who seek information." Sign up online for a free digital copy of this magazine. Free registration is required. For customer service: (212) 624–3760.

Journals (Magazines) and Newspapers with General Health Sections

Many major newspapers and consumer-oriented magazines/journals have excellent health and science sections, usually written by journalists/reporters whose main focus is health care and medicine, containing consumer-friendly condensed versions of the latest peer-review published or professional meeting–presented studies that are of interest to most of its readers. Heart diseases are well represented. While every related newspaper and magazine cannot be listed, a sampling of well-respected Pulitzer Prize–winning newspapers and journals was selected. (Note: The authors of this book did not receive any money or other benefits for endorsing these newspapers or journals.)

➤ Academy of Nutrition and Dietetics—"EatRight." http://www.eatright.org/.
Under the section "Public," the Academy of Nutrition and Dietetics offers consumer information on nutrition, food safety, food labeling, food shopping, meal planning, what a registered dietitian is, and under the heading, "Disease Management and Prevention" a section on diet and heart health. There are also videos.

➤ *BusinessWeek* (weekly journal)—"Science and Research" (daily news). http://www.businessweek.com/technology/science-and-research; alternate path:

http://www.businessweek.com/, click on the category "Technology," and then click on the section title "Science and Research."

With many categories to choose from, users can read up-to-the minute health reports and health care industry announcements. To keep informed, free smartphone apps are available for download.

➤ *The Economist* (weekly journal)—"Science and Technology." http://www.economist .com/science-technology; alternate path: http://www.economist.com/, click on the category "Science and Technology."

Scroll through the topics for up-to-the minute health reports and health care industry announcements. Subscribe to *The Economist's* free e-mail newsletters (e.g., health) and alerts; follow *The Economist* on Twitter and/or Facebook. (A limited number of free articles are available without a paid subscription.)

➤ *Financial Times* (for United States; daily newspaper)—"Health: Companies." http://www.ft.com/companies/health; alternate path: http://www.ft.com/home/ us, click on the category "Companies," and then scroll down to click on the title "Health."

Read up-to-the minute health reports and health care industry announcements. To receive health care–related daily updates, scroll down to "Tools and Services" and click on "Daily Briefings." Sign up for free briefings on health topics by clicking on news alerts, e-mail summaries, or RSS feeds. (A limited number of free articles are available without a paid subscription.)

➤ Kaiser Health News (KHN). http://www.kaiserhealthnews.org/.

According to its website, KHN "is a nonprofit news organization committed to in-depth coverage of health care policy and politics. KHN's mission is to provide high-quality coverage of health policy issues and developments at the federal and state levels. In addition, KHN covers trends in the delivery of health care and in the marketplace. . . . KHN accepts no advertising and all original content is available to partner news organizations and the public free of charge. Neither KHN nor the Kaiser Family Foundation is affiliated with the health insurance company Kaiser Permanente." KHN offers a free e-mail subscription for health news, including state and federal health policies and reform.

➤ *Los Angeles Times* (newspaper)—"Health." http://www.latimes.com/health/; alternate path: http://www.latimes.com/, click on the category "Health."

Read up-to-the-minute articles on a wide variety of health reports. Stay connected with Twitter, @latimeshealth; Facebook at L.A. Times Health; an e-mail newsletter, *The Health Report*; and/or RSS feed, "Health."

➤ Medical News Today (MNT)—"Heart Disease News." http://www.medicalnewstoday .com/sections/heart-disease/; alternate path: http://www.medicalnewstoday.com/, search for "heart disease," and then click on "Heart Disease News."

According to its website, MNT "brings you hourly health news from well-regarded sources such as *JAMA* [*Journal of the American Medical Association*], *BMJ* [*British Medical Journal*], *Lancet*, BMA [British Medical Association], plus articles written by our own team."

➤ *New York Times* (newspaper)—"Health." http://www.nytimes.com/pages/health/; alternate path: http://www.nytimes.com/, scroll down and select the category "Health."

Read a large volume of up-to-the minute health reports on topics including research, fitness and nutrition, money and policies, the Food and Drug Administration, and wellness; also browse the Times Health Guide ("More than 3,000 topics described, illustrated and investigated"), which contains an A to Z list of health topics with information available. There are several columns, including one called *Consults* with "Your Health Questions Answered," as well as one called *Personal Health* and *Well*, a blog. Plus, under the heading "Science" you can subscribe to *Science Times*, podcast. You can sign up for free with the link "Follow Us on Facebook"; some health articles are posted to share freely on Facebook. (A limited number of free articles are available without a paid subscription.)

➤ *Philadelphia Inquirer* (newspaper)—"Health." http://www.philly.com/philly/health/; alternate path: http://www.philly.com/, click on the heading "Health."

On this website, you'll find up-to-the minute health reports and interactive health tools with updated information, including a doctor finder, a hospital guide, regional hospital data, Food and Drug Administration product safety news, and recalls. Click on "Latest Blog Posts" for most recently published content. There are also health sections on "Special Reports" and a calendar (click on the heading "Calendar") listing what is happening locally in the Philadelphia, Pennsylvania, area, including "Wellness Community" events. Click on the heading "Forums" for links to health-related discussion groups including "Heart Disease," "Women's Health," "Men's Health," "Wellness," "Fitness," "Alternative Medicine," and "Health Insurance." Click "Like" on the Facebook icon on of the "Health and Science" webpage for Philly.com's Health, Science, and Medical News.

➤ Reuters News Service. http://www.reuters.com/news/health; alternate path: http://www.reuters.com/, mouse over the heading "Life," and then click on the category "Health."

Read up-to-the minute health reports, including news on heart and cardiovascular disease. There is also a category called "Healthcare Reform," which may be of some interest to patients. Reuters is part of Thomson Reuters, which according to its website "is the world's leading source of intelligent information for businesses and professionals. We combine industry expertise with innovative technology to deliver critical information to leading decision makers in the financial, legal, tax and accounting, healthcare, science and media markets, powered by the world's most trusted news organization." Reuter's Health News is also available by e-mail updates, by clicking "Like" on its Facebook icon, and by following the organization via Twitter.

➤ *Time Magazine* (journal)—"Healthland—A Healthy Balance of the Mind, Body, and Spirit." http://healthland.time.com/; alternate path: http://www.time.com/time/, click on the heading "Health."

Time, a weekly magazine, has a health website that includes categories such as medicine (e.g., women's health, latest health news, health prevention), diet and fitness (e.g., "Enjoy! Chocolate Is Good for Your Heart" and "To Lose the Beer Gut, Try the Treadmill, Not the Dumbbells"), and policy and industry (e.g., drug recalls, safety rules, health care, government health policies). Sign up for *Time*'s health newsletter, and follow *Time* on Twitter, Facebook, Google+, and other popular social media.

➤ *U.S. News and World Report* (journal)—"Health." http://health.usnews.com/; alternate path: http://www.usnews.com/, click on the main category "Health."

U.S. News and World Report is a weekly magazine. The health section of its website includes current information on health articles (e.g., a plant-based diet to cut bad cholesterol), health conditions (e.g., heart health), health decisions (e.g., decoding doctor-speak: translations of common medical terms), health plans, rankings, and featured videos. Follow *U.S. News and World Report* Health on Facebook and Twitter.

➤ *Wall Street Journal* (*WSJ*; newspaper). http://online.wsj.com/.
  • "Health." http://online.wsj.com/public/page/consumer-health-wellness.html; alternate path: http://online.wsj.com/, under the heading "Life and Culture" click on the subheading "Health." Read up-to-the minute health reports. Also, scroll down to the category "Columns," where several columnists specialize, including links to "Heart Beat," "Health Journal," "Informed Patient," and "In the Lab." Also available is a searchable "Health Blog" (http://blogs.wsj.com/health/; alternate path: search for "blogs," scroll down to "WSJ Blog Archive," and click on "Health Blog") that is written by a *WSJ* staffer offering "news and analysis on health and the business of health." At the bottom of the page, under "Tools and Features," click on "e-mails and alerts," then click on the subcategory "Life and Culture," and click on "The Health Edition." Sign up for free daily e-mail, with links to the latest health reports on *WSJ*. Free registration is required. Follow *WSJ* on Facebook, Twitter, and Google+.
  • *Health Industry.* http://online.wsj.com/public/page/news-health-industry.html?mod=WSJ_topnav_na_business; alternate path: http://online.wsj.com/, under the heading "Business" click on the subheading "Health." Read up-to-the minute reports on the health care industry's announcements. Health discussion groups are available. Scroll down to "More Industries" for

related categories such as "Pharmaceuticals and Biotech." Access to some articles is limited without being a *WSJ* subscriber.

> *Washington Post* (newspaper)—"Health and Science" and "Wellness." http://www
.washingtonpost.com/national/health-science and http://www.washingtonpost
.com/lifestyle/wellness; alternate path: http://www.washingtonpost.com/, under
the heading "National" click on the topic "Health and Science"; also scroll
under the heading "Lifestyle" to click on the topic "Wellness."
Read up-to-the minute health and wellness reports by clicking on categories and
columns, including "Health News," "The Checkup," "Eat, Drink, and Be Healthy,"
"How and Why," "AnyBODY," "Medical Mysteries," and health videos. To keep
informed, subscribe free to "get a dose of nutrition and fitness news delivered to
your inbox every Wednesday from the Lean & Fit electronic newsletter." You can
also follow *Washington Post* health notes on Facebook and Twitter.

Websites

> AARP: Health—"Heart Disease Learning Center: Heart Disease." http://healthtools
.aarp.org/learning-center/heart-disease; alternate path: http://www.aarp.org/, click
on the heading "Health," scroll down and click on the category "Learning Centers,"
and then click on the title "Heart Disease."
The AARP section on heart disease offers a consumer-friendly wealth of topics on
specific heart diseases as well as heart research news. With membership to AARP,
you will receive a monthly magazine and monthly AARP bulletin, which includes
current health information focusing on those age 50 and older. Available are videos,
blogs for discussion, and a newsletter concerning the latest health care issues,
including federal health care law updates. Follow AARP on Facebook and Twitter.

> Academy of Nutrition and Dietetics—"It's about Eating Right." http://www
.eatright.org/Public/; alternate path: http://www.eatright.org/, click on the heading "Public."

Online Search Tips

- If you click on a link (e.g., a title) and nothing happens, try this: right-click on
that link and then left-click on the option "Open in new window."
- If you experience problems with PDF documents, you can download the latest
version of Adobe Reader for free at http://www.adobe.com/products/reader.html
or by going to http://www.adobe.com/ and searching for "adobe reader."
- Adobe Flash Player, required to view most short videos, is available as a free
download at http://get.adobe.com/flashplayer/; alternate path: http://www
.adobe.com/, choose the "Download" tab on the menu bar, and select the
Adobe Flash Player link.

The Academy of Nutrition and Dietetics (formerly the American Dietetic Association) offers consumer information on nutrition, food safety, food labeling, food shopping, meal planning, and locating a registered dietitian. Under the heading "Diseases, Allergies, and Health Conditions" is a section on food and heart health. There are also videos on nutrition-related topcis. To find a registered dietitian who works with heart disease patients in your area, at the top of the screen click on the "Find a Registered Dietitian" button, then type in your zip code and click "Search Now," and then click "Refine Search." Under the heading "Expertise Area," check off "Heart Health," and click on "Update Map." According to its website, the "Academy of Nutrition and Dietetics is the world's largest organization of food and nutrition professionals. The Academy is committed to improving the nation's health and advancing the profession of dietetics through research, education and advocacy."

> Administration on Aging (AoA)—"Health, Prevention, and Wellness Program." http://www.aoa.gov/AoARoot/AoA_Programs/HCLTC/Evidence_Based; alternate path: http://www.aoa.gov/, search for "wellness program," and click on the title "Health, Prevention, and Wellness Program."
> The Administration on Aging, a division of the U.S. Department of Health and Human Services (DHHS), states that the "need for programs that enable older adults to learn and practice healthy behaviors is critical. . . . Through collaboration with [DHHS] Agencies, the National Council on Aging (NCOA), and philanthropic organizations, AoA has created national partnerships that have addressed the need for community-based health, prevention, and wellness programs."

> Aetna InteliHealth—"Living Well with Heart Failure." http://www.intelihealth .com/IH/ihtIH?d=dmtHMSContent&c=358633; alternate path: http://www .intelihealth.com/, search for "heart failure," and then click on the resource title.
> This website offers ways of living well with heart failure, including such topics as energy and mood boosters, ways for patients to save energy, eating a heart-healthy diet, and monitoring the heart. Aetna InteliHealth, a subsidiary of Aetna, is reviewed by the faculty of Harvard Medical School and University College of Dental Medicine. According to its website, "Aetna InteliHealth maintains absolute editorial independence. That means that Aetna InteliHealth makes decisions about the information on our site free of outside influence." Under "Healthy Lifestyle," Aetna InteliHealth also offers free health-related e-mail subscriptions.

> AgingCare.com: Connecting People Caring for Elderly Parents—"Heart Disease." http://www.agingcare.com/Heart-Disease; alternate path: http://www.agingcare .com/, under the category "Elder Care," scroll under "Health Conditions" to click on "Heart Disease."
> AgingCare.com offers heart disease information related to older adults and their caregivers, including their parents. AgingCare.com also offers information on

the most common health-related issues, including senior living, elder care, financial issues, insurance, and legal matters. Readers can subscribe to receive an e-mailed newsletter from this website. Also, under the menu heading "Caregiver Forum," there are several ways to connect with others: through question and answer forums, discussion boards, reading the stories of caregivers, participating in polls, and more; the website describes it as a "place where you can ask questions, give answers, exchange messages and get support from other caregivers who understand exactly what you're going through."

➢ The AGS (American Geriatrics Society) Foundation for Health in Aging—"Home Care: Basic Facts and Information" and "Eldercare at Home: Caregiving." http://www.healthinaging.org/aging-and-health-a-to-z/topic:home-care/ and http://www.healthinaging.org/resources/resource:eldercare-at-home-caregiving/; alternate path: http://www.healthinaging.org/, click on the heading "Home and Community," and then click on "Home Care."
The AGS Foundation is a nonprofit organization that focuses its information on older adults. This website also has information for caregivers of older patients. Patients and health care providers can share their stories online so that the "real-life experiences of older adults and their family caregivers will help the public, policy makers and others recognize the urgent need for better care." Sign up for a free newsletter on elder care. A blog, *Health in Aging*, provides thoughtful posts and allows readers to share "issues concerning older adults." Also on the "Home Care" page, click on "Caregiving How-To's," and for information on heart disease and the elderly, search for "heart disease" and click on related topics for specific heart conditions.

➢ American Academy of Family Physicians (AAFP)—"Health Coaching Dramatically Lowers Patients' Systolic Blood Pressure" and "Health Coaching for Patients with Chronic Illness: Does Your Practice 'Give Patients a Fish' or 'Teach Patients to Fish'?" http://www.aafp.org/online/en/home/publications/news/news-now/practice-professional-issues/20120704annalshealthcoaches.html and http://www.aafp.org/fpm/2010/0900/p24.html; alternate path: http://www.aafp.org/, search for "health coach" and then click on each title.
These articles, on the American Academy of Family Physicians website, clearly explain what a health coach is, the positive outcomes of cardiovascular disease when guided by a health coach, who can be a health coach, specific roles of a health coach, two models of health coaching, and the business case for health coaching in primary care.

➢ American Medical Association (AMA)—"DoctorFinder" (to find a local heart or cardiovascular specialist). https://extapps.ama-assn.org/doctorfinder/recaptcha.jsp; alternate path: http://www.ama-assn.org/ama/, under the heading "Popular AMA Links," click on "Doctor Finder."

From this tool from the AMA is a directory of medical doctors (MDs) and osteopaths (DOs) practicing in the United States. Scroll down to "Search by Physician Specialty," and then under the category "Specialty" select "Cardiology" from the drop-down list. For location, select from the drop-down lists your state, city, or ZIP code, click the "Search" button, and then click on the "View Non-Members" button for a comprehensive list of physicians in your area. Click on a physician's name for details, including primary specialty, location, telephone number, address, and any American Board of Medical Specialties certifications. You can also search by physician name.

➤ Brigham and Women's Hospital (BWH) (Boston, MA)—"Cardiac Wellness Service." http://www.brighamandwomens.org/Departments_and_Services/medicine/services/cvcenter/cvwellness; alternate path: http://www.brighamandwomens.org/, scroll under the heading "Departments and Services" to the category titled "Centers of Excellence," click on the title "Cardiovascular," and then under the heading "Cardiovascular Medicine," scroll down to click on the category "Cardiac Wellness Service."
Brigham and Women's Hospital's Cardiac Wellness Service offers several plans to help prevent heart disease and encourage a healthy heart lifestyle. Click on the titles under the category "For Patients" for numerous links, including heart disease basics, risk factors, signs and symptoms, screenings, knowing the numbers (understanding the results), and educational videos.

➤ British Heart Foundation (BHF)—"Recovery." https://www.bhf.org.uk/heart-health/recovery.aspx?; alternate path: http://www.bhf.org.uk/, search for "recovery," and then click on the title "British Heart Foundation—Recovery."
The British Heart Foundation website on recovery includes readings on cardiac rehabilitation, caring for a heart patient, counseling, driving, holidays and travel, insurance, money issues, returning to work, seasonal influenza (flu), and sex and heart conditions. There is also a section called "Hope for Heart Failure," a link to a nine-minute video called "On Leaving the Hospital," and a section called "Community: Share Experiences with Others." Under the section titled "Related Links" are such topics as caring for someone with a heart condition, support groups, and booklets and DVDs.

➤ Family Caregiver Alliance (FCA). http://www.caregiver.org/.
Although this nonprofit organization is not specific to heart disease (there is, however, information on stroke), a person with cardiovascular disease can have a chronic and disabling health condition and therefore be in need of a caregiver. According to its website, Family Caregiver Alliance "seeks to improve the quality of life for caregivers through education, services, research and advocacy. FCA's National Center on Caregiving offers information on current social, public policy and caregiving issues and provides assistance in the development of public and

private programs for caregivers." Click on the menu heading "Groups" at the top of the screen to see a list of several support groups for caregivers and their loved ones. Caregiver advice and tips are also available in Spanish and Chinese.

➤ Harvard University–Harvard Medical School (Boston, MA)—*Harvard Heart Letter*. http://www.health.harvard.edu/newsletters/Harvard_Heart_Letter; alternate path: http://www.health.harvard.edu/, scroll under "Harvard Newsletters," and click on the title.

The *Harvard Heart Letter* is a consumer-friendly paid monthly subscription newsletter that offers the latest heart information, including:

- hypertension guidelines, including how low blood pressure should be and what you can do to lower yours;
- the good and the bad of cholesterol and steps you can take to manage cholesterol levels—and just how low your cholesterol target should really be;
- how best to prepare for a cardiac emergency;
- eating fish and whether it really helps prevent heart disease;
- the connection between poor sleep and heart trouble; and
- whether chelation therapy is all it's cracked up to be.

In addition to health newsletters, Harvard publishes consumer-friendly special health reports (e.g., "Heart Disease," "Heart Health and Nutrition," "High Blood pressure," and "High Cholesterol") and health books (e.g., *Smart at Heart, The Harvard Medical School Guide to Lowering Your Cholesterol*, and *Mind Your Heart: A Mind/Body Approach to Stress Management, Exercise, and Nutrition for Heart Health*). Also available from Harvard Medical School are free weekly *HEALTHbeat* e-newsletters with specific topics such as heart health, hypertension, and stroke, along with heart-healthy lifestyle change topics, including healthy eating, stress management, healthy aging, and diet and weight loss. There is a Harvard health blog (Harvard health publication experts answer questions written by nonprofessionals) and a column called *Ask Doctor K*, where "Each day [Dr. Anthony L. Komaroff, professor of medicine at Harvard Medical School] answers readers' questions about a wide range of health concerns."

➤ Harvard University–Harvard School of Public Health (Boston, MA)—"The Nutrition Source." http://www.hsph.harvard.edu/nutritionsource/; alternate path: http://www.hsph.harvard.edu/, search for "nutrition source," and click on the resource title.

The Harvard School of Public Health offers an extensive nutrition source website with a wealth of nutrition information, including links to detailed descriptions of the "Healthy Eating Plate" (based on the latest U.S. Department of Agriculture's MyPlate guide), healthy food choices, and current nutrition news. Click on the topic "Healthy Food Service" for "guidelines, recipes, and other resources for creating and promoting healthy, delicious foods in schools and at work sites." Also click on the topic "Your Questions Answered" for a list of questions with answers requested by "consumers, journalists, and health professionals" and a section called "Ask the Expect" to write to "Professors from the Department of Nutrition at Harvard School of Public Health [who] answer questions about their area of expertise."

➤ HealthDay: News for Healthier Living. http://consumer.healthday.com/.
HealthDay is a consumer-friendly, expertly written health website that is updated several times a day. To search for archived heart disease articles, under the heading "Archive Search," in the "By Category" drop-down list, click on the topic "Heart/Cardiovascular," click "Go," and then select from a variety of heart disease topics for recent articles. You can select using the "By Topic" drop-down list to locate heart disease–related topics, including high blood pressure and numerous other topics beginning with the word *heart*. The HealthDay website also produces video clips that can be accessed by clicking on the menu heading "Health-Day TV" at the top of the screen. Visit the website for a "daily [Monday thru Friday] video recap of the latest consumer health research . . . for insight into the latest news published in major medical journals and new research presented at medical conferences. Dr. Haines explains the news with short, easy-to-understand commentary that translates highly technical language into a concise and compelling report for medical consumers." A free, weekly HealthDay newsletter is available at http://www.healthday.com/. The newsletter can be customized to include heart health and many other conditions.

➤ Healthfinder.gov—"Eat Healthy." http://healthfinder.gov/HealthTopics/Category/health-conditions-and-diseases/heart-health/eat-healthy; alternate path: http://www.healthfinder.gov/, under "Health Topics" click on "Health Conditions and Diseases," then click on the title "Heart Health," and then click on "Eat Healthy."
Healthfinder is sponsored by U.S. Department of Health and Human Services. Choose from a variety of titles, including getting your blood pressure checked, getting your cholesterol checked, reducing your risks of stroke, and learning heart-healthy conversation starters. Each topic has a "Basics" section describing the topic and a "Take Action" section explaining what patients can do proactively to manage their heart health. Topics include ways to manage stress, get active, eat healthy, get more out of doctor visits, and improve shopping lists (low sodium foods and heart-healthy foods). You can follow health information from Healthfinder on its Facebook and Twitter pages. Sign up for e-mail updates.

➤ HeartHub for Patients—"Take Control: Caregiver." http://www.hearthub.org/hc-caregiver.htm; alternate path: http://www.hearthub.org/, scroll down to the section titled "Health Centers," and then click on the title "Caregiver."
HeartHub, a division of the American Heart Association (AHA), is a patient-support portal for information, tools, and resources on caregivers, including the

heart of the caregiver, rights, responsibilities, reality check, healthy recipes, how to get help on the phone, lining up your team, you're not alone, caregiver journal pages, and top 10 tips for caregivers. You can also subscribe to a caregiver e-newsletter.

➤ TheHeart.org. http://www.theheart.org/.
TheHeart.org, owned and produced by Medscape, "provides information on caring for people with disorders of the heart and circulation, and on preventing such disorders" and is written by a staff of experts in the field. Keep up with the latest studies in myriad heart and cardiovascular diseases and disorders. Free registration is required.

➤ Johns Hopkins Hospital (Baltimore, MD)—"Clinical Exercise Physiology and Cardiac Rehabilitation" (Clinical Services). http://www.hopkinsmedicine.org/heart_vascular_institute/clinical_services/specialty_areas/cardiac_rehabilitation.html; alternate path: http://www.hopkinsmedicine.org/, search for "clinical exercise physiology and cardiac rehabilitation," and then click on the resource title.
Johns Hopkins Clinical Exercise Physiology and Cardiac Rehabilitation Center "offers comprehensive, medically supervised programs designed to teach people how to exercise safely and manage heart disease risk factors." This website describes three areas: individualized exercise prescriptions, types of exercise equipment, and comprehensive metabolic fitness and body composition testing. Also, at the top of the screen, click on the heading "Clinical Trials" for links to current trials in various heart and cardiovascular conditions.

➤ KidsHealth.org. http://kidshealth.org/.
The Nemours Center for Children's Health Media provides current information on conditions afflicting children, written for both children and parents. Information is available in English and Spanish. Some webpages contain a "Listen" button that you can click on to hear the text read aloud. Weekly age-appropriate e-mails are available to offer relevant health information. You can also follow KidsHealth on Facebook, Twitter, and Google+.

- *For Kids:* http://kidshealth.org/kid/health_problems/index.html#cat141, scroll down the "Health Problems" list to click on "Heart and Lungs" or "Birth Defects and Genetic Problems"; alternate path: http://kidshealth.org/, click on "For Kids," scroll down to click on "Health Problems," then scroll down to click on "Heart and Lungs" or "Birth Defects and Genetic Problems." Topics are designed to help parents discuss the heart condition with their child, including living with various heart conditions.
- *For Parents:* http://kidshealth.org/parent/medical/index.html#cat141, scroll down to "Heart and Blood Vessels"; alternate path: http://kidshealth.org/, click on "Parents," scroll down to click on "Diseases and Conditions," and

then scroll down to click on "Heart and Blood Vessels." Topics discussed include monitoring treatment, caring for the child, finding safe activities, and knowing when to call the doctor.

- *For Teens:* http://kidshealth.org/teen/diseases_conditions/#cat141, scroll down to "Heart and Cardiovascular System"; alternate path: http://kidshealth.org/, click on "For Teens," scroll down to click on "Diseases and Conditions," and then scroll down to click on "Heart and Cardiovascular System."

➤ Massachusetts General Hospital (MGH) (Boston, MA)—"Cardiovascular Disease Prevention Center." http://www.massgeneral.org/heartcenter/services/treatmentprograms.aspx?id=1012; alternate path: http://www.massgeneral.org/, search for and then click on the title "Cardiovascular Disease Prevention Center"; or click on "Centers and Services," then click on "View All Departments," then click on "Heart Center," then click on the heading "Treatments and Services," and then scroll down to click on the title.

The Cardiovascular Disease Prevention Center at the Massachusetts General Hospital Heart Center website offers links to comprehensive information in several categories. "Our Approach" includes an overview of their team approach with a description of their four prevention programs, treatments and procedures, and links to each medical expert (with profiles, e.g., specialty, medical board certification, education). "About This" describes the benefits, commitment, and goals of using these four prevention programs at MGH to reduce cardiovascular disease. "Conditions and Diseases" has links to detailed information on several conditions and diseases that affect the heart and cardiovascular system. "Support and Wellness" offers several wellness series, including nutrition classes and relaxation classes, as well as a patient guide, *Patient and Family Guide to the Heart Center.* "Clinical Trials" has links to several MGH trials and research studies that are currently seeking participants. "News and Events" includes the latest information on related topics, and "Multimedia" contains videos.

➤ Mayo Clinic (Rochester, MN)—"Lifestyle and Home Remedies." http://www.mayoclinic.com/health/heart-disease/DS01120/DSECTION=lifestyle-and-home-remedies and http://www.mayoclinic.com/health/heart-disease/DS01120/DSECTION=coping-and-support and http://www.mayoclinic.com/health/heart-disease/DS01120/TAB=multimedia; alternate path: http://www.mayoclinic.com/, search for "heart disease," click on the title "Heart Disease—Mayo Clinic," scroll down to the section "Lifestyle and Home Remedies," click on "Coping and Support," and then click on the tab "Multimedia."

This section of the Mayo Clinic's website covers stopping smoking, controlling blood pressure, checking cholesterol, keeping diabetes under control, getting moving, eating healthy, maintaining a healthy weight, managing stress, practicing good hygiene, and getting a flu shot. Scroll down to the section called "Slide

Shows," where there are links to heart-healthy recipes, including vegetable recipes and the Mediterranean diet. Scroll down to "See Also" for other sections that offer detailed information, including eating grass-fed beef; omega-3 in fish; eating nuts for heart health; menus for heart-healthy eating: cutting fat and salt; heart-healthy recipes; heart-healthy diet; butter versus margarine; chocolate; low-fat diets; and the Atkins diet.

➤ MedPage Today—"Cardiovascular Information Center." http://www.medpagetoday .com/Cardiology/; alternate path: http://www.medpagetoday.com/, scroll under the heading "Specialty," and click on the topic "Cardiovascular."
The MedPage Today webpage on cardiovascular disease offers daily medical news updates on a variety of subtopics, including acute coronary syndrome, arrhythmias, atherosclerosis, congestive heart failure, heart transplantation, hypertension, metabolic syndrome, peripheral artery disease, strokes, and venous thrombosis. While according to its website, "MedPageToday.com is a trusted news service for physicians that provides a clinical perspective on the breaking medical news that their patients are reading," it may offer new information patients might want to discuss with their physician. "Co-developed by Med-Page Today, LLC and the Perelman School of Medicine at the University of Pennsylvania, each article alerts the reader to breaking medical news, presenting that news in a context that meets their educational practice needs." A free daily e-mail newsletter on cardiology is available.

➤ MyFitnessPal. http://www.myfitnesspal.com/.
MyFitnessPal offers numerous apps and tools for tablets or smartphones to help monitor lifestyle changes, including counting calories, making informed food choices, types of exercises, burning calories, and monitoring pulse rate. Available are numerous message board topics.

➤ National Heart, Lung, and Blood Institute (NHLBI)—"How Does Smoking Affect the Heart and Blood Vessels?" http://www.nhlbi.nih.gov/health/health -topics/topics/smo/; alternate path: http://www.nhlbi.nih.gov/, search for "smoking heart," and then click on the title "How Does Smoking Affect the Heart and Blood Vessels?"
The National Heart, Lung, and Blood Institute, a division of National Institutes of Health (NIH) from the U.S. Department of Health and Human Services, website extensively explains the effects of smoking on the heart. Click on topics, including how does smoking affect the heart and blood vessels, risks, benefits of quitting, strategies for quitting, healthy lifestyle, and clinical trials.

➤ SuperTracker. http://www.supertracker.usda.gov/.
This website might help patients develop a heart-healthy lifestyle food regimen. According to this interactive consumer website from the U.S. Department of

Agriculture, on this website you can "get your personalized nutrition and physical activity plan, track your foods and physical activities to see how they stack up, and get tips and support to help you make healthier choices and plan ahead." You can create a personalized profile, use a general plan, and sign up for a virtual coach.

➢ Texas Heart Institute (Houston, TX). http://www.texasheartinstitute.org/.
From the homepage, you can find the following resources through a title search or by going to the Heart Information Center, clicking on "Healthy Heart Guide," and then scrolling down to click on the title of choice.

- "Exercise." http://www.texasheartinstitute.org/HIC/Topics/HSmart/exercis1 .cfm. This webpage offers information on exercise including what to do before starting an exercise program; what kinds of exercise to do; information about cardiovascular exercises, strength-building exercises, and flexibility exercises; and preventing exercise injuries. There also are charts for target heart rates by age and a project about the heart with activities for the classroom. There is also a section called "Ask a Texas Heart Institute Doctor" for questions and answers. There is an easy-to-print format available.

- "Healthy Heart Guide." http://www.texasheartinstitute.org/HIC/Topics/ HSmart/index.cfm. The Heart Information Center gives an overview on how a healthy lifestyle can help keep the heart healthy.

- "Nutrition." http://www.texasheartinstitute.org/HIC/Topics/HSmart/ nutriti1.cfm. This webpage offers a definition of nutrition, as well as information including food and nutrients, carbohydrates, sugars, starches, fiber, proteins, types of fats, vitamins, minerals and trace elements, body shape, snacking tips, holiday tips, and the U.S. Department of Agriculture Food Pyramid.

- "Obesity and Overweight." http://www.texasheartinstitute.org/HIC/Topics/ HSmart/obesity.cfm. This webpage offers a definition of obesity, a body mass index calculator, as well as information including causes, risks, and treatment.

➢ UCLA Ronald Reagan Medical Center (Los Angeles, CA)—"In-Depth Reports" on lifestyle changes. http://www.uclahealth.org/body.cfm?id=592, scroll down to the heading "In-Depth Reports," then click on the word "More"; alternate path: http://www.uclahealth.org/, under the heading "For Patients and Visitors," scroll down and mouse over the category "Health Resources," then select "Heart Health Center," scroll down to the heading "In-Depth Reports," and then click on the word "More."
UCLA Ronald Reagan Medical Center's Heart Health Center provides several in-depth reports on lifestyle changes to lower risk of heart disease. Sections include highlights, introductions, risk factors, symptoms, diagnosis, prevention, treatment, medications, surgery, and resources. Click on links to in-depth

reports, including "Diet—Heart Health," "Dieting," "Exercise," "Heart-Healthy Diet," "Obesity," "Weight Control and Diet," and "Weight Loss." The UCLA Heart Health Center (http://www.uclahealth.org/body.cfm?id=592) provides animations related to various conditions. Scroll to the bottom of the page and select "More" under "Animations." (Note: To view the animation, you might be asked to allow the installation of a common Internet plug-in called Shockwave Player by Adobe, available for free at http://www.adobe.com/products/shockwaveplayer .html.) Also on the Heart Health Center website, under the heading "Health Assessments," you can sign up for "personalized messages to improve your [heart] health and lifestyle" by clicking on one of these categories: "Diet and Nutrition," "Fitness," "Heart Attack," or "Stress and Anxiety." For patient services in various cardiology programs, return to the UCLA Health homepage (http://www.uclahealth.org/), under the heading "Medical Departments" scroll down and click on "Medicine," and then scroll and click on "Cardiology." Included is a list of programs and links to physicians and specialists (with profiles, e.g., specialty, medical board certification, education). To possibly participate in a clinical trial at UCLA, if available, visit http://clinicaltrials.ucla.edu/ (or on the homepage type "clinical trials" in the Search box, and then click on "Clinical Trials").

➤ *U.S. News and World Report*—"Best Diets for 2013." http://health.usnews.com/best-diet; alternate path: http://www.usnews.com/, click on the main category "Health," and then scroll down to click on the title "Best Diets."
Click on the title "Best Diet Rankings," or click on the title "Best Diet Overall." Click on the diet name (e.g., DASH diet, TLC diet, Ornish diet, Weight Watchers, Mediterranean diet) for a description, pros and cons, do's and don'ts, how the diet works, whether the diet has cardiovascular benefits, whether it causes weight loss, if it helps control diabetes, if it is easy to follow, health risks, and whether it conforms to accepted dietary guidelines. To learn about how *U.S. News and World Report* ranks diets, click on the title "How We Rank Diets." To find out who the experts are behind the rankings, click on the title "The Experts Behind It All." Links to other up-to-the minute diet information are available.

➤ USA.gov—"Caregivers' Resources." http://www.usa.gov/Citizen/Topics/Health/caregivers.shtml; alternate path: http://www.usa.gov/, search for "caregivers resources," and then click on the title "Caregivers' Resources—USA.gov."
For caregivers of senior citizens with serious heart disease issues, this webpage offers a comprehensive list and links to government agencies and other organizations that provide services and programs for seniors, including health and housing for seniors, long-distance caregiving, medical benefits for seniors, programs to help pay medical expenses, legal matters, and end-of-life issues, There is also a section with comprehensive lists of resources devoted to "Support for Caregivers." You can subscribe to free e-mail updates about this topic on this webpage.

Guides to Health Care Costs and Comparisons

➤ Healthcare Blue Book: Your Free Guide to Fair Healthcare Pricing. http://www
.healthcarebluebook.com/.
According to this website, which is free to consumers, "The Healthcare Blue Book
price represents a fair price to pay for a service or product when the patient is
paying cash at the time of treatment. It represents a payment amount that many
high-quality providers accept from insurance companies as payment in full, and it
is usually less than the stated 'billed charges' amount." Click on the headings,
including "Hospital," "Physician," "X-Ray Imaging" (e.g., angiography), "Labs"
(e.g., cardiovascular), and "Resources for Patients." Type in your ZIP code in the
Search box at the top of the screen for health care pricing averages in your area.
Check out updates on their Facebook or Twitter website or get smartphone apps
(iPhone or Android).

➤ Medicare.gov. http://www.medicare.gov/.
This is the official U.S. government website for Medicare-related information.
The homepage includes links for Medicare services, plan comparisons, and find-
ing out whether a test, item, or service is covered by Medicare.

- "Caregiving." http://www.medicare.gov/campaigns/caregiver/caregiver
.html; alternate path: http://www.medicare.gov/, search for "caregiving"
and then click on the title "I'm a Caregiver—Medicare.gov." This website
includes information on cardiovascular screening, heart and vascular diseases, and heart disease in women. Click also on the headings "Manage
Your Health," "Medicare Basics," and "Resource Locator."

- "Hospital Compare." http://www.medicare.gov/hospitalcompare/. This
tool from the U.S. Department of Health and Human Services provides, by
location (ZIP code or city and state), pricing comparisons for services and
patient safety measures. Included is a section titled "Who Can Help Me If I
Have a Complaint about the Quality of My Hospital Care?"

Patient Support Groups and Organizations

➤ Facebook—"American Heart Association" and "American Heart Association
Nutrition Center." https://www.facebook.com/AmericanHeart and https://www
.facebook.com/heartofhealth; alternate path: https://www.facebook.com/, search
for the group by name, and then click on the group name with the largest
number of people.
Participate and learn from experts. On these very popular webpages, you can
find tips to help you live healthier through various means (e.g., choosing nutritious foods, heart-smart cooking, healthy diet goals, and becoming physically
active) as well as the tools and resources to support you in making the best nutrition choices for you and your family. Facebook requires free registration.

➤ U.S. Hospital Finder. http://www.ushospitalfinder.com/.
Ask your health care professional or call hospitals in your area to ask if they have
or know of a cardiology support group that meets regularly. You can also search
on this website for "support groups." Using this U.S. Hospital Finder, you can
find the names of hospitals by ZIP code, city, state, or your address. A map is
displayed with directions.

➤ WebMD—"WebMD Heart Disease Community." http://exchanges.webmd.com/
heart-disease-exchange/; alternate path: http://www.webmd.com/, search for
"heart disease health center," scroll down and click on the title "Heart Disease
Health Center," and then scroll down to "WebMD Heart Disease Community"
(WebMD Community).
Click on the title "Community Experts Support" as well as the links under "Discussions," "Expert Blogs," and "Community." Join the WebMD heart disease
community (WebMD moderated), which includes tips, resources, and support.
According to the WebMD heart disease community, "WebMD's heart experts
and other knowledgeable members are here to share help and guidance about
everything from diagnosis and treatment to getting back on track with a heart-
healthy lifestyle." To search for other health topic communities, visit http://
exchanges.webmd.com/, "Be Part of the WebMD Community." You can also
scroll down to the "Create Your Own Community" section for easy instructions
on starting your own group.

Webliography

Academy of Nutrition and Dietetics. "Heart and Cardiovascular." Accessed May 28,
2013. http://www.eatright.org/Public/list.aspx?TaxID=6442452082/.

American Academy of Home Care Physicians. "Assisted Living Programs Substitute
for Skilled Home Care Services." Accessed April 8, 2013. http://www.aahcp.org/
displaycommon.cfm?an=1&subarticlenbr=49.

American Heart Association. "Cardiac Rehabilitation." Accessed April 8, 2013.
http://www.heart.org/HEARTORG/Conditions/More/CardiacRehab/Cardiac
-Rehab_UCM_002079_SubHomePage.jsp.

———. "HeartHub for Patients: Take Control." Accessed April 8, 2013. http://www
.hearthub.org/.

———. "Lifestyle Changes." Updated January 23, 2013. http://www.heart.org/
HEARTORG/Conditions/HeartAttack/PreventionTreatmentofHeartAttack/
Lifestyle-Changes_UCM_303934_Article.jsp.

———. "Physical Activity—Get Moving." Accessed April 8, 2013. http://www.heart
.org/HEARTORG/GettingHealthy/PhysicalActivity/Physical-Activity_UCM
_001080_SubHomePage.jsp.

————. "Stress Management." Accessed April 8, 2013. http://www.heart.org/ HEARTORG/GettingHealthy/StressManagement/Stress-Management_UCM _001082_SubHomePage.jsp.

————. "What Is Cardiac Rehabilitation?" Updated August 14, 2012. http://www .heart.org/HEARTORG/Conditions/More/CardiacRehab/What-is-Cardiac -Rehabilitation_UCM_307049_Article.jsp.

Bennett, H. D., et al. "Health Coaching for Patients with Chronic Illness: Does Your Practice 'Give Patients a Fish' or 'Teach Patients to Fish'?" *Family Practice Management*, 17, no. 5 (2010): 24–29. http://www.aafp.org/fpm/2010/0900/p24.html.

Brubaker, Harold. "IBC Hiring 100 Nurses as Health Coaches." *Philadelphia Inquirer*, March 18, 2013. http://www.philly.com/philly/health/20130318_IBC _hiring_100_nurses_as_health_coaches.html.

Caregiver Action Network. Accessed April 8, 2013. http://caregiveraction.org/.

Centers for Disease Control and Prevention. "Healthy Eating for a Healthy Weight." Updated October 25, 2012. http://www.cdc.gov/healthyweight/healthy_eating/ index.html.

————. "Losing Weight." Updated August 17, 2011. http://www.cdc.gov/healthyweight/ losing_weight/index.html.

————. "Physical Activity." Updated August 7, 2012. http://www.cdc.gov/physicalactivity/ index.html.

————. "State Heart Disease and Stroke Prevention Program Addresses Cardiac Rehabilitation." Reviewed December 20, 2010. http://www.cdc.gov/dhdsp/data _statistics/fact_sheets/fs_state_cardiacrehab.htm.

Chicago Tribune. "Types of Nutritionists." March 21, 2013. http://articles .chicagotribune.com/2013–03–21/health/ct-met-nutritionist-types-20130128_1 _medical-nutrition-therapy-food-and-nutrition-nutrition-professionals.

Commission on Dietetic Registration. "Not All Nutrition Certification Programs Are Created Equal" and "Latest News/Information." Accessed May 28, 2013. http://cdrnet.org/.

Deardorff, Julie. "How to Find Good Nutrition Advice." *Chicago Tribune*, January 28, 2013. http://articles.chicagotribune.com/2013–01–28/health/ct-met-nutritionist -tips-20130128_1_nutrition-public-health-advice.

————. "Who Gives the Best Nutrition Advice?" *Chicago Tribune*, January 28, 2013. http://articles.chicagotribune.com/2013–01–28/health/ct-met-nutrition-advice -20130128_1_dietitians-health-coach-nutrition.

Educational Blog: How to Eat Well. December 28, 2012. http://www.cochinpages .com/how-to-eat-well/.

Estruch, R., et al. "Primary Prevention of Cardiovascular Disease with a Mediterranean Diet." *New England Journal of Medicine*, 368, no. 14 (2013): 1279–1290. http://www .nejm.org/doi/full/10.1056/NEJMoa1200303?query=featured_home&.

FamilyDoctor.org. "Caregiver Health and Wellness." April 2012. http://familydoctor
.org/familydoctor/en/seniors/caregiving/caregiver-health-and-wellness.html.
———. "Caregiver Stress." February 2012. http://familydoctor.org/familydoctor/en/
seniors/caregiving/caregiver-stress.html.
Gearon, Christopher J. "How Healthcare Is Changing—For the Better." *U.S. News
and World Report*, October 18, 2012. http://health.usnews.com/health-news/
articles/2012/10/18/how-healthcare-is-changingfor-the-better.
Guliksson, M., et al. "Randomized Controlled Trial of Cognitive Behavioral Therapy
vs. Standard Treatment to Prevent Recurrent Cardiovascular Events in Patients
with Coronary Heart Disease: Secondary Prevention in Uppsala Primary Health
Care Project (SUPRIM)." *Archives of Internal Medicine*, 171, no. 2 (2011): 134–140.
http://archinte.jamanetwork.com/article.aspx?articleid=226464.
"How to Eat Well." *ShopSmart*, January 8, no. 1 (2013): 55–56. http://www.cochinpages
.com/how-to-eat-well.
Koeth, R. A., et al. "Intestinal Microbiota Metabolism of l-Carnitine, a Nutrient in
Red Meat, Promotes Atherosclerosis." *Nature Medicine*, 19 (2013): 576–585. http://
www.nature.com/nm/journal/vaop/ncurrent/full/nm.3145.html.
Kolata, Gina. "Mediterranean Diet Shown to Ward Off Heart Attack and Stroke."
New York Times, February 26, 2013. http://www.nytimes.com/2013/02/26/health/
mediterranean-diet-can-cut-heart-disease-study-finds.html?pagewanted=1&_r
=0&smid=fb-nytimes&adxnnlx=1361815470-ekhMy%2FbE5FmxcWmYKGMgBg
&pagewanted=all.
Lagiou, P., et al. "Low Carbohydrate–High Protein Diet and Incidence of Cardiovascular Diseases in Swedish Women: Prospective Cohort Study." *British Medical
Journal*, 344 (2012): e4026. http://www.bmj.com/highwire/filestream/591596/
field_highwire_article_pdf/0/bmj.e4026.
Landro, Laura. "Giving More Support to Support-Group Leaders." *Wall Street Journal*, April 19, 2012. http://online.wsj.com/article/SB1000142405270230443270
4577347841297047380.html.
Margolius, D., et al. "Health Coaching to Improve Hypertension Treatment in a
Low-Income, Minority Population." *Annals of Family Medicine*, 10, no. 3 (2012):
199–205. http://annfammed.org/content/10/3/199.full.pdf+html.
Mayo Clinic. "Cardiac Rehabilitation." August 19, 2011. http://www.mayoclinic
.com/health/cardiac-rehabilitation/MY00771.
———. "Home Care Services: Questions to Ask." May 25, 2011. http://www
.mayoclinic.com/health/home-care-services/HO00084.
———. "Lifestyle and Home Remedies." Updated January 16, 2013. http://www.mayo
clinic.com/health/heart-disease/DS01120/DSECTION=lifestyle-and-home-remedies.
McDowell, Dimity. "Move Over Book Club, Fitness Parties Are Hot." *Health*, 26,
no. 9 (2012): 55–56. http://www.health.com/health/article/0,,20637701,00.html.

Medicare.gov. "Nursing Homes." Updated August 3, 2012. http://www.medicare
.gov/nursing/alternatives.asp.

MedlinePlus. "Cardiac Rehabilitation." Updated May 24, 2013. http://www.nlm.nih
.gov/medlineplus/cardiacrehabilitation.html.

———. "Caregivers." Updated March 27, 2013. http://www.nlm.nih.gov/medlineplus/
caregivers.html.

———. "Heart Disease in Women." Updated April 29, 2013. http://www.nlm.nih
.gov/medlineplus/heartdiseaseinwomen.html.

———. "Heart Diseases—Prevention." Updated May 24, 2013. http://www.nlm.nih
.gov/medlineplus/heartdiseasesprevention.html.

———. "Heart Failure." Updated May 24, 2013. http://www.nlm.nih.gov/medlineplus/
heartfailure.html.

———. "Heart Surgery." Updated May 24, 2013. http://www.nlm.nih.gov/medlineplus/
heartsurgery.html.

———. "Home Care Services." Updated May 13, 2013. http://www.nlm.nih.gov/
medlineplus/homecareservices.html.

National Cancer Institute. "Caring for the Caregiver." June 29, 2007. http://www
.cancer.gov/cancertopics/coping/caring-for-the-caregiver.

National Heart, Lung, and Blood Institute. "Heart and Vascular Diseases." Updated
August 2011. http://www.nhlbi.nih.gov/health/public/heart/index.htm.

———. "How Does Smoking Affect the Heart and Blood Vessels?" Updated December 20, 2011. http://www.nhlbi.nih.gov/health/health-topics/topics/smo/.

———. "Talking with Your Doctor" Updated April 22, 2013. http://www.nia.nih
.gov/health/publication/talking-your-doctor-guide-older-people.

———. "What Is a Heart Attack" Updated March 1, 2011. http://www.nhlbi.nih.gov/
health/health-topics/topics/heartattack/.

———. "What Is an Implantable Cardioverter Defibrillator?" Updated November 9,
2011. http://www.nhlbi.nih.gov/health/health-topics/topics/icd/.

———. "What Is Cardiac Rehabilitation?" Updated February 22, 2012. http://www
.nhlbi.nih.gov/health/health-topics/topics/rehab/.

———. "What Is Cholesterol?" Updated September 19, 2012. http://www.nhlbi.nih
.gov/health/health-topics/topics/hbc/.

———. "What Is Heart Failure?" Updated January 9, 2012. http://www.nhlbi.nih
.gov/health/health-topics/topics/hf/.

———. "What Is Heart Surgery?" Updated March 23, 2012. http://www.nhlbi.nih
.gov/health/health-topics/topics/hs/.

———. "What Is Physical Activity?" Updated September 26, 2011. http://www.nhlbi
.nih.gov/health/health-topics/topics/phys/.

National Public Radio. "Red Meat's Heart Risk Goes Beyond the Fat" (transcript).
Talk of the Nation, April 12, 2013. http://www.npr.org/2013/04/12/177029247/
red-meats-heart-risk-goes-beyond-the-fat.

3

Reinberg, Steven. "'Atkins'-Type Diets May Raise Risk of Heart Problems: Study." HealthDay. June 27, 2012. http://consumer.healthday.com/Article.asp?AID=666110.

Roberts, Timothy. "Searching the Internet for Health Information: Techniques for Patients to Effectively Search Both Public and Professional Websites." Hospital for Special Surgery. April 30, 2010. http://www.hss.edu/conditions_techniques-patients-search-health-websites.asp.

U.S. News and World Report. "2012–2013 Best Diets." August 2012. http://health.usnews.com/best-diet.

Wang, Z., et al. "Gut Flora Metabolism of Phosphatidylcholine Promotes Cardiovascular Disease." *Nature,* 472 (2011): 57–63. http://www.nature.com/nature/journal/v472/n7341/full/nature09922.html.

WebMD—Heart Disease Health Center. "Cardiac Rehabilitation—Topic Overview." Updated April 25, 2011. http://www.webmd.com/heart-disease/tc/cardiac-rehabilitation-topic-overview.

———. "Heart Disease and Cardiac Rehabilitation." Reviewed February 15, 2012. http://www.webmd.com/heart-disease/guide/heart-disease-cardiac-rehabilitation.

———. "Heart Disease Resources." Reviewed July 14, 2012. http://www.webmd.com/heart-disease/guide/heart-disease-resources.

———. "Heart Failure: Activity and Exercise." Updated July 30, 2010. http://www.webmd.com/heart-disease/heart-failure/activity-and-exercise-for-heart-failure.

WomensHealth.gov. "Patient Education (for Women)." Accessed April 6, 2013. http://www.womenshealth.gov/heart-truth/clinical-resources/patient-education.cfm#d.

Chapter 8

Heart Disease in Women

Salted in among the previous information on heart disease is information about women's specific issues with heart disease. To make things more clear and accessible, we compiled women's heart issues in this chapter. *See this chapter's final section,* RESOURCES FOR FURTHER INFORMATION ON HEART DISEASE IN WOMEN, *for all references on heart disease in women.*

Heart health in women is affected by both biological (sex) and behavioral (gender) factors. Women have identical heart and circulatory structures to men. Yet women have smaller hearts and coronary arteries than men. On average, a woman's heart weighs about eight ounces (approximately two ounces less than a man's) and is about the size of a clenched fist. It pumps more than eight pints of blood throughout a woman's body every minute. Other sex-based differences include hormones, pregnancy, smaller vessels, a higher incidence of diabetes in women, and obesity as a higher risk factor for women than men. Microvascular disease is also more common in women, who have different biological responses to emotional events (sometimes known as "broken heart" syndrome) than men. Gender differences include a higher incidence of depression in women, more prescription drug use, barriers to health care, different use of available treatments, and less clinical trial evidence supporting how to diagnose and treat heart disease in women.

Heart risk factors of particular concern for women, according to the American Heart Association, include cardiovascular disease (CVD), diabetes, peripheral artery disease, and renal disease. Various forms of heart disease, which include coronary artery disease (CAD), high blood pressure, atherosclerosis, heart failure, and heart attacks, cause more than 250,000 deaths a year among women. It is estimated that about one woman per minute dies from cardiovascular disease. The rate of women who die from cardiovascular disease (43 percent of all female deaths) is much higher than for those who die from breast cancer. Of those who die suddenly of heart disease, 64 percent had no previous symptoms. More women than men will die within the first year after they suffer a heart attack.

To learn more, visit the **National Heart, Lung, and Blood Institute** of the National Institutes of Health at http://www.nhlbi.nih.gov/health/health-topics/topics/hdw/. This webpage includes an illustration of a heart with muscle damage and a blocked artery. Part A shows the heart muscle death caused by a heart attack. Part B shows plaque buildup in an artery and the resulting blood clot.

Risk Factors for Heart Disease in Women

The average lifetime risk of having heart disease in women is one in two. In addition, having one or two disease risk factors increases the risk of heart disease close to three times, while having three factors will increase the risk almost six times. The key risk factors of heart disease in women include age, menopausal status, smoking, family history of premature coronary disease, depression, sedentary lifestyle, metabolic problems, and obesity. African American and Hispanic American/Latina women have higher risk factors than white women. These risk factors are the same for men and women other than menopause and sex hormone–related risks, but they differ in their degree of associated risk for heart disease (e.g., diabetes is a greater risk in women than in men).

In 2007, the American Heart Association (AHA) changed the cardiovascular disease risk classification for women. High-risk classification now includes women with known coronary disease, diabetes, and peripheral arterial disease, as well as those with chronic renal disease and a 10-year Framingham risk score (which includes age, gender, smoking, blood pressure, and cholesterol levels) of more than 20 percent.

Controllable Risk Factors

Anemia

Anemia, which is a below-normal level of red blood cells, increases women's risk for heart disease problems. Red blood cells carry oxygen throughout the body. A lower-than-normal level of red blood cells is thought to slow the growth of the cells needed to repair damaged blood vessels.

Birth Control Pills

Low-dose (20 to 30 micrograms of estrogen) birth control pills or birth control patches are not a risk factor for heart disease in women who do not already have serious heart disease risk factors. Such risk factors include women who smoke; have high blood pressure; are overweight or obese; have diabetes; have a diagnosis of heart disease, have had a stroke, or have had blood clots; or have a family history of heart disease.

Diabetes

Diabetes, both type 1 and type 2, increases the risk for heart disease. The excess sugar in the blood causes blood vessel problems, increasing the possibility of developing high blood pressure, atherosclerosis, and blood clots. Women with diabetes are three to seven times more likely to develop heart disease than women without diabetes (compared to two to three times in men). Women with diabetes are two to five times more likely to die of heart disease than women without diabetes. Women who have heart disease and have had diabetes for more than 15 years are 30 times more likely to die sooner than women with neither condition.

Diet

Too much sugar can lead to weight gain, and foods high in saturated fat can lead to increases in cholesterol and triglyceride levels in the blood. Too much alcohol can lead to weight gain and an increase in blood pressure.

Emotional Conditions (e.g., Stress and Depression)

Stress increases blood pressure, which in turn increases risk for heart attack. Stress can cause arteries to constrict and decrease blood flow to critical organs. Depressed people have an increased risk in developing coronary heart disease. Depression occurs twice as often in women as in men.

Hormone Therapy

Hormone replacement therapy (HRT) is prescribed to women to reduce symptoms of early menopause, such as hot flashes, anxiety, and depression. For numerous years there have been major controversies over long-term use of HRT, which has been suspected of causing serious health risks, including heart attack, stroke, and breast cancer. Results of a 10-year, randomized controlled trial, published in the *British Medical Journal*, involving 1,006 "recently Postmenopausal" women, those with perimenopausal symptoms, and those who had undergone hysterectomy (aged 45 to 58, average age: 50), indicated that the use of HRT may lower women's risk of death, heart attack, and heart failure "without any apparent increase in risk of cancer, venous thromboembolism, or stroke." The study results included an additional six years after stopping the use of HRT (Schierbeck et al., 2012). Previously, a Women's Health Initiative randomized, double-blinded, placebo-controlled trial of 16,608 healthy women (aged 50 to 79, average age: 63, and all participants were at least 10 years postmenopausal) found that HRT users had a slightly higher risk of heart disease, blood clots, and stroke than women who did not receive HRT. In addition, a combination of estrogen and progestin provided no protection from heart attack, stroke, or heart disease, as reported in the *Annals of Internal Medicine* (Toh et al., 2010). The trial was stopped early because women taking-hormone therapy also began to show an increased risk of breast cancer. The main difference between the two randomized controlled trials was the use of HRT since menopause began.

Lack of Exercise

Lack of exercise can lead to poor cardiovascular circulation, high blood cholesterol and triglyceride levels, high blood pressure, being overweight or obese, and diabetes.

Metabolic Syndrome

Metabolic syndrome (also called dysmetabolic syndrome, insulin resistance syndrome, and syndrome X) occurs in patients who are overweight or obese and are inactive and have other risk factors, including abdominal obesity, high triglyceride blood level, low blood level of high-density lipoprotein (HDL) cholesterol, high blood pressure, and high fasting blood sugar. Being inactive means that one is getting little or no physical exercise (e.g., walking, jogging, bicycling, aerobics, swimming, sport activity). Women with metabolic syndrome have twice the risk of developing heart or cardiovascular disease.

Although metabolic syndrome occurs basically equally among Caucasian women, African American women, and Mexican American women, women are more likely to have metabolic syndrome than their male counterparts. Whereas family history cannot be altered, lifestyle changes in diet and exercise can reduce the risk or prevent heart and cardiovascular disease from occurring. (*See also* CHAPTER 3: METABOLIC SYNDROME.)

Obesity

As a woman's body mass index (BMI) increases, so does her risk of dying from heart disease, according a Nurses' Health Study of more than 115,000 women published in the *Archives of Internal Medicine* (now *JAMA Internal Medicine*; Wilson et al., 2002). In this study, obese women had about four times the risk of dying from heart disease as normal weight women. Being overweight or obese can also affect the risk of heart disease indirectly by increasing the likelihood of developing risk factors for heart disease. *Overweight* is the term for a person with a BMI higher than 25 but lower than 30. *Obese* is the term for a person with a BMI higher than 30.

Pregnancy

In a study published in 2006 by James and colleagues, researchers searched pregnancy-related discharge records from approximately 1,000 hospitals nationwide. During 2000 to 2002, there were about six heart attacks per 100,000 deliveries. The risk was about 30 times higher for women 40 years and older compared with younger mothers. Women with inherited blood-clotting problems had 25 times higher risk of heart attack. High blood pressure increased the risk almost 22 times. Pregnant smokers were eight times more likely to have a heart attack than nonsmokers. African American women older than 35 years appeared to have the highest risk, but this was likely because they were more likely to have high blood pressure.

A woman who has a history of heart disease, heart murmur, rheumatic fever, or high blood pressure should talk with her physician before she decides to become pregnant. A woman who has congenital heart disease has a higher risk of having a baby with some type of heart defect. Sometimes women with normal hearts experience cardiac abnormalities during pregnancy, including heart murmurs, which are usually caused by extra blood flowing through the heart; arrhythmias, which are fast or slow heartbeats that may be regular or irregular and may cause symptoms such as palpitations, dizziness, or lightheadedness; and high blood pressure (hypertension), which is a serious complication. When very high blood pressure occurs with rapid weight gain, swollen ankles, and protein in the urine, this condition is called preeclampsia, which is the leading cause of premature birth in the United States.

Sleep Apnea

Sleep apnea is a chronic sleeping disorder in which breathing intermittently stops; this pause can last from a few seconds to minutes at a time. Breathing typically starts again. However, these stoppages can happen from a few times to more than 30 times an hour. If not treated, sleep apnea can lead to high blood pressure or heart attack. In women, sleep apnea occurs more often after menopause.

Smoking

Of all lifestyle risks, smoking tobacco, even one cigarette per day, is one of the worst. Continued exposure to secondhand smoke is another high risk. The carbon monoxide from smoking displaces oxygen in the blood, which causes plaque to build up in the arteries, narrowing the vessels. Also, blood clot formation (thrombus) increases in these arteries.

Uncontrollable Risk Factors

Age

Women tend to develop heart disease 10 to 15 years later than men do and, therefore, are usually older and more likely to have diabetes when they have their first heart attack. As a result, they are not able to undergo invasive procedures as often and are more likely to die.

Family History

A family history of early heart disease means that a parent, brother or sister, or child was diagnosed with heart disease or died suddenly from heart problems before age 65 in women or before age 55 in men. Genetic factors and lifestyle factors (such as smoking, diet, and exercise) determine the risk of developing heart disease. Women with a family history of early heart disease are three times more likely to have a heart attack and five times more likely to die from heart disease than women without a family history of heart disease.

Menopause

The risk of heart disease is higher for women after age 55. Women's hearts are thought to be protected by estrogen. Levels of estrogen in the body drop after menopause, which usually occurs in the mid-fifties. Estrogen affects the levels of cholesterol and fat in the blood, changes the way blood clots, varies how well blood flows, alters how blood vessels respond to their environment, and affects many factors related to the buildup of fatty plaques in the arteries.

Some risk factors for clotting problems include C-reactive protein, inflammation, some inflammatory diseases (e.g., lupus and rheumatoid arthritis), high blood pressure, high cholesterol, low bone density, infection, metabolic syndrome, and mental health. (*See also* CHAPTER 5: RISK FACTORS.)

Women's Heart Disease Issues

As noted, women are different from men. When women have heart problems, these also differ from what happens to men. For example, a woman's smaller heart probably makes her more likely to develop coronary microvascular disease, which is very difficult to detect. Other issues are presented in the sections that follow.

Arrhythmia

To determine heart rhythm irregularities, an electrocardiogram (ECG) is used to measure the electrical activity of the heart; however, the measurement of the QT interval is always shorter in men than in women. Therefore ECG stress test results are less accurate in women. In women who have a genetic disorder called congenital long QT interval, the condition becomes more pronounced over time than it does in men.

Broken Heart Syndrome or Stress Cardiomyopathy

Broken heart syndrome or stress cardiomyopathy primarily affects women who are middle-aged or elderly (average age about 60 and most are postmenopausal). It can, however, occur in young women and also in men.

Intense emotional or physical stress can cause sensations of chest pain or heart attack. A temporary condition, it can occur after emotional stress (such as grief, fear, anger, or surprise) or after physical stress (such as stroke, seizure, difficulty breathing, or severe bleeding). A surge of stress hormones may cause sudden, severe heart muscle weakness. Patients usually make a rapid and complete recovery within a few days or months.

In May 2005, Ilon Wittstein, assistant professor at the Heart Institute of the Johns Hopkins University School of Medicine, published a breakthrough study in the *New England Journal of Medicine* (*NEJM*) describing how to distinguish between a heart attack and broken heart syndrome. This study has helped prevent prescribing aggressive treatment as for a heart attack. Sudden broken heart syndrome is not caused by blood clot or narrowed arteries and can be diagnosed simply by using heart angiography. According to this *NEJM* report, in Japan the heart condition was "referred to as 'takotsubo cardiomyopathy,' named for the fishing pot with a narrow neck and wide base that is used to trap octopus." Wittstein notes, "In this country, a more apt description might be that of a boxing glove with the strings pulled tight. It was a shape of the heart we had never seen before." Currently, studies with large numbers of patients are under way to help answer the question of what increases the risk for stress cardiomyopathy.

Cardiac Syndrome X (Microvascular Angina)

Also known as microvascular angina, cardiac syndrome X is when a patient (70 percent are women) feels sudden chest pain similar to angina but does not have the blocked or narrowed arteries that usually cause angina (a major risk factor of a heart attack). Angiography or radiography is used to diagnose this condition. The cause of cardiac syndrome X is not known, but the syndrome is also not a risk factor for heart disease. Studies have indicated that cardiac syndrome X occurs most often after menopause, so it has been suggested that one cause might be the drop in estrogen levels that occurs at this time. Another suspected cause is having small blood vessels (known as microvascular dysfunction), which can reduce oxygen flow, particularly triggered by exercise. Cardiac syndrome X can be confused with the condition known as metabolic syndrome (formally known as metabolic syndrome X); however, unlike with cardiac syndrome X, the group of risk factors associated with metabolic syndrome can cause cardiovascular disease.

Coronary Microvascular Disease

Coronary microvascular disease (CMVD) is a disease of the heart's tiny coronary arteries (arterioles). Diagnosing CMVD is difficult because standard tests used to diagnose heart disease look for blockages in large coronary arteries. These same tests used in women with symptoms of heart disease often show that they have "clear" arteries.

To learn more, visit the **National Heart, Lung, and Blood Institute** of the National Institutes of Health at http://www.nhlbi.nih.gov/health/health-topics/topics/hdw/. This webpage includes an illustration of CMVD. Part A shows the small coronary artery network (microvasculature) with a normal artery and a CMVD artery. Part B shows a large coronary artery with plaque buildup.

CMVD is a newer concept that is currently being studied as a possible cause of heart disease in women, according to the National Heart, Lung, and Blood Institute. Women may be at risk for CMVD if they have low levels of estrogen at any time as an adult. (This refers to estrogen that the ovaries produce, not estrogen used in hormone replacement therapy.) Lower than normal estrogen levels in women before menopause also can put younger women at higher risk for CMVD. Low estrogen levels in younger women may be caused by stress or problems with the ovaries. As mentioned in the section on menopause, women tend to have more of the traditional risk factors for atherosclerosis after menopause, putting them at higher risk for coronary CMVD at that stage in life.

Health Outcomes

Heart disease is one of the most studied conditions in which sex- and gender-based differences in health outcomes have been found, according to *Literature Review on Effective Sex- and Gender-Based Systems/Models of Care*, produced for the Office on Women's Health, U.S. Department of Health and Human Services. This report found that:

- diagnostic mistakes are made more frequently in women than in men;
- women tend to die more often after coronary bypass surgery and angioplasty;
- women with heart failure are more likely to have a lower quality of life with more frequent depression compared with men; and
- women with acute heart attack die in the hospital more frequently than men.

Obstructive Coronary Artery Disease

Obstructive coronary artery disease (CAD) is when one or more coronary arteries (2 mm in diameter or larger) are 70 percent or more blocked (stenosis). The main symptoms are angina (chest pain), pressure, and tightness of the chest, symptoms that have been considered more "typical" in men than women. If these symptoms are present, a coronary angiogram should be performed to diagnose obstructive CAD and allow for treatment to help prevent a heart attack, stroke, or death. However, contrary to what has been believed, according to lead researcher Catherine Kreatsoulas, PhD, of the Harvard School of Public Health, in a study published in *JAMA Internal Medicine* (May 2013), most women do experience these same three major symptoms and in similar percentages (chest pain: 82 percent of men and 84 percent of women), pressure (54 and 58 percent, respectively), and tightness (43 and 58 percent, respectively). To accompany this article, Rita Redberg (2013), MD, of the University of California, San Francisco, an editor for *JAMA Internal Medicine*, wrote, "It is likely that atypical symptoms represent women who do not have ischemic [obstructive] CAD. These findings should be a great relief to the many women who have been concerned that they could be having a myocardial infarction unbeknownst to them because they would not get the typical warning symptoms of chest pain."

Symptoms of Heart Attack

Women experience different symptoms of a heart attack than men do. These symptoms are described as aching, tightness, or pressure but not pain over the left chest. Women do experience mid-back, shoulder, or arm pain, and they may also experience shortness of breath and sweating (symptoms also experienced by men). Many women also experience an early warning of intermittent symptoms that increase in frequency and severity more than a month before a heart attack. Unfortunately, women and their physicians often fail to recognize these symptoms as a warning or onset of a heart attack. Also, these symptoms are often undertreated even if they are recognized. For example, women are less likely to have an ECG performed within 10 minutes of hospitalization. It is also more common for women to have a silent heart attack in which few, if any, symptoms are experienced.

Some symptoms experienced by women are often called atypical, although this is a misleading label because these symptoms are relatively common in women. Atypical symptoms include back, neck, or jaw pain; nausea and vomiting; indigestion (similar to acid reflux or gastroesophageal reflux disease); weakness; fatigue; and dizziness and light-headedness. Women experience more of these "atypical" symptoms at the time of a heart attack than men. According to the American Heart Association's section "Heart Attack Symptoms in Women," although for both men and women the major symptom of a heart attack is chest pain, women are more likely than men to experience "shortness of breath with or without chest discomfort, nausea/vomiting, and back or jaw pain."

Resources for Further Information on Heart Disease in Women

Books

> American Heart Association. *American Heart Association Complete Guide to Women's Heart Health: The Go Red for Women Way to Well-Being and Vitality.* New York, NY: Clarkson Potter, 2011. Print.
> American Heart Association's book focuses on empowering women with knowledge about heart disease. The book is divided into four sections: what everyone needs to know, choosing a heart-healthy lifestyle (each chapter divided by age ranges), heart care (diagnostic tests and treatments), and resources (e.g., screenings, warning signs, how to talk to your doctor).

> Elefteriades, John A., and Teresa Caulin-Glaser. *The Woman's Heart: An Owner's Guide.* Amherst, NY: Prometheus, 2008. Print.
> Two heart specialists focus on the complexity of a woman's heart from anatomy and physiology to why some procedures and surgery are not as effective in women as in men. The book explains heart risks during different phases of a woman's life, recognizing a heart problem, the connection between emotions and heart risks, genetics, and the female heart. Chapters also cover living with heart disease, increasing strength and staying healthy, and answers to frequently asked questions.

This 304-page book is written in everyday language and prepares readers to monitor their own heart health.

> Goldberg, Nieca. *The Women's Healthy Heart Program: Lifesaving Strategies for Preventing and Healing Heart Disease.* New York, NY: Ballantine Books, 2006. Print.
> Goldberg's book explains how physiology of a woman's heart, symptoms of heart disease, and signs of impending heart attack are different for women than for men. The book also offers age-specific programs to help women recognize, treat, and prevent heart disease.

> Gulati, Martha, and Sherry Torkos. *Saving Women's Hearts: How You Can Prevent and Reverse Heart Disease with Natural and Conventional Strategies.* Mississauga, Ontario: Wiley, 2011. Print.
> Gulati is a cardiologist and an associate professor of medicine at the Ohio State University; she specialize in heart disease prevention in women. Torkos is a pharmacist. Their book describes symptoms, screening and diagnosis procedures, treatment options, and prevention of heart disease specifically in women.

> Kastan, Kathy. *From the Heart: A Woman's Guide to Living Well with Heart Disease.* Cambridge, MA: Da Capo Press, 2007. Print.
> Kastan is president of WomenHeart: The National Coalition for Women with Heart Disease and chair of the board of the Memphis American Heart Association. Kastan, who at age 42 had emergency bypass surgery, explains through personal experience what she endured, how she recovered, and how she moved forward in managing her heart health. As a therapist, she learned from other women who have heart disease how they survived and shares what she learned in this book.

> Latrella, Margaret, and Carolyn Strimike. *Take Charge: Woman's Guide to a Healthier Heart.* Indianapolis, IN: Dog Ear Publishing, 2008. Print.
> Written by two cardiac nurse practitioners, this easy-to-use reference and workbook explains how to prevent heart disease and stroke by adopting good health habits. The book covers risk factors and women's issues, including menopause, birth control pills, polycystic ovary syndrome, inflammation, periodontal gum disease, and sleep. The section on nutrition offers tips for dining out, managing portion control, food shopping, and reading food labels. A worksheet helps readers determine their risk scores, and a checklist prepares them for doctor visits. Additional worksheets cover topics such as knowing your numbers, logging in your daily food intake and physical activity, charting blood pressure, and writing down important medical information. *Take Charge* is available as a Google e-book at http://books.google.com/books/about/Take_Charge.html?id=lJajbuFbe2IC.

> Roberts, Barbara H. *How to Keep from Breaking Your Heart,* 2nd ed. Sudbury, MA: Jones and Bartlett, 2009. Print.

Roberts, who is the director of the Women's Cardiac Center at the Miriam Hospital, presents a detailed, easy-to-understand, patient-friendly book on heart disease that focuses on risk factors, prevention, and treatment.

Brochures, Booklets, and Other Short Print Publications

➢ American Society of Nuclear Cardiology Patient Awareness Initiative—"Women and Heart Disease" (Brochure). http://www.asnc.org/imageuploads/PatientInfoBrochure -Women031709.pdf; alternate path: http://www.asnc.org/, search for "women and heart disease," click on the title "Patient Awareness Brochures," and then scroll down to click on the brochure "Women and Heart Disease."
This brochure covers risk factors, risk reduction, screening for heart disease including myocardial perfusion imaging, and women and heart disease. This full-color, trifold brochure can be downloaded.

➢ British Heart Foundation (BHF)—"Women and Heart Disease" (Booklet). http:// www.bhf.org.uk/publications/view-publication.aspx?ps=1000711; alternate path: http://www.bhf.org.uk/, search for "women and heart disease," click on the title "British Heart Foundation—Women and Heart Disease," click on "Women and Heart Disease," and then scroll down and click on "Women and Heart Disease: Download Our Booklet."
The BHF offers a free booklet on women and heart disease. The website notes that "many women aren't aware that they are three times as likely to die from heart and circulatory disease, than from breast cancer."

➢ Illinois Department of Public Health, Office of Women's Health. "Women and Heart Disease" (Brochure). http://www.idph.state.il.us/about/womenshealth/ pubs/HeartHealthybrochure.pdf; alternate path: http://www.idph.state.il.us/, click on "W," and then scroll down to click on "Women's Health." Then click on the topic "Publications," and then scroll down to the publication title "Women and Heart Disease."
This brochure from the Office of Women's Health covers heart attack risk factors, heart attack and stroke warning signs, and preventing heart disease. It is available as a trifold, two-color PDF.

➢ National Heart, Lung, and Blood Institute (NHLBI). *The Healthy Heart Handbook for Women.* http://www.nhlbi.nih.gov/health/public/heart/other/hhw/, then click on the title to download; alternate path: http://www.nhlbi.nih.gov/, search for "healthy heart handbook women," and then click on the title "Healthy Heart Handbook for Women."
NHLBI is a division of National Institutes of Health from the U.S. Department of Health and Human Services. This handbook presents information on women's heart disease and on how to live a healthier and longer life. Practical information

includes steps for preventing and controlling heart disease risk factors. The handbook also provides a guide for developing an action plan for heart hearth, including following a nutritious eating plan, tailoring a physical activity program to personal goals, quitting smoking, and getting the family involved in heart-healthy living. *The Healthy Heart Handbook for Women* is part of The Heart Truth for Women, a national public awareness campaign for women about heart disease sponsored by the NHLBI and many other groups. The 6-inch-by-9-inch, 122-page handbook can be downloaded for free. A printed copy can be ordered for $4.00 via the NHLBI website.

> National Institute of Nursing Research (NINR). "Subtle and Dangerous: Symptoms of Heart Disease in Women" (Booklet). http://www.ninr.nih.gov/sites/www .ninr.nih.gov/files/subtle-and-dangerous-symptoms-heart-disease-in-women -booklet.pdf; alternate path: http://www.ninr.nih.gov/, search for "symptoms heart disease women," and then click on the resource title.
NINR is a division of the National Institutes of Health (NIH) from the U.S. Department of Health and Human Services. This brochure covers heart disease risks for women, subtle symptoms of heart attack, recovery and rehabilitation after heart attack, chronic angina, peripheral artery disease, and factors that increase heart disease risk. This 15-page, two-color booklet can be downloaded as a PDF.

> National Women's Health Resource Center. http://www.healthywomen.org/.
The National Women's Health Resource Center is a nonprofit, national clearinghouse for unbiased and accurate health information for women.
  • "Fast Facts for Your Health: Women and Stroke: Knowing Saves Lives" (Brochure). http://www.healthywomen.org/sites/default/files/FastFactStroke_0.pdf; alternate path: http://www.healthywomen.org/, search for "fast facts women and stroke," click on the title, and then scroll down to the "Download" link to view and/or print this brochure. This free brochure focuses on stroke in women, including warning signs, risk factors, and what to do quickly if you think you are having a stroke. You can order print copies from this website; shipping charges are added when you order more than two items.
  • "Heart to Heart: High Blood Pressure (Talk about It)" (Booklet). http://www .healthywomen.org/sites/default/files/HearttoHeartBooklet.pdf; alternate path: http://www.healthywomen.org/, search for "high blood pressure talk," scroll down to click on the resource title, and then scroll down to the "Download" link to view and/or print this brochure. This free brochure focuses on women and high blood pressure. You can order print copies from this website; shipping charges are added when you order more than two items.
  • "Women's Health Updates: Women's Heart Health News" (Brochure). http:// www.healthywomen.org/sites/default/files/HealthUpdHeartHealth.pdf;

alternate path: http://www.healthywomen.org/, search for "women's heart health news," click on the resource title, and then scroll down to the "Download" link to view and/or print this brochure. This free brochure discusses heart disease in women, prevention, questions to ask, and resources. You can order print copies from this website; shipping charges are added when you order more than two items.

➢ Preventive Cardiovascular Nurses Association (PCNA)—"Living Guidelines for Women: 2011 Heart Disease Prevention Guidelines for Women." http://pcna.net/patients/women-heart-disease; alternate path: http://pcna.net/, search for "living guidelines women," and click on the title "Living Guidelines for Women."
"The American Heart Association, in collaboration with national organizations dedicated to women's health, have released new life-saving guidelines for the prevention of heart disease." A brochure, with lists and a chart, details women's heart disease risk levels from low risk to at risk to high risk. Scroll down to download the print version.

➢ WomensHealth.gov. http://www.womenshealth.gov/.
WomensHealth.gov is a division of the U.S. Department of Health and Human Services. This website offers many brochures focused on heart-healthy living.
 • "Heart Healthy Eating Fact Sheet." http://www.womenshealth.gov/publications/our-publications/fact-sheet/heart-healthy-eating.html; alternate path: http://www.womenshealth.gov/, search for and then click on the title "Heart Healthy Eating Fact Sheet." This website features a downloadable PDF version of this brochure as well as several other heart-healthy-eating publications.
 • "How to Talk to Your Doctor or Nurse." http://www.womenshealth.gov/publications/our-publications/talk-doctor-how-to.pdf; alternate path: http://www.womenshealth.gov/, search for "talk to doctor nurse" and then click on the brochure title or click on the section titled "A–Z Health Topics," then scroll down and click on the title "Heart Health and Stroke," scroll down again to "Features," and then click on the brochure title. According to WomensHealth.gov, "This print-and-go guide can give you tips on talking to your doctor or nurse."

Websites

➢ Administration on Aging. "Heart Disease in Women." http://www.aoa.gov/AoARoot/Press_Room/Social_Media/Widget/Statistical_Profile/2011/7.aspx; alternate path: http://www.aoa.gov/, search for and then click on the title "Heart Disease in Women."
This website from the Administration on Aging, a division of the U.S. Department of Health and Human Services, is designed to assist senior citizens by

Online Search Tips

- If you click on a link (e.g., a title) and nothing happens, try this: right-click on that link and then left-click on the option "Open in new window."
- If you experience problems with PDF documents, you can download the latest version of Adobe Reader for free at http://www.adobe.com/products/reader .html or by going to http://www.adobe.com/ and searching for "adobe reader."
- Adobe Flash Player, required to view most short videos, is available as a free download at http://get.adobe.com/flashplayer/; alternate path: http://www .adobe.com/, choose the "Download" tab on the menu bar, and select the Adobe Flash Player link.

listing federal agencies and several health organizations that offer information and resources for women on preventing heart disease and how to protect health.

➤ American Heart Association (AHA). http://www.americanheart.org/, type "women" in the Search box at the top of the screen to browse a variety of information on women and cardiovascular disease. See also the following resources.

- "Caregiver." http://www.heart.org/HEARTORG/Caregiver/Caregiver_UCM _001103_SubHomePage.jsp; alternate path: http://www.heart.org/, search for and then click on the title "Caregiver." This AHA section focuses exclusively on the caregiver, offering "Top 10 Tips to Refresh Yourself," as well as links to "[Caregiver] Rights," "Responsibility [as a Caregiver]," "Reality Check [for a Caregiver]," "Refresh [Yourself as a Caregiver]," "Rejuvenate [Yourself as the Caregiver with Physical Activity for Mental and Physical Health]," "Replenish [by Eating Well]," "Reach Out" [when communicating "with family, friends, co-workers, employers, healthcare professionals, insurance companies—and a loved one"], and "Resources."
- "Go Red for Women." http://www.goredforwomen.org/. Go Red for Women is an educational program of the AHA. Sections under the tab "Healthy at Any Age" include prevention, know your numbers, live heart healthy, ask our specialists, taking heart—together, and heart-healthy recipes. This website offers an easy-to-use interactive heart checkup that takes less than 10 minutes to complete. Based on the results of the checkup, this AHA website provides a risk report that provides information about the user's risk of developing heart disease in the next 10 years. The user can print this report and take it to her doctor. The site also provides action plans based on the online heart checkup.
- "Heart Attack Symptoms in Women." http://www.heart.org/HEARTORG/ Conditions/HeartAttack/WarningSignsofaHeartAttack/Heart-Attack -Symptoms-in-Women_UCM_436448_Article.jsp; alternate path: http:// www.heart.org/, search for and then click on the title "Heart Attack

Symptoms in Women." This American Heart Association website offers the latest list on heart attack signs in women, along with an animation of a heart attack. Links to other heart attack topics include warning signs, understanding risks, diagnosis, treatment, and prevention. Available is an e-mail sign-up for the AHA's Heart-Health E-news, with several heart topics from which to choose.

➤ British Heart Foundation (BHF)—"Women and Heart Disease." http://www.bhf .org.uk/heart-health/conditions/women-and-heart-disease.aspx; alternate path: http://www.bhf.org.uk/, search for "women and heart disease," and then click on the title "British Heart Foundation—Women and Heart Disease."
The BHF website on women and heart disease includes discussions on recognizing the symptoms of a heart attack and angina, as well as protecting yourself against heart disease. You can also take a free lifestyle check. There is also a link to a podcast on five things to do to lower cholesterol. Available is a section called "Community: Share Experiences with Others."

➤ Centers for Disease Control and Prevention (CDC), Division for Heart Disease and Stroke Prevention (DHDSP)—"WISEWOMAN (Well-Integrated Screening and Evaluation for WOMen Across the Nation)." http://www.cdc.gov/ wisewoman/; alternate path: http://www.cdc.gov/, search for "wisewoman," and then scroll down to click on "CDC—WISEWOMAN Index—DHDSP."
According to the CDC, a part of the U.S. Department of Health and Human Services, the "WISEWOMAN program provides low-income, under-insured or uninsured women with chronic disease risk factor screening, lifestyle intervention, and referral services in an effort to prevent cardiovascular disease. The priority age group is women aged 40–64 years."

➤ Cleveland Clinic (Cleveland, OH). "Heart Failure and Women." http://my .clevelandclinic.org/heart/disorders/heartfailure/hfwomen/women.aspx; alternate path: http://my.clevelandclinic.org/, under the category "Institutes and Services," click on "Heart and Vascular," then click on the category "Diseases and Conditions," then scroll down to the title "Heart Failure," and then click on the "Heart Failure and Women" link in the text.
The Cleveland Clinic provides comprehensive patient-friendly information on heart failure in women, including definitions, causes, symptoms, diagnosis, treatments, prognosis and outlook, and a link to the Center for Women and Heart Disease. The Cleveland Clinic also offers a link to "Chat Online with a Heart and Vascular Nurse." To participate in a clinical trial at the Cleveland Clinic Heart Center, go to http://my.clevelandclinic.org/heart/research/clinicalresearch.aspx; or click on the category "Research and Innovations," and under the category "For Patients" click on the title "Clinical Research," and then click on "Search for a Clinical Trial."

➢ HeartHealthyWomen.org. http://www.hearthealthywomen.org/.
HeartHealthyWomen.org is a joint project of the Cardiovascular Research Foundation, the Office on Women's Health of the U.S. Department of Health and Human Services, and WomenHeart: The National Coalition for Women with Heart Disease. HeartHealthyWomen.org provides sections on cardiovascular disease, risk factors, signs and symptoms, tests and diagnoses, health and wellness, and resources and links. It also offers feature stories in a magazine-style format, as well as an opportunity to ask an expert a question. See also the following resource:

- "Cardiac Syndrome X." http://www.hearthealthywomen.org/cardiovascular -disease/cardiac-syndrome-x/cardiac-syndrome-x.html; alternate path: http:// www.hearthealthywomen.org/, click on the heading "Cardiovascular Disease," and then click on the topic "Cardiac Syndrome X." This HeartHealthyWomen .org webpage describes this syndrome, how it differs from other types of chest pain, causes, why women are more likely than men to have cardiac syndrome X, diagnosis, treatment, prevention, and prognosis.

➢ Hospital of the University of Pennsylvania (HUP) (Philadelphia, PA)—"Women's Heart Health Program." http://www.pennmedicine.org/heart/patient/clinical -services/womens-heart-health/; alternate path: http://www.pennmedicine.org/, click on the "Departments and Services" icon (or search for "departments and services"), scroll down to click on the category "Cardiology and Cardiac Surgery," scroll down under the heading "Clinical Services" and click on "View All Clinical Services," and then click on "Women's Heart Health."
HUP offers at its Penn Heart and Vascular Center website patient services in the Women's Heart Health Program, which includes links to "Overview" (combating cardiovascular disease in women); the "Team," with links to each physician and specialist (with profiles, e.g., specialty, medical board certification, education); "Penn Difference" (program described, patient experiences, unique capabilities and expertise, and hospital highlights); and "Physician Interviews" (videos).

➢ Insidermedicine. http://www.Insidermedicine.com/.
The physician-led Insidermedicine Project "allows patients, doctors and medical students to keep up on the latest medical information by watching" videos created each weekday by their team of medical experts, allowing anyone to receive daily evidence-based health and medical updates. Previously created videos are available and free to view or download. Under the heading "Programs," click the category "By Disease or Symptom," scroll through the list of conditions, and click on a heart or cardiovascular topic. Also under the heading "Programs," click on "Universities and Hospitals" for links to "University and Hospital News Segments." From the homepage, you can find the following resources by searching for the videos by title or by part of the title.

- "Low Risk Lifestyle Reduces Risk of Sudden Cardiac Death in Women" (Video). http://www.Insidermedicine.com/archives/Low_Risk_Lifestyle _Reduces_Risk_of_Sudden_Cardiac_Death_in_Women_Video_5368.aspx. In this video, a medical specialist speaks in patient-friendly language on recommendations for managing cardiac arrest. Previously created videos on this website are free to view or download. There are several other videos on sudden cardiac death available for viewing.
- "Risk of Congenital Heart Abnormalities Raised When Mother Is Overweight and Smokes during Pregnancy" (Video). http://www.insidermedicine.com/ archives/Risk_of_Congenital_Heart_Abnormalities_Raised_When_Mother_is _Overweight_and_Smokes_During_Pregnancy_Video_5857.aspx. This video includes an interview with a medical specialist discussing fortified folic acid foods and supplements use during pregnancy to lower risk for congenital heart defects. Previously created videos on this website are free to view or download. There are several other videos related to congenital heart defects available for viewing.
- "Young Women More Likely to Suffer a Heart Attack Without Chest Pain" (Video). http://www.insidermedicine.com/archives/Young_Women _Who_Suffer_A_Heart_Attack_Without_Chest_Pain_At_Increased_Risk _of_Death_Video_5912.aspx. In this video, a cardiologist speaks about the importance of calling 911 when suffering a heart attack, symptoms (men versus women), and treatments. Previously created videos on this website are free to view or download. There are several other videos on heart attack available for viewing.

➢ Johns Hopkins Hospital (Baltimore, MD)—"Women's Cardiovascular Health Center" (Clinical Services). http://www.hopkinsmedicine.org/heart_vascular _institute/clinical_services/centers_excellence/womens_cardiovascular_health _center/; alternate path: http://www.hopkinsmedicine.org/, search for "women's cardiovascular health center," and then click on the title.

The Johns Hopkins Women's Cardiovascular Health Center of offers a "unique cardiovascular health program [that] combines advanced medical treatment with a whole-body approach to preventing and managing heart disease. Our multidisciplinary team combines experienced cardiologists from the Johns Hopkins Heart and Vascular Institute with fitness, nutrition, and mental health experts." For comprehensive information on women and heart disease, click on such categories as risk factors, services (including evaluation and disease management, lifestyle management, diagnostic testing, and treatment), patient information (including articles about heart health and accessing cardiovascular risk assessment tools), and research published by cardiovascular staff members of Johns Hopkins. Click on videos from the Women's Cardiovascular Health

Center. Also, click on the heading "Clinical Trials" for links to current trials in various heart and cardiovascular conditions.

➤ Massachusetts General Hospital (MGH) (Boston, MA)—"Corrigan Women's Heart Health Program." http://www.massgeneral.org/heartcenter/services/treatmentprograms .aspx?id=1011; alternate path: http://www.massgeneral.org/, search for "Corrigan Women's Heart Health Program" or click on "Centers and Services," click on "View All Departments," then click on "Heart Center," click on the heading "Treatments and Services," and then scroll down and click on the topic.

The Corrigan Women's Heart Health Program at the MGH Heart Center website offers links to comprehensive information in several categories. "Our Approach" includes an overview of their multidisciplinary team approach created especially for women with heart disease, guiding the patient through tests and procedures, and links to physicians with their profile. "About This Program" describes the benefits and the team's commitment as "advocates for preventing heart disease" in women at their Corrigan Women's Heart Health Program at MGH. "Conditions and Diseases" has links to detailed information about heart conditions and diseases that might be treated within this program, including aortic aneurisms, angina pectoris, arrhythmias, atrial fibrillation, cardiac sarcoma, cardiomyopathy, chest pain, congenital heart defects, coronary heart disease, heart attack and heart failure, heart valve disease, high blood pressure, pericarditis, and rheumatic heart disease. "Support and Wellness" offers patient guides, including "Understanding and Preparing for a Catheterization Procedure" and "Frequently Asked Questions about Cardiac Anesthesia." "Clinical Trials" has links to numerous MGH trials and research studies that are currently seeking participants. "News and Events" includes the latest information on related topics with event dates, and "Multimedia" contains video demonstrations.

➤ Medicare—"Heart Disease and Women." http://www.medicare.gov/Pubs/pdf/11294 .pdf; alternate path: http://www.medicare.gov/, search for "heart disease and women," and then scroll down to click on the topic.

Also, click on the title "Ask Medicare," for caregiver information. This website includes information on cardiovascular screening, heart conditions, and vascular diseases. Click also on the headings including "Manage Your Health," "Medicare Basics," and "Resource Locator." Click on the heading "Home" for links to other Medicare services and plan comparisons.

➤ MedicineNet.com—"Heart Disease in Women." http://www.medicinenet.com/ script/main/art.asp?articlekey=11014; alternate path: http://www.medicinenet .com/, click on the major topic "Diseases and Conditions," click on "H," and then scroll down to the topic.

MedicineNet is owned and operated by WebMD and is a part of the WebMD Network. According to its website, MedicineNet "provides easy-to-read, in-depth, authoritative medical information for consumers via its robust user-friendly, interactive website." In-depth information on risks for women, smoking cigarettes, cholesterol treatment, diagnosis of heart attack, treatment of heart attack, estrogen and coronary heart disease in women, HERS (Heart and Estrogen/progestin Replacement Study trial results), WHI (World Health Initiative) trial results, and recommendations for the use of estrogens plus medroxyprogesterone (progestin) in women. The medical information is written and edited by a nationally recognized group of more than 70 U.S. board-certified physicians. The website contains a "Symptom Checker," with symptoms of disorders listed in alphabetical order as a guide to "pinpoint your pain." MedicineNet's homepage lists links to articles on sections titled "Health News of the Week" and "Daily Health News." Also available is a health newsletter signup.

➤ Medscape Reference (Drugs, Diseases, and Procedures). "Takotsubo Cardiomyopathy [Broken Heart]." http://emedicine.medscape.com/article/1513631-overview; alternate path: http://emedicine.medscape.com/, search for "takotsubo," and then click on the resource title.
  Written by Eric B. Tomich et al. for Medscape, this is a comprehensive report on what takotsubo cardiomyopathy is (broken heart syndrome or stress cardiomyopathy). Although written for the health care professional, it might be helpful for interested laypersons. Medscape Reference, whose articles are written by medical experts in their field, states, "Our rigorous literature survey process allows us to rapidly integrate new practice-changing information into the relevant topics by systematically reviewing the major medical and pharmacy journals, news announcements, and important practice guidelines." Free registration is required.

➤ National Women's Health Resource Center—"Heart Disease." http://www.healthy women.org/condition/heart-disease; alternate path: http://www.healthywomen.org/, search for and then click on the title "Heart Disease."
  The National Women's Health Resource Center (Healthy Women Organization) is a nonprofit, national clearinghouse for unbiased and accurate health information for women. The section on heart disease in women gives overviews on heart disease, diagnosis, treatment, prevention, facts to know, questions to ask, and lifestyle tips.

➤ Texas Heart Institute (Houston, TX)—"Women and Heart Disease" (Heart Information Center). http://www.texasheartinstitute.org/HIC/Topics/HSmart/women.cfm; alternate path: http://www.texasheartinstitute.org/, search for and then click on the title "Women and Heart Disease"; or scroll down to the heading "Heart Information Center," click on "Heart Smart," and then click on "Women and Heart Disease."
  The Heart Information Center at the Texas Heart Institute website has numerous topics on women and heart disease, including women and heart attacks, estrogen and heart disease, and risk factors in women. There is an easy-to-print format

available. One section is called "Ask a Texas Heart Institute Doctor," where users can submit questions and read answers to questions that have already been asked. To participate in a clinical trial, if available in your cardiology condition, at the Texas Heart Institute Research Laboratory, go to http://www.texasheartinstitute.org/Research/hfresearch.cfm (or return to the Texas Heart Institute homepage, click on the heading "Research," and then click on the title "Heart Failure Research Laboratory"). Scroll down to the section "Research Projects," and click on the title "FDA-Approved Clinical Trials." Under the heading "About Us," click on "Professional Staff Directory" to view a list of physicians and specialists (with profiles, e.g., specialty, medical board certification, education).

➤ Women's Heart Foundation (WHF). http://www.womensheart.org/.
The WHF's goal is "to provide for the education of women as consumers concerning heart disease as it affects them economically, culturally, physiologically, psychologically and spiritually; to provide for the education of health professionals concerning the unique needs of women with heart disease; to advocate for research into the diagnosis, prognosis, treatment and outcome of heart disease as it affects women, particularly minority women; and to support women as caregivers." Check out the following resource.

- "Cardiac Arrhythmia Management: Why Women Are Different from Men." http://www.womensheart.org/content/HeartDisease/cardiac_arrhythmias.asp; alternate path: http://www.womensheart.org/, under the heading "Heart Disease," click on the topic "Arrhythmia Management." This WHF webpage explains why diagnostic techniques should be measured and analyzed differently for women and men and why these results matter.

➤ WomensHealth.gov. http://www.womenshealth.gov/.
WomensHealth.gov, a division of the U.S. Department of Health and Human Services, provides comprehensive information on prevention, risk factors, and signs of both heart attack and stroke. Also of interest is the WomensHealth.gov brochure "Heart Healthy Eating Fact Sheet" discussed earlier in this chapter.

- "Government in Action on Heart Health and Stroke." http://www.womenshealth.gov/heart-health-stroke/government-in-action/; alternate path: http://www.womenshealth.gov/, search for "heart health and stroke," and then click on the resource title. This webpage offers numerous links to "National Campaigns" (e.g., National Women's Health Week, National Women's Checkup Day, and Women's Heart Day Campaign), "Programs Targeting Minorities" (e.g., Generations, to prevent heart disease in African American women), and "Evaluation Programs" (e.g., Comprehensive Women's Heart Health Care Program).
- "Heart Disease and Stroke Prevention." http://www.womenshealth.gov/heart-health-stroke/heart-disease-stroke-prevention/; alternate path: http://

www.womenshealth.gov/, search for "heart health and stroke prevention," and then click on the resource title. This webpage offers expanded information for heart disease prevention for women with such topics as physical activity, healthy eating, understanding test numbers, and healthy living, along with numerous articles and publications.

- "Heart Disease Fact Sheet." http://www.womenshealth.gov/publications/our-publications/fact-sheet/heart-disease.html; alternate path: http://www.womenshealth.gov/, search for and click on the title "Heart Disease Fact Sheet." For "Interactive Features on Heart Disease and Stroke for Women," scroll down to the section titled "Features." Here are several interactive activities to help empower the female patient in understanding and managing her heart, including taking the Heart Attack Quiz to test knowledge of the symptoms of a heart attack in women, using the "Body Mass Index (BMI) Calculator [which] is a number calculated from a person's height and weight. This calculator can help you find out what your BMI is and whether it is in the healthy range"; using the chart called "Physical Activity for a Healthy Weight—There are many different activities that can help you raise your fitness level. This chart tells you which activities burn the most calories during an hour of activity"; trying out the "Screenings and Immunizations Wizard—Use this womenshealth.gov tool to find out which screenings and immunizations you should be getting"; and reading about "What Happens When You Quit Smoking?—This womenshealth.gov tool shows you how your health begins to improve right away when you stop smoking."
- "Heart Disease: Know Your Risk." http://www.womenshealth.gov/heart-health-stroke/heart-disease-risk-factors/index.html; alternate path: http://www.womenshealth.gov/, search for and then click on the title "Heart Disease: Know Your Risk." This website offers numerous articles and publications focusing on types of risk factors for heart and cardiovascular disease in women that can and cannot be altered, along with action plans.

Patient Support Groups and Organizations

➢ Facebook—American Heart Association (AHA). "Go Red for Women—American Heart Association." https://www.facebook.com/GoRedforWomen?fref=ts; alternate path: http://www.facebook.com/, search for "go red for women-american heart association" (include the quotation marks), and then scroll down and select this title "(from Dallas, TX)," or search for just "go red for women" (in quotes) and select from a variety of cities.

Participate and learn at the official "AHA—Go Red for Women" Facebook webpages, help women fight heart disease, and "take control of their heart health."

➤ Friends' Health Connection. http://www.friendshealthconnection.org/.
According to its website, the Friends' Health Connection's goal is to "work with hospitals and other nonprofit organizations to complement their program offerings and connect people with resources and support that can enrich their lives." Join the free online community, which "features free talks by some of the world's top thought-leaders, authors, self-help experts and celebrity guests who share their insights and life experiences." Membership is free; first, start "by answering a questionnaire about you or your family's health condition. After completing the questionnaire, search for other members with heart disease or other medical condition. As the website says, 'Find a Heart Friend . . . who can truly relate to your own situation.'"

➤ Mended Hearts. http://mendedhearts.org/.
Not just for women, Mended Hearts is a national nonprofit organization affiliated with the American Heart Association. This organization provides support groups, educational resources, and a newsletter. According to the American College of Cardiology's CardioSmart website, "as part of the CardioSmart National Care Initiative, the American College of Cardiology has partnered with Mended Hearts to expand a network of cardiovascular patient support and care."

➤ National Heart, Lung, and Blood Institute (NHLBI)—"The Heart Truth." http://www.nhlbi.nih.gov/educational/hearttruth; alternate path: http://www.nhlbi.nih.gov/, search for "heart truth," and then click on the resource title.
NHLBI is a division of National Institutes of Health from the U.S. Department of Health and Human Services. This consumer-friendly website has many sections devoted to learning about women and heart disease, as well as educating others and participating in events. Click on the topic "Lower Heart Disease Risk" to browse sections including "Tools" (to empower the patient and family), "Resource Links," and "Risk Factors." The category "Get Involved" discusses ways to become active in this health awareness program, including by partnering with the campaign, joining the health action community, and providing event ideas and event support tools. The heading "Campaign Materials and Resources" contains an online toolkit, health professional materials, a faith-based toolkit, a speaker's kit, a National Wear Red Day toolkit, and a newsletter. There are also categories on "Campaign Partners" and "Media Room."

➤ Sister to Sister: The Women's Heart Health Foundation. http://www.sistertosister.org/.
The free Sister to Sister online community is an opportunity for women to join discussions, including best and worst eating habits, meeting sisters in the local area, submitting questions for experts at upcoming roundtables, and accessing personalized health tools. Members share experiences and exchange health tips through forum posts and blogs. Also offered are annual women's heart health fairs (type "heart health fairs" in the Search box at the top of the screen). This interactive website provides a daily health tip, heart health news, and sections such as

heart facts, healthy living, and health tools (e.g., map my walk, screening locator, heart risk assessment, BMI calculator, and recipes). Check your local hospital for a patient support group that may be sponsored by or meet at the hospital.

➤ WomenHeart: The National Coalition for Women with Heart Disease. http://www.womenheart.org/ and http://www.inspire.com/groups/womenheart/; alternate path: http://www.inspire.com/, click on the heading "Group," search for "women heart," and then click on the title "WomenHeart."
WomenHeart is a nonprofit, 501(c)(3) patient advocacy organization, which was founded by three women who had heart attacks in their forties. WomenHeart provides education for women and health professionals concerning the unique needs of women with heart disease and also advocates for research into the diagnosis, prognosis, treatment, and outcome of heart disease as it affects women—particularly minority women. The section titled "Support for Women" includes an online community, survivor stories, and topics such as living with heart disease, prevention, and early detection. The section titled "Take Action" includes hot topics, current policy statements, legislative priorities, and how to influence public policy.

Webliography

American Heart Association. "Angina in Women Can Be Different Than Men." April 15, 2013. http://www.heart.org/HEARTORG/Conditions/HeartAttack/WarningSignsofaHeartAttack/Angina-in-Women-Can-Be-Different-Than-Men_UCM_448902_Article.jsp.
———. "Heart Attack Symptoms in Women." Updated April 15, 2013. http://www.heart.org/HEARTORG/Conditions/HeartAttack/WarningSignsofaHeartAttack/Heart-Attack-Symptoms-in-Women_UCM_436448_Article.jsp.
———. "Metabolic Syndrome." Accessed April 6, 2013. http://www.heart.org/HEARTORG/Conditions/More/MetabolicSyndrome/Metabolic-Syndrome_UCM_002080_SubHomePage.jsp.
———. "Physical Activity Improves Quality of Life." Updated July 24, 2013. http://www.heart.org/HEARTORG/GettingHealthy/PhysicalActivity/StartWalking/Physical-activity-improves-quality-of-life_UCM_307977_Article.jsp.
Finks, S. W. "Cardiovascular Disease in Women." In *Pharmacotherapy Self-Assessment Program*, 7th ed., Book 1: *Cardiology*, edited by Judy W. M. Cheng, 179–199. Lenexa, KS: American College of Clinical Pharmacology, 2010. http://www.accp.com/docs/bookstore/psap/p7b01sample03.pdf.
James, A. H., M. G. Jamison, M. S. Biswas, L. R. Brancazio, G. K. Swamy, and E. R. Myers. "Acute Myocardial Infarction in Pregnancy: A United States Population-Based Study." *Circulation*, 113 (2006): 1564–1571. http://circ.ahajournals.org/content/113/12/1564.full.pdf+html.

Kreatsoulas, C., H. S. Shannon, M. Giacomini, et al. "Reconstructing Angina: Cardiac Symptoms Are the Same in Women and Men." *JAMA Internal Medicine,* 173, no. 9 (2013): 829. Accessed May 13, 2013. http://archinte.jamanetwork.com/article.aspx?articleid=1675875#ref-ild130002-5.

Mayo Clinic. "Heart Disease in Women: Understand Symptoms and Risk Factors." January 11, 2011. http://www.mayoclinic.com/health/heart-disease/HB00040.

MedlinePlus. "Heart Disease in Women." Updated March 26, 2013. http://www.nlm.nih.gov/medlineplus/heartdiseaseinwomen.html.

National Heart, Lung, and Blood Institute. "How Can Heart Disease Be Prevented?" (Heart Disease in Women). Updated September 26, 2011. http://www.nhlbi.nih.gov/health/health-topics/topics/hdw/prevention.html.

———. "How Does Heart Disease Affect Women?" Updated September 26, 2011. http://www.nhlbi.nih.gov/health/health-topics/topics/hdw/.

———. "How Is Heart Disease Diagnosed?" (Heart Disease in Women). Updated September 26, 2011. http://www.nhlbi.nih.gov/health/health-topics/topics/hdw/diagnosis.html.

———. "Living with Heart Disease" (Heart Disease in Women). Updated September 26, 2011. http://www.nhlbi.nih.gov/health/health-topics/topics/hdw/livingwith.html.

———. "What Are the Risk Factors for Heart Disease (in Women)?" Updated February 29, 2012. http://www.nhlbi.nih.gov/educational/hearttruth/lower-risk/risk-factors.htm.

———. "What Are the Signs and Symptoms of Heart Disease?" (Heart Disease in Women). Updated September 26, 2011. http://www.nhlbi.nih.gov/health/health-topics/topics/hdw/signs.html.

———. "What Causes Heart Disease?" (Heart Disease in Women). Updated September 26, 2011. http://www.nhlbi.nih.gov/health/health-topics/topics/hdw/causes.html.

———. "What Is Coronary Microvascular Disease?" Updated November 2, 2011. http://www.nhlbi.nih.gov/health/dci/Diseases/cmd/cmd_whatis.html.

———. "What Is Metabolic Syndrome?" Updated November 3, 2011. http://www.nhlbi.nih.gov/health/health-topics/topics/ms/.

———. "Who Is at Risk for Heart Disease?" (Heart Disease in Women). Updated September 26, 2011. http://www.nhlbi.nih.gov/health/health-topics/topics/hdw/atrisk.html.

Neale, Todd. "Angina? Heartache Is Same in Men and Women." MedPage Today. April 8, 2013. http://www.medpagetoday.com/Cardiology/Atherosclerosis/38317.

NIH News. "WHI Study Data Confirm Short-Term Heart Disease Risks of Combination Hormone Therapy for Postmenopausal Women." February 15, 2010. http://www.nih.gov/news/health/feb2010/nhlbi-15.htm.

Poirier, P., et al. "Obesity and Cardiovascular Disease: Pathophysiology, Evaluation, and Effect of Weight Loss." *Arteriosclerosis, Thrombosis, and Vascular Biology,* 26, no. 5 (2006): 968–976. http://atvb.ahajournals.org/content/26/5/968.full.

Redberg, Rita F. "Debunking Atypical Chest Pain in Women: Editor's Comment on 'Reconstructing Angina: Cardiac Symptoms Are the Same in Women and Men.'" *JAMA Internal Medicine,* 173, no. 9 (2013): 752. http://archinte.jamanetwork .com/article.aspx?articleid=1675873.

Regnante, R. A., et al. "Clinical Characteristics and Four-Year Outcomes of Patients in the Rhode Island Takotsubo Cardiomyopathy Registry." *American Journal of Cardiology,* 103, no. 7 (2009): 1015–1019. http://www.ajconline.org/article/ S0002–9149(08)02215–7/abstract.

Schierbeck, L. L., et al. "Effect of Hormone Replacement Therapy on Cardiovascular Events in Recently Postmenopausal Women: Randomised Trial." *British Medical Journal,* 345 (2012): e6409. http://www.bmj.com/highwire/filestream/607291/ field_highwire_article_pdf/0/bmj.e6409.

Toh, S., et al. "Coronary Heart Disease in Postmenopausal Recipients of Estrogen Plus Progestin Therapy: Does the Increased Risk Ever Disappear? A Randomized Trial." *Annals of Internal Medicine,* 152, no. 4 (2010): 211–217. http://annals.org/article .aspx?articleid=745597.

Wilson, P. W., R. B. D'Agostino, L. Sullivan, H. Parise, and W. B. Kannel. "Overweight and Obesity as Determinants of Cardiovascular Risk: The Framingham Experience." *Archives of Internal Medicine,* 162, no. 16 (2002): 1867–1872. http://archinte .jamanetwork.com/article.aspx?articleid=212796.

Wittstein, I. S., et al. "Neurohumoral Features of Myocardial Stunning Due to Sudden Emotional Stress." *New England Journal of Medicine,* 10, no. 352 (2005): 539–548. http://www.nejm.org/doi/full/10.1056/NEJMoa043046.

WomenHeart: National Coalition for Women with Heart Disease. "Resources." Accessed April 6, 2013. http://www.womenheart.org/?page=Resources_Intro.

Women's Heart Foundation. "Cardiac Arrhythmia Management: Why Women Are Different from Men." Accessed April 6, 2013. http://www.womensheart.org/ content/HeartDisease/cardiac_arrhythmias.asp.

WomensHealth.gov. "Heart Health and Stroke." Updated February 1, 2009. http:// www.womenshealth.gov/heart-health-stroke/index.html.

———. "The Heart Truth: Patient Education" (for Women). Accessed April 6, 2013. http://www.womenshealth.gov/heart-truth/clinical-resources/patient-education .cfm#d.

———. "Literature Review on Effective Sex- and Gender-Based Systems/Models of Care." January 30, 2007. http://www.womenshealth.gov/archive/owh/multidisciplinary/ reports/GenderBasedMedicine/FinalOWHReport.pdf.

Glossary

ACE (angiotensin-converting enzyme) inhibitors: A class of drugs that expand blood vessels and decrease blood flow resistance by lowering the blood level of the peptide angiotensin II, thereby making blood flow more easily and reducing the workload on the heart. *See* ANGIOTENSIN-CONVERTING ENZYME INHIBITORS IN CHAPTER 5 (p. 275).

alternative therapies: Products, techniques, theories, or practices which fall outside conventional medicine and which are used instead of conventional medicine. *See* COMPLEMENTARY AND ALTERNATIVE THERAPIES IN CHAPTER 5 (pp. 268, 270).

anemia: Lack of sufficient red blood cells or lack of sufficient hemoglobin to carry oxygen to the body's cells.

aneurysm: A balloon-like bulging of an artery wall. Certain disease conditions cause the normally thick muscular artery wall to weaken and allow a bulge. The bulge can rupture or dissect. With rupture, the artery wall tears open and bleeds out into the surrounding tissue (e.g., brain aneurysm). With dissection, the layers of the artery wall are delaminated, which can block blood flow or cause a bulge. In either case, the problem can be fatal or at least disabling if not rapidly addressed with surgery.

angina pectoris (or angina): Severe chest pain caused by heart muscle ischemia. It is a symptom of coronary artery disease. Worsening angina, angina while resting, or angina that lasts for more than 15 minutes suggests an oncoming heart attack.

angiogram: A radiograph or series of pictures of the heart used to determine the state of the arteries, valves, chambers, and blood flow in the heart. *See also* IMAGING TESTS IN CHAPTER 5 (pp. 284–287).

angioplasty (coronary angioplasty): A surgical procedure used to open clogged or blocked coronary arteries by compressing plaque (balloon angioplasty), stenting the artery open, or removing the plaque (arterectomy) that is clogging or blocking the artery. Cardiac catheterization is a surgical procedure in which a long tube (catheter) is inserted into a patient's blood vessel to examine or treat heart and vascular problems. *See* ANGIOPLASTY IN CHAPTER 5 (pp. 263–264).

angiotensin II receptor blockers: A class of drugs that prevent angiotensin II from being sensed by blood vessels, thus preventing blood pressure from rising. *See* ANGIOTENSIN II RECEPTOR BLOCKERS IN CHAPTER 5 (pp. 275–276).

anticoagulants: Drugs used to prevent blood from clotting. They are used during surgeries and with some disease states to reduce the risk of blood clots causing tissue damage. *See* ANTICOAGULANTS IN CHAPTER 5 (p. 276).

antiplatelet agents: Drugs used to prevent platelet (a blood component) from breaking down and starting the clotting process. *See* ANTIPLATELET AGENTS IN CHAPTER 5 (p. 277).

aorta: The main artery leading from the heart to the rest of the body. It curves up and over the heart and descends down the thorax next to the spinal column; branches from the aorta connect to all parts of the body. *See* CHAPTER 2 (pp. 15–18).

aortic dissection: An emergency condition in which the layers of the aorta delaminate under pressure from the heart. The dissection may proceed along the length of the aorta and thereby block blood flow or may cause an aortic aneurysm to form. In either case, failure of the aortic wall can lead to rapid bleed out into the thorax and death unless the problem is quickly surgically controlled. *See* MARFAN SYNDROME IN CHAPTER 4 (pp. 213–221).

arrhythmia: An irregular heartbeat, such as slow (bradycardia); fast (tachycardia); and fast, irregular, and unsynchronized (fibrillation). *See* ARRHYTHMIAS IN CHAPTER 3 (pp. 25–43).

arteriosclerosis (also atherosclerosis): A disease condition in which plaque forms in the arteries, narrowing the arteries and causing them to harden. Arteries need to be elastic to respond to blood pressure changes and body needs. Hardened arteries prevent this and lead to other problems such as coronary artery disease, carotid artery disease, and ischemia. *See* CORONARY ARTERY DISEASE *and* PERIPHERAL ARTERIAL DISEASE IN CHAPTER 3 (pp. 59–77, 180–190).

atria: The receiving chambers of the heart. In the right atrium, blood is collected from the vena cava before being pumped into the right ventricle. In the left atrium, blood is collected from the pulmonary vein before being pumped into the left ventricle. *See* CHAPTER 2 (pp. 15–18).

atrial septal defect (ASD): A congenital defect that is a hole between the atria. This hole allows oxygenated and unoxygenated blood to mix. The mixture provides insufficient oxygen to tissues, resulting in a blue appearance of the patient. *See* SEPTAL DEFECTS IN CHAPTER 4 (pp. 235–238).

beta-blockers: A class of drugs that prevent stress hormones (e.g., adrenaline) from being effective. *See* BETA-BLOCKERS IN CHAPTER 5 (p. 277).

bicuspid aortic valve: The two-leafed valve between the left ventricle and the left atrium, also called the mitral valve. *See* CHAPTER 2 (pp. 16–17).

blood pressure: A measure of how well the heart is pumping blood. A blood pressure of 120 over 80 is considered normal. *See* HIGH BLOOD PRESSURE *and* LOW BLOOD PRESSURE IN CHAPTER 3 (pp. 135–148, 162–166).

blue baby: A symptom of many congenital heart defects in which the blood is not properly or fully oxygenated, causing the infant to have a bluish tint. *See* DIAGNOSING CONGENITAL HEART DISEASE IN CHAPTER 4 (pp. 272–273).

BMI (body mass index): A measure of how much fat is present in the body. BMI is equal to the person's height in meters divided by his or her weight in kilograms. A BMI below 25 and above 18.5 is considered as normal. BMI between 25 and 30 is considered as being overweight. A BMI above 30 is considered obese. *See* OBESITY, BEING OVERWEIGHT, AND ANOREXIA IN CHAPTER 6 (pp. 326–327).

bradycardia: A type of arrhythmia in which the heart rate slows. *See* ARRHYTHMIAS IN CHAPTER 3 (pp. 25–43).

Brugada syndrome: A genetic disease indicated by an abnormal electrocardiogram and a risk of sudden cardiac death from ventricular fibrillation.

CABG (coronary artery bypass grafting; also bypass surgery): Surgery in which a segment of an artery or vein is transplanted to feed blood around a blocked coronary artery thereby restoring blood flow to the affected portion of the heart. The surgery can be open chest with heart–lung bypass for more extensive grafting or can be done percutaneously with endoscopic surgery through several incisions in the chest wall for minor grafting. *See* CORONARY ARTERY BYPASS GRAFTING IN CHAPTER 5 (pp. 270–272).

calcium channel blockers: A class of drugs that reduce the contractility of cardiac and smooth muscle, thus preventing high blood pressure and lowering the heart's workload. *See* CALCIUM CHANNEL BLOCKERS IN CHAPTER 5 (p. 277).

cardiac arrest: An event that occurs when an arrhythmia causes the heart to stop pumping. The condition can be fatal if not treated quickly with cardiopulmonary resuscitation or defibrillation. *See* CARDIAC ARREST IN CHAPTER 3 (pp. 43–49).

cardiac catheterization: A surgical procedure in which a small diameter tube (catheter) is inserted into the heart. The tube can be one of several different types to allow various examinations and treatments of the heart and coronary arteries. *See* CARDIAC CATHETERIZATION AND MYOCARDIAL BIOPSY IN CHAPTER 5 (pp. 262–266).

cardiac nerves: The nerves that control the heart and how it pumps. They are part of the autonomic nervous system (working without conscious effort) and have sympathetic and parasympathetic components (complementary systems) that increase and decrease heart rate. There are superior, middle, and inferior cardiac nerves that connect from several levels of the spinal cord to the heart. Inside the heart, the nerves connect to the heart's internal nervous system, which causes the chambers of the heart to contract in such a way as to move the blood through the heart and lungs and to the body. This internal nervous system includes the sinoatrial node, the atrioventricular tracts, the bundle of His, and the left and right bundle branches. *See* CHAPTER 2 (pp. 15–18).

cardiac rehabilitation: The process used to restore a cardiac patient to his or her best functionality. *See* CARDIAC REHABILITATION IN CHAPTER 7 (pp. 350–351).

cardiomyopathy: A condition in which the heart walls become thickened or otherwise diseased. *See* CARDIOMYOPATHIES IN CHAPTER 3 (pp. 49–59).

caregiver: A person, usually with some nursing degree or training, who provides basic care for a patient who cannot do his or her own routine activities of daily living. A caregiver helps the patient with such tasks as dressing, bathing, exercising, preparing and eating food, taking medicine, and moving about. *See* HOME HEALTH CARE (CAREGIVERS) IN CHAPTER 7 (pp. 352–353).

cholesterol: A type of waxy, steroid metabolite normally found in all animals. It has many bodily functions, including ensuring proper performance of cell membranes and as an ingredient in making bile acids, steroid hormones, and several vitamins. Too much blood cholesterol can lead to plaque formation in the arteries and heart disease. *See* HIGH CHOLESTEROL IN CHAPTER 3 (pp. 148–161).

cholesterol-lowering drugs: Several classes of drugs that lower low-density cholesterol and triglyceride levels to help prevent plaque formation. *See* CHOLESTEROL-LOWERING DRUGS IN CHAPTER 5 (p. 278).

clinical trials: Tests of new products, techniques, theories, or practices to determine their safety and effectiveness. *See* CLINICAL TRIALS IN CHAPTER 5 (pp. 267–268, 269).

CMVD (coronary microvascular disease): A disease in which the smallest arteries (arterioles) become damaged and limit the blood flow to small portions of the heart, which can damage the heart muscle. *See* CORONARY ARTERY DISEASE

IN CHAPTER 3 (p. 60) *and* CORONARY MICROVASCULAR DISEASE IN CHAPTER 8 (pp. 391–393).

complementary therapies: Products, techniques, theories, or practices which fall outside conventional medicine and which are used in addition to conventional medicine. *See* COMPLEMENTARY AND ALTERNATIVE THERAPIES IN CHAPTER 5 (pp. 268, 270).

computed tomography: *See* CT SCAN.

congenital: A condition that exists at or before birth. *See* CHAPTER 4 (pp. 203–204).

coronary arteries: The blood vessels that supply the heart. There are three main coronary arteries: left descending, right descending, and left circumflex. They are supplied with blood directly from the aorta and are the first arteries branching from the aorta. *See* CHAPTER 2 (pp. 15–18).

coronary artery bypass grafting: *See* CABG.

coronary microvascular disease: *See* CMVD.

C-reactive protein: A substance released by the liver when certain chemicals are released from fat cells in response to inflammation. *See* C-REACTIVE PROTEIN BLOOD LEVEL IN CHAPTER 6 (p. 324).

CT (computed tomography) scan: An imaging procedure in which X-rays are used to image the body's interior. The X-ray device spins around and spirals along the body. The information from this scan is processed by a computer to produce a three-dimensional image. The detail achieved approaches (and some may exceed) that of magnetic resonance imaging. CT scans of the heart are often done to get a precise image of the heart and identify any structural problems it may have. *See* IMAGING TESTS IN CHAPTER 5 (pp. 284–286).

defibrillator (also automatic external defibrillator; defibrillator monitor): A device used to provide an electric shock to the heart in an attempt to stop an arrhythmia and restart a normal heartbeat (called defibrillation or cardioversion). It can be implanted with leads to the heart or external with paddles or pads applied to the chest. An automatic external defibrillator (AED) is an easy-to-use defibrillator that can be used by laypersons on a person having a heart attack. AEDs provide audible and visual directions on how to apply and use the device. AEDs are placed in many public areas such as malls, hotels, stadiums, and some workplaces. Defibrillator monitors are used to track a patient's heartbeat, sound and display an alarm should an irregular heart occur, and deliver an electric shock to the heart in an attempt to stop an arrhythmia and restart a normal heartbeat. These devices may be used alone or may be connected to

a central monitoring station. *See* PACEMAKER OR DEFIBRILLATOR IMPLANTA-
TION IN CHAPTER 5 (p. 288).

dextrocardia: A congenital defect in which the heart is on the right side of the
body, displaced from the left. It can also be caused by disease or surgery.

diabetes: A disease in which the body does not produce enough or properly use
insulin, resulting in a high blood sugar level. *See* DIABETES IN CHAPTER 6 (p. 325).

DiGeorge syndrome: The result of a genetic defect on chromosome 22 that causes
various bodily defects, including heart defects (such as truncus arteriosus, ventricular septal defect, and tetralogy of Fallot), poor immune system function,
cleft palate, poor function of the parathyroid glands, and behavioral disorders.

digitalis: One of the first heart drugs ever used. It increases the heart's contractility
and helps control the heart rate. *See* DIGITALIS IN CHAPTER 5 (pp. 278–279).

diuretics: A class of drugs that cause the body to produce more urine, which
reduces blood volume and edema. *See* DIURETICS IN CHAPTER 5 (p. 279).

double inlet left ventricle: A congenital heart condition in which both the right and
left atria are directly connected to the left ventricle. The left ventricle is typically
enlarged.

double outlet right ventricle: A congenital heart condition in which the pulmonary artery and the aorta are both connected to the right ventricle. The size and
position of the blood vessels can vary, and the defect is usually associated with a
septal defect. Physiologically, the condition can resemble the tetralogy of Fallot.

dysautonomia: Also called autonomic dysfunction, this term describes any disease or malfunction of the autonomic nervous system (the part of the nervous system that works automatically) that causes light-headedness, fainting,
or loss of consciousness. This problem includes many disorders, such as postural orthostatic tachycardia syndrome, inappropriate sinus tachycardia,
vasovagal syncope, mitral valve prolapse dysautonomia, neurocardiogenic
syncope, and neurally mediated hypotension. Dysautonomia is associated with
some other diseases, notably Marfan syndrome. *See* TILT TABLE TESTING IN
CHAPTER 5 (p. 290).

Ebstein's anomaly: A congenital heart defect in which the tricuspid valve is near
the apex of the right ventricle. This causes other defects such as an enlarged right
atrium, defects in the valve, an opening between the atria, and arrhythmias.

echocardiograph: A machine that uses ultrasonic waves to noninvasively determine various characteristics of the heart. *See* ECHOCARDIOGRAPHY IN CHAP-
TER 5 (pp. 281–282).

electrocardiography: A test that measures the electrical performance of the heart's nervous system. It produces an electrocardiogram that shows the PQRST wave, which corresponds to the heart chambers' contractions. Deviations from the normal wave shape indicate specific disease processes. *See* ELECTROCARDIOGRA-PHY IN CHAPTER 5 (pp. 282–283).

electrophysiologic studies: Examinations of the heart's nervous system to determine if irregularities exist and the locations of nerves in the heart. Electrocardiography uses external connections while an electrophysiologic catheter is used inside the heart. *See* CARDIAC CATHETERIZATION AND MYOCARDIAL BIOPSY IN CHAPTER 5 (pp. 262, 264).

endocarditis: An inflammation of the interior lining of the heart, its valves, and associated blood vessels. *See* ENDOCARDITIS IN CHAPTER 3 (pp. 85–90).

fibrillation: A condition in which the heart or a part of the heart contracts irregularly. Atrial fibrillation is the most common form. Because of the irregular contractions, the heart will not pump blood properly, which can lead to chest pain, stroke, and heart failure. *See* ARRHYTHMIAS IN CHAPTER 3 (pp. 25–43).

foramen ovale: A hole in the septum between the atria. This is sometimes present in fetuses to allow blood to bypass the nonfunctioning lungs but typically closes during or shortly after birth. If it does not close, it is called a patent foramen ovale. *See* THE FETAL HEART IN CHAPTER 2 (p. 18).

heart attack: A myocardial infarction or acute myocardial infarction, in which part of the blood supply to the heart is interrupted, leading to death of heart muscle. It is typically caused by blockage of one or more coronary arteries. *See* HEART ATTACKS IN CHAPTER 3 (pp. 90–103).

heart augmentation: A surgical procedure in which the heart is assisted in pumping blood by adding a device to the left ventricle or aorta. It is a transitional procedure, used until a replacement heart can be found. *See* HEART AUGMENTATION AND REPLACEMENT IN CHAPTER 5 (p. 284).

heart block: A condition in which part of the heart's nervous system is blocked, causing the heart to pump ineffectively. *See* HEART BLOCK IN CHAPTER 3 (pp. 103–108).

heart failure: The inability of the heart to supply sufficient blood flow to the body. It has various causes and is different from a heart attack. *See* HEART FAILURE IN CHAPTER 3 (pp. 108–122).

heart murmur: The sound made by the heart valves during heartbeat. Normally a lub-dub, the normal sound is changed by valve disease states. *See* HEART VALVE DISEASE IN CHAPTER 3 (pp. 122–135).

heart replacement: A surgical procedure in which a patient's failed heart is replaced with a donor heart or a mechanical heart. *See* HEART AUGMENTATION AND REPLACEMENT IN CHAPTER 5 (p. 284).

home health care: Caring for a patient at his or her home. This may require specialized equipment and professional caregivers, but the patient's family can also provide the needed care in familiar surroundings. *See* HOME HEALTH CARE IN CHAPTER 7 (pp. 352–353).

hospitalization: The act of placing a patient in a hospital where he or she can receive more and varied care than can be had elsewhere. *See* CHAPTER 5 (pp. 259–260).

Kawasaki disease (also Kawasaki syndrome): A disease in children and infants, mostly of Japanese and Korean descent (80 percent are under five years old), that, if left untreated (usually with medication), causes vasculitis (inflammation of blood vessels all through the body) and can then develop into coronary heart disease. *See* CORONARY ARTERY DISEASE IN CHAPTER 3 (pp. 59–77).

lipids: Substances that include fats, waxes, sterols (e.g., cholesterol), fat-soluble vitamins (such as vitamins A, D, E, and K), monoglycerides, diglycerides, phospholipids, and others.

long QT syndrome: A rare congenital heart defect in which the heart cells are unable to process ions (such as calcium, sodium, and potassium) properly; the name refers to part of the cardiac waveform. *See* LONG QT SYNDROME IN CHAPTER 4 (pp. 211–212).

magnetic resonance imaging: *See* MRI.

Marfan syndrome: A genetic disorder that affects the body's connective tissue and results in (among other defects) several possible heart defects, including heart palpitations, angina, valve murmur and prolapse, dilated aorta, and aortic dissection. *See* MARFAN SYNDROME IN CHAPTER 4 (pp. 213–221).

mitral valve: The valve between the left atria and ventricle. It is also called the bicuspid valve because its two flaps are shaped like a miter. *See* CHAPTER 2 (pp. 16–17).

mitral valve prolapse (also Barlow's syndrome): A condition of the mitral or bicuspid valve in which the valve flaps are too floppy. Thus when the left ventricle contracts, one or both flaps of the mitral valve is pushed back (prolapses) into the left atrium. This can prevent the valve from forming a tight seal and may cause backflow from the ventricle into the atrium. *See* HEART VALVE DISEASE IN CHAPTER 3 (pp. 122–135).

mitral valve stenosis: A disease conditions that occurs when the valve flaps become calcified or otherwise damaged and do not fully close. *See* HEART VALVE DISEASE IN CHAPTER 3 (pp. 122–135).

MRI (magnetic resonance imaging): A system that uses a large, strong magnet with a smaller wiggler magnet to produce a three-dimensional image of the heart. The strong magnet aligns atoms in the body. The wiggler magnet causes a momentary misalignment of the atoms. As the atoms realign with the strong magnet, they emit radiation that can be detected. The emissions vary with the type of tissue. A computer processes the emission information to produce the image, which contains great detail. *See* MAGNETIC RESONANCE IMAGING IN CHAPTER 5 (p. 286).

pacemaker: A device, usually implanted, that delivers an electrical pulse to the heart to make it contract in a normal rhythm. *See* ARRHYTHMIAS IN CHAPTER 3 (pp. 25–43) *and* PACEMAKER OR DEFIBRILLATOR IMPLANTATION IN CHAPTER 5 (p. 288).

patient: A person who has an injury or disease that needs medical treatment.

pentalogy of Cantrell (also thoraco-abdominal syndrome): A congenital syndrome that causes defects involving the diaphragm, abdominal wall, pericardium, heart, and lower sternum. Patients typically have three of the defects but may have all five.

pericarditis: An inflammation of the pericardium. *See* PERICARDITIS IN CHAPTER 3 (pp. 174–180).

pericardium: A tough, three-layer sac that surrounds the heart to reduce friction of the heart on surrounding tissues and protect the heart from injury. *See* PERICARDITIS IN CHAPTER 3 (pp. 174–180).

PET (positron emission tomography): A three-dimensional imaging method that uses a radioisotope-tagged chemical to show which parts of the heart are working properly. *See* POSITRON EMISSION TOMOGRAPHY IN CHAPTER 5 (p. 286).

plaque: A substance that causes swelling of the arterial wall and contains cells, cellular debris, cholesterol, fatty acids, calcium, and fibrous connective tissue. *See* CORONARY HEART DISEASE *and* HIGH CHOLESTEROL IN CHAPTER 3 (pp. 59–77, 148–161).

positron emission tomography: *See* PET.

pre-eclampsia: The term for a set of symptoms sometimes occurring during pregnancy that includes hypertension, protein in the urine, and possible kidney and liver damage. The cause is believed to be chemicals released by the placenta that damage the endothelial cells lining the blood vessels.

pulmonary hypertension: A disease in which the blood pressure in the lungs is too high. *See* PULMONARY HYPERTENSION IN CHAPTER 3 (pp. 191–197).

radionuclide imaging: A three-dimensional imaging method that uses a radioisotope-tagged chemical to show which parts of the heart are working properly. *See* RADIONUCLIDE IMAGING OR NUCLEAR HEART SCAN IN CHAPTER 5 (p. 287).

scimitar syndrome: A congenital heart and lung defect in which the venous return from the right lung enters the inferior vena cava instead of the left atrium.

septum: A wall of tissue that separates chambers of the heart. *See* CHAPTER 2 (p. 17).

Shone's syndrome: A set of four congenital cardiac defects: a membrane above the mitral valve, an abnormally large (parachute) mitral valve, a subaortic stenosis, and coarctation (stenosis) of the aorta. In essence, the defect is an obstruction of the inflow and outflow of the left ventricle.

stent: A small diameter, cylindrical cage that is placed in a clogged artery and then expanded by a balloon catheter. The expanded stent is intended to hold open the clogged artery. Stents can have a drug coating or radioisotopes to prevent in-growth of tissue through the stent into the artery. *See* ANGIOPLASTY (AND USE OF A STENT) IN CHAPTER 5 (pp. 263–264).

stress: The body's response to physical or emotional threats. For example, a release of adrenaline on experiencing a physical threat enables a person to fight or take flight. Long-term or chronic stress can cause physical changes to the body that can lead to various diseases. *See* STRESS IN CHAPTER 6 (p. 327).

stress test: A method of working and examining the heart to see how well it responds to strenuous exercise. *See* STRESS TESTING IN CHAPTER 5 (p. 289).

stroke rehabilitation: The process used to restore a stroke patient to his or her best functionality. *See* RESOURCES FOR FURTHER INFORMATION ON STROKE IN CHAPTER 3 (pp. 77–84).

tachycardia: A heart arrhythmia in which the heart rate speeds up. *See* ARRHYTHMIAS IN CHAPTER 3 (pp. 25–43).

tetralogy of Fallot: A set of four congenital heart defects: a narrowing of the outflow tract from the right ventricle, connection of the mitral valve to both ventricles, an opening in the wall between the ventricles, and a muscular right ventricle. It is one cause of cyanotic heart defect and blue baby syndrome. *See* CONGENITAL HEART DISEASE IN CHAPTER 4 (pp. XX–XX).

total anomalous pulmonary venous return: A congenital defect in which none of four of the veins returning blood to the heart is connected to the left atrium. It is often associated with a septal defect and cyanosis. *See* MULTIPLE CONGENITAL HEART DEFECTS IN CHAPTER 4 (pp. 221–226).

transmyocardial revascularization: A surgical procedure in which small holes are "drilled" through the heart wall in an attempt to cause new blood vessels to grow in sections that have reduced blood flow from coronary artery disease. *See* TRANSMYOCARDIAL REVASCULARIZATION IN CHAPTER 5 (p. 290).

transposition of the great vessels: A group of congenital heart defects in which the large blood vessels associated with the heart are misconnected or misplaced. *See* ABNORMALITIES OF THE HEART IN CHAPTER 4 (pp. 204, 209–211).

tricuspid atresia: A congenital heart condition in which the tricuspid valve is not present. It usually occurs during fetal development and leads to a diminished right ventricle, an atrial septal defect, and improperly oxygenated blood. *See* NARROWED HEART VALVES IN CHAPTER 4 (pp. 226–227, 231–233, 234).

truncus arteriosus (also persistent truncus arteriosus): A congenital heart condition in which the embryonic heart does not properly form an aorta and a pulmonary artery. *See* NARROWED HEART VALVES IN CHAPTER 4 (pp. 226, 233–234).

valve disease: A condition in which the heart valves do not function properly, causing leaking, stenosis, or retroversion of the valve leaves. *See* HEART VALVE DISEASE IN CHAPTER 3 (pp. 122–135).

valvuloplasty: A surgical procedure in which the heart valves are repaired or replaced. *See* VALVULOPLASTY IN CHAPTER 5 (p. 290).

vasodilators: A class of drugs that cause the blood vessels to relax, which decreases the heart's workload and gets more blood to the heart. *See* VASODILATORS IN CHAPTER 5 (p. 281).

vena cava: The main vein bringing blood from the body to the heart. The superior vena cava brings blood from the upper part of the body to the upper part of the right atrium, and the inferior vena cava brings blood from the lower part of the body to the lower part of the right atrium.

ventricle: A large pumping chamber of the heart. The right ventricle pumps blood to the lungs through the pulmonary artery. The left ventricle pumps blood to the body through the aorta. The left ventricle is typically larger than the right ventricle because it pumps to the entire body, whereas the right pumps only to the lungs. *See* CHAPTER 2 (pp. 15–18).

Wolff-Parkinson-White syndrome: An arrhythmia in which the ventricles are stimulated at the wrong phase of the heartbeat. The condition is caused by an abnormal nerve connection between the atria and the ventricles.

X-ray: An imaging method that uses a shortwave electromagnetic radiation to image the interior of the body. Depending on the type of X-ray machine used, still (radiography), moving (fluoroscopy), or three-dimensional (computed tomography) images are produced. *See* X-RAY FLUOROSCOPY IN CHAPTER 5 (p. 287).

About the Authors

Jeanette de Richemond, MLIS, AHIP, is completing her doctoral dissertation on the concept of having "enough information" to make a clinical diagnosis. She has immersed herself in learning how doctors come to conclusions so that they can act to help patients. She hopes that what she learns about "enough information" can be applied in practice to improve the speed with which such needed information is distributed in many fields. She has been a journalist, a public relations consultant, and an expert medical researcher. She is also a mother and grandmother with dogs and cats and a husband to care for. In writing this book de Richemond used, and added to, a lifetime of knowledge on heart disease collected from various projects in which she has been involved: as a reporter for a newspaper, as a public relations consultant for many heart health care clients, and as an expert medical researcher for a nonprofit organization. Basic knowledge about the heart and heart disease is fairly well known by nurses and physicians but much less so by the general public. This is despite the multitude of pamphlets, books, journals, webpages, medical device information, drug information, heart treatment center outreach programs, and many other private, nonprofit, and governmental information sources. She learned much from these sources and hopes the reader will too through this book.

Terry Paula Hoffman, BS, ME, has been a professional medical literature researcher for a nonprofit health care organization (ECRI Institute), for the pharmaceutical industry (Merck and Co., Inc.), and as an independent consultant. Hoffman searches medical databases, the Internet, and libraries for answers across all medical product lines, therapeutic areas, and diseases for evidence-based medicine for the professional and consumer. At Merck, Hoffman received an award of excellence in recognition for outstanding technical assistance in bringing the *Women's Health on CD* program to completion. As a product development chemist (Quaker Chemical Corporation and E. F. Houghton Corporation) Hoffman created new and revised currently used chemical products to lessen the need for oil for manufacturing metal and paper products. Hoffman also developed a chemical product that received a U.S. patent for a permanent-wave treatment for hair, along with a related abstract published in the professional journal *Soap/Cosmetics/Chemical Specialties*. Hoffman, who has a permanent teaching certificate in Pennsylvania, was a secondary science teacher in chemistry, physics, and biology. She participated in a special project to include her students' help in an ongoing research study through the Temple University Medical School Pharmacology Department (Philadelphia, PA), which involved the practical and beneficial use of guppies in developing anesthetic drugs. Hoffman graduated from Temple University, where she studied toward undergraduate and graduate degrees in secondary science education, majoring in chemistry. She is also a wife and mom who loves photography, organic gardening, creating and baking delicious healthy treats, and doggy-sitting "Teddy Hacker" and "Peppi Koman."

Index

CPSIA information can be obtained at www.ICGtesting.com
Printed in the USA
LVOW07s1514280913

354570LV00004B/14/P